Thank you for choosing Re
as your companion for your PMP®

Our mission is to assure project management certification success while ensuring that the readers become practically empowered for real-world projects as well.

The material in this book is based on *A Guide To The Project Management Body Of Knowledge, (PMBOK®)*, Sixth Edition, 2017, Seventh Edition, 2021, Latest Examination Content Outline (ECO), PMI Approved PMP Prep. Guide, Standards For Agile, Standards for Change Management and Standards for Requirements.

Terms And Conditions.

On buying this book you have consented towards not copying, scanning, reproducing, sharing or picking up phrases and/or images from any part of this book.

Author: Maneesh Vijaya

Second Edition.

ISBN: 9798842845170

Table Of Contents

Read And Pass Notes For PMP® Exams

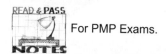

1 Why I Wrote This Book?

It has been some time since I completed my PMP® certification. The foremost issue that I faced those days was the conspicuous absence of any suitable book that could be used for preparing for PMP Exams. Even the training was not conducted well and there was no way to contact the trainers to take their guidance, once the training was concluded. My trainer just directed me to buy a book written by a famous "US-based author". When I went through the book it was absolutely clear that the author had not worked in the real world projects at all, and what really put me off was that the book only talked about "How to clear the exams". It did not explain what a specific concept meant, how that concept helped in the real world projects; instead it simply stated things like "If you get this question.... Answer this". For me, such an approach is very dangerous and absolutely meaningless. Thankfully I did not use that book.

Any training or any book that directs a candidate to only concentrate on passing the exams and study only for the exams are not only missing the entire point about PMP certification but also passing on this irresponsible behavior to the candidate as well which in turn would affect the career of the project managers.

Since then many new books have come into the market and there are a lot more trainers in the exciting world of project management, however, the methodology adopted by most of them, more or less, remains the same. This is so sad.

And this is the precisely the reason I am writing this book.

I truly believe in PMP® and its power to set you on a very powerful trajectory concerning your career in project management. I too experienced this after obtaining the PMP® certification. But now when I look at so many PMP® certified professionals who do not seem to be doing anything better or not really going anywhere, career-wise, I reflected on what the successful PMP®'s did differently compared to what is being "Widely" done. This reflection brought me to the conclusion that most of the participants just clear the PMP® exams, just for the sake of it, without understanding the concepts of Project Management from a practical perspective which prevents them from harnessing the powers of and enjoying the benefits of applying them in their real-world project management scenario.

When I conduct training on this subject I continually get people who had failed in the PMP® earlier having trained under some other training provider. And it's these very persons who come up to me immediately after the training and exclaim "This is the first time I truly understood what project management is all about". I see the light of confidence and clarity in their eyes and their behavior. Passing the exams becomes a side effect for them as their main focus becomes practical project management.

Through this book, I wish to not only help you pass the exams but more than that I want it to show you the amazing world of project management by ensuring that you understand everything about the foundational concepts of project management.

It is my attempt here to present you a book/series of books on PMP® exams and project management that is not only practical but easy to understand and everything is explained in a way that you can apply in real world.

I am writing this book because, quite frankly, there is no book like this in the world on this subject. Well at least for now.

2 About PMP® And Project Management

The reason that you have bought this book is that you are already aware of what is PMP® (Project Management Professional) certification and the institute called the Project Management Institute (PMI).

One of the larger challenges in Project Management has been to identify the competency of a Project Manager especially while interviewing him/her. Usually, once a person is hired and given a project to manage, it's only then that the organization becomes aware of the competency of the project manager. However, by then, it could be too late. Hence PMI came out with a certification which benchmarks the Project Management competency and knowledge of project professionals. This helps recruiters/businesses and others to hire/place "Competent" Project Managers at the helm of a project. The PMP Certification.

However, like any other professional exams, it's unable to cover every single aspect of it. The huge area of "Interpersonal Skills" and "Leadership" have not been covered in as many details as they are needed in real-world projects. Despite this shortcoming, PMP® is now the de-facto standard for Project Management Competency around the world and is among the most popular global certifications. PMP® is based on PMBOK® (Project Management Body Of Knowledge) which is the standard for Project Management around the world. This is the most researched project management guide and gets revised every 4 to 5 years to keep it as relevant to the real world and the changing environment, as possible.

This particular book is based on The PMBOK® Guide 6th as well as 7th Edition along with scores of other reference material that PMI has earmarked for PMP exams.

I guess you can see the importance of this certification.

Not only this, this guide applies to every single industry, domain, cultures, and verticals where projects are undertaken, hence the PMP® Certification makes a project manager industry/domain agnostic. This is exactly what happened to my career. During my days of employment I could easily jump from one vertical/industry/domain to another without any qualms, and now that I am an independent consultant I am moving between verticals and domains more than ever. I owe this ability to this certification.

There is a big difference in how I passed PMP® compared to how most of the people pass the PMP® exams. Just passing the PMP® exams is meaningless if you do not understand and appreciate the processes contained therein and are unable to relate them to the real world. This is where most of the other trainers and other books on PMP® seriously lack. Don't get me wrong. There are so many other books out there which are simply amazing from the point of view of just passing the exams but this is the only book that focuses not only on passing the PMP® but also on the practical aspects of the concepts of project management. This way not only a person can pass the PMP® but also become practically effective at it.

3 About The Author

Maneesh Vijaya, PMP

Chief Consultant, Mentor, Coach, and Trainer on Strategy, Portfolio, Program and Project Management with 28+yr Experience

Founder of PM-Pulse, global consulting and training organization on Strategy, Portfolio, Program, Project Management and Related Interpersonal Skills.

Founder of "Read & Pass Notes" publication.

Founder of the exams simulation site "Exam.pm-pulse.com" and PM audio sites "PMDhwani.PM-Pulse.com".

Trained over 44,000 professionals from almost every domain and industry, on Strategy, Program, Portfolio and Project Management including project management tools and techniques across 18 countries spread over 3 continents using traditional as well as virtual modes of training.

Provides consultation to some of the largest Automotive companies, shipping undertakings, construction and infrastructure organizations, financial institutions, IT Majors, Railways, Aviation Companies, Microsystem companies, Telecom Majors, Manufacturing mammoths and Defense establishments.

Usually consult on Organizational Structure, Organizational Changes, Project Management Office Set Up (PMO), Process GAP analysis for Process Enhancement as well as complete Re-engineering, Project Management Discipline establishment, Productivity Matrix Creation and Research, Project Piloting for enhanced processes, Project Management Robust processes adoption, Creation of the Project Based Organization (to support projects in a functional organization), Launch of products, Use of Project Management among Marketing and sales forces of organizations, Scheduling tools selection and rollout, Launch of products/services, Establishing estimation practices, Pre-sales checklists to ensure clarity of scope during project execution, RFP scanning practices, Establishment of Business Analysis Practices, Template creation for organizations, and even hiring project managers, product managers, business analysts and portfolio managers.

Having visited over 72 countries Maneesh has a very strong command over "Global Etiquettes" and several companies have used this to their advantage for establishing "Best Practices" for their Global teams to ensure the teams work together with least amount of confusions and conflicts as possible.

Maneesh loves to do wood carving using traditional tools (no power tools) and is now getting requests by hotels and corporates for lobby and centerpieces. Maneesh is also a very avid nature photographer and since his daughter is an avid bird-watcher, he usually accompanies her as her photography assistant. Maneesh has been a beer expert and is fondly called "Beer Baba". He is using this pseudo-name to write a comprehensive book on beer which will be launched soon.

4 A quick word about the illustrations in this book.

Being fed up of excessively serious-looking books with serious illustrations, I decided to write books for PMP® just like we used to make notes during our school and university days. I have used a lot of illustrations throughout the entire series to make it fun, colorful and informative for you.
All the illustrations are handcrafted by myself using traditional art paper and fine pens as well as Microsoft Surface Pro 4.0 and MS Surface Pro. 7 Plus using its famous stylus on an application called Sketchable. I am not an artist of any kind hence do not expect mind-blowing artwork here. However one thing I can guarantee and that is, each of these illustrations would be easy to read, interesting to relate to and create a lasting impression in your mind.

There are some anchor illustrations throughout the book which I should explain now.

This illustration, font and font color is meant to show/draw attention to the common mistakes, traps, and pitfalls in project management certification.

This illustration and font color is meant to show/draw attention to some amazing exams tricks and insights that you could remember to ace your PMP® exams.

This illustration is to draw attention to some exercise and drills that will help you to recall, retain and remember important concepts in a chapter/book.

All Examples (e.g.,) are colored brown and italicized for easy identifications.

All Processes are ***FORMATTED LIKE THIS.***

All Tools & Techniques as well as Outputs / Outcomes / Artefacts **would be in bold format**.

5 About PMBOK Guide 7th Edition.

PMI made some radical changes (as they claim) in their 7th Edition of PMBOK Guide which was released on 1st July 2021. It was slated to be released way back in August 2019 but it missed the target and then got further delayed because of the immense global problems created due to the Chinese virus. Something that is affecting us till date.
This version of PMBOK Guide 7th edition completely does away with the concept of structured processes (Not sure if this was actually a practical move or just a business oriented move) as well as the Knowledge Areas. Instead it is now claimed to be a Project Management Guide that is based on "Principles". This ends up giving it a rather fluid structure which is creating havoc with many of the candidates and professionals who are trying to understand it, let alone use if for preparing for the PMP Exams.

The current PMBOK 7th Edition has the following overall structure: -

A. The Standard For Project Management and
B. A Guide To The Project Management Body Of Knowledge

The section "Standard For Project Management" lays down the overall principles and some framework related information as under:

A. The Standard For Project Management
    a. Introduction
    b. A System for Value Delivery and
    c. Project Management Principles

The section "A Guide To The Project Management Body Of Knowledge" has been structured as under:

B. A Guide To The Project Management Body Of Knowledge
    a. Project Performance Domain
    b. Tailoring
    c. Models, Methods and Artefacts

However the thing to remember from this structure are the following: -

1. Project Management Principles (12 in total)
    1.1. Be a diligent, respectful and caring steward
    1.2. Create a collaborative team environment
    1.3. Effectively engage with stakeholders
    1.4. Focus on value
    1.5. Recognize, evaluate and respond to system interactions
    1.6. Demonstrate leadership behaviors
    1.7. Tailor based on context
    1.8. Build quality into processes and deliverables
    1.9. Navigate complexity
    1.10. Optimize risk responses
    1.11. Embrace adaptability and resiliency
    1.12. Enable change to achieve the envisioned future state

2. Project Performance Domain (8 in total)
    2.1. Stakeholder
    2.2. Team

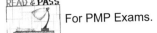

2.3. Development approach and lifecycle
2.4. Planning
2.5. Project work
2.6. Delivery
2.7. Measurement
2.8. Uncertainty

Now this is where it gets a bit complex for most people. While PMP is based on some content from 6th edition and some from 7th edition, the exams is still structured around 3 domains of People, Process and Business Environment as per the ECO. And this is the reason why this kind of structure becomes rather difficult to understand and comprehend. And this is precisely the reason why I have painstakingly created a book that is made following a logical structure that would not only be extremely easy to go through and understand but it would also contain each and everything that is mentioned in the PMBOK Guide 6th and 7th edition (and other earmarked resources and sources) which are important for PMP Exams. Basically this book makes it super easy for you to understand the entire content of the PMBOK Guide 6th & 7th edition along with other reference material, without having to go through that confusing structure that is creating havoc with the minds of those who are trying to understand it by reading all the different PMI resources.

My sincere (and I am not being arrogant here) suggestion for you would be to simply adhere to the content of just this book (without going through any of the official content suggested by PMI for PMP) and you will be absolutely safe, both from a practical understanding standpoint as well as from acing the PMP Exams, point of view.

The overall structure of this book would be in the same manner (more or less) in which we conduct a real project. Viz., Initiation, Planning, Execution, Monitoring and controlling and finally Closing.

I know what you are thinking, “But Maneesh, what about agile projects, there is massive focus on Agile in PMP now, what about that?”. Well to be honest Agile too is conducted in the same IPECC manner with the main exception of the Planning, Execution and Monitoring and controlling being repeated cyclically for each of the iterations, the Initiation and the Closing remaining absolutely the same. I have spent a lot of time thinking through all this to ensure that when you start reading this book, you do not get confused one bit, and understand it easily and be easily be able to shift your mindset between Predictive (traditional) Project Management and Adaptive Project Management. However before we get started with the flow, we need to first understand the overall basic project management concepts which is provided in the following chapter, viz., Project Framework.

The way I will be writing this book from here on, may once in a while refer to the 12 principles, but at no place would it refer to any of the Performance Domains. The reason is twofold. One, the PMP exams does not care whether you can relate the content with the relevant performance domain or not, they just want you to be able to understand the content of the guide and apply it in answering the question, and two, since the PMBOK Guide 7th edition's structure itself is confusing, hence replicating the same here would defeat the very purpose of writing this book. Besides, PMP Exams is still based on the earlier 3 domains mentioned in the ECO.

One request, though, please go through this entire book in the exact order in which it has been written, well at-least the very first time to ensure understanding. Later on, it would be up to you to read from whatever point you wish to.

All right then, let us get started.

6 Project Framework

Project Framework is not one of the Performance Domains. However, this chapter has a lot of importance as it helps to lay down the important project related definitions and terms which are commonly misunderstood. This chapter helps lay the foundation for understanding the rest of the Project Management journey. From exams point of view, a good amount of questions in the exams usually are from framework as well, thus making it worth the while to include a complete section on it in this book.

6.1 Understanding Project

The first thing we need to know is that there are only two kinds of work in this whole wide world, whether its personal work or professional work. The two categories of work are **Projects** and **Operations**. There is no "Third" category whatsoever.

Official Definition (as per PMBOK® Guide) of a Project is, "A temporary endeavor undertaken to create a unique product, service or result."
This definition brings out 3 main elements that constitute a "Project". They are "Temporary", "Unique" and "Endeavor" (which can also be stated as "Progressive Elaboration").

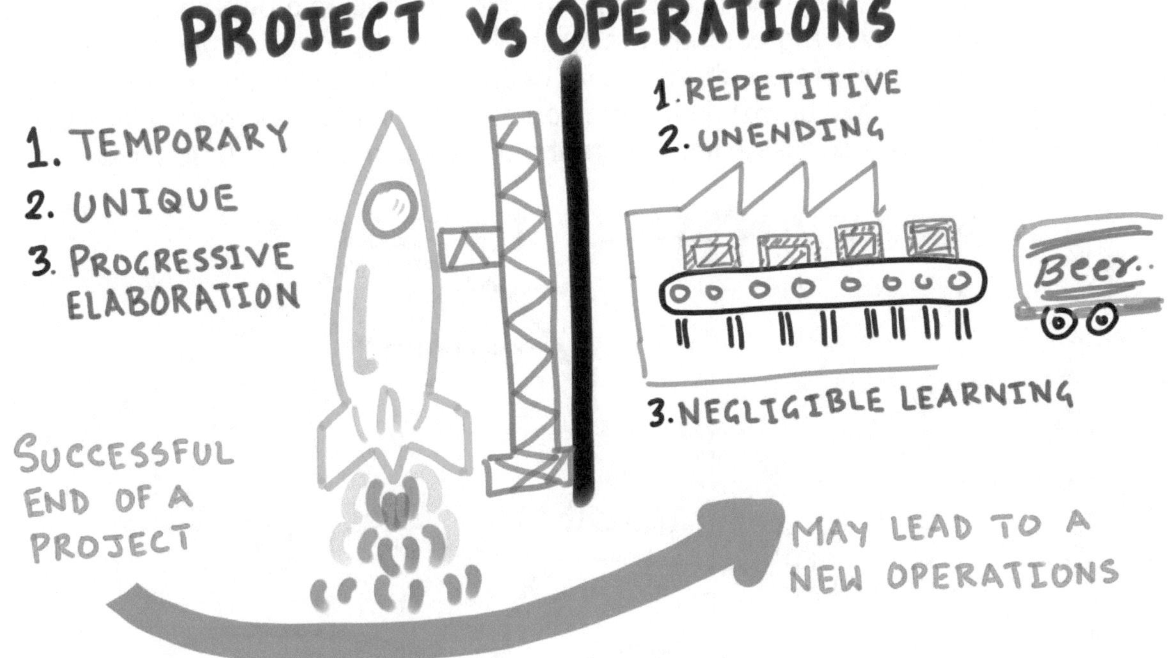

When you are assigned any new work or initiative, you need to ask only three questions about the new work. If the answer to **all** three of them are yes, then for sure you are working on a project. However if the answer, even for one of the three questions, is "**No**" then the work assigned to you is not a project but Operations. Yes, it's just as simple as that. And yes, this is the very trick you may use to ascertain what the question scenario is talking about, during exams. These questions are:
One – Is the work temporary? You need to understand if the work has an end in mind. The exact end date may or may not be known but there is a clear intention to end the work at a particular point of time. Remember that Operational work is not supposed to ever end. They may end due to some external factors like change in technology, or change in market

demand or a better product/service launched by your competitor and so on, but you never start Operations with the intention of ending them yourself. Hence if the answer to this question is "Yes". One hurdle is completed for the work to be a project. There are two more hurdles to go.

Two – Is the work unique? You need to ask yourself if what you are doing/assigned to you, has not been done in the organization before or are you using a completely new set of plans to do something that has been done before. Let us say your organization is a civil construction organization and has created a "Residential Housing Building". This building has been so successful in every way that your organization is planning to construct another building which is almost a copy of the previous one. You have been assigned this work. Since this is an exact copy of something that has been done earlier do you really think this is "Unique" in any way? The answer is that if you make a new plan for this assignment and provide for the challenges of the new locations, new regulations, ensuring that you do not repeat the mistakes made while executing the earlier project and as such trying to optimize investment in this new work, than you have been assigned "Unique" work.

And Finally, **Three – Is there "Progressive Elaboration" during this work?** Progressive Elaboration means that the understanding of the work improves as you spend more time in the work. This is hardly prevalent in operations. In fact, one gets into operations once the work has been completely "Progressively Elaborated". Projects are uncertain by nature. During the beginning of the project, there is a lot of uncertainty, however, understanding improves (uncertainty comes down) during the course of the project as more things become clearer. The elaboration is complete just before the project is handed over to the operations.

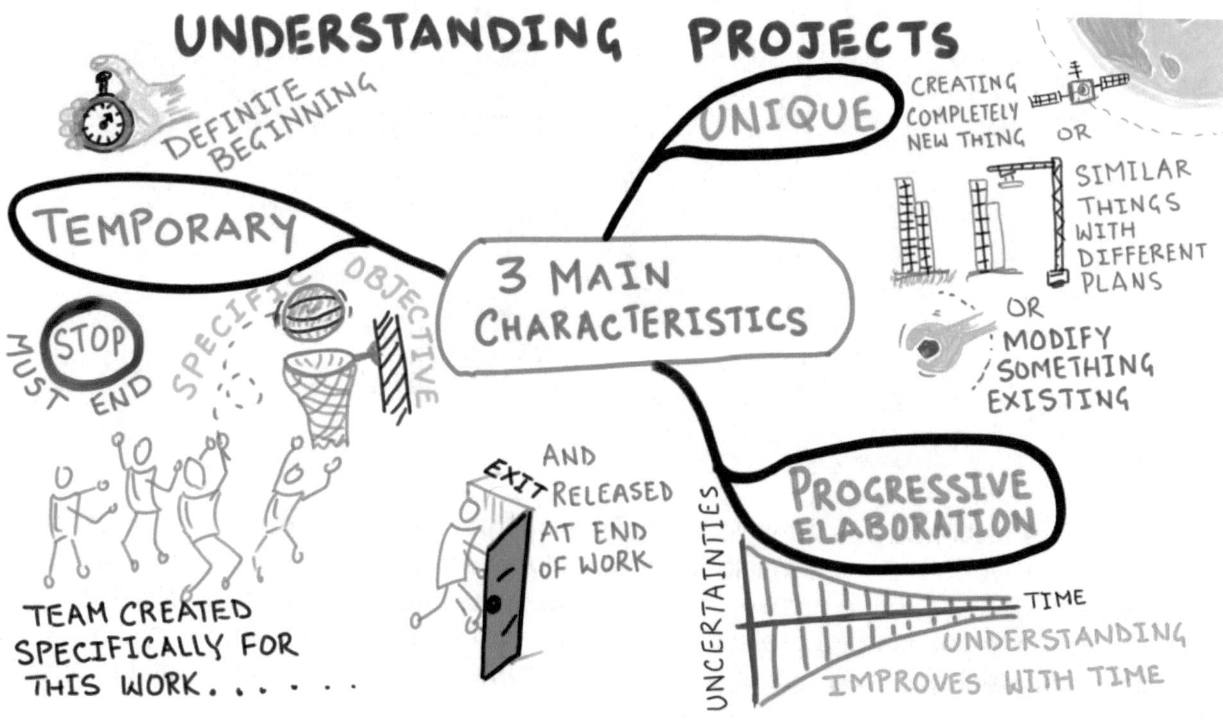

Please understand that Projects can be huge, like setting up an offshore oil drilling platform or sending another mission to Mars, or it could be rather small like holding a conference on "Soft Skills" for your employees with an external speaker. A project could be connected to

your professional world like "Green Belt Six Sigma Project to reduce the number of latent defects found by your customer" or connected to your personal life like organizing a birthday of your 4 years old child at your own home where all friends of your child are invited.
A project could have a physical and tangible end product like a 10 story hotel building or it could be intangible service like "Process improvement which would create a much better brand recognition and goodwill in the market for your soap brand".

There are only two ways for a Project to officially end. One is "Termination" and other is "Handover to Operations". Termination of a project can happen at any stage.

Let us look at some examples of Projects and Operations.

- Sending your kid to school every single day. **Operations**.
- Getting your kid admitted to a new school. **Project**.
- Each of the rocket launches for putting satellites in orbit by NASA, ISRO or ESA. **Project.**
- Daily publication of a newspaper. **Operations.**
- Special news publication edition, dedicated to the upcoming Olympics event. **Project.**
- Running standard workshops on PMP® by the training organization **PM-Pulse**. **Operations**
- Organizing a customized session for a corporate entity on Project Management to target their specific needs and improvement areas. **Project.**
- Soap Manufacturing. **Operations.**
- Creation of the first prototype soap. **Project.**
- Software maintenance. **Operations.**
- Software Enhancement. **Project.**
- Renovation of an existing building. **Project.**
- Routine financial audits. **Operations.**
- Implementation of a new financial and taxation system. **Project.**
- Extension of an existing building by adding two new rooms. **Project.**
- Installing a product on the client/customer side. **Project**.
- Running of a Help Desk set up. **Operations.**
- Installation of a new Help Desk set up. **Project.**

If for each of the examples you have applied the "Three Question Test" explained above, I am sure you have a very clear picture of what is really a project and what is not.

6.2 Reason For Projects

Projects are initiated/authorized within an organization for a variety of strategic reasons, some of them are:

1. **Market demand:** This refers to a general demand for a kind of product in the market which is large enough to warrant the effort for trying to meet that demand. (*e.g., A computer manufacturer initiates a project to create a hybrid computer which works as a full-fledged computer as well as a touch screen tab to harness a huge market demand for devices that are both portable and yet pack a lot of features*).
2. **Business need or Strategic Opportunity**: This refers to a need within an organization which needs to be met to help it attain some elements of the overall organizational strategy or it refers to a new opportunity which needs to be capitalized

on, to meet its organizational objectives. (*e.g., A car manufacturing organization which has 5 yrs. strategy to be the largest supplier of non-commercial vehicles in the entire Asia-Pacific region authorizes a project to create an "Electric Car" to help achieve their strategic goals faster.)*

3. **Social Need:** This refers to the initiatives for social work. Such projects are mostly done by Governmental bodies or Non-Governmental bodies (NGO's) and Charitable Associations. (*e.g., The Ministry of Health initiated a project for a 500-bed "Diabetes" specialty hospital to be built up in an area which has shown an alarming rise in the number of Diabetes patients*).
4. **Environmental Considerations:** This refers to initiatives to help restore environmental balance in an area or to reduce the effect of environmentally harmful emissions or to reduce the emissions of environmentally harmful substances. (*e.g., City Municipality authorizes a drive for planting a million trees within the city limits to help recycle the carbon dioxide produced by various sources within the city.*)
5. **Customer Request:** This refers to a specific demand from a specific customer to get something created which is not otherwise available off the shelf. (*e.g., A hotel chain has hired one of the top construction companies to build a 5-star deluxe hotel right next to the new international airport. Hence the Construction Company has authorized a construction project due to specific customer demand.*).
6. **Technological Advances:** Refers to "Migration and upgrade" initiatives which are related to the technological advances thus allowing more to be done which was not possible earlier. Such initiatives are triggered by the advancement in the technology itself. (*e.g. A Bank initiates a project to replace its "Legacy" core banking system to most recent "Core Banking Engine" that has much more flexibility, availability, speed, security, and modularity.*)
7. **Legal Requirement:** This refers to the initiatives being undertaken solely to meet government regulations. (*e.g., A paper manufacturing plant authorizing a project for installing "11 Water treatment and sedimentation plants" to clarify its industrial sewage before releasing it into the river to meet the new regulation initiated by the environmental ministry*).
8. **Competitive Forces:** This refers to a project sanctioned by an organization to meet or supersede competitive forces. (*e.g., A soap manufacturing company initiating a project for developing a low-cost organic ingredient soap with lesser chemicals and more plant and fruit-based extracts to counter a new launch by a rival company to corner the new urban middle-class market which has now become increasingly conscious of the harmful chemicals in regular soap.*)
9. **Material Issues:** This refers to the projects that are initiated to repair or redo damaged or flawed parts of the project due to wrong, substandard or insufficient material that may have been used during the development stage of the project. Such projects also get initiated to find a substitute for a material that may have become too expensive, rare or redundant. (*e.g., A road construction company launching a new project to find the substitute for regular asphalt for road construction at high altitudes and which would withstand the extreme weather and slow-moving traffic better and last longer than asphalt.)*
10. **Political Changes:** Some projects are initiated due to changes in political office bearers to either undo what had been done earlier or to start a brand new project or to start a new version of the project that has been going on, to further their political interests. (*e.g., A newly elected minister of a state initiating a project for creating a public grievance resolution system where each of the grievances towards public*

utilities and services would be tracked and assigned to specific government bodies and officials and tracked to completion and closure.)

11. **Economic Changes:** Certain new projects may get started because of changes in national or international economic conditions. (*e.g., Due to better financial situation and recovery from the economic meltdown, the company started the project for acquiring a new company, something it had kept on hold during the economically adverse conditions*).
12. **Stakeholder Demands:** Some projects may get created by some specific stakeholder's demands or ideas put forth by some important stakeholders. (*e.g., The managing director of the organization initiating a Six Sigma project to reduce the number of defects found by the customers by 65% with the dual idea of building confidence among the customers as well as reducing costs of failure in the organization.*)
13. **Business Process Improvement:** Some projects are created to improve the existing processes which may be either too wasteful, costly or just too slow and error-prone. Usually, a re-engineering project is created to change a process, pilot it and then release it into operations. (*e.g., The administrative wing of defense initiating a project to automate the stationary and consumables procurement system to reduce the delays and mistakes that are made in the current manual system.*)

There are chances that you may get confused between projects that are initiated due to stakeholders with those created for a specific customer demand; or between projects created due to social need with those created due to political changes. It is important to read the question carefully to see which specific reason for project creation does the scenario fall in. It is also to be noted that in most of the cases the creation of the project is due to one or more of the above-stated reasons for project creations.

While each of the strategic reason why a project may come into being, has been defined individually, it mostly happens that a project may be such that it would seem that it's because of more than one of these strategic reasons. However one has to see the "Primary Intent" of the project and that would help understand as to which specific strategic reason is being met in the given project.
(e.g., A car manufacturing organization starts to produce electric cars. In this case, it seems that strategic reasons could be "Business need", "Environmental Considerations", "Market Demand" and "Technological Advances". However, if the Primary Intent of the organization was to fill a strategic gap they had vis-à-vis a competitor which seemed to have cars for all segments, then this would mean that the strategic reason for this project was "Business need or Strategic opportunity").

6.3 Project Management

Now that we have understood the meaning of the term "Project", let us take the next step and that is to understand the term "Project Management".
The official definition of the term "Project Management", is the application of Knowledge, skills and tools and techniques to project activities to meet the project requirements.
Just like "Operations Management" is for Operational work, "Project Management" is for Project work.

PROJECT Vs OPERATIONS MGMT.

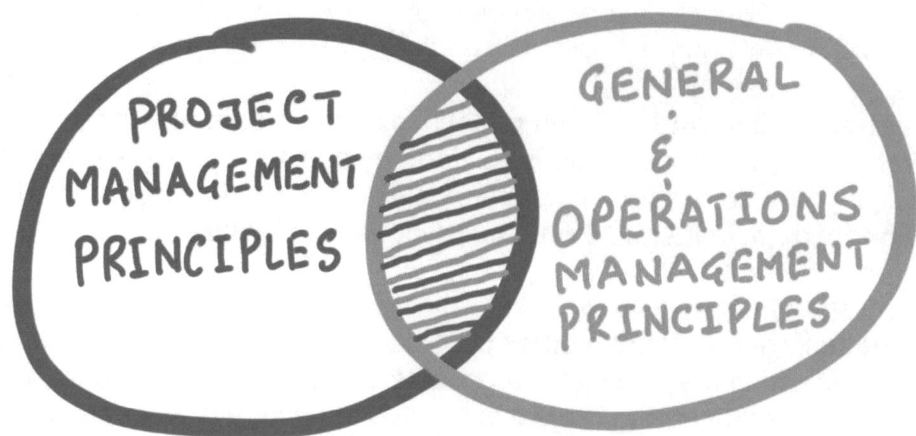

Project Management is the science of conducting projects from their beginning to end. This would mean the use of specific tools and techniques, specific project-related knowledge as well as some people skills, to get the project work accomplished.
Since this book is fully aligned to PMBOK® guide, Project Management would also mean the practical application of the applicable processes of Project Management, as listed in the guide, and in the manner as mentioned therein. It also means, and includes, all the 12 principles (something we will discuss in the following paragraphs) mentioned in the PMBOK Guide.
It is important to note that though the processes of the Project Management would remain the same, the application of it would depend on a variety of things like Industry, Domain, Organizational Structure, Approval Mechanism, Work Culture, Regulations and so on. Therefore Project Management simply means the "Best Possible" or the "Most Apt" implementation of the project management processes on a given project, using a specific project lifecycle, given the surrounding environment and circumstances and suitably tailored to meet specific needs and situations.

It should be noted here that the project management principles and concepts have to be within the limits of the Code of Ethics and Professional Responsibility. These are basically based on four values viz.,

1. Responsibility
2. Respect
3. Fairness and
4. Honesty

6.3.1 Importance of Project Management

With trillions of dollars' worth of projects are being undertaken in all the industries and domain across the world in any given year, highlights the importance of Project Management.
It is usually seen that the absence of proper project management in projects (hence poorly managed projects) give rise to several issues: -

6.3.2 Project Management Principles

As per the PMBOK guide the entire project management is based on 12 overall principles. This allows the project manager a lot of flexibility for situational tailoring without compromising the tenets of project management, as long as the project manager sticks to these 12 principles.

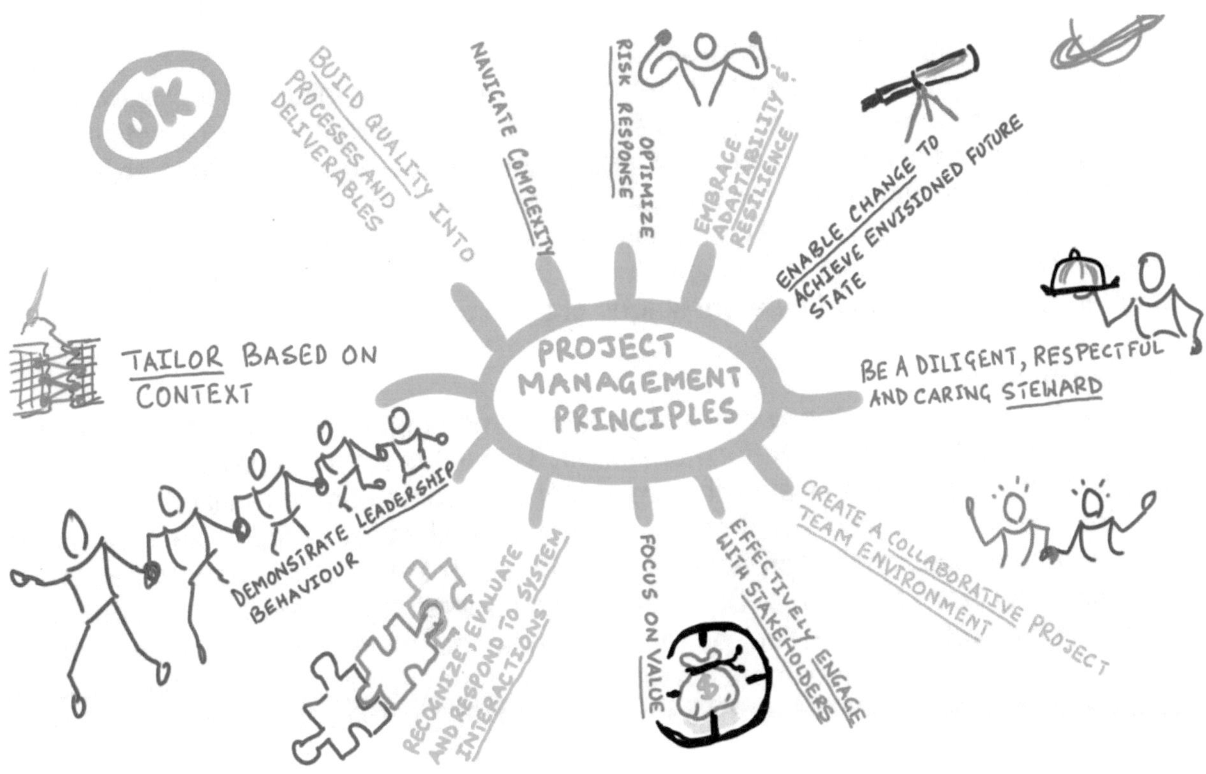

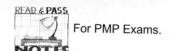

Let us quickly go through each of these 12 principles.

1. **Be a diligent, respectful and caring steward.**
   Stewardship is a loaded term. It means carrying out your responsibilities with integrity, ethics, care, and trustworthiness while being mindful of the external and internal forces, limitations and factors affecting your work. Here, when we use this term in connection to a project manager, it also includes understanding of financial, business, social as well as environmental aspect of the project. This principle basically talks about the quality that an effective project manager must possess. Being respectful has more to do with people, cultures and communities and the project manager must ensure that there is harmony and integration among cross cultural teams. Being trustworthy and being in compliance with customer or regulatory framework is also included as a part of this principle.

2. **Create a collaborative project team environment**
   This principle is another quality that a project manager must possess. The quality to build effective teams, that work in a collaborative manner (even in a virtual team environment), to meet project and organizational objectives. This principles includes the apt culture, use of specific tools and techniques, apt skills as well as the right kind of team members with the required personalities to create a team that works within the organizations value system as well as the organizational culture to deliver the project objectives. The main components that help in building an effective and collaborative team environment could be listed as:
   a. Team Agreements
   b. Organizational structures / Team structures
   c. Processes and
   d. Clarity of roles and responsibilities.

3. **Effectively engage with stakeholder**
   Stakeholders contribute as well as determine the success or failure of a project. Hence it is important for the project manager to ensure that the stakeholders are identified, analyzed in terms of their engagement level, prioritize and engaged with in an effective manner to ensure success of the project. This principle of project management revolves around interpersonal skills and communication skills. Since stakeholders affect each and every aspect of the project (or get affected by it), it is important to ensure apt engagement of different stakeholders at different stages of the project.

4. **Focus on value**
   Value is the worth, importance or usefulness of something. Every project is undertaken to provide a value to the organization / customer. This value from the project can be ascertained completely only after the project, but the value can be realized in parts during the lifecycle of the project. The project manager as well as the entire project team must keep an acute focus on the "proposed value" for which the project is undertaken. This also helps the team maintain a "Big Picture" and understand the strategic advantage / fitment of the project in question. As far as possible the value of the project must be defined unambiguously and in quantitative terms. Some aspects of the project value may also be defined in Qualitative terms as well. The main documents where the proposed value of the project is written are
   a. Business Need document
   b. Business case for initiating the project and

c. Benefits management plan document

5. **Recognize, evaluate, and respond to system interactions**
A project is a system. There are various methodologies that are used under different circumstances to achieve the project objectives. Keeping a systems view allows the project manager as well as the team to maintain a holistic view of the project and how the project fits into the overall organizational portfolio and finally the organizational strategy. There are other systems, like programs and operations in place within the organization, and thus it would make sense for the project team to understand the interfaces this project has with elements of other systems in play within the organization.

6. **Demonstrate leadership behaviours**
A project is all about people. Team Members, stakeholders and end users are all humans. Humans are complex, unlike the machines and tools. Hence, in order to work well with a diverse group of humans connected to the project, the project manager as well as the project team must demonstrate "Leadership Behavior". Remember, Leadership is the ability to influence people without authority. Leadership has various styles that need to be displayed during different situations. Leadership and its components would be discussed later in this book.

7. **Tailor based on context**
Each project being unique and is to be planned and executed under differing circumstances, the project manager must tailor the project processes and principles based on the specific requirements of the project as long as the project objective are met. Tailoring means alteration of the processes.
When a project is tailored with the involvement of a team the following benefits may occur:
    a. Deeper commitment among project team
    b. Reduction in waste due to unnecessary and non-value adding processes
    c. Customer oriented focus
    d. More efficient use of resources due to focused approach
    e. Increased innovation, efficiency and productivity
    f. More practical lessons learned that may give rise to better handling of future projects and better tailoring of projects in future
    g. Helps in creating a unique and more practical methodology for the organization
    h. Better integration among all components and artefacts as well as project teams since the project has been tailored specifically in favor of meeting project objectives and taking into account specific circumstances.
    i. Creates a culture of adaptability across the organization regarding projects

8. **Build quality into processes and deliverables**
Quality simply means conformity to requirements along with fitness of use. The end result quality cannot be obtained till the processes used for executing those deliverables follow quality principles themselves. The main focus of this principles is on two major tenets. One, Quality is not just the result of inspection but has to be planned in. And two, prevention is better than cure.
For each project just the apt quality metrics must be used and maintained. Quality is dependent on the level to which the requirements have been met and requirements are of

various kinds. Hence this principle would also include that each type of requirements are duly documented and provided for.

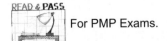

The major benefits of this principle are:

a. Moving the deliverables to delivery faster and with lesser rework and
b. Preventing defects by identifying them earlier in the development process

9. **Navigate complexity**

Complexity of the projects are getting higher now a days. The project manager must know how to navigate through complexity. But, what is complexity? Complexity is the result of human behavior, system interactions, uncertainty and ambiguity.

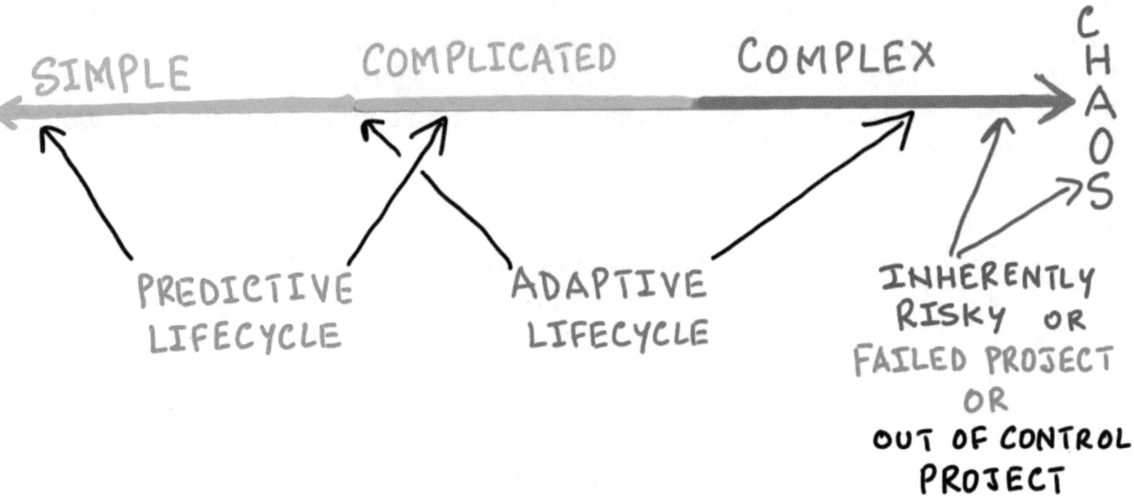

Complexity is also due to VUCA world that exists today.

Mature organizations have a method of calculating the complexity of a project and thereby tailoring the project accordingly. This allows a lot better control over the project under uncertainties. Different methodologies are needed for different levels of complexity. Some of the commons sources of complexity are:

a. Human behavior
b. System behavior
c. Uncertainty and ambiguity
d. Technological innovation

10. Optimize risk responses

Risk is any uncertain event that has an impact on the project. This impact may be positive or negative for the specific project. Hence a risk may be an opportunity as well as a threat. Response to the risk is what the project team would do about that risk depending on whether the risk is an opportunity or a threat.

This principle basically focuses on the following:

a. Responses to the risk must be appropriate and timely based on the significance of the risk
b. Responses to the risk must be cost effective
c. Responses must be realistic
d. Responses must be agreed to by the stakeholders / key stakeholders and
e. Responses must be owned by specific individuals

11. Embrace adaptability and resiliency

Adaptability is the ability to respond to changing situations. A focus on outcomes rather than outputs facilitates adaptability.

Resilience is the ability to absorb impacts and to recover quickly form a setback or failure. It has been generally seen that the following capabilities or actions tend to enhance adaptability ad resilience in a project:

a. Short feedback loops from stakeholders and customers
b. Project teams with broad skill sets coupled deep specific skills
c. Regular audits and inspections
d. Diverse project teams from varied experiences
e. Open and transparent planning
f. Small-scale prototypes
g. Ability to leverage new way of thinking
h. Process design that balances velocity of work and stability requirements
i. Open organizational conversations
j. Effectively using past learnings

12. Enable change to achieve the envisioned future state

Change is the new constant. It is the new normal. Business globally has become more volatile. Organizations need to keep evolving to stay relevant. Hence a project may be created just to bring about an organizational change. However, even within a project a lot of changes may be expected because of project complexity and ambiguity. Hence a good control as well as adaptability towards change is essential to keep course correcting to ensure that the vision is achieved.

6.4 Project Team, Project Management Team and Cross-Functional Team

This is also a good time for us to clearly lay down what exactly is Project Team. Project Team consists of a group of people who work towards meeting the Objectives of the project. Yes, it is as simple as that. This means that the Project Team includes Project Manager, Team Members (part time, full time or hired temporary team members or even virtual team members) and also includes vendors.

The project team is a superset and contains the Project Management team. A project management team is the group of people who guide and help the Project Manager to plan and control the project and they are dedicated to the work of project management.

The project team has many roles and constituents:-

THE PROJECT TEAM

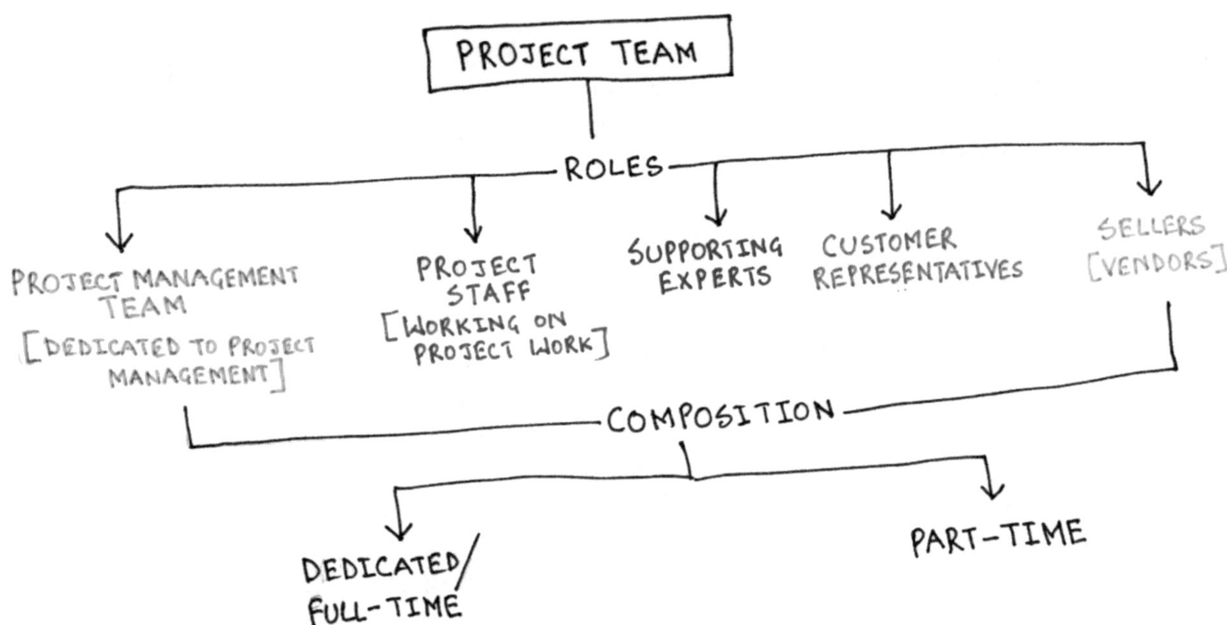

6.5 Sponsor

The very first thing to know is that a "Sponsor" is not the same as a "Customer" or "Client". I wanted to get rid of the biggest myth that people have, at the very outset.

So what is a sponsor? Sponsor is the person (or a body of persons) who helps provide resources, finance and other support to the Project Manager as well as the Project (or a Program as well) to ensure that the project is done in a manner that was originally agreed upon. The Sponsor is the person who is held "Accountable" for the Project while the Project Manager is "Responsible" for the Project.

This sponsor could be within the same organization where the project work is being conducted (a most common scenario) or could be outside the organization (not a common scenario).

It's important to note here that the Sponsor does not always "themselves" provide the finance or resources to the project but mostly arrange it and make it available to the project manager. This is very much like what the "Producers" of a movie do. They do not always put in their own money in a movie but arrange from multiple sources and financial institutions and make it available to the "Director" of the movie. This is the reason why the "Producers are more concerned about the Movie than the Director". If there is anything that is beyond the scope of work of the Director of the movie, the director simply escalates it to the Producers. Producers do not interfere with the movie direction unless they feel that the direction is not as per the original intent of the movie. The directors have to give a regular update to the producers who mostly keep a check on the three main elements of movie production, "Scope, Time and Cost". If you fully understand this about Movie making and the relationship between the

Producer and the Director than reread this paragraph and replace "Producer" with "Sponsor", "Director" with "Project Manager" and "Movie" with "Project" and you will obtain absolute understanding of the Role and function of a "Sponsor".

It's not necessary that the sponsor has to be a single person. It is common to have a body of persons to be a sponsor as well. A "Body of Sponsors" is sometimes also known as "Management Council" or "Steering Committee". This usually happens in the case of larger and more complex projects and programs.
In certain disciplines like "Six Sigma" a Sponsor is called a "Champion" as they are also supposed to promote the project among the senior level stakeholders, garner support for the project, and help create a positive atmosphere among the resources concerning the project and basically "Champion" the cause and purpose of the project at hand.

From the exams point of view the best way to understand from a given situation as to who is the "Sponsor", remember the simple rule Viz., "Sponsor is the person (or group) who (that) appointed you as the project manager of the project". This rule would never ever fail. This also means that the Sponsor would be at least one level higher in the hierarchy to the project manager and would be held accountable for the project. The Project Manager has only one line of "Escalation" and that is the "Sponsor". One of the common questions in the exams is giving a situation where the project manager has to escalate a situation or a problem and the question gives you options like "To senior management", "to group acting as sponsors", "to customer" or "to project management team" and asks who should the project manager escalate to. And well now you know…it's only the sponsor or "to a group acting as sponsors".

Sometimes a "Sponsor" is also called a "Business Sponsor" or "Executive Sponsor".

A quick look at the various things done by a "Sponsor" vis-à-vis a project: -

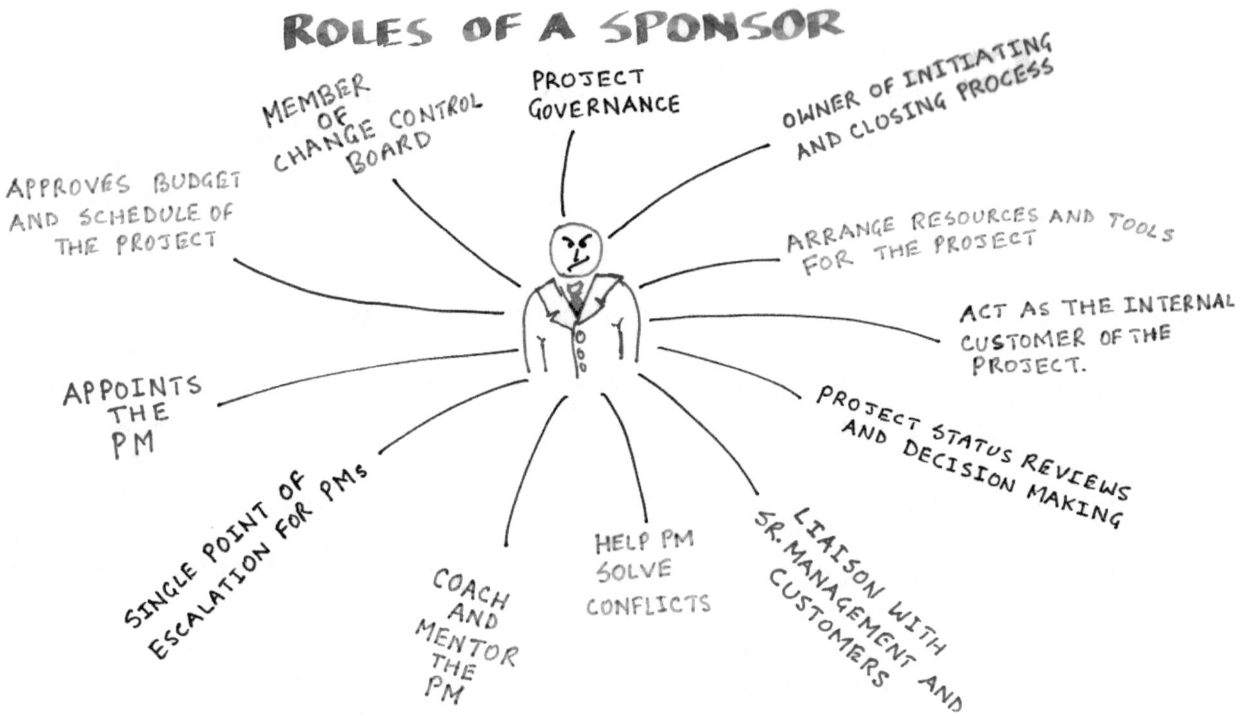

The content of the doodle above can also be treated as "what to expect from a Sponsor" or even the "behavior of the sponsor". This is so, because the questions in the exams my use any of the terms to define a situation involving the Sponsor.

The main areas where a sponsor supports and helps the team are:

1) Help the project manager and the team understand the ***Business Value*** from the project as well as the ***Vision*** of the project at hand. This keeps the project aligned to the bigger picture expected from the project.
2) Help the project team maintain focus on the Customer and what is it that they want. It is natural for the team to lose the customer focus while working on the absolute details of the project and hence it is the duty of the Sponsor (with the help of the project manager) to remind or reiterate that the team needs to keep a ***Customer Focus***.
3) From time to time, during the lifecycle of the project, there are several stages at which decisions have to be taken in the project. ***Decisions*** that are outside of the jurisdiction of the Project Manager has to be taken by the Sponsor promptly and without wasting much time.
4) Sponsor is ***Accountable*** for the project. And this is the reason the sponsor keeps ensuring that the project team is not deviating from the original intent and vision of the project at hand.
5) The sponsor also helps the team by ***motivating*** them from time to time. The project team must feel that they are making a difference and the fact that there is something in it for them. This duty of sponsor is usually executed through the project manager.

Sponsorship can also flow downwards in hierarchy as well. Say a "Sponsor" appointed a "Program Manager" for a Program. Once the program starts the program is subdivided into multiple projects and program manager appoints the project managers of those individual projects. Which means that the Program Manager becomes the "Sponsor" for the Project Managers that she appointed. If there were sub-projects and the Project Managers appointed Project Leads for each of those Sub-projects, then the Project Manager becomes the sponsor for those Project Leads.

6.6 Program Defined

Program is a grouping of multiple projects which are interrelated in a way such that they all come together to help achieve a strategic objective. A program may also have some elements of "Operations" in them.

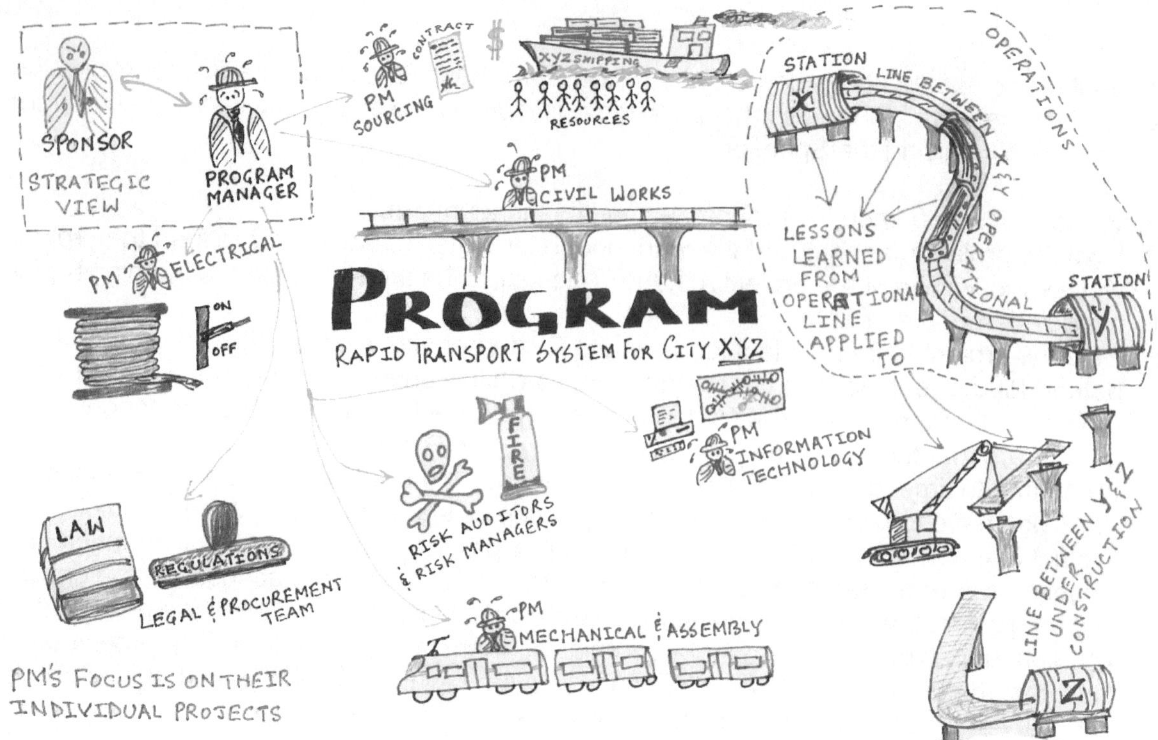

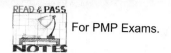

Programs are closer to the strategy of the organization than individual projects. What you must understand is that there is no specific reason or size constraint beyond which a project becomes a program. Bluntly speaking every single program can be executed as a single project. Most of the time a large or complex project is broken down into multiple projects to reduce complexity, reduce cost, optimize resource utilization, reduce risk, increase flexibility to change, work with changing requirements and such other reasons. Sometimes a project, when it becomes too large for a single project manager to handle and track, it can be broken down into sub-projects. In which case the main project becomes the program and the sub-projects become individual projects within the program.

Just because a lot of projects in your organization have shared resources and shared vendors and shared resources and even common project manager, does not necessarily make them a part of a program. In order for the multiple projects and sub-projects to be considered a part of the program, they need to be connected in such a way that they together help deliver a strategic or business objective for the organization. Because of the fact that programs are made up of multiple projects and once started, different projects would start and finish at different times, it does happen that some of the earlier projects in the program, get handed over to operations while the other projects are still in execution or even planning. In some programs, the learnings from the "Operations" are applied to the other projects in the programs, while those projects are still going on.

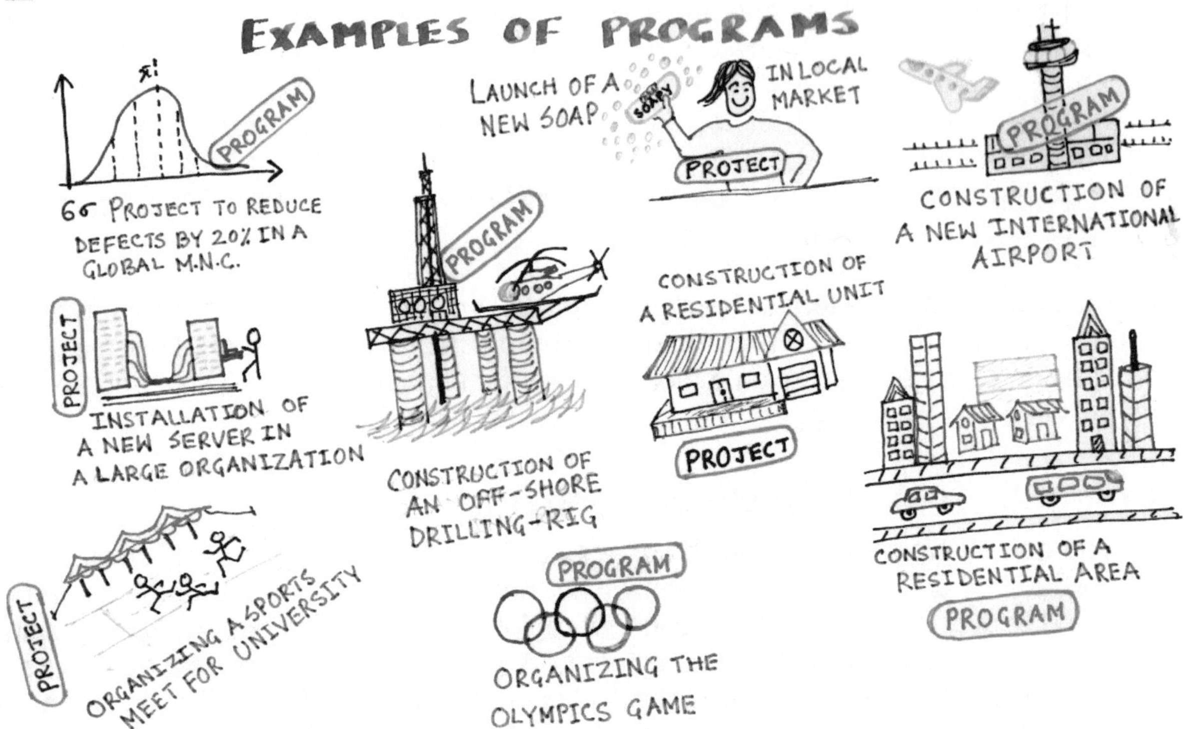

As a general rule, programs are more closely related to organizational strategy than the projects and hence there is more organizational focus and oversight on programs compared to a project.

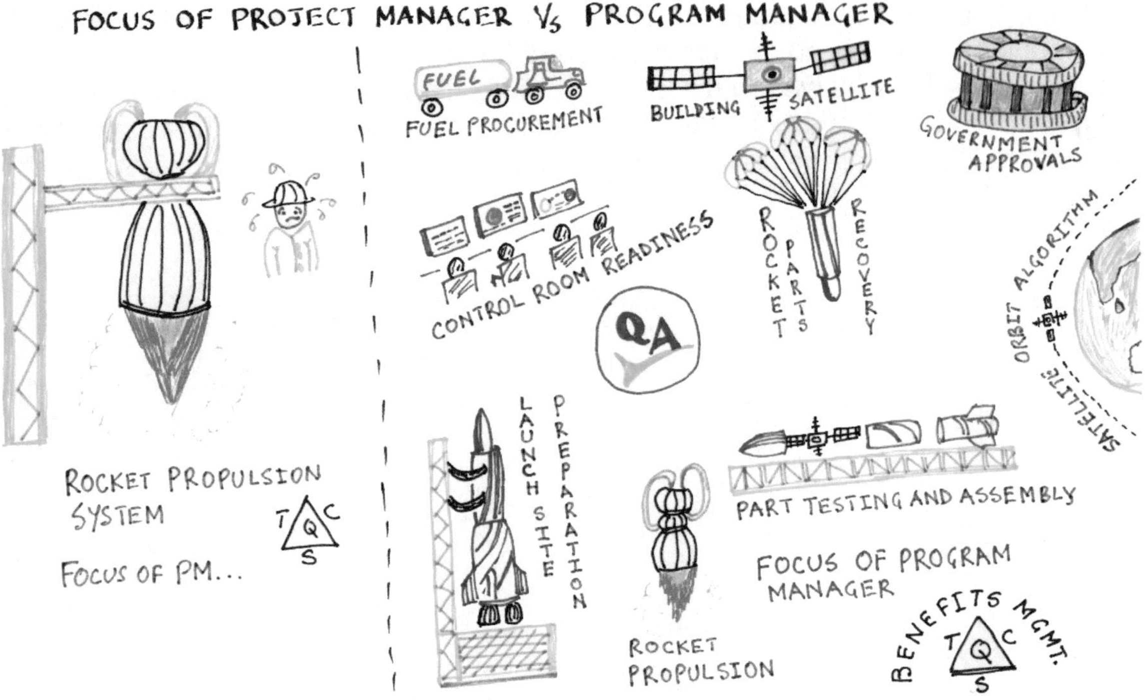

The focus of a project manager is on the objectives and targets for his specific project. The focus of the program manager is on the overall strategic objectives and strategic benefits that the program is expected to deliver. For a program manager, even if a project (within a program) does not deliver the project-specific objectives, it's of no major concern as long as the overall program objectives and strategic benefits are not negatively affected. *E.g., While the project manager of the Project "Propulsion unit", tasked with finding a cheaper fuel combination for a cryogenic engine, may fail to deliver the project objective but the program would not be too adversely affected if there is a provision to buy a cryogenic propulsion system from another space agency. As long as the entire "Satellite Launch" program meets the overall strategic benefit of placing a long-term geo-stationary thermal imaging and geo-mapping satellite successfully.*

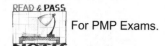

Please remember that the terms Program and Sub-Projects are relative terms and not absolute terms like a Project. Program and Sub-projects are always in relation to a project or a combination of projects and would mean different things based on the size and complexity of the initiative.

6.7 Project Management Office (PMO)

When you go to a typical airport which services a City, you will find a control tower. Ever wonder what they do? They are the ones who coordinate the takeoff and landings and parking and sequencing of all air traffic in that region, especially the airport. Now imagine, can you think of landing an aircraft at a city airport, which is rather busy, without the help of the control tower. Though the control tower does not fly the aircraft, the pilot does that, but the pilot has to work with the Control Tower to get the ground reality, has to follow its advice to ensure a safe landing or takeoff, to ensure there is no mishap, and such other things. I am sure you cannot imagine any scenario where it would be prudent to land any aircraft at a busy airport without collaborating with the control tower. Now let us change the scenario. Have you ever been to an airport (rather an airstrip) where you would find not more than 2 aircrafts landing or taking off through the entire day? They do not have a control tower. It's not really needed as there is no danger because of hardly any air traffic.
You must be wondering why we are discussing Control Towers when we are supposed to be discussing PMO's. Well, that's what a PMO is, actually, to all the projects flying around within the organization. PMO's are the control tower of the projects and programs within an organization.

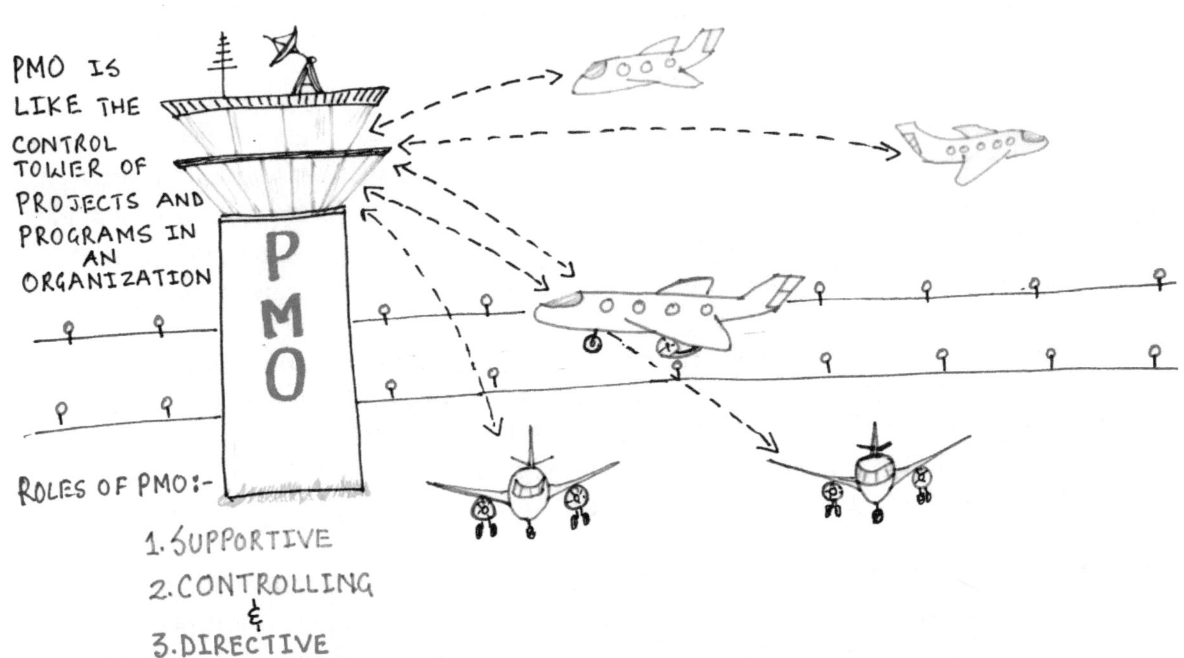
PROJECT MANAGEMENT OFFICE [PMO]
PMO IS LIKE THE CONTROL TOWER OF PROJECTS AND PROGRAMS IN AN ORGANIZATION
PMO
ROLES OF PMO:-
1. SUPPORTIVE
2. CONTROLLING
&
3. DIRECTIVE

PMO is an organization/division/ unit which standardizes processes, governance, project tracking, project dashboards etc., among the various projects and also becomes the central repository for resources, templates, process assets and learnings including historical data. PMO has three distinct roles and they are

1. Supportive
2. Controlling and
3. Directive.

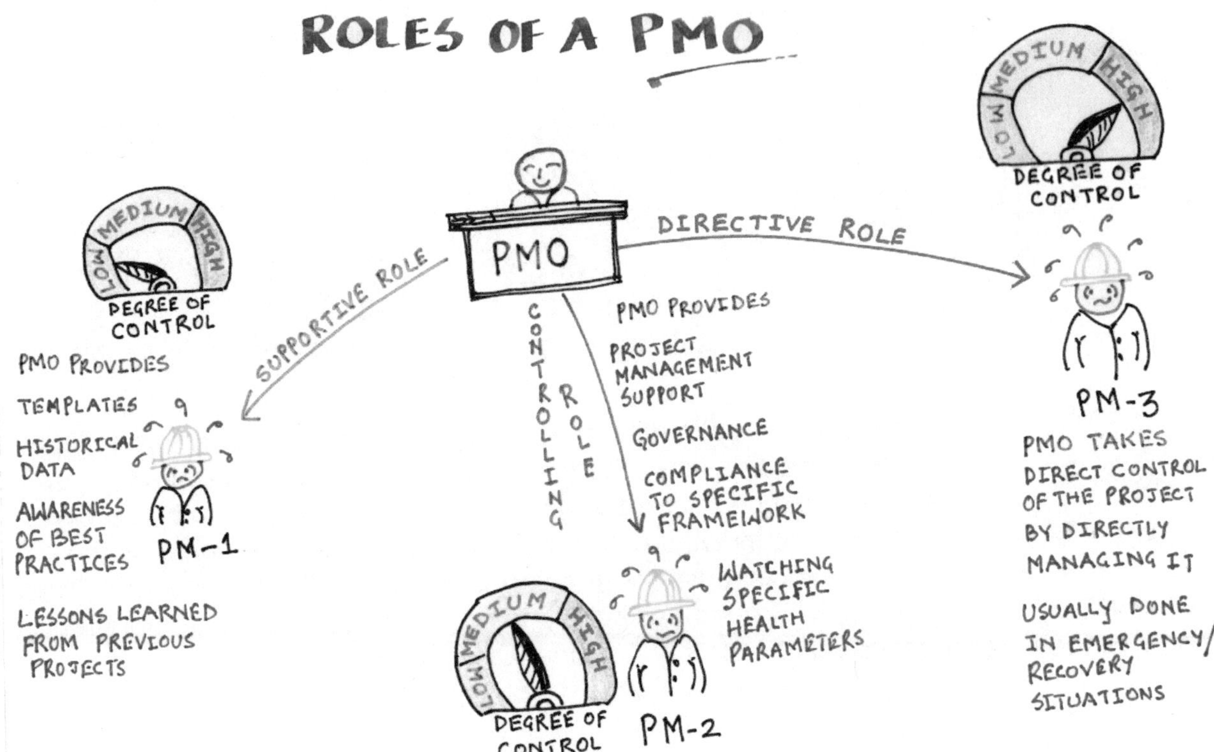
ROLES OF A PMO
PMO
SUPPORTIVE ROLE
CONTROLLING ROLE
DIRECTIVE ROLE
LOW MEDIUM HIGH
DEGREE OF CONTROL
PMO PROVIDES
TEMPLATES
HISTORICAL DATA
AWARENESS OF BEST PRACTICES
LESSONS LEARNED FROM PREVIOUS PROJECTS
PM-1
PMO PROVIDES
PROJECT MANAGEMENT SUPPORT
GOVERNANCE
COMPLIANCE TO SPECIFIC FRAMEWORK
WATCHING SPECIFIC HEALTH PARAMETERS
PM-2
PM-3
PMO TAKES DIRECT CONTROL OF THE PROJECT BY DIRECTLY MANAGING IT
USUALLY DONE IN EMERGENCY/ RECOVERY SITUATIONS

The PMO is also responsible to make a dashboard for the Portfolio and decision makers, about how the investments are being used in projects and programs and how the various strategic objectives are being achieved and at what cost.

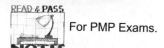

Project Management Office (PMO) should not be confused with Program Office which is basically the office of the Program Manager for a program which is entirely focused on the projects and sub-projects being planned and executed within that program. Program Offices, ultimately report to or obtains guidance and consulting from PMO. One organization – One PMO is the usual norm, however, in an organization, there may be multiple Program Offices based on the no. of programs that are being undertaken there.

PMO's are needed in an organization only when a substantial investment is made in Projects and Programs and hence they need to be planned, executed and tracked in a consistent and uniform manner. However, PMO's are not really needed where the number of projects done is very few and far in between. Remember the analogy about why a Control tower is not needed in an airport which has hardly any traffic.

In certain larger (read that mammoth) organizations there is even a hierarchy of PMO structure. At the Portfolio level there is the "Enterprise-level Project Management Office" (EPMO). And then for different divisions or even, at times, different departments there would be PMO's that would have to work within the overall oversight of the EPMO. This is very much like a distributed "PMO" architecture.

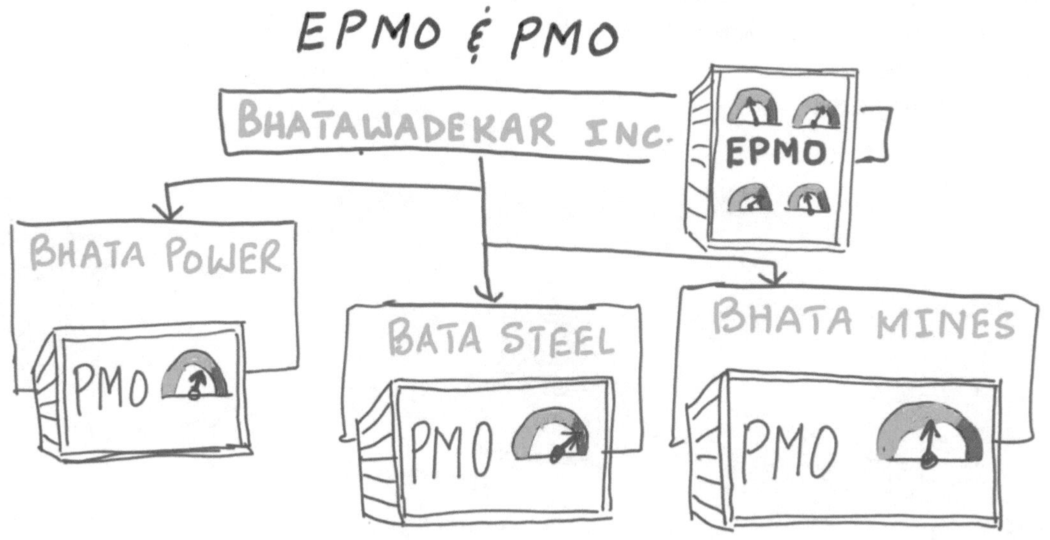

If you consciously keep in mind the analogy of "Control Tower" and Flights vis-à-vis the PMO and Projects, chances of you making any mistake in answering the question would be minimized. Remember the relationship that a Control Tower has with the individual aircraft is almost exactly the same as they have in PMO and Projects. Just like in a very serious condition the Control Tower takes the control of the aircraft (Ground assisted landing) the PMO also takes up direct control of the Project under very serious conditions (Directive Role).

Organizations which have adopted Adaptive Methodologies like Agile as their primary value delivery methodology, they tend to have "Agile Center of Excellence" (ACoE) or "Value Delivery Office" (VDO), instead of PMO. These bodies have more or less the same role as that of a PMO, just they have a different name. Since Agile methodologies mostly work with Self Organized teams, ACoE / VDO tend to only have supporting role and not directive or controlling roles.

If you try and generalize / summarize the key contributions that a PMO / ACoE / VDO make towards organization then we can identify three major contributions:-

1. Promoting healthy project management practices by fostering delivery and outcomes-oriented capabilities.
2. Keeping the "Big Picture" perspective by ensuring that all projects and programs are in line to the overall strategy of the organization through governance. And
3. Continually improving, sharing knowledge and supporting change management.

6.8 Portfolio And Portfolio Management

Let us say that you like to invest your money for the growth of your wealth. For this you may invest all your money in one single investment opportunity. This would usually be considered excessively risky (All eggs in one basket). Therefore, you would like to distribute your money over multiple kinds of investments with different levels of "Risk Vs Return" factors. This distribution of your investible money over multiple investments, for the growth of wealth, is called your "Portfolio". This same concept, when applied to the entire investment of an organization, is called the "Organizational Portfolio" or "Portfolio of the Organization". Therefore it's obvious that each and every Program, Project and Operations that are being undertaken by the organization is part of the organizational portfolio. Simply put, every single investment made by the organization is part of the overall portfolio of the organization.
For most organizations, the portfolio managers tend to be the top-most management who take strategic investment decisions, usually the "Board of Directors" or group of persons with such decision-making capacity.
A portfolio may also be broken down into "Sub-portfolios" based on the size and structure of the organization. *E.g., A large organization may have a global organization portfolio which may be broken down into sub-portfolios like Healthcare, Lighting, Artificial Intelligence, and White Goods. These sub-portfolios may be even further broken down to sub-sub-portfolio like "Healthcare Africa", "Healthcare Asia Pacific", "Healthcare North America" and so on.*

Portfolios could also be made in larger organizations based on "Lines of business" or "Verticals".

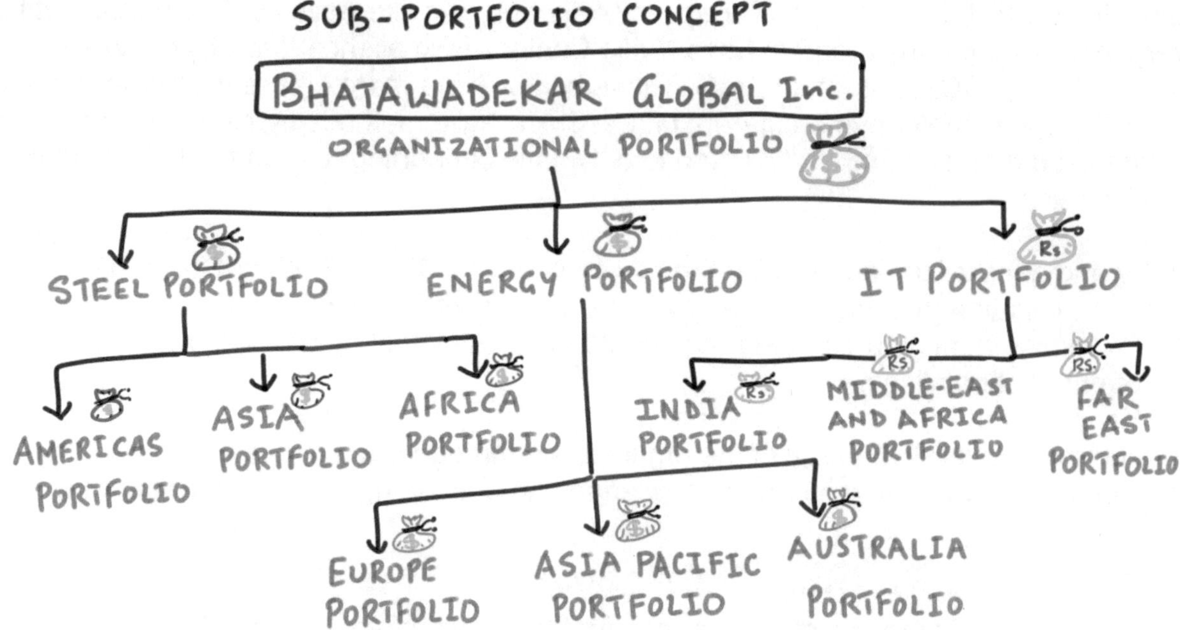

Portfolio Managers are usually the same persons who have the responsibility of fixing the "Strategic Direction" of the organization. Portfolio managers are "Accountable" for organizational strategic achievements.

There is a chance that in your organization you may be using a totally different meaning of the term "Portfolio and Portfolio Manager", this is so because this term is rather abused in the management world and tends to mean different things for different organizations and management institutes. It has a vastly different meaning in "Marketing Management Circles". Do not be confused with those other meanings. When it comes to Project Management as well the original meaning of this term, whatever that has been stated above is the only meaning that you should subscribe to.

Portfolio Management is the constant monitoring and controlling of the Portfolio investment and changing investment decisions (if need be) to keep on aligning all the benefits from all the organizational investments to the overall "Organizational Strategy". Different priority is also given to different projects, operations and or programs based on their importance in the overall portfolio and hence the overall organizational strategy.

6.9 Portfolio, Programs, Projects, and Operations – How they stack up.

Having gone through the differences between projects, program, and operations along with understanding what a PMO is, it's time to have a look at how do they actually stack up together in an organization. This stacking up would be different in different organizational structure. What is being shown here is how projects, programs, operations, and PMO stack up in a "Balanced Matrix".

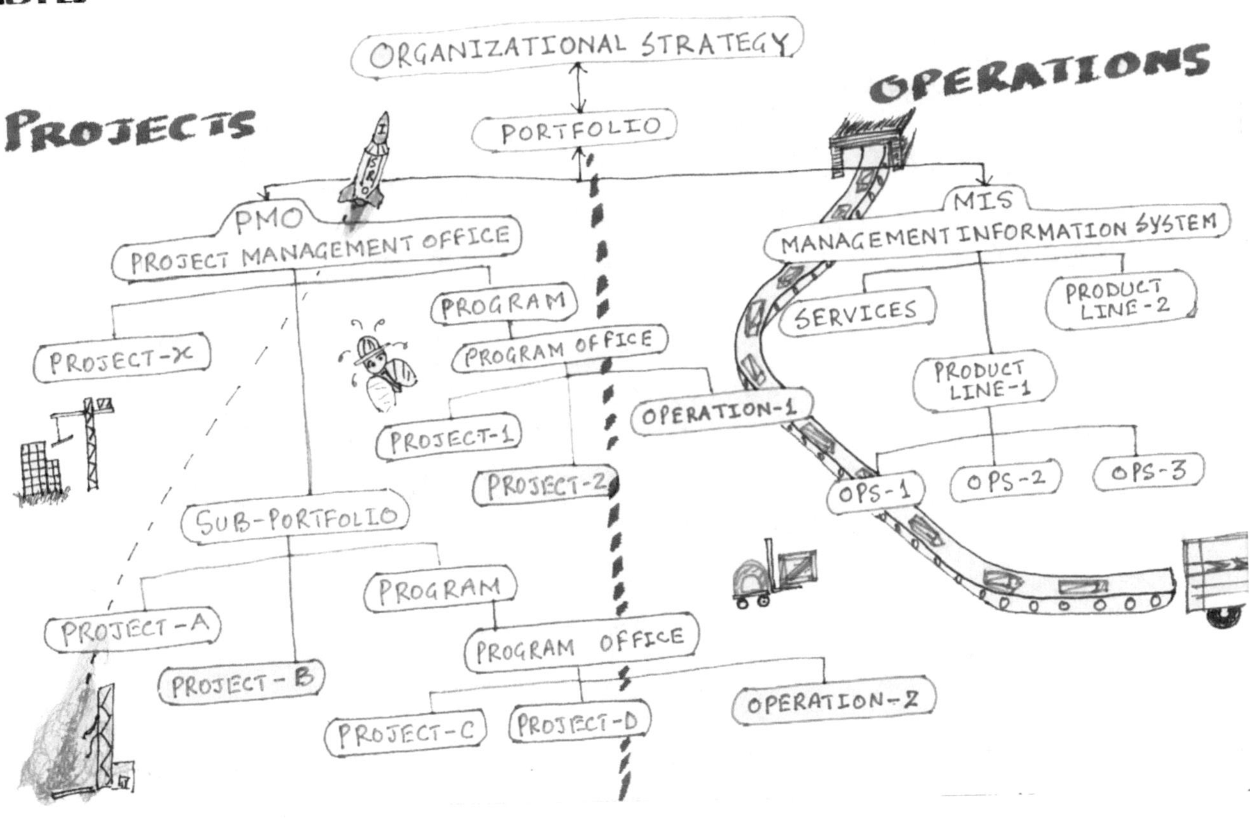

6.10 Five Distinct Stages Of A Project

It is important to understand here that every single project, no matter what methodology, will always follow the 5 distinct stages of a project. These stages are:-

1. Initiation
2. Planning
3. Execution
4. Monitoring & Controlling and
5. Closing

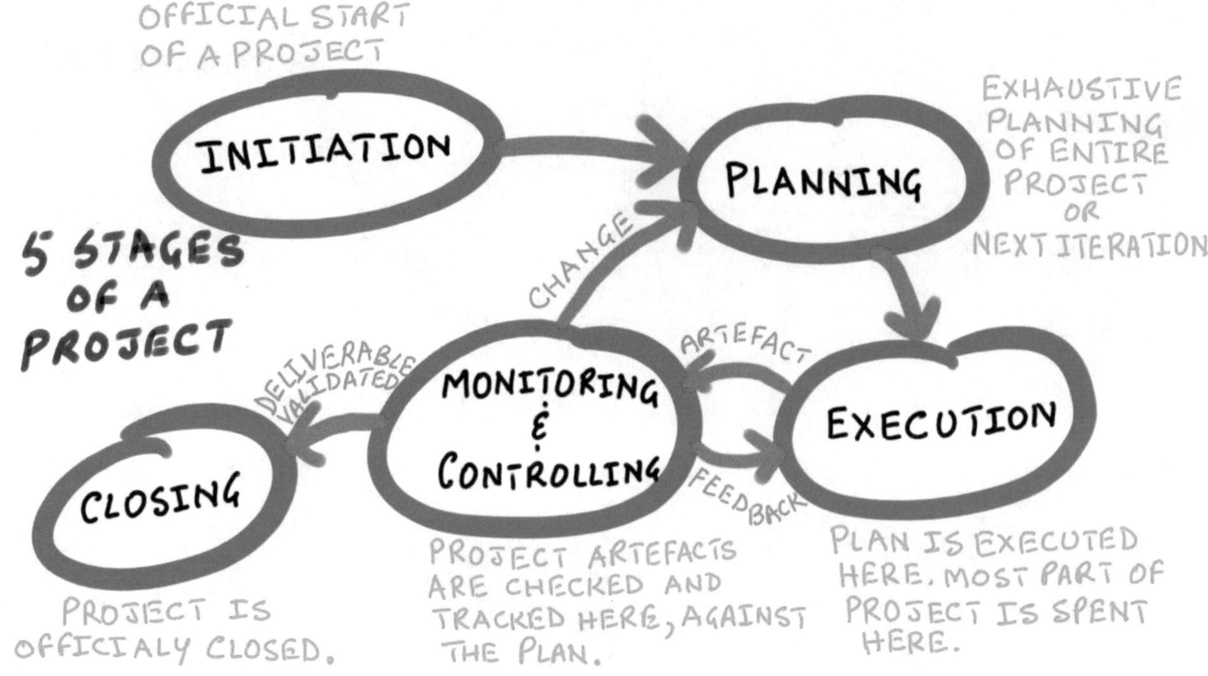

Let us have a look at how these 5 stages apply to the typical predictive project management (Waterfall Project) connected to a civil construction project.

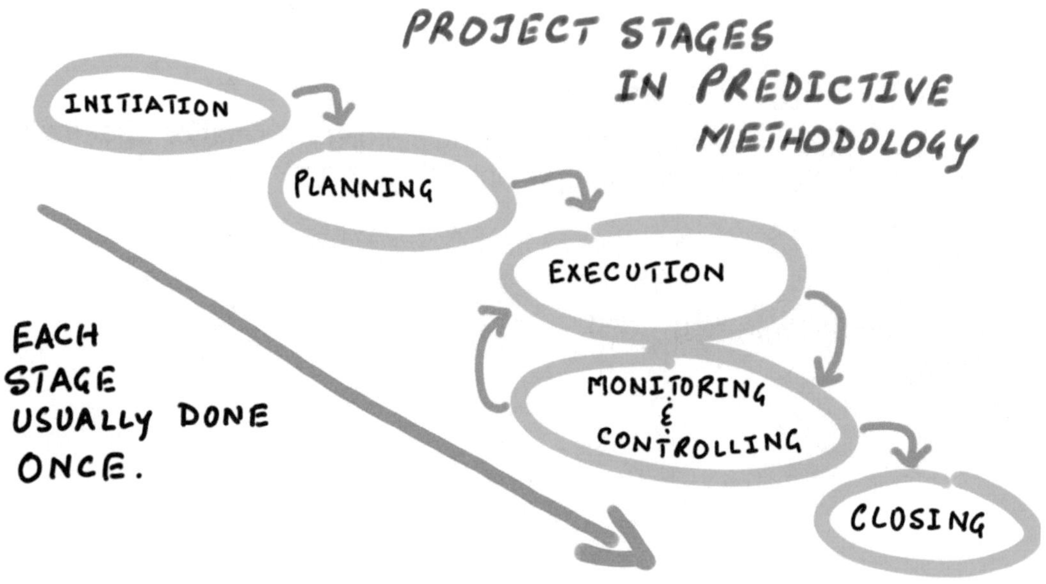

Some of us may feel that these 5 stages of the project many not apply to "Adaptive" lifecycles". Well, that is incorrect. Every single project methodology (something we will understand in further details little later in this book) is nothing but the manipulative implementation of these very 5 stages of a project.
Let us have a look at a typical Agile project using SCRUM (do not worry if you do not understand these terms yet, you will become a master of these topics in the very next chapter), for a typical software development project.

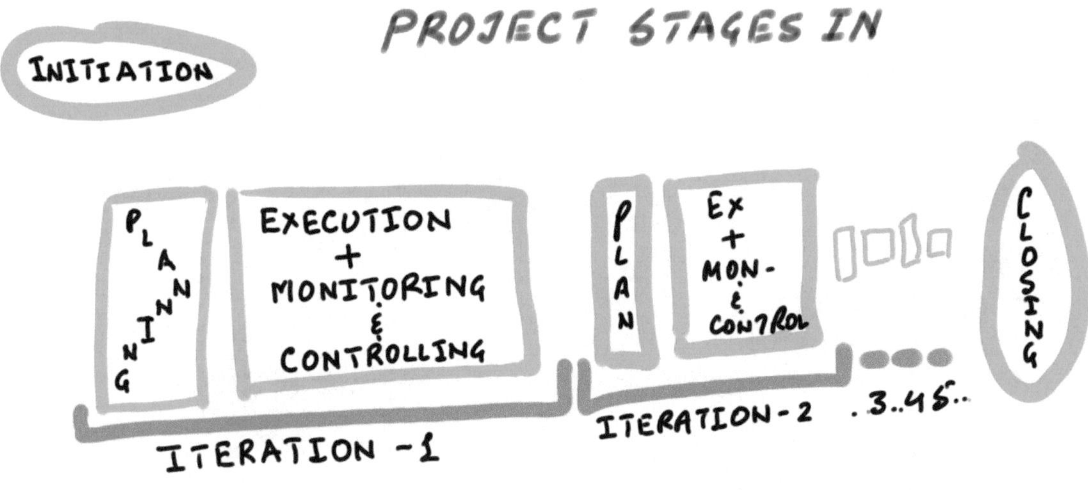

ADAPTIVE PROJECTS

While we discuss the 5 stages of the project, it is important to note a few things. Execution and Monitoring & Closing are clubbed together and called “Implementation”. These 5 stages are also called the “Project Lifecycle” in general. In a predictive project the least amount of money and resources are used during panning. The maximum amount of resources and costs are expended during Implementation stage and the costs and the resources quickly reduce during project closure. This means that in order to keep the overall cost of the project within budget it is important to keep the duration of “Implementation” as short as possible. This is because the more time you spend in implementation means more time the resources are fully assigned and hence the more time you are spending when you are spending the maximum amount of costs. The only way to keep the implementation as short as possible is by planning comprehensively. Hence if you spend good amount of time planning it does not cost much but it also helps you to keep the overall cost of the project down since comprehensive planning ensured shorter Implementation stage. However this brings to light another concern. The later in the lifecycle of the project a change is introduced the more expensive it would be to implement.

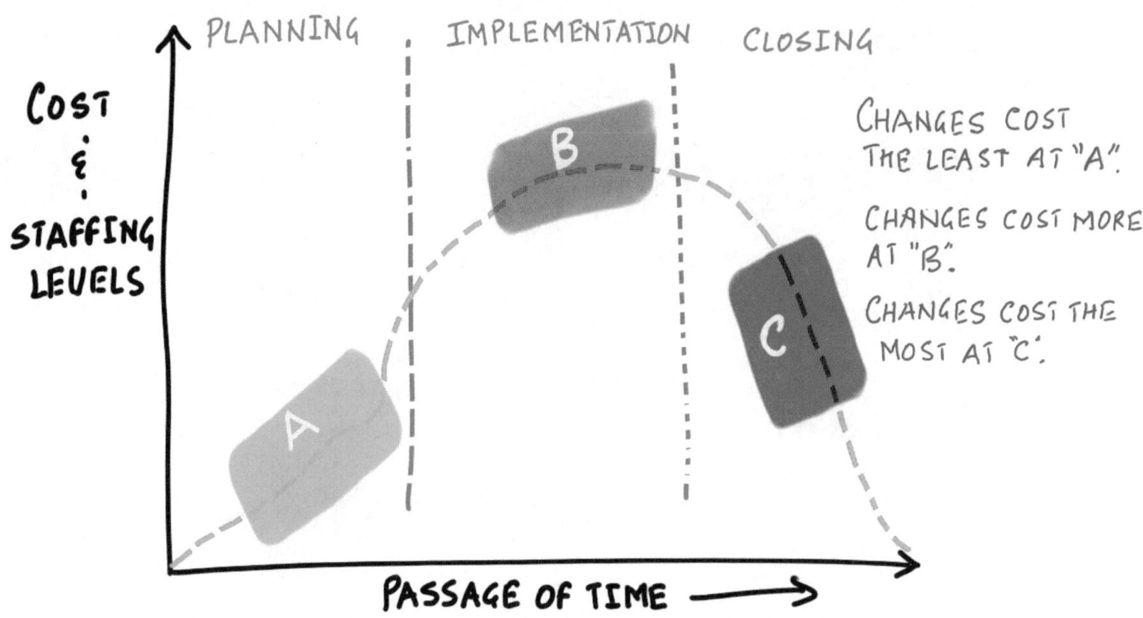

This is precisely the reason why it is not a good idea to use Predictive lifecycle when a lot of changes are expected in a project. To handle frequent changes one of the 3 adaptive methodologies could be used depending on the circumstances. These methodologies would be discussed a bit later in this book. Actually the very next chapter.

6.11 The Product Lifecycle

There is one more lifecycle that you should be aware of and that is the Product Lifecycle. Product lifecycle is the lifecycle of "Operations". Yes, operations have a lifecycle too.
Let us take the example of a new bathing soap that you wish to introduce in the market. You feel that there are some specific qualities in a soap that are currently not being catered to by any of the existing soap sellers and you wish to use this gap to introduce your new soap.
To be able to sell soap you need to manufacture them and before you can manufacture you would need to know exactly how to make this soap. You would also have to set up the plant for manufacturing and start a marketing and sales initiative etc.

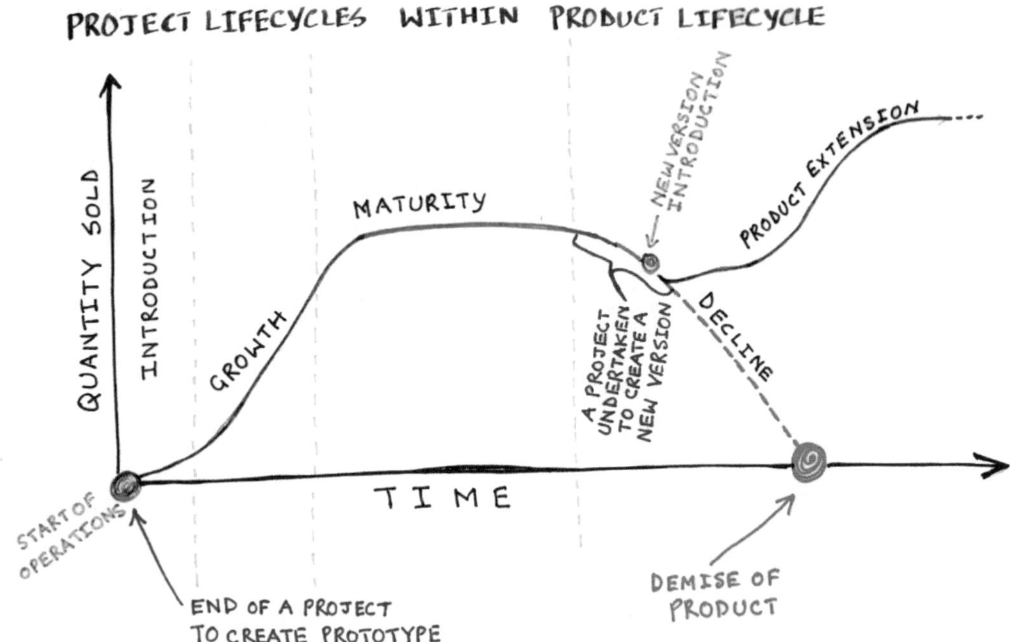

Clearly, you need to have a project that will find the correct formula of ingredients which would be used for manufacturing. You would also have to erect the plant for manufacturing soap. Once these projects are handed over to the operations team they start to manufacture and sell. The operations have started and so has the product lifecycle. Every day more and more soap are sold which means that your operations or product lifecycle are in a growth phase. At some time in the future, you will find that over a week or month similar quantity of soap are sold which means that your operations have reached “Maturity / Stagnation / Plateau”. However, over the period, you realize that less and less of your soap is being sold either due to shifting in market taste or due to competitor activity, which means that your product lifecycle or operations are in a “Decline Phase”.
In case you wish that your operations/product lifecycle gets back on track you may decide to create another project for enhancing the soap or create a new project for fresh marketing and sales blitz.
What you will realize that within every operations/product lifecycle there are multiple projects. A product lifecycle could also exist within a program since some programs do have operations in them.

Simply said, Each And Every Project Or Program Is Either Undertaken To *Create* A New Operation (Product Lifecycle) or To *Enhance* An Existing Operation.

6.12 Projects, A System For Delivering Value

The term “Business Value” is a strategic term and hence thought of and defined at a Strategic level. Every organization (whether involved in business/trade related work or not) has “Business Value” which is the sum total of all tangible and intangible elements of that organization. Some tangible elements are product base, services offered, patents, buildings, fixtures and so on. Some intangible elements could be “Brand value”, “Goodwill”, “Social Benefit” and so on. Hence it can be seen that even Non-Governmental Organizations

(NGO's) have a Business Value. Each organization has to undertake some projects and programs to try and reach its Business Value targets. Projects and Programs contribute to the overall Business Value.

If this sounds very much like the "Portfolio" do not be surprised as that's what it basically is. The strategy of the organization is to achieve certain Goals. These Goals would deliver certain Business Value. Portfolio devises the investments in Projects and operations to help deliver those strategic goals and hence help achieve organizational Business Value.

PROJECT AS A VEHICLE FOR CHANGE...

A system that spans the entire length of the organization cannot work effectively without clear and apt communication as well as an effective information system. When a strategy is converted into projects, programs and operations by the portfolio layer it is not necessary that all decisions taken at all levels would be correct and accurate. Hence the importance of feedback. Every layer below must give timely and concise feedback to the layer above about every single initiative. This information tends to take a more holistic shape as it trickles up the layers of the organization to ensure that the apt layer could decipher the information and act accordingly.

ORGANIZATIONAL INFORMATION FLOW

SENIOR LEADERSHIP
STRATEGY
PORTFOLIO
TACTICS, VALUES & OBJECTIVES
PORTFOLIO PERFORMANCE INFORMATION
PERFORMANCE & PROGRESS
OUTCOMES & BENEFITS
TRANSITION & MAINT.
PROGRAM & PROJECTS
OPERATIONS
FIXES & ENHANCEMENTS

6.12.1 Project Management Business Documents

Since each of the projects has a business value the projects must start due to some strategic reason. And since the projects have a strategic reason (Justification) they must ultimately result in certain business/strategic benefits.
Hence, the projects start because of two documents viz., Project Business Case (which documents the reason / justification / financial feasibility for starting the project) and Project Benefits Management Plan (which documents the way the expected benefits from the project would be obtained and maximized during the lifecycle of the project and after the project is handed over to operations). Both these documents are created before the start of the project.

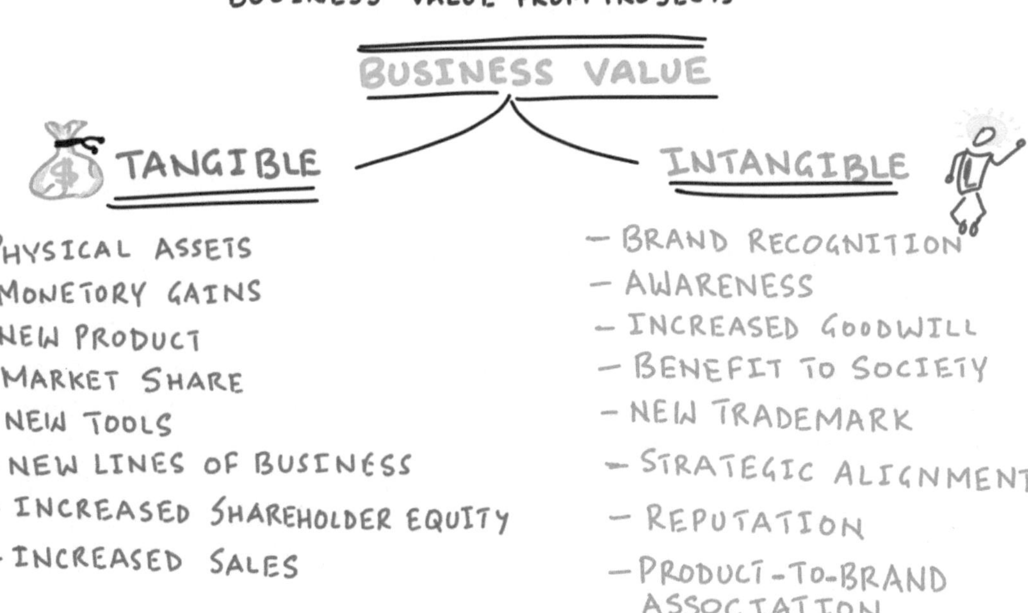

The **Benefits Management Plan** is created before the start of the project. However, the benefits management plan continues much after the end of the project as well. A benefits management plan is used to see if the operations are finally realizing the benefits the project was initially targeted to achieve. The usual contents of Benefits management plan are: -

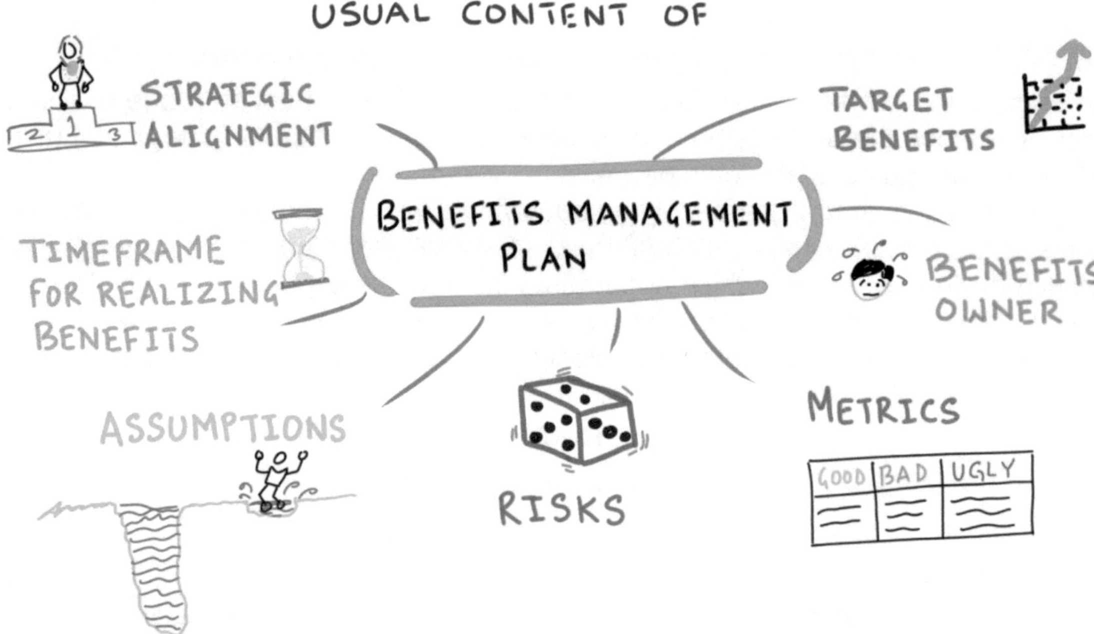

EXAMS SPECIAL

Remember the differences:
Objectives = What is to be done in a project? What is the end goal of the project?
Business Case = Why are we doing the project? What is the financial justification, strategic justification, business need for this project?
Benefits Management Plan = What strategic benefits would we get once the project is over? What kind of matrices would be used to track the quantum of targeted benefits achieved? What are the assumptions taken for the establishment of targeted benefits for this project?

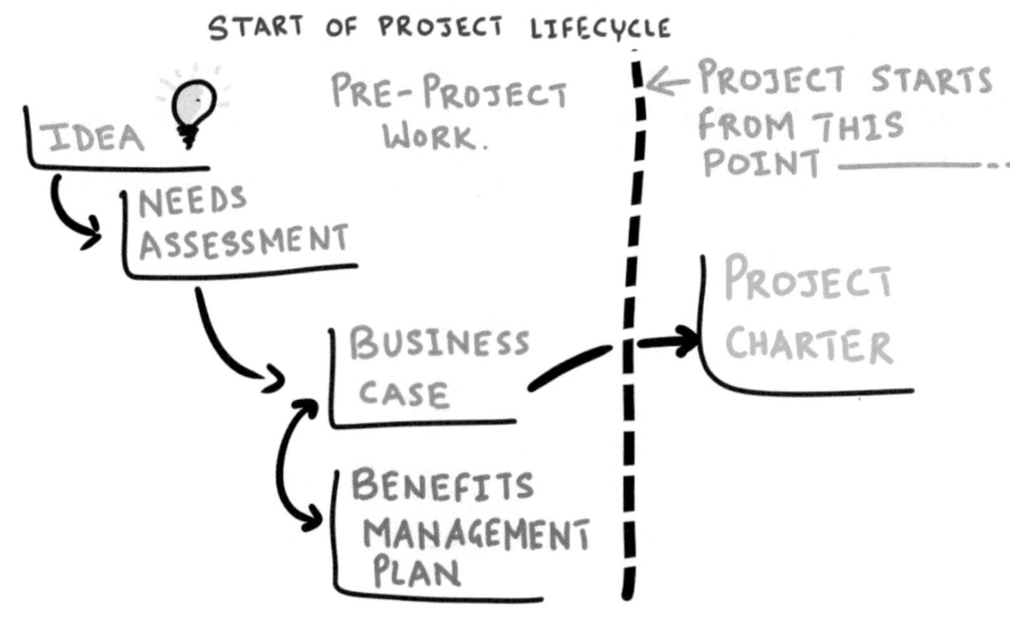

6.13 Environmental Factors And Organizational Process Assets

Just like a human being is shaped by factors like family values, language, religion, country, culture, population, economic conditions, tools of education at his disposal, employment opportunities provided, availability and access to schools and knowledge etc., after his birth till his death, a Project once initiated is also affected (positively or negatively) by the presence or absence of certain factors, which are mostly out of direct control of the project team. These factors affecting the project are collectively called the "Environmental Factors or Enterprise Environmental Factors".

Environmental factors have an effect on the project and therefore the project manager and the team must always identify and acknowledge the environmental factors affecting their specific project, so that they are ready for them, plan accordingly or include them in their "Risk Management and Response".

Different projects would have different environmental factors and hence need to be identified afresh for each of the projects.

One of the first things to be done by a project manager is to identify and list as many (if not all) environmental factors affecting the project.

Some examples (not an exhaustive list) is given hereinbelow.

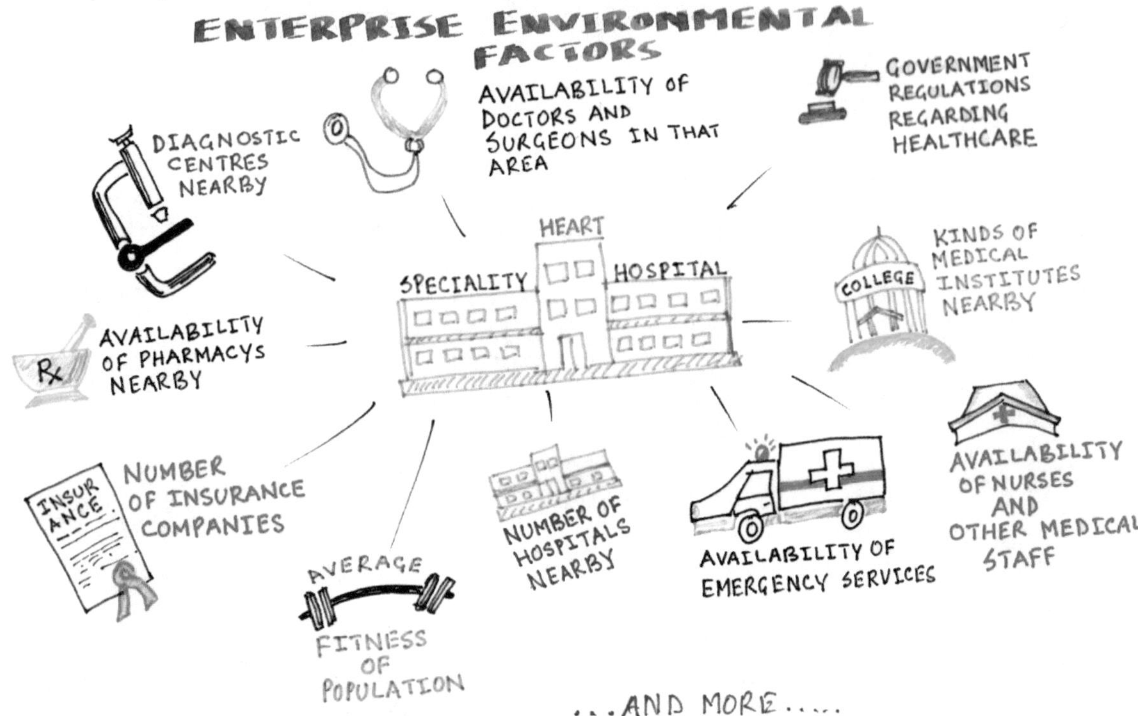

It is important not to get confused between Enterprise Environmental Factors and Organizational Process Assets.

Process Assets are just like Assets, things that are owned or created by the organization and could be reused in a project and would always help positively towards the project. E.g. Email Tool bought and implemented within the organization is called an Asset and not an environmental factor. On the other hand, if your organization has to follow the "Six Sigma Benchmarks" due to industry regulations or standards then this becomes an Environmental factor. However, the fact that in the last "Six Sigma Green Belt Project" in your organization has left you with very good "Templates" and "Processes" and could be reused in this project, therefore they are your "Assets".

On the other hand, Organizational Process Assets are the processes, tools, methodologies, historical data, technical literature and project templates, which, like assets, can be used repeatedly in projects. Project Managers must realize that they do not have to reinvent the wheel each time they work with a new project. Mature organizations have lots of "Process Assets" which could be reused thus bringing consistency as well as reducing efforts in a project.

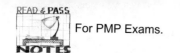

Sometimes people cannot distinguish between cases of Organizational Process Assets and Enterprise Environmental Factors. This diagram would help you distinguish the two clearly.

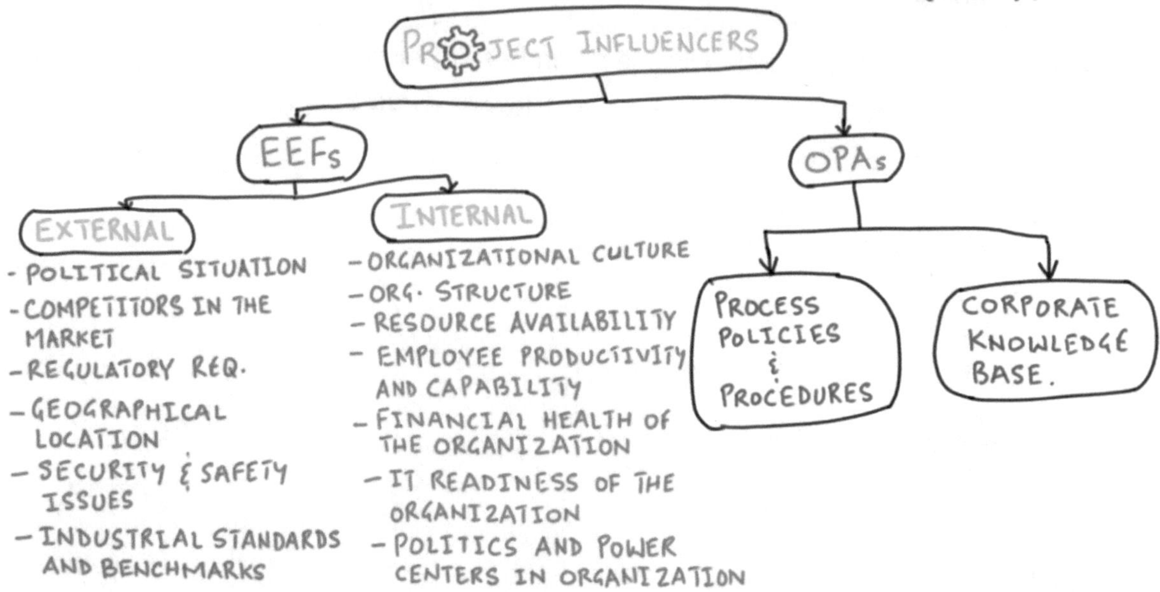

6.14 Organization Structures

This is a topic that needs more than usual attention as it is best to understand this concept rather than just mugging it. For some inexplicable reason, this is one of those topics in project management which is never explained properly either in training or in books published on the subject, barring just a couple.

It is important that you understand the basics of the topic well so that you do not have to mug up permutations and combinations of the questions that show up in exams pertaining to this topic. If you understand this topic well you would not make any mistake in the exams irrespective of the complexity and numbers of questions asked in the exams on this topic.

Organization structure is one of the environmental factors which have a very serious effect on the project. The way a project would be conducted would be based on the organizational structure of the organization where the project is being undertaken.
It is important to note here that though this topic is not specifically mentioned in the PMBOK Guide 7th edition, there almost total certainty that the PMP Exams based on 7th edition would have questions around this topic. Besides, the main purpose of this book is to make you practically effective as well, apart from just acing the PMP Exams, hence this topic has been added in complete details.

Every organization is created to conduct business. Based on the kind of business the entire organization is designed to best suit that specific business so that the organization could meet its strategic objectives.
However, we already know that there are only two kinds of work in this world and they are "Operations" or "Projects". This means that there could only be three kinds of basic business that an organization could have and they are "Business based completely on Operations" or "Business based completely on Projects" or "Business Based on a combination of both".

Let us take an example. If there is an organization that is completely based on buying and selling products (like a large departmental store or chain of stores) in that case their business is 100% operations. They are not into creating something new, they just want to buy and sell. Such organizations whose "Business is based completely on Operations" are called "Functional" organizations. They are called functional (they are also called "Departmental") because each and every resource in that organization is assigned to a function. The function (or a department) is led by a Functional Manager (also called "Head of Department"). Such organizations are created as Functional so that they can maximize the quantum of operations and reducing costs as well. This is based on the famous concept of "Economies of Scale through Division of Labor". Hence an organization is made into a "Functional Organization" so that they can maximize profits when their business is 100% Operations. Departments / Functions like Accounting, Finance, Marketing, Works, Design, Quality Assurance, Purchases, Supply Chain etc., are created and staffed with super-specialized professionals in that specific field of work and work in that department/function, more or less, independent of the other departments/functions. They report to their respective departmental/functional head.

However if, on the other hand, there is an organization which only undertakes consulting assignments from its customers and clients then they are only doing projects and absolutely no operational work. This organization would not have any departments/functions because they are not undertaking any Operations whatsoever. All the employees within the organization would be identified by the "Teams" or "Projects" they are associated with and not any department. This is the kind of organization which has "Business based completely on Projects" and is termed as "Projectised Organization. Such organizations usually have a skeleton permanent employees and hire staff as and when they have projects. Many infrastructure and consulting companies have "Projectised Organization Structure" as their business is 100% Projects.
When such organizations do not have any projects they usually end their contracts with the employees. There is no "Bench" (as there are no departments/functions to go back to for the employees) in between projects, in such organizations.

Most of the organizations have a business model that is a mix of both Projects and operations. They undertake some projects and also have some regular business lines. Which means that their "Business depends on a combination of Operations and Projects" and they are termed as "Matrix" organizations. It's called matrix as employees here are assigned to specific departments/functions and do report to a departmental/functional head but when a project is initiated the project team is taken on loan from these very departments and for the duration of the project report to the project manager. This is the reason why an employee within such organizations usually feels that it reports to "Two" managers.
You can see from the real world organizations that all "Matrix" organizations do not undertake the same numbers of projects. Some hardly undertake projects, some have an equal distribution of investment between projects and operations and some undertake much more projects than they invest in operations. Matrix organizations which have fewer Projects are called "Weak Matrix" (as project management is weak in it), Matrix organization which has more projects is called "Strong Matrix" (as project management is strong there) and Matrix organizations where they have more or less similar amount of investment in Projects and Operations are called "Balanced Matrix or just "Matrix".

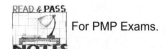

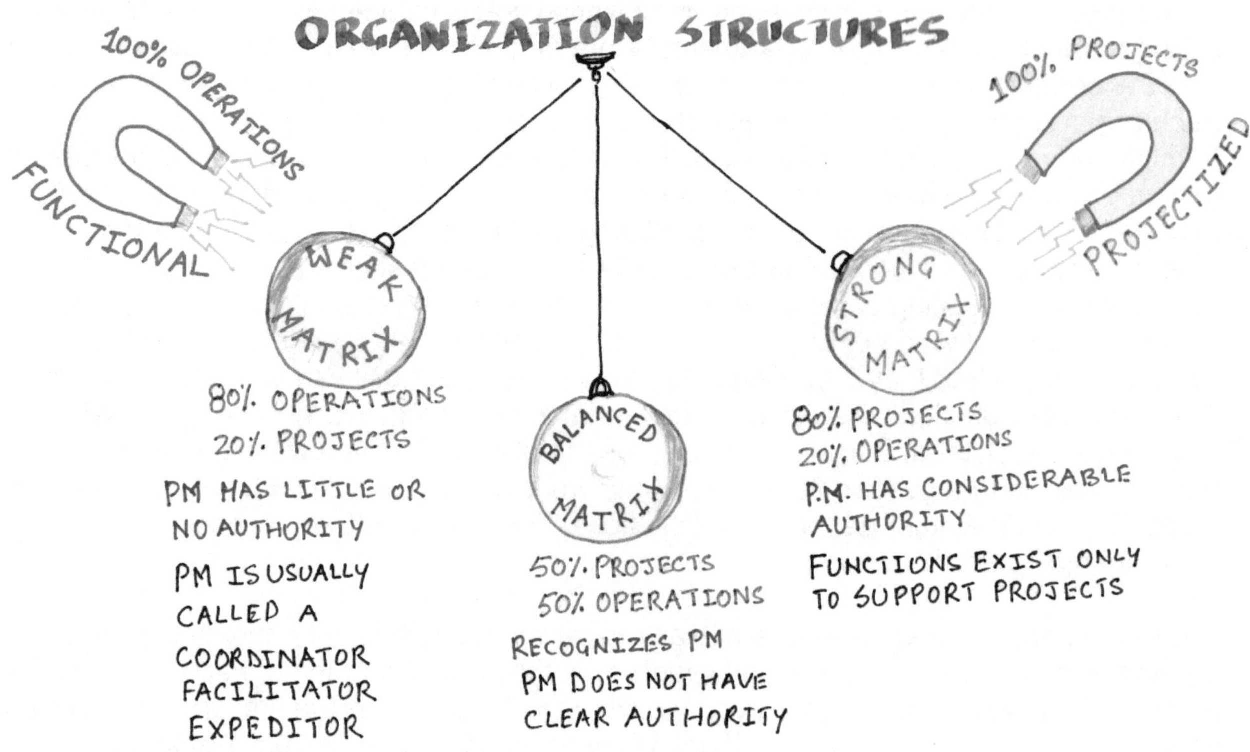

Just by understanding the 5 kinds of organization structures which exist, it's quite obvious that there would be challenges in conducting Projects in some of them just because of the power distribution among Project Managers and Functional/Departmental Heads.

6.14.1 Functional / Departmental

In a Functional/Departmental organization, the Functional/Departmental Head has all the power and full command over the resources. Since projects do not even exist in that organization, the project managers are not even thought of. Every person is known by the department/function they are assigned to.

6.14.2 Projectised/Project Oriented

In a Projectised organization, on the other hand, the Project manager has almost total power over resources and since there are no departments, there is no position of "Functional / Departmental head within that organization". Most of the employees are contractual in nature and once the project finishes the project team is not only dismantled they also have to move out of the organization as well. There is no department or a "Bench" for them to go back to.

6.14.3 Weak Matrix

In a "Weak Matrix", since there are so few Projects the business value is mostly derived from operations, the balance of power is in favor of the Functional / Departmental head. The project manager is usually not even called a project manager in such organizations. They are usually referred to as Coordinator, facilitator or expeditor.

6.14.4 Strong Matrix

In a "Strong Matrix", since there are very few Operations, the balance of power is in favor of the project manager. Here Project Manager takes all important decisions and functional/departmental heads just provide support to the project as directed to them by the project manager. There are departments and those departments have department heads as well but they do not have much powers/authority over the resources or decision making.

6.14.5 Matrix / Balanced Matrix

In a "Balanced Matrix or Matrix" organization the Project Managers and the Functional / Departmental heads have equal power over resources and decision making. This creates certain complexities in communication in a matrix organization as well as creates situations that are prone to conflicts and confrontations. Most employees feel that they are stretched between the demands of the Projects and the operations.

In the exams, you might be given a situation where they show that the project manager does not seem to have many rights or the project manager is not being taken seriously by the team or all the decisions for a project are being taken by the functional/departmental head. You can see that this situation would be about "Weak Matrix". This is because though there are projects (hence it's not a case of Functional Organization) in this organization the project managers do not have much power or say in decision making. If the exam question mentions terms like "Project coordinator", "facilitator" or "expeditor" it is talking about "Weak Matrix". If the question says something like "There is no "**home**" for the team to go back to or there is no Bench for the team" the question is talking about a "Projectised" organization because in this organization there are no Functions or Departments whatsoever. "Balanced Matrix" has most conflicts and communication is complex.

In exams sometimes you will get to see only the term "Matrix" which might confuse you because there are actually three kinds of matrix viz., Weak, Balanced and Strong matrix. If this happens than just assume that "Matrix" is "Balanced Matrix". Just using the term "Matrix" is the same as "Balanced Matrix".

6.15 Organizational Culture

Peter F. Drucker had once said, "Culture Eats Strategy For Breakfast". Take a moment to re-read this line. It has a very strong and relevant message which laced with heavy dose of reality.

How many times we have seen that an organization architect a new strategy to deal with the evolving directions and technologies in the business world only to see all efforts and millions of dollars go to waste because the people in the organization had a different or contrasting value systems that they were subscribing to. How many times we have seen "Corporate Governance policies" failing in most organizations. How many times have we seen modernization and digitization of several government agencies fail miserably. Why do such things fail? Why do so much of money and investments go down the drain?

The answer is the "Culture" of the organization. Yes! Organizational culture is that strong. This is the reason why Peter F. Drucker made that statement.

The obvious next question is, what this "Organizational Culture" is made of. Well, let us look at some of the components of the organizational culture.

1) Shared vision, mission, values, beliefs and expectations
2) Organizational regulations, rules, policies and procedures
3) Motivation and reward system
4) Risk tolerance
5) View of leadership, hierarchy and authority relationships
6) Code of conduct, work ethics and working hours
7) Operating environment

Culture is made of all these above factors because these factors tend to align the overall behaviour and thinking of the employees. This is the reason why every organization needs to align their purpose, culture, organizational structure with organizational strategy. If there is any misalignment among these elements the organization would be bound to have more misses than achievements.

Culture adoption starts from the top and takes time to percolate throughout the organization. Culture has to be kept consistent for a period of time (usually linked to the duration of the strategy of the organization) to see its effectiveness.

Any project or initiative undertaken in an organization which does not align with the organization culture is bound to fail.

One of the most glaring example of how projects and initiatives fail because of organizational culture was when Apple fired Steve Jobs and concentrated on manufacturing and selling Apple – 1. Apple was supposed to conduct R&D on newer versions but that never happened because the values, rules, rewards, regulations all favoured "Operations" and not "Innovation". Apples culture was reset and very soon everything started to go down. When Steve Jobs got back Apple, his main focus were two, Realignment of Organizational Culture to organizational Strategy and restructuring the organization to support innovation and project culture. And the rest is, as they say, history.

6.16 The Triple Constraint

This term called the "Triple Constraint" does not officially exist in PMBOK® Guide 7th Edition, however, this concept is important for understanding project management as well as for the exams.

The triple constraint is shown as a triangle because all the three elements are interrelated. The three elements of Triple Constraint are Scope, Time and Cost.

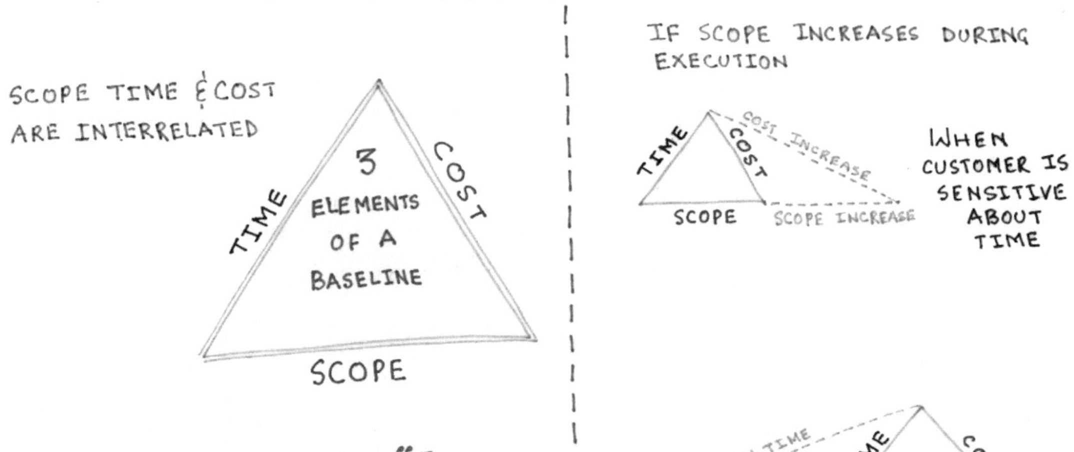

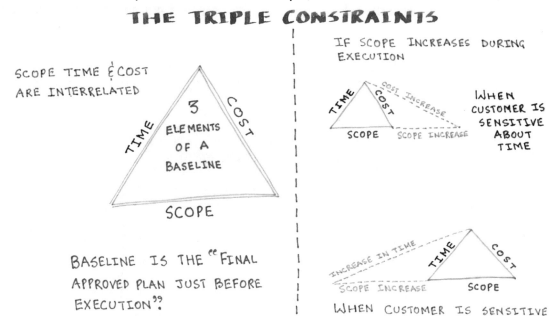

You will also notice that the area that is enclosed within the triple constraint is called "Quality". However "Quality" is not an element of the Baseline. Baseline is only made up of Scope, time and cost. Quality is an outcome of the three elements.

One way to understand this is to compare the Quality of one of the cheapest cars in the world made by Tata Motors with that of Ferrari GTC4 Lusso. Most of us simply jump to the conclusion that "Oh come on….. Ferrari has a lot better quality….". But take a moment to think a little more and you will realize that comparison of quality amongst the two is not even possible. They both belong to different market segments and hence they both belong to different grades. These grades are created by the size of the triangle created by the three elements of triple constraints viz., Scope, Time and Cost, for each of the cars.

Baseline is the combination of these three elements. Baseline is mentioned in the document "Project Management Plan". Baseline is the final approved project plan just before execution. In Agile projects, though it is not called so, baseline is created just before executing every iteration. Sometimes in exams there is mention of "Performance Measurement Baseline". This too is considered a baseline. Hence if you come across a question that talks about "Performance Measurement Baseline" it is actually a baseline. However this is rather rare and most of the time questions stick to "Scope, Schedule and Cost" as baselines.

6.17 Organizational Governance And Project Governance

Organizational Governance refers to organizational structures and arrangements at all levels of an organization designed to determine and influence the behavior of the personnel. Organizational Governance is tuned into the overall strategy of the organization such that all the personnel, working in different projects, programs and operations behave in a manner that helps the organization achieve its strategy. Governance is the tool to achieve the strategy of the organization by influencing the behavior and actions of the personnel of the organization.

Governance is at multiple levels. One is at the Organizational Level (which is also called "Portfolio Level Governance"), one is at Project and Program Levels and one is at Operations levels.

The usual elements of Organizational Governance are (Though they may vary from organization to organization and from industry to industry): -

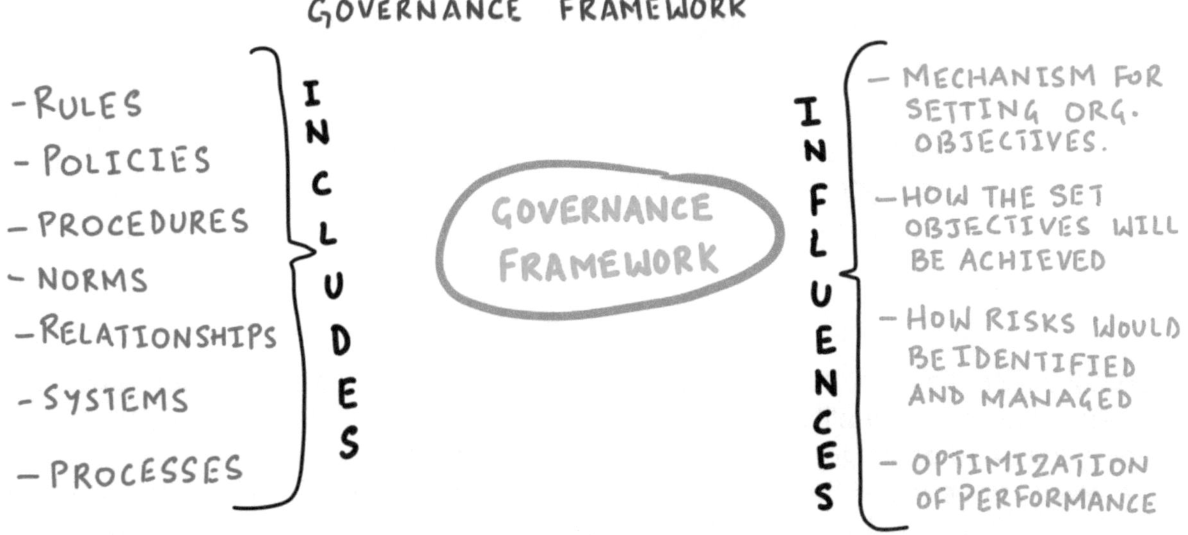

Project Governance is much more than just the Monitoring and Controlling of Project execution. Governance is an oversight function and is part of the overall "Enterprise-wide organizational Governance".

In an organization there would be multiple projects of different kinds and complexities and yet there has to be some consistency in initiating projects, estimating projects, tools, and techniques to be used, ensuring that the projects that do not fit the overall organization strategy are not undertaken, lessons learned are documented, project tracking is done using prescribed templates etc. This overall framework of consistency and tools and techniques and ensuring which projects are tracked more closely than others etc. is called organizational governance model. PMO is a Part of organizational governance. When governance is applied to a specific project it's called Project Governance.

Governance is not the same as PMO. PMO is a part of the Organizational Governance framework.

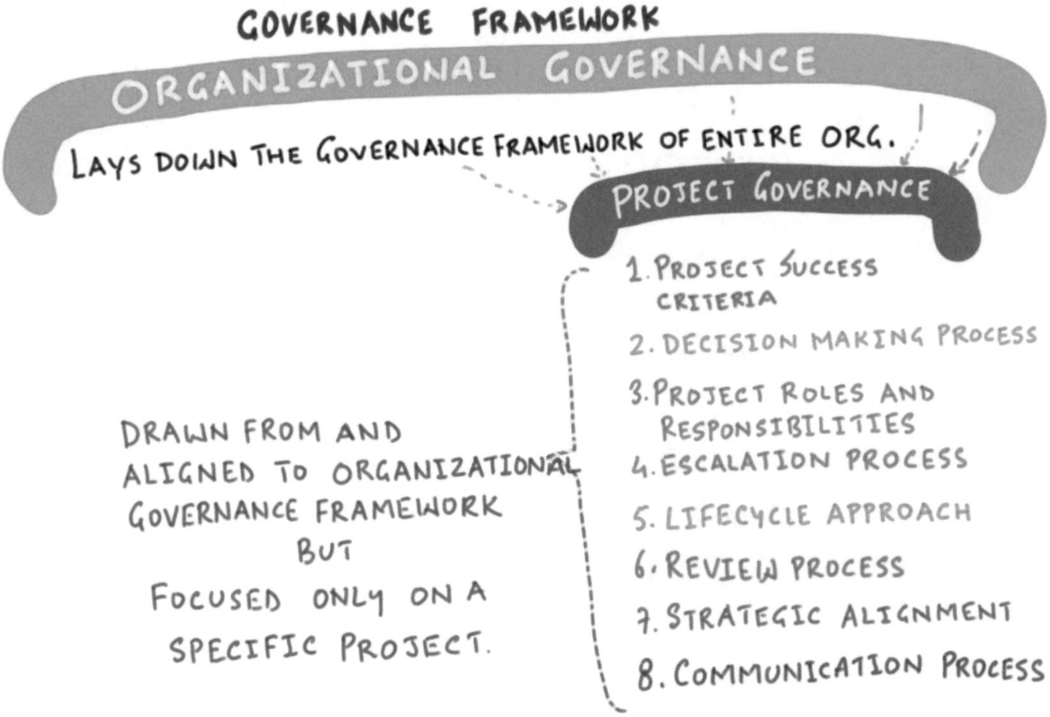

GOVERNANCE FRAMEWORK

ORGANIZATIONAL GOVERNANCE

LAYS DOWN THE GOVERNANCE FRAMEWORK OF ENTIRE ORG.

PROJECT GOVERNANCE

1. PROJECT SUCCESS CRITERIA
2. DECISION MAKING PROCESS
3. PROJECT ROLES AND RESPONSIBILITIES
4. ESCALATION PROCESS
5. LIFECYCLE APPROACH
6. REVIEW PROCESS
7. STRATEGIC ALIGNMENT
8. COMMUNICATION PROCESS

DRAWN FROM AND ALIGNED TO ORGANIZATIONAL GOVERNANCE FRAMEWORK BUT FOCUSED ONLY ON A SPECIFIC PROJECT.

6.18 Organizational Change

There are two levels of changes. Changes that affect an entire organization and change within a project. This section deals with the former, viz., changes that affect the entire organization. Organizational change is done to ensure that the organizational business and its way of working is relevant to the changing business world that affects that organization. Changing or revising the organizational strategy is also one of the kinds of Organizational Change.

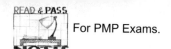

REASONS FOR ORGANIZATIONAL CHANGE

Organizational Change is usually effected through one or more projects. The biggest challenge is transition and adoption of changed organization by the employees. No one likes change and change is always uncomfortable. Despite all that, organizations must change to keep relevant.

E.g., Seeing how the market and the infrastructure for reliable electric passenger vehicles is developing around the planet, several traditional car manufacturing organizations are now embarking on developing in-house talent and facility for developing saleable electrical vehicles of their own. This is easier said than done. Let us look at what kind of organizational level change that is involved in such transition. The organization structure itself would have to be changed from a "Weak Matrix" to "Strong Matrix" so that more power is provided to the project managers such that none of the electrical car projects is delayed. The culture of the organizational staff has to change from operational mindset to a more R&D mindset. The traditional car production would have to be scaled down to ensure some income while still freeing most of the resources for new development. Almost the entire vendor partners would have to be changed. The quality testing, checklists, assembly line, government regulation compliance etc., all would need to change. I guess you can see now, why many organizations, when they try organizational change, are unable to transition to the changed form due to cascading effect of the changes and above all, the resistance to change. I am also sure, that now you can see why certain erstwhile world leaders like Nokia and Toys R Us, have become completely irrelevant now because of not changing or not changing fast enough.

The framework for managing change in an organization is made up of 5 interconnected elements.

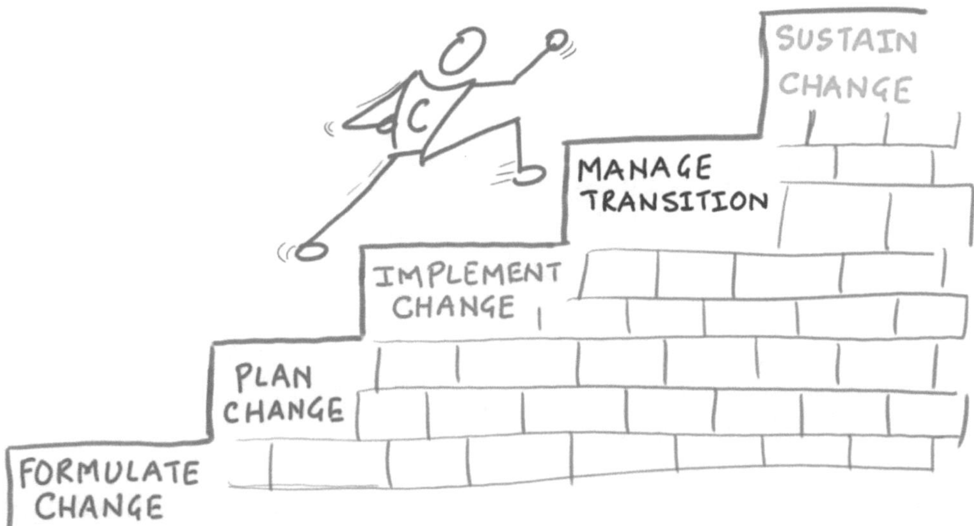

Let us look at what happens in each of the stages mentioned in the doodle above:

1) **Formulate Change**: This is where the justification and rationale for the proposed organizational change is created and fine-tuned. All the background information, relevant data and justification are documented to later impress upon just how the organization would benefit post successful transition from this proposed change.
2) **Plan Change**: At this stage the people and managers championing this change as well as the change agents would create a detailed plan (similar to a full-fledged project plan) that would be required to shift organization from "AS-IS" to "To-Be" state.
3) **Implement Change**: This is where the entire change plan (documented and created in the previous step) is executed and monitored & controlled. The whole purpose of this stage is to focuses on demonstrating the future state capabilities, checking to ensure the capabilities are having the intended impact, and making necessary improvements or adaptations in response. This stage is iterative in nature.
4) **Manage Transition**: This is the stage where the human element is looked into more deeply. The purpose of this stage is to manage expectation and to answer questions connected to change once the change is implemented. Many new questions and challenges emerge post implementation of change and this is the stage where those questions and hurdles are addressed.
5) **Sustain Change**: This is the stage or step that ensures that the people within the organization keep on working with the changed processes or situation and do not relapse to the pre-change behavior.

When an organizational level change actually occurs, the people within the organization go through a noted pattern while adapting to the change. This pattern is explained in something known as the ADKAR model which was created by Jeff Hiatt. This can be applied to personal as well as professional change.

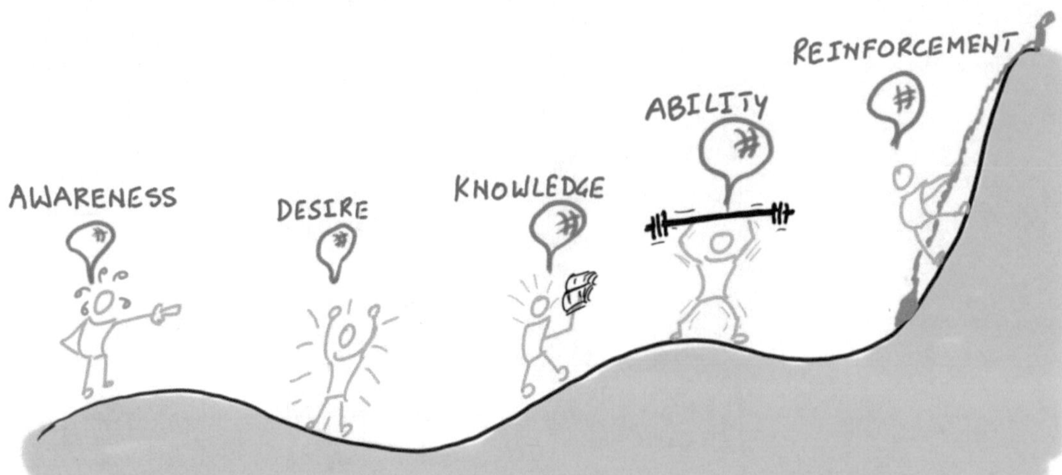

As you can see the ADKAR model is a short form for the names of the stages. Let us explain each of these stages for you to get a better grasp and appreciation for this model:

1) **Awareness**: At this stage the people become aware of the change and this is where their fears of change need to be replaced with the need and the justification for change. This is aimed at creating a positive awareness and the need for change.
2) **Desire**: Once the awareness is created among the people with sufficient effort, the people develop a desire towards that change. This desire helps them overcome the fear of the change.
3) **Knowledge**: Once the desire for change has been created among the people, it is important for them to know "How to change?". Change agents must let the people know all the different trainings, processes, documents that they could go through to understand the mechanics of getting involved in the change process and arm themselves with the knowledge and know-how of adapting to the chage.
4) **Ability**: Once the knowledge is available to the people, they would need some hand-holding, mentoring, coaching or even guidance to develop the necessary abilities to work with the changed processes and conditions. This could even mean getting to acquire new skills.
5) **Reinforcement**: This is the stage the cements the change in the minds of the people. By rewarding early adopters, contributors and people who support and champion the change a healthy adoption practice is created among the people vis-à-vis the change. Obtaining feedback and necessary matrices from people also helps in reinforcement of change.

There is another model created by John Kotter, called the "The 8 – Step Process For Leading Change". This model (basically just a series of steps) that the leadership of an organization must take to ensure that the change is properly implemented and the organization actually gets transformed.
The 8 Steps are listed as under:

1. **Create Urgency** for the need of the change by clearly stating the threats due to not changing as well as the opportunities for changing.
2. **Form a powerful coalition** with all the change leaders and organizational influencers and ensure that they understand the importance of the change and help spread the transformation across the organization.

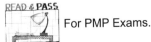

3. **Create a vision** for change by not only stating what a realized vision looks like but also create a plan / strategy to realize that vision.
4. **Communicate the vision** across the length and width of the organization and also among the vendor partners associated with the organization. Ensure that the change leaders and influencers are also communicating the vision to their area of influence.
5. **Remove obstacles** that are coming in the way of transformation. Obstacles in the form of human resistance, organizational structure, roles and responsibilities, process re-engineering etc., all need to be identified, prioritized and addressed in a timely manner to ensure that the transformation is not held up.
6. **Create short-term wins** instead of going for a big-bang concept. Breakdown the entire transformational program into multiple important milestones and then celebrate and communicate each milestone as it is achieved thus reducing the organizational ambiguity and enhancing organization wide buy-in towards the change.
7. **Build on the change** incrementally. Milestone after milestone and win after win, the entire organization would get transformed.
8. **Anchor the changes in the corporate culture**. Transformation alone is not enough. Maintaining transformation has also to be done till the transformed organization and the changed way of working becomes the norm over a period of time.

Organizational change is not easy to cope with for the organizational staff. In fact no one likes change. (Just so that you understand the phenomenal resistance to change do any of the following, change the location of the beer cans in the refrigerator where your friend, spouse or live-in partner usually keeps it or change the order in which the coffee / tea container and the sugar container is kept in the kitchen or start leaving the WC seat up in a house which is occupied by a lady or start leaving the WC seat down in a house which is occupied by a dude, and see what happens. Now, if such a minor change can evoke such emotions, just imagine what can be expected among hundreds of employees who are used to working in a certain way for years, are now asked to change their working style.) Therefore Virginia Satir created a model of how to cope with changes and what to expect from the employees during the organizational change. This model is called the “Virginia Satir Change Model”.

This model has 6 distinct stages and they are:

1) **Late Status Quo**: People are well trenched into existing processes and way of doing things.
2) **The Foreign Element:** The change is regarded as a foreign element and is feared just as much. This comes in the way of the usual way of working for the people.
3) **Chaos**: This change brings people into an unfamiliar territory and this also results in noticeable drop in the overall productivity of the affected people. Chaos is not necessarily a bad thing always. Many people try to adjust to change by inventing novel ideas or way of doing things.
4) **The Transforming Idea**: People come to a point where they come up with an idea that helps them make sense of the situation. They begin to see how they can find a way out of the chaos and cope with the new reality. Work performance begins to increase.
5) **Practice and Integration**: This is where people start applying their understanding and knowledge to work with the changed situation. This can also lead to allowable

mistakes and hence some guidance, mentoring and training helps them start working within the changed situation better.

6) **New Status Quo**: Over regular practice people settle down to this new ways their regular way of working and this now becomes the new normal.

At this moment of time it would make sense to distinguish between a change and transition. Change is something that is material. However when the organizational staff has adopted it and internalized it, only then it would be called a transition.

E.g., The organization has spent over a million dollars in rolling out a new ERP system to replace the manual workflow management system. This is a change. However till all the organizational staff that is affected by this change or works on the workflow management system, do not start using it and till the time they get used to it, it would not be called a Transition.

Therefore, a Change cannot be a success till it has been transitioned.
William Bridges' Transition Model (only applicable to transition and not just the change) identifies three stages of transition and they are:

1. Ending, losing and letting go.
2. The Neutral zone
3. The New beginning

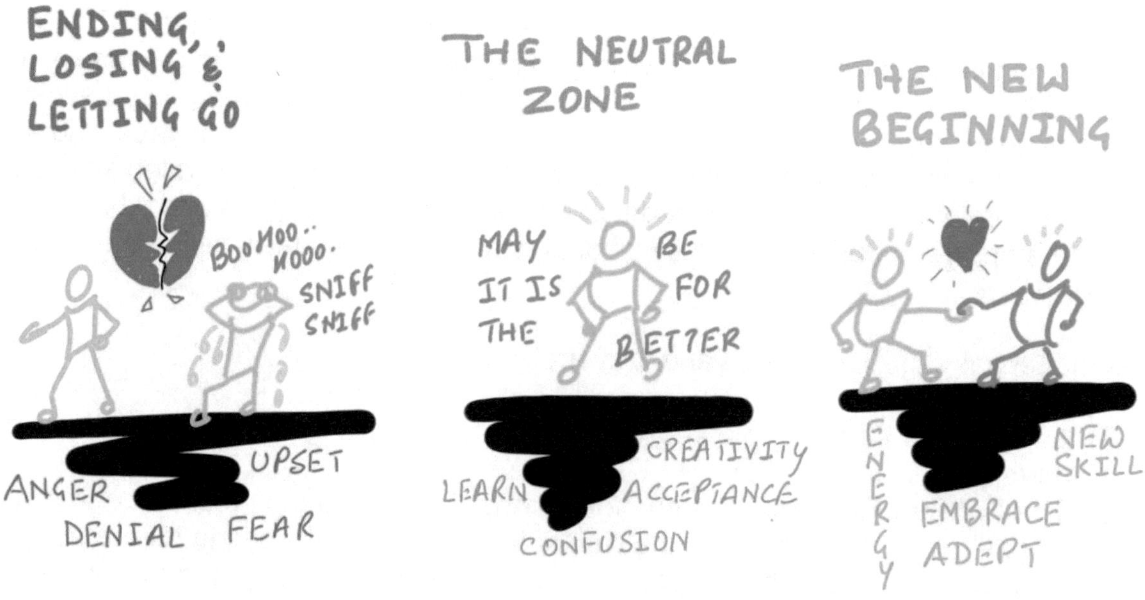

In exams you may find it difficult from the scenario question or even the general question, as to which specific model the question is actually talking about when it comes to Organizational Change. To ensure that you do not get confused, just follow the following rules. If the question is talking about how the organization must ensure change, or what the leaders are supposed to do to ensure that the change is adapted within the organization or how to roll out a change within an organization, the question is talking about the John Kotter's 8 Step Process for transforming organizations.

If the question is talking about how the people must cope with the organizational change, the question is talking about the Virginia Satir Change model.
If the question is talking about what are the steps that lead to adaption of a change or steps of adoption, the question is talking about ADKAR model by Jeff Hiatt.
However if the question has clearly mentioned the term "Transition" then the question is talking about the William Bridges' Transition Model.

The downside to constantly making organizational changes or engaging in a prolonged organizational change is the "Change Fatigue" that the organizational employees may experience. Hence changes must be done in smaller steps as well as unwind time must be provided to work in a changed environment and settle down.

6.19 Project Management Roles and Skills Needed

This goes without saying that the role of the project manager is "Strategic" in nature. Project Managers, in general, have a widespread influence and this can be observed from the image herein below: -

The Project Manager needs to have specific competencies.
To be a successful project manager one needs to have Knowledge of Project Management Concepts, must be Performance oriented and know which tool and technique to use when and must have strong Interpersonal skills. The combination of all these three important traits makes a "perfect" project manager.

The PMBOK® Guide 6th Edition presents a PMI Talent Triangle to showcase the needed skills of an effective project manager. This was not continued in PMBOK Guide 7th Edition. However it would be important to still understand the overall skill requirements from a Project Manager. Understanding this will also allow you to tackle real world project situations as well as dealing with scenario based questions in PMP Exams.

The “PMI Talent Triangle” consists of Technical Project Management, Leadership, and Strategic and Business Management.

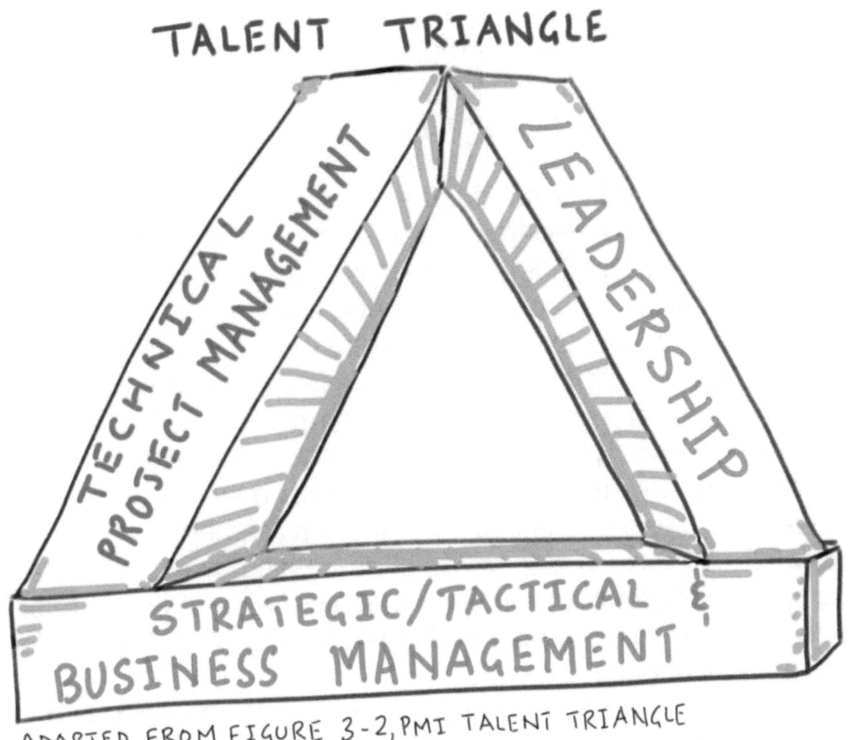

1. **Technical** Project Management Skills are effective project management skills and knowledge of project management processes, lifecycle, project methodologies, and project governance.
2. **Strategic** And Business Management Skills are the abilities and skills required to understand and work towards the overall strategy of the organization using the project at hand and constantly negotiating with, influencing and managing others to ensure that the project is executed in a manner to align with the overall strategy of the organization. This skill is sometimes referred to as "Business Acumen" in certain organizations.
3. **Leadership** Skills are the abilities to guide, motivate and direct a team. This involves critical thinking as well as working with complex projects and under uncertainties.

Project Manager is expected to know how to deal with people, influence them and also be able to understand office politics and power distribution (formal as well as informal) within the organization. The project manager must traverse through the political and power maze to get the work done. This means that the project manager must also be a very keen observer.

There are various forms of power that the project managers must be aware of or even use to get things done.

1. **Formal Power/Position Based Power/Legitimate Power**: This comes from the very appointment of a project manager and the formal designation that has been assigned to him within the organization. This is generally the very first form of power that a project manager applies when working for a new company or a new project with a new team or taking over a project from another project manager. This is, however, not the best form of power for longer duration.

2. **Informational**: This is a short term power where the project manager wields power over others because of the information possessed by him. This form of power never lasts long and should not be a long-term strategy for influencing others.
3. **Referent**: It refers to the ability of a project manager to influence a follower because of the follower's loyalty, respect, friendship, admiration, affection, or a desire to gain approval. This power is created generally due to the admiration, trust that the manager may have earned from his team by treating them fairly, by giving timely advice and by ensuring that he comes through as a credible manager.
4. **Situational**: This kind of power over people/team gets created due to specific situations and lasts only as long as the life of that situation. Let us say that there was a crisis in the project where the approvals from customs authorities were not taken now the shipment has arrived and all clearances have to be obtained on a war footing. During this situation (Crisis) the team member with better understanding over "Customs rules" will automatically have power over the team and the team will simply do whatever is being suggested by that team member.
5. **Personal**: This power is also called charismatic power. Because of a person's charm, the perception of grandeur a person may hold a lot of power over the team. This kind of power is usually long-lasting and usually ends when the charismatic person does something less popular.
6. **Relational**: This kind of power is generated by developing relationships through Networking and creating alliances. To wield this power one needs to continually foster and strengthen relationships.
7. **Expert**: This power refers to the experience, certification, specialization or specific training that a person may possess thus making the others look up to him for direction and guidance. An experienced project manager with a PMP® certification will find it easy to use his "Expert Power" over the team and other stakeholders.
8. **Reward-oriented**: This is by far the best power for a project manager. The power to reward, praise and grant recognition is the most healthy and long-lasting method of influential power over the team and other stakeholders.
9. **Punitive or coercive**: This refers to the power using fear of negative effect over people. This power is not the best method and should be used only as a last measure. Use of this power generates negativity.
10. **Ingratiating**: Commonly known as "Buttering" and "Kissing **s". Flattery goes a long way to get some work done. But this is not all that repetitive. However people, being what they are, this method works more often than not, at least for the first time with almost everyone.
11. **Pressure based**: This refers to creating multiple ground rules and stiffer compliance to processes thus bringing about pressure on the team and this could also help get power over them. This too is not an ideal method of exercising power, however, this kind of power becomes important for mission-critical situations or projects (*E.g., special ops by armed forces, nuclear power plants troubleshooting, satellite launch projects and so on*).
12. **Guilt based**: This refers to the concept of reverse psychology to hold power over a team of stakeholders, by generating a feeling of Obligation, or a sense of duty, or awareness of dereliction of duty or not doing what they should have done and such, to have power of molding direction of work and thus having power over the team. This too is not the best method as it may tend to be used for manipulation as well. Hence it must be used as one of the last measures and not a regular form of power.

13. **Persuasive**: This form of power is based on logical arguments, logical and technical facts and evidence for the direction which the team must take. This is one of the few forms of power that can be used among a team of peers (teams without hierarchy). This form of power, though one of the positively good ones, tend to take much longer to exercise. This also requires that the project manager have good articulation skills.
14. **Avoiding**: This is not even power. This is the worst form of power. This is where the project manager refuses to be part of the decision or direction that the team is going in, to persuade to change their decision or direction. This is one of the negative powers and is considered the worst, even though there are times when there is no other method left but to exercise this power.

There are 5 bases of social power and they are: -
Coercive
Reward
Legitimate
Expert and
Referent.
The best power is “Rewards”, the first power to apply is “Formal” the worst power is “Avoid” and “Coercive”.

The project manager needs to display some of the Leadership Skills about dealing with people. They can be listed as under.

1) **Visionary**
Being able to understand the objectives, end results, product of the project, themselves and be able to articulate the same to the team and other stakeholders as well. Remember, the PM has to be the Visionary Leader for the team.

2) **Positive outlook and optimistic attitude**
Keeps the team and other stakeholders motivated even in the most trying and difficult situations. Being positive in all situations is one of the prime leadership skills that generates a following without authority.

3) **Working with others / Collaborative**
Making use of participative management within a project and taking work and project related decisions through collaboration and consensus creates a very strong buy-in and sense of commitment towards the project as well as the project team.

4) **Managing and handling** conflicts to build relationships can be done by the following actions and focus areas. Conflicts are a way of life in projects and it should be the aim

of the Project Manager to ensure that there are "Healthy Conflicts" but fewer "Negative Conflicts".

5) **Communication Skills,** like some of the skills and actions shown in the diagram below, helps overall communication within the team. Let us not forget that Communication is by far the most important "Leadership" and project management skill (the project manager is supposed to spend around 90% of his time doing it).

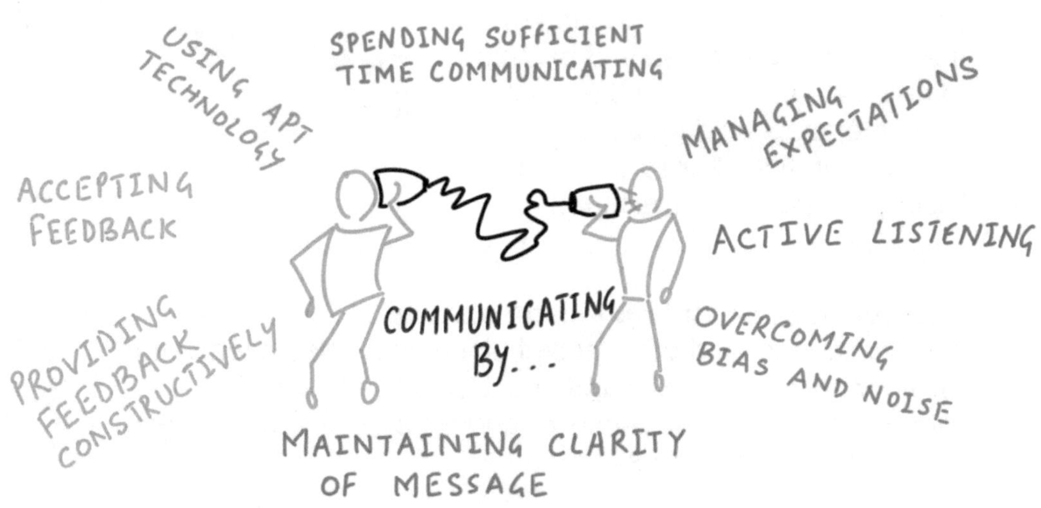

6) **Respectful and Courteous**
Respectful behavior is one of the leadership traits. Bestowing apt respect to the team members and other stakeholders as well as being courteous to all, creates a very good feeling of professionalism which helps everyone work with ease. This behavior also includes leadership traits of being ethical, honest, loyal and friendly.

7) **Integrity** is to have an inbuilt "Moral Compass" and the ability to follow that moral compass in all walks of life. Having strong integrity is crucial for anyone to look up to "you" as a PM as well as to accept you as a guide and a leader. This is something that the leader (PM) has also to bring it out in others as well.

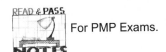

8) **Cultural Sensitivity**
Cultures do not only change based on geographies, but they could also change from function to function. As a global leader who is be able to have an influence on cross-functional teams as well as cross-cultural teams, the project manager must display adequate cultural awareness and sensitivity. This helps diverse team members to gel well together.

9) **Ability to constantly learn and adapt**
One of the worst things that can happen to a Leader is to become irrelevant in their respective field. Constantly updating themselves with changes, new developments and new processes are crucial for a project manager to maintain influence over others.

10) **Giving credit where due and being fair**
One of the most motivating thing for the team is to be recognized for the work done. Apt and timely credit to the right person or team for stellar work done helps everyone to develop a sense of healthy competition and helps bring out the best in everyone else.

11) **Work prioritization and focus on important things**
A good leader knows that not all work can ever be finished as well as the fact that not all work should be treated as equal. Evaluating the priority of tasks as well as ensuring that the team engages in priority tasks first ensures a clear focus on practicality as well as a focused approach. One of the key habits of a successful project manager is to constantly prioritize work.

12) **Critical thinking and problem-solving abilities**
A project would always beget some issues and problems. The experience, as well as the competence of a Project Manager,  is ascertained by how well appropriate problem-solving techniques is applied to the problems and issues at hand. Mostly this is done in collaboration with the team.

13) **Ability to build effective teams**
Project work happens through teams. How team member's work as a "Team" has a direct effect on the outcome of the project. Hence, as a good leader, one of the leadership skills the project manager must have is to be able to create performance oriented teams from various kinds of stakeholders.

14) **Ability to have a holistic view of the project**
Should be able to ascertain Enterprise Environmental Factors affecting the project at hand and be able to factor them in during planning.

There are a variety of leadership styles available for the project manager to use during their project.

There is a very important development in the PMBOK® Guide (something we have been talking about since ages in all our practical project management training) and that is the understanding of and use of "Organizational Politics" to get the work done. For some reason, people tend to frown at the term "Politics". Many people consider it bad and "Villainous". The point to ponder is that if politics were really that bad then how come there are university courses called "Political Science". Politics is essential and necessary and practical. What people must understand is that it's the "Manipulation" which must not be used. I guess now the question is what is the difference between "Politics" and "Manipulation"?
Politics is dealing with and influencing people using various means for the benefit of meeting organizational or project objectives, without stepping outside of moral fiber, organizational

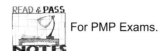

rules and code of conduct as well as the rule of the land. However, Manipulation is about dealing with and influencing people using various means for the benefit of one's own interests over and above that of the organizational objectives or project objective. I guess the difference is clear.

6.19.1 Situational Leadership

While we are talking about Leadership, it is important (both from exams point of view as well as from the real world engagement) to also talk about "Situational Leadership". Again, even this topic we will understand it in a manner that you will become practically effective as well as understand it so well that no matter what kind of question they throw at you, you will be able to answer them with ease.
Ken Blanchard and Paul Hersey created this model in 1969. It was clear that the concepts of Leadership and Managership cannot apply to all the team members in "One Size Fits All" manner. Based on the competence, situation, trust etc., one's leadership style must alter. Overall this model talks about 4 situations in general. These situations are based on the "task" to be performed as well as the "team" performing it. A seasoned leader (and for that matter, even managers) would weigh these factors before figuring out the most apt kind of leadership to be adopted for the situation. For ease of application and understanding, Ken and Paul created 4 possible situations and called them S1, S2, S3 and S4.

These 4 situations are created from the combination of two attributes about individual team members. These two attributes are "Competency" to get the work done and "Commitment" to get the work done. Hence based on the 4 different situations of Competency and Commitment of the team members, the manger / leader would use different techniques to manage or lead them.

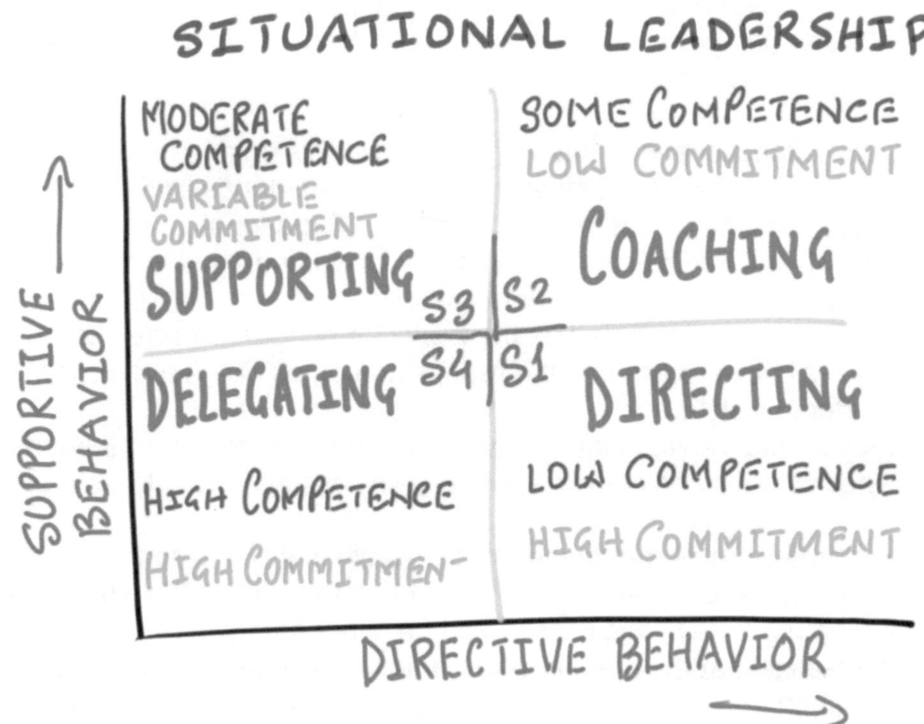

As you can see in this image above, that for Situation S1 you, as a leader, will show more ***Directive Behavior***, where you simply instruct the team member without seeking much feedback or their participation, but will support them less for actually getting the work done. It would be more a of a one-sided instructions from the manager's side.

When it comes to Situation S2, you will not only show high amount of directive behavior but also provide a high amount of support to the team member. This is exactly what is called "**Coaching**". Coaching would be needed to make the team member understand the importance of the work at hand. How it enhances her skill or how the work is related to his career. This will shore up the team member's commitment to work. Directing part in coaching will help the team member here to get the work done even though her competence level may be low.

When it comes to Situation S3, you will be high on supporting and low on directive behavior. This is basically the "**Supporting**" situation. This is because you as a manager, would be more interested in getting the work done from a team member whose competence may be moderate while commitment is not low but reasonably in place.

And finally, Situation S4 is where you will be low on Directive Behavior as well as low on Supporting the team member. This situation is just called "**Delegating**". A manager or a leader's target should be able to develop as many of the team members to ultimately be in the S4 category.

Before we get into these 4 situations, we also need to understand that there is a difference between a person's "Competences" in getting that work done and "Commitment" towards getting that work done. It's not necessary that a competent person would also have commitment or vice versa and all other combinations of these two terms. Again, we categorize our team members based on 4 levels of "Commitment" and "Competence" and they can be shown as under:

In exams you can expect scenario based question on this topic. The question may describe a situation that loosely places the Situations and / or Competence and Commitment levels of the team and you would be asked to choose the apt "Situational Leadership" style to choose from. Leadership styles are Directing, Coaching, Supporting and Delegating. Let me give you some scenarios to show you how easy this actually is.
Let us say, you have been appointed as the project manager for a new team working on a new project. You will have to assume the team situation as D1. And hence you will begin with a "Directing" leadership style.
Let us say, that you later realize that the team has some commitment towards the project but lacks certain specific skills and competence, you will assume them to be a D2 level and start coaching them.
But what if you come to know that the team is actually highly skilled for this kind of work but are struggling due to the requirements of this new project, you will assume them to be at D3 Level. Your leadership style in this case would be "Supporting".
However, if you realize that the team is very comfortable with what they need to do as well have a lot of commitment towards the work at hand, you will realize that the team is at D4. Your leadership style would be "Delegating".

See, not that difficult. Things are much easier when they are understood.

As I had suggested before, please stick only to the content of this book, which will ensure that you would be safe. Some books and resources on PMBOK Guide 7th Edition are showing the older version of Situational Leadership. The older version labels are not in use today and different from the labels I have listed above. Besides, PMBOK Guide 7th Edition only subscribes to the "Situational Leadership" model II, which is what has been discussed here.

6.19.2 OSCAR Model

OSCAR Model is purely a Coaching and a Problem Solving model. I have been using this very often during consulting in various countries as well as coaching my daughter on life's lessons. It is a very powerful technique / model.

Overall this Coaching and Mentoring Model 5 Steps as under:

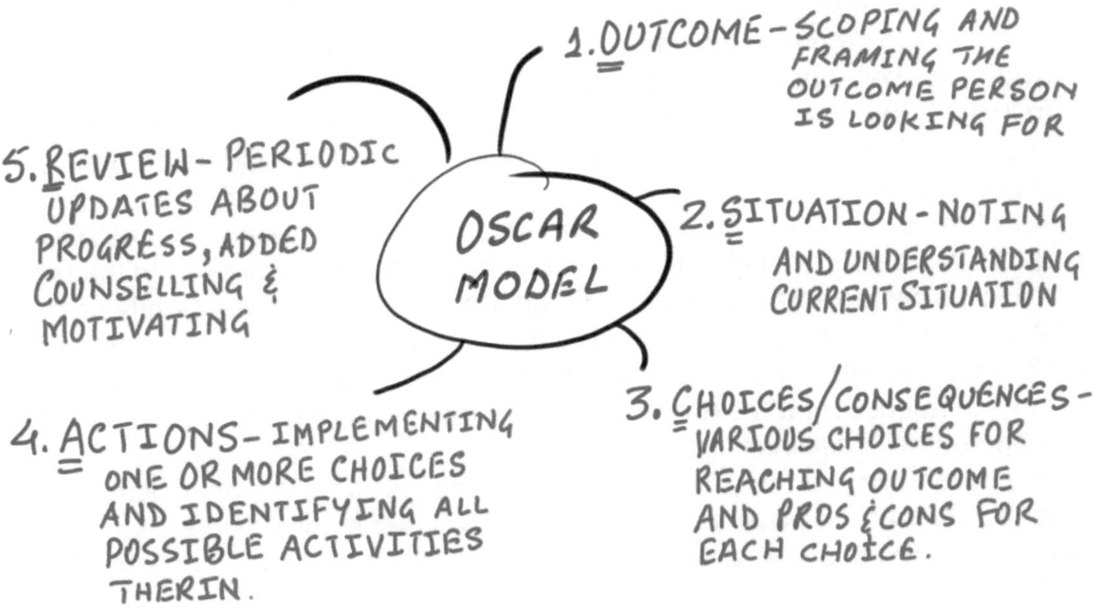

This model first focuses the attention of the coached persons target or vision. Clearly ensuring that the "Outcome" is well defined and specific. As far as possible the outcome should be SMART. If the outcome or vision is not clear nothing that one does will take you there. By starting with defining and focusing on the outcome, puts the person being coached in a very positive state of mind and that itself helps with the rest of the steps.

Next is the understanding of the "Current Situation". The skills, conditions, capabilities, education etc., that you have right now. By clearly defining your current situation one understands the exact "Gap" between where you are and what you want to be. This clarity of gap is what is needed for the rest of the steps in this model to work towards.

Next step is "Choices" that they have in filling that gap along with the consequences for each of the choices. This helps in separating practical approach from a dreamy or knee-jerk approach. This also helps understand which approach or choice of filling this gap between current situation and the vision, will suite best to the coached person.

Once the choice of path is chosen, this path is broken down into a series of "Actions". Nothing should be left out from it. Make it as detailed and granular as possible. This clearly shows the exact work and actions to be taken to reach the vision using a path that has the least negative consequences for you. And finally the "Review" and "follow-up" that a mentor has to do with the coached person during regular intervals to understand the progress as well as the impediments to the progress.
I regularly use this model for coaching the 30 coached persons that are always there under my direct mentorship, to help them solve specific personal problems as well.

6.20 Project Success Defined

One of the many confusions around project management is "Exactly when is a project successful?" Simply said, the project is successful if it meets its objective that brought it into existence in the first place.
For example if a hydropower electricity generation Dam project was to be built for providing uninterrupted power supply to 100,000 homes and if the actual dam is only able to supply the same to just 50,000 homes than the project was unsuccessful (while some would call it partially successful) even if this project was completed in less cost, before time and meeting the full scope of work.
This clearly showcases the immense importance of having a clearly defined "Objective" of the project even before a single action is taken in the project. However, in the real world, there are so many projects which either do not define the objectives clearly or they do not define it at all. Which is also one of the biggest reasons why there is so much confusion around project success. Once the project objectives are well documented and the boundaries (Project Scope) established then it's the Project Manager's responsibility to fix and then meet the "Baselines".
Hence from Portfolio point of view, a Project Success is when the objectives for the same have been achieved. However from the Project Manager's point of view, the Triple constraints viz., the baseline as last established, is fully achieved.

6.21 Project Performance Domain Overview

Before we move to the next chapter in this book, it would make academic sense, if not practical sense, to talk about the way PMBOK Guide 7th Edition states the 8 Performance Domain. They are not really important for the PMP Exams. I am just putting it here so that you understand how the PMBOK has been structured in general.

Performance Domain are created to group together those project activities, tools and techniques that have the same genetics under one heading. For example, if you wanted to know all the things connected to Stakeholder Management that is usually done in a project (irrespective of when and how many times those activities are performed in different projects and methodologies) connected to Stakeholders and managing them, you just need to go through the Performance Domain called "Stakeholders".
Performance Domain are just that. Nothing more and nothing less. It is a suitable way of classifying and categorizing information. It has no practical purposes nor asked in exams. But it is essential for understanding and comprehension. For those who have seen the

PMBOK Guide 6th edition or for that matter, any of the previous PMBOK editions, you can easily relate these Performance Domains to what the earlier editions called as “Knowledge Areas”.

However there is a huge catch. In PMBOK Guide 7th edition, there are no defined processes. Remember 7th edition is about project management principles rather than processes. Now, not having processes, presented another book compilation problem. Since the projects are not conducted in the Performance Domain sequence, they are performed in the Initiation, Planning, Execution, Monitoring and Controlling and finally Closing, steps, and since there are no defined processes in 7th edition, there was no way to explain as to which activities, tools and models need to be applied during which stage of the project. In 7th edition this has been done by creating a series of tables on pages 193, 194 and 195 to give a general idea of what needs to be done when and during which stage of the project. However, as I meet more and more people who have tried to unravel 7th edition, I find almost all of them were highly confused.

And this is the biggest reason I wrote the book in this manner. The way you would undertake a real project. This way, in a logical manner, you will see what comes when and what tools have to be used when. This way you not only understand the entire content of the 7the edition with ease, you do not get confused one bit. All this information will appear to you rather “logical”. And that is what is needed to ace both, your exams, as well as your real world projects.

The 8 performance domain are listed herein below and their names are rather self-explanatory themselves.

1. Stakeholders
2. Team
3. Development Approach and Life Cycle
4. Planning (by introducing this performance domain you can see the amount of confusion that has been created because most of the other performance domain you do have some work that is also done in planning).
5. Project Work (people are also confused between this performance domain naming and how is it different from the performance domain called “Delivery”)
6. Delivery
7. Measurement and
8. Uncertainty

From the PMP Exams Point of view please remember that the ECO still applies where the domain are just three viz.,

1) People
2) Process
3) Business Environment

The PMBOK Guide 7th Edition is also based on 4 values and 12 principles. Though I am listing them down here just to satisfy your academic curiosity, do not make it your life’s ambition to know all of these principles in details.

I have highlighted those principles that sometimes show up in PMP Exams. I have also provided some explanations. Keep this point in mind while going through these 12 principles.

The 4 Values first (this is something that you should know for PMP Exams):

1) Responsibility
2) Respect
3) Fairness and
4) Honesty

These 4 values spawn 12 Principles.

1) **Be A Diligent, Respectful And Caring Steward.**
   Being a Steward means being entrusted with the care of something. Here it is the Project and the Project Team.
   PM has to guide the project team in tandem with all internal processes and compliances as well as all relevant external guidelines and regulations to the project done in a manner that is conducive to project environment while maintaining respect within the team.
   a) PM has to display
   b) Integrity
   c) Care
   d) Trustworthiness
   e) Compliance and
   f) Transparency

2) Create A Collaborative Project Team Environment
   This principle is focused on supporting a project culture that enables diverse individuals to work together and provide synergistic effects from interactions.
   This means focusing on the following
   - Team Building
   - Team Agreements
   - Team Structure (Organizational Structure)
   - Processes (that ensure work is done properly through clarity on R&R, by focusing on) :
     - Authority
     - Accountability
     - Responsibility

3) Effectively Engage With Stakeholders:
   Stakeholders are persons or body of persons that can either affect the outcome of the project or get affected by it, positively or negatively and directly or indirectly.

   Involves
   - Detailed stakeholder identification
   - Stakeholder analysis
   - Planning stakeholder engagement
   - Engaging with stakeholders
   - Ensuring that the stakeholder engagement was effective and helped project
   - Remove or Resolve stakeholder issues and conflicts

4) **Focus On Value**
Value is the "Business Outcome" of a project from the perspective of the User or the Customer.
A project manager has to ensure that the project is being conducted in a manner that assures "Value" from the project to the relevant stakeholders.
This can be done by aligning to the "Business Case" of the project, which consists of:
- Business Needs
- Project Justification
- Business Strategy

5) Recognize, Evaluate and Respond To System Interactions
Projects are not independent of the systems (internal and external) that they are born within.
Project teams need to have "Systems Thinking"
Systems Thinking entails taking a holistic view of how project parts interact with each other and with external systems
Systems are constantly changing requiring consistent attention to internal and external conditions
Being responsive to systems interactions allows project teams to leverage positive outcomes

6) Demonstrate Leadership Behaviors
Leadership is the ability to influence people without authority.
Leadership is not only the domain of the project manager, any of the team members can demonstrate it.
Leadership styles need to be adapted to the situation at hand.
Leadership is a learnable quality and comes with practice.
Leadership behavior helps team jell better and help in team coordination.

7) **Tailor Based On Context**
Each project is unique
Lean management in Project Management
Adapting processes and methodologies to the project instead of creating a bureaucratic environment
Tailoring approach is iterative and hence it is a continuous process throughout the project.

8) Build Quality Into Processes And Deliverables
Quality ensures satisfaction by focusing on "meeting acceptance criteria for deliverables".
The intention here is for the team to minimize waste while maximizing probability of attaining desired outcome. This results in:
- Faster delivery that meets success criteria and
- Preventing defects and errors thus reducing rework

Includes focus on Quality assurance as well as Quality control.

9) **Navigate Complexity**
Complexity is the level of difficulty of doing something due:

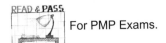

- Human behavior
- System behavior
- Uncertainty and ambiguity
- Technological innovation

Project Manager and project team members must understand how to decipher complexity as well as how to navigate through it.
Project complexity could be nascent or latent.

10)Optimize Risk Responses
Risk is any uncertain event that has an impact on the project.
A project manager and the project team must understand all the risks applicable to the project and act according to the risk appetite and risk threshold of the organization.
Every project is inherently risky.

11)Embrace Adaptability and Resiliency
Change is the only constant.
Adaptability is the ability to respond to changing conditions.
Resilience is the ability to absorb impacts and to recover quickly from a setback or failure.
A focus on outcome, rather than outputs, facilitates adaptability.

12)Enable Change To Achieve The Envisioned Future State
Changes can come from anywhere.
Enabling changes can be challenging as not all stakeholders embrace change.
A structured approach to change is helpful
Attempting too much or to many changes may result in “Change Fatigue” or “Resistance”.

6.22 Ninja Drill – Project Framework

You will find a Ninja Drill which lists the most important points you must remember for the exams, as far as that Knowledge Area is concerned.

S. No.	Drill Points
1.	Project is a temporary endeavor to undertake the creation of a unique product service or result.
2.	The three questions for something being a project or not are 1. Is the work Temporary? 2. Is the work Unique? And 3. Does the work involve Progressive Elaboration? If the answer is yes for all the 3 of the questions then the work is a Project.
3.	In a Generic project lifecycle … cost and staffing levels are low at the beginning of the project, maximum during mid phases or execution phases and drop rapidly as the project comes to a closure.
4.	The later you make a change in the project lifecycle the more expensive it becomes to implement it.
5.	Modifying or enhancing something existing is a project.
6.	Software maintenance work is operations.
7.	Progressive learning / elaboration is also called "The Cone of Uncertainty".
8.	Projects have to be formally closed whether they are terminated or successfully completed
9.	Can "Material Issue" give rise to a project? Yes! It can.
10.	There are only two ways for a project to end, viz., Termination or Successful Completion.
11.	Project Manager and Project team cannot "Convince" anyone to avoid termination once the formal termination order has been passed.
12.	A rumor for a possible termination cannot be the grounds for the PM to change anything they are doing as per the plan.
13.	Project Management is the application of knowledge, skills, tools, and techniques to project activities to meet the project requirements.
14.	The 4 Values of project management are: 1. Responsibility 2. Respect 3. Fairness and 4. Honesty
15.	These 4 values are broken down into 12 Principles. (You do not have you know / remember their names for the PMP Exams)
16.	Project Team is the collection of all the personnel who work in a project either full time or part time to help the Project Manager achieve the project objectives.
17.	Project Management Team is a subset of the Project Team and its main purpose is to help the Project Manager Plan and control the project.
18.	Sponsor is anyone who appointed you as a project manager. A sponsor is sometimes called a "Champion".
19.	A "Group Sponsor" is usually called the "Steering Committee" or "Management Council" or "Leadership Council".
20.	The Project Manager is responsible for the project but the Project Sponsor is Accountable for the project.
21.	A program is a collection of multiple projects and sub-programs which are interconnected in such a way as to generate a strategic benefit and a program may also have operations in them.
22.	A project may not be part of a program but a program would always have projects in them.
23.	A program may have elements of operations in them.
24.	The program manager is the sponsor for all the projects under that program.
25.	A PMO = Project Management office. The three kinds of roles or structures of PMO in an organization are…Supportive, Controlling and Directive.
26.	PMO = VDO (Value Delivery Office). VDO is a term that is more popular in organizations that heavily

	invest in Agile projects.
27.	EPMO = Enterprise Project Management Office
28.	Program Office is not the same as PMO.
29.	Portfolio is a collection of programs, projects and sub-projects and even operations managed as a group to achieve a specific objective.
30.	In large organizations an Enterprise Portfolio may be subdivided into "Sub-Portfolios".
31.	The five distinctive stages of a project are: 1. Initiation, 2. Planning, 3. Execution, 4. Monitoring & Controlling and finally, 5. Closing.
32.	A product lifecycle can have projects and programs supporting it.
33.	A product lifecycle can exist within a program.
34.	There are 5 base kinds of organization Structures. Functional also called Departmental, Projectised, Balanced Matrix, Strong Matrix, and Weak Matrix
35.	Value / Business value is the estimated health and well-being of a business by measuring concrete and abstract elements such as monetary assets and utility and employee, customer, supplier and societal value.
36.	Project is the "Vehicle" for achieving business value.
37.	Value / Business Value can be Tangible or Intangible.
38.	Enterprise Environmental Factors (EEF) are the conditions and constraints not under the immediate control of the team, that influence, constrain or direct the project, program or portfolio. EEF could be both, internal (within the organization) and external.
39.	Organizational Process Assets (OPA) are plans, processes, policies, procedures and knowledge bases that are specific to and used by the performing organization.
40.	Enterprise Environmental Factors could be Internal as well as external. But Organizational Process Assets are always Internal.
41.	The project manager in a Weak Matrix is called as a facilitator, expediter or a Coordinator. A coordinator is more powerful than Expediter and an Expediter is more powerful than a Facilitator.
42.	Most conflicts exist in Balanced Matrix.
43.	Communication is most complex in a Balanced Matrix.
44.	In Projectised organizations, the team members do not have a home to go back to.
45.	PBO's or Project Based Organizations are a temporary division created within Functional and Weak matrix organizations which are dedicated to projects which are immune to the hierarchy of the organization so that the project work is completed efficiently.
46.	OPM = Organizational Project Management = EPMO.
47.	Organizational Culture is shaped by people's common experiences such as: 1. Shared visions, missions, values, beliefs and expectations 2. Regulations, policies, methods and procedures 3. Motivation and reward systems 4. Risk tolerance 5. View of leadership, hierarchy and authority relationships 6. Code of conduct, work ethic and work hours 7. Operating environment
48.	A project is considered completed when it's handed over to the Operations team.
49.	Organizational Governance is the organizational or structural arrangements at all levels of an organization designed to determine and influence the behavior of all personnel of the organization to meet the strategic objectives of the organization.
50.	Project Governance is an oversight function that encompasses the entire lifecycle of the project. It provides a comprehensive and consistent method of controlling the project and ensuring its success or help take an early decision about its termination.
51.	There are three elements of a baseline viz., Scope Baseline, Schedule Baseline and Cost Baseline. (Sometimes PMP Exams talk about "Project Performance Baseline" and if you see it in exams, consider it as the 4th element of the Baseline).
52.	The Project Management (or PMI) talent triangle is made up of three elements viz., 1. Technical

	Project Management, 2. Leadership and 3. Strategic And Business Management.
53.	Organizational change are those changes that affect the entire organization. Project level change is a change that only affects that specific organization.
54.	Steps for managing organizational change: - 1) Formulate Change 2) Plan Change 3) Implement Change 4) Manage Transition and 5) Sustain Change
55.	ADKAR = Awareness, Desire, Knowledge, Ability and Reinforcement.
56.	What is the purpose of ADKAR? ADKAR is the 5 step process that every individual has to go through to embrace change, personal or professional.
57.	The 8 Step Process for leading change: 1) Create urgency 2) Form a powerful coalition 3) Create a vision 4) Communicate the vision 5) Remove obstacles 6) Create short-term wins 7) Build on the change and 8) Anchor the change in the corporate culture.
58.	Virginia Satir model has 6 steps: (how people cope with change) 1) Late status quo. 2) The foreign element. 3) Chaos. 4) The transforming idea. 5) Practice and integration. 6) New status quo.
59.	The William Bridges' Transition model is 1) Ending, losing and letting go. 2) The neutral zone 3) The new beginning
60.	A project manager has to be the visionary manager / leader.
61.	In Situational Leadership, you will "Delegate" work to those who have High Commitment and High Competence.
62.	As a Situational Leader, you will "Direct" those who have Low Competence and High Commitment.
63.	"Coaching" needs to be provided to those with Some Competence and Low Commitment.
64.	OSCAR = Outcome, Situation, Choices (Consequences), Actions and Review.
	End Of Ninja Drill

7 Project Development Methodologies

Not all projects are alike and hence they also need to be planned and executed differently. This chapter dives into different methodologies (different ways of conducting a project) for Project Management.
What must be understood that different methodologies are not competitors to project management or alternates to project management, they are just different ways of doing the project under different situations and different levels of complexity.

PMP exams or real world, this is one of those areas that each of the project managers must understand so well that they are able to counsel and consult customers, clients as well as their own management / leadership to apply the most apt combination of project management methodologies for specific situations.

7.1 Project Management Vs Methodology

Methodology is a "Way of conducting a project in a specific situation, industry or domain". Which means that while you may do project management to manage projects but you would have to use a specific set of "Templates", "Rules", "Tools" and even "specific sequence of phases" in certain industries or specific organizations. This would mean that there are various "Methodologies" within the overall umbrella of project management and these methodologies may be specific to certain industries, domains or even to a specific organization. *E.g.; In six sigma projects you may use only one methodology viz., DMAIC (Define, Measure, Analyze, Improve and Control)*. The project management practices of PMBOK® would be used here but they would be used in the sequence as set by this methodology of DMAIC.

Though we would be discussing the "Project Lifecycles" separately, it's important to understand that the term "Project Lifecycle" is not exactly the same as a methodology. One methodology may have one or more project life cycles. However in cases where a methodology has only one lifecycle under it than the terms "Methodology" and "Project Life cycle" become interchangeable. *E.g., Six Sigma has only one Methodology, which is DMAIC, and hence DMAIC is also called the Six Sigma Lifecycle. However Agile is a Methodology and it has multiple project lifecycles under it viz., FDD (Feature Driven Development), SCRUM, and XP (Extreme Programming).*

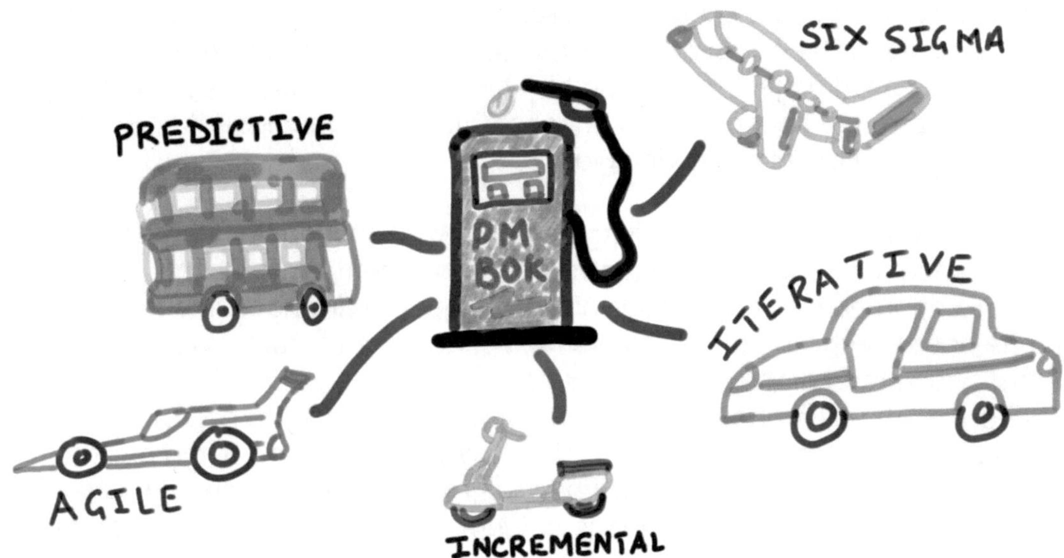

The methodology for "Process Improvement Projects" usually follow the "PDCA" (Plan – Do – Check – Act) from TQM (Total Quality Management) or it could also be from Six Sigma called DMAIC. Some white goods and engineering organizations have created their own "Project Management Methodology" and they even give that methodology a name like, "Robust Engineering Model" or "Project Excellence In Execution" or even "Project Forward". I once worked in an organization which called its Agile Development Methodology as "Shinkansen" (Bullet Train). Fancy Eh! What we need to understand is that "Project Management" is the fuel that drives different methodology. Different methodologies are just different implementation of Project Management based on different situations and different domain.

I hope this puts into perspective how Project Management, Project Methodology, and Project Life Cycles are related or interrelated.

7.2 Project Phases And The Project Lifecycle

In the case of a small project, one could just write all the "Project Activities" down and then track them. However when the project is a medium size or larger or even very complex, just writing all activities would be impossible to track. Hence, what is logically done is that all activities are first identified and then activities are segregated based on their overall relation. Each group of these segregated activities are given a name and these "Group Heads" are called "Phase". Hence a project is normally divided into Phases and each of the phases consists of related activities that together deliver one or more deliverables of the project. Hence a **Phase** = Collection of logically connected project activities culminating into a deliverable or a measurable milestone. *E.g.'s of Phases are "Initiation, Initial Planning, Requirements Generation, Architectural Designing, construction, Audit, Commissioning and so on.*

Now when this is the meaning of phase then it's also quite obvious that the numbers of Phases and the names of these phases, as well as the sequence of these phases, would be

different in different industries, domain, and organizations. Even within the same organization, different categories of projects could have different phases.
This collection and sequence of phases determine the “Lifecycle” of the project. **Hence a Project Lifecycle is the collection and the sequencing of the project phases.** Project lifecycle is also called project methodology. Therefore a methodology is nothing but the sequence and arrangement of project phases. Different arrangement and sequence of phases result into different methodologies.

There are various kinds of Project Lifecycles that exist as industry standards and they are: -

1. **Predictive / Sequential Relationship (also called Waterfall)**
   In this approach, all the Phases of the project are arranged in such a way such that one phase ends and only then the next phase would start and so on, all the way till the last phase (end of the project). They are done, usually, in a non-overlapping manner where each of the phases has to be completed before the next phase can be started. This kind of “Lifecycle” can be used only where the scope of the project is not only clear but also fairly stable. This lifecycle is flexible and hence any “Change” during the lifecycle results into a tremendous amount of rework and time and cost impact.

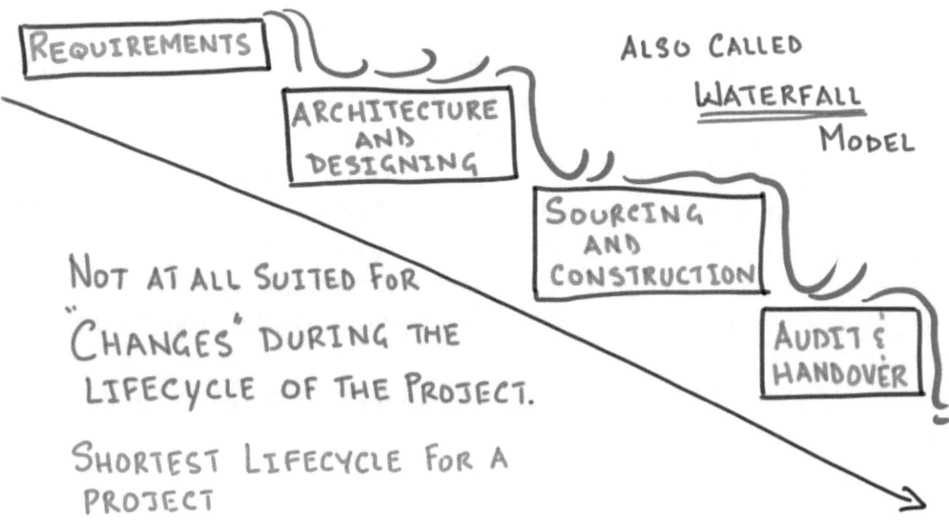

2. **Overlapping Relationships**
   In this approach, the sequential phases are just overlapped to save time. This approach may need more resources and assume more risks than the sequential approach. This is essentially a Predictive / Waterfall lifecycle where the phases overlap the previous phases (every single phase does not have to overlap) to overcome time constraints. This lifecycle is also not very open to “Changes” and has a higher risk because of overlapping phases. This is usually done to overcome the time constraint.

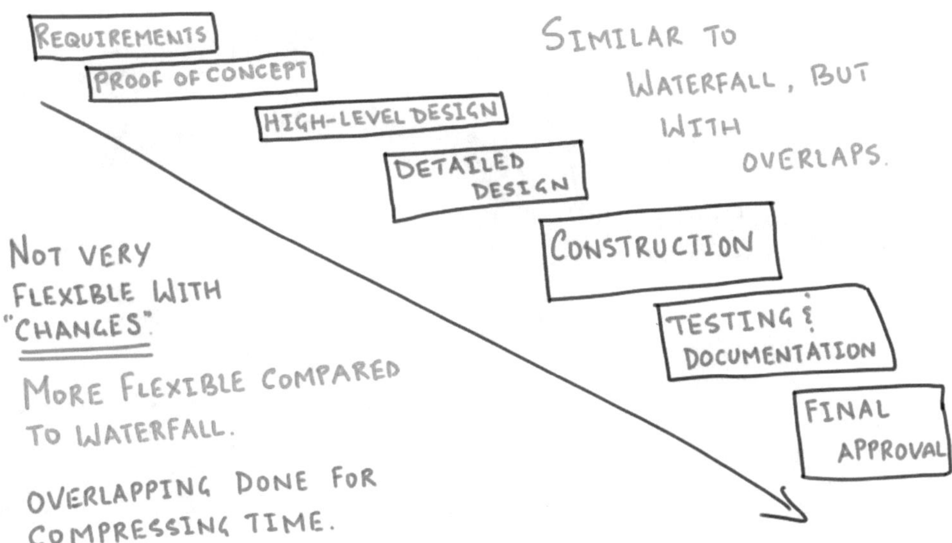
OVERLAPPING RELATIONSHIPS
REQUIREMENTS
PROOF OF CONCEPT
HIGH-LEVEL DESIGN
DETAILED DESIGN
CONSTRUCTION
TESTING & DOCUMENTATION
FINAL APPROVAL
SIMILAR TO WATERFALL, BUT WITH OVERLAPS.
NOT VERY FLEXIBLE WITH "CHANGES"
MORE FLEXIBLE COMPARED TO WATERFALL.
OVERLAPPING DONE FOR COMPRESSING TIME.

3. **Iterative (Adaptive)**

Have you ever wondered how the Vaccine was made to counter Chinese Virus? This was a Research and Development Project. In R&D projects you do not even know if you will be successful or not. Now when the several pharmaceutical giants set out to create the vaccine for the Chinese Virus they were not even aware of the full details about the virus itself, let alone the vaccine for the virus. As you can see such projects turn out to be highly risky. But then a question comes to mind. Is there a way to reduce the risks? Is there a way to come to know earlier on that the project may not be successful and walk out of the project without any further losses? Well, this is where the project life cycle / methodology called "Iterative" comes into picture. Iterative is one of the "Adaptive Life Cycles", meaning this lifecycle would be more adaptive to changes and uncertainties during the life of the project.

Now let us understand this lifecycle taking the example of how the Vaccine was developed.

Let us say you own a pharmaceutical lab that undertakes research for others. You have accepted the project for developing the vaccine for a nation. Since you have done R&D before you know you have to have a methodology that helps you move forward in steps and allows you to make changes as more information is available to you as well as allows you to exit the project or even go back to the drawing board if the results are not moving in the right direction.

For this what you will do is you will do this entire project in a series of iterations. Each iteration would be small R&D project itself. There would not be any deliverable for use at the end of each of the iterations. At the end of each iteration you would come to know either you are in the right direction, or you need to go back to the drawing board and change the way you work or you may decide to quit. Your entire project would be done in the following manner:

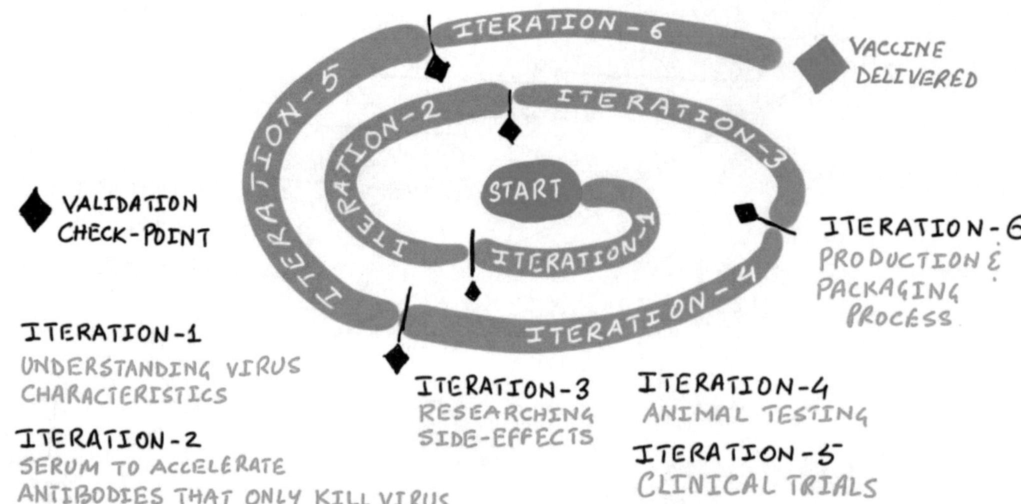

You can see how this methodology allows you to change your plan as well as your design for the next iteration based on the previous iteration. Every iteration helps you understand the project better. It lowers your risk because you are not trying to attempt the entire project in one shot. You may have also seen that none of the intermittent iterations provide any kind of usable deliverable. The final deliverable is the only one that could be used. It would be important to mention here that the diagram as well as the entire explanation in PMBOK about Iterative is wrong. This may be an oversight by the reviewing committee or other learned persons but they have received massive feedback on this mistake hence it is best that you stick to the description and explanation here in this book.

Remember, Iterative is an adaptive methodology and is best for R&D kind of projects. It is applied for R&D projects in every single domain and not just the pharma industry. Several industries call the Iterative methodology as “Spiral Life cycle”.

4. **Incremental (Adaptive)**
Have you seen how the railway lines are laid across the entire country? How the highways are repaired? How you get your house renovated while living in the same house? If you have seen, observed or experienced any one of the above, you already know what Incremental Methodology is. Let us take a real world example that is rather common.
Let us say you want to build a farmhouse at a beautiful ancestral land left to you by your parents. You being a salaried person you may not have all the money to get it done upfront. You also do not wish to take a larger loan because you already have a loan for the apartment that you are living in. Therefore what you do is, first you make a pan as well as a design and then estimate and budget for only getting the entire piece of land fenced or boundary-walled. You hire a contractor, fix a price, provide the specifications and get started. The contractor will then execute as per the plan and once done, will invite you to inspect to see if the wall and the main entry gate along with a security guard room has been created as per your satisfaction. If you are satisfied you will pay the contractor and thus your very first iteration of the project "Farm house" is done. You might think, "hey wait a minute, isn't that Iterative Methodology?" Well! No. It is not. Because after this iteration you have a usable deliverable which, in this case, is the boundary wall. Iterative methodology does not have intermittent deliverables. Now, after sometime, when you obtain some more funds, you decide that you should build a two room house with bath and a kitchen. You can plan for the building structure with an architect, obtain the necessary permissions and get utility connections and again hire a contractor to build you the house as per your specifications. Once the contractor is done and you are satisfied, you now have the end of the second iteration of the project. After this second iteration you have the boundary wall as well as the house for you to live in. I guess, now you can see, where I am going with this. You are incrementally building your farm house one iteration at a time. The amazing thing about this methodology is that, you do not have to have all the funds at the same time, you have the flexibility to keep changing

the design of the deliverables from the next iteration. You also see that each of the iterations have to be estimated, budgeted, scheduled and planned afresh. The overall scope of work remains the same and yet it affords you amazing elbow space to keep on making changes as you proceed.

Iteration - 1

Iteration - 2

Iteration - 3

Iteration - 4

Iteration - 5

Take the example of renovating your home while you are living in it. You get one room renovated completely and only then shift to that room and then get the other room renovated and so on, incrementally. Incremental projects can be used in every single domain for a variety of reasons. However it is never used for R&D projects. Remember, in Incremental methodology at the end of each iteration there would be some usable deliverable but in Iterative methodology there are no intermittent usable deliverables. In iterative methodology the final usable deliverable is only available at the end of the project.

5. **Agile (Adaptive)**
Agile is combination of Iterative and incremental. Like incremental, agile gives intermittent deliverables and just like the iterative lifecycle, agile also evolves the project and can be used for those projects where the scope is not clear.
After the initial planning, smaller iteration with specific phases are created for faster delivery of deliverables and then releasing to customer or market while continuing on the next smaller iteration working on a separate set of deliverables. In between or during the small iterations the scope could be changed and the requirements could be re-prioritized which would become part of the next available small iteration. Agile allows all kinds of changes in the project at any point of time including changes retrospectively (Meaning even redoing the artefacts that have already been delivered as earlier deliverables).
This approach needs a lot of oversight and needs agile processes to help work in this approach.

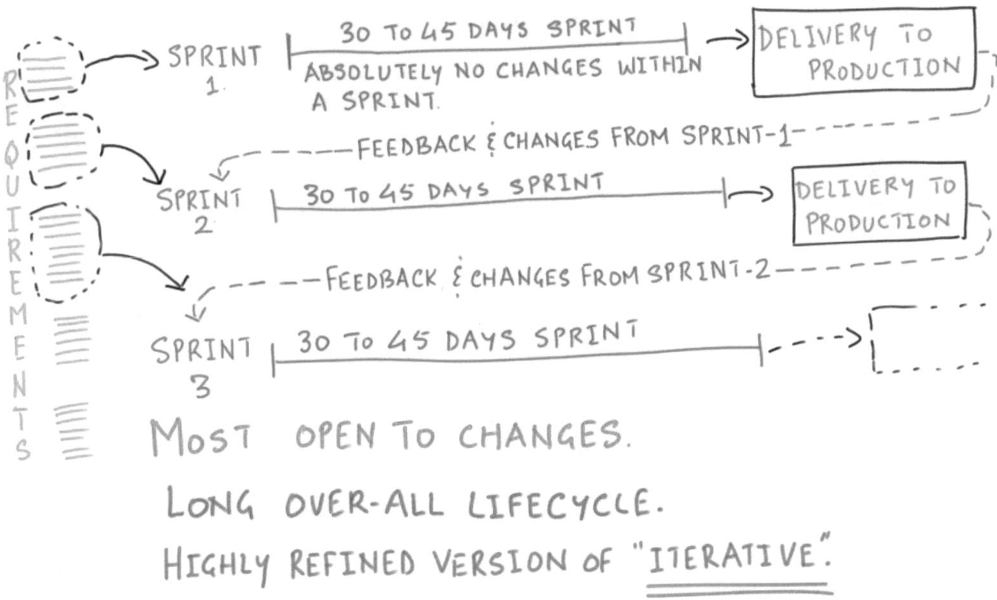

Agile is actually a suite of methodologies. There are multiple flavors of methodologies in this overall umbrella of Agile. Listing a few of them herein below.

1. **SCRUM** – The most popular and also the methodology that PMI has adopted
2. Feature Driven Development (FDD)
3. eXtreme Programming (XP)
4. Lean
5. Crystal
    - Crystal Clear
    - Crystal Yellow
    - Crystal Orange
    - Crystal Red
    - Crystal Maroon

Almost all PMP exams questions around agile would be from SCRUM. Some of the exams questions would be on Flow Based Agile which has been explained later in this book.

6. **Hybrid**
This lifecycle (as the name suggests) is a mix of predictive and adaptive lifecycle. This lifecycle is used in cases where the project starts in an evolving mode and then later, with a better understanding of the scope, the project lifecycle is changed to predictive. Let me give a real-world example. I lead a team in Japan where we were hired by the leading bank there to try and create the very first ever "Suspect Fraud Detection Engine". The engine was to look at all transactions and flag suspect patterns which could lead to fraud thus detecting frauds before they actually happen. No one had any requirements and we did not know of any other such engine in the world to apply as a benchmark at that time. Hence, we started the project in an adaptive iterative lifecycle where we toyed with some ideas and built upon it to see if it worked and so on. In

about 5 months' time, we reached a level where we could fully understand what is needed to be done for such engine for Retail and ATM banking. Therefore, with this finalized scope, we converted the project lifecycle into a predictive / waterfall lifecycle.

No matter which methodology that is used, each phase must be formally closed before moving on to the next one, such that the benefits, deliverables or outputs of one phase is received completely and approved before moving on to the next phase.
These phase-end formal approvals are also just the apt points for "Killing" a project if it is seen that the progress of the project is not in the desired direction. This helps in taking a termination decision earlier on in the project rather then later, thus saving money, effort, and resource usage.

In the exams questions these formal "review and closure of a phase" can be called as "Phase Review" or "Phase End Review" or "Go-No-Go Decision" or "Kill Point" or even "Toll Gate". They all mean just "Formally closing a phase in a project".

7.3 All About Agile

I have added this section for a specific reason. Among the professionals who plan to attempt the PMP exams, many of them are from industries and domain where agile methodologies are not applicable and they may not be well aware of agile. However, for clearing PMP exams a good understanding of agile is a prerequisite. Therefore, instead of taking the agile understanding for granted, I have included this section that walks you through the entire concept of agile in an easy, logical and relatable manner. At the same time, this section would also help those professionals who may have a mixed understanding about agile concepts. It would be important for me to point out here that when it comes to agile methodologies there are just too many misconceptions that are being floated around. This seems to further confuse people. Even if you are software professional and have done some work using agile, it would still be advisable for you to go through this material here to get a practical hold of this subject and also get the authentic explanation that you can rely on.

I guess the best way for you to understand the necessity as well as the benefit of using agile is by providing you how I used it for creating one of my platforms. This will also ensure that you get to know the correct overview and concepts around agile.

A few years back I got an Idea that I should make the very first Audio Platform solely dedicated to project management. Such a platform would be the very first one on the planet, and for some reason it is still the only one till date. Since there was no other platform out there, I had no idea how to start. I had no idea what the look and feel would be. In fact, I did not even know if anyone would like it. After all, people prefer videos and not audios. And yet, I was convinced about the idea. I called my developer who has been making my sites and platforms since the last 8 yrs or so, and told him my idea. We spent an hour discussing my ideas and yet we realized that both of us only ended up having a huge list of ideas around this platform but not one single requirements. We both were not sure if this idea itself would work. We decided to proceed by using agile. Since I did not even know what I wanted in terms of requirements, the best way was to proceed iteratively but at the same time, since the budget for this was not too lavish, we also wanted to get the benefits of intermittent deliverables which we could launch in the market and make some money, as well as test if the market appreciates this idea. Agile being a combination of iterative and incremental, we decided that it would suite us the best, given the circumstances.

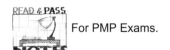

The very first thing that the developer did was to document all my dreams and ideas about this proposed audio platform in an excel sheet. We called that document the "Product Backlog" or just the "Backlog". Backlog is a document that captures all the high-level requirements. These high-level requirements are also called "Epics". We spent a lot of time writing all possible high level requirements / capabilities / epics in the backlog and once we realized that they were enough for the time being (we could add to backlogs at any time during the project), we decided to move to the next stage of the project.

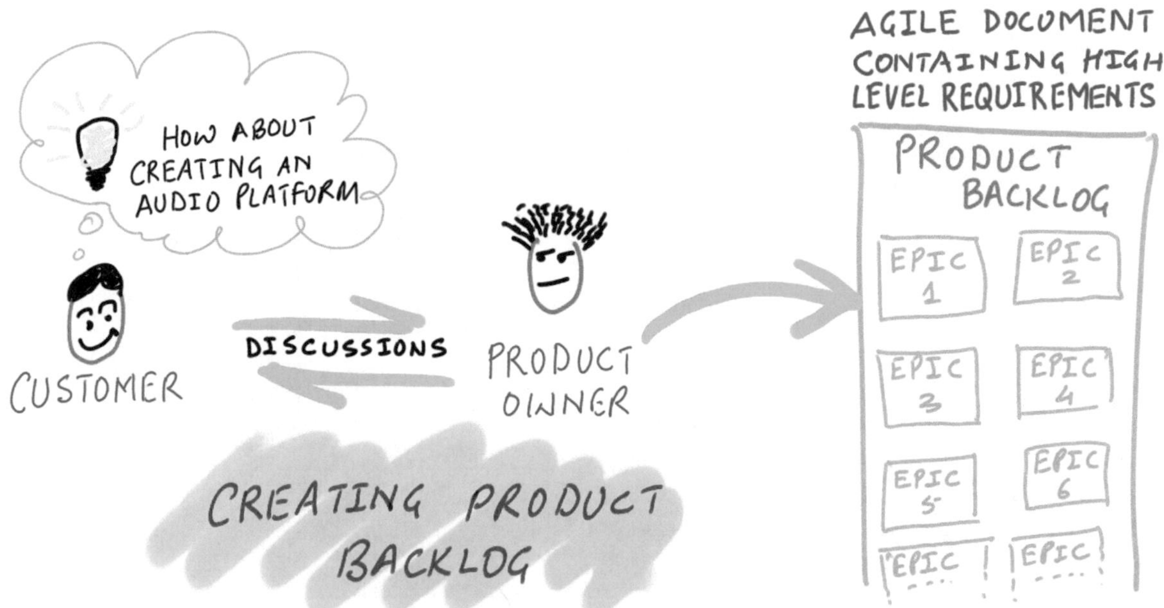

Now if you look at the roles in Agile project, I was the customer while my chief developer was playing the role of a "Product Owner". Frankly a product owner is nothing but a typical Business Analyst and nothing more. They do exactly what a BA does in other methodologies. Just that the role of a BA is called as "Product Owner". If you keep in mind that "Product Owner" = "BA" you will never have any problem with any of the scenario questions about this role, no matter how complex they try to make the question.
Coming back to my audio platform, after populating the backlog it was time to take the next step. The product owner (my chief developer) started to discuss about what I envisioned about the sequence in which my ideas should be implemented. Basically what the product owner was doing was to prioritize the backlog. See the backlog is made up of ideas / epics / high level requirements, but you need to put them in order of the sequence in which the customer would like to see them happen in reality. For my Audio platform, I was not even sure if this platform will be appreciated by my intended user base. Hence it made sense that the very first release (a deliverable or a set of deliverables that can be put into production) should help me test the waters. For this I chose the idea of "Free Audios". This release would be done first to test if people like it. If they do not, I will then stop any further development on this platform. However, if people provide a positive feedback, I will then move to the next release. The next release would be the "Paid Audios". This release would contain features about loading audio packages which people could subscribe to and then listen to the audios

for a specific number of days. The idea was, that if the second release also became successful, then I could use the revenue generated from this release to finance the rest of the releases. Hence this platform would help me build itself and at the same time, I had the flexibility to remove any feature that did not work well with people or stop the entire platform at any stage depending on how people reacted to it. Basically what the product owner was trying to do was to make an overall "Road Map" or "Product Vision" for this platform.
Road Map / Product Vision = The high level sequence of Releases that you envision for your entire project.

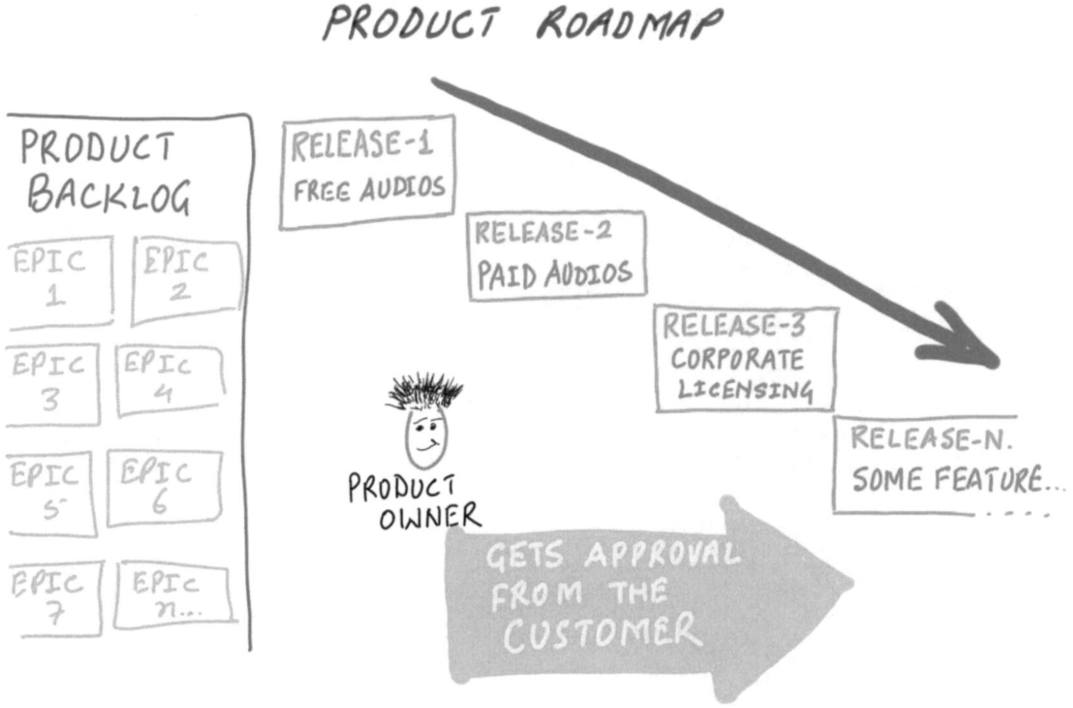

Now it was time to get serious about coding. The product owner created a team of a few developers and presented the first idea (Release) of "Free Audios" to them. Since I had no clue myself how to present the free audios list to the intended users, I asked the product owner to provide some suggestions. The team got together to only focus on the first release viz., Free Audios. The high level requirements connected to the Free Audios were taken from the Backlog and posted in another document called the "Release Backlog". A release backlog is a document that contains the list of High Level Requirements / Epics / Ideas that are going to be created in that specific release. Which means, that while the Product Backlog / Backlog is only one for the entire agile project, there would be one Release Backlog for each of the releases. The requirements still remain high level here. They are just parked the epics here to indicate which high level requirements are being created in which release. Once the team did this, they now set about planning for the entire release of Free Audios. They decided to present the entire first release using three distinct Iterations. Iterations are called "Sprint" in SCRUM (the most popular methodology among Agile suite of methodologies). Remember, "Sprint" = Iteration. You can use them interchangeably as far as PMP is concerned. The very first iteration / sprint was for creating the look and feel of the page where the Free Audios would be listed. Along with it would be the overall look of the platform itself. Based on my reaction and suggestion on the look and feel, the second iteration was for creating the actual front end coding for the user functionality of sorting, listening to and searching for specific audios. And the third sprint was for creating the backend of the platform to allow me to record and upload as well as delete or modify audios that are meant for the Free Audios listing. The team estimated 2 weeks for Sprint 1, 3 weeks for sprint 2 and 3 weeks for sprint 3.

Once this overall planning was done they presented this plan to me via the Product Owner. This plan is called the "Agile Release Plan" or "Release Plan". A release plan is about how the release would be created. How many iterations and in which sequence those iterations would be done and how much time each of the iterations would take as well as the requirements that would be delivered from each of those iterations. Remember, each Release has several iterations. Since our project was not that big or complex, we did not have to have a separate iteration only for planning. This planning iteration is called "Iteration 0". In complex and very large releases, a more comprehensive planning is done with the team. The time taken for planning for this release is adopted as an Iteration itself and hence this iteration which is only meant for planning is called the Iteration 0. It is not necessary that each of the release plans have to have an Iteration 0.

When the team decided on the 3 sprints that they will take to create my first release, they also worked with the product owner to create three different documents, one for each of the iterations, called the "Sprint Backlog" or the "Iteration Backlog". The sprint backlog contains the absolute detailed requirements of all that is going to be created in that iteration. These requirements are so detailed that in Agile they are referred to as "User Stories". User stories are nothing but the detailed requirements written in a detailed narrative manner as if telling a story to the person reading that document. The high level requirements parked in the Release Backlog are broken down into detailed requirements, called user stories, and documented in Iteration Backlog. Iteration backlog only contains the user stories for only those features that are going to be created in that specific iteration.

Now we know, that there are three kinds of Backlogs and they are:

1. Product Backlog
2. Release Backlog and
3. Iteration Backlog

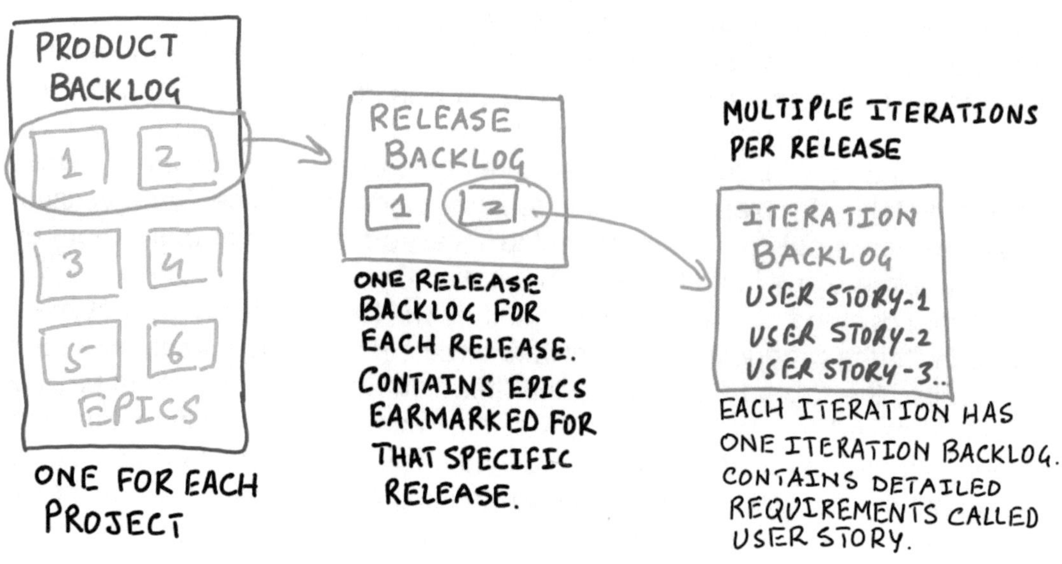

Product Owner is the person responsible for all the backlogs.

Many times in exams scenario question only the term “Backlog” is mentioned. This presents a problem to the candidate because there are 3 different kinds of backlogs and they are unsure which one to assume for the question at hand. In such a case please always assume that “Backlog” = “Product Backlog” and you will never get the answer wrong.

While the team works on the different iterations, the customer can keep altering the content of the product backlog with the help of the product owner. The order in which the releases have to be made can be changed in the product backlog by reprioritizing the content of the backlog. The sequence in which the high level requirements are written in the product backlog decides the sequence in which they are to be released. The customer may end up deleting some earlier ideas, or add some new high level requirements in the product backlog. This alteration of the backlog can be done at any time, irrespective of what is going in the project. This act of constantly updating and altering the Product backlog is called “Backlog Grooming” or “Backlog Refinement”. There is actually a slight difference between Backlog Grooming and Backlog Refinement but it is not something that is required for PMP.

Just before each of the iteration, the team gets together to plan it out very carefully. User stories are created and understood as well as estimated. User stories could be estimated using a variety of ways, and they will be discussed in details at the appropriate location in the planning section later in this book. Sometimes points are allocated to show the relative size of the user story and those points are actually called “Story Points”. Estimation helps the

team understand how many of the user stories could be completed in the given iteration or even decide on the length of the iteration required to finish the given user stories. Schedule is also crated to show the sequence in which the user stories would be developed in that given iteration. Basically, all elements of planning are planned out here for that specific iteration.
It would be important to note here that the Agile team is a “Self Organized Team”. What it means is that once the scope of work is explained to that team, the team decide, among themselves, who will do what and who will assume which role. The team tries to solve the problems and take all development based decisions themselves. Among the team members there is one role called the “Project Leader” or “Agile Leader” or “Agile Manager” or “Scrum Master”. All these varied names are nothing but the role of a Project Manager in Agile. If you see these terms in any of the questions in PMP Exams, the question is basically talking about the Project Manager in Agile project.
Since the agile team is a self-organized team the role of the project manager becomes more of a supporting role. This supporting role of a project manager in agile projects is known as “Servant Leadership”. It is important to note that though the term is “Servant Leadership” it is not one of the “Kinds of leadership”. It is still a management style but instead of giving instructions, delegating work and monitoring work, the role of a supportive manager is to help the team overcome any impediments that come in the way of their working and also mentoring them to grow their ability to work. Hence the name “Servant Leadership”. I was shocked to note to see that some of the books and some of the trainers actually take this term literally and say things like, “Servant Leader” get coffee and cookies for the team, helps them clear their desk etc. Well it is nothing like that. This is just an indicative term to signify that the management style in this team would be more from a mentoring and supporting kind of way rather than instructing and controlling manner. A matured agile team may also change the role of a project manager amongst them intermittently. During these planning meetings conducted by the agile team, the product owner only contributes from the point of ensuring that the backlogs are documented properly and to clarify user story prioritization as well as to ensure that the team understand the user stories well.

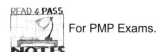

Once the team finishes panning, they let the product owner know the duration of the sprint. In my case the very first sprint was for 2 weeks. Once the team confirmed that, this sprint becomes “Timeboxed” for 2 weeks. What this means is that if, let us say, 4 user stories were earmarked to be finished in the 2 weeks of sprint, and when those 2 weeks are over and one user story was still pending, the sprint will still be ended. The pending user story would have to be done in some other subsequent sprint. That is the meaning of the concept of Timeboxing. Your PMP Exams is timeboxed for 230 mins. Which means if you do not finish your exams in that time you exams will still be considered over. The reason why this is done, is to have some kind of work ready in the promised time to show to the product owner and the customer to obtain feedback. The entire idea of Agile is to make something faster and show it to the customer and understand if the team is on the right direction or not and accordingly move forward. By making bit sized functionality in shorter periods, it is easy to reject the deliverables without costing the customer a lot, if the customer does not like those deliverables. This also allows for constant changes as and when they occur. These changes can also be applied retrospectively.
In SCRUM there is a strong suggestion that the minimum duration of the iteration is for 1 week while the maximum duration is 4 weeks. Remember this is not a hard and fast rule but a strong suggestion as such.

At this time it is important to know the meaning of two important terms that form the backbone of "What needs to be delivered in a Release?" These terms are MVP and MBI. MVP = Minimum Viable Product (I hope you will not confuse it with the NBA MVP concept so popular in US Sports scene), while the MBI = Minimum Business Increment.
Both these terms are not explained properly in PMBOK Guide 7th Edition, but they do show up in exams in scenario questions.

Minimum Viable Product (MVP) is a concept that is associated with the very first release of a new product. In order to test the real market, the very first release of your proposed product should contain only the most basic and yet logically meaningful set of functionality for the intended users. This is done so that proper feedback is obtained from the real users and the rest of the product development may be altered or changed accordingly. This saves the customer to put a lot of money at stake in the very first go and also allows the customer to reach out to the customer earlier with minimum but meaningful functionality to obtain their feedback. In my case of developing the first Audio Platform dedicated to project management, the MVP was the "Free Audios". The feedback I got on it helped my next release drastically.

Minimum Business Increment (MBI) has multiple meanings but in this book we will only understand it from the point of view of kinds of agile questions on PMP exams. MBI is the minimum and yet meaningful increment to the functionality, already in production, that makes business sense and would be meaningful even from the point of the users. Simply put, MVP is about the content of the first release of a new product and MBI is the content making up the subsequent releases. Hence if you look at it from the point of the Audio Platform, while "Free Audios" was MVP, the paid audios was the MBI, followed by another MBI of "Corporate Licensing" and so on. When it comes to MBI, you need to understand that your agile project does not have to be always about creating a new product development. It could also be about enhancing an existing running product. In which case you will never have an MVP, but each of releases content would be based on the concept of MBI. What is the minimum business features that can be released that would be meaningful for the users and provide value to the customer? This concept of MBI helps in not locking up too many functionality in a large release after taking months, only to come to know that your release were not acceptable.

MVP & MBI

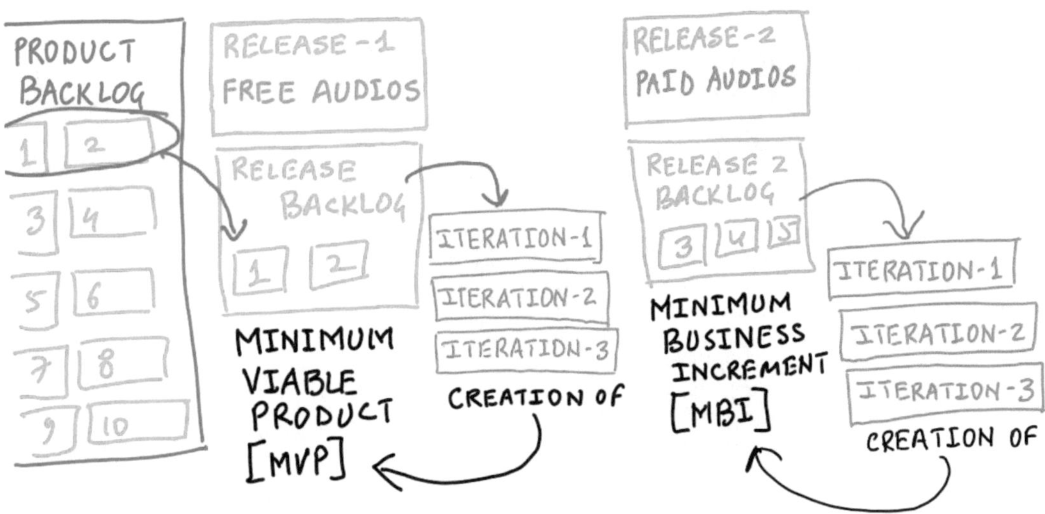

As the agile team starts to code during the iteration the project manager wants to ensure that the project team is not facing any impediments and the fact that the project work is progressing as per the plan. However, this health checking would not be done at the end of a week or fortnight, as is done in most other methodologies. In Agile the iteration is just 1 to 4 weeks long, hence it is imperative that a daily stock taking is done. This is what is called the "Daily Stand Up Meeting" or the "Daily SCRUM". In Toyota, where this concept was invented, the meeting happens in person and at the shop floor and it is a literally stand up meeting. However when this is transported into Agile the team does not have to engage in a literal stand up meeting until all the team members are in the same physical location. Else, it is just a daily meeting. Since this meeting is done daily, it cannot take much time else this meeting itself will end up becoming the biggest disruptor in the flow of work. A rule has been created that states that the daily scrum cannot take more than 15 minutes. Remember, this meeting is not a "Status Review" meeting. It is just a stock taking meeting. In this meeting only three questions are discussed: -

1. What has been done since the last meeting? Any variance there?
2. What has to be done till the next meeting?
3. Any impediment or obstacle being faced or expected to be faced by the team in doing their work?

This meeting is only to understand the progress and usually during these meetings Burn-up charts / Burn-down charts are used for tracking.
However it is important to note that these daily meetings are not for "solving the problems" or finding the exact "cause of variance". Different subsequent meetings with different stakeholders can be done for solutions and recovery or analysis. The daily meeting is done with each and every team member and hence it is just a stock-taking meeting no exceeding 15 minutes. This is one part most of the actual agile practitioners get wrong in real world projects. 45 minutes to 2 hrs of meeting are conducted by project managers with all the team members to solve problems and further analysis and still call it "Daily Stand Up" meeting. This act creates an innate resistance and aversion towards meetings of any kind, among the team members.

DAILY ~~BORING~~/STAND UP MEETING

During the iteration the code is developed, quality controlled and unit tested. Once the iteration is done, whether all the user stories earmarked for that iterations has been completed or not, the iteration would have to end at the expiry of the duration assigned during its planning. Whatever that is produced during this iteration would have to be validated by the product owner and / or customer. This validation process is called the "Iteration Review" / "Sprint Review". Validation basically means ensuring if the finished deliverables are as per the requirements or not. Usually the iteration review is done by the agile team demonstrating the functionality to the product owner, this Iteration / Sprint review is also called "Demo".

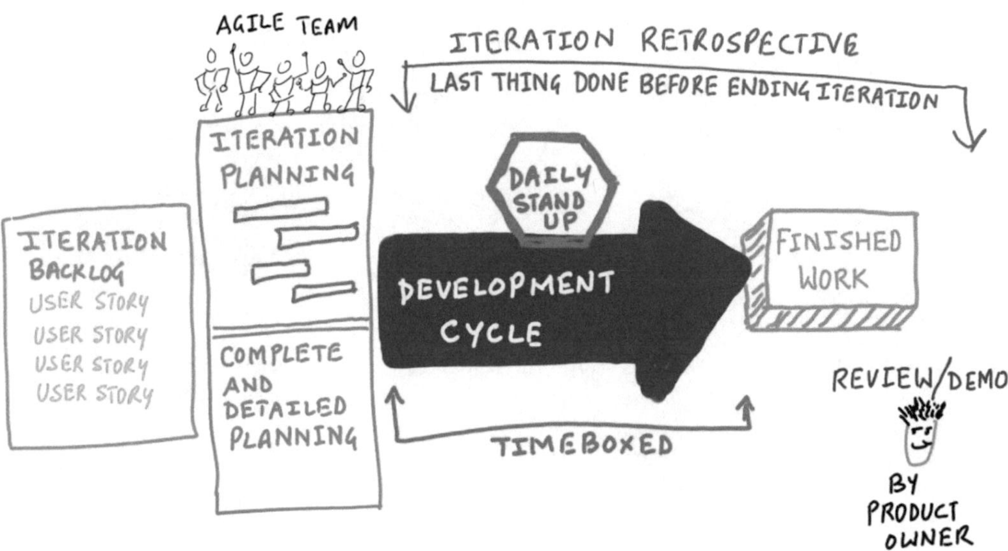

Once the sprint review is done and the observations from that review are documented, there is one last thing that is done before we can say that the sprint is completed. The "Sprint / Iteration retrospective". Retrospective is nothing but lessons learned. A lessons learned meeting is conducted at the end of each iteration, immediately following the sprint review, to understand "what are some of the great things they learnt that should be replicated in other iterations?" and "what are some of the things that must not happen in subsequent iterations?" Once all these learnings are documented, they are then prioritized and the top 4 or 5 priority learnings are agreed upon to be applied from the next iteration. Some of these learnings may be connected to the way of doing things or may be connected to some requirements and hence in such cases the Product Backlog will be updated with this new work ascertained from this Sprint Retrospective meeting. This step means that the sprint is officially completed.

This cycle of iteration after iterations is repeated till there is nothing left in the product backlog. As long as there is an item pending in the product backlog, the agile project keeps going on. Remember, an agile project ends the moment there is nothing left in the product backlog.

This constant bit by bit building up of the product through multiple releases is called the "Continuous delivery".

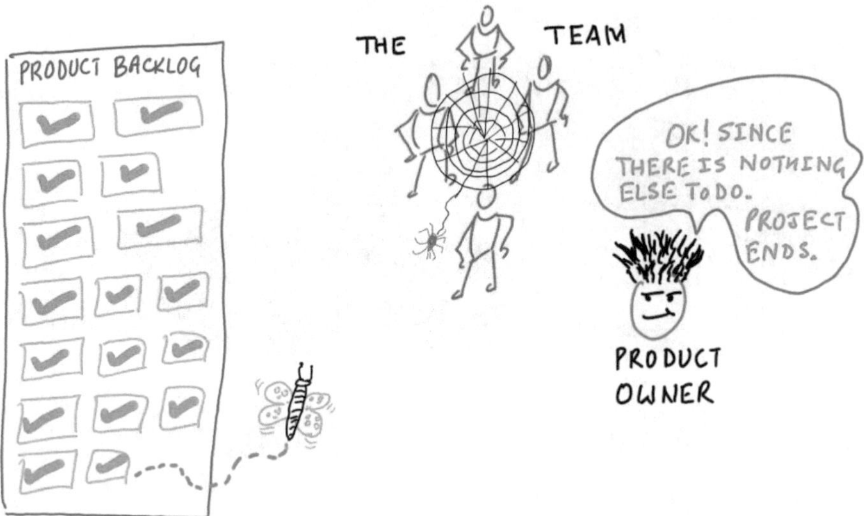

Whatever that we have discussed about agile so far is a rather detailed summary of what is done in an agile project and how it really happens. This will not only practically help you with Agile projects in real world, it will also help you ace most questions on Agile that show up in PMP Exams. I know you must have caught on to the word "most" and wondered, ok what about the rest? Well, these previous paragraphs discussed the agile methodology in details but the detailed tools and techniques would be discussed throughout this book at appropriate places. This book takes us through the life of a project and will constantly alter between predictive and adaptive methodologies at appropriate places and stages of the project. Hence, to prevent you from getting confused, we discussed agile before starting with project management. Now when you read the rest of the book you will easily know when I am talking about predictive methodology and when I am talking about adaptive and agile methodologies. As I said, every aspect of this book has been deliberated in detail before writing it to make it easily understandable by all.

There are a few additional definitions that you must know before moving forward.

7.3.1 Agile Practitioner

Agile Practitioner Is anyone who has an agile mind set. Person with an agile mind set is someone who can work in uncertain conditions and handle changes. A person who understands the concept of evolutionary projects and knowns that agile projects are created because they would have a lot of changes going forward. The Agile mind set is opposite to the "fixed mind set". A fixed mind set is nothing wrong or unwanted. It is just how people think and what kind of work they are comfortable with. My father being a project manager from the 1950s till the 80s, he always worked on projects that had a fixed scope. He would not take kindly to anyone who would keep changing the requirements and stop his work till the stakeholders agreed on what they really wanted before proceeding forward. In his line of work there was no concept of adaptability. However, now with growing uncertainty around the requirements and the birth of evolutionary projects, in certain industries, professionals like you and I need to be comfortable in working with limited and ill-defined scope as well as in volatile situations as well. Even today there are a lot of industries where Fixed Mind set is highly celebrated. Remember, agile mind set is not a qualification. It is just an ability.

7.3.2 Servant Leader

Though we have talked about servant leader concept earlier, we need to discuss this a little more to ensure you understand all aspects around it. Irrespective of what any other trainer or book may have told you about servant leader, just stick to the concepts and explanations below and you will be absolutely safe.

The project manager has to be a servant leader in agile projects. The explanation of why that is needed has already been explained earlier while explaining the agile concept.

I am putting all of this in the form of points so that it would be a lot easier to understand and remember.

1. The most important contribution of a servant leader is to remove impediments (also called obstacles, hurdles and challenges) for the team or help and guide the team remove those impediments.
2. Servant leader must help the team members grow individually as a person as well help grow their abilities and skills.
3. Servant leader must help their team members become healthier, wiser, freer, and more autonomous. This is also called "Empowering" the team members.
4. Servant leaders must groom some team members to become servant leaders in due time.
5. Servant leader must be proactive by anticipating risks and future possible impediments and plan for appropriate prevention.
6. Servant leader must ensure that all team members understand the "Vision" of the product.
7. Servant leaders protect the project team from internal and external diversions that redirect the project team from the current objectives, and help them keep focus.
8. The servant leader also provides tools and encouragement to keep the project team satisfied and productive.
9. Facilitate team's discovery and definition of agile.
10. Help define "Why" of the project
11. Promote self-awareness
12. Listening / Active Listening
13. Serving team members
14. Helping team and certain other stakeholders grow
15. Coaching instead of controlling
16. Promoting safety respect and trust
17. Promoting energy within the team and certain stakeholders
18. Promote collaboration and communication within the team
19. Act as impartial bridge builders (among team as well as among stakeholders)
20. Remove or resolve impediments
21. Celebrate team success
22. Remove work barriers encountered by the team
23. Educate the stakeholders about the processes being followed
24. Celebrate the team's accomplishments

If you go through these points a couple of times you will realize that you do not have to remember them. Just imagine that as a servant leader you are a coach and a mentor, hence as a mentor and a coach, how would you behave with the team. Being a typical "confidence building and empowering" father figure is what this is all about and once you understand this simile, you will not need to remember these points specifically.

A product owner is not expected to be a servant leader but a project manager must portray behaviour of a servant leader in agile projects.

7.3.3 Agile Release Plan

Agile Release Plan is a schedule plan that shows how the specific release is going to get delivered. Agile release plan is almost always made for only one release at a time. Rarely if the project is much smaller or there are two or more smaller releases, can an agile release plan show the schedule of more than one releases.
Basically this plan documents and presents the numbers of iterations as well as their sequence and their individual durations along with the list of deliverables that each of those iterations would generate to deliver the capability and functionality promised in the specific release in question.
Agile release plan is made multiple times in an agile project, moving from one release to another in the sequence as documented in the "Overall Road Map" or the Project Vision.

Remember, iteration 0 is a planning iteration.

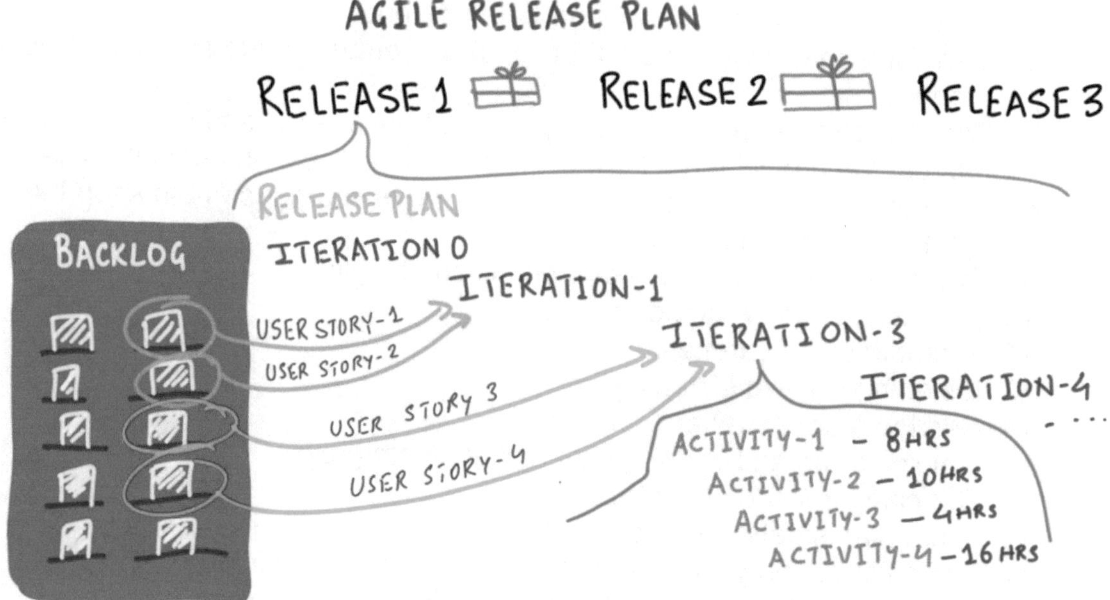

7.3.4 Iteration Based Agile Vs Flow Based Agile

Though PMBOK Guide 7th edition does not specifically discuss this topic, the exams would expect you to know this to correctly answer certain kinds of scenario based questions. This has been explained lightly in the PMI Agile Standards (Part of PMBOK Guide 6th Edition).
We know what iterations are. They are mini "waterfall" lifecycles to help develop a small set of deliverables. Basically, if you have understood agile well, agile is made up of several iterations (mini waterfalls) to progressively develop and deliver the project over time. However the way the iterations are managed in an agile project decides whether the

project is following the "Iteration based Agile Methodology" or the "Flow Based Agile Methodology".
In iteration based methodology each iteration in the project is of the same timeboxed duration. At the beginning of the project it may be decided with the customer, that the team will deliver something every 3 weeks. Which means for each iteration only the amount of user stories would be picked up which could be done in 3 weeks. This way the customers would also be aware and be ready to receive something every 3 weeks. This creates a flow of expectation across all stakeholders and maintains a rhythm of delivery. Simply put, all iterations in the "Iteration based agile" will have the same timeboxed duration.

On the other hand, in a Flow based agile each of the iteration durations is derived based on the numbers of specific user stories that are required to be delivered in each of the iterations. The customer (through the product owner) prioritizes and also dictates which user stories need to be delivered in which specific iteration and based on this the team estimates the amount of time they would need to finish those user stories in that iteration. Simply put, in Flow based agile the iterations have different timeboxed durations. Basically, for the Iteration based project we choose the user stories that could be done in the fixed duration iteration while in the flow based iteration we estimate the duration of the iteration based on the numbers and kinds of user stories that need to be delivered in that iteration.

ITERATION Vs FLOW BASED AGILE

ITERATION BASED AGILE

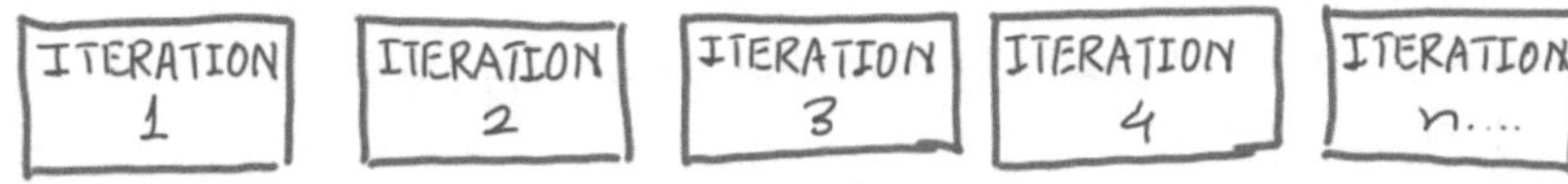

HERE DURATION OF EVERY ITERATION IS EXACTLY THE SAME.
HAS REGULAR CADENCE

FLOW BASED AGILE

HERE DURATION OF EACH ITERATION IS DIFFERENT.
HAS IRREGULAR CADENCE.

The reason we need to know the difference between the two is because these two methodologies use different information radiators (something explained later) for managing the projects.

Remember that the common information radiators used in "Iteration based agile" are Burnup / burndown charts. To understand the average speed of team progress,

productivity measures like "Velocity" and "Throughput" are calculated. These terms are explained later.
However, in "flow based agile", Kanban charts are used. Burndown and burnup charts could also be used in Flow based agile but from the exams point of view remember that if the question is talking about burnup / burndown chart then the question is referring to Iteration based agile. The productivity measures common for flow based agile projects are "Lead Time" and "Cycle Time". These two are explained in the section where Kanban is discussed later.

7.3.5 Information Radiators

Just as the name suggests these are a group of chats and tools that provide information to the team members at all times. Information radiators are also called the "Big Visible Charts (BVC)" (Yes! US citizens like to keep things simple, don't they). These charts are placed at prominent places of work and meeting locations of the team members. In virtual teams these charts are dynamically updated page that constantly shows the progress of the project.
The purpose of these radiators / charts is to allow the team to ascertain the up-to-the-minute key information about the project and particularly the iteration in execution. The biggest benefit that these radiators serve is that information is available to the team without disturbing them from their work to attend meetings or updates or to look at emails.

The most popular information radiators are:

1. Burndown Chart
2. Burnup Chart
3. Velocity Chart
4. Iteration Cumulative Flow Diagram
5. Kanban Chart
6. Variance Analysis Reports
7. Traffic Lights (Red Amber Green – RAG Charts)
8. EV Reports
9. Bar Charts

Some of these charts would be explained in the subsequent paragraphs and some would be explained later at appropriate places in this book.

7.3.6 Burnup, Burndown and Combined Burn Chart

One of the most popular charts (both in exams as well as in real projects) are the Burnup and Burndown Charts. These Charts typically show the overall progress in an iteration in terms of the work done. These charts usually show the numbers of "User Stories" completed or pending in a given iteration. In those projects where estimation method of "Story Points" are used, these charts could also show the numbers of story points finished or number of story points pending in a given iteration.
A burndown chart shows the numbers of user stories or story points remaining against the time left in the said iteration.

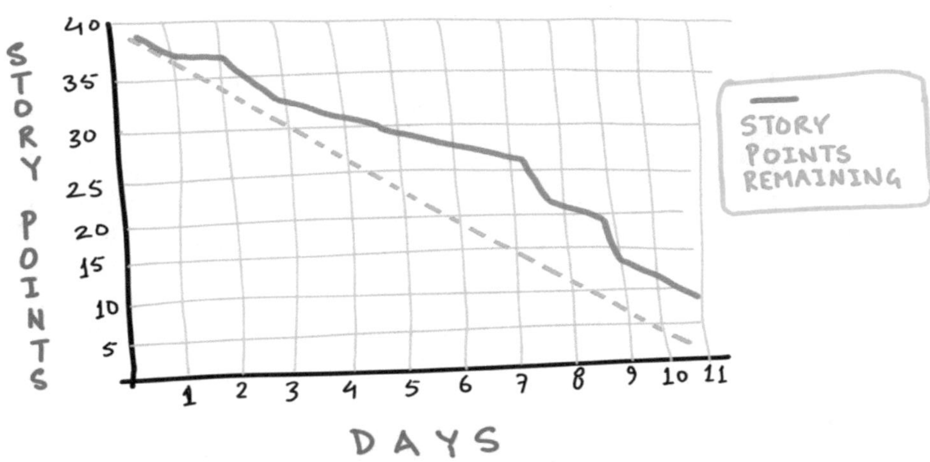

While the Burnup chart shows the numbers of story points or user stories pending against the time left in the given iteration.

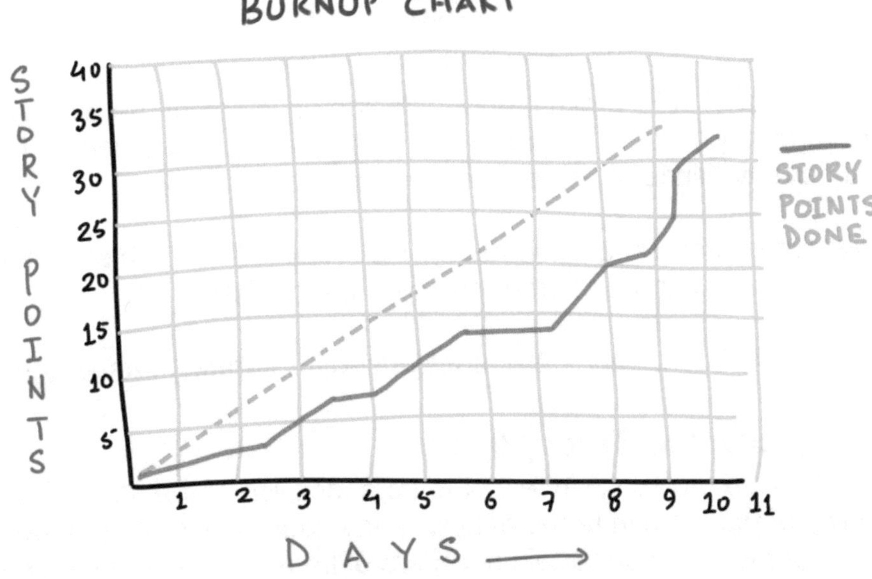

The "combined burn chart" shows both burndown chart as well as the burnup chart in a single chart. It also shows the stability of requirements / user stories during the length of the iteration. Any disturbance in stability of the user stories (like adding, deleting or modifying user stories) during the iteration must be correlated with the resulting blimps in the burnup and burndown lines.

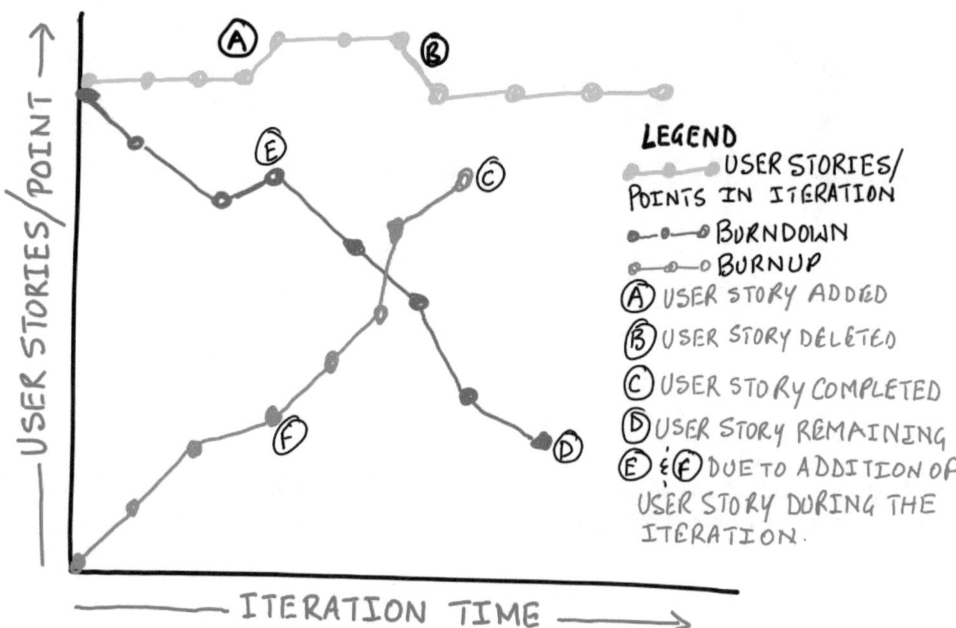

Generally in a real agile project, teams decide on which of the burn charts to use and stick with it throughout the project. This is done to avoid confusion of "Glass half full or glass half empty" kinds of perceptions among team members.

In exams sometimes the questions only state "Burn Chart", this term is the same as either burndown chart or burnup chart or combined burn chart.

Do not forget that burn charts are mostly used in "Iteration based agile projects".

7.3.7 Velocity and Throughput

In iteration based projects, since all the iterations are of the same duration, the productivity of the team in terms of how many user stories or story points are being conducted per iteration. A certain numbers of iterations must have been done by the team to start understanding their rate of finishing the user stories or story points per iteration. This productivity measure is what is called the Velocity. Needless to say this kind of productivity measure cannot be used in a flow based project because the iterations would not be of equal length.

The Throughput is a more granular version of the Velocity. A throughput sates the productivity of the team against a specific unit of time. E.g., User stories completed per week or Per day or per fortnight.

Velocity is calculated against the iteration duration and throughput is measured against a unit of time (which may not be the same as the length of the iteration).

When the velocity or throughput are plotted on a chart against each of the iterations, it shows if the team is getting more productive over time or not. This chart is called the Velocity Chart or the throughput chart.

7.3.8 Kanban Board / Kanban Chart

Kanban board is used in mostly Flow based projects. This board / chart shows the status of the individual user stories in that given iteration. This is one of the information radiators and shows the overall progress of the iteration vis-à-vis the user stories earmarked for that iteration. These charts also help the team quickly identify impediments and obstacles that is preventing the progress of certain user stories.
The time it takes for a user story once it is placed on the Kanban chart till it is completed and meets with all the points in the "Definition of done" for that user story, is called the Lead Time. However the Cycle time is the time difference between a user story is being placed in development (different than placing it on the board) till it is completed and meets all the points in the definition of done for that user story.

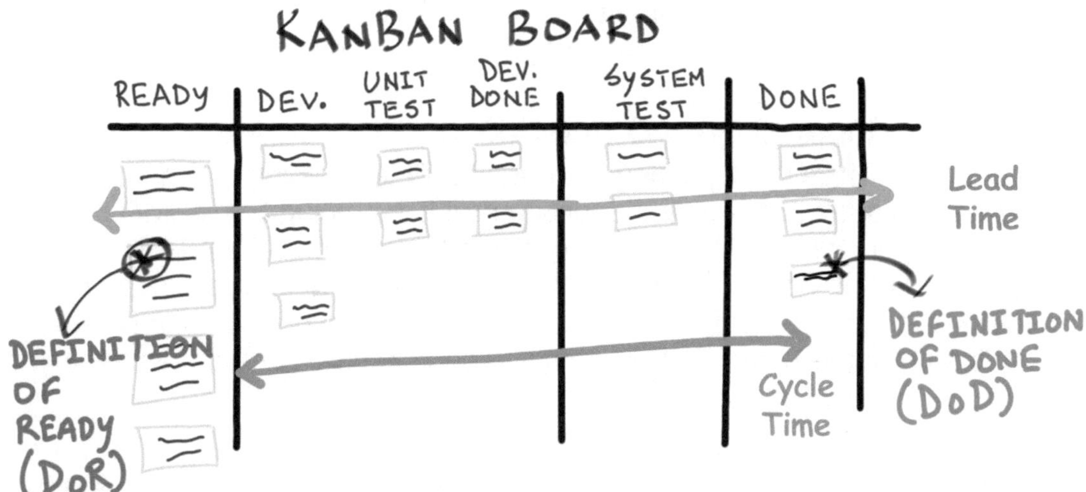

Lead time is useful to understand cycle time from the first look at a particular feature to the length of time it took to release it to the customer. The work in progress (WIP) limits at the top of each column, shown in boxes here, allows the team to see how to pull work across the board. When the team has met its WIP limits, the team cannot pull work from the left into the next column. Instead, the team works from the right-most full column and asks, "What do we do as a team to move this work into the next column?" This leads to improving productivity as well as removing impediments if any.

7.3.9 Definition of Ready (DoR) and Definition of Done (DoD)

Definition of Ready (DoR) is basically a checklist to ensure that all the information that is needed for the targeted user stories, is available with the team such that they can start working on it without having to come back to product owner or the customer midway in their work to understand more about the user story they are working on. DoR is a very important tool to remove assumptions about a user story that a team may have which may result into missed information that may hinder progress when the team actually starts to work on it. Iterations and sprints are for a short duration and while executing a sprint if some team members get stuck due to lack of information connected to a user story, it may derail your entire iteration. Hence DoR ensures that the team has all that they need about user stories before they start working on those user stories in an iteration.

Definition of Done (DoD), on the other hand, is a checklist of all that needs to be completed, checked and validated before the deliverables can be said to be completed and ready for use as per the customer. This too removes any assumption that may lead to any kind of difference in expectation.

7.3.10 Agile Ceremonies

Agile ceremonies are nothing but the regular intermittent meetings and team collaboration events in the course of delivering the deliverables to the customer.
There are 4 Agile ceremonies and they are:-

1. Sprint / Iteration Planning
2. Daily stand up meeting / Daily SCRUM
3. Sprint Review / Iteration Review / Demo and
4. Sprint / Iteration Retrospective

Each of these ceremonies and meetings have been discussed earlier.

7.3.11 Value Driven Office (VDO)

Value Driven Office (VDO) is nothing but a PMO, something that has been explained earlier in this book. But then the question is, if it is nothing but a PMO then why does it have a different name? Well in organizations that use more of adaptive methodologies they tend to refer to their PMO as VDO. VDO usually maintains a supporting and mentoring roll and in most cases do not ever assume Controlling or Directive roles ever. From the purposes of the PMP Exams you can simply treat them as the same as PMO.

7.3.12 Epic, User Story, Story Map and Story Points

The term Epic has been one of the most abused term in the management world connected to agile. Almost every book and every other trainer has a different meaning and explanation about what it means. Some of these wrong explanations have over 30K views in youtube and thus it becomes scary about the potency of a well-made video that explains things wrongly and still finds so many viewers that believe it. I guess that is a problem with just about every other topic that is discussed on youtube, be it health, exercise or finance and not just management.
Let us understand why the term EPIC was introduced in the Agile circles. This will help with your understanding in a way that you will never ever forget it. Agile alliance people were looking for alternate words to describe “High Level Requirements” and “Detailed Requirements” for Agile. They needed different terms because they wanted to differentiate themselves from the rest of the existing authorities on “Requirements” like IIBA and PMI. This is also the reason they have a different term for almost everything that already exists. Unsuspecting people take this difference in terminology as a literal difference and try to split hair trying to prove a difference between agile and project management terms. If you look at stories like “Mahabharat” (for those who are not Indians please search the internet and understand why it is the largest historically proven story ever told on the planet) and Bible, they are always called as Epic. An epic is a huge story that spawns several stories. Taking this metaphor further, Agile called all the high level requirements or capabilities or ideas as “Epic” and the detailed requirements that are derived from this epic as “User Stories”. Hence you will find that the Epics are written in Product Backlog and parked for specific releases, in the Release Backlog, but the User stories are documented in the Iteration backlog.

Story Map is nothing but a diagram like “Story board” or “Use Case Model” or “Flow diagram” that explains the overall flow of the requirements and how different aspects of the high level requirements as well as detailed requirements are interconnected. In the exact words of PMI, “A story map is a visual model of all the features and functionality desired for a given product, created to give the project team a holistic view of what they are building and why”. Again, as you can see, a different name for an existing terminology.

Now the term “Story Points” have been loosely fashioned on a very scientific software estimation methodology developed by IFPUG in Europe viz., Function Points. However unlike Function Points there is nothing scientific about Story Points. These are just point system decided among the team members (it is not an international standard or benchmark and hence each team may have their own measurements) to be allocated to a user story to signify its relative size. This is the reason why “Story Points” are called Relative Estimates. These points would then be used for estimating the effort and duration needed for completing it. When it comes to user stories, they are not all the same size therefore instead of making it purely qualitative like “Simple”, “Moderate” and “Complex” (a method which is still globally very popular in software circles), a certain amount of rationality and quantitative element is being brought in by giving “relative size number points” to each user story. Usually these numbers are based on a modified “Fibonacci Series” where a smaller number like 1 or 2 or 3 indicate a user story that has very small size while a higher number would indicate it to be a much larger story that would result in greater effort and duration. This makes it a bit more mathematical in measuring team productivity against “Story Points” instead of against “User Stories”. More details about exactly how these Story points are allocated would be discussed during scheduling later in the book.

7.3.13 Swarming and Mobbing

I know this term sounds like people going crazy over stuff in departmental stores during major sales or during “Black Friday” and slugging it out over few remaining items. It also brings ugly memories, thanks to TV News, of radicalized religious people mobbing a group of people from any other faith. But, thankfully, when it comes to agile, they do not mean that. Nor do they have such violent and aggressive tones. These terms are taken from the way insects Swarm together (also called mobbing) to overcome a difficult situation. This is not an agile specific term. These terms have been in use since the turn of the century to build team dynamics. I am sure you may have seen those heart-warming videos generally showing a kid being unable to do some difficult jump or exercise or gymnastic move and then suddenly all his team members would swarm around him to give him encouragement, provide directions and motivation and post that suddenly that kid is able to perform that task, or about a group of individuals who are not able to scale a tall wall individually but suddenly they make human ladder and together they are able to scale a wall. That is exactly how it is used in Agile. Certain difficult codes or issues or impediments could be solved by “Swarming” around it and solving it together. Remember swarming is the same as mobbing. However one must understand that swarming is only done once the person responsible for the work has tried their best and still are unable to solve the problem. Swarming is not to be done as a default measure to solve problems.

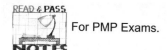

7.3.14 Cadence

This term is important only from the point of understanding the scenario question if this term shows up in PMP Exams. Many organizations refuse to use this term as it tends to confuse people. However, it is a term that is used a lot in PMI (PMP as well as ACP). Cadence simply means "a rhythm of doing something". If your day is more or less similar every single day, you have a cadence in your daily work. In agile it simply means the rhythm of delivering artefacts to the customers. Which means if in your project it has been decided that each of the iteration is for, say, 3 weeks, then you have created a cadence for delivery. Every 3 weeks, like clockwork, you will deliver something to the client and the client would give their feedback and this cadence will continue till there is nothing left in the product backlog.
Flow based projects cannot really have a regular cadence, since the iterations would all have a different duration. Hence in exams if the term "regular cadence" shows up then just assume that the question is talking about an Iteration based agile project.

This takes care of agile in a manner that would ensure that you have a proper and practical understanding of Agile methodologies.

Once you have gone through this, you would now appreciate the 4 values that make up the Agile Manifesto. I decided to show it only once you understood the agile practically so that you can now understand and appreciate these values in their true context.
Let us go through them.

1. **Individuals and interactions** over processes and tools.
2. **Working software** over comprehensive documentation.
3. **Customer collaboration** over contract negotiation.
4. **Responding to change** over following a plan.

All these four values only show the priority and do not replace what is shown in the right side of each statement. Processes and tools are important and necessary but they cannot replace nor should be put above individual observations, suggestions and network in agile projects. Each of these 4 statements need to be remembered since they form the backbone of the agile methodologies. Now that you know about agile, understanding these 4 values would not be confusing at all. Having read them before understanding agile ends up confusing a lot of people. This is the reason why some people mistakenly think that "There is no documentation at all in agile". Yep! Not kidding. This is because someone just took the value no. 2 literally without understanding anything about agile and why and when it is needed.

From the exams point of view these 4 values need to be well remembered because several scenario questions are presented to test your understanding of these values. The scenario may talk about how your team members are talking about what is mentioned in the contract and what is not and on the other hand one of the users at the customer side is putting forward a new requirement. In such cases go for an answer-option that is nearest to the value no. 3. Viz., Customer collaboration over contract negotiation. Once you remember these rules you will find many such agile based scenario questions so easy to answer. If you are from an industry where agile is not used and you have to understand agile only so that you can obtain PMP certification, in such cases it becomes imperative that you make it a habit of applying these 4 values rather deliberately to each and every scenario question on agile in the exams. This is to counter your traditional mindset that would automatically engage while answering such agile questions and you may thus end up answering it wrongly.

Irrespective of what you read anywhere else or no matter which kind of project expert promise applicability of Agile in different kinds of domain and industries, please note that Agile Methodologies can only be applied for Software development and certain services and nothing else. Many authors and trainers say that agile can even be applied to construction and infrastructure, please do not take that seriously. Such authors and trainers tend to assume that anything that is not predictive (waterfall) is agile. This is a wrong assumption and a very dangerous one at that. Some infrastructure and civil work is done using Incremental methodology (Most temple complexes in India some of which are over 10,000 yrs old, Pyramids and even the Roman aqueducts were constructed in increments, over a long period of time using incremental methodologies) which is not Agile. Remember, apart from Agile there are Incremental and Iterative methodologies which form part of Adaptive. Everything in Adaptive is not Agile.

7.4 Ninja Drill – Project Methodologies

You will find a Ninja Drill which lists the most important points you must remember for the exams, this chapter is concerned.

S. No.	Drill Points
1.	Methodologies = Arrangement of phases in a project.
2.	What is the appropriate methodology for Research and Development [R&D] project? Iterative.
3.	When the requirements are very clear and are not expected to change much, which the most appropriate methodology? Predictive
4.	What is the best methodology when the project scope is clear but the entire project cannot be undertaken because of risk exposure or funding issues? Incremental.
5.	If your customer wants an evolutionary software development and wants to you constantly check with him to understand if the project is moving in the correct direction? Agile.

6.	Categories of Project Methodologies are:
	• Predictive
	• Adaptive
	  o Iterative
	  o Incremental
	  o Agile
	• Hybrid

7.	Any question in exams which talks about "Iteration" means it is talking about some kind of Adaptive project.
8.	Hybrid is when more than one methodology is applied within one project lifecycle.
9.	Predictive methodology is not supportive of changes in a project
10.	Adaptive methodology are adaptive to changes in a project.
11.	Predictive and Iterative methodologies do not have any intermittent deliverables.
12.	Incremental and Agile methodologies have intermittent deliverables.
13.	There are two kinds of Agile projects, viz., Iteration based and Flow based.
14.	In iteration based agile all the iterations have the same duration.
15.	In flow based agile different iterations would have different durations.
16.	There is no change management plan or change management system in Agile (unless you wish to make changes within a running iteration).
17.	The values in Agile Manifesto are: 1. **Individuals and Interactions** OVER Processes and Tools 2. **Working Software** OVER Comprehensive Documentation 3. **Customer Collaboration** OVER Contract Negotiations 4. **Responding To Change** OVER Following A Plan
18.	Roles in Agile projects are: 1. **Project Manager** / Project Leader / Scrum Master / Team Leader 2. **Product Owner** (responsible for all backlogs) 3. **Agile Team** 4. **Agile Consultant** / Coach (External or Internal)
19.	**Product backlog** contains high level requirements called Epics.
20.	**Product backlog** can be updated by Product Owner at any time.
21.	All the requirements in product backlog are prioritized for development.
22.	Agile project delivers to the client through a series of "Releases".
23.	The way and the sequence in which the releases would be made in is called Road Map.

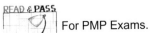

24.	Each release would contain several iterations.
25.	Each iteration has an iteration backlog associated to it.
26.	Iteration backlogs have detailed requirements called "User Stories".
27.	**Minimum Viable Product [MVP]** is the very first release that contains the least amount of features and requirements that would still make business sense for the customer and provide business value.
28.	Every following release after MVP is called **Minimum Business Increment [MBI].**
29.	Each iteration is timeboxed (meaning the iteration has to end at the decided time whether all the requirements / user stories have been completed or not).
30.	Daily standup meeting / daily scrum is conducted for 15 minutes.
31.	3 questions of Daily Standup meeting. 1. What did you do since the last daily standup? 2. What is planned to be done till the next daily standup? 3. Any impediments or challenges faced by you?
32.	Daily standup is not the right forum for solving problems or removing impediments.
33.	Daily standup meeting is attended by all team members.
34.	After iteration ends the working software is shown to the customer or product owner and feedback is obtained and this meeting is called the Iteration Review / Sprint Review / Demo.
35.	The last thing done in an iteration before moving on to the next iteration is the Iteration Retrospective.
36.	After retrospective the team may prioritize their learnings and even update the backlog with the help of Product owner, with required priority.
37.	Only the product owner can cancel an iteration / sprint.
38.	There are three kinds of Backlogs and they are: 1) Product Backlog 2) Release Backlog (Not important from PMP exams Point of view) and 3) Iteration Backlog
39.	Story point signifies the relative complexity of the user story in terms of difficulty, time and effort needed to complete it.
40.	Agile teams are supposed to be cross-functional and self-organized and self-managed. They can decide the roles of the team members amongst them.
41.	By providing the agile team to make some local decisions on their own the servant leader can Empower the team.
42.	The most important role of a Servant leader is to remove or help remove obstacles, impediments or hurdles that the team faces or may face.
43.	The detailed planning of a release showing the further details of the iterations and user stories to be developed within each of the iterations and in what sequence, is what is called the Agile Release Plan.
44.	Iteration "0" is a planning iteration.
45.	Efficiency tools used in Iteration based agile are: 1. Burnup and burndown chart (also combined burn chart) 2. Velocity 3. Throughput
46.	Efficiency tools used in flow based agile are: 1. Kanban board 2. Lead time 3. Cycle time
47.	Kanban board / chart is visualization tool that shows work in progress to help identify bottlenecks and over commitments, thereby allowing the team to optimize the workflow.
48.	Cadence is the rhythm or pattern of iterations and deliveries made.
49.	Definition Of Ready (DoR) means that the team has all the necessary information about a user story to start working on it.
50.	Definition of Done (DoD) a checklist of all the criteria that needs to be met before the user story can be considered completed to the extent that it could be delivered to the customer for them to use it.

51.	Common agile ceremonies: 1. Sprint / Iteration Planning 2. Daily Stand up / Daily SCRUM 3. Sprint Review / Demo 4. Sprint Retrospective
52.	Tailoring is the deliberate adaptation of approach, governance, and processes to make them more suitable for the given environment and the work at hand.
53.	An Agile project finishes once there is nothing left in the Product Backlog.
54.	Tailoring involves altering leadership and management styles based on the situation at hand.
55.	Usual aspects of tailoring are: • Life cycle and development approach selection, • Processes, • Engagement, • Leadership / Management styles • Tools, and • Methods and artefacts.
56.	**When your project produces poor quality deliverables** then tailor your project to add more feedback verification loops and quality assurance steps.
57.	**When your team members are unsure of how to proceed or undertake their work** tailor your project to add more guidance, training, and verification steps.
58.	**In case you have to wait longer periods for obtaining authorizations and approvals** then tailor the project by streamlining approval decisions through fewer people authorized to make decisions up to certain value thresholds.
59.	**If your project is producing too much scrap or work in progress** then tailor your project to use techniques like value stream mapping and Kanban boards to visualize the work, identify the issues, and propose solutions.
60.	**If you experience detached stakeholders or they are providing negative feedback** then first evaluate whether sufficient information is being shared with stakeholders and then based on the outcome tailor the project for more feedback loops and deeper engagement instead of just communicating.
61.	**If your team is constantly challenged by issues which they seem unprepared for** thus engaging in more firefighting than actual work, the first thing to do is to evaluate your risk management as well as conduct a root cause analysis on your existing processes and then tailor your project processes to close the gap.
62.	Agile Facilitator is usually the same as the Agile Project Manager.
End Of Ninja Drill	

8 Initiating A Project

The very first thing that we do in project is the Initiation. A project officially starts the moment it is initiated. Some domain call project initiation as "Start Up". Essentially there are two main documents made during initiating a project viz., Project Charter (also called Initiating document) and the Stakeholder Register.
However, before a project gets initiated, there are several things done or decided upon. These things done before initiation are not part of the project.

There is usually some confusions about, exactly when does a Project Start. What is the starting point of a project? The answer is "the moment a project charter is created". All the steps that were taken until the time the project charter was created (*e.g. Pre-sales, contract vetting, proposal writing*) are not part of the project. A project starts the moment a "Project Charter" is created.

WHEN DOES THE PROJECT ACTUALLY START?

PRE-PROJECT WORK	PROJECT INITIATION	PROJECT PLANNING	PROJECT IMPLEMENTATION	CLOSING / H.O.	OPERA-TIONS
-PROJECT ACQUISITION -PRE-SALES -IDEATION -BUSINESS CASE -BENEFITS MANAGEMENT PLAN.	-PROJECT CHARTER -STAKEHOL-DER IDENTIFI-CATION	ALL PROJECT PLANS	PROJECT EXECUTION AND CONTROL	-LESSONS LEARNED -HANDING OVER -ARCHIVE	OPS.. START

PROJECT START AND END

◆ = TOLL GATE/ GO-NO-GO

A project may get acquired through a sales effort. All the work that was involved in creating the proposal, making presentations, signing the contract etc. are not part of the project initiation, but steps leading to initiation.

A project idea must also go through some kind of technical feasibility analysis based on the current capability of the organization as well as the current capability of the technology itself, before financial feasibility and other financial analysis is done.

Before committing to a project the organization would also like to ascertain if the proposed project would fit in their overall strategy or not or would the project provide any strategic benefit, and if yes, when and how.

Hence, there are two major documents that need to be made to ascertain if the proposed project should be allowed to get initiated, and they are “Business Case / Justification” and “Benefits Management Plan”.

The business document called “**Business Case**” (also called Justification) comes from the Sponsor or sponsor body. Business case / Justification explains the economical reason why this project is being done, is it for making money, is it for gaining experience in a specific technology, is it for a short term gain, is it for a stop gap arrangement for keeping “on bench” employees busy, is it for entering a completely new market segment, is it for making the organization more competitive, is it an excuse for making a product and so on. A good project manager knows that just the objective is not enough for a practical plan, he must also know ***why*** the organization is undertaking this project. *E.g. if the project has been under-quoted to enter a completely new business area to gain experience and this experience could help make the organization more money in subsequent projects in this new business area. Now, if the project manager is not aware of this justification than his planning and project tracking would be focused on saving costs whereas the organization would not want him to do that as the “Reason / Justification” for the project is something else. This may lead to defeating the very purpose of why the project was undertaken in the first place.*

Making a business case is a complete domain in itself. PMI would not get into absolute details of it. However, it does ask questions to ensure that the candidate understands the various kinds of Business Case / Justification / Project Selection techniques. Please note that once the project charter is made there is no longer an option “Whether to do the project or not” hence the term “Project Selection” / Justification or Business Case only means “Why” this project is being undertaken by this organization.

There is some financial/economic justification and then there are some qualitative justifications.
Let us talk about Financial / Economic justification first.

1. **Present Value (PV):** This is an investment justification concept. Basically, it is a crude way to answer the question “Is it worth investing in this?” A project is an investment too, hence PV could be used to understand whether it is worth investing in this project. PV is the present value of future cash flow. Say you have Rs100/- today and you invest it for 10% and therefore get Rs110/- in one year. Now if the inflation rate is 5% than the PV of Rs110/- that you will get one year later, in today’s price it would be RS 104.76 which as you can see is more than Rs100 and therefore a good investment but if you invested in something like a mutual fund which would give you Rs105/- one year later than its PV would be Rs99/-which is less than Rs100/- thus making it a bad investment.

PRESENT VALUE [PV]

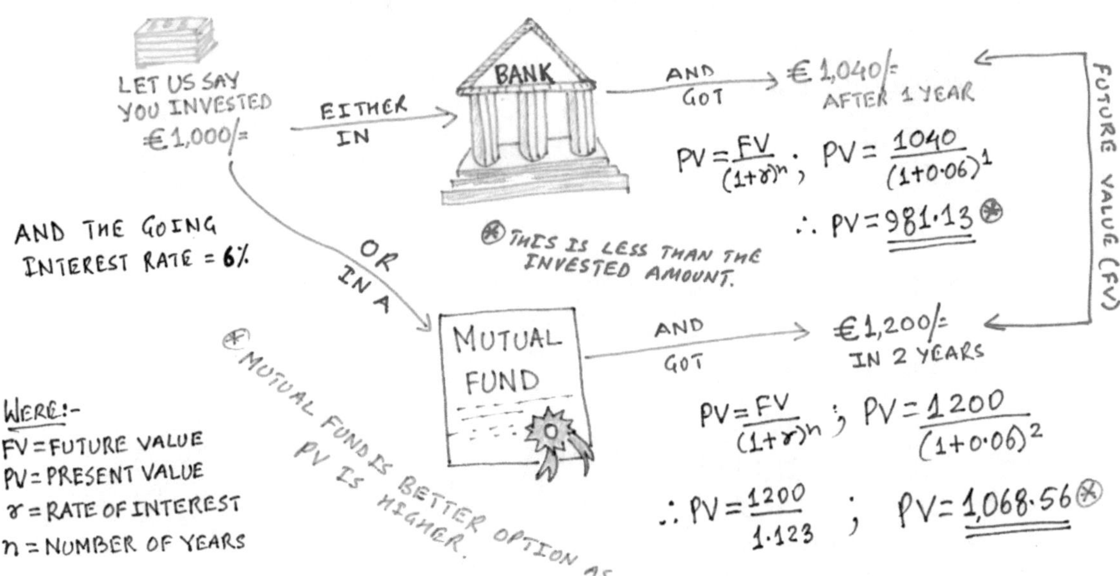
LET US SAY
YOU INVESTED
€1,000/=
EITHER
IN
BANK
AND
GOT
€ 1,040/=
AFTER 1 YEAR
PV = FV / (1+r)^n ; PV = 1040 / (1+0·06)^1
∴ PV = 981·13
THIS IS LESS THAN THE
INVESTED AMOUNT.
AND THE GOING
INTEREST RATE = 6%
OR
IN A
MUTUAL
FUND
AND
GOT
€1,200/=
IN 2 YEARS
FUTURE VALUE (FV)
PV = FV / (1+r)^n ; PV = 1200 / (1+0·06)^2
∴ PV = 1200 / 1·123 ; PV = 1,068·56
MUTUAL FUND IS BETTER OPTION AS
PV IS HIGHER.
WERE:-
FV = FUTURE VALUE
PV = PRESENT VALUE
r = RATE OF INTEREST
n = NUMBER OF YEARS

As you can see the higher the PV the better it is. Hence if you get a question which shows multiple projects with their PV's all you have to do is pick the one that has the highest PV. Yes…its that simple. Would you get calculations in the exams for calculating PV? No.

2. **Net Present Value (NPV):** Similar to PV in concept but a little more refined and hence considered more appropriate and meaningful than PV. When more information about the investment is available then NPV is a measurement of the profitability of an undertaking that is calculated by subtracting the present values (PV) of cash outflows (including initial cost) from the present values of cash inflows over a period of time. Incoming and outgoing cash flows can also be described as benefit and cost cash flows, respectively.

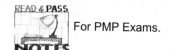

NET PRESENT VALUE-[NPV]

WHICH PROJECT IS FINANCIALLY SMARTER?

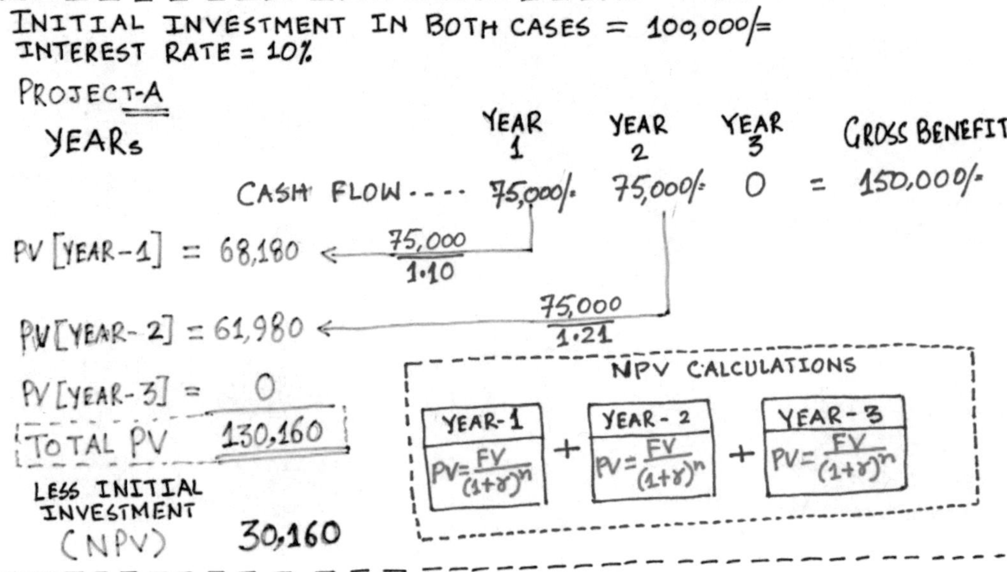

INITIAL INVESTMENT IN BOTH CASES = 100,000/=
INTEREST RATE = 10%
PROJECT-A
YEARS
YEAR 1
YEAR 2
YEAR 3
GROSS BENEFIT
CASH FLOW ---- 75,000/- 75,000/- 0 = 150,000/-
PV [YEAR-1] = 68,180
75,000 / 1.10
PV [YEAR-2] = 61,980
75,000 / 1.21
PV [YEAR-3] = 0
TOTAL PV 130,160
LESS INITIAL INVESTMENT
(NPV) 30,160
NPV CALCULATIONS
YEAR-1
PV= FV/(1+r)^n
+
YEAR-2
PV= FV/(1+r)^n
+
YEAR-3
PV= FV/(1+r)^n

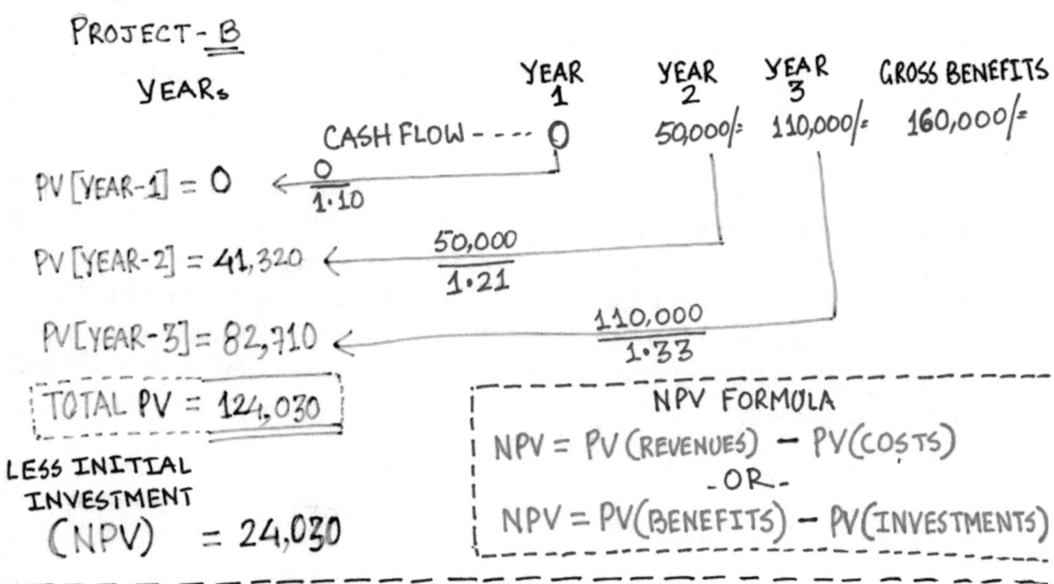

BASED ON NPV, PROJECT-A IS A SMARTER INVESTMENT.

Again, you do not have to calculate the NPV during the exams all you have to do is select the best project in terms of NPV from the given options. All you have to remember that when all projects in the question are compared in NPV simply select the "Highest One". Sometimes you might get a question where some projects are shown in PV while others are shown in NPV, in such cases just select the "Highest NPV" and completely disregards PV. This is done because PV is a very crude calculation whereas NPV is a much more refined calculation and makes projects more certain.

3. **Internal Rate of Return (IRR):** IRR is also sometimes called the "Discounted Cash Flow Rate Of Return" (DCFROR). The official definition is, the IRR of an investment is the discount rate at which the net present value of costs (negative cash flows) of the investment equals the net present value of the benefits (positive cash flows) of the investment. Usually, to calculate this you need the full projected cash flows and complete information about inflows over a period of time. One usually needs a software application to calculate the IRR and yes it does get complex. Aren't you glad that you are not expected to calculate IRR in exams? In exams, questions are about various projects with their IRR mentioned and you have to select the best option. And yes, the project with the higher IRR is better. Always.

Exams rules for PV, NPV, and IRR. Check out the image below and commit it to memory.

RULES CONNECTED TO PV, NPV & IRR QUESTIONS

RULE#1: IF IN THE QUESTION ALL PROJECTS ARE IN PV, THEN SIMPLY SELECT THE HIGHEST PV.

EXAMPLE: WHICH OF THE FOLLOWING PROJECTS SHOULD BE SELECTED?

PROJECT-A: PV = 10,000/-
PROJECT-B: PV = 15,000/-
PROJECT-C: PV = 40,000/-
✓ PROJECT-D: PV = 50,000/- ✓

RULE#2: IF IN THE QUESTION, PROJECTS ARE A COMBINATION OF PV AND NPV, THEN SIMPLY SELECT THE HIGHEST NPV. (EVEN IF ONLY ONE PROJECT IS IN NPV)

EXAMPLE: WHICH OF THE FOLLOWING PROJECTS SHOULD BE SELECTED?

✓ PROJECT-A: NPV = 70,000/- ✓
PROJECT-B: NPV = 50,000/-
PROJECT-C: PV = 100,000/-
PROJECT-D: PV = 170,000/-

RULE #3: IF IN THE QUESTION, PROJECTS ARE A COMBINATION OF PV, NPV & IRR, THEN SIMPLY SELECT THE HIGHEST IRR. (EVEN IF ONLY ONE PROJECT IS IN IRR)

EXAMPLE: WHICH OF THE FOLLOWING PROJECTS SHOULD BE SELECTED?

PROJECT-A: PV = 60,000/-

✓ PROJECT-B: IRR = 10% ✓

PROJECT-C: NPV = 50,000/-

PROJECT-D: PV = 100,000/-

4. **Return On Investment (ROI):** Also called the Return On Capital (ROC), it measures the percentage efficiency of net income (Revenue – operating costs) against the capital invested for the project. Hence the higher the ROI the better the investment. When ROI is compared amongst multiple projects, it makes sense to choose a project with a highest ROI percentage. Though the calculation for ROI would not show up in exams but for the sake of clarity of understanding let me provide a real world example.
E.g., Let us say you have some money and wish to invest in transportation business. You have the option of investing in trucks for goods transportation or in passenger busses for passenger transportation. When you conduct a detailed financial analysis you realize the following:
If you invest INR 10,000,000/- in trucks your yearly expenses would be INR 600,000 and your revenue from transporting goods would be INR 2,000,000/-. This means a net income of (2,000,000 – 600,000) = 1,400,000. Hence the ROI for this would be
*(1,400,000 / 10,000,000) X 100 = **14%***
However,
If you invest INR 10,000,000/- in passenger busses for long routes your expenses would come to INR 1,000,000/- per year and your revenue would be INR 3,200,000/-. Hence your Net Income would be (3,200,000 – 1,000,000) INR 2,200,000/-. Therefor the ROI for this would be
*(2,200,000 / 10,000,000) X 100 = **22%.***
Therefore, purely going by ROI, investing in Passenger busses is better.

5. **Benefit-Cost Ratio, BEP and Payback:** Another set of financial/economic justification for projects is Benefit Cost Ratio (B:C or BCR), Break Even Point (BEP) and Payback Period. Let us start with B:C or BCR. Benefit-Cost Ratio is a simple calculation where you take all the "Measurable Revenue" and call it Benefits and put all the "Measurable Expenses and costs" of the project as Costs. Now the Benefits are divided by Costs. This gives a ratio. Now if the value is more than 1 then it means that your project is yielding more benefits than incurring costs at this point of time or in other words a value of more than 1 is good. Corollary to the same, a less than 1 value would be bad because then the expenses would be more than the benefits from the project. Now if the BCR or B:C ratio gives exactly 1 then it means, that this is the point of no profit (benefit) or loss; which is also known as "Break Even Point" (BEP). BEP is the point at which cost or expenses and revenue are equal: there is no net loss or gain, and one has "broken even". In other

words BEP = when BCR = 1. Payback Period is the amount of time it takes the project to reach its BEP. Which means the shorter the Payback period the better it is.

BENEFIT/COST RATIO, BREAK EVEN POINT & PAYBACK PERIOD

$$\frac{\text{BENEFIT}}{\text{COST}} = \frac{B}{C} = BCR = B:C$$

WHERE: B = BENEFITS
& C = COSTS

∴ B:C RATIO of > 1 IS GOOD
B:C RATIO of < 1 IS BAD
&
B:C RATIO of = 1 IS BEP

BEP = BREAK EVEN POINT
WHICH IS THE POINT OF NO PROFIT AND NO LOSS
OR
BEP = WHEN B:C = 1.

NINJA TAXI COMPANY BOUGHT A CAR

INITIAL INVESTMENT $10,000
RUNNING COSTS PER YEAR $4,000
REVENUE GENERATED PER YEAR $8,000

NO. OF YEARS BY WHICH NINJA TAXI WILL REACH BEP. 2.5 YRS.

∴ PAYBACK PERIOD OF THIS NEW CAR = 2.5 yrs.

THE SHORTER THE PAYBACK PERIOD THE BETTER IT IS.

6. **Opportunity cost:** This has always been a troublesome subject because there are multiple meanings of this term. It's basically an economics term which, in some books, is defined as "When you choose one project/investment than the opportunity cost of that chosen investment is the investment cost of the "Next" best alternative. While in some cases it has been defined to mean "When an investment is chosen then the opportunity cost of that investment is the sum of all the other options/choice of investments that we did not take." This does not show up so regularly in the exams anymore. However, if you do see a question please sum up the value of all the investment choices that were not chosen and that would be your answer.

Now on to the non-financial and qualitative justification/business case criteria.

1. **Murder Board:** This method uses the "Negativity of people" and uses it for selection. (it is not only used for selecting projects, it is used for selecting vendors as well as candidates for crucial and top posts.) Here all the decision makers are asked to only list out "Why project should not be undertaken". No positive comments can be presented. The project opportunity which eventually has the least numbers of Negative statements is chosen. This shows that the project selection has gone through fire.
2. **Scoring Model / Organizational Fit:** Some organizations have a template where all the projects are compared against certain predefined strategic and financial objectives and a score is provided to each of the project opportunity. The project that scores the most in total is eventually selected. This is also called Organizational fit because the projects are selected based on what is best for the "Strategy" of the organization.

3. **Risk Analysis:** Certain kind of organizations and in certain domain the project is also subjected to Risk Analysis to understand how risky the project is. Usually, there is a threshold which needs to be met before a project is selected for going ahead.
4. **Net Promoter Score (NPS):** This is usually a measure / rating on a scale of 0 to 10 (sometimes it is 0 to 100) which essentially shows the likelihood that your existing customers are going to recommend your products to others. Some might think that NPS has more to do with operations and sales hence may end up questioning, "What has NPS got to do with initiating a project?" Well, let us take the example of a car that I drive. It is a mid-sized car called Tata Nexon. It has gone on to create some new and impressive records in sales as well as around standards on Safety and sturdiness. The reason it became an overnight success is because the customers are literally forcing others to buy this car. Seeing this TATA realized that they have a ready market for new models for Nexon and hence they initiated projects for making electrical versions of this car. The very reason they were able to invest in such an expensive project which involved so much R&D was simply because they had a ready market due to their high NPS rating. No wonder their Electric version has sold so much that some of the biggest names in electrical cars manufacturing in the world are finding it hard to enter India.

From the point of view of practicality, though there are many economic and qualitative business case methods it must be understood that depending on the situation a combination of various business case method could be used to justify why the project has been selected.

Let us now move on to the next pre-project document viz., **Benefits Management Plan**. Benefits Management Plan states the overall set of actions to be taken to help obtain the "Strategic Benefits" that the organization hopes to meet once the project is over. The content of this document is included in Project Charter (the very first document ever created in any project) and this is done to ensure that the project manager is fully aware of exactly where and how this project fits into the overall strategic scheme of things. The strategic benefits which are expected to be obtained from this project helps the project manager plan accordingly and chose relevant decisions throughout the project. This Benefits Management Plan also contains the necessary milestones or checkpoints through the project lifecycles to take stock whether the project is proceeding in such a way that the "Strategic Benefits" would actually be met or not when it completes. These checkpoints or milestones would have to be taken into account by the Project Manager during the project planning.
Remember, Business Case provides the "Financial Justification" or Financial Why, whereas Benefits Management Plan provides the "Strategic Justification" or the strategic "why" for the project at hand.

BUSINESS CASE
FINANCIAL WHY
Rs
-FINANCIAL AND ECONOMIC JUSTIFICATION FOR DOING THE PROJECT

- FINANCIAL & TECHNICAL FEASIBILITY
- GROUNDS FOR STARTING THE PROJECT

STRATEGIC WHY → BENEFITS MANAGEMENT PLAN

- WHAT STRATEGIC BENEFITS WOULD BE OBTAINED BY DOING THIS PROJECT.
- IS THERE A STRATEGIC NEED FOR THIS PROJECT.
- HOW TO OBTAIN BENEFITS DURING AND AFTER THE PROJECT.

Once the Business Case and the Benefits Management Plan has been created the leadership may decide not to go ahead with the project. But, on the other hand, if they decide to approve the project, then the project is officially started in the phase called "Initiation" and the very first document that is created by the project sponsor is the "Project Charter".

8.1 Project Charter (Create Project Charter)

Project Charter is the very first document that is ever created in any project. The moment the management or anyone takes the decision that a project has to be done the first document (that establishes the project existence itself) is the project charter. Therefore the process that is dedicated to creating the project charter is also the very first Process that is undertaken in any project whatsoever. This process is called *CREATE PROJECT CHARTER*.
A Project Charter is the very first document that authorizes the start of a project and also appoints a project manager and empowers him to apply resources to the project.

This brings to light another question; "Who makes the Project Charter?"
Since the project manager has not been appointed until this moment it's the project Sponsor who makes the project charter. "Remember anyone who appoints the project manager is the project sponsor" and the project manager is appointed in this document by the sponsor.
A project manager may take part in making the project charter (and he should, because this is a prime document) but is not called the owner or creator of the Project Charter. The owner and creator of the project charter is the "Sponsor" or "Sponsor Committee" (as the case may be) because they are the ones who sign/approve the project charter.
So, what is the purpose of the project charter? Project Charter is the initial documentation that lays down some high level but important initial elements of a project. These initial elements become indispensable during detailed planning. Just imagine if this document is the very first document ever created for a Project and is made by the sponsor, what elements should it contain to give a clear picture to the Project Manager about expectations from the project and at the same time provide all the inputs for a practical detailed plan later on, in the project.

Project Charter creates a direct link between the project and the strategic objectives of the organization.

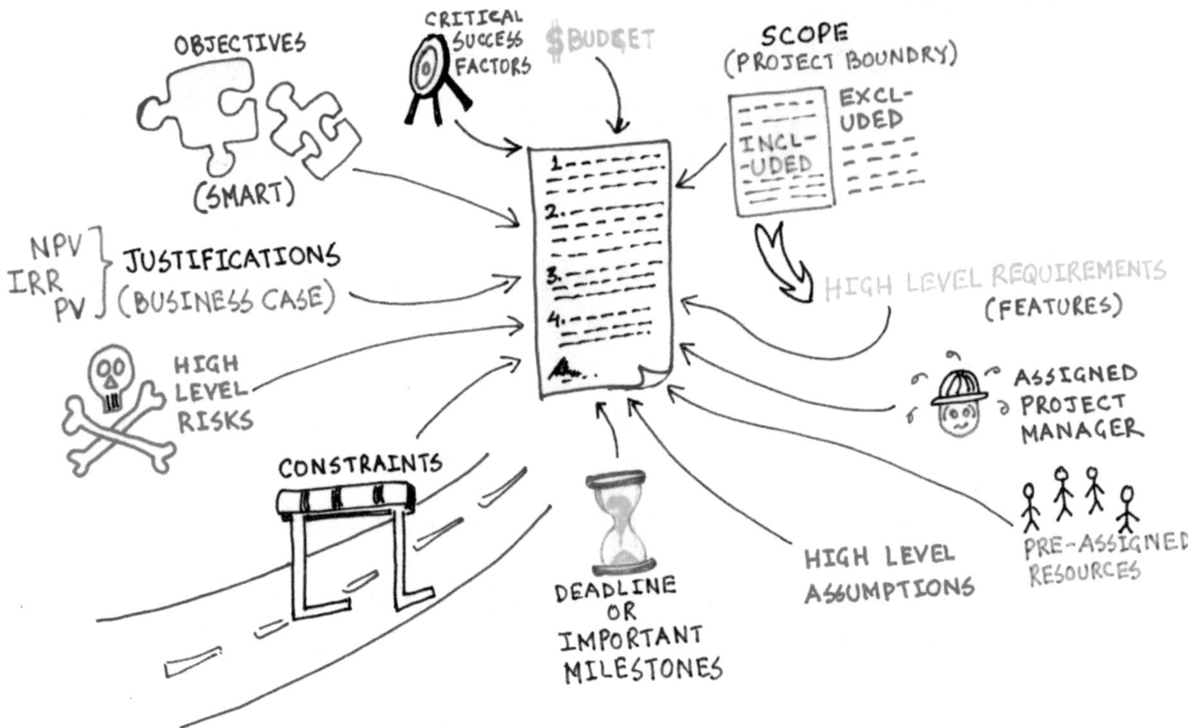

The project charter is created by the sponsor which would mean that it could be created by, PMO (Project Management Office), Steering Committee (which is a Sponsoring body instead of an individual sponsor), Program Manager (the program manager sponsors all the projects under its program) or the representative from the organizations Portfolio layer.
One must clearly understand that a Project Charter is not an external contract or agreement. It is an internal agreement between the sponsor and the project manager about expectations from the project. Formal agreements/contracts are used between the Client organization and the performing organization but the Project Charter is to be used only internally by the performing organization. In fact, for all practical purposes, a project charter is not shared with the client/customer. Project Charter is not an Agreement or Contract technically as it does not contain any form of consideration or a "legally binding" relationship.

You may find questions in the exams which present a scenario where a project manager is being asked to start the project without the presence of a Project Charter. In such questions always go for the option that talks about insisting for a project charter or pushing back with the sponsor about the importance of a Project Charter. Remember "No Project Charter = No Project".

Please note that the Project Charter "Does NOT" contain any "Detailed" plan or a detailed list of resources or schedule of the project. Project Charter is made once in the project. Project Charters do not change in the same project. Changing the project charter means creating a new project.

It is important to note that no matter which kind of methodology that the project may apply, in all cases a project charter has to be made first. In Agile projects the project charter is usually an informal document.

During the creation of the Project Charter it is also usually decided (and it makes sense to do so at this stage) about the specific methodology that would be used for the project at hand. The methodology selection is done while preparing the project charter.

At times a project is created because of an Agreement that a vendor may have entered into with a customer. Hence the terms of the contract / agreement would need to be stated in the Project charter as well.

Though this is not clearly explained nor expressly stated in the PMBOK® Guide, but from exams point of view you must know that the agreements also usually contain “Statement of Work (SOW)”. Statement of work is the write-up from the client perspective about what is it that they want to get done. This is usually high level but at times (though rare) this can be so detailed that they can be treated as “Project Requirements”.

A project charter must also contain risks and opportunities or constraints because of the Environmental Factors. **Enterprise Environmental Factors** contains all the factors (internal and external) that would affect this project. Some examples could be Organizational Structure, availability of resources of that technology in the market place, applicable regulations or industrial standards, countries, and cultures where work would be done and so on.

Organizational Processes Assets are things like internal processes, templates, authorization processes, historical data, past learnings, intelligence about the market place, survey results etc. These are documents, knowledge and information that is with the organization and can be reused in various projects. The whole idea is to “Not Reinvent the entire wheel” but look for things which are existing within the organization which could be reused, thus bringing down effort and cost. This is one of the biggest reasons why every professional organization places so much stress on “Lessons Learned”.

Every project is based on some assumptions from the moment it is initiated. Assumptions must be clearly documented to ensure that we get rid of as many of them during the journey of the project. These assumptions are documented in a log called the Assumptions Log and this document is also created along with the Project Charter. This is because, usually at the start of the project there are more assumptions.
Assumption Log contains all the assumptions on which the project has been based on. Assumptions are very dangerous and they need to be actively tracked across the lifecycle of the project to ensure that new ones are identified while the older ones are relooked at, to ensure if the assumptions can be removed. There are bound to be assumptions at the beginning of the project but in a healthy project (due to progressive elaboration) the assumptions should reduce at the project progresses. The idea is that the project manager

must always keep in view the assumptions taken for the project and look for evidence to ensure that those assumptions are removed as soon as possible. Baseless assumptions end up giving rise to the most critical risks. *E.g., During initiation of a project, it came to light that the project would need some special resources (like developers for "Lotus Notes") that do not exist in the organization. If the management assumes that during execution the organization would be able to find and hire/take on contract the necessary numbers of the lotus notes professionals, but have not done any kind of survey to verify their assumption till execution. Then this assumption becomes a critical risk for the project.* This is a serious assumption and the success of the project depends on it. A proactive project manager would try to connect with Human Resource Managers to test the assumption to see if there are some professionals on Lotus Notes in that geographical area and if yes, then would their compensations be within the budget. The Project manager can only do that provided if those assumptions were properly logged and tracked on the document called "Assumption Log". Else, "Out of sight and out of mind".

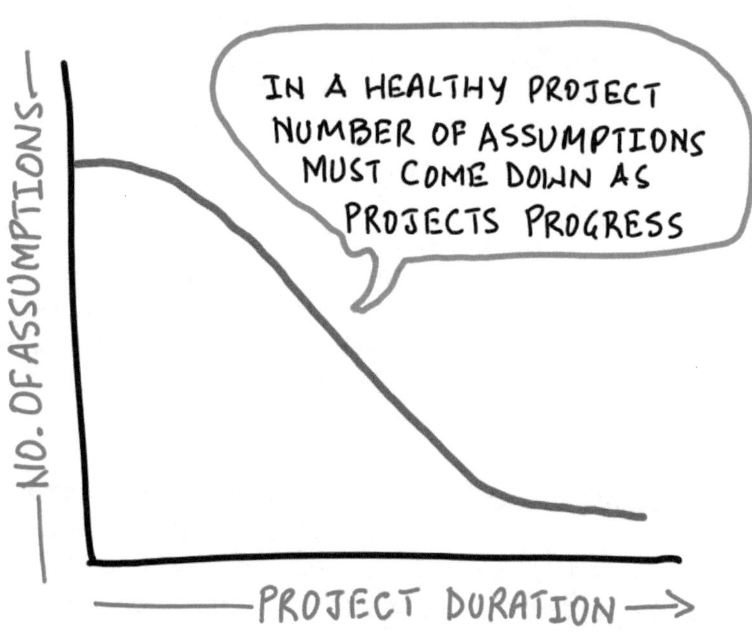

Depending on the kind of methodology that you may be using for the project in question as well as the management language adopted within the organization there are some additional documents that are also created along with the project charter.

1. Business Model Canvas: This is a one-page visual document that shows the overall strategy of the organization. This model is used mostly for the projects in a startup. This model has 9 pillars or elements or sections and they are: -
    i. Key Partners.
    ii. Key Activities.
    iii. Key Resources.
    iv. Value Propositions.
    v. Customer Relationships.

vi. Customer Segments.
vii. Channels.
viii. Cost Structure.
ix. Revenue Streams

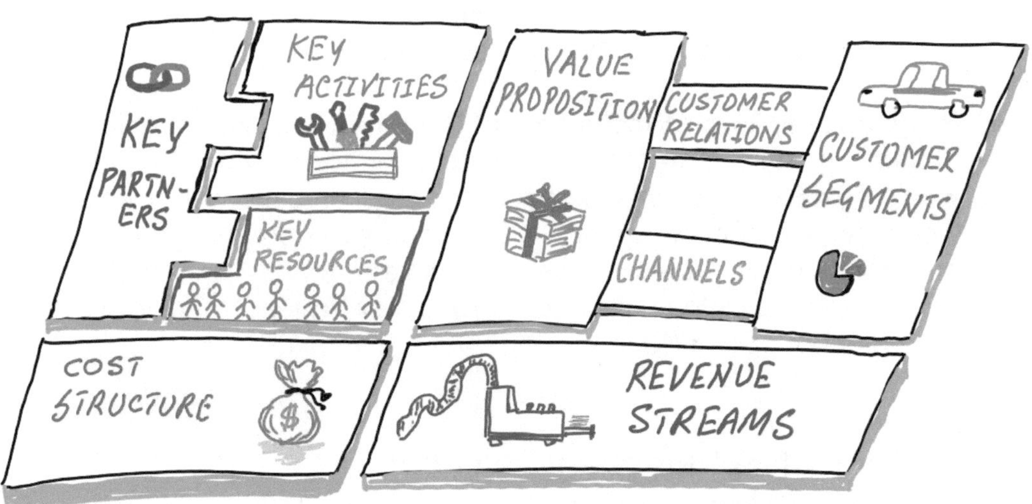

This model is also used to understand the strategic importance of the project. If the project is internal to the performing organization then it is important to see which of the elements of Business Model Canvas of the organization it relates to. On the other hand, if the project is external to the organization, then the Business Model Canvas of the customer organization is seen to understand the strategic importance of this outsourced project to the customer.

2. **Project Brief**: This is a summarized overview of the project that explains the "What", "Why" as well as the benefits from the project. It is a short and sweet way to explain the need for the project and what it hopes to achieve. In some organizations this is prepared in the same manner as though a marketing information would be written on the box of a product. No wonder this term is also called the "Product Box Statement" in certain organizations. More common alternate terminology for the same are, "Project Overview" and "Executive Summary". Project Brief is very important to create a buy-in among the diverse stakeholders without getting too much in details with each of them.

3. **Project Vision Statement:** Very similar to the project brief, this statement is meant to inspire the project team to participate in the project at hand. It is supposed to create an emotional as well as technical connect towards the project. This document is a concise, high-level description of the project that states the purpose, and inspires the project team to contribute to the project. There are some additional statements I have listed below to give you further insights into the concept of vision. These statements would also help you answer questions in exams connected to vision.

- Vision is a desired end-state, often described as a set of desirable objectives and outcomes.
- Vision is not the scope of the project.
- Vision is more from the point of view of what the customer should be able to do from a business standpoint after the entire project is done.
- Vision must be clearly understood by the team.
- Project Charter is a document while Vision is a team understanding. They both are connected.
- Vision must work as a "Guiding Star" for the team while the various components of the project keep changing.

4. **Project Road Map / Product Road Map:** has different meaning for different kinds of projects. In agile, it means the overall sequence in which the product backlog ideas would be released as well as a rough overall timeline within which those releases would be provided. However, when it comes to non-agile projects, it means the overall milestones of the project, decision points and their timelines. When it comes to PMP Exams if the question talks about Product or Project Road Map then that question is talking about agile initiation.

8.1.1 Project Methodology Selection

Initiation is also the time for selecting the methodology that would be used for the conducting of the project. Based on the complexity, situation and the requirements from the stakeholders the most apt methodology has to be chosen.

We have already discussed the details for each of the methodologies earlier, therefore let us revise the same through situational discussions. Go through each of the situation and think why this situation would need the methodology mentioned next to it.

S. No.	Situation	Methodology
1	Projects in a complex environment where the end product is not fully known and user feedback is very valuable.	Agile
2	Scope and Requirements are very clear and change would be expensive.	Predictive
3	Fixed Price Contract	Predictive
4	Projects with dynamic requirements and activities are repeated until they are deemed correct.	Iterative
5	Where scope is clear but intermittent deliveries are needed.	Incremental
6	Customers have an unclear scope but want to move to a fixed price contract as soon as possible.	Hybrid

Questions do show up on this topic in PMP Exams and they are all scenario based questions. However if you understood the methodologies and the reason why they are undertaken, these questions would be one of the easiest to answer.

8.2 Project Stakeholders

A "Stakeholder" is a person or a body of persons (like an organization, association, NGO, Government Body) who can either affect the outcome of the project or get affected by the outcome of the project, either positively or negatively or directly or indirectly. The stakeholders also include all those who have a "perception" that they may be affected by the outcome of the project.
It is important to note here that the term "Stakeholders" is a very wide term and includes only Humans but not Animals, plants, flora and fauna, atmosphere, environment etc. They may be represented through a Human body of stakeholders or an individual stakeholder but they cannot be stakeholders themselves.

As you can see that "Stakeholders" are not just the "Project Team", as is understood by most managers, professionals and PMP® Books. It is a much wider term.

Some of the Stakeholders may have a negative effect on the outcome of the project or some stakeholders may be affected by the outcome of the project negatively or perceive that they are / could be negatively affected by the project outcome. They are called Negative Stakeholders.

Remember that a negative stakeholder is not a negative person by nature. It's just the effect of the project outcome on them or their effect on the project, determines if they are negative or positive stakeholders. Negative stakeholders are equally important to be identified so that plans could be made to reduce, eliminate or counter their negative effect on the project or the negative effect of the project on them. Negative Stakeholders are also referred to as "Resistant Stakeholders".

From exams point of view, understanding and mastering the concepts around all aspects of Stakeholders would bear rich dividends.

The stakeholders have to be identified across the lifecycle of the project. However, identifying as many of them (if not every one of them) at the very beginning of the project is crucial simply because stakeholders have the "Highest Impact on the project during the beginning of the project and this impact becomes progressively less as the project progresses through its lifecycle".

In Adaptive projects the stakeholders need to be identified just ahead of each of the iterations.

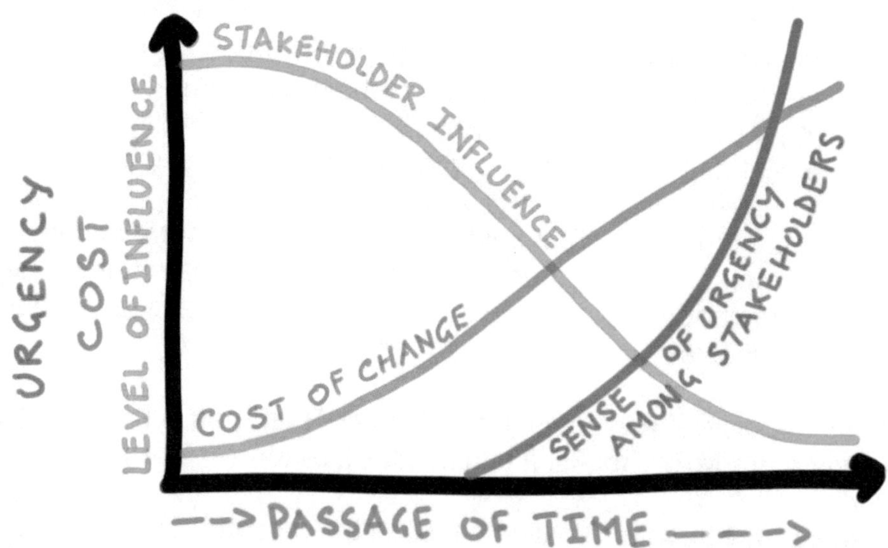

If you look carefully at this graph you will notice that the "stakeholder influence" is the highest at the beginning of the project. Their influence dips as the project progresses. As the project progresses the cost of any change to the project increases as well (this fact is not applicable to Agile projects because Agile methodology is all about adapting to changes as and when they are introduced). Which means that if you do not identify and collect requirements from all the key stakeholders early in the project, it would be excessively difficult and expensive to implement any changes suggested by a key stakeholder who was left out earlier. This means that the best impact of "Stakeholder Management" is felt at the very beginning of the project and not later. Interestingly from the stakeholder's standpoint, they do not find it worthwhile to spend quality time in a project during its beginning, they start showing urgency and interest after substantial time has elapsed in the project. Stakeholders do not realize that by showing interest and urgency later in the project does not solve anything and tend to make the project chaotic, expensive and delayed. I am sure you will be able to relate this phenomenon with this "Classic Real World Situation". I am also sure you are beginning to appreciate the importance of stakeholder management and their early involvement.

The best way to prevent unnecessary changes in a project is to conduct a thorough stakeholder identification during the early stages of the project. This also means that the biggest reason for unnecessary changes in a project is due to shoddy stakeholder identification.

It is important that you should know that not all the stakeholders have the same priority. Some are called Key Stakeholders because of their high priority in the project. The priority of the stakeholders changes over the lifecycle of the project.

Stakeholder Management involves: -

- Identifying Stakeholders
- Identifying the "influence factor" of the stakeholders
- Understanding their needs and interests and expectations from the project

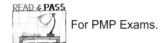

- Assessing their Knowledge and Skills
- Analyzing the project to ensure that their needs are met
- Mapping of Stakeholders to Project Phases

Now that we know what is stakeholders, their importance as well as the concept of stakeholder management, it is time for us to understand what is done vis-à-vis the stakeholders during project initiation.
Three thigs are done, to be precise.

1. Stakeholder Identification
2. Stakeholder analysis and prioritization and
3. Creation of Stakeholder Register

8.3 Identify Stakeholders:

This process viz., *IDENTIFY STAKEHOLDERS*, is an important process in project management and if done improperly it would have cascading effect all through the rest of the project.
It is also important to point out that the Initiation phase of the project has only two processes viz., *CREATE PROJECT CHARTER* and *IDENTIFY STAKEHOLDERS*. The process *CREATE PROJECT CHARTER* is always done before *IDENTIFY STAKEHOLDERS*.

What is done in this process is to first identify every single stakeholder of the project and then using a scientific management grid they are prioritized. The outcome of this process is a "Stakeholder Register" with the list of all stakeholders along with their priority vis-à-vis the project.

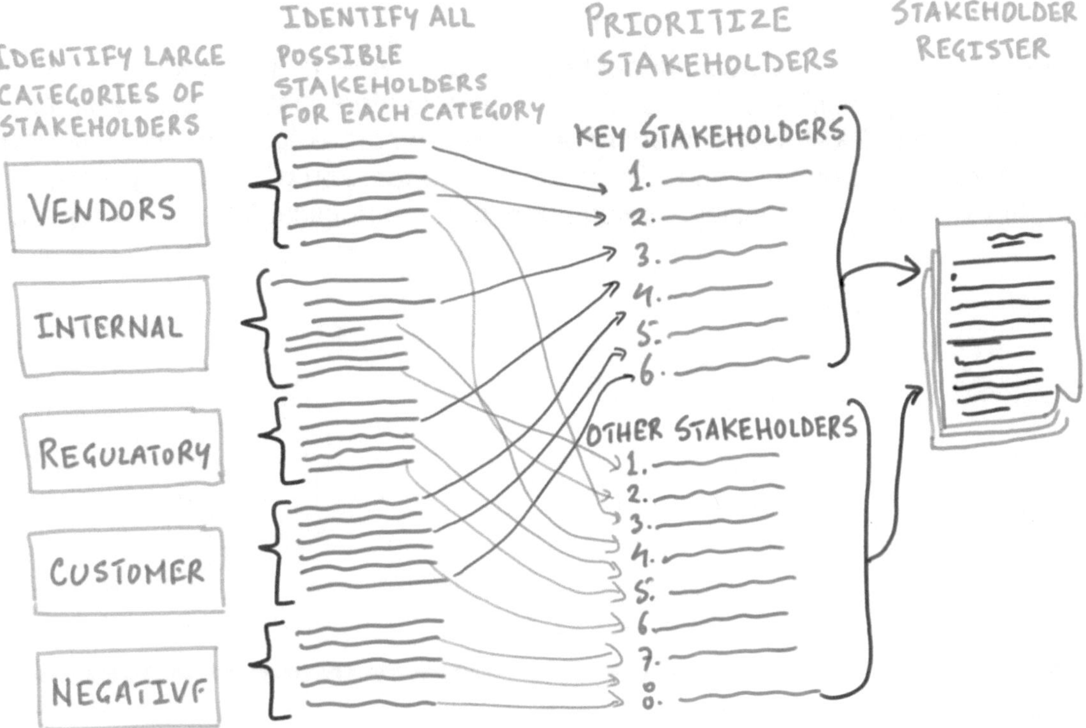

It is important to note that this process is not done only once in the project, it is done at every phase end as well. If engaged in iterative projects, it is imperative to ensure that this process of Identification of stakeholders is done during "Iteration Planning" before each of the iterations. However, the best results are got when it is done in details at the very beginning of the project.

Some of the usual documents that are referred for identifying all possible stakeholders are

1. **Project Charter**
2. **Project Vision**
3. **Business Map Canvas** shows the various strategic footprint of the project. This allows to ascertain the various internal leadership stakeholders as well as some external stakeholders like competitors and other players in the same space etc.
4. **Business Case**
5. **Agreements or Contracts** contain all the terms of the contract as well as the overall scope and requirements of the project. This gives a lot of idea about the categories as well as the sources of stakeholders that are applicable to this project.
6. **Organizational Process assets** like an existing and often used "Stakeholder Prioritization Grid", list of Stakeholders from a previous similar project, template for the Stakeholder Register and lessons learned about stakeholders from previous similar projects would also help the project manager in the current project to identify stakeholders.
7. **Environmental factors** like Government Regulations, Customs, multi-geographical work, cross country work, cross-cultural work etc. give the project manager more inputs for identifying relevant stakeholders. E.g. if some work has been outsourced to Korea then new stakeholders like Embassy, Courier Companies, travel agents, language translators, local hotel and travel organizations also become stakeholders of the project.

In order to identify all possible stakeholders, it is advisable to first make comprehensive list of all possible "Categories" and "Sources" of the stakeholders that are applicable to your project. And then pick up each category or source and break it down into all possible stakeholders. Once you are done with all the categories, you will end up having a comprehensive list of all possible stakeholders that are applicable to your project.

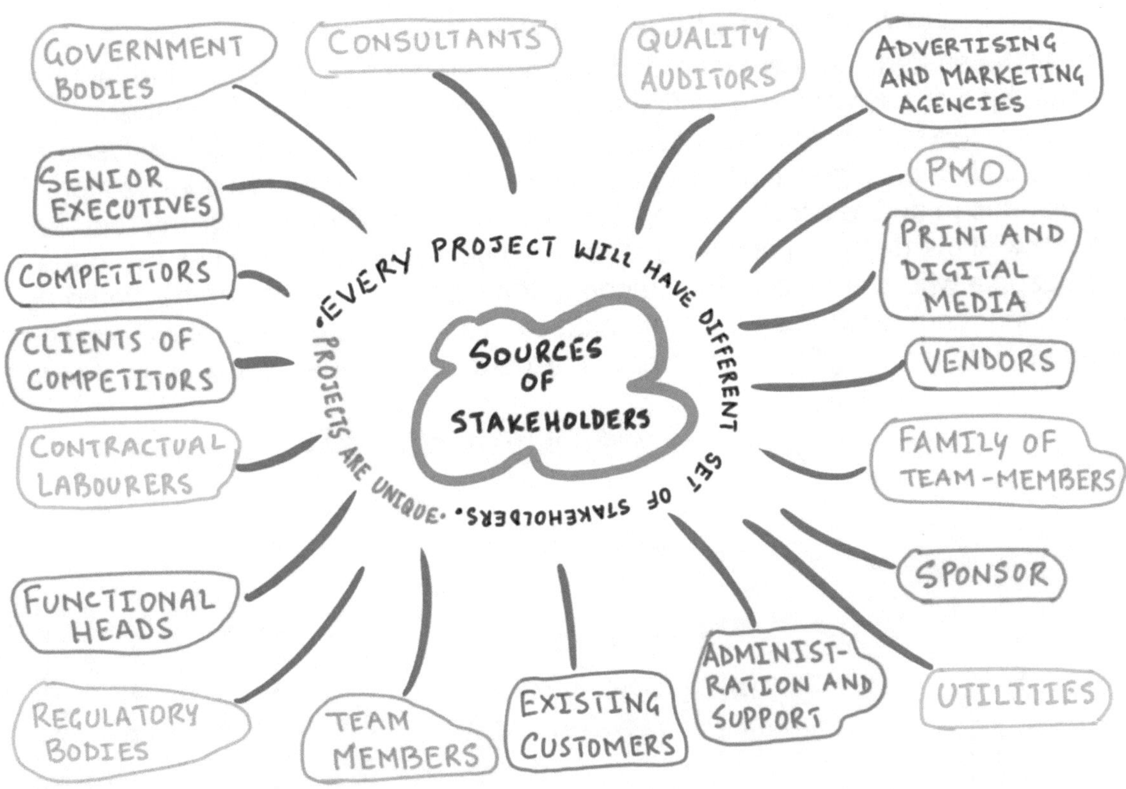

The larger the list at this stage, the better it is. However its important at this step to ensure that only the relevant stakeholders should be identified otherwise the non-relevant stakeholders would serve to distract your attention. *E.g., for an internal cost-cutting project listing Customs, Environment Ministry and Health Ministry would not make any sense whatsoever.* Though the list of stakeholders at this step has to be as long as possible but all of them have to be relevant. Indirect stakeholders are fine but not irrelevant ones. Many matured organizations have “Stakeholder Checklists” or “High-Level Categories” that could be used for identifying granular level stakeholders. Another important thing to watch out in this step is that the listing of the Stakeholders should be as specific as possible. *E.g., Instead of writing “Government Regulations”, which is a very generic term, specific Government Regulatory bodies applicable to your project should be listed like, Direct Taxation Department, Environmental Ministry, Labour Tribunals and so on.*

It is also a very good idea for the project manager to take the help of whatever other team members and stakeholders, already connected to the project, to identify all possible stakeholders. In certain cases, where the organization is engaging in one of its kind project (also called First In Kind (FIK)), an external consultant could be hired to help identify all possible stakeholders for the project at hand.

Questionnaires and surveys can be used to connect with distributed team to identify stakeholders, as well.

8.3.1 Stakeholder Analysis and Prioritization

Once all the stakeholders are identified, the next step is to understand the requirements and other aspects of each of the identified stakeholders and finally prioritize them.
In this step, the stakeholders identified from the previous list would be analysed and finally prioritized. Usually, a grid is used for a more practical and scientific prioritization. There are various grids to do the same. The most popular one is the "Power Vs. Interest" grid.
If you look at the definition of the stakeholders you will notice that it has two parts. One is about people who can "Impact the outcome of the project", which can be stated as "Power" and second, people who can get "Impacted by the outcome of the project", which can be stated as "Interest". A grid can be created using these two elements of power and interest.

PRIORITIZING STAKEHOLDERS

TWO QUESTIONS FOR EACH OF THE STAKEHOLDERS

1. HOW MUCH "POWER" DOES THE STAKEHOLDER HAVE ON THE OUTCOME OF THE PROJECT?

AND

2. HOW MUCH "INTEREST" DOES THE STAKEHOLDER HAVE IN THE OUTCOME OF THE PROJECT?

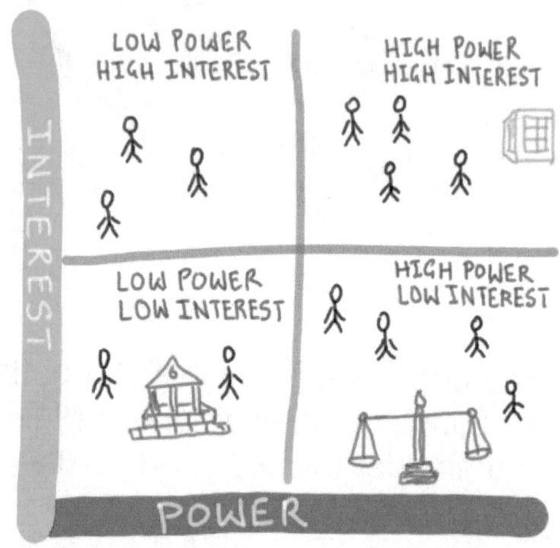

STAKEHOLDER PRIORITIZATION GRID

EACH OF THE STAKEHOLDERS ARE PLACED ON THE GRID BASED ON THE ANSWERS TO THE TWO QUESTIONS AND THEN DEALT ACCORDINGLY.

E.g., In a project where your organization is getting a new office building constructed from one of the most reputed builders and later you will shift into that building once it's ready and completed in all respects, the stakeholders may be placed on the grid as under.

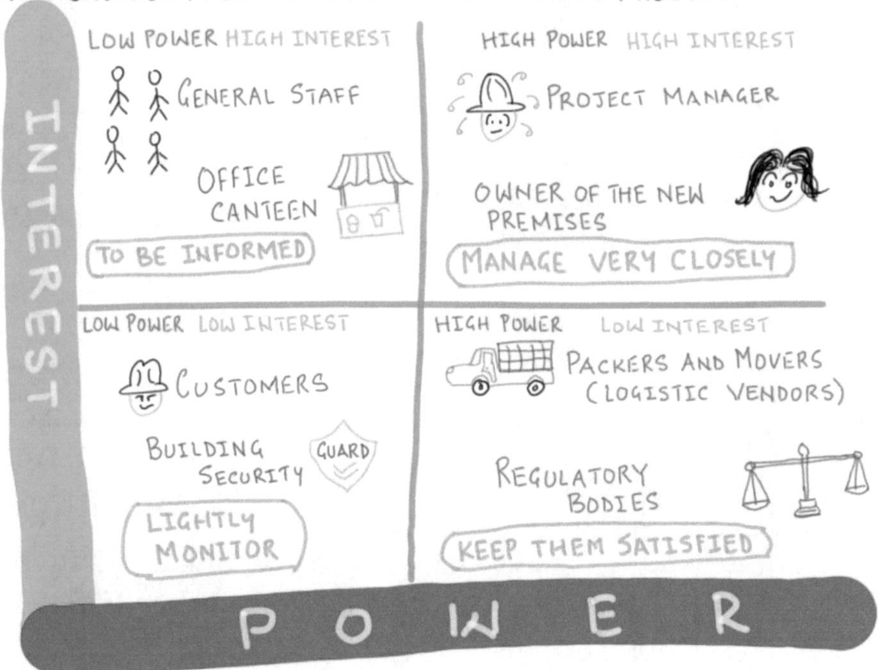

Owners of the new premises are interested in the shift as it affects their business and at the same time, they have a lot of power in the way, time and the process of shifting. Hence they have the power too.
Regulatory bodies have a lot of power. If the project manager does not meet the stated compliance this project to move would be stopped or postponed till compliance. But they are not really interested in the outcome of the project. They have nothing to gain or lose from this project. Hence regulatory bodies are in High Power and Low-Interest Quadrant.
The General staff is interested in the project as it affects them a lot. However, at the same time they cannot really affect the way office is being shifted or whether to shift or not or change anything in the plan. Thus they do not have any power in the project. Therefore the General staff is shown in the High Interest – Low-Power quadrant.
I am sure you will be able to guess the reason why in this project the Building security is in Low Power and Low-Interest Quadrant.
Remember, this stakeholder grid has to be created for each and every project separately as the circumstances and the stakeholder influences on each of the project are different.

There are some popular questions in exams about how to deal with the stakeholders. Such questions have the Power-Interest Grid as the main background. And therefore, always remember that, “High Power – High Interest” have to be “Managed Closely”. The stakeholders falling in “High Power – Low Interest” have to be “Kept Satisfied”. The stakeholders falling in “Low Power – High Interest” have to be “Kept Informed” and stakeholders falling in “Low Power – Low Interest” have to be “Lightly Monitored”.

The stakeholders falling in different quadrants have to be handled differently. The term “Key Stakeholders” are those that fall in the “High Power and High Impact” quadrant.

DEALING WITH STAKEHOLDERS

INTEREST

LOW POWER - HIGH INTEREST

SOME OF THEIR REPRESENTATIVES TO BE INVOLVED IN REQUIREMENTS.

TO BE KEPT INFORMED.
LESS FREQUENCY OF COMMUNICA--TION.

NOT ALL CONFLICTS HAVE TO BE TO BE RESOLVED.

HIGH POWER - HIGH INTEREST

KEY STAKEHOLDERS.
MAXIMUM COMMUNICATION.

NO DIPLOMACY NEEDED.
FAST CONFLICT RESOLUTION.

ALL OF THEM NEED TO BE IDENTIFIED UP-FRONT ELSE TOO MANY CHANGE REQUESTS.

MUST BE PART OF REQUIREMENTS.

LOW POWER - LOW INTEREST

POLITE INDIFFERENCE.

COMMUNICATION ONLY TO INFORM OR SEEK SUPPORT.

NO NEED FOR RESOLVING CONFLICTS.

HIGH POWER - LOW INTEREST

LEADERSHIP AND DIPLOMACY TO BE USED.

THEIR HIDDEN AGENDA TO BE UNDERSTOOD BEFORE INVOLVING THEM IN REQUIREMENTS.

LESS COMMUNICATION AND FORMAL COMMUNICATION ONLY.

SWIFT DISMISSAL OF CONFLICTS.

P O W E R

The stakeholders are placed in the grid based on their possible impact on the project and the level as well as the kind of expectations they have from the project.
The stakeholder prioritization grid must be made separately for each of the project based on its own unique set of circumstances. While one could copy the list of stakeholders from previous similar project, the prioritization grid placements must never be copied because the circumstances may have changed.
It is this grid that would be used for making a plan as well as a strategy to deal with the stakeholders.

The other grids and prioritization methods are: -

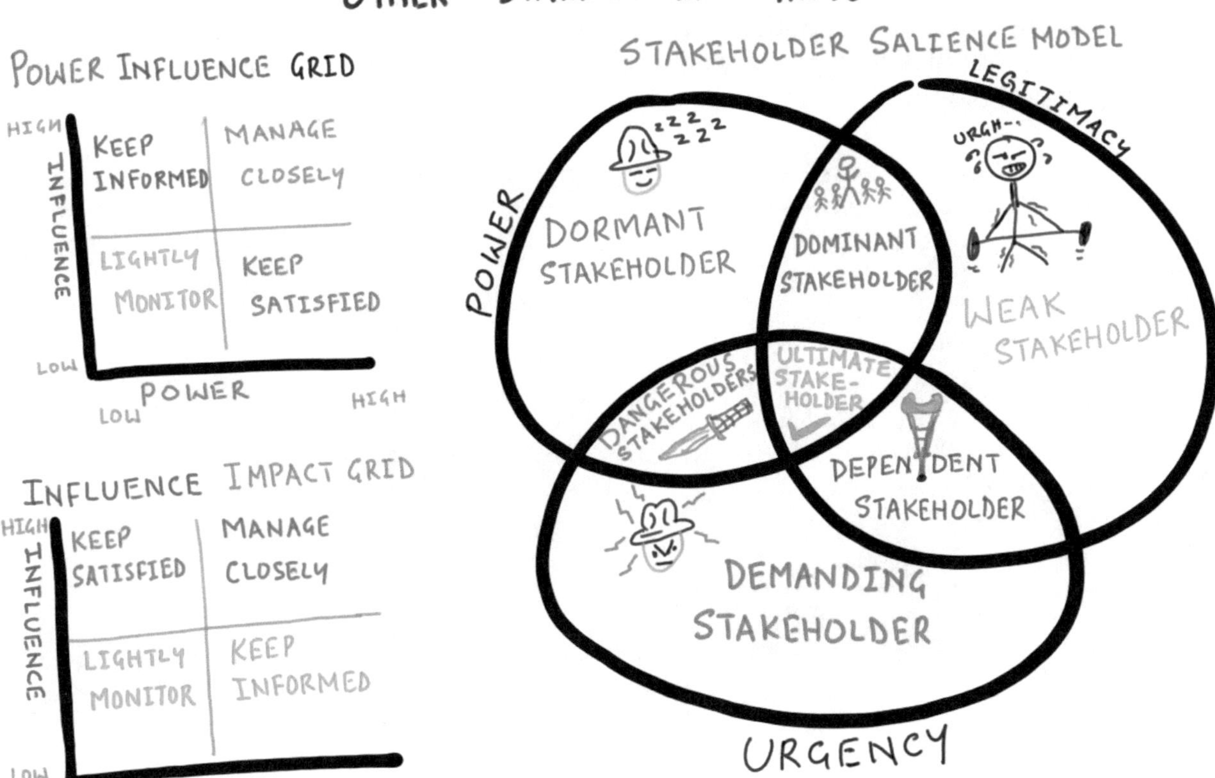

While the other grids are very similar to the "Power – Interest" grid, let me provide some explanation about the Salience Model. First of all this model is not a prioritization method. This method simply categorizes the stakeholders. To do that it uses three major categories viz., Power (within the organization and not just on the project), Legitimacy (those who are directly connected with the project in one way or the other) and Urgency (those who show or have urgent requirements vis-à-vis the project). Once the stakeholders have been identified then we place them in the salience model van-diagram. The reason why the intersection of all three categories is called the "Ultimate Stakeholders" because these stakeholders have Power to get things done within the organization, they are legitimate stakeholders and connected directly to your project and also have Urgency towards the project. They will get a lot of things done on their own and within time. Compared to this look at the interaction of only the categories of "Legitimate" and "Urgency". Here the image of a "Crutch" is shown. A crutch is a device that one places under their armpit to relive pressure on one's leg if they have hurt or injured their legs. Basically a crutch is a sign of dependency. These stakeholders are directly connected to the project but they do not have any power to get things done while having a lot of urgency towards the project. Since they cannot get their own work done they will pile up on you (the project manager) to get the work done for them. The more the stakeholders in this area the more you would have to do other peoples work for them. With this basic knowledge of how to use Salience Model, please revisit the diagram above and understand the rest of the entries in that diagram. It will provide you clear understanding of the same.

There is another method for prioritizing stakeholders which is gaining a lot of ground of late viz., Stakeholder's Cube.
This model is a 3d model and works on three parameters to prioritize the stakeholders.

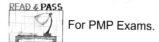

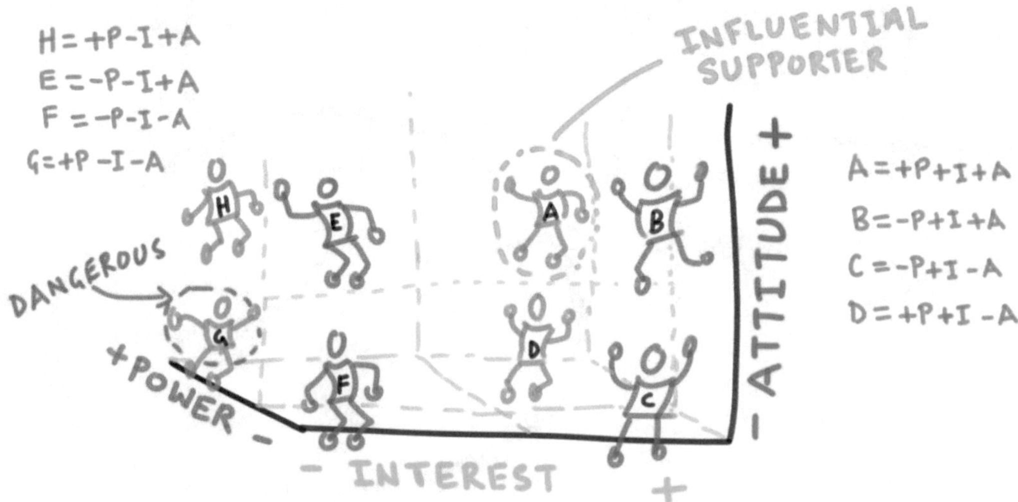

Power and Interest is just like the 2D Power-Interest grid. However this third attribute of Positive attitude vs Negative attitude makes a big difference. In the diagram the stakeholder labelled as "A" is marked as an "Influential Supporter" because this person has "High Interest" as well as "High Power" in the project and has a "Positive Attitude" towards the project. Compare A with D now. D has high power, high interest but a negative attitude towards this project. Hence D would be marked as an "Influential Blocker or Resistor". I guess you can see the picture now. Cool, isn't it?

Directions Of Influence: This means the direction in which the Project Manager would have to "Influence" the different groups of stakeholder. Senior managers who can affect the project from the point of view of their authority and higher hierarchical positions are called "Upward" because the project manager would have to "Influence" those who are higher up in hierarchy to meet the project objectives. Since the project manager would also have some team members who would report to him and other such project contributors and he would have to influence them too to meet the project objectives, this is termed as "Downward" direction of influence. Obviously, the strategy would be different for Downward and different for upward direction of influence of the stakeholder groups. The third category of the stakeholders is those who are outside the realm of the organization *e.g., Government Bodies, Regulatory Bodies, Advertising firms, external consultants, end users, and suppliers.* This group of stakeholders is called "Outward" direction of Influence. And the fourth group is the "Sideward" direction of influence stakeholders. These are the "peer" level stakeholders like other project managers, Quality Assurance department heads, other managers competing for the same group of resources and Operational heads (depending on the kind of organizational structure).

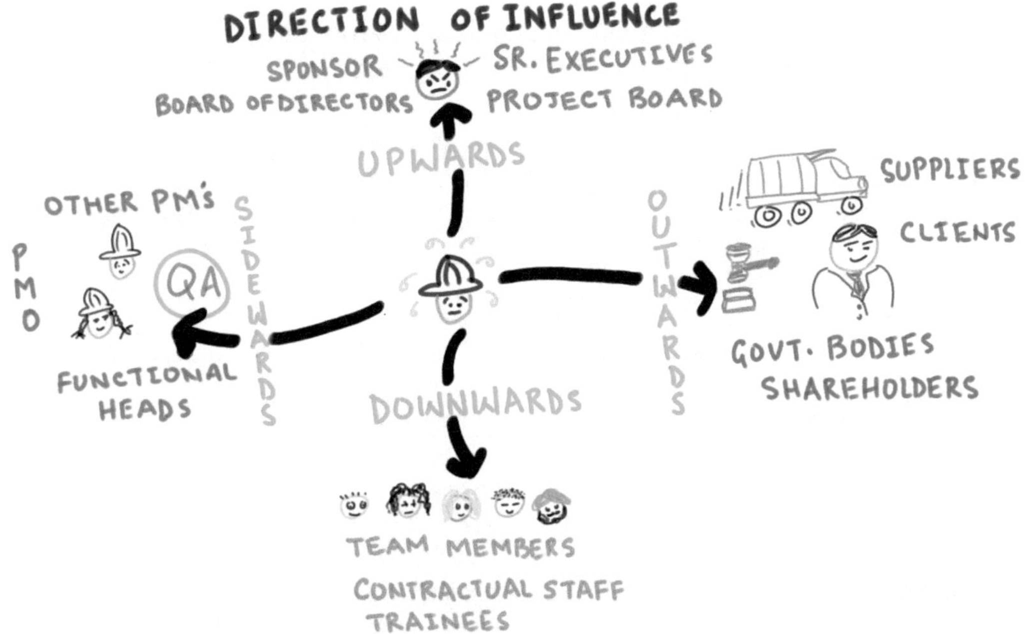

8.3.2 Outputs, artefact or outcome of the process IDENTIFY STAKEHOLDERS:

Stakeholder Register, being the main output of this process, contains all details about the stakeholder duly prioritized based on the classification that was used to prioritize them in the first place. There could also be some additional notes about the stakeholders that could come in handy during communication planning or something that would help create a more practical strategy for dealing with them.

STAKEHOLDER REGISTER

PROJECT NAME = KUCH 2 KAR || PM = JOE B CARVALHO || PROJECT STAGE = INITIATION

NAME	ROLE	CONTACT	CATEGORY	POWER	INTEREST	REQUIREMENTS	EXPECTATIONS
T. TOTELER	SPONSOR		INTERNAL	HI	HI		
U-R JAKED	GOVT. REGUL.		EXTERNAL	HI	LOW		
RAFU CHAKKAR	VENDOR		EXTERNAL	HI	LOW		
R2D2	PROC. DEPT.		INTERNAL	LOW	LOW		
M.E. MANGTA	CLIENT		EXTERNAL	HI	HI		

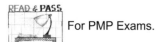

8.4 Ninja Drill – Initiation

You will find a Ninja Drill which lists the most important points you must remember for the exams, this chapter is concerned.

S. No.	Drill Points
1.	Project Charter is always created before identifying and analyzing stakeholders.
2.	All the work done before the creation and approval of Project Charter is called "Pre-Project Work" and is not part of the project as such.
3.	No Project Charter = No Project.
4.	The Sponsor signs and hence authorizes the project charter.
5.	Project Charter has to be formal document for all methodologies except agile, where just an email can suffice as a Project Charter.
6.	Business Case is the financial justification for undertaking the project.
7.	Benefits Management Plan contains the strategic benefits that would be obtained through the project.
8.	Business Model Canvas is an artifact which is a one-page visual summary that describes the value proposition, infrastructure, customers, and finances. These are often used in lean start-up situations.
9.	All the assumptions taken at the project start (initiation) must be documented in an Assumption Log to ensure that these assumptions become less and less during the life of the project.
10.	Agile methodology would be needed for projects in a complex environment where the end product is not fully known and user feedback is very valuable.
11.	Hybrid methodology should be used for a situation like where customers have an unclear scope but want to move to a fixed price contract as soon as possible.
12.	Vision is a desired end-state, often described as a set of desirable objectives and outcomes. Project Charter is a document while Vision is a team understanding. They both are connected.
13.	Overall scope of the project is documented in Project Charter.
14.	The main purpose of the process Identify Stakeholders is to not only identify all possible stakeholders of the project at hand but also prioritize them.
15.	The stakeholders have the highest effect (influence) on the project during the early stages of the project. Their influence diminishes as time passes in the project.
16.	The best way to reduce unnecessary changes in the project is to conduct comprehensive Stakeholder Management.
17.	The most popular method for prioritizing the stakeholders is called the "Power – Interest" Grid.
18.	**High Power – High Interest** Stakeholders need to be "Managed closely". **High Power – Low Interest** stakeholders need to be "Kept Satisfied". **Low Power – High Interest** stakeholder need to be "Kept Informed". **Low Power – Low Interest** stakeholders need to be "Lightly Monitored".
19.	Salience Model has three parameters viz., Power, Urgency and Legitimacy.
20.	The main outcome / output / Artefact of the process "Identify and Analyze Stakeholders" is the **Stakeholder Register.**
End Of Ninja Drill	

9 Project Planning

Planning a project is the most structured as well as the biggest section in Project Management. This is where each element of planning is done at a granular level to ensure that execution of the project is meaningful and delivers the results that was hoped for. Execution is nothing but the working of the plan. Hence more forethought has to be put into planning.
However, the way planning is done for Predictive projects is slightly different from the way it is done for adaptive projects. In adaptive projects planning is progressively done in pieces, again and again, just before each of the iterations. This repetitive planning is called the "Rolling Wave Planning".

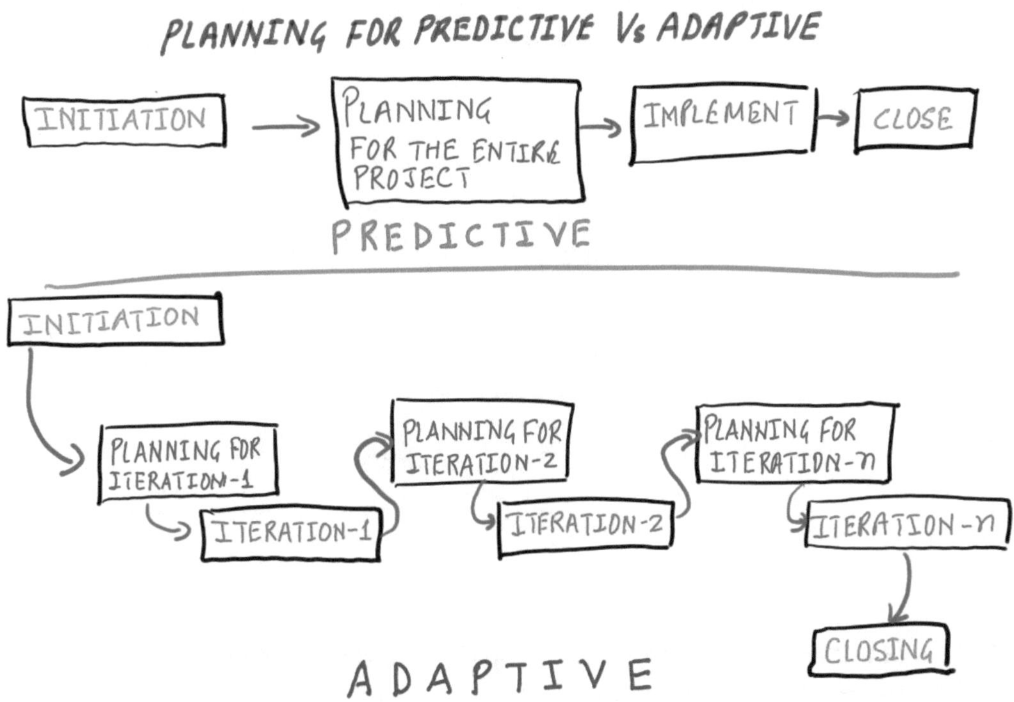

Irrespective of whether the planning is done once or progressively, the overall concepts are exactly the same.

9.1 Scope Management Plan And Requirements Management Plan

Scope is something that lays down the overall boundary of the project by clearly stating what needs to be done as well as stating what is not included. Establishing a scope ensures that you do all the work required and ONLY the work required, to complete the project successfully.
But why "ONLY"?
In a real-world project, it's very dangerous to provide anything outside the scope of the project, with the hope that the customer would be delighted. Terms like "Customer Delight", "Customer Extras", "Value Added" etc., are open to all kinds of interpretations and they all tend to take away the focus of the project team from the actual scope of the project.
There is actually a derogatory term for giving anything extra to the customer outside the scope of the project, it's called "Gold Plating". Gold Plating should be avoided and the project manager is responsible to ensure that there is no gold plating.

Some credible school of thoughts also suggest that overall "Customer Satisfaction" is achieved if 75% of the stated requirements have been met. Now with nearly 50% to 60% of the projects failing across all industries and countries, most of them are not even able to achieve even 75% of the customer satisfaction let alone giving something extra. This should be food for thought.

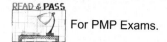

I hope you do remember that there are 3 elements that constitute the baseline which are Scope, Time and Cost. In the next few processes the "Scope Baseline" is going to be established. The control processes would all be in the Implementation section.

PROJECT SCOPE MANAGEMENT

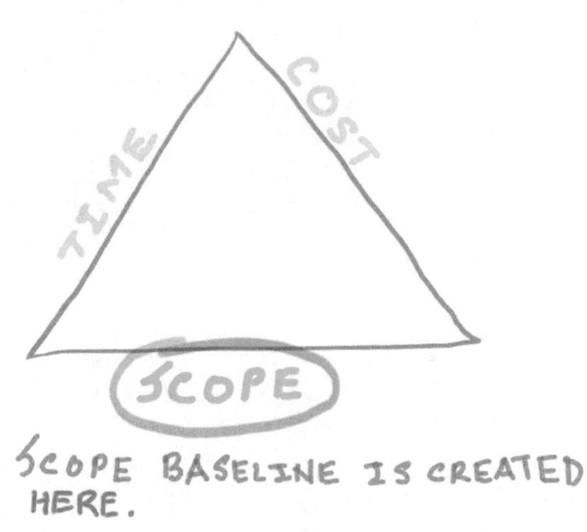

At this time it is important to know that "Scope" is made up of two parts. One is "Product Scope" and the other is "Project Scope". This much information is good enough for now as this concept would be explained in detail in the section where the WBS would be discussed later.

Total Scope = Product Scope + Project Scope
(Remember this well).

Before moving forward, it is important to know some terms. There are four terms which are always ascertained in a specific sequence, while working with customers, and they are, Needs, Scope, Requirements, and Specifications. They are always in this order. The diagram below explains this concept in details.

Needs come from the customer and they are never very clear. The needs have to be converted into "Scope" which basically states, at a high level, "what is included in the project and what is not". Specifically stating and documenting what is "not included" is very important.

All the things that are "Included" within the scope have a term for it viz., "Features". Each of these features has to be detailed out in the form of requirements. Requirements are the most detailed "Business rules and logic" and there is nothing technical about it. The whole purpose of Requirements is to capture, in absolute details, each and every business rule forming part of the "Scope" of the project. Finally, since the product of the project is either in the form of technical deliverables or services, hence each of the requirements has to be broken down and interpreted into "technical" terms and that's what "Specifications" are.

It is important for you to recall that "Scope" of the project is mentioned in the document "Project Charter". Hence in this knowledge area, there would not be any process where scope would be documented as it's already stated in the document Project Charter. Also remember that there is no overall scope, but only vision, in the Project Charter for Agile Projects.

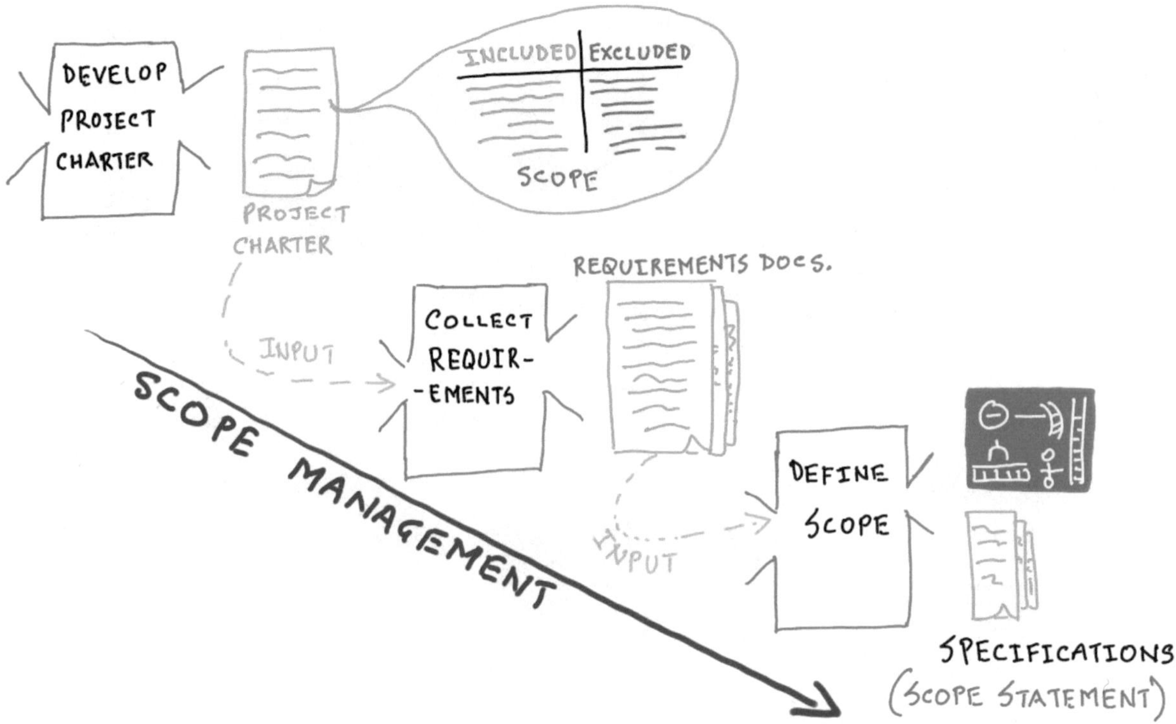

Over some time now a specialization in the field of project scope management has generated a much-needed role called "Business Analyst" and their main job is "Business Analysis". Traditionally the role and work of the BA was usually performed by the PM (I too have done that in the older days). However, now with the projects getting more complex and the expectations of the customers getting more challenging most organizations tend to create a separate role called "Business Analyst. Many people do get confused between the roles of the PM Vis-à-vis the BA.

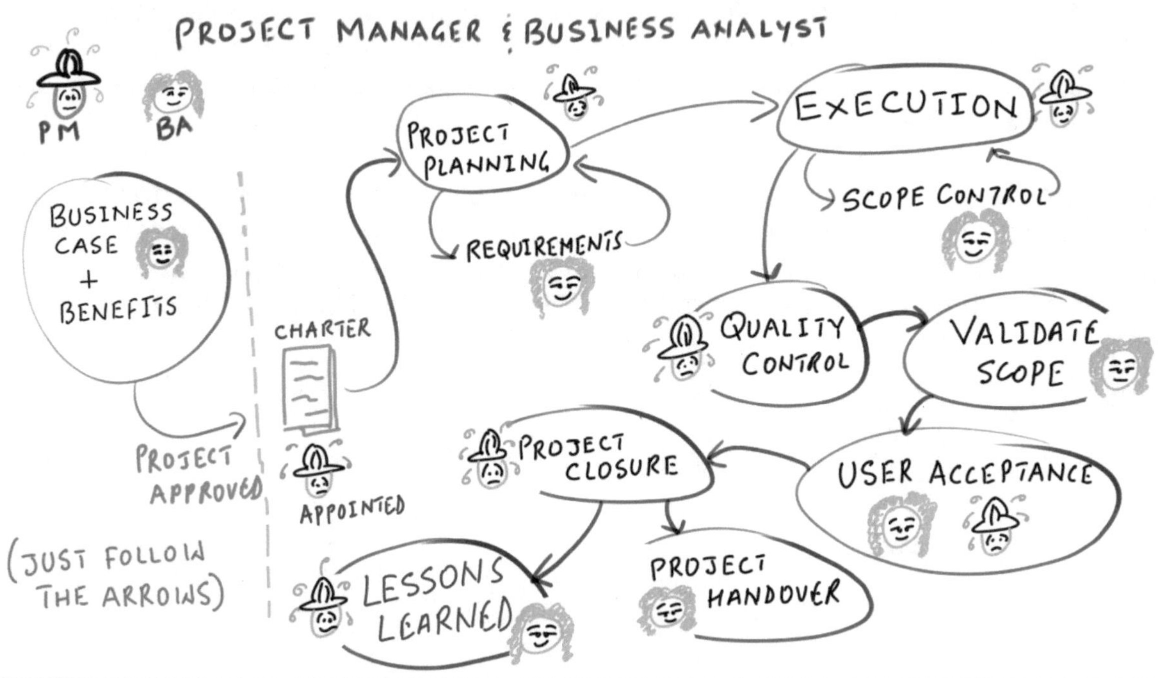

Remember, in Agile a BA is called a Product Owner.

9.2 Planning For The Project Scope

This is the first thing we do in planning. Understand and plan how the scope and requirements of the project would be addressed through the lifecycle of the project. This is the stage where we create two important plans (Subsidiary plans that make up the overall Project Management Plan) viz., the "**Scope Management Plan**" and the "**Requirements Management Plan**". This process is officially called *PLAN SCOPE MANAGEMENT*.

How do you eat an elephant? (My apologies to the vegetarians and the vegans, it is just a and age old African phrase) Correct answer, "One portion at a time". And that's precisely how practical project management works. It does not help you make one large mammoth (pun intended) plan, but several mini plans that can be clubbed together to, ultimately, make a mammoth plan. The entire project management plan is not made at one go, instead, it is divided into multiple subsidiary plans and each of them is made individually and compiled into the overall project management plan document.

There are basically two major kinds of projects. One is generally called "Predictive" and the other is called "Adaptive" (covered earlier where we talked about project lifecycles). A predictive lifecycle is where all the requirements are clearly documented at the very beginning of the project, hence requirements are documented, converted to specifications and then executed. After execution, the scope is validated to ensure that all the requirements have been met. This kind of lifecycle assumes that there would not be many changes to the scope of the project during the course of the project.

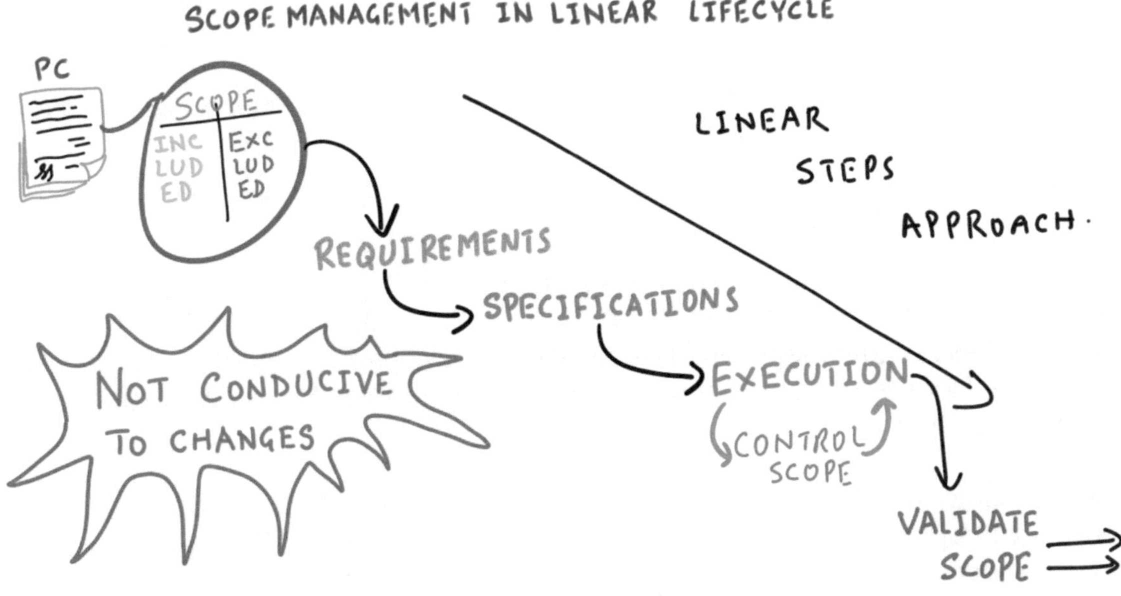

The adaptive lifecycles (like agile) are undertaken because the scope of the project is not very clear or not fixed at the early stage of the project. The journey itself is expected to unravel more requirements. Which means that these lifecycles are open to "Changes". In these lifecycles, for each of the iteration/sprint/cycle the requirements are generated from the backlog and documented, converted to specifications, executed and finally the scope is validated before releasing the product. These steps are constantly repeated for each of the iteration/sprint/cycle till everything in the backlog is completed.

There is a difference between Scope and Requirements. Something that was discussed a bit earlier in this chapter. Scope is the boundary of the project and requirements are the detailed business rules for each of the elements that is contained within the scope of the project. Which essentially means that you can have changes in requirements without affecting the scope of the project. A change in scope of a project is a huge change. And this is the reason why two separate subsidiary plans are provided in PMBOK to draw attention to this major difference between the two. In real projects most of the time they are not two separate documents but even in that document the scope and requirements management plan are written separately.

Scope Management Plan contains details about how the scope of the project would be documented and defined and changed if required. This plan has wider and bigger implications than the other subsidiary plan called the Requirements Management Plan. A change in scope has a much larger implication on the project than a change in requirements. In fact, the subsidiary plan "Requirements Management Plan" is more or less a sub-part of this plan. Scope management plan is concerned with the overall maintenance of the scope (boundary) of the project as well.

Requirements Management Plan is only concerned with how the Requirements would be elicited, documented, structured, prioritized, verified and approved by the customers / key stakeholders. This plan would list down the template for the requirements documentation, stakeholders needed to elicit the requirements, frequency of review, format of traceability matrix and approving authority for the requirements.

Needless to say that these two plans are not created at all during the Agile projects.

9.3 Eliciting And Documenting Requirements (Collect Requirements)

This process, ***Collect Requirements***, is dedicated to eliciting requirements and documenting them. Requirements form the very basis of the entire project and the final deliverables are based on these requirements and therefore this activity set assumes a certain level of importance. Needless to say that most of the projects which fail got their requirements elicitation botched.

"Requirements" are the business rules that represent a condition or a capability that the product of the project or service, must have. These are the detailing of the features that form part of the overall scope.

FEATURES TO REQUIREMENTS

SCOPE

INCLUDED	EXCLUDED
1. FEATURE A	X.
2. FEATURE B	X.
3. FEATURE C	X
4. FEATURE D	

EACH ELEMENT INCLUDED IN SCOPE IS A FEATURE

1. FEATURE - A

1.1

1.2

1.3.

EACH FEATURE IS DECOMPOSED INTO DETAILED BUSINESS RULES... ...WHICH ARE... REQUIREMENTS.

BY MAPPING FEATURES TO REQUIREMENTS, REQUIREMENTS WILL BE IN SCOPE.

The better the requirements are collected the higher the chances of the project success. It is as simple as that.
In agile projects the Features are the same as high-level requirements as well as the same as Epics while requirements are the same as user stories.

The overall process of collecting requirements is..

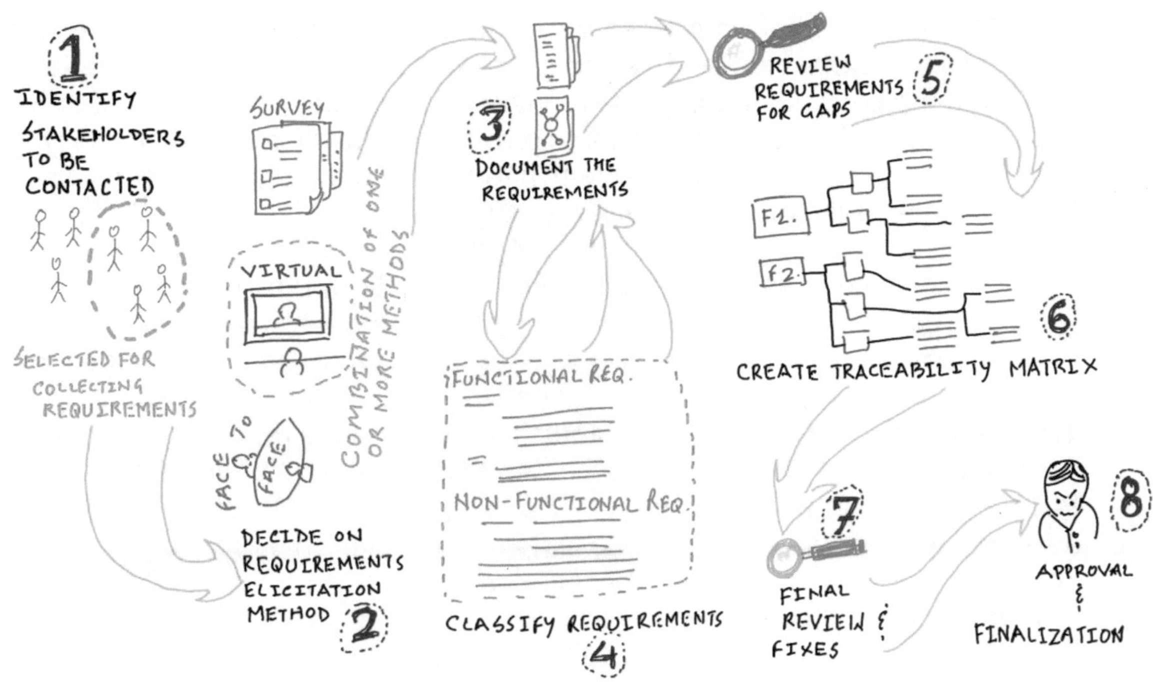

There are various categories of requirements. These categories are needed to ensure that we are not missing out any specific category of requirements. The reason for this is that by covering all categories of requirements the chances of missing out requirements would be significantly reduced.

Some of the commonly used categories are as under:-

1. **Business Requirements**: these are slightly high-level requirements which basically state the reason why the project is being undertaken. *E.g. The bank has decided to opt for internet banking as the customers are moving on to other banks. However, to protect the high-value transactions of the corporate banking, internet-based Retail Banking would be introduced first.*
2. **Regulatory requirements**: these are the requirements that have been enforced because of the government regulations affecting the project. *E.g. All the waste flow from the paper mill must be first cleaned and separated using clarifiers and stored in sedimentation tanks for 2 days before releasing it downstream in the river.*
3. **Stakeholder Requirements**: These requirements are those which are connected to specific groups of Stakeholders and affects those groups. *E.g. There must be a helipad on the drilling platform that must accommodate two concurrent 10 seater helicopters for the board of directors and senior management visiting for inspections and getting journalists and government visitors to the platform for "goodwill" building.*
4. **Solution Requirements**:
    a. *Functional Requirements*: These requirements constitute most of the requirements documentation and contain a detailed level breakdown of each of the features mentioned in the scope. They are always non-technical in nature even for the most technical projects. *E.g., The hospital surgery room must have a 10 square feet of changing room where the surgeons can change into surgical gowns and apparels. This room must have lockers for the surgeons to carefully store their belongings and every surgeon must have a designated locker with lock combination given to him. Each locker must be 2 feet high, 1.5 feet wide and 3 feet deep.*
    b. *Non-Functional Requirements*: This category is more popularly used for IT, electronic/electrical and Telecom projects/products. It is applicable for most other projects as well. These requirements basically do not provide a solution to any business requirements or provide any functionality. However, they state the expectation from the system in terms of Load, ruggedness, reliability, serviceability, maintainability. *E.g., **IT Example:** At any given 10,000 concurrent users must be able to log into the system without reduction in their experience of speed of access. **Electronic Example:** The switch must be able to withstand 1million "off – on" operations with half kg pressure on the switch knob for each operation. **Engineering Example:** The car engine should not need any kind of servicing or oil change before 10,000 km of running.*
5. **Transition / Transitory Requirements**: These are those requirements which are usually done once in the project, just at the time of transition from "As – Is" to "To – Be" state (Handing-over phase). *E.g. **IT Example:** Before the new financial software is rolled out in the finance department, last two years financial data has to be entered into the system before the features of the application can be used. **Civil Construction Example:** Before the office building is handed over to the operations team all the security and the key stakeholders have to be trained on emergency evacuation process.*

At this time one must also be very clear about the stated requirements vs unstated requirements vs implied requirements. Stated requirements are the ones that are explicitly documented. Implied requirements are part of the "Stated" requirements and they do not have to be explicitly documented. If you want to get a door built for your office, you would have to provide explicit requirements like material, size, décor details etc. However as a part of these explicitly stated requirements, the implied requirements would be that the door should open and close, it should stop people from coming in when closed, and so on. However, wherever there is a choice available and the choice has not been explicitly stated than that becomes an example of unstated requirements.

IMPLIED VS UNSTATED REQUIREMENTS

REQUIREMENTS
FOR A CAR
THAT YOU JUST
ORDERED.
IMPLIED
- ACCELERATOR
- WHEELS ROTATING
- LIGHT SWITCHING ON
- STEERING TURNING THE CAR
- SHOCK ABSORPTION SYSTEM
PART OF STATED REQUIREMENTS AND DO NOT HAVE TO BE MENTIONED EXPLICITLY
UNSTATED
- SHOULD BE 4X4
- BLUE IN COLOR
- MILEAGE
- SHOULD SEAT 6 PEOPLE
- CONVERTIBLE
UNSTATED CHOICES
OR
ASSUMPTIONS

Remember, in Agile the high level requirements are called Epic and the detailed requirements are called User Stories. Irrespective of what requirements are called, the elicitation process as well as the techniques used for them would be more or less the same.

9.3.1 Tools and Techniques For Requirements Elicitation -

There are multiple tools and techniques for eliciting the project requirements. One can pick and choose the most apt tools and techniques for the situation at hand.

A good project manager or a business analyst must be aware of the various barriers to the requirements collection and plan for overcoming them.

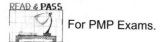

These tools help with a structured way of eliciting requirements as well as help overcome barriers to requirements elicitation. Some of the barriers to the requirements elicitation could be depicted as under:

Let us now get to know and understand the tools and techniques of the process *COLLECT REQUIREMENTS*.
There are a lot of tools and techniques in this process. Hence let us go through groups of these tools and techniques based on what they do.

9.3.2 Tools that help in collecting requirements:

- **Brainstorming:**
  Whenever we need to find out new ideas from stakeholders, one of the most productive techniques is "Brainstorming". This is a meeting (real or virtual live) among the stakeholders where the facilitator lays down the subject of discussion and then all the participants give ideas, suggestions, requirements etc. The rules are simple, no one is judged, no one is stopped from speaking as long as they are speaking within the scope, healthy conflict is promoted and the brainstorming can continue as long as participants do not run out of things to say or the time runs out (in time-boxed meetings). The prioritization of ideas or selection of the idea is not done in Brainstorming. The whole purpose of Brainstorming is to come out with ideas. Brainstorming may be vocal or silent. In silent brainstorming the ideas are written on paper or post-its and pasted on walls for others to read it and then have multiple rounds of finding and writing more pertinent ideas without having conflicts and aggression. One example of Silent Brainstorming is "Crawford Slip Method".

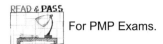

It is important to note that Brainstorming is only used when no one has requirements with them. Requirements have to be thought up by the participants of brainstorming. If the requirements are available with certain stakeholders, brainstorming would not be required.

No tool and technique is perfect. Each tool has certain pros and cons.

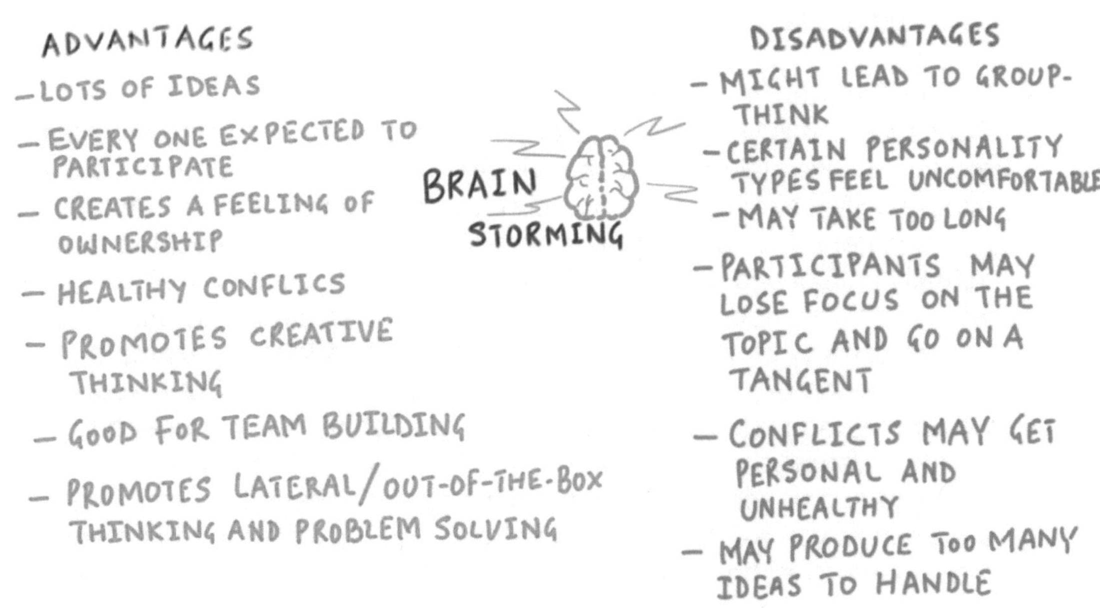

ADVANTAGES
- LOTS OF IDEAS
- EVERY ONE EXPECTED TO PARTICIPATE
- CREATES A FEELING OF OWNERSHIP
- HEALTHY CONFLICS
- PROMOTES CREATIVE THINKING
- GOOD FOR TEAM BUILDING
- PROMOTES LATERAL/OUT-OF-THE-BOX THINKING AND PROBLEM SOLVING
BRAIN STORMING
DISADVANTAGES
- MIGHT LEAD TO GROUP-THINK
- CERTAIN PERSONALITY TYPES FEEL UNCOMFORTABLE
- MAY TAKE TOO LONG
- PARTICIPANTS MAY LOSE FOCUS ON THE TOPIC AND GO ON A TANGENT
- CONFLICTS MAY GET PERSONAL AND UNHEALTHY
- MAY PRODUCE TOO MANY IDEAS TO HANDLE

- **Interviews**
  Interviews are usually the most popular requirements collection method. What it means is that requirements are collected from the pertinent stakeholders face to face or over virtual platform but always directly. The number of interviewees can be more than one and so is the case with interviewers. This requires interaction of questions and answers and hence is termed as the interview method. This method is also used to develop a networking relationship with certain stakeholders.

  Advantages of the interview method of collecting requirements: -
  - Respondents are usually very comfortable with the interview process
  - Interviewer can adjust to the individual style of communication and deal with unexpected information and revelations
  - Interviews are usually fairly easy to arrange in the normal workplace
  - Interviews use a flexible format, allowing follow-up of new points and interesting lines of discussion if time permits
  - Interviewing encourages buy-in from participants

  Disadvantages of interview of collecting requirements: -
  - One-on-one interviews can be time-consuming
  - Subsequent analysis can be time-consuming
  - Interviewer must guard against focusing on routine aspects of the task or situation

- Personal biases may affect the interview, depending on the relationship established between the interviewer and respondent
- What people say is often very different from what they do
- Interviewer may need to acquire domain knowledge in order to know what questions to ask and to understand the responses

An interview method of collecting requirements is a time taking process hence its best used when the numbers of stakeholders from whom the requirements have to be collected are few.

- **Focus Groups**

Focus Group is yet another tool and technique for collecting requirements. Focus groups involve stakeholders, customers, prospective customers, subject matter experts (SME's) and so on, who can give an opinion about what they think of a product, service or offering. The person who wants to collect the requirements would actually collect and document the views and suggestions of all the participants and later use those documented views and opinion to come out with requirements. This is an indirect way of collecting requirements. Let us take an example. You wish to launch a new version of a cellphone/smartphone in the market. For a successful launch, you would need to understand what people feel/felt about your previous cellphone/smartphone. Therefore, you invite some "Shop owners", some past customers, and some cellphone/smartphone geeks or let's say Tech-Experts. Once all are present you ask them to "Focus" on what they liked in the previous cellphone/smartphone. You record their statements and ensure that no one is going off topic. Then you ask them to "Focus" on the things that they did not like about the cellphone / Smartphone and why. Again you record their statements. This is exactly what a focus group is. Later, these recorded statements may be used for finding the actual requirements for the new version of cellphone/smartphone.
As you can see this is more of an "Observation and Suggestions gathering" session where the communication is mostly one way, from the participants to the person recording the observations.

Advantages of Focus Group method of eliciting requirements: -

- Can capture a lot of information quickly
- Allow participants to compare and contrast their perceptions, priorities, and needs
- Allow the analyst to obtain rapidly a wide variety of views from a range of people with different, but relevant, perspectives

Disadvantages of Focus Group method of eliciting requirements: -

- Must be skillfully facilitated to prevent off-topic tangents and open conflict among participants
- Can become a destructive activity (whine session) rather than a constructive one
- May lead to inaccurate results due to peer pressure

Again, these focus groups could be in person at a common physical place or over a virtual live platform. These focus groups could also be either Homogenous (where similar kind of pre-qualified participants are invited) or Heterogeneous (where different kinds of pre-qualified participants are invited).

- **Questionnaires And Surveys**
  Sometimes the number of the stakeholders could be so many that neither interview nor focus group or facilitated workshops can be conducted. In such cases, the best option would be to obtain requirements through **"Questionnaire and Survey"** method. This method is an impersonal method where carefully designed survey with questionnaires and rating charts are circulated to all the stakeholders who are then expected to fill them up and return it for analysis within the prescribed time limit. This is best suited for a large number of stakeholders or stakeholders who are geographically distributed or when the results need to be analyzed statistically.

  Advantages of Questionnaire method of collecting requirements:-
  - Are quick and relatively inexpensive to administer
  - Can be distributed simultaneously to a large group of people
  - Can prevent tangential issues from being introduced
  - Can produce answers that can be rated for reliability and consistency if statements and rating scales are used correctly

  Disadvantages of Questionnaire method of collecting requirements: -
  - May or may not be filled out by respondents
  - May not be accurate if respondents are not committed to giving correct answers and are influenced by what they think they should answer
  - Require a large, identifiable user pool that is prepared to complete and return the questionnaire
  - May not gain as much information as other techniques, especially in the area of subjective insights

- **Benchmarking**
  In certain organizations like Construction, Infrastructure and Software Development it makes sense to look at the way requirements are documented and elicited in other organizations which have become industry leaders. This is called "**Benchmarking**" and this also helps in requirements elicitation. However, this concept tends to inhibit own team's creative thinking and abilities. This must be done with a lot of care and understanding so that it does not translate into abject copying of requirements and requirement processes without taking into consideration local environmental factors as well as the uniqueness of the organization itself. You can see that of late most cellular phone devices companies use the features present in Samsung or Apple (iPhones) as a benchmark and try to provide similar or even superior features.

- **Document Analysis**
  I and my team once got a huge project with the administrative wing of the Indian Army. We had to collect requirements for, develop and implement the customized workflow management system across all locations of the Indian Army bases. Our first step was to collect requirements from the key stakeholders. After the initial overview and expectation setting discussions with the top brass of the Army Administrative unit at Sena Bhawan, New Delhi, we were handed box loads of rule books, instructions, procedures and rulings by the army brass. Though, at that time the entire workflow management system was done through manually handled paper and file trails, they

had extensive documentation about everything that Army does in terms of Administration services. We were able to glean nearly 60% of all our requirements from these documents alone. This is what is known as Document Analysis. Many industries and domain have extensive documentation that could be perused to obtain a substantial part of requirements. Some kinds of projects are heavily regulated by government regulations, hence a large part of their requirements come from these well documented regulations. This also includes documents like Agreements, Contracts, Statement Of Work and any other project documents that have already been made till this stage in the project. Their perusal also helps in obtaining some requirements for the project.

- **Observation And Conversation**
When the detailed requirements are not easily available from a stakeholder or the stakeholder finds it difficult to articulate the requirements then one of the possible ways to understand the process is to "**Observe or Job Shadow**" the stakeholder and make detailed noting of what they are physically doing. The observer may even try to validate the requirements collected through observation with the help of the observed by showing, in practice, what he could learn from observation (this is called "Reverse Job Shadowing"). This is not possible in all circumstances. Despite the fact that it helps with understanding the process flow but it only captures the AS-IS process and not the TO-BE process. The requirements seeker may even try to participate in executing the process himself (Participant Observer) to uncover some shortcuts (that are different from the documented processes) or some hidden requirements which are not otherwise easily visible. There is a variant to the Observation or Job Shadow Technique called "Verbal Protocol" which is mainly used in research and scientific analysis. Verbal Protocol is basically "on the job requirements collection". This is usually done for mission-critical projects and initiatives.

- **Facilitation**

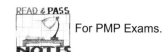

  Facilitation is the skill for ensuring participation and engagement among the participants and attendees to a meeting or an initiative. This skill is important to get the participants involved in the decision making process or requirements elicitation process to help ensure that the elicitation process is thorough and successful.
  From PMP point of view, the term facilitation is usually linked with the "Facilitated Workshops" for requirements elicitation.
  Though the concept of "Facilitated Workshop" is not specifically written in the tools and techniques of this version of PMBOK® Guide, you must still know what it is. Questions on this topic still shows up in PMP Exams. **Facilitated Workshops** are highly interactive sessions where all those stakeholders who could provide requirements for the project are invited by the facilitator who records the requirements suggested and also records the differences among the stakeholders. These sessions are usually intensive and may have multiple sessions instead of just one and tend to be longer. These sessions have to be very well planned in order to be successful. This session, if properly conducted, can build trust among the various stakeholders, improves communication and lays down clear expectations from the project among the various stakeholders. These sessions would directly result in documented requirements duly prioritized and categorized.
  E.g., You have already recorded the suggestions from the participants of the focus group and now you wish to create the requirements for the new version of cellphone/smartphone. For this, you have requested the Product Manager, Head of Legal Department, Technical leaders, A freelance software and platform consultant, Works Manager, Quality Manager, Top Dealers, and the Marketing and Sales head to be present at a meeting at an appointed time. You have prepared slides about the various suggestions from the focus group and you are now inviting these participants to give their requirements about features and functionality that should be present in the new version of the cellphone/smartphone. There is a lot of discussions and a lot of ideas are thrown at you. Some of these ideas are rejected by the technical leader as not feasible. The dealers want the new launch to be in pink and beige and not just black, silver and white, because he knows that certain colors are more preferred by different genders.

  You can imagine how difficult it would be to manage such vibrant sessions. Well, this is what happens in a Facilitated Workshop. The communication is not only two way among the participants but also promotes healthy conflict.

  Agile development methodologies usually use Facilitated Workshops to list down User Stories and develop backlogs.

  I guess this clearly differentiates what is a Focus Group and what is a Facilitated workshops.

  EXAMS SPECIAL In exams, most of the time, questions on this topic ask about examples of Facilitated workshops in different kinds of industries. You need to remember the following. Joint Application Development (JAD or JAD Session) is an example of Facilitated Workshops in IT and Software Development Industry. Quality Function Deployment (QFD) (which uses Voice of Customer (VOC) survey system as inputs to it) is an example of Facilitated workshop in Manufacturing based industries. Design of Experiments (DOE) is an example of Facilitated workshops in Research and Innovation based industries.

- **Delphi or Wide-Band Delphi:**
There is yet another method of facilitation and it's called the "**Delphi Technique**". ***Delphi*** is a technique where you obtain the consensus of stakeholders on certain points. Various rounds of discussions are done and debates are also done till most of the attendees reach a consensus. Many times this is done without the stakeholders coming to know who the other stakeholder was. Which means this is done anonymously. For some reason if the requirements cannot be collected upfront (maybe because of bias, hierarchy issues, political issues, sensitivity of the project) face to face and the stakeholders are not comfortable knowing who said what and who gave what information, then the best way to go forward is to apply the Delphi method. In this technique, each of the participating stakeholders is approached separately and anonymously. However, whatever is suggested or documented by one stakeholder is available for view and review to each of the other participating stakeholder without divulging the identity. This way when stakeholders go through the documents of the others, without knowing the identity, they either correct themselves or correct others and after some rounds of this most of them end up agreeing on similar things viz., arriving at a consensus.

9.3.3 Tools and Techniques for confirming requirements:

- **Prototype and Beta:**
Experienced Project Managers and Business Analysts know that stakeholders tend to articulate requirements slightly different from what they have imagined it in their minds. This human limitation poses serious threat to the project. To overcome this the concept of "**Prototyping**" was invented. A prototype is a "Mock-up" or a slightly working, model which has been created in line with the requirements collected so far. This model, when placed in front of the stakeholders would help refine the requirements and also elicit hidden requirements from the stakeholders. This can be done once or multiple times in a project. *E.g., Mock up screens created (without any kind of processing behind it or sometimes partial processing) to show to the customer how their online banking solution would look like and how the user would be able to use it and what would be the navigation.* This would prompt the stakeholders to come out with better requirements and hidden requirements and even gaps in understanding of requirements. *E.g., The architect builds a 3D computer model or a physical scale model of the building requirements of the customer.* The customer may look at it and realize that how he imagined the rounded balconies to be, do not look as great in reality and hence would correct the requirements and may even prompt him to suggest gaps in his requirements; like Solar Panels on roof, guard room location, store room etc.
In the cinema and advertising industry, the concept of **Storyboarding** was used to lay down the sequence of proposed events and shooting sequence on boards and paper to show how the idea would look. A variant of the same Storyboarding is a regular "Prototype" feature in most Agile development engagements.

Every once in a while the exams talk about the difference in “Beta” and Prototyping. The main difference between the two is that Beta is a working model and is released to some stakeholders for obtaining feedback and suggestions which would help create a better, more practical final release. Some organizations even call a Beta Release as “Safe Release”. Many famous hotels go for a “Soft opening” before opening it for all. Hence Beta is a working and a release version albeit not a final version. The prototype is just a mock up or a partially working model but is never released. Google Mail was on Beta version for several years obtaining feedback and suggestions from some customers, before releasing the final version to everyone.

9.3.4 Tools and Techniques for Representing Requirements:

- **Affinity Diagram**
  Affinity Diagram is a tool that is used typically after a brainstorming session. Once you have a lot of ideas they are grouped together by similarity or functionality under headings. Once all the ideas are grouped under headings the team than looks for any missing “Headings” or “Broad Functionality”. Having done that the team then looks for ensuring that no points are missed out under each of the headings. This is one way of filling gaps and fishing out hidden functionality. Sometimes the group headings are broken down into sub-groups for better structure. The affinity diagrams could then be later used as direct inputs for a cause and effect diagram or an NGT could be used for prioritizing the requirements. Affinity Diagram is one of the common ways of finding out the various Epics (Features) in a proposed software and then later broken down into “Stories” in an Agile Methodology. Most people/organizations use multi-colored post-it for this and some use software that simulates the same.

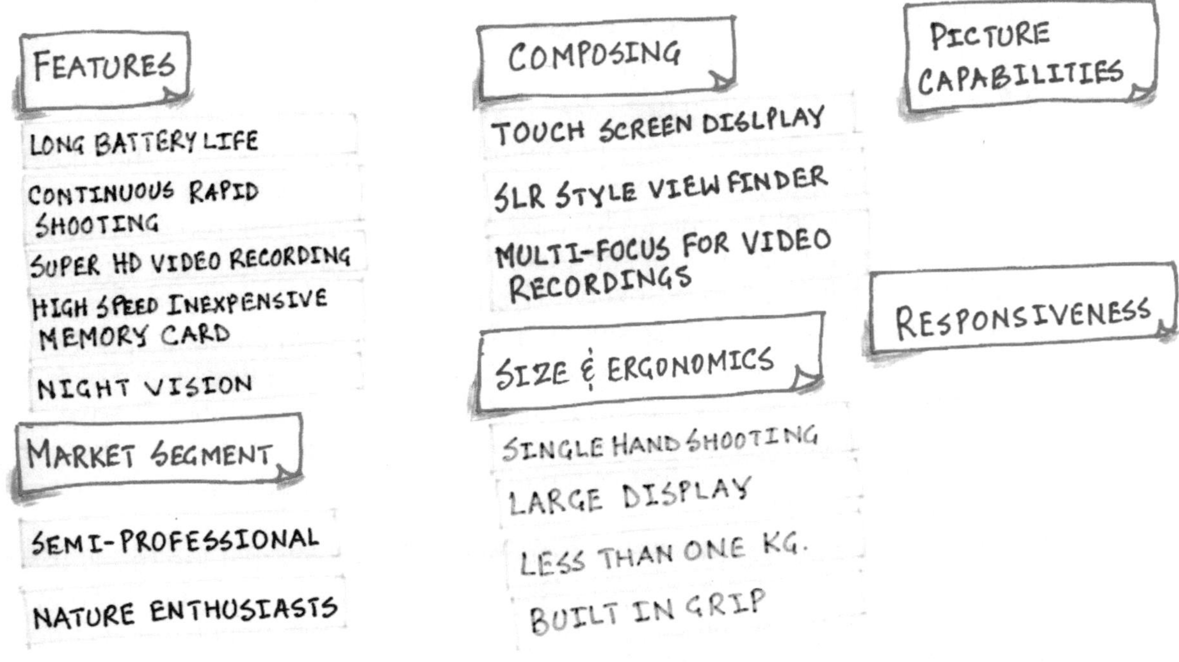

- **Mind Mapping**
  Mind mapping or Idea mapping is a graphical technique to expand a central idea. This is done by using paper or mind map software. This should be done with stakeholders to get more perspective instead of doing it alone. This is basically a tool and could be used even during Brainstorming to map out all the ideas generated. I guess the best way to understand it would be for you to see an example.

Mind Maps help you find all aspects of requirements connected to an idea. This helps you take a holistic approach and chances of missing requirements are a little less. Usually, this method is used to expand upon a new idea.

9.3.5 Tools and Techniques for Requirements Prioritization:

Prioritization of requirements are more popular in Agile projects. The reason for that is because the Product Backlogs have to be constantly prioritized because only the most prioritized Epics get earmarked for next release. The bigger reason why requirements prioritization is popular in Agile projects is because of the fact that each of the iterations in agile are “Time Boxed”. This presents a problem to the team. Let us say they have earmarked 10 User stories to be developed in the next sprint / iteration. Let’s say the iteration is for 3 weeks. Since the moment 3 weeks are over, whether or not the team has been able to develop all the user stories, they will have to demo the working software to the customer. Hence, to ensure that at least the most important user stories get developed first within that iteration, the user stories need to be prioritized.

However, at the same time, it is a misconception to think that the requirements are to be prioritized only in Agile Projects. Requirements need to be prioritized in every methodology. When it comes to Predictive methodology, prioritization is done to ensure that the development focus and testing focus is largely on requirements that are closer to the heart of the customer. Requirements that would be used more often and considered crucial by the clients would have a higher prioritization. In Predictive projects these high priority requirements are called "Critical To Acceptance (CTA)" or "Critical To Quality (CTQ)". These terms essentially mean those requirements which are critical to acceptance and any defect in them would lead to rejection of the deliverables.

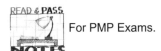

Let us have a look at some of the requirements prioritization techniques:

- **MoSCoW**
  This is by far the most common requirements prioritization technique in the world when it comes to IT industry. MoSCoW essentially stands for:
    - **Mo** = Most Important / Must Have
    - **S** = Should Have
    - **Co** = Could Have and
    - **W** = Won't Have (for now or in this iteration)

  "Won't have" is not something that the customer does not want at all. It simply means that the requirements marked as "Won't have (yet)" do not need to be provided in the release or iteration in question. These may be provided in the subsequent iterations when they obtain higher priority.
  The whole purpose of having MoSCoW prioritization is to figure out the minimum business functionality that would actually make crucial difference to the customer that could be developed in an iteration. This is what is actually called the MVP / MBI, something that has been explained earlier.
  An iteration is timeboxed, which means that the iteration would end whether all the user stories assigned to it are completed or not. To be able to prioritize the user stories even within the iteration itself, the "Must Haves" would be developed first, followed by "Should haves" and finally the "Could Haves". Now if some of the "should haves" and "Could haves" do not get completed in the iteration, the MBI is not adversely affected because the "Must Haves" have been developed anyway.

- **Voting / Cluster Voting**
  Voting is probably the most simplistic method of prioritization. Similar to the democratic voting system, each of the stakeholders involved in prioritization of requirements, would be given one vote to cast it on the requirements / user story he thinks is the most important for the project or the specific iteration. Once everyone has cast their votes, the requirements or the user stories with the most vote count will be considered the highest priority, while the one with the next highest vote count would be considered the next highest priority and so on. The requirements which have not received any votes whatsoever would be eliminated from the requirements of the proposed product itself.

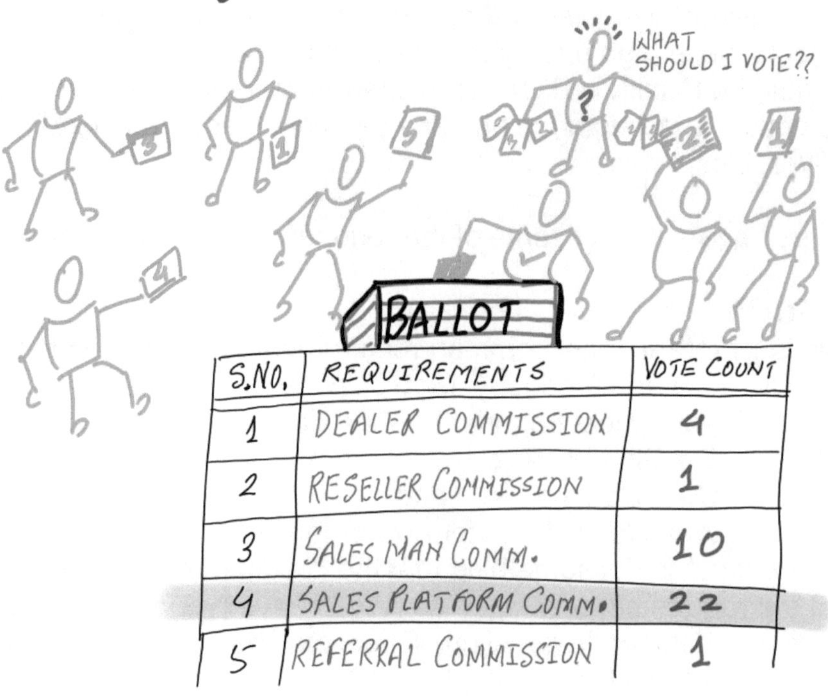

Once the voting is done there are several ways to interpret the votes. ***Unanimity*** is when all the stakeholders agree to a specific course of action. This usually happens without much convincing or discussions. ***Consensus***, on the other hand, is slightly different where unanimity is achieved after a lot of discussions and convincing and debate. Sometimes when consensus or unanimity is not achievable a simple ***Majority*** of the stakeholders decide what to do. When even a clear majority is not visible than simply the largest group decides what needs to be done which is called ***Plurality***. However, if one person takes all the decision for the entire group it's called ***Dictatorship***. Sometimes one person can take a decision on behalf of the entire group of participants and this is called ***Autocratic*** decision making. There is a difference between Dictatorship and Autocratic. Dictatorship is through coercion, power play, and force. While Autocratic is usually through giving such powers expressly to someone to make decisions for and on behalf of them.

There is a variation of voting called the "Cluster voting". In this case a certain numbers of votes (say 10 votes) are provided to each of the stakeholders involved in requirements prioritization. Each of the stakeholders may then distribute these votes across the various requirements or user stories. A stakeholder may decide to vote all his votes to just one single requirements or he may provide different numbers of votes to different requirements. The stakeholder may decide to even spread all his votes by giving each requirements one vote. This makes the requirements prioritization process even more democratic and rational instead of binary method of single voting.
Once cluster voting is all done, the highest prioritization requirements is the one with most votes and so on.

- **100 Points**
  This a variant of cluster voting. The only difference is that here the numbers of votes per stakeholder, involved in requirements or user story prioritization, is exactly 100.

Rest is just like the cluster voting. Several times there are some additional rules laid down during such voting, like, "Not more than 50 votes can be assigned to a single requirements" or "100 votes need to spread over at least 10 different requirements".

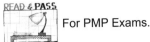

100 POINTS METHOD DISTRIBUTION

REQ.S	BUSINESS CONSULTANT	MARKETING HEAD	DEALER REP.	IT MANAGER	TOTALS
DEALER DISCOUNTS	10	2	40	1	53
LOYALTY POINTS	10	30	20	9	69
CUSTOMER REG.	20	30	10	20	80
ORDER TRACKING	60	38	30	70	198
TOTALS	100	100	100	100	400

- **Nominal Group Techniques**
  Once you have many ideas or requirement suggestions from Brainstorming or Silent Brainstorming, one way to select an idea or prioritize the requirements is to do a voting system called ***Nominal Group Technique (NGT)***. Though NGT is mostly about voting but it also involves gathering opinions of all the participants, rounds of discussions and then voting. NGT is NOT Just Voting.
  There are usually 4 steps on NGT.

EVERY ONE WRITES DOWN MULTIPLE IDEAS

MODERATOR PUTS ALL IDEAS ON THE WALL
THIS CYCLE IS REPEATED TILL ALL IDEAS ARE COMPLETELY EXHAUSTED

ALL IDEAS ARE MADE ABSOLUTELY CLEAR TO EVERY ONE

EVERY ONE VOTES ON IDEAS
BALLOT BOX
* MOST VOTED IDEA WINS *
NGT IS A 4 STEP PROCESS

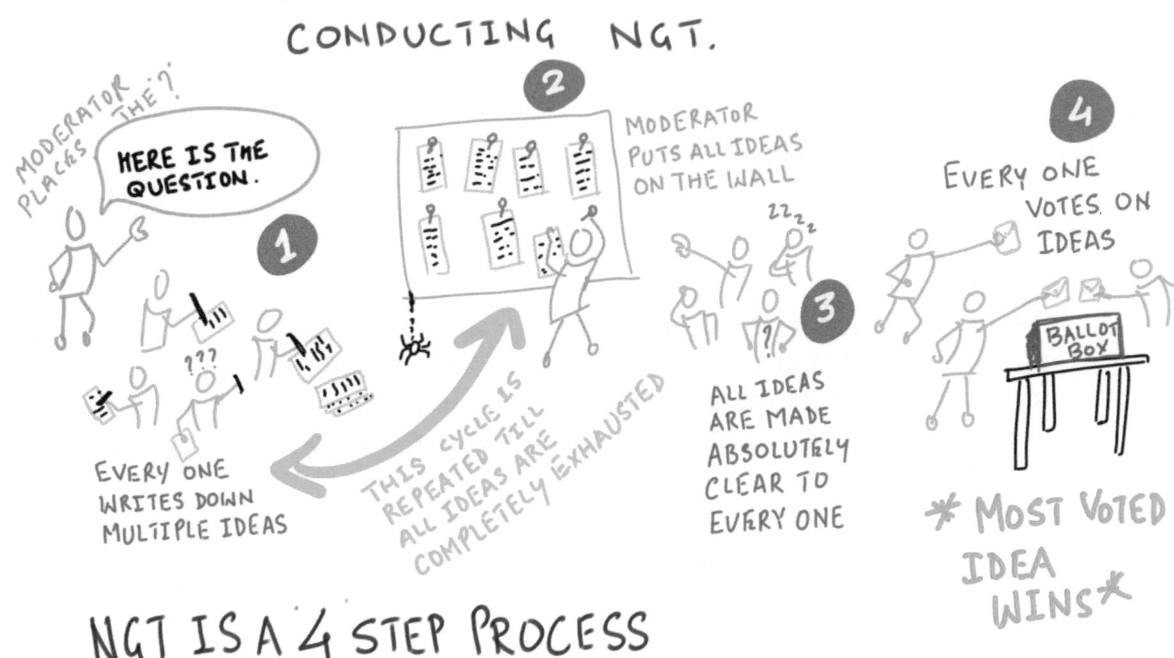

CONDUCTING NGT.
MODERATOR PLACES THE ?
HERE IS THE QUESTION.

- **Multicriteria / Weighted Method / Multi Criteria Decision Making (MCDM)**
  Multicriteria prioritization is essentially, as its name suggests, a decision making process where conflicting criteria about the project at hand are taken and compared. *e.g., Number of features vs Maintainability, Cost vs quality, Return on Investment vs Time taken to be profitable, and so on.* These MCDM can also be used for requirements and understanding the optimal level to which we can achieve keeping the tradeoffs as low as possible. Simply put, multicriteria is the name for what we have been using all the while called, Weighted Decision Making or Weighted Ranking. I guess an example below will help you understand.
  Let us say that you are trying to prioritize some requirements based on certain "Criteria" and these criteria themselves are ranked against each other on a scale of 5. Now each of the requirements are ranked against each of the criteria and total average is calculated. The requirements with the highest average would have the highest priority and so on. This is just one of the uses of MCDM, albeit the most common in agile and other iterative development lifecycles.

MULTI CRITERIA DECISION ANALYSIS

S.NO.	REQUIREMENTS	COST 2	TIME TO IMPLEMENT 5	EASE OF IMPLEMENTING 3	CLEAR 4	TOTAL	AVG.
1	REQ - 1	5	2	5	3	47	11.75
2	REQ - 2	3	2	2	2	30	7.5
3	REQ - 3	2	3	4	2	39	9.75
4	REQ - 4	5	5	3	4	60	15
5	REQ - 5	2	1	2	1	19	4.75
6	REQ - 6	1	2	3	1	24	6
7	REQ - 7	4	4	3	4	53	13.25

CALCULATION E.g., REQ-1 = 5×2 + 2×5 + 5×3 + 3×4 = 47 ; 47÷4 = 11.75
(YEP IT'S MULTIPLICATION BEFORE ADDITION)

- **Kano Model**
  As the name suggests this model was developed by Dr Noriaki Kano. Realistically speaking, this model is not really a prioritization model. It is a model to categorize the features and requirements of the proposed product.
  This model categorizes all the proposed user stories and requirements into 3 broad categories.

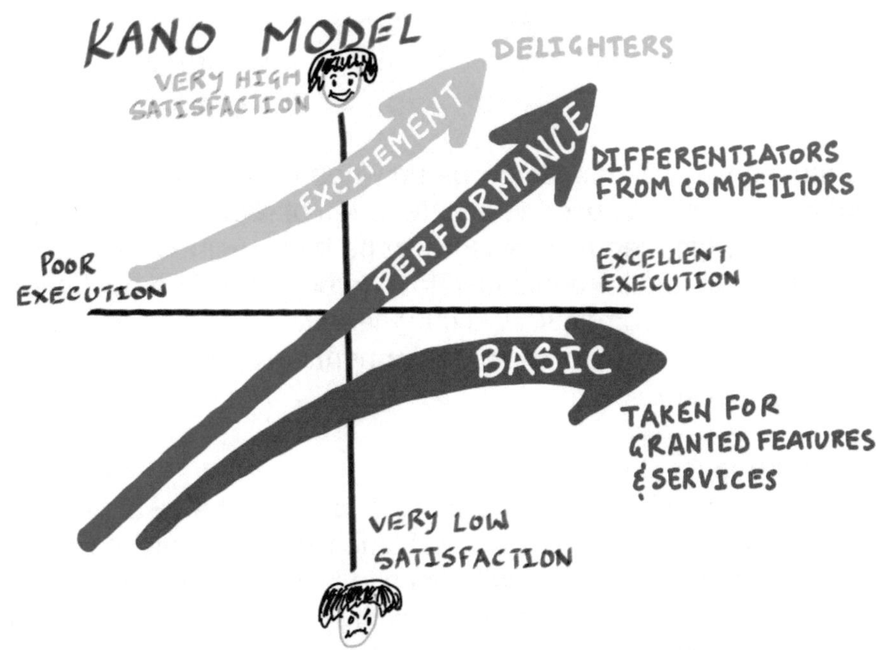

The basic requirements are those that are usually taken for granted from a product. Their presence will never excite the customer, no matter who well you develop them. However their absence or lack of quality would lead to immense customer dissatisfaction.

E.g., The ability to make phone calls from a new cell phone is now a basic feature. No matter how rich this feature is provided in the cell phone, it would not excite anyone. It is taken for granted. However if the new cellphone has bad sound quality while talking on phone or it does not have conferencing features to patch in different calls together, it would highly dissatisfy the user.

Performance requirements are those requirements which are used as comparison points with the product of your competitors. The better such requirements are provided the more the user would be exited and find your product better in comparison to that of your competitors. The vice-versa is true as well.

E.g., The comfort of the seats, the timeliness of departure and the ease with which you get to board the aircraft are some of the performance requirements when it comes to the commercial airlines. Launch of a new airline would have to consider the level of requirements provided by their competitors and accordingly provide such features in this category that are considered more exiting to the customers in comparison to those from your competitors.

Excitement requirements are those requirements that are not expected by the customer in the product or the service you propose to offer. Which means if they are not present in the product they would not dissatisfy the customers at all. However their presence would excite the customers.

E.g., In a compact SUV car segment, which is very popular in regions like Europe, Japan and India, no one expects 5 star safety features nor the feature of choosing driving modes. However if one company launches its new model of compact SUV with driving mode selection features as well as 5 star rated safety features, it would create major excitement among the customers of that grade of vehicles. On the other hand, if this new model did not have these features, it would not make anyone dissatisfied, because it was not really expected in the first place.

The reason why this model shows up when we are discussing "prioritization of requirements" is because these categories of requirements could be used to understand which requirements "must be implemented" and which ones could be optional. Basic requirements just have to be there. The next priority would be for the performance requirements. And they need to be well done to create the differentiation. And, once all the performance requirements are met, the Excitement requirements could be provided.

- **Comparative Ranking**
  Comparative ranking is by far the most comprehensive method of prioritization. This prioritization would also be the most time taking as well. In this method each of the requirements are compared with each of the other requirements individually and then decided by the stakeholders as to which requirement is more important. Once each of the requirements are compared with each of the other requirements, we would simply count the instances where any requirement was more important than the one it was compared to. Once we have all the counts of all the requirements we get the numbers of times each of the requirements was considered more important than the other requirement it was compared with. The requirements with the highest such count number would be the highest priority requirements and so on.

COMPARITIVE RANKING

S.No.	REQUIREMENTS	A	B	C	D	E	F	G	H	I
A	APPRECIATION		A	A	A	A	A	A	A	A
B	ACHIEVEMENT			C	B	B	B	G	B	B
C	WORK CONDITION				C	C	C	G	C	C
D	POWER					D	D	G	D	I
E	CREATIVITY						F	G	E	I
F	INTEREST							G	F	I
G	FISCAL BENEFITS								G	G
H	RELATIONSHIPS									I
I	SELF DEVELOPMENT									
	COUNT	8	5	6	3	1	2	7	0	4
	RANK	1	4	3	6	8	7	2	9	5

9.3.6 Tools and Techniques for Requirements Documentation

- **Context Diagram**
  "A Picture is worth a 1000 words", so the saying goes and for good reason too. If the entire requirements documents are written in words the document would become rather bulky and tedious to review. However, if there were well-illustrated diagrams within the document then, not only the document would become less bulky, they would become easier to review and validate. This is the purpose of "**Context Diagrams**". Every industry has some kind of established / commonly used diagramming techniques for use during requirements documentation and the same must be used to increase readability and structure of the document.

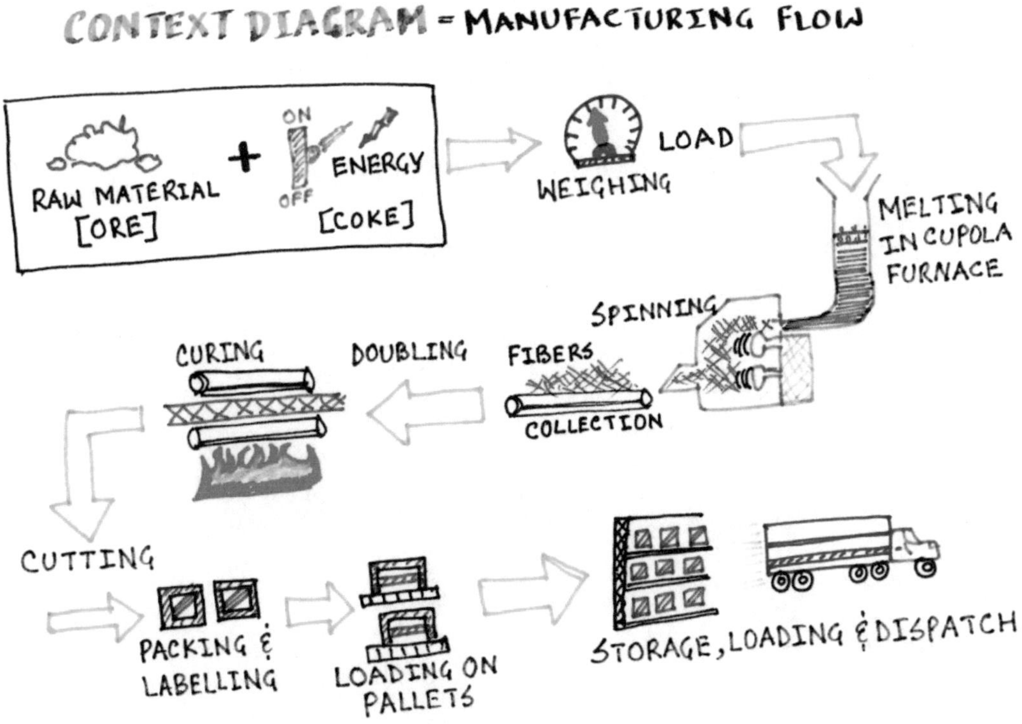

CONTEXT DIAGRAM = MANUFACTURING FLOW

RAW MATERIAL [ORE]
+
ON
OFF
ENERGY [COKE]
WEIGHING
LOAD
MELTING IN CUPOLA FURNACE
SPINNING
FIBERS
COLLECTION
DOUBLING
CURING
CUTTING
PACKING & LABELLING
LOADING ON PALLETS
STORAGE, LOADING & DISPATCH

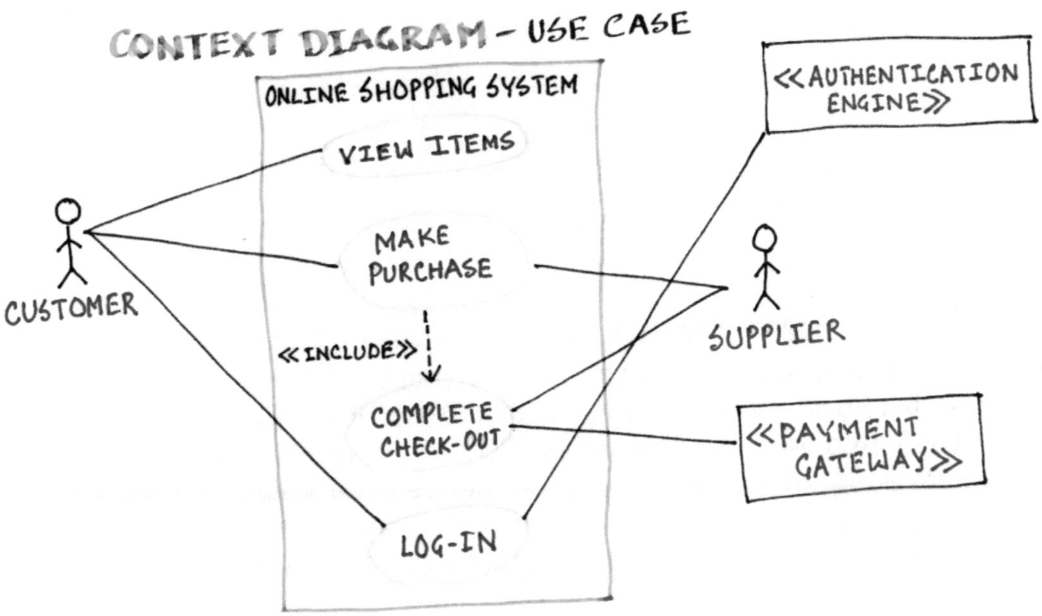

CONTEXT DIAGRAM - USE CASE

ONLINE SHOPPING SYSTEM
VIEW ITEMS
MAKE PURCHASE
<<INCLUDE>>
COMPLETE CHECK-OUT
LOG-IN
CUSTOMER
SUPPLIER
<<AUTHENTICATION ENGINE>>
<<PAYMENT GATEWAY>>

- **Story Map**
  This is a technique where the user stories are pictorially shown exactly how they are connected to each other, when they would be available and how do they stack up, thus providing the holistic view of the entire proposed product.
  This story map is created by putting up the major features, tasks or epics, as per the users, at the top. Specific user stories that are connected to each tasks are put up below that task and this way one gets to see how each user story fits into the entire scheme of things. It also shows the user stories that make up a task. This can also help identify gaps in functionality or identification of missing user stories.

  This helps even when new functionality or user stories are added by the customer. It becomes easier to adjust the new additions among the entire big picture thus understanding the complete impact of addition to the overall sequence as well as design of the user stories.

  Story map can also help prioritize the requirements / user stories.

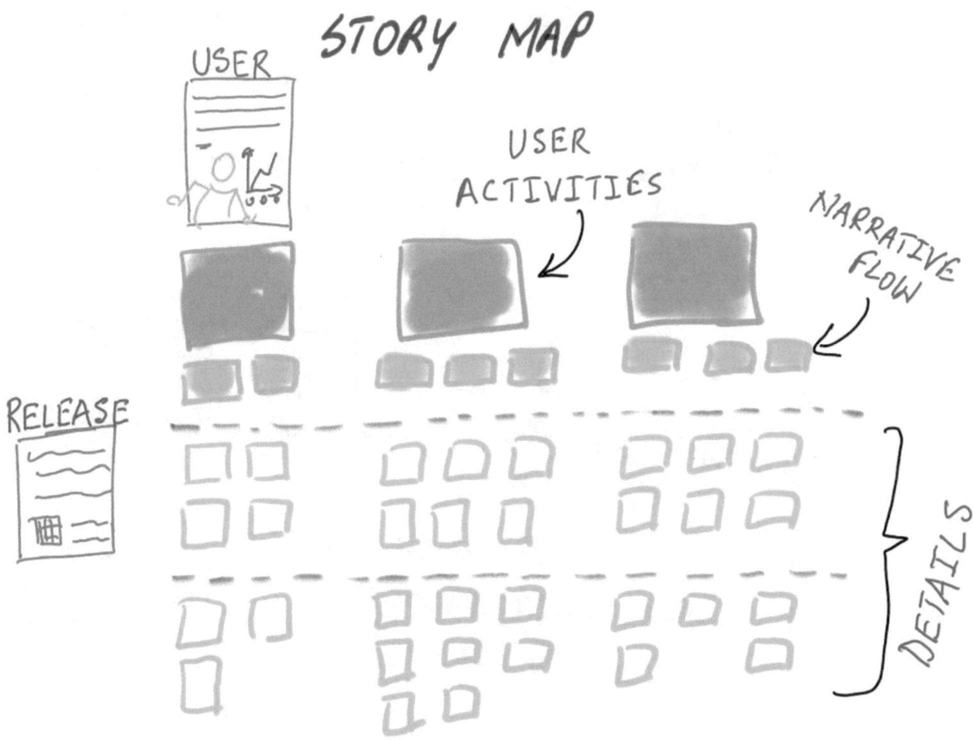

9.3.7 Outcome / Artefacts / Outputs of Collect Requirements

Requirements Documentation (called by different names in different industries and organizations, like Business Requirements Document (BRD), Functional Specification Document (FSD), Requirements Document (RD), and Project Requirements Document (PRD)) is where all the requirements collected needs to be written down in a structured manner and duly categorized so that the same can be reviewed and approved. This document becomes the reference point for all requirements for the project at hand.

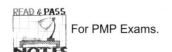

Different organizations have different templates for the same. A template for this document also works as a checklist and helps consistency in documentation.
This document must also have relevant tables, glossary, index and good use of diagrams to reduce number of pages along with increasing readability.
This document should also try and categorize the requirements based on the groups of stakeholders who provided it.
While making this document the Project Manager or the Business Analyst must make a conscious attempt to balance the competing interests of the stakeholders as far as requirements are concerned.
Requirements must also be prioritized and the "Critical To Acceptance (CTA) / Critical To Quality (CTQ)" must be clearly stated. CTA / CTQ are those requirements in this project without which the customer would reject the product of the project. They are the highest priority requirements.

For agile projects the essential project document is the "Product Backlog". This has been explained earlier in this book. Agile is a methodology that embraces changes. Hence the product backlog is a live document that constantly undergoes additions and modifications throughout the lifecycle of the project. The product backlog is populated with high level requirements which are prioritized such that the high priority requirements are kept at the top of the product backlog. The highest priority requirements are broken into detailed requirements (user stories) in a document called "Iteration Backlog". These user stories are earmarked for getting constructed in that iteration. However, while the work is going on in Iteration, the customer and the product owner may keep updating the product backlog with new ideas, epics and reprioritization. This is called Product Backlog "Grooming". This is also called "Backlog Refinement".

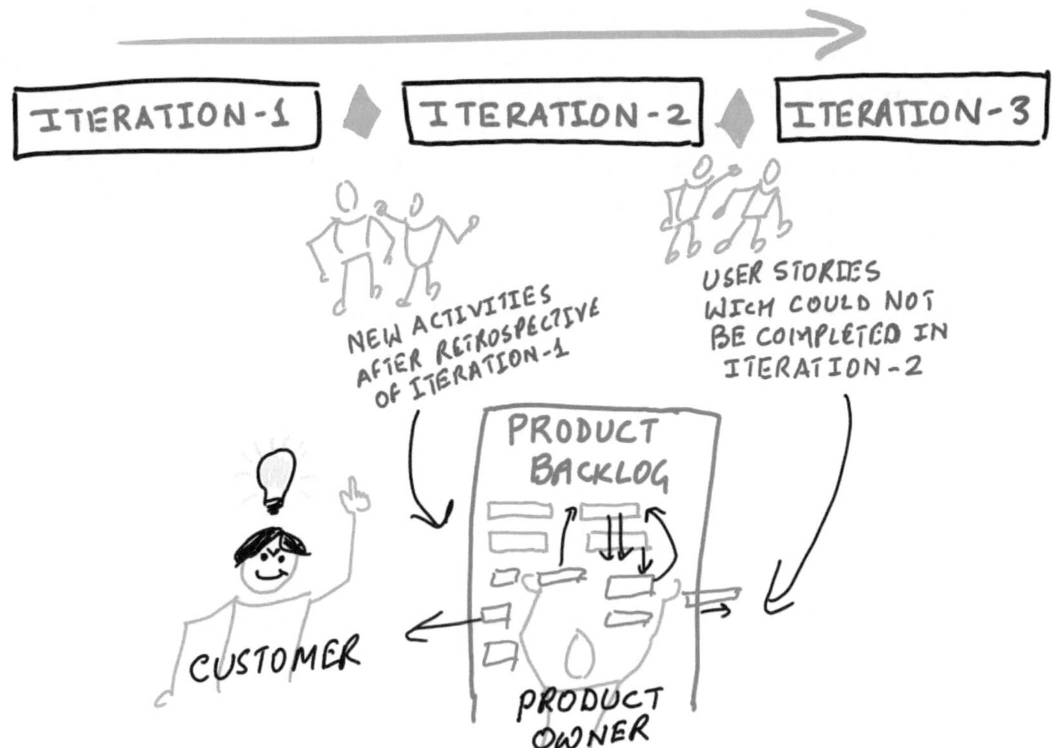

While documenting the requirements / User stories particularly for agile projects, each of the user stories must also have additional documentation, usually in the form of a checklist, which are called “Definition of Ready (DoR)” and “Definition of Done (DoD)”.

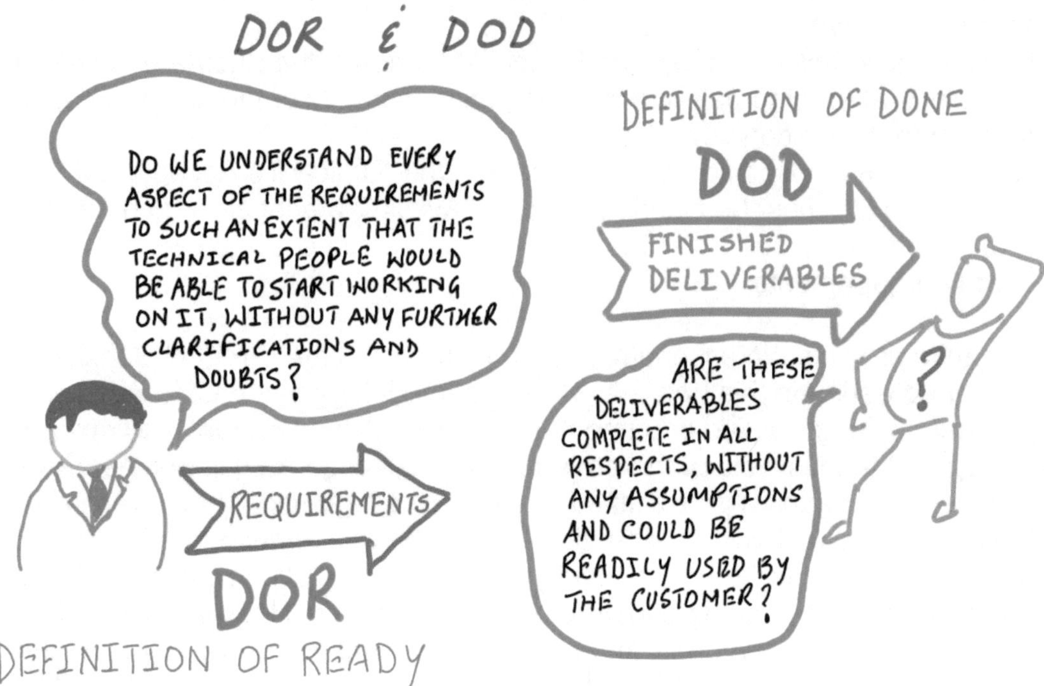

What we have to understand is that one feature from the Scope of the project may translate into hundreds of requirements. One line of requirements may be translated into Hundreds of lines of Specifications. Then there are the test cases, test scenarios and test conditions connected to the requirements. In such multiple documentation, it’s quite possible to miss out something. Hence a numbering system or a separate tracking system called “**Requirements Traceability Matrix (RTM)**” is required to ensure that nothing is missed while decomposing scope to requirements, requirements to specifications, Specifications to test cases, requirements to test scenarios and back. Basically, it’s a numbering system or a separate table/grid like numbered structure that links project requirements right from “Scope” to all the way to individual “artifacts” or “deliverables”.

Traceability matrix is very useful during managing changes and for configuration management.

TRACEABILITY MATRIX

SCOPE	BRD*	DETAILED DESIGN	TEST CASES	- - - ->
1. ACCESS CONTROL	1.1. LOGIN	1.1.1. LOGIN PAGE	TC 1.1.1 LOGIN	
	1.2. MEMBER REGISTRATION	1.1.2. LOGIN PROCESS	TC 1.1.2. LOGIN	
2. PRODUCT DISPLAY	1.3 VALIDATION	1.1.3. LOGIN EXCEPTION	TC1.1.3 LOGIN EXCEPTION	

* BRD = BUSINESS REQUIREMENTS DOCUMENT.

NOTICE THE NUMBERING SYSTEM.

In exams if you come across a question where one of the stakeholders is asking for evidence that the requirements provided by him are actually being developed. Basically, how do you prove to anyone that the requirements are being developed as documented in requirements document, even though the deliverables are not ready. The answer in all these cases is to show Traceability Matrix to the stakeholder.

9.4 Define Scope / Define Specifications

We already know how needs are converted to specifications. Specifications are the technical interpretations for each and every requirement that has been detailed out and documented. This process is done once in a predictive methodology, but in adaptive methodologies this process is done as a part of overall planning before each of the iterations.
The main document that is created here is the "Scope Statement". Remember, scope statement contains the "Specifications" of the project. The process ***Define Scope*** deals is all about listing down all the specifications for the project / iteration.

This step is supposed to do three distinct kinds of work: -

1. Ensuring that all the requirements that have been collected are within the scope of the project or not. (Remember scope is mentioned in the Project Charter)
2. Further detailing out and breaking down the requirements into technical specifications or the absolute detailed level of business rules and specifications and design that define the product of the project….. and
3. List down risks, assumptions and constraints (connected to requirements and specifications) that become apparent during such details and attempt are made to address the same.

A lot of people get confused between the name of this process and the "Scope" that is stated in the "Project Charter". Some of us are not too happy with the name of this process but nevertheless, that is the name given by PMI. Hence I would suggest you to condition your mind such that when you see the terms "Project Scope", "Total Scope", "Scope", "Project Boundary" than remember that the question is talking about "The scope mentioned in the Project Charter". However when you see the term "Define Scope" just substitute it in your mind with "Define Specifications" and you will be just fine.

9.4.1 Tools And Techniques Of This Process:-

- **Alternatives Analysis** This analysis is used for finding out the various manner in which the requirements could be met, meaning, this technique is aimed at finding the various alternative specifications for a given set of requirements. That's all. The actual selection of a specific alternative is part of the following tools and techniques. Say you are involved in making a stretch of road in a rainforest area. Now the road could be made of Asphalt, Cement, Rubberized rubble, Stones and so on. These are the various options. What you know is that this road would be mostly used by heavy goods vehicles at low speeds thus increasing the wear and tear on the roads. You also know that it's going to rain a lot in this area thus you have to provide for erosion and vehicle skidding off the road. Besides this road would be very difficult and expensive to maintain. Hence you decided to go for Cemented roads with vertical grooves to counter erosion, reduce maintenance and skidding. Asphalt gives better driving experience but needs maintenance and is rather slippery during rains and has a tendency of getting eroded by rains as well. Rubberized Rubble provides excellent control and practically zero skidding but is very prone to getting uprooted and hard to maintain and very susceptible to temperature swings. A decision would have to be made from the various alternatives, a decision which has the least amount of tradeoffs.
  Alternatives Analysis also uses Life-Cycle Costing. LCC uses various combinations of alternatives of ways to construct the product/deliverable and chose the one that best meets the expectation given the constraints and objectives. LCC also takes into account the overall cost of the product or deliverables including maintenance and helps you choose those alternatives that have lower LCC.
  Another concept associated with alternatives analysis is called "Value Engineering". This essentially means looking for more economical technical or material related alternatives for the development of the deliverables without adversely affecting its quality in anyway.

- **Product Analysis** is all about finding out what technical features and details make up the end product of the project. Every organization and industry have some proven ways of converting requirements into technical and physical/measurable deliverables and artifacts and that's what the concept of Product Analysis is. Techniques like Value Engineering, Product Breakdown, System Engineering, and Value Analysis are used as a part of Product Analysis. Let us understand them. Value Engineering understands that the "Value" is a Function to Cost ratio. Hence Value can be increased by either reducing the cost for the same functionality or increasing the functionality at the same cost. Value engineering also applies to products which have a decided small lifecycle, like a cell phone. Here the choice of material being used is made to last only a specific amount of use. This gives high functionality to the user without adding cost on material that lasts a long time. Value Engineering is also called Value Analysis. Of late another concept is getting more popular and that is "Life Cycle Assessment". This is an assessment to figure out the total impact of the project or product on the environment across the entire lifecycle of the product of the project till its discarding.

Product Breakdown usually uses a tool called the **Product Breakdown Structure** which essentially breaks a product down into main features/artifacts and then subdivides each of these features/artifacts into smaller and more well-defined features to ensure that nothing, even the smallest of functionality or technical specs, is missed out. This is very popular in mechanical engineering and electrical/electronic products development.

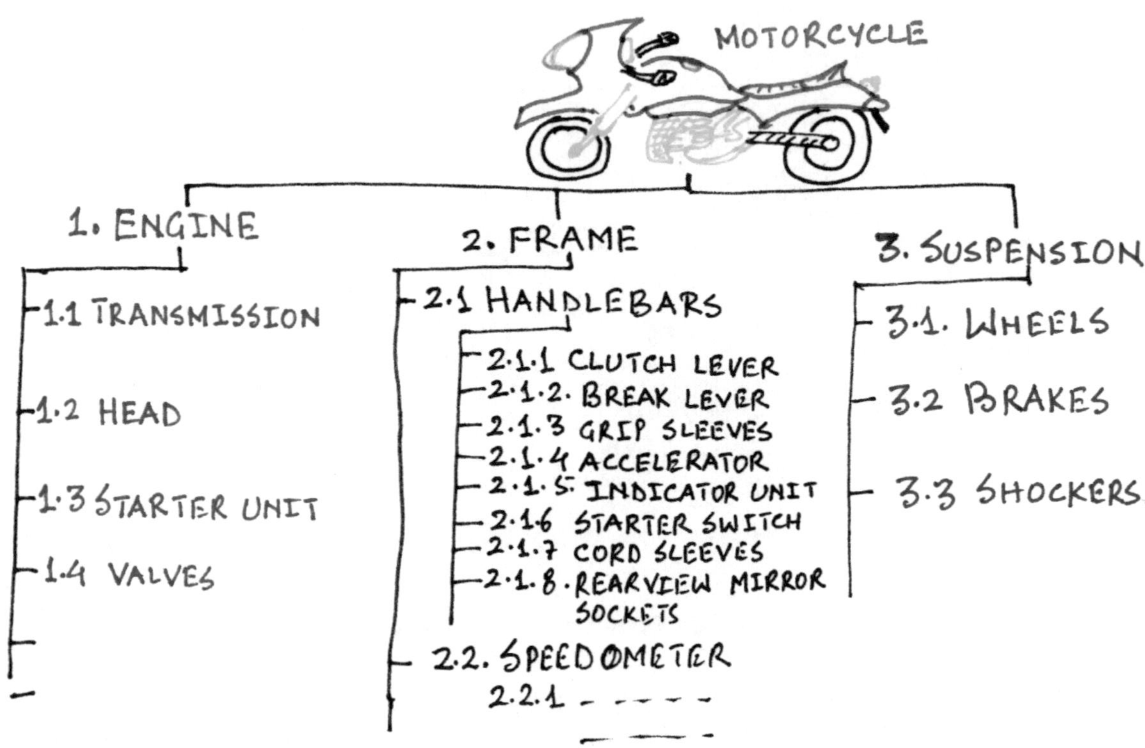

- **Themes** represent large groups of customer value reflected as user stories associated by a common factor, such as functionality, data source, or security level. Themes is a term used only in Agile methodology. Themes are a very high level concept that just groups similar high level requirements of proposed functionality together under a heading. This is done to keep an eye on those related user stories that make up a theme. The ability to track which user story leads into which specific theme helps in ensuring nothing is missed out as well as a way to ensure if an entire high level capability (theme) has been completed or not.
  E.g., While implementing a banking solution using Agile methodology, the themes could be, core banking, retail banking, corporate banking and so on. Each of these are higher than high-level requirements or Epics. For retail banking theme, one of the epics could be Fixed Deposits. This epic would have to be broken down and detailed into user stories like "choosing fixed deposit policy", "interest calculation", "maturity of fixed deposit" and so on.

Now each of these user stories would have to be converted to specifications. Hence these specifications would need to be grouped as per themes to ensure consistency of coding as well as ensuing understanding with the customer that a specific Theme has been delivered. This also helps in complete impact analysis across the entire Theme if a requirement has been updated by the customer at any level in the given theme.

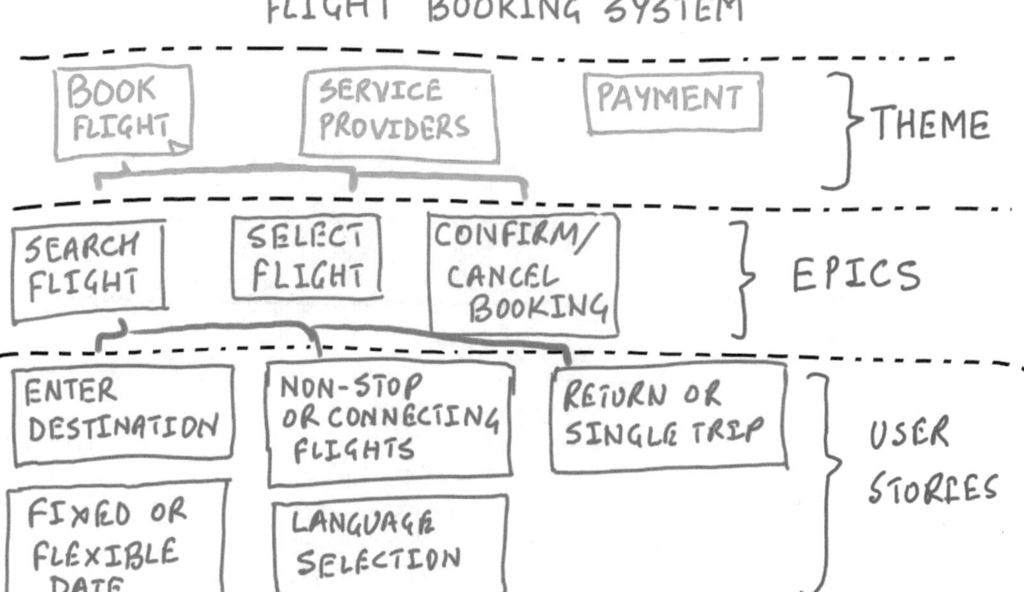

9.4.2 Artefact Of The Process Define Scope:

- **Project Scope Statement** contains all the specifications of the project. Completion of deliverables is an important part of Scope Statement. Irrespective of which methodology is being used. It explains clearly when a deliverable would be considered completed in all respects.
    - ***Acceptance or completion criteria***. The criteria required to be met before the customer accepts the deliverable or before the project is considered complete are often documented in a scope statement.
    - ***Technical performance measures***. The technical specifications for a product may be documented in a separate specifications document, or they may be documented as an extension to the WBS. This extension, known as a WBS dictionary, elaborates the information for each deliverable (work package) in the WBS.
    - ***Definition of done***. The definition of done is used with adaptive approaches, particularly in software development projects. It is a checklist of all the criteria

required to be met so that a deliverable can be considered ready for customer use.

9.5 Create Work Breakdown Structure (WBS)

Let us say that you planned for the birthday of your family member or your friend. You planned for it very well and looked into details of each of the possible activities you can think right now and you are satisfied that you have covered just about everything. On the day of the birthday, however, things are different. Suddenly everyone around is in a heightened state of chaos. The cake has arrived from the bakery but the size of the cake is too large to fit into the refrigerator shelves and now you are wondering if the icing on the cake would melt if kept outside. There are so many kids around and it just occurs to you that no games have been planned for the kids and they are getting bored and cranky. Just when the cake is brought out for cake cutting you realize that you forgot the small decorative candles, or you forgot the cutting knife, or you forgot where you have kept the camera to record this event and so on. Some of your friends are making urgent trips to the local store for cold drinks, disposable cups and plates, tissues and so on to help you out during the "B'day" party. Sounds familiar. Happens even with the most careful persons among us. Now, imagine such a thing happening in a professional project at your workplace. Happens all the time.
How do such things happen? Why do we forget so many things despite such careful planning? Why is there chaos in each of the projects which require gallant firefighting? These things happen because we are unable to identify all possible activities up front. Now, just because we could not identify them, does not mean we will not have to do them. Since we did not identify them, we could not plan for them, since we could not plan for them we did not estimate duration and cost for them. When the execution starts these unplanned / unidentified activities become due and you have to leave everything else and focus on these urgent unplanned activities as soon as possible. Since they were not planned you have no clear idea of how you will do it and so on. And this is nothing but chaos. This is the reason why in almost all projects there is chaos and firefighting towards the end of the project as more and more unidentified and unplanned activities become due.

All this can be handled by a concept called "Work Break Down Structure (WBS)". WBS helps you identify all possible activities upfront and hence makes your plan more practical, reliable and chaos-proof.

Ok! So let's now talk a bit about WBS. WBS, as the name suggests, is a hierarchical decomposition of the overall scope and deliverables of the project. Bigger or major deliverables are progressively broken down into smaller deliverables. These deliverables are also called 'Work". The idea is to keep breaking down the Work into smaller pieces until it cannot be broken down any further. This is done pictorially just like shown as under: -

To make a practical and realistically usable WBS one has to follow the rules as laid down in the "Standard for WBS" from PMI. These rules will not only help you understand the WBS so that you can start creating one yourself in your real-world projects, but also help you correctly answer just about any questions you get in the exams on this topic. And well, you do get quite a few questions in the exams on this topic. So here we go.

Rules of WBS:

1. **WBS Is always pictorial/hierarchical in documentation.**
   The core idea of WBS is that it is a pictorial display and always in a hierarchical chart form. This is based on the inherent reaction of humans to pictorial diagrams compared to just texts and tables. This form always generates higher focus and better contribution from the stakeholders participating in creating the WBS.

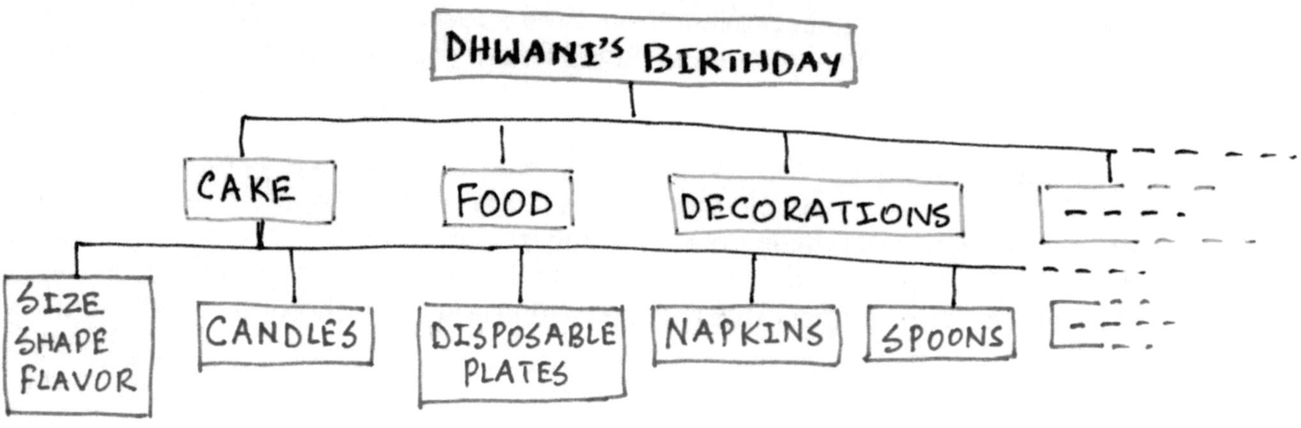

2. **There are no activities in WBS**
   This may sound opposite to what we said earlier as to what WBS is used for. Yes; WBS is used for identifying all possible activities but within WBS there are no activities. Only Work / Deliverables are broken down further and further into smaller

deliverables and not activities. Basically larger "Nouns" are broken down into smaller "Nouns" and at no time would any "Verbs" (Activities or Tasks) are identified. The concept behind this is that all the deliverables are accounted for or identified before we move on to the task level granularity. What usually happens without WBS is that people identify certain areas and get into too many details and even jot down all activities in that area but in turn overlook an entire set of phases or deliverables completely, and this, in turn, gives rise to chaos.

3. **The first level of WBS is always the major deliverables / Work / Phases of the project.**
   The first level is the level that immediately follows the name of the project. This level can either be names of the Phases of the project or the Major Deliverables or major chunks of work.

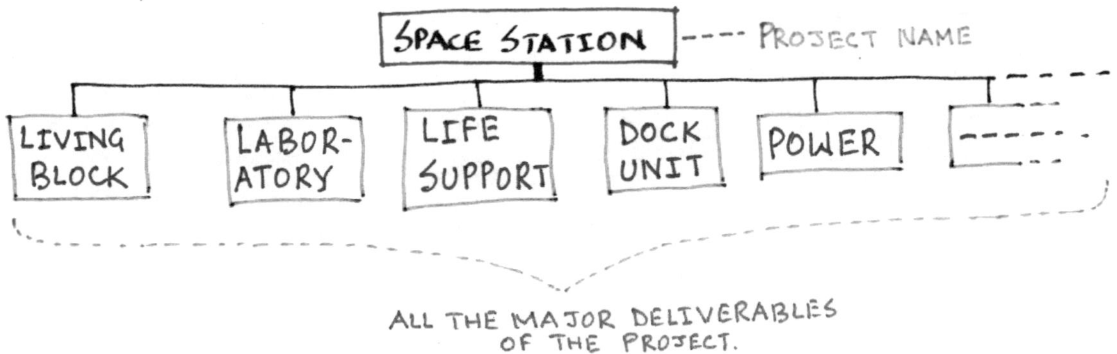

4. **Each of the main deliverable / Work / Phase needs to be broken down individually and completely before moving on to the next Deliverable / Work / Phase.**
   This first level of WBS has to be broken down in a disciplined manner. There is no rule for deciding which major deliverable to be broken down first. Anyone can be selected. But the rule is that one major deliverable has to be broken down at a time. This generates a clear focus among the participating stakeholders. When everyone focuses on one topic, instead of jumping from one topic to another, the output is more relevant and complete. This also allows the project manager to invite a different set of stakeholders to decompose different major deliverables and at different times.
5. **The Project Manager does not make the WBS alone, he makes it with the help of Stakeholders**
   One of the most dangerous things a Project Manager may do is to try and make the entire WBS alone. This would defeat the very purpose. This has to be made with not just the team members but the stakeholders in general. All inputs should be invited from the participating stakeholders to ensure that nothing is missed as far as possible. The idea is to involve as many of the key stakeholders as possible.
6. **WBS prevents work from slipping through the fingers/gaps/cracks**
   The whole idea of WBS is that it prevents work from slipping through your fingers. What it basically means is that with the WBS in place the chances of missing out any work is less to negligible.
7. **WBS of a similar past project can be reused in a new project**
   The entire WBS or at least a part of it can be reused. If a project was done in the past, using a WBS, and that projects is similar to a current project, then the WBS of that

previous project can be reused completely or partially to find all the deliverables in this current project. This increases the speed of planning, prevents reinvention of the wheel and works as a checklist. Now, just imagine if most of your projects had WBS created then how much of reuse could happen, saving a substantial amount of effort while ensuring nothing is forgotten.

8. **The lowest level in a WBS is called WorkPackage.**
   When a major deliverable is broken down completely, then the lowest levels to which it has been broken down into, are called "Workpackages".

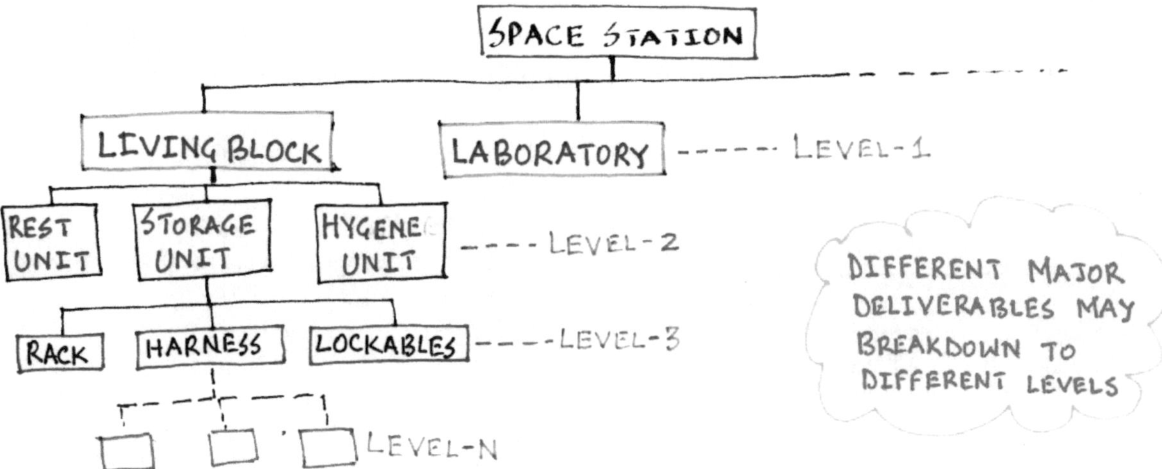

However, the main question is, how do you know that you have reached the lowest level or the smallest work. This is where the science of project management comes into effect. One of the rules of creating a WBS is that there are no activities in WBS. When the deliverables have to be broken down further and further a point would be reached beyond which one cannot breakdown without converting deliverables into activities. This lowest "non-activity" or the smallest deliverable is the Workpackage. It's called a workpackage. This is because all further planning, estimating and resourcing happens using these workpackages.

Some well-known authors and books and youtube videos say that a work package level is achieved when a work can be done in 80 to 100 hrs or it can be assigned to a single person. Such statements are absolutely and unequivocally incorrect. Different projects would have different levels of granularity. In many construction and infrastructure project, a work package may become a complete project for a vendor while, in other projects like events management, work packages may be as granular as "Flower Décor" or "Cutlery" where a single resource may handle more than one work package.

9. **All Workpackages are associated to a Control Account.**
   Since the WBS is in a hierarchical pattern, certain components of the WBS could be used for "points of control or costing or accounting". These are called control accounts. The Control accounts become points of control for all the work packages under it. Accounting and costing for the project can also be done using the names of

those components. Remember; a control account may have several work packages under it but a work package would be under one and only one control account.

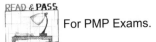

10. **WBS is a very good stakeholder communication tool.**
Since the WBS clearly and pictorially as well as hierarchically depicts the entire project, it works well as a communication tool to show the big picture, impact analysis, control accounts, estimation and so on. Hence it's considered a very good communication tool for stakeholder. WBS can also be used for expectations setting of the stakeholders.

11. **WBS can be used to generate the Resource Assignment Matrix (RAM).**
Based on the kind of deliverables and the skills required for specific workpackage, a project manager can easily ascertain the kind of functions, organizations, vendors and cross-functional teams that would be needed to complete that workpackage. Workpackages may be put in a tabular form later to show, who, which function or team would be involved in that specific workpackage. This is nothing but a high-level RAM (Responsibility Assignment Matrix).

12. **Each of the major deliverables of the WBS may get broken down to different levels**
Each of the major deliverables needs to be broken down till they reach the smallest deliverable (Workpackage Level). Now, this may happen at 3rd level or 10th level or even more. Different major deliverables would be broken down to their work packages at different levels. Some people and even some books wrongly suggested that all the major deliverables are broken down to the same level in a WBS and that's why I have included this rule here.

13. **Each of the components of the WBS has to be suitably numbered.**
Each of the WBS components must be numbered so that each of them can be uniquely identified and even related to their downline or upline components. One of the best forms of numbering is the "Outline" numbering system.

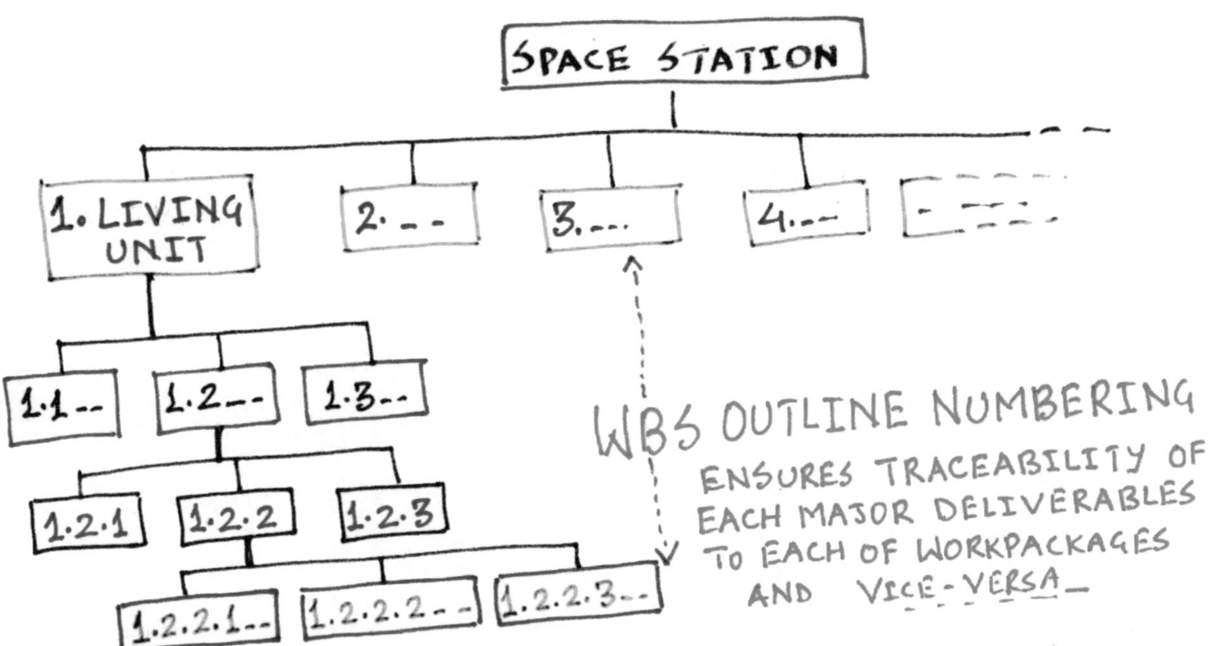

14. **Work packages are not activities or tasks**
    Under no circumstances, the work package would be an activity or a task. Please note that tasks and activities mean the same. Different cultures use one or the other to mean the same. Task = Activity.
    However, the Workpackages are used later (in other processes) to find all possible activities for the project but Workpackages themselves are NOT activities.
15. **WBS is not used for Sequencing.**
    Since work packages are not activities, no portion of WBS can show or depict any kind of sequencing of work. It only shows the hierarchical decomposition.
16. **When WBS is used for any kind of estimation it's called "Bottom-Up Estimating".**
    As can be seen that since WBS breaks down the entire project into smallest of deliverables, the WBS can be used for estimating costs and resources. Since all the estimation is done at the work package level and then aggregated upwards to the control account level or the major deliverable levels, such estimations that use WBS are called generally as "Bottom-up estimating".
17. **WBS breakdown must follow the 100% rule.**
    The 100% rule means that when a component of the WBS is broken down into multiple components than the basic validation should be done to show that all the sub-components must fulfill the 100% of the work of the main component and none of the sub-components should be outside the scope of work of the main component. This self-validation rule has to be applied every time any component of the WBS is broken down. This maintains sanity and avoids duplication and avoids any kind of "Gold Plating" as well.

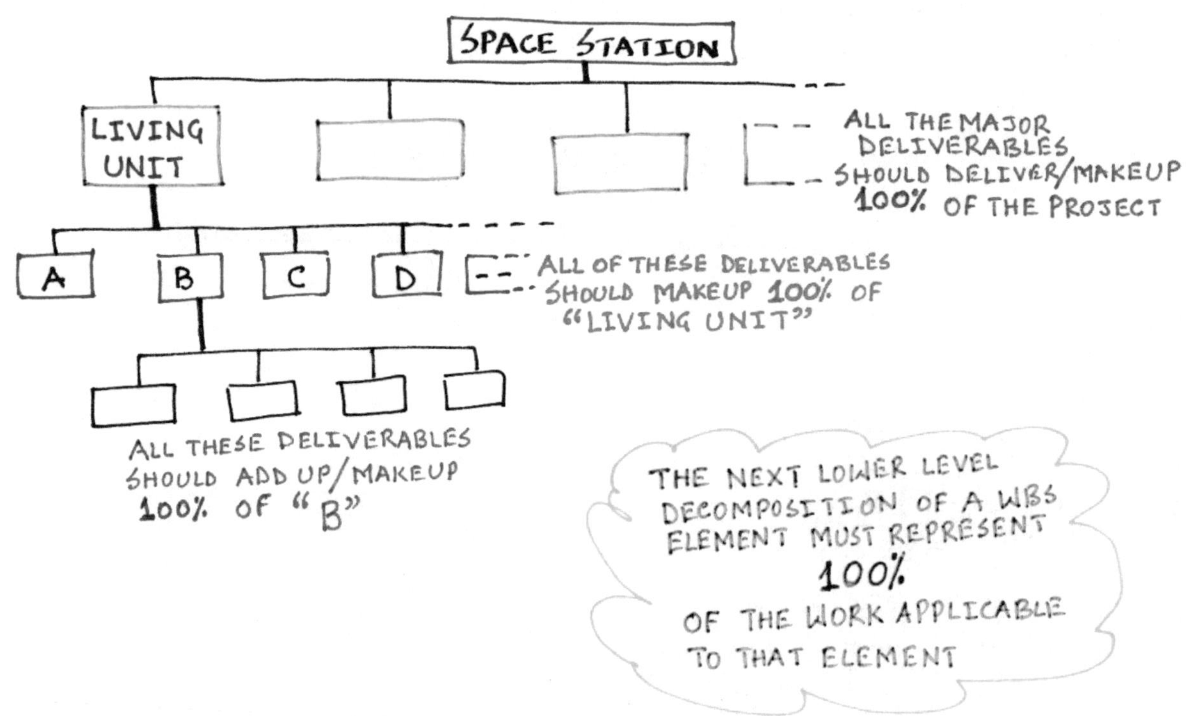

18. **Anything not mentioned in the WBS is officially not a part of the project.**
    The whole purpose of WBS is to find everything that needs to be done in the project even at the minutest level. This also means that anything not mentioned in the WBS is not considered part of the project.
19. **WBS can be used for understanding the impact of a Change Request.**
    Since the WBS presents the entire big picture of the project even down to the smallest deliverables. Thus it is the best tool to simulate the impact on the project of any change request by seeing how many work packages increased or decreased and so on.
20. **In an iterative project, all Work/Major Deliverables may not be decomposed upfront.**
    There is something called "Rolling Wave Planning". This method of planning does not identify all work packages and activities and schedule upfront. In iterative and exploratory lifecycles it's not possible to breakdown each and every major deliverable completely. Some are broken down and some are broken down later on and so on. Hence it's not necessary that in all cases all the major deliverables of WBS would be broken down to work packages level upfront.

9.5.1 Main Tools & Techniques – Create WBS:

The main tools & techniques of the process *CREATE WBS* is **Decomposition**. It means breaking down something. In this process it is breaking down large deliverables into smaller deliverables.

9.5.2 Outcome or Artefact of the process Create WBS:

The most important outcome / output / artefact of the process Create WBS is **Scope Baseline.**

TOTAL SCOPE OF PROJECT

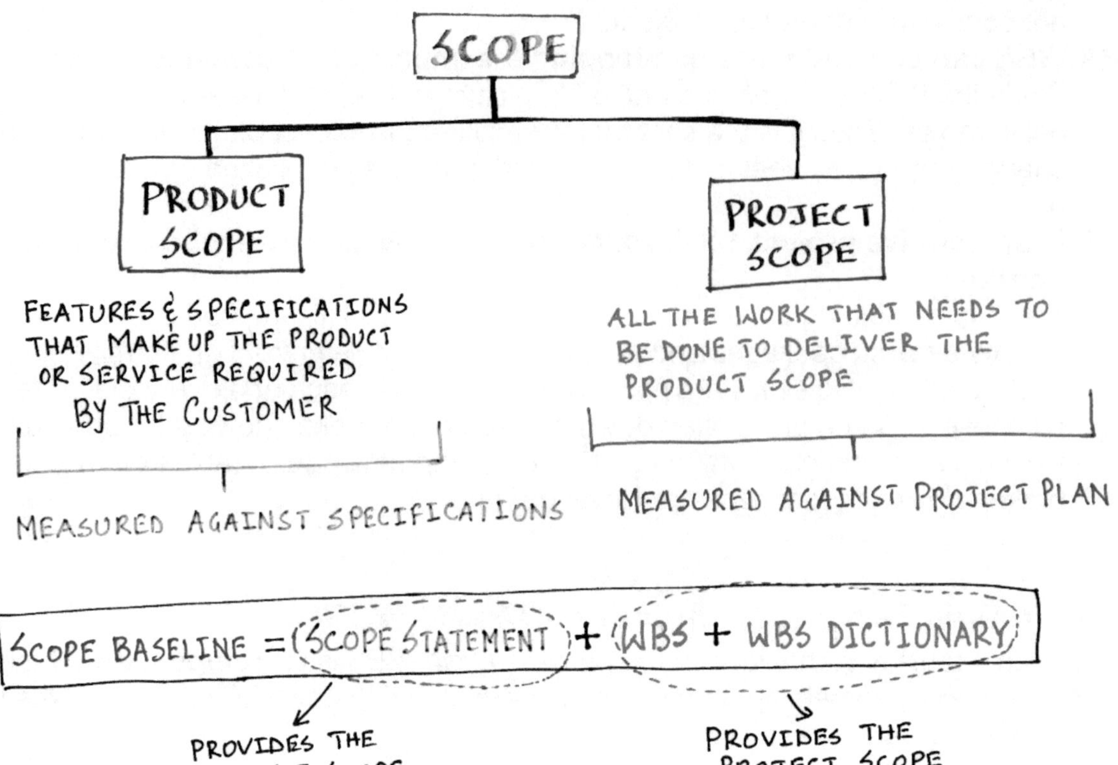
SCOPE
PRODUCT SCOPE
FEATURES & SPECIFICATIONS THAT MAKE UP THE PRODUCT OR SERVICE REQUIRED BY THE CUSTOMER
MEASURED AGAINST SPECIFICATIONS
PROJECT SCOPE
ALL THE WORK THAT NEEDS TO BE DONE TO DELIVER THE PRODUCT SCOPE
MEASURED AGAINST PROJECT PLAN
SCOPE BASELINE = SCOPE STATEMENT + WBS + WBS DICTIONARY
PROVIDES THE PRODUCT SCOPE
PROVIDES THE PROJECT SCOPE

9.6 Ninja Drill – Planning - 1

In this Ninja Drill you will find the most important notes and pointers that are important from the point of PMP Exams and covers, Plan Requirements Management, Collect Requirements, Define Scope and Create WBS.

S. No.	Drill Points
1.	Process Plan Requirements Management produces two plans (project management plan components) and they are Scope Management Plan and Requirements Management plan.
2.	In predictive projects an attempt is made to ascertain all possible requirements of the entire project upfront, while in Adaptive projects it is done repetitively for each of the releases and iterations.
3.	Business Analyst = Product Owner (in Agile)
4.	Remember, in predictive projects, Scope is originally mentioned in the Project Charter.
5.	A requirement is a condition or capability that is necessary to be present in a product, service, or result to satisfy a business need.
6.	High level requirements are also called "Epics or Features"
7.	Detailed requirements are also called "User Stories or Use Cases"
8.	Important Tools & Techniques for collecting requirements: 1. Interview Method (Traditional as well as Virtual) 2. Wideband - Delphi 3. Brainstorming 4. Focus Group (Homogeneous or Heterogeneous) 5. Questionnaire And Surveys 6. Benchmarking 7. Document Analysis 8. Observation And On The Job Requirements Collection
9.	Wideband Delphi is a method of connecting with the experts and obtaining consensus through multiple rounds. Could be Anonymous as well.
10.	Facilitated workshops in IT organization are called Joint Application Development [JAD].
11.	Facilitated Workshop in manufacturing organizations is called Quality Functional Deployment [QFD].
12.	Benchmarking is the comparison of actual or planned products, processes, and practices to those of comparable organizations to identify best practices, generate ideas for improvement, and provide a basis for measuring performance.
13.	Observation / Conversation is also called Job Shadowing.
14.	Reverse Job shadowing is when the person observing the other person demonstrates understanding to that other person.
15.	Important Tools & Techniques for confirming requirements: 1. Prototype / Wireframe / Storyboard / Mock Up 2. Beta / Proof Of Concept / Working Prototype / Safe Release / Soft Release / Demonstrations
16.	Prototype is a mock up and not a working model.
17.	Beta Release is a working model but not a final deliverable.
18.	Important Tools & Techniques for representing requirements: 1. Affinity Diagrams 2. Mind Mapping
19.	Affinity diagrams are for classifying and grouping requirements or ideas (after a brainstorming) into various logical heads for further analysis.
20.	Mind Mapping is a graphical representation technique that is usually used for ideation during the brainstorming.
21.	Affinity Grouping is the process of classifying items into similar categories or collections on the basis of their likeness.
22.	Important Tools & Techniques for prioritizing requirements: 1. Voting / Cluster Voting 2. 100 Points

	3. MoSCoW 4. Paired Comparison / Comparative Ranking
23.	100 points is like cluster voting where each person is provided exactly 100 points to spread across various requirements to indicate which requirements are higher priority according to him.
24.	**MoSCoW** is another way of prioritization (the most common among Agile project teams) requirements where Mo = Most Essential or Must have, S = Should have, Co = Could have and W = Wont have (for this iteration or this sprint).
25.	Paired Comparison involves comparing each and every requirement with every other requirement individually and stating which one of them is higher on requirements among the two. Once this is done with all the requirements, the requirements that had the maximum number of cumulative votes would become the highest priority.
26.	For agile projects each user story must have Definition of Ready [DoR] as well as Definition of Done [DoD].
27.	Product Backlog is a live and continuous document in Agile projects. They can be updated and modified and the requirements therein could be reprioritized at any time by Product Owner at the behest of the customer. This act is called "Backlog Grooming" or "Backlog Refinement".
28.	The main outputs / outcomes / artefacts of the process "Collect Requirements" are: 1. Requirements Documentation 2. Requirements traceability matrix 3. Story Map
29.	Traceability Matrix is used for investigating or providing evidence of the existence of specific requirements and artefacts.
30.	Story Map is a visual model of all the features and functionality desired for a given product, created to give the project team a holistic view of what they are building and why.
31.	The main Tools & Techniques of the process "Define Scope" is Alternatives Analysis.
32.	**Value Engineering**: Where the method chosen to meet the specifications is less expensive while maintaining the quality and performance. (A kind of Alternatives analysis)
33.	**Lifecycle Costing**: Where the method chosen to meet the specifications ensure that the cost of "ownership" is as low as possible and not just the cost of construction. (A kind of Alternatives analysis)
34.	**Life Cycle Assessment:** This is an assessment to figure out the total impact of the project or product on the environment across the entire lifecycle of the product of the project till its discarding. (A kind of Alternatives analysis).
35.	Total Scope = Product Scope + Project Scope.
36.	The main outcome / output / artefact of the process "Define Scope" is the Project Scope Statement which is essentially the Product Scope.
37.	Most important rules of WBS (from Exams point of view) 1) WBS is created with the help of the Stakeholders and never alone by the Project Manager 2) WBS of a similar past project can be reused in a new project 3) The lowest level in a WBS is called Work Package. 4) WBS can be used to generate the Resource Assignment Matrix (RAM). 5) When WBS is used for any kind of estimation it's called "Bottom-Up Estimating". 6) In an iterative project, all Work/Major Deliverables may not be decomposed upfront. 7) Prevents work from slipping through the cracks / fingers 8) WBS creates buy-in among teams and stakeholders.
38.	The main outcome / output / artefact of the process "Create WBS" are: 1. WBS 2. Scope Baseline 3. WBS Dictionary
39.	Remember, the sequence of processes connected to Scope: 1. Plan Scope Management 2. Collect Requirements 3. Define Scope and 4. Create WBS

End Of Ninja Drill

9.7 Developing A Schedule

This is the planning stage where the project schedule is developed and baselined (Time Baseline) to be used during execution. A schedule is a model of exactly how the work would be accomplished in a project or an iteration and how much time it would take.

The entire Schedule is developed in the following steps, whether it is being made for a predictive project or for an iteration in an adaptive project:

- **Step – 1**: Plan how the schedule would be crated and approved in this project.
- **Step – 2**: Decompose all possible activities from the work packages and document those activities.
- **Step – 3**: Sequence all these identified activities in a way that represents logical progression as well as real world constraints.
- **Step – 4**: For each of the activities, estimate the kinds and numbers or resources needed to complete it.
- **Step – 5**: For each of the activities, estimate the duration, keeping in mind the resources estimated for it. And finally,
- **Step – 6**: Bring all the elements together, optimize against constraints and objectives and baseline the schedule.

The structured approach above is exactly what the 6 steps that we are going to go through next.

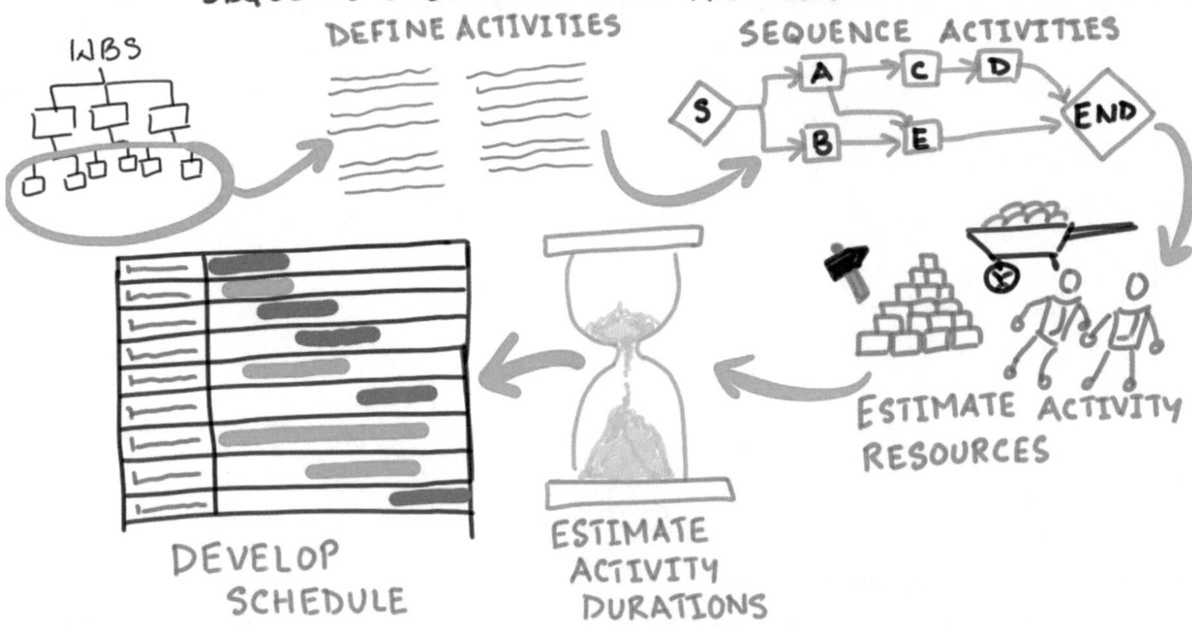

9.8 Plan Schedule Management

This process is responsible for making a mini plan (subsidiary plan) about the way the schedule would be made in this project, who all will participate in making it, what templates would be used, what unit of duration measure would be used, what kind of thresholds would be used, who will approve and how it would be reviewed and what is the frequency in which this schedule would be monitored in this project.
All this is documented in a plan called the "Schedule Management Plan".

This plan details out exactly how, by whom and by when the project schedule would be developed. The plan also details out exactly how it would be reviewed and approved and later, during execution, the frequency and time for monitoring and controlling the schedule.

Usual elements of this plan would be: -

1. Unit of measure: Hours, Days, Weeks or Months would be the unit of measure for the activities or decisions like "Effort would be measured in Hours and Duration would be measured in Days", are stated under this head.
2. Level of accuracy: Would there be some acceptable variance like + - 2 days for activities or would the scheduled activities have to be dead accurate. Larger projects tend to have some range of accuracy.
3. Variance thresholds: states the amount of delay that would be considered worrisome and trigger corrective or preventive actions. The plans could also lay down "Slippage Thresholds" for the schedule.
4. Scheduling Methodology/Lifecycle and Tool to be used
5. Organizational templates and procedures to be used

6. Method for updating and tracking and changing the schedule: like tracking them only on phase ends or tracking them weekly.
7. Rule for performance measurement: states if Earned Value (will be discussed in detail in Cost Management Knowledge Area) or the straightforward percentage completion method. Some companies decide that activity completion can be given only as 0%, 50%, and 100%.
8. Frequency and format of reporting

9.9 Define Activities

A real-world practical schedule can only be as good as the number of activities of the project that have been identified. Missing out activities would make the schedule less practical and less realistic, thus making it ineffective, in both planning as well as tracking the project. The purpose of this process is to identify all possible ***activities*** in suitable granularity and list them. Essentially in this process, the technical team and other Subject Matter Experts (SME) would take a Work package from the Scope baseline and list down all activities needed to finish that specific work package. This is done for each of the work packages thus generating a very comprehensive and near-complete list of all activities needed to complete the project. The project manager may use different people and experts for different work packages depending on the kind of expertise required for each of the work packages.

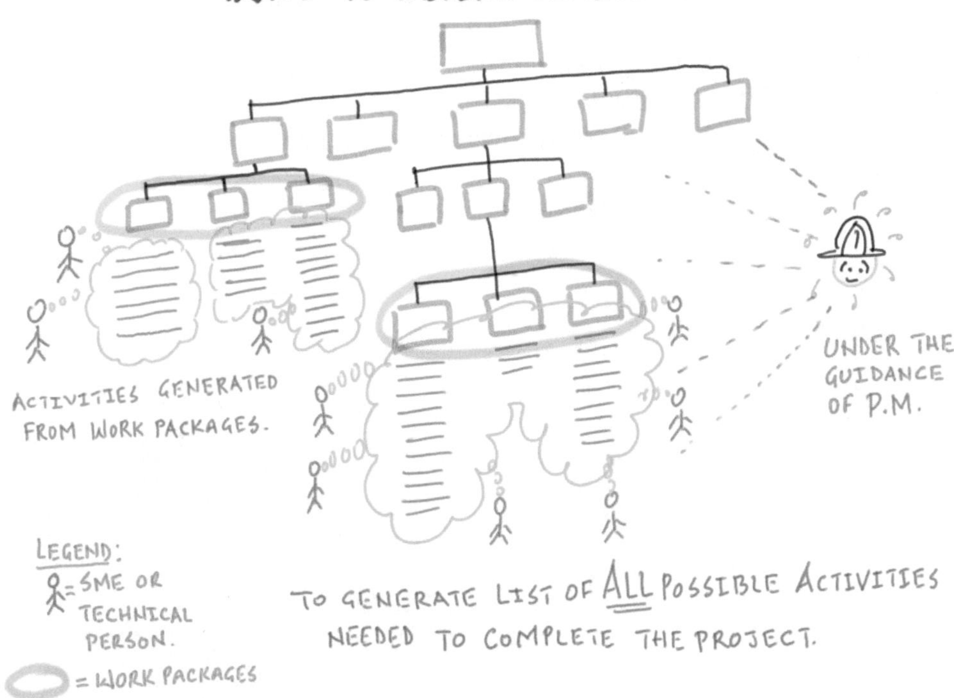
WBS TO DEFINE ACTIVITIES
ACTIVITIES GENERATED FROM WORK PACKAGES.
UNDER THE GUIDANCE OF P.M.
LEGEND:
= SME OR TECHNICAL PERSON.
= WORK PACKAGES
TO GENERATE LIST OF ALL POSSIBLE ACTIVITIES NEEDED TO COMPLETE THE PROJECT.

This process is the very foundation of all the other following steps as far as creating a schedule is concerned.

Let us get into the nitty-gritty of this process.

9.9.1 Main Tools & Techniques of the process Define Activities:

Decomposition is the technique which breaks down the work packages into activities. Decomposition was used in the process *CREATE WBS* as well, but here this technique would be used for breaking deliverables into activities or let's say from Nouns to Verbs. The idea here is to identify and document every conceivable activity that may be needed in this project or iteration.

Sometimes, in an evolutionary and iterative project lifecycle, the entire WBS and all the work package are not available or identifiable upfront. They are decomposed progressively. This is also very popular in Agile lifecycles. In adaptive lifecycles, some deliverables are decomposed into Work packages and hence only those work packages are decomposed into activities. The other deliverables are visited later in the project in increment cycles. Hence the name "**Rolling Wave Planning**". This term Rolling Wave Planning is a very generic term and covers every iterative and evolutionary lifecycle in every domain and industry in the project management world.
Let me give you a real-world example. One of my first projects in Japan was to create an engine that monitors every single transaction in a bank and predicts if a fraud, illegal activity or any such nefarious activity is about to take place. Now a bank is made up of Retail Banking, Core Banking, Corporate Banking, Loan Banking and so on. This was the first project of its kind in the world and hence we did not have any kind of requirements. Therefore we decided to start with the simplest and smallest scope viz., ATM. Once we started working on it and after some trial and error we began to understand several things. Once we were about to finish with ATM our understanding of Retail Banking fraud detection improved and we started detailing out the same. When we were midway in "Anti-Fraud" for Retail Banking we got some great ideas for Corporate Banking and hence started planning for that. I guess you can see the concept of rolling wave planning. Agile is also one of the implementations of Rolling Wave Planning.

ROLLING WAVE PLANNING

INITIATION
PLANNING
EXECUTION
MONITORING & CONTROLLING
CLOSING
DELIVERY = 1.

I P E M/C C
DELIVERY = 2.

I P E M/C C
DELIVERY = 3.

ONE PROJECT IS BROKEN DOWN INTO MULTIPLE PHASES AND DONE IN MULTIPLE WAVES

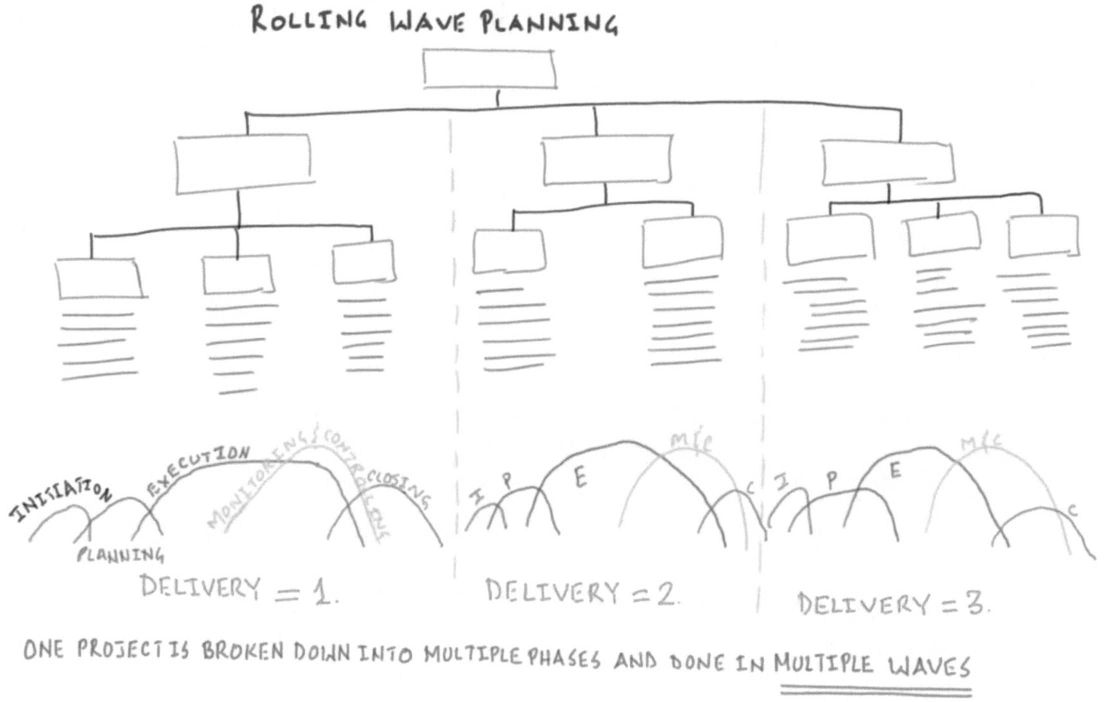

From the point of view of exams it is important to note that the technique of Rolling Wave Planning is unique to this process, viz., *DEFINE ACTIVITIES*. You will not find it in any other process. Which essentially means if in exams question you see this term, then the question is taking about this process and nothing else.

9.9.2 Main Outcomes of the process Define Activities:

The very purpose of this process is to produce a list of every possible activity that would be needed for the successful completion of the project at hand. This list is basically called the "**Activity List**". If the activity list is actually decomposed from the WBS then this list also has a structure of Summary Tasks and Phases where each of the activities is listed.

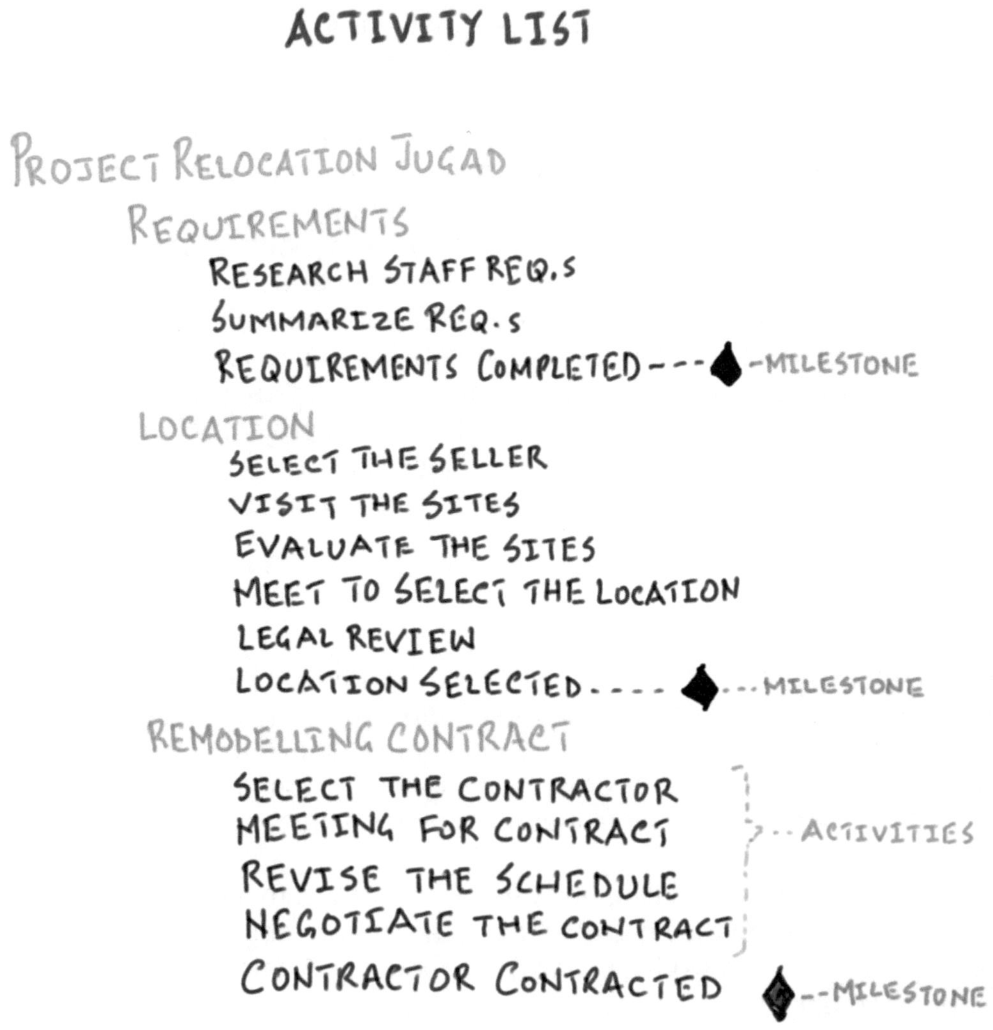

ACTIVITY LIST

- PROJECT RELOCATION JUGAD
  - REQUIREMENTS
    - RESEARCH STAFF REQ.S
    - SUMMARIZE REQ.S
    - REQUIREMENTS COMPLETED --- ◆ - MILESTONE
  - LOCATION
    - SELECT THE SELLER
    - VISIT THE SITES
    - EVALUATE THE SITES
    - MEET TO SELECT THE LOCATION
    - LEGAL REVIEW
    - LOCATION SELECTED .... ◆ ... MILESTONE
  - REMODELLING CONTRACT
    - SELECT THE CONTRACTOR
    - MEETING FOR CONTRACT
    - REVISE THE SCHEDULE
    - NEGOTIATE THE CONTRACT
    - (the four above) } -- ACTIVITIES
    - CONTRACTOR CONTRACTED ◆ -- MILESTONE

Activity Attributes: Along with the list of activities, there could be some activity attributes that may get identified as well and they need to be recorded with the corresponding activities. While identifying activities, certain aspects (Attributes) of the activities may also get identified like kind of resources needed for that activity, any specific kind of sequencing information for that activity, regulatory compliance needed for certain activities, duration related constraints for certain activities, risks associated with executing certain activities and so on. It's not necessary that each and every activity would have to have some attribute, but many of them tend to have it. In a real-world project, the outputs Activity List and Activity Attributes are indistinguishable but they are shown separately in the process to remind the project manager's that attributes of the activities also have to be thought through.

Milestone List: In a mature schedule, along with activities, there should be some progress points called Milestones that must be identified along with the list of activities. Just like a real-world milestone, that shows exactly how far you have progressed in your journey, these schedule based milestones are sprinkled across the schedule at control points for comparing the progress against, during the project execution. It's important to remember that these milestones are no activities and no resources have to be assigned to them as well as the duration of the milestones is "0" (only activities can have durations).

Milestones typically mark completion of a Phase or a group of activities or an initiative. E.g., Design Completed, Kick off Achieved, Requirements Completed, Vendors Appointed, Customs Clearance Obtained, Ready to Manufacture and so on.
The milestones can be of two kinds, Mandatory and Optional. The mandatory milestones are those provided by the Senior Management, Customers, Regulatory Bodies, listed in the terms of the contract and Key stakeholders of the project; whereas the optional milestones are the ones included by the Project Manager and the Project Team for internal tracking purposes and for better granularity while tracking the schedule.

9.10 Sequence Activities

Once you have identified and recorded all the activities in the previous step, they cannot all be done together nor can they be done haphazardly. They need to be sequenced in such a way as to ensure that the sequencing represents a model of reality. The purpose of sequencing is to bring logical order of doing things during execution as well as to obtain optimum efficiency within the constraints provided.

The entire concept of scheduling has been borrowed from the engineering process originally, therefore you may find PMI using terms from engineering field. The most prominent being the "Network Diagram". Sequencing creates the network diagram of interconnected activities. These activities are related to each other through arrows, which in turn, represent relationships.
Network diagrams take the form shown as under:

PDM - EXAMPLE-2: ANSWER

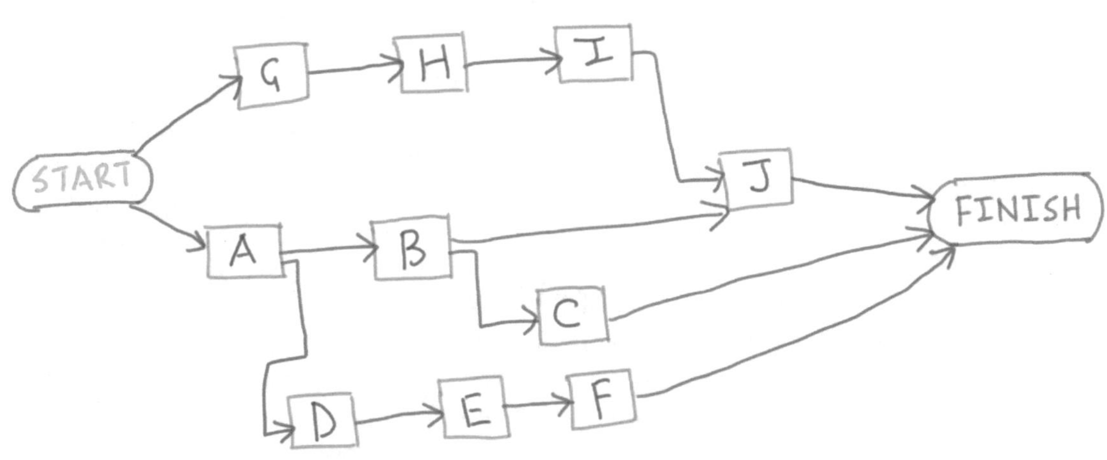

Essentially there are 4 possible kinds of relationships that can exist between two or more activities. Each activity has a start date and a finish date. The only way one activity may be connected to any other activity is through the permutations and combinations for these "Start Date" and "Finish Dates". This is the reason why we have 4 different possible relationships between activities.

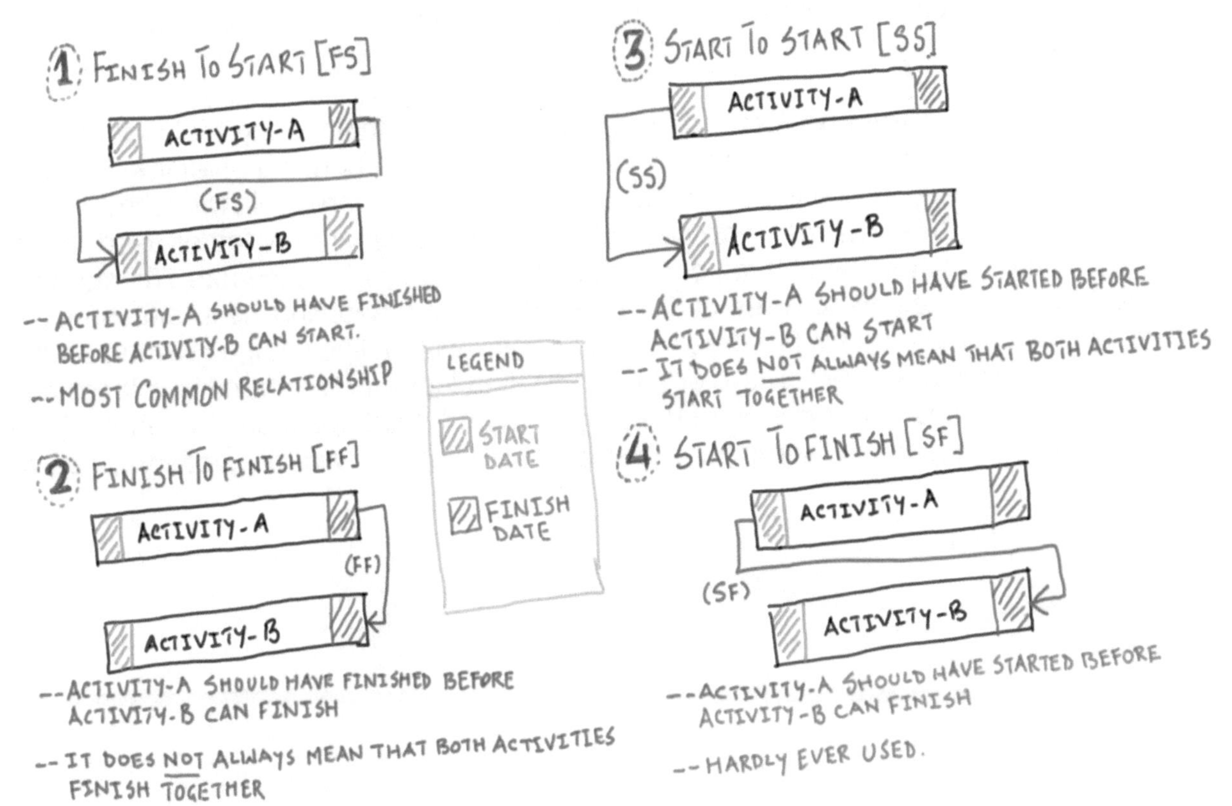

Example of **Finish to Start (FS)** is "Lay foundation" and "Build Pillars"; where the activity "Lay Foundation" must be finished before "Build Pillars" activity can be started. Example of **Start to Start (SS)** is "Campus Hiring" and "Departmental induction"; the activity "Departmental Induction" can only start if the activity "Campus Hiring" has started. They are related to each other by their start dates. But even here focus should be on "which activity depends on which". Example of **Finish to Finish (FF)** is "Handover of software product" and "Training of users on software product" (assuming that the scope validation or the User Acceptance Testing has already been done); where the larger activity of "Handover of software product" cannot finish till the activity "Training of users on software product" is finished. I will desist from giving an example of **Start to Finish (SF)** even though there is one mentioned in some project management books. What you must know is that there is no feasible example of this relationship type and you must never use it. This is only used as a default relationship type when people do a "Backward Scheduling" where the scheduling is worked backward from the end date of the project. Backward scheduling itself is a dangerous philosophy and has been proven historically that most projects done on Backward Scheduling have been largely delayed. Hence, in the real world, projects always go for a "Forward Scheduling" and use only 3 of the relationships viz., FS, FF and SS. But for exams, there are 4 kinds of relationships.
As a basic rule of validation, each and every activity and milestones, other than the first and the last and all Summary Activities, must be linked/related to at least one other activity. This may not hold true in all circumstances but it's a good rule to validate your sequencing.
Ok time to look into the innards of this process.

9.10.1 Main Tools & Techniques of Sequence Activities:

Sequencing uses some techniques as well as some tools. Let us get acquainted with some of them.

Precedence Diagramming Method (PDM) is a matured engineering tool that has been in use since ages and was the de-facto tool for creating sequencing of all the activities in a project, especially before the advent of sophisticated software tools for scheduling. I used to visit the "War Rooms" (now called Project Office) where my father used to plan out the entire construction of large paper manufacturing plants in the late 70s and the early 80s. There was no software during those days for scheduling. This war room had huge walls and over the walls were pieces of paper (with activity names written on them) pasted with arrows connecting two or more activities together and forming a fascinating network of activities from the start of the project to end. I did not know then that this tool was called "Precedence Diagramming Method (PDM)" or just Activity Network Diagram.

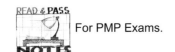

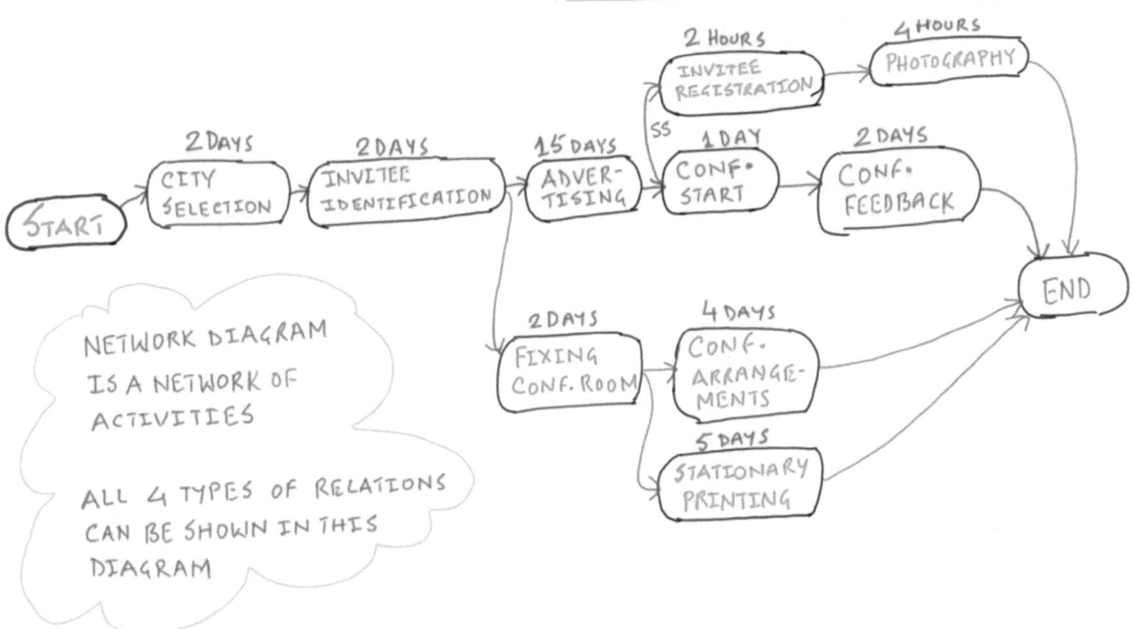

This PDM is also called “Activity on Node (AON)” as the nodes of the network diagram represent the activities and the arrows represent the dependency/relationships.

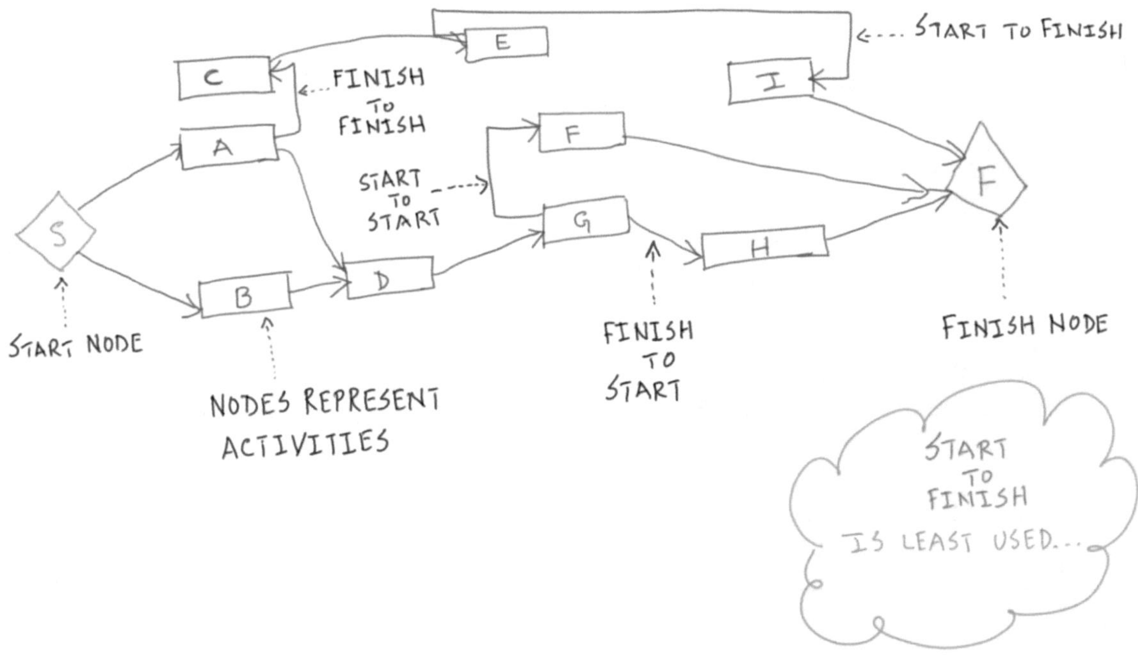

The PDM / AON represents all 4 kinds of relationships. It is important to note that every single project scheduling tool in the world uses the rules of PDM in the background processing to present the schedule that you model on the scheduling tool.

In exams, you would be asked to make or read a PDM and hence you must be good at doing the same. Though in exams even calculation of "Critical Paths" are asked, something we will cover later in this book. Right now it's important to know how to create a PDM from the instructions given. There are two kinds of instructions, namely, tabular form and paragraph form. You must be good with both as you never know which kind of question shows up in the exams. Unfortunately, most of the books on PMP® scare the readers about this section, whereas, actually this is a very easy section and we just need to understand it.

Exams cannot give a case study because it would take too much time, they just want to know if you know the concept well. This method of sequencing is not needed in the real world projects as now we have sophisticated software tools that help us do the same.

Example – 1: Paragraph Style.

You have a project with the following activities: Activity A takes 40 hours and can start after the project starts. Activity B takes 25 hours and should happen after the project starts. Activity C must happen after activity A and takes 35 hours. Activity D must happen after activities B and C and takes 30 hours. Activity E must take place after activity C and takes 10 hours. Activity F takes place after Activity E and takes 22 hours. Activities F and D are the last activities of the project.

If you made the network diagram correctly than it would look like this.

PDM - EXAMPLE -1 : ANSWER

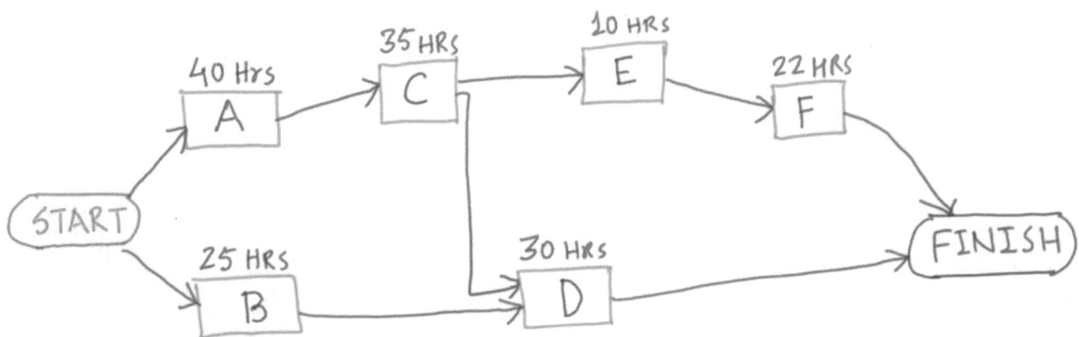

Example – 2: Table Style.

Task Name	Predecessor
Start	--
A	Start
B	A
C	B
D	A
E	D
F	E
G	Start
H	G
I	H
J	B,I
Finish	F,J,C

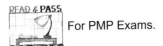

Draw the PDM / Network diagram for the same.

If you got it correct the network diagram would look like this.

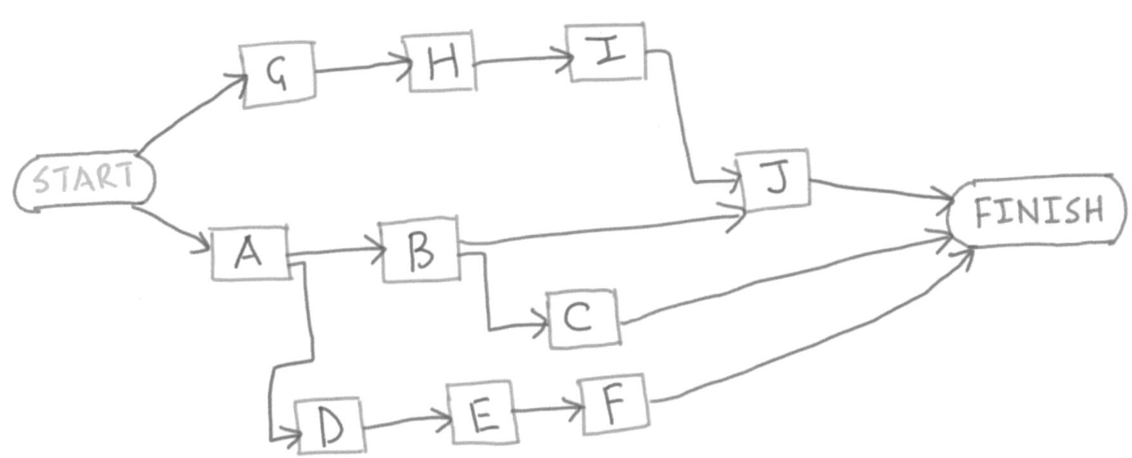

When you get a question in exams where you have to make a Network Diagram on the rough paper provided to you, or on the virtual whiteboard, you must retain that diagram as you continue with the rest of the questions in the exams and this is because usually in the same exams more questions show up relating to the exact same network diagram. This way you save the effort and consequently the time.

Dependency Determination And Integration is a technique to figure out what mix of relationship would be best suited for a set of activities. This technique looks at the four possible relationships Viz., Finish to Start (FS), Start to Start (SS), Finish to Finish ((FF) and Start to Finish (SF) and decides which represents the most **real to life** relationship. However, we have already seen the details of these relationships. Dependencies can also be either "Mandatory (hard logic) or Discretionary (Soft Logic)" and "Internal Dependency or External Dependency". This makes every relationship/dependency one of the following four dependency attributes: -

1. Mandatory – External
2. Mandatory – Internal
3. Discretionary – External and
4. Discretionary – Internal.

Over and above the 4 kinds of dependencies and the 4 dependency attributes there are **Leads and Lags** that can be applied on the dependencies to make the schedule even closer to reality.
Lag is the amount of time a successor activity is delayed after the predecessor activity. The best example is curing of cement pillars for bridges. For a bridge to be built, cement pillars are erected and after that, the slabs are put on top of them to connect the pillars.

But if you erect a pillar and immediately put the slabs on top of them the pillars will simply disintegrate. For the cement to convert into stone, it has to be left for atmospheric curing for say 15 to 20 days (in a warm climate zone) before the slabs can be mounted on them. This “Leaving of the pillar for curing” is called lag. And the relationship between these two activities would look like this.

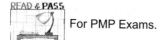

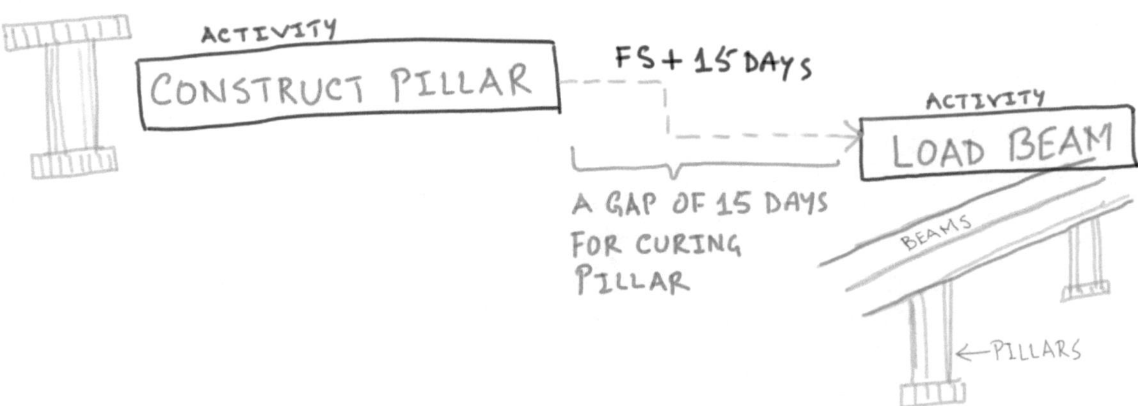

Let us look at more examples of Lag.
Say your team is developing a software product and soon this product would be functionally tested by the Customers before accepting the same. Now the technical writer’s team is going to work on the User Manual. The problem is that though the User Manual can be started at any time but cannot be finished till UAT (User Acceptance Testing) is completed because the known issues and training issues from such testing would have to be documented in the User Manual. This clearly is a Finish to Finish relationship. However, there is a catch. See, the User Manual cannot finish on the very same day the UAT finishes. A couple of days would be needed, after the end of UAT to update and finalize the User Manual with the findings from the UAT. Therefore the best way to show this relationship would be:-

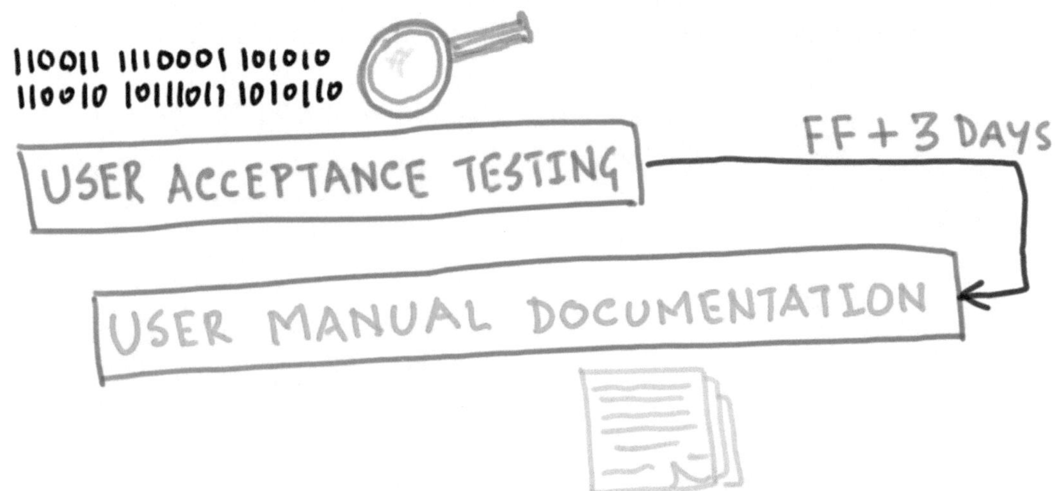

Another example, the most common example but a really apt one, of lag, is when you have to paint a room with enamel. You have to paint the primer and then the enamel. So it's an example of Finish (paint primer) to Start (Paint Enamel) relationship. However, you know that you cannot simply paint on top of primer the moment you finish painting primer. You have to wait for the primer to dry up before you can paint the enamel. Thus there is a lag for drying the primer between the two activities.

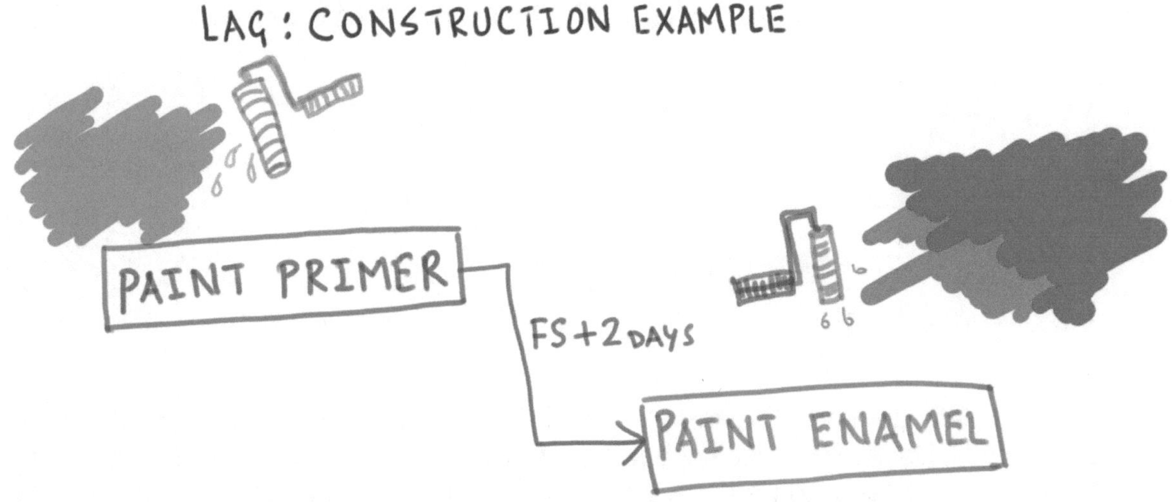

Ok, so that does it for Lag (Delay). Now let us move on to Lead. Lead is just the opposite of Lag; literally. While Lag is a Delay, the Lead is an Overlap.
In relationships which are discretionary, a succeeding activity can be overlapped with the preceding activity to gain some time or to represent the real world situation. I guess an example would do the trick.
Say, in your project one piece of work is to create a cemented floor for the entire banquet hall. After that, you have to put up marble tiles on top of that cemented floor. Now technically speaking the activity of cementing the floor has to be done and only then the tiling of the floor with the marble tiles have to start. However, you may be running behind

time so what you can do is that you can overlap the activities by a few days so that before the entire floor of the banquet hall is completed the tiling can start from the other end where the cementing has already been done. Tiling does not need cement to completely dry hence there is no effect on quality. This overlap is called "Lead".

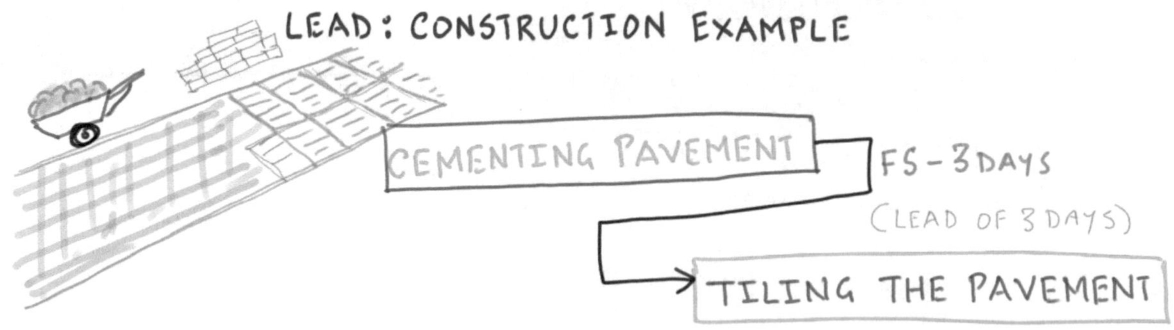

Another real-world example. You are going to custom build a set of soft toys and hence one of the activities in making the soft toys would be to sew the eyes on to these soft toys. However, the seamstress needs the **eyes** in their inventory bin at the beginning of the day. So obviously the act of "Sewing Eyes" and "Inventorying the Sewing line" have a start to start relationship. There is no doubt about it. If the sewing starts the inventorying has to start. However, there is a catch. The Inventorying has to be done one day in advance of each day of sewing. Hence the real relationship, as it turns out, is that the inventorying has one day LEAD on the activity of Sewing Eyes.

Another, really common IT example, which I have been guilty of doing 100s of times during my IT Days. Technically speaking, the complete Software Architecture and structure design have to be done before the software project construction and coding can start. Obviously a text book example of FS relationship. However, confident project managers try to overlap the Coding / Construction part a little on to the Designing activity. So the activities around Coding would start even before the activity of Designing is absolutely complete.

Please remember that Leads and Lags can be applied to every relationship kind. Also, in a real-world scheduling these three tools and techniques, viz., PDM, Dependency Determination and Leads and Lags are not applied separately in steps, they are usually done together.

When it comes to adaptive projects, sequencing is done incrementally, one iteration at a time. In fact there are two levels of sequencing that is done in adaptive projects. One is a high level and another at the iteration level. A typical release plan shows the high level sequence in which the release would be built. The detailed sequence is made at the iteration level. Just before the iteration the team estimate all the activities that are needed to complete each of user stories earmarked for the said iteration. And then go about sequencing them. All that we have understood in sequencing, so far, would apply here as well. However this is done just for the iteration. Once this iteration is over, a detailed planning and hence the sequencing would be done just before the next iteration as well, and so on. Remember Rolling Wave Planning?

9.11 Estimating Activity Resources

Now that all the activities have been sequenced, the next step is to estimate all the resources or the kinds of resources that are needed to ensure completion of individual activities. This step is best accomplished by involving team members including vendors if some of your work is outsourced.
Basically this is one of the steps where we conduct an estimation activity. Estimation is done only for three distinct things in a project and they are 1. While estimating resources, 2. While estimating durations and lastly 3. While estimating costs.
I guess this is a good time for us to get acquainted with the term Estimating.

An Estimate is a quantitative assessment of the likely amount or outcome of a variable, such as project cost, resources, effort or duration. Estimation is nothing more than a structured, refined and evidence based guess work. And therefore this guess work would tend to become better as one progresses through the project and when more details become apparent.
As one progresses through the project, this progressive elaboration (remember this discussion at the very beginning of this book?) tends to impact four aspects of the estimation process:

1. As the project progresses and with more details becoming available the "**Range**" of your estimation tends to become smaller. This range would be a lot higher during the early stages of the project but becomes narrower as the project progresses.

E.g., During the initiation phase of the construction project about building a house, you may estimate that the project would need about 2 tons of concrete (plus – minus say 50%). However during designing you may have much better knowledge and you could then estimate that the project would actually use 2.5 tons (plus – minus say 25%). However when you make a detailed WBS and activity based analysis you may realize that you actually need 2.2 tons of concrete (plus – minus say 5%). This range may vary from project to project based on domain, industry, size and complexity.

2. Because of the above, obviously as the project progresses your estimates also become more and more accurate. **Accuracy** is how close your estimates were from what actually happened. Obviously when your range in estimating becomes narrower your accuracy also tends to improve. Accuracy is also connected to taking into account the risks that may affect it.
3. Estimating is also dependent on another concept called "**Precision**". Precision is different from Accuracy. Precision is consistency. The best way to explain this is to say that, a person who is consistently missing the target by say 20% is better than a person who is accurate once in a while. This means that a person or a process or a system that is more "Precise" can be understood and later made to be more accurate but anything that is not precise, it is difficult to understand how to correct it. Hence, as the project progresses you and your team may find that you may be getting more consistent or "precise".
4. Estimating is also based on **confidence**. Confidence on the quality of your historical data, confidence on your teams understanding, confidence on your experience, confidence on your ability to use the correct technique for the correct situation to estimate. If you and your team has done certain kinds of projects several times your confidence on the estimates would be high. On the other hand when you and your team find yourself estimating for a new kind of project or a very complex project your confidence on the estimate would be a lot lower.

9.11.1 Main Tools & Techniques of the process Estimate Activity Resources:

When it comes to estimating resources for the activities there are some tools and techniques that could be used.

Bottom Up Estimating is basically using WBS (Work packages) or even further subdividing work packages into activities and steps to such a level where the resources are estimable at a very granular level. This is generally called Bottom up estimating as the estimates are done at the lowest decomposed work or activity and rolled up or aggregated to higher levels of the WBS components.

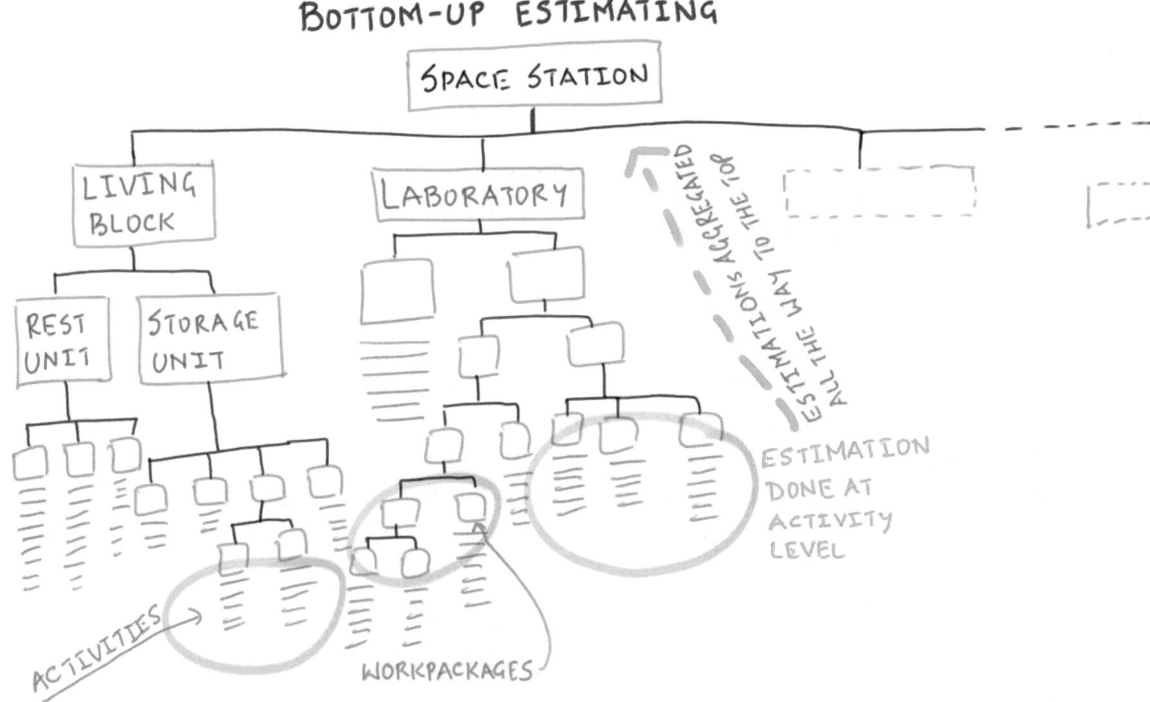

Analogous Estimating is when you use the information from a similar previous project or projects from the organization's historical data, to estimate the different kinds, skills, numbers, and quality of resources needed for this current project. This is one of the "Top-down" estimates where such estimates are made without getting into too many details of the project.

Parametric Estimating is when the historical data from the previous projects have been analyzed and converted into parameters for straightforward calculations. *E.g., You ask a contractor how many people, cement, bricks, grit (small stones that are mixed with cement to make it into concrete), sand, mixers, grinders, trucks, and forklifts would he need to make you an office of 2,000 square meters spread across 3 floors and with a basement for parking 20 vehicles. The contractor asks you for the covered area and open areas, carpet area and developed area and such, and after that right in front of you, tells you he would need 32 workers, 1 supervisor, 1000 meters of piping, 3000 meters of wiring, 2 tons of cement, 500kg of sand and grit and so on.* I guess you get my drift. This could be done so easily by the contractor that he has converted all his historical data into variables and parameters which can tell him the different resources he would need for the kind of work involved. In fact, in some industries (specifically Infrastructure) there are published estimating data to help for such kind of estimation. Such data are usually published by engineering and other technical journals.

When it comes to Adaptive projects this same techniques could be used for estimating the resources needed for each of the iterations based on the work and the requirements that need to be achieved in that iteration. The only difference is, while in predictive projects this kind of estimates is done for the entire project upfront, but in adaptive projects this is done just before each of the iterations and only for the iteration in question.

9.11.2 Main Outcomes of the process Estimate Activity Resources:

Predictive or adaptive or hybrid, whenever and at whatever level, once you have estimated the resources for the project or iteration or phase, it is also advisable to create a "Resource Breakdown Structure (RBS)".

Resource Breakdown Structure (RBS) presents the breakdown of the various categories of resources, tools, and material required for the project. This is not a "Per-activity" table but a hierarchical chart showing the breakdown of the main categories of the resources into sub-categories to show the various kinds of resources that are required for the project at hand. These subcategories may also have some additional information about the quality and skill parameters as well as the quantities. At a broad level, the RBS shows the different categories of resources that are needed for the project at hand.

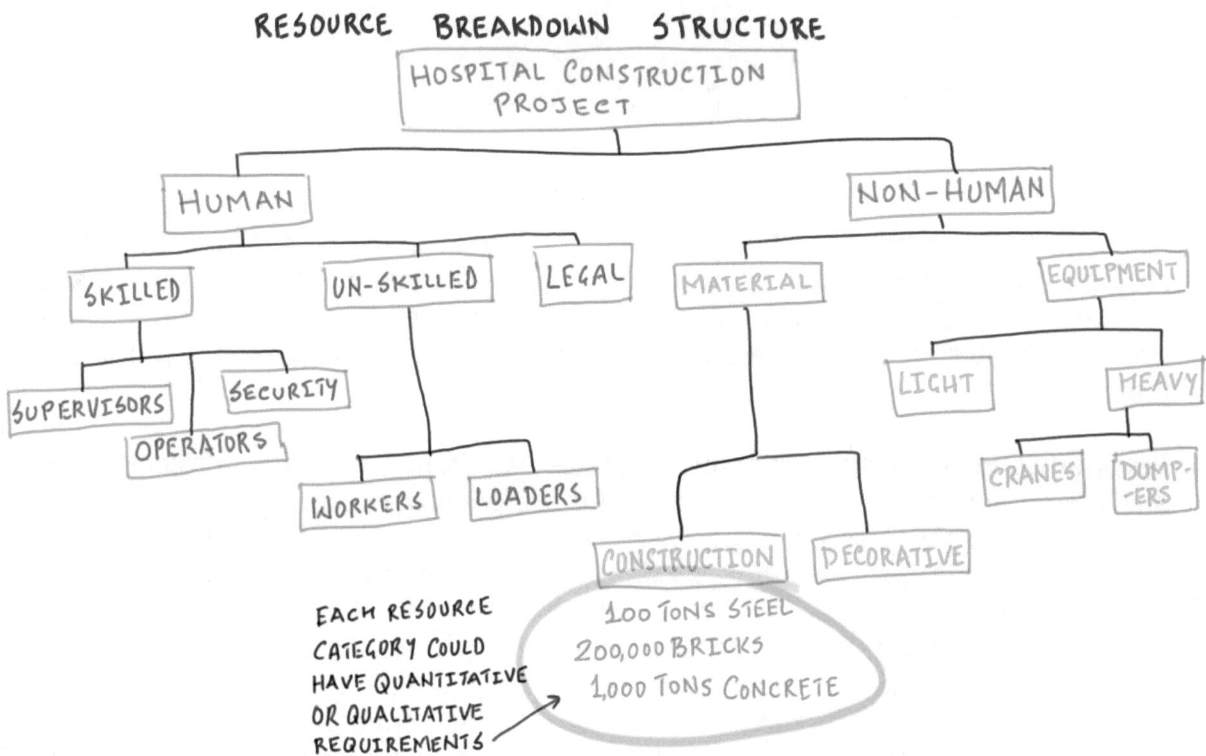

9.12 Estimate Activity Durations

The main purpose of this step is to estimate the number of "Time Units" needed to complete each of the activities. Time units could be "Days", "Hours", "Weeks" and even "Minutes" (Yes! Even minutes. I have worked, only once in my life, with Minutes as a unit of measure when I had to create a schedule to optimize on idle time on an assembly line of one of the foremost automotive company in the country). The time units to be used in a project are dependent on the Schedule Management Plan. It's not necessary that all the activities in a project have to have the same unit of time (though it is desirable). Different project activities may be estimated using different time units, however, that is not

recommended because comparing activities and updating them during execution and tracking them may become a challenge. This duration estimate is also based on the numbers of resources assigned to a specific activity. At this time it is also important to know the difference between Effort (Also called “Work Effort”) and Duration. Effort is the energy required to finish the activity in a given duration. Effort is what is used for calculating the cost of resources as well.
The standard formula used during this portion of schedule is:

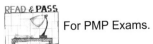

SCHEDULING BASE FORMULA

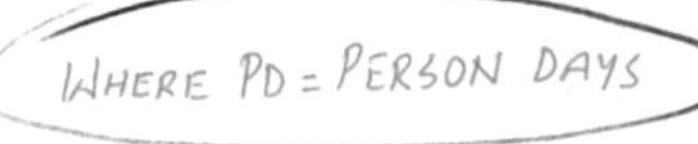

VARIATIONS OF THE BASE FORMULA

⇒ WHEN YOU WANT TO KNOW "DURATION?" FOR AN ESTIMATED EFFORT WITH GIVEN RESOURCES:

$$\text{DURATION} = \frac{\text{EFFORT}}{\text{RESOURCES}} \quad \text{Eg: } 4_{\text{DAYS}} = \frac{40\text{PD}}{10\text{ PERSONS}}$$

⇒ WHEN YOU WANT TO KNOW THE NUMBERS OF "RESOURCES?" REQUIRED TO COMPLETE AN EFFORT IN GIVEN NUMBER OF DAYS:

$$\text{RESOURCES} = \frac{\text{EFFORT}}{\text{DURATION}} \quad \text{Eg: } 8_{\text{PERSONS}} = \frac{40\text{PD}}{5\text{ DAYS}}$$

9.12.1 Tools and Techniques for Estimating

There are some techniques and some tools that are used for estimating the duration of the activities.

Affinity Grouping: Do you remember the time when during group photographs in school a generalized grouping was created where tall kids would be asked to stand at the back, the medium height kids will stand in the middle row and the short kids will stand right in front. This was not perfect but kind of worked. If you tried to create a generalized group on these three affinity groups viz., tall, medium and short, from this very same group, a few days later, you might have a different composition of each of the rows. Though hardly scientific in nature, this kind of classification kind of works. When this grouping of similar things are used for estimating anything, it is called Affinity Grouping Estimation.
In software industries this was very popular earlier, where requirements were simply grouped as Simple, Medium or Complex. These groupings were not very scientific but more or less worked in estimation. This method is somewhat popular in civil construction as well. Let us say that a 20 km elevated road has to be constructed over undulating topography. This would mean different heights of pillars would have to be constructed. Let us say that in this project, 5 different sizes of the pillars have been identified. The team would then use their historical data to ascertain, in general, how much time units

would each of these 5 pillar sizes would take. Once this unit is known for one pillar for that specific size, it would be multiplied by the number of pillars counted for that pillar size. And so on. It goes without saying that the actual pillar construction time would depend on the soil structure on which it is being constructed, challenges and approachability of the specific spot where it is constructed and other such factor. But for estimation purposes, this grouping more or less works.

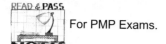

Bottom Up Estimating is when the WBS is used to find the work packages and from the work packages the individual activities are identified and then the duration estimation is done at the individual activity level and then aggregated all the way to the project level. This kind of estimate tends to be closer to accuracy than any other estimation method. However, this method ends up taking a lot of time. Most accurate but takes a lot of time.

Analogous Estimating is a technique which uses the data from the past similar projects for estimating durations for the current project. **Analogous Estimating = Historical Data Based Estimating**. It's as simple as that. The historical data could be used as-is or it could be factored up or down using any established complexity scale within the organization to provide for complexity or size. Analogous estimating can be done for the entire project or it could be done only for some specific portion of the project. Usually, this estimating method is used when not much of detailed information about the elements of the project is available. Needless to say that this method is easy to apply and does not take much time however, it's also less accurate. It is important to note here that if your organization had not undertaken a similar project (in relation to your current project) then you simply cannot use Analogous Estimating.

In some organizations and industries, the historical data are compiled and converted into mathematical formulas, variables and parameters which can be scaled up or down based on the project situation. Unlike the analogous estimating method, this technique bother about the fact if the data is from a similar project or not. This is a much more refined version of the Analogous estimate method and is called the **Parametric Estimating.** This kind of estimating method is not prevalent in every kind of industry or domain. In the infrastructure and civil construction domain, this method of estimating is almost a standard practice.

For example.

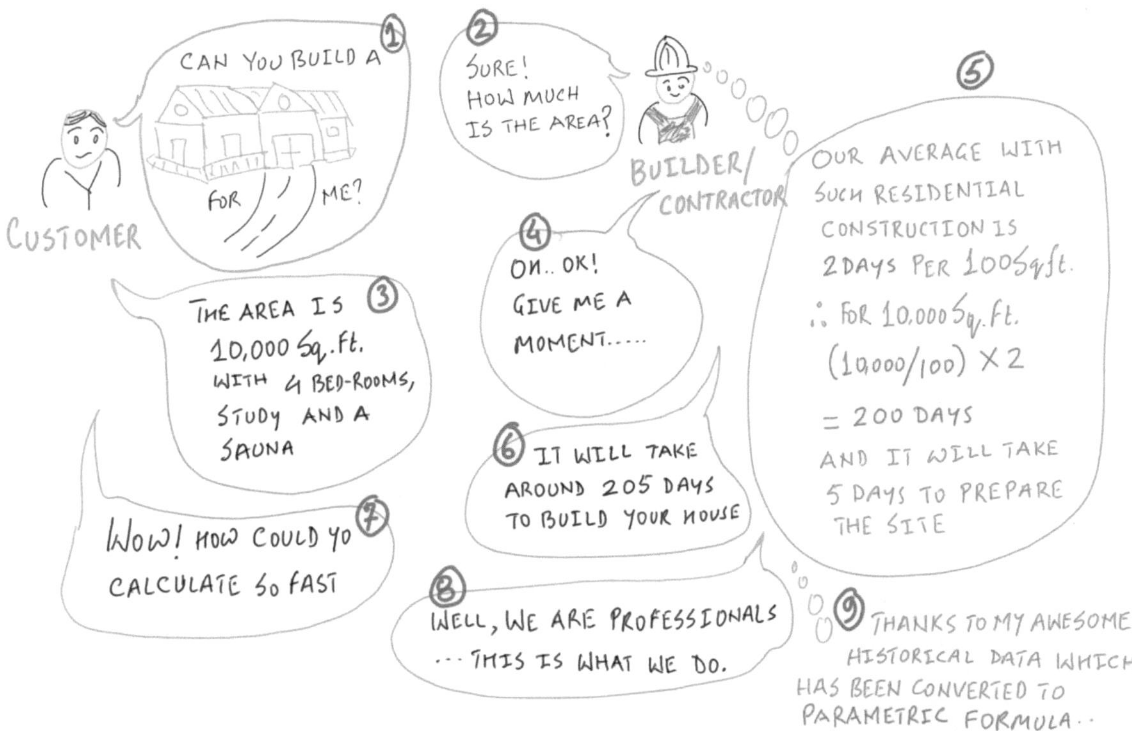

Single Point Estimating: This is an estimate which may use an experienced Subject Matter Expert's estimate or from that of a consultant or by using Function Point method, to arrive at a single estimate for an activity or work. Bottom up estimating is also a type of "Single Point Estimating".

Multipoint Estimating (Three Point Estimating): method is a method for validating duration estimates or minimizing the risk element from duration estimates produced using other estimating methods. There is usually a degree of variance in most estimates which makes these estimates have an element of risk. The Three Point Estimating method (also called PERT Formula) has been used over the ages for reducing the risk associated with duration estimates. What it does is that it uses three estimates for each of the elements to be estimated. The longest of the three is called "Pessimistic" estimate, the shortest of the three is called the "Optimistic Estimate" and the third is called the "Most Likely / Middle Value" estimate. These three are used in a formula as under.

$$D = \frac{P + 4M + O}{6}$$

WHERE:
P = PESSIMISTIC
M = MOST LIKELY/MIDDLE VALUE &
O = OPTIMISTIC
D = DURATION

Eg: LONGEST DURATION = 20 DAYS
MOST LIKELY DURATION = 11 DAYS &
SHORTEST DURATION = 7 DAYS

$$\therefore D = \frac{20 + 4(11) + 7}{6} \qquad \therefore D = \frac{20 + 44 + 7}{6}$$

$$\therefore D = \frac{71}{6} \qquad \therefore D = 11.8 \text{ DAYS or } 12 \text{ DAYS}$$

The outcome is a single estimate which is least risky. This formula is called the "Beta Distribution". There is another variation to this formula and it is called the "Triangular Distribution" where the following formula is used: -

$$D = \frac{P + M + O}{3} \qquad \text{Eg: } D = \frac{10 + 6 + 4}{3} \quad \therefore D = \frac{20}{3} \quad \therefore D = 6.66$$

It is important to note here that it's the "Beta" formula that actually reduces the risk while the "Triangular" formula only provides an average and is not as widely used as Beta distribution formula.

The "Beta" distribution formula is also used for finding out the best possible estimate in the given situation by estimating the worst case scenario (longest duration or Pessimistic situation where all known risks actually happen) duration estimate for the element and then estimating the best case scenario (shortest duration or optimistic situation where none of the risks happen and the work happens without a hitch) duration estimate and finally the most likely scenario (most likely duration or Middle value) duration estimate is found out. After this, the Beta distribution is applied to find the safest estimate from among the options.

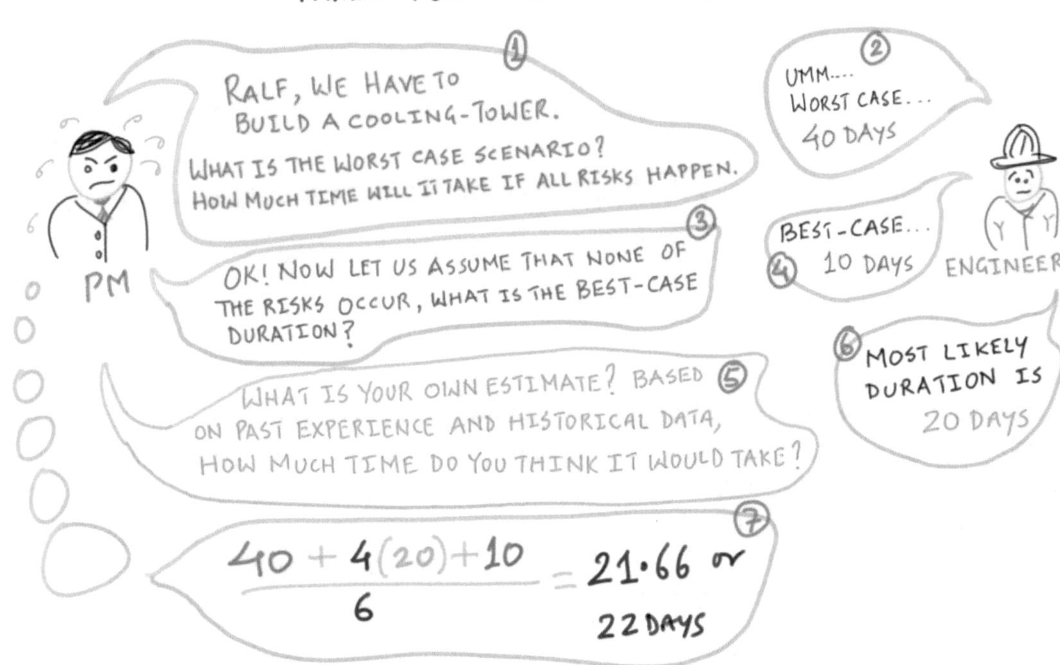

The Beta Distribution may also get affected by irregularities over time and hence it has a self-validation formula to find the suspect cases using its own version of Standard Deviation. The formula for standard deviation is

STANDARD DEVIATION

$$\text{STANDARD DEVIATION} = \frac{P - O}{6} \qquad \text{Eg: } \frac{40-10}{6} = \frac{30}{6} = 5$$

Technically this standard deviation is used for the very same reason why the traditional standard deviation is used in statistical values, which is, to look for statistical outliers or suspect cases which need to be estimated again or investigated for variance.

EXAMS SPECIAL

Sometimes in the exams it's not very clear if they want us to use the Beta Distribution or the Triangular distribution formula. For this, please remember the following rules and you will never go wrong:-

If in the exams question you do not see any description like Beta or Triangular formula to be used, then only use Beta.

$$D = \frac{P + 4M + O}{6}$$

If in the exams question its mentioned PERT formula than use only the BETA formula

$$D = \frac{P + 4M + O}{6}$$

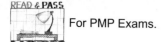

If in the exams question asks for which is the safest or least risky duration estimate than use Beta Formula

$$D = \frac{P+4M+O}{6}$$

Use Triangular formula only if it's specifically asked for average or triangular formula in the question.

$$D = \frac{P+M+O}{3}$$

In many organizations (specifically critical infrastructure projects) the Beta Formula is used for generating three overall schedules viz., Worst Case Schedule (where each of the activity on the schedule would display only pessimistic durations), Best Case Schedule (where each of the schedule activities would only display their optimistic durations) and Target case Schedule (where each of the scheduled activities would only show Most likely durations calculated through the use of Beta Distribution formula).

Remember, Three Point Estimating is also now called the "Multipoint Estimating".

Estimating techniques that are used specifically in software projects are specifically discussed here. These are also used for Agile projects as well.

- **Relative Estimating:** This estimating is not at all scientific in any manner whatsoever. Just that this method kind of, works in Software development world and is rather common at that this is the reason why it is showing up here. Remember school photography people arrangement that was discussed a few pages earlier. Well this is similar to that. In software development some teams simply compare the user stories or requirements amongst themselves and classify them as "Complex", "Medium" and "Simple". Not at all perfect and just as scientific as "gut-feel" estimates. But it kind of works because of the inherent flexibility and labor intensive work involved in software development. Just imagine if this was used in construction industry we would be estimating it like this, "The larger room will take 50 days to complete and the smaller room will take 25 days to complete". Would you ever use this estimation without knowing the actual size and dimensions of the room? Definitely not. Well that is why you will not find this kind of estimation in industries where there is unit of measure already in place. "T-Shirt Sizing", "Story Points" and "Simple, Moderate, Complex" are some examples of Relative Estimating.

- **Modified Fibonacci Using Agile Poker:** This is one of the "Relative Estimating" techniques. This means that it is not really a scientific technique that could be used over a period of time to understand productivity or even estimating accuracy. In this method a set of cards are provided to all the team members who are going to work on the user stories / requirements in the given iteration. There are several versions of this Agile Poker and users of each version claim that theirs is the best and authentic method. The truth is that this is not a scientific method and hence its rules can be bent a bit, but as long as whatever rules you are using are used consistently across the entire project, it would work reasonably well.

The version that I liked best is detailed as under. Each team member is provided a series of cards. These cards are partially based on the Fibonacci sequence. (Fibonacci sequence starts with 1 and 2 as the initial two digits and then the third digit is found by adding the previous two digits, thus the next digit after 1 and 2 would be 3. After three we would add 3 and 2 and get 5 and so on). However in Agile poker the cards given to each of the team members are “0, 1, 2, 3, 5, 8, 13, 21, 30, 40, 50 and 100”. Hence you can see that this is a Modified Fibonacci sequence. For each of the user stories placed in front of the team, each of the team members will throw down three cards. One card for the best case scenario, one card for the worst case scenario and one card for what they think it to be. (Very similar to 3 points estimation). At least one number must match for each of the team members. If one number is common among all the team members, that User Story would be given that number as the “User Story Point”. User story point does not refer to the duration but to the size of the user story as the team views it in comparison to the other user stories in that iteration. If none of the numbers match, the user story would be discussed again and then the team members would throw their cards again. This process will continue till at least one card is common among all team members. Any team member who throws a card with a number “0” only means that the team member does not understand the user story or that he has several questions and queries about that user story. If any team member throws the card bearing the number “100” it means that he thinks that the user story is way too big and needs to be broken down into smaller user stories.

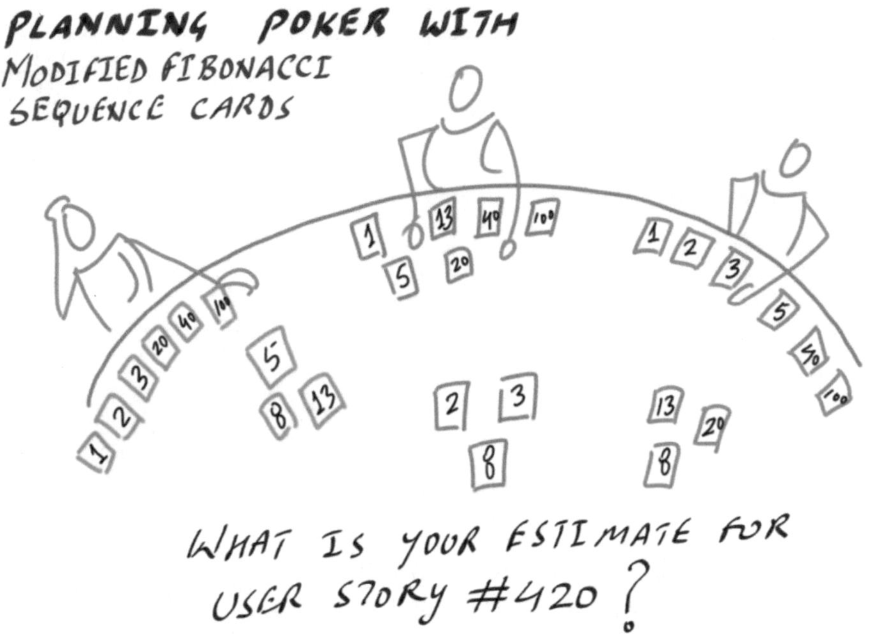

PLANNING POKER WITH
MODIFIED FIBONACCI
SEQUENCE CARDS
WHAT IS YOUR ESTIMATE FOR
USER STORY #420 ?

There are several versions to this game. One version is with each team member throwing one number each and the average of each of those card numbers are taken as the User Story point. Another version is that each team member throws one card each and it would continue till each of the users get exactly the same numbers. There are even more variations. The main point is that these details are not asked in PMP Exams but they do ask what this technique is used for as well as when this technique is used.

Since this is a sizing technique that provides “Story Point” to each of the user stories, these points are then converted, either using a parametric formula or consensus among team members, into durations.

- **“T” Shirt Sizing**: This too is an unscientific, relative estimating technique. In this method an even more generalized method is used for grouping the various user stories in an iteration, into different sizes. These sizes are usually labelled as “Small (S)”, “Medium (M)”, “Large (L)”, “eXtra Large (XL)” and “eXtra eXtra Large (XXL)”. This too does not provide any kind of duration but just the relative size of the user stories or the requirements. Again these “Sizes” have to be converted into durations using parametric methods or even past velocity or lead time or cycle time achieved for such user story sizes in the previous iterations of the same project. In fact this is the reason why speeds like “Velocity” and “Throughput” are calculated for Iteration based agile and “Cycle Time” or “Lead Time” are calculated for the Flow based agile. This speed is used for converting Story Points or User Story sizes of next iterations into expected durations.

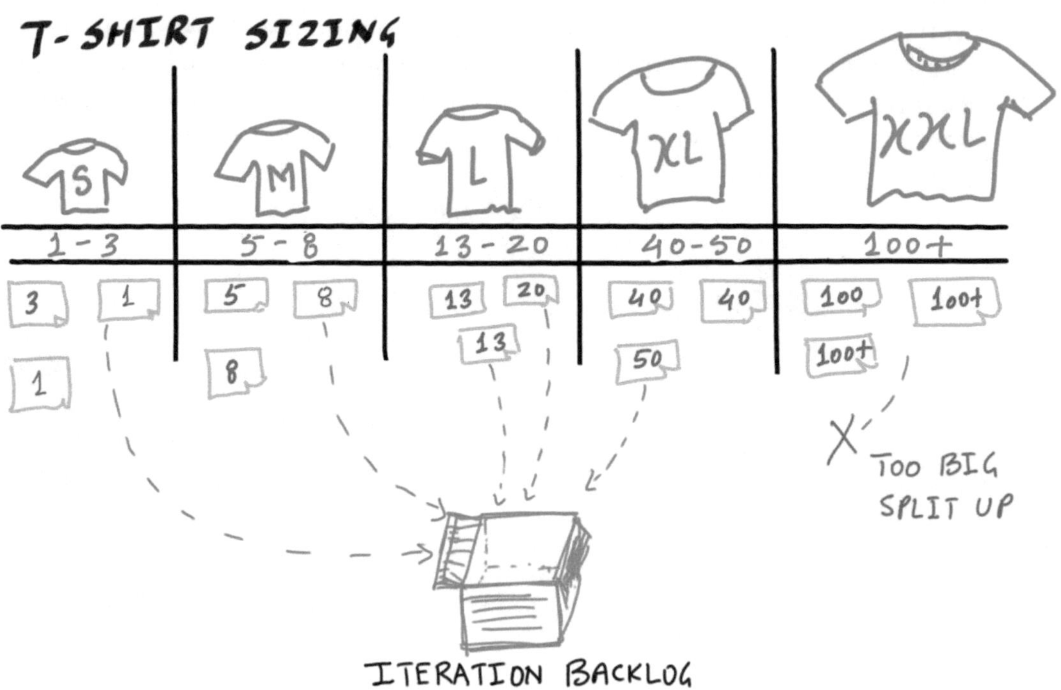

Sizes that are XXL simply mean that the User Story is way too complex or huge and needs to be broken into smaller User Stories.

- **Wide Band Delphi**: In this method of estimation the team members are all asked to estimate the user story or the requirements at hand, individually, and present to others. Once each of the team members have presented their estimates, the team members with outlier estimates are asked for rationale. Once everyone has heard them and seen others estimates as well, they go for another round of estimating. This is repeated till all team members have estimates which are either the exact same or very close to each other. If this sounds very similar to Agile poker (Estimation Poker), well it is. The only difference is that in Agile Poker the relative size of the user stories are estimated, while in Wide Band Delphi the durations could be directly estimated.

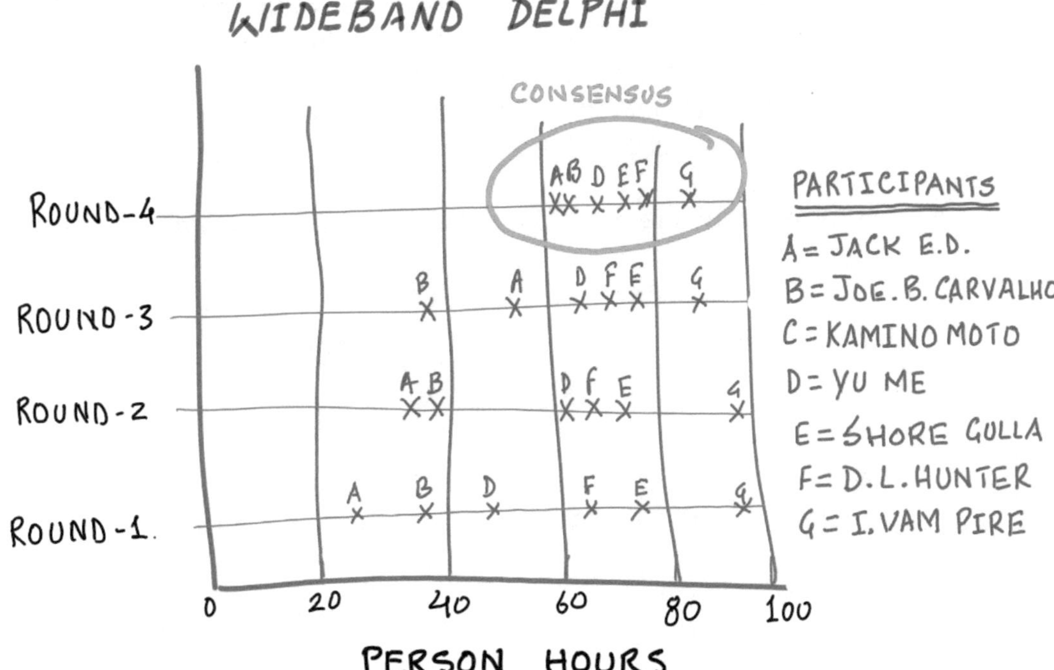

Wide Band Delphi can also be done in an anonymous manner (I have done it twice when I worked for a crack anti-terrorist unit as a civilian delegate) where the participants would not be introduced to each other and their identities would be kept hidden but all participants would get to see what was the input of everyone else. Rest is the same. Multiple rounds are done with the anonymous participants till you find some kind of consensus in their inputs.

- **Function Point Estimating**: This is a scientific estimating method that estimates the size of the requirements. They are based on global benchmarks that give tabulated sizes to various aspects of requirements and user stories based on the underlying characteristics. In fact I have used this method a lot and trained some of the top software organizations on this topic. It is probably the only scientific sizing technique in the world of software development. Once the size of the requirements are estimated, it is then converted to “Effort” based on the past productivity factors connected to the software platform to be used. This effort can then be easily converted into cost estimates as well as durations based on the numbers and kinds of resources that you would wish to use for these requirements.
  At this point it is really important to know that what “Sizing” and “Relative Sizing” means. If I were to describe two rooms that you are expected to paint where “One is small” and the other one is “medium”. This is not very scientific is it? There is no way to truly understand how big the room actually is without using a scientific metric system. This is what is called the “Relative Sizing”. As you can see from the example provided about rooms, why this method would be rarely used in traditional industries. However it “kind of works” in Software circles. Hence this is used mostly in Software development and software services. On the other hand if I was to tell you that one room has a covered area (for painting) of 220 sq meters and the other rooms covered area is 450 sq meters. Now, this is something that you can easily estimate and easily

understand as well. This is called sizing. Traditional industries cannot estimate without sizing. The only sizing technique in software development is "Function Points" (and it's variants like "Full Function Point" etc.) I truly hope this clarifies very well the difference between sizing (scientific method) and relative sizing (unscientific method). At this point it is important to note that Function Point is only used for Software Estimation. In fact it is the only scientific method for estimating and sizing software projects.

Let us summarize all the estimating methods for your review and quick classification.

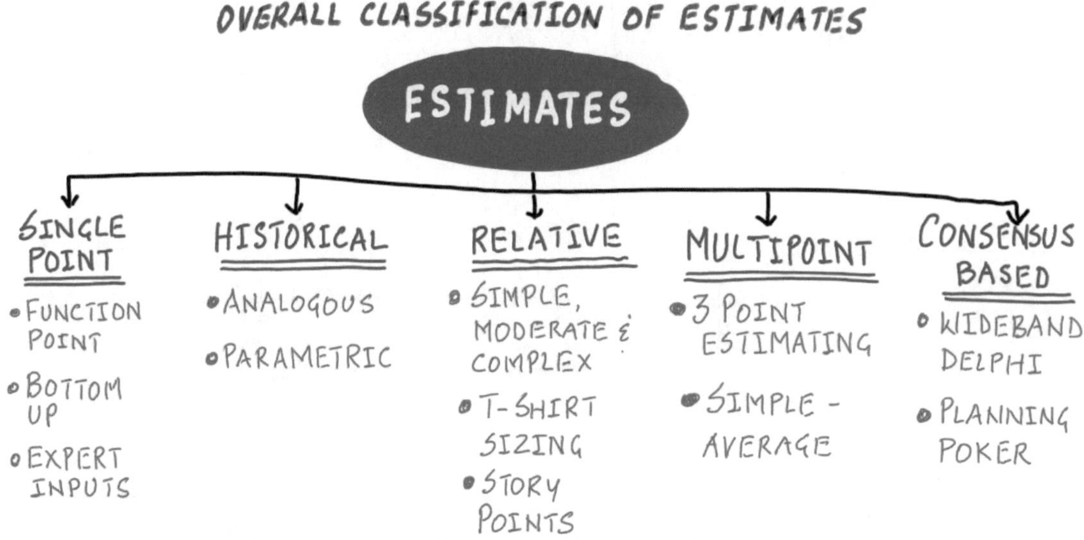

"**Reserve Analysis**". Reserves are created to provide for Risks. In this process, however, only the "Duration Reserve" is being discussed. The Cost reserves would be discussed later in this book. Risks are basically of two kinds viz., Identified Risks (also called Known – Unknowns) and un-identified risks (also called Unknown – Unknowns) and hence the reserves would also be of two kinds. When duration reserves are kept for Identified Risks (Known – Unknowns) the reserve is called "Contingency Reserve" whereas if the reserve is kept aside for Unidentified Risks (Unknown – Unknowns) it is called "Management Reserve".
The contingency reserve is usually put against specific activities or schedule elements so that the reserve is only utilized by that activity or element and not by any other element or activity. Whereas the management reserve is kept at the overall project level as no one knows for which risk would the extra time be used.

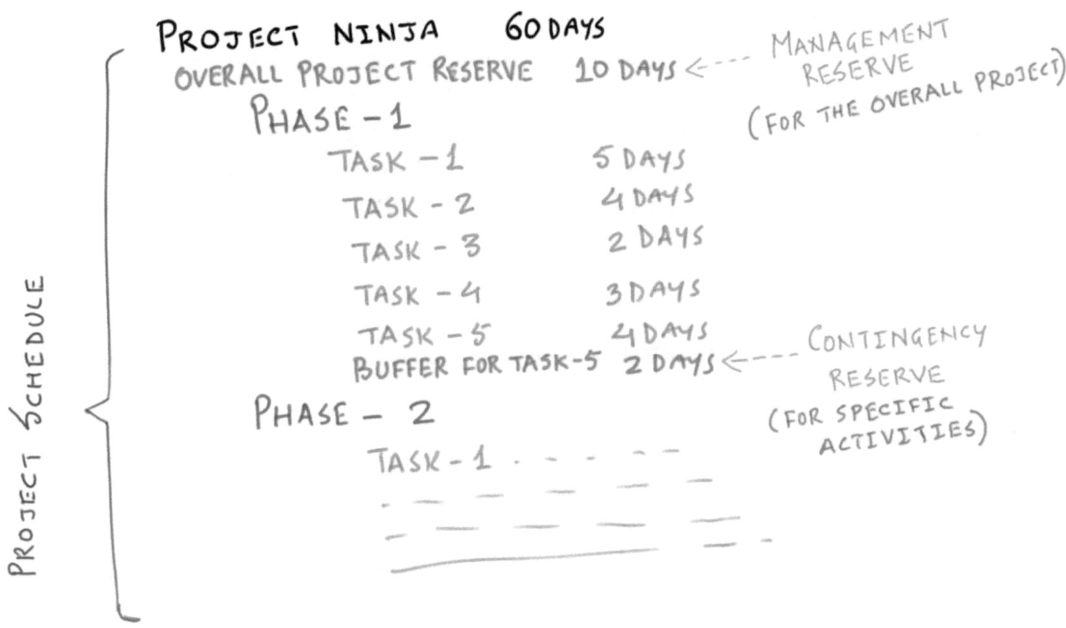

There are two ways in which the reserves are provided for a specific activity, in a schedule. One is the correct way and the other is, well….. , a convenient way. One is called “Buffer” and the other is called “Padding”. Let us look at how the two are done.

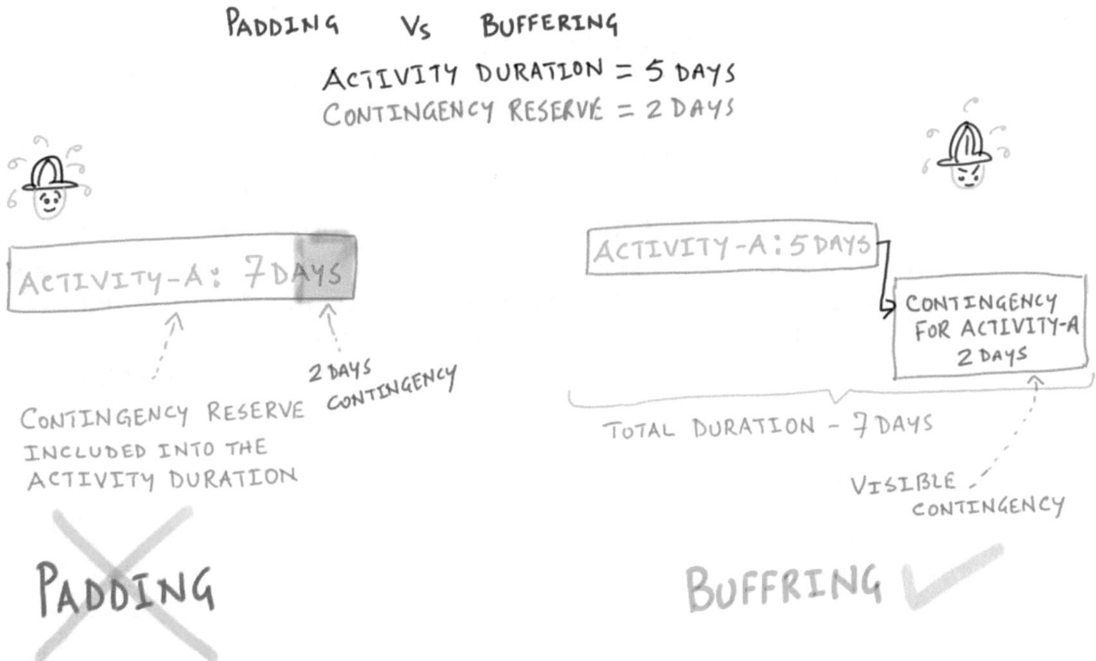

Now that we know that Buffer is nothing but a visible contingency reserve a lot of us might think that it may not be a good realistic way to show the reserves. Many people would fear that the management or the customer or even their own sponsors may ask them to remove the buffers to save on time. But going for padding is a very dangerous thing to do. In organizations where padding of estimates is rife, the sponsors tend to arbitrarily cut, say, 10% off the estimate to do away with the padding kept by the project managers. This brings about a feeling of distrust among the team members. Not only this. A padded estimate becomes a historical data, at some point of time, which cannot be reused because no one clearly knows as to how much the estimates have been padded. The worst thing about padding is that since the reserve is hidden the entire duration (including reserves) would always get utilized unlike buffers where the contingency is visible and hence can be tracked and may not always be fully used up.

EXAMS SPECIAL

In exams sometimes they used to ask about which of the methods of keeping a ***reserve*** is an ***illegal*** method, please remember its "***Padding***". Management Reserves are not usually a part of the project schedule baseline, but contingency reserves are always a part of the project schedule baseline. As more and more information becomes available on the project (across the lifecycle of the project due to progressive elaboration) the contingency reserves may be reduced or even eliminated or increased.

Decision Making is a tools and technique that you are very well acquainted with as we have discussed them so many times in the past. Techniques like voting and cluster voting and similar other techniques have already been discussed. I will use this space to discuss some other methods for taking a decision about project duration estimates. They are both from the stable of "Agile" techniques.

- **Fist To Five (or Fist of Five)** Yeah yeah…it sounds so similar to that Hollywood blockbuster called "Fast Five", I know…. I am a movie buff myself. In this method (again very popular in Agile methodologies) the team members and team contributors come together in a room and for each of the features/activity/story point, the PM would state a duration. As a reaction to this duration, all those present have to raise their hands and hold up fingers (1 to 5) or no fingers (making a fist). People who hold up less than 3 fingers are not really supportive of this estimation. However, if more people hold up more than 3 fingers the duration is approved. If more people hold less than 3 fingers then a discussion is held and voted again. This process is repeated until most of them either pass it or block it or revise it.

FIST-TO-FIVE

Why does it remind me of the childhood game called "Rock – Paper – Scissors?" ☺

Fist-to-five is a group decision making technique and it is not only used for understanding team reactions to duration estimates. It could be used for bouncing proposed decisions and ideas with the team and obtain a quick feedback. It could even be used for the team to decide on what kind of food and beer would work best for their next team outing.

9.12.2 *Main Outcome of the process Estimate Activity Durations:*

The main artefact of this process is Duration Estimates. For a predictive project these duration estimates are for all the activities that make up the project. For adaptive projects this is done for all the activities only for the next iteration.

9.13 Develop Schedule (Optimizing Schedule)

This is the step where whatever that has been done earlier in preparation of a schedule, all comes together in the form of a Project Schedule. In this process, the schedule is put together and any adjustments or corrections needed to make the schedule more realistic, are done.
The moment the schedule is approved and finalized, it becomes the "Time Baseline" or the "Schedule Baseline". Hence it is this process viz., DEVELOP SCHEDULE, which provides the "Time (Schedule) Baseline" for the project at hand.

Ok let us get into the internals of this process.

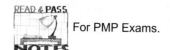

9.13.1 *Main Tools & Techniques of the process Develop Schedule:*

Schedule Network Analysis is a comprehensive set of scheduling analysis techniques to help understand, refine and optimize a given schedule. This involves things like Critical Path Method Analysis, Critical Chain Method (Theory of Constraints), Path Convergence (where multiple paths converge on to a specific activity or scheduling element thus making it risky) as well as Path Divergence and even things like "What-if analysis" and precedence analysis (study of dependencies among the schedule activities). The objective is to look for the best "sequence" of activities that would provide optimum results for the project at hand.

Critical Path Method (CPM) is an analysis technique which analyses the Critical Path/(s) of a project schedule. So what is a critical path?
Let us spend some time understanding clearly what a Critical Path is and how it is formed and why is it so important.
You are already aware of how a Network Diagram is created. When dependencies / relationship is created among the project activities a network of activities is created which are called a network diagram. This was the "Pre-software" way of scheduling. Now that we have software, in real world, actually creating a network diagram is not all that necessary. However, the concept of Critical Path is best understood using a Network Diagram.
In a network diagram, there are more than one paths from start to end of a project.

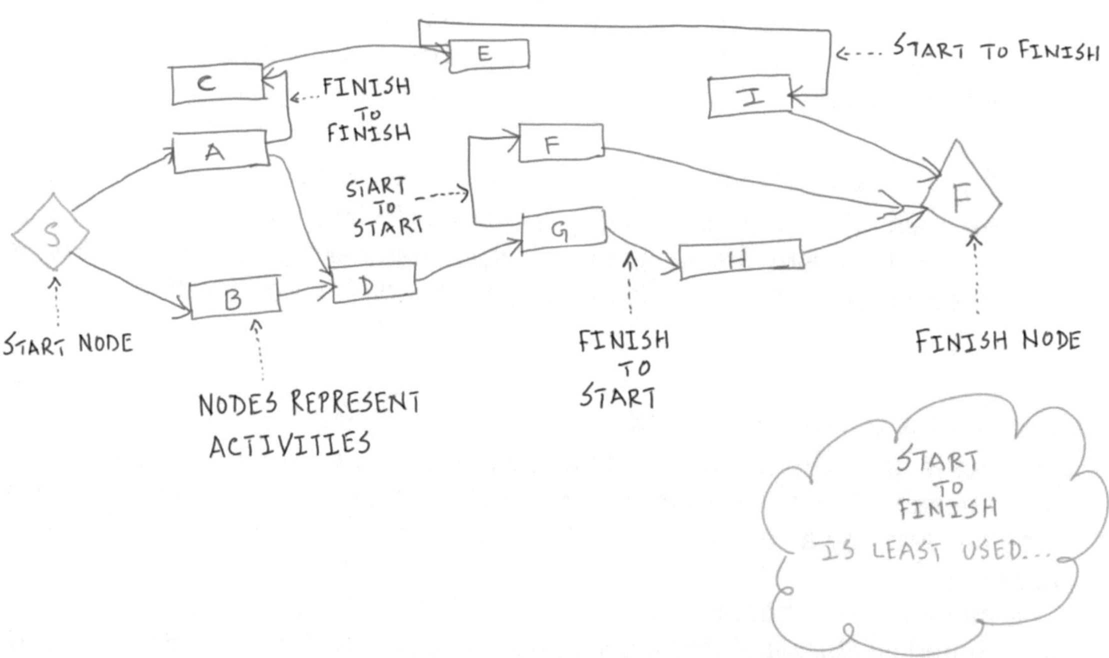

Each of the activities has durations and hence if you add up the duration of each of the activities on a path you end up getting the duration of the entire path. Once you have the duration of each of the paths than the path with the longest duration is called the critical path.

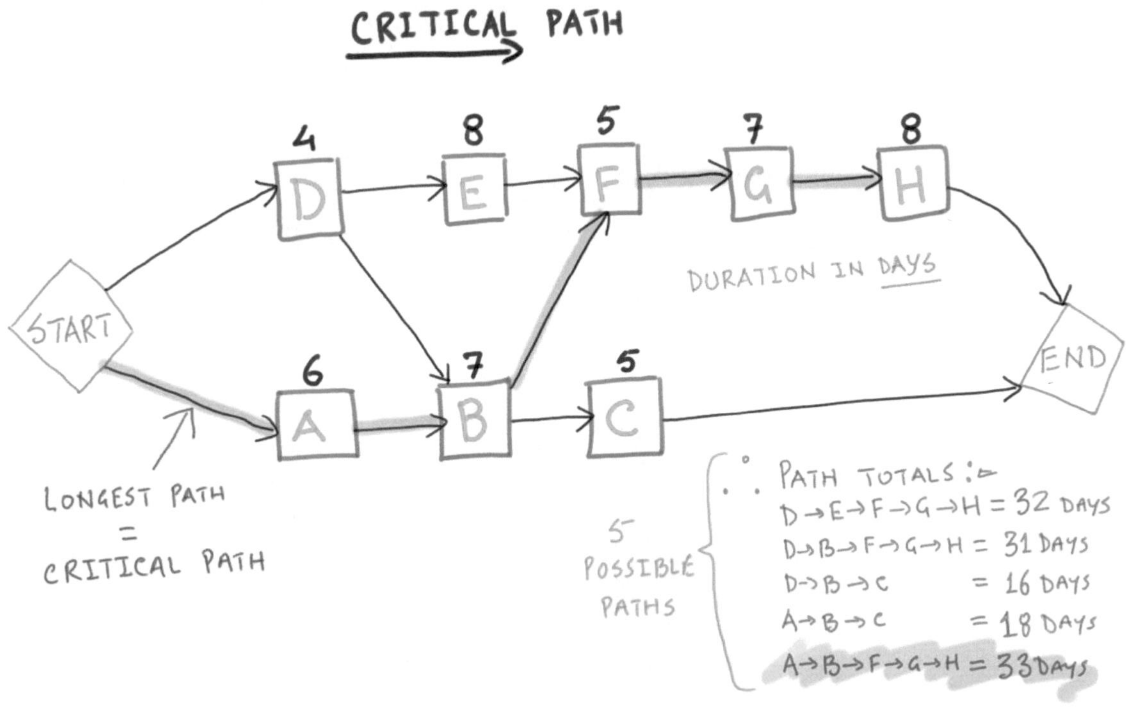

A lot of people get confused (as they may have read it somewhere else) as to what is the real definition of Critical Path. Is it the longest path or the shortest path in a network diagram? Well, it's the **Longest Path** in the project schedule or the network diagram. However, the reason why some people get this wrong is that there is another definition of Critical Path and it is "The **Shortest Duration in which the project can finish**". If you read both the definitions carefully you will realize that they both mean the same. The longest path decides the total duration of the entire project. If the Critical Path is 250 days than the entire project duration is 250 days. It's as simple as that. It's the critical path that decides the total duration of the project. Now, this also means that the project cannot finish before these 250 days. Which also means that the earliest that this project can finish is 250 days. Hence remember the definition **"Longest Path Duration / Shortest Project Duration"**.

Now, the question is why do we really call this path the critical path? Look at it this way. If this path decides the total duration of the project than any activity on this path, if it is delayed for even a single day, it would end up delaying the entire project. Each of the activities on the Critical path is called a "Critical Activity". Therefore, if you want to ensure that the project is not delayed just concentrate on the critical path and ensure that none of the activities on the critical path are delayed.

Obviously, the question in your mind would be "If we cannot delay the critical activities than does it mean that the non-critical activities/activities not on the critical path, can be delayed?". Yes, they can be, but there is a limit to which they can be delayed. This flexibility of the Non-Critical activities to be delayed within a limit, without delaying the project is called "Float" or "Slack".

Let us look at the example given here and see what the float on the activity "B" is.

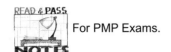

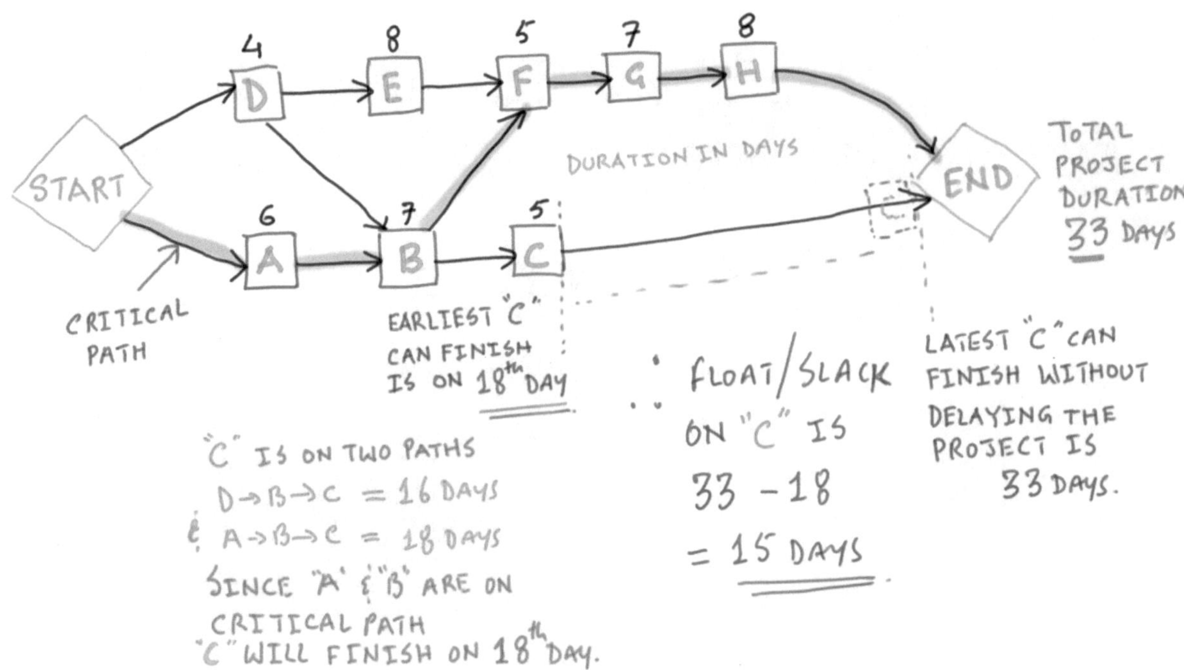

EARLIEST "C" CAN FINISH IS ON 18th DAY

"C" IS ON TWO PATHS
D→B→C = 16 DAYS
& A→B→C = 18 DAYS

"C" WILL FINISH ON 18th DAY.

If you use a project scheduling tool you will be able to find out your critical path and the float on non-critical activities in just a couple of clicks. However in the exams, one must know the traditional method of calculating the Float/slack on a non-critical activity. Imagine that each of the nodes of the network diagram shown above looks like this and has a naming convention for each of the 4 corners of the node.

NAMING CONVENTIONS - NODE

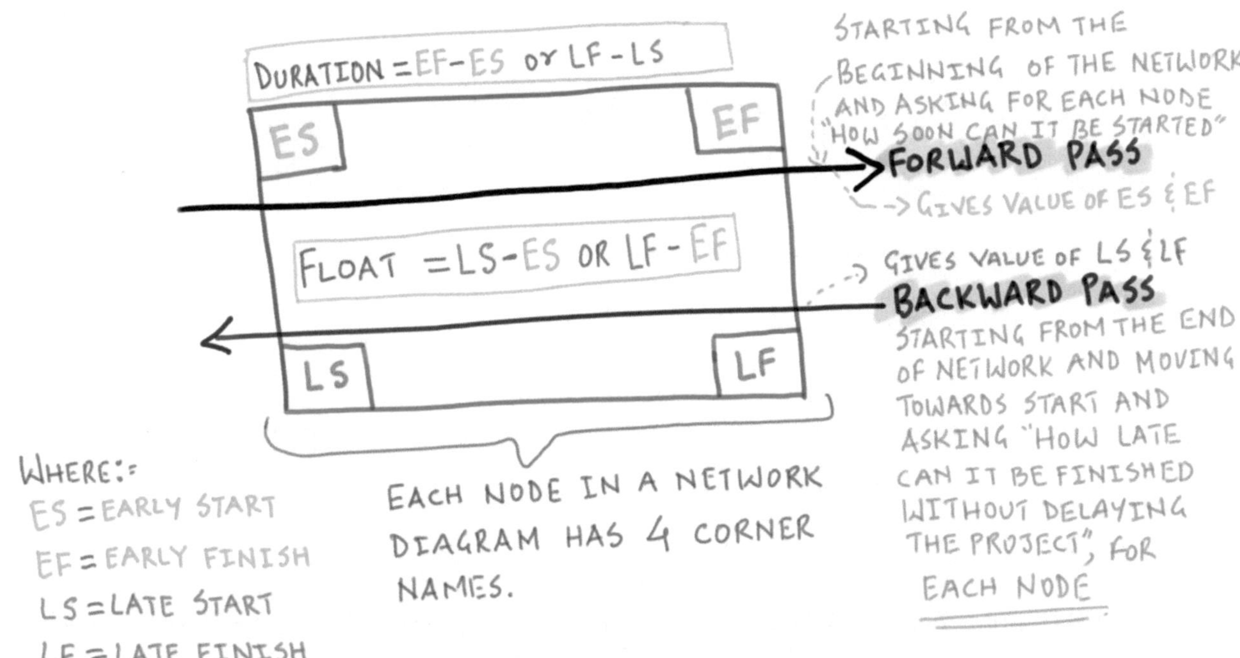
DURATION = EF - ES or LF - LS
ES
EF
FLOAT = LS - ES OR LF - EF
LS
LF
STARTING FROM THE BEGINNING OF THE NETWORK AND ASKING FOR EACH NODE "HOW SOON CAN IT BE STARTED"
FORWARD PASS
GIVES VALUE OF ES & EF
GIVES VALUE OF LS & LF
BACKWARD PASS
STARTING FROM THE END OF NETWORK AND MOVING TOWARDS START AND ASKING "HOW LATE CAN IT BE FINISHED WITHOUT DELAYING THE PROJECT", FOR EACH NODE
WHERE:-
ES = EARLY START
EF = EARLY FINISH
LS = LATE START
LF = LATE FINISH
EACH NODE IN A NETWORK DIAGRAM HAS 4 CORNER NAMES.

Now, let us use the same network diagram shown earlier, to calculate the Float / Slack on Activity "B" but this time using the traditional method.
As a first step let us calculate the ES and EF of each of the activities using Forward pass. A forward pass is when we start from the beginning of the project and keep asking "What is the earliest we can start this activity and hence what is the earliest we can finish this activity?" for each of the activity.

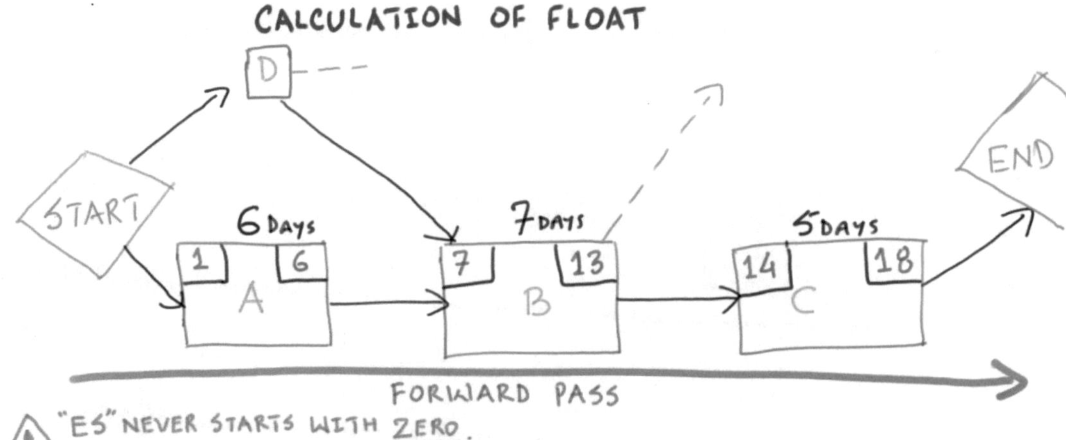

⚠ "ES" NEVER STARTS WITH ZERO.
"ES" OF FIRST NODES WILL ALWAYS START WITH "1" IN FORWARD PASS
FORWARD PASS "INCLUSIVE" COUNTING HAS TO BE DONE.
∴ ALWAYS USE THE FORMULA $EF = (ES + DURATION) - 1$
∴ FOR FIRST NODE $ES = 1$ HENCE $EF = (1+6)-1 = 6$

You might have noted that the ES of the very first activities are "1" and not "0". This is because time and date are never 0. There are many PMP® books where the first activity's ES starts with "0" and they are absolutely incorrect. Though this difference looks small, but if you carefully observe, you will notice that the calculation changes drastically. Notice the first node "A" it's ES is "1" and its duration is "6" hence its EF must be (ES + Duration) = "7". But actually, the EF of A is "6" because the ES of "1" is also included in the work duration. To make it simple for you to never go wrong in calculating EF in exams, use this formula in forward pass viz., **EF = (ES + Duration) – 1.** You will never go wrong with this. Let us apply this rule on activity "B". Its ES would be "7" as "6" was utilized in activity A. The EF of activity "F" would be 7 + 7 = 14 minus 1 which would give EF of "13".

Practice this formula on the other activities as well and you will get a clear picture of why the ES and EF of the activities are those numbers shown. I am sure now you can calculate the ES and EF of activity "C".

Now, let us move to the backward pass to calculate the LS and LF of each of the activities. Backward pass is just the inverse of the Forward Pass where you start from the "Finish" of the project and start going backward, activity by activity, and asking the question "What is the latest this activity can finish without delaying the project or the next activity, and hence what would be the latest it can start?" for each of the activities. Let us put this into practice starting with activity "B".

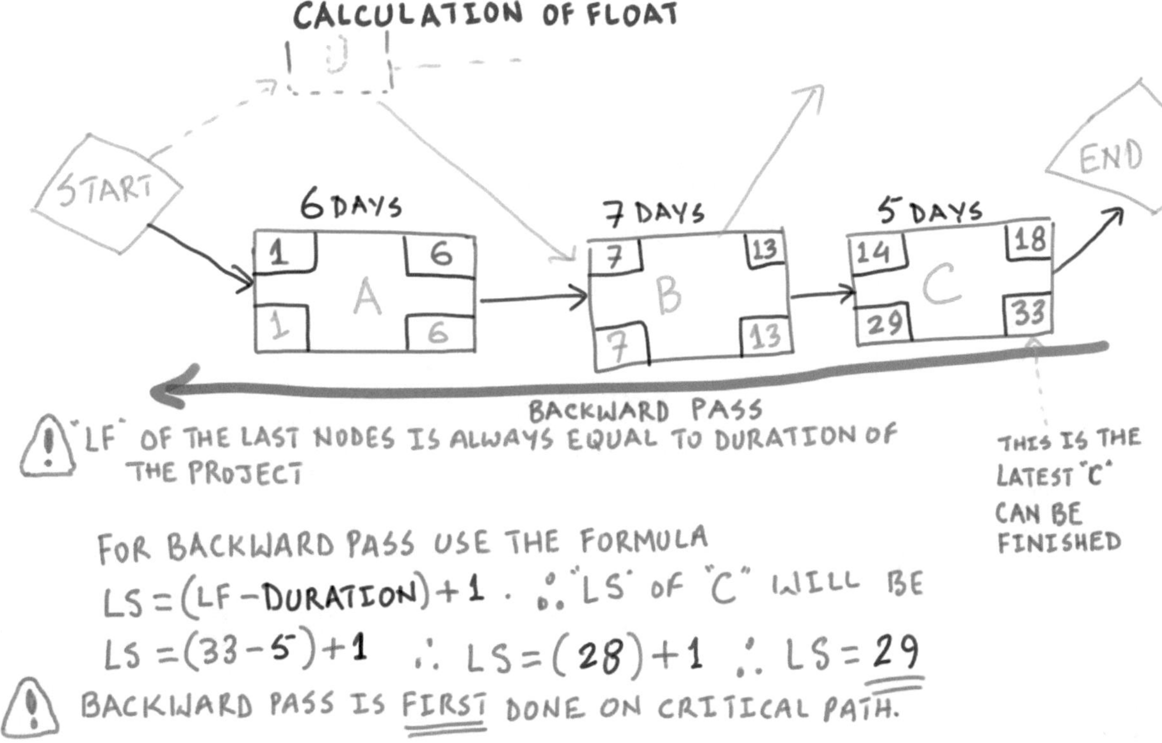
CALCULATION OF FLOAT
START
END
6 DAYS
7 DAYS
5 DAYS
A
B
C
1
6
1
6
7
13
7
13
14
18
29
33
BACKWARD PASS
"LF" OF THE LAST NODES IS ALWAYS EQUAL TO DURATION OF THE PROJECT
THIS IS THE LATEST "C" CAN BE FINISHED
FOR BACKWARD PASS USE THE FORMULA
LS = (LF − DURATION) + 1 . ∴ "LS" OF "C" WILL BE
LS = (33 − 5) + 1 ∴ LS = (28) + 1 ∴ LS = 29
BACKWARD PASS IS FIRST DONE ON CRITICAL PATH.

Since the total duration of the project is 33 Days the LF of activity "B" would be 33. The duration of activity "B" is 5, therefore, LF – Duration or 33 – 5 = 28. Hence LS should be 28. But that is not true. Remember we are doing inclusive counting. Hence we would add "1" to this and LS which would make it 29. Simply use the formula **LS = (LF – Duration) + 1**. Let us apply this again in activities "C, H, G, F and A". The Keep on using the backward formula. Did you notice something that on the critical path the ES = LS and EF = LF this is why there is no float/slack on the critical path activities? But notice on activity "C" the EF is not the same as LF and ES is not the same as LS. LS – ES = Float and so is LF – EF. Hence the float on activity C is 15 days.
Go back and do this again to hone your skills.

EXAMS
SPECIAL

A network diagram can have more than one critical path and the duration of them would be the same. The activities on the critical path (Critical activities) cannot have a positive float but can have a negative float which would mean that the project is running behind schedule. Float means exactly the same thing as Slack which means the amount of time-units you can delay any activity without delaying the project. A critical path is not created by the scheduler. The critical path is created by the way predecessor/dependencies/relationships are created among activities and need to be found out by the scheduler. The ES, EF, LS, and LF should always be calculated on the critical path first. The simplest way to see if any activity is on critical path or not is to see if there is a difference in values of ES and LS or EF and LF. If there is a difference than the activity is NOT on critical path.

Ok, let us practice this just one more time. Given below is a small network diagram where some of the ES, EF, LF, and LS have been filled in. You have to fill in the empty ones and calculate the float.

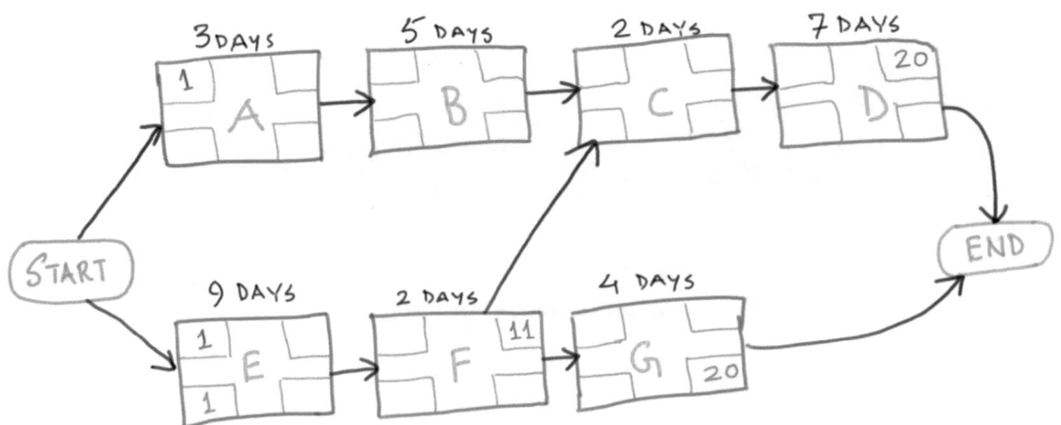

In case you found some difficulty in this than remember that the critical path has to be found out and the forward pass must be done on that first followed by the other non-critical activities. And same is the case with Backward pass which has to be first done on the critical path before working on any other activity. And well you must remember to use the Forward pass formula and the backward pass formula.
Check your answer with the completed network diagram shown below.

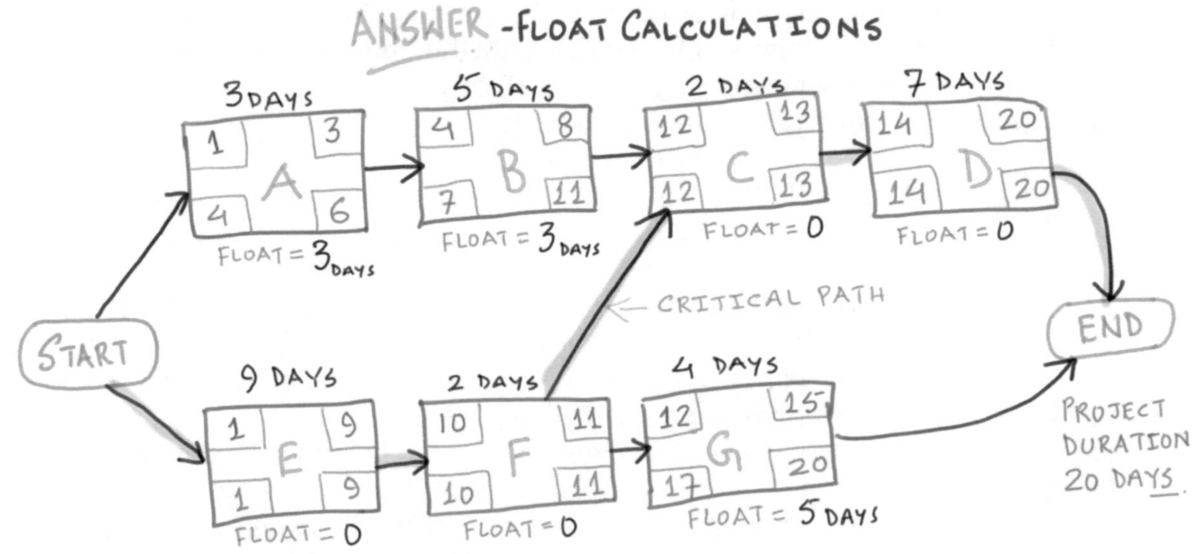

* THE TRICK/RULE IS TO DO FORWARD PASS ON CRITICAL PATH FIRST. LATER DO THE OTHER PATHS.

* DO EXACTLY THE SAME IN BACKWARD PATH.

It is important to note here that critical path must be found out even in the schedule made for an iteration in adaptive methodology projects.

A variant of the Critical Path Method is **Critical Chain Method,** (does not show up in PMP Exams these days) it is a method which was propagated by a genius by the name of Eliyahu M. Goldratt and this concept is basically based on the "Theory Of Constraint" (TOC). Though this tool is not specifically mentioned in PMBOK® Guide but there are chances that it may show up in exams. And besides, there is nothing wrong with knowing a few things more around scheduling and project management. This concept builds upon the Critical Path Method with the assumption that there would not always be enough resources available all the time. In theory, if there is an unlimited supply of resources to be used in the project as and when required with apt competency, than the Critical Chain would be the same as Critical Path Method. However in reality when you assign limited resources on your project you find that because of limited resources your Critical path may change (Critical path may also change due to resource leveling). This is an advanced concept and is basically outside the scope of the level of understanding we need at PMP® level. However, since this is a very important theory it needs mentioning.

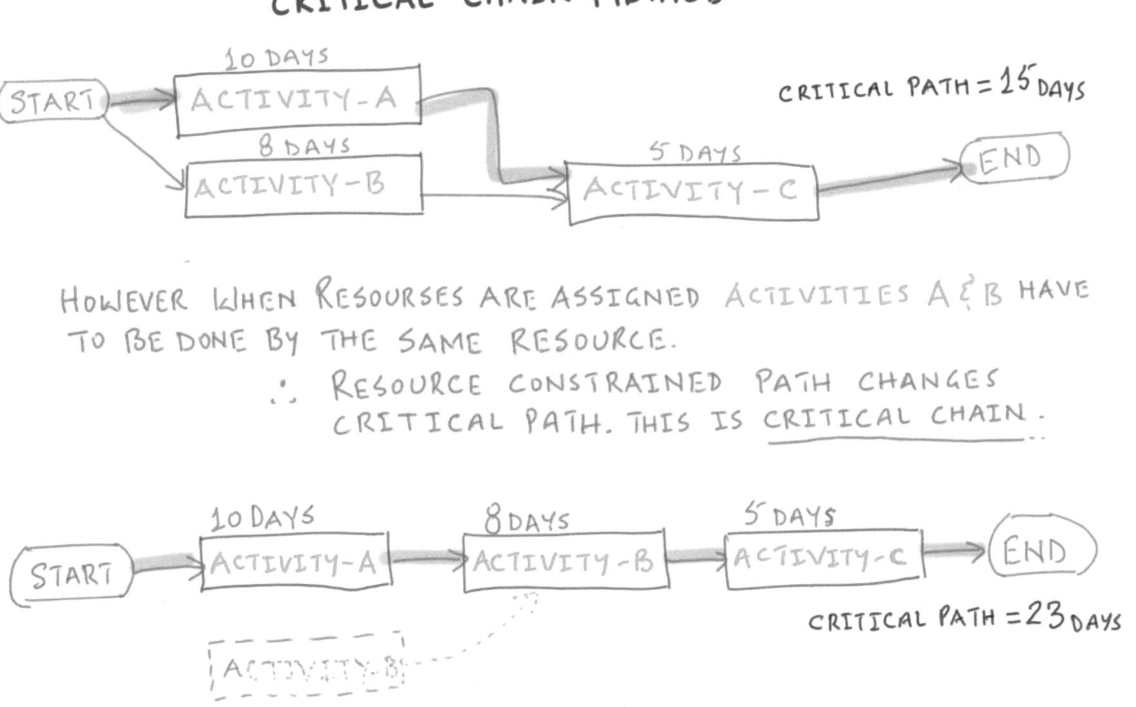

A duration is assigned to each task. Some software implementations add a second duration: one a "best guess," or 50% probability duration, and a second "safe" duration, which should have a higher probability of completion (perhaps 90% or 95%, depending on the amount of risk that the organization can accept). Other software implementations go through the duration estimate of every task and remove a fixed percentage to be aggregated into the buffers.

Resources are assigned to each task, and the plan is resource leveled, using the aggressive durations. The longest sequence of resource-leveled tasks that lead from beginning to end of the project is then identified as the critical chain. The justification for using the 50% estimates is that half of the tasks will finish early and half will finish late so that the variance over the course of the project should be zero.

Recognizing that tasks are more likely to take more time than less time due to Parkinson's law, Student syndrome, or other reasons, Critical Chain Method uses "buffers" to monitor project schedule and financial performance. The "extra" duration of each task on the critical chain—the difference between the "safe" durations and the 50% durations—is gathered in a buffer at the end of the project. In the same way, buffers are gathered at the end of each sequence of tasks that feed into the critical chain. The date at the end of the project buffer is given to external stakeholders as the delivery date. Finally, a baseline is established, which enables financial monitoring of the project.

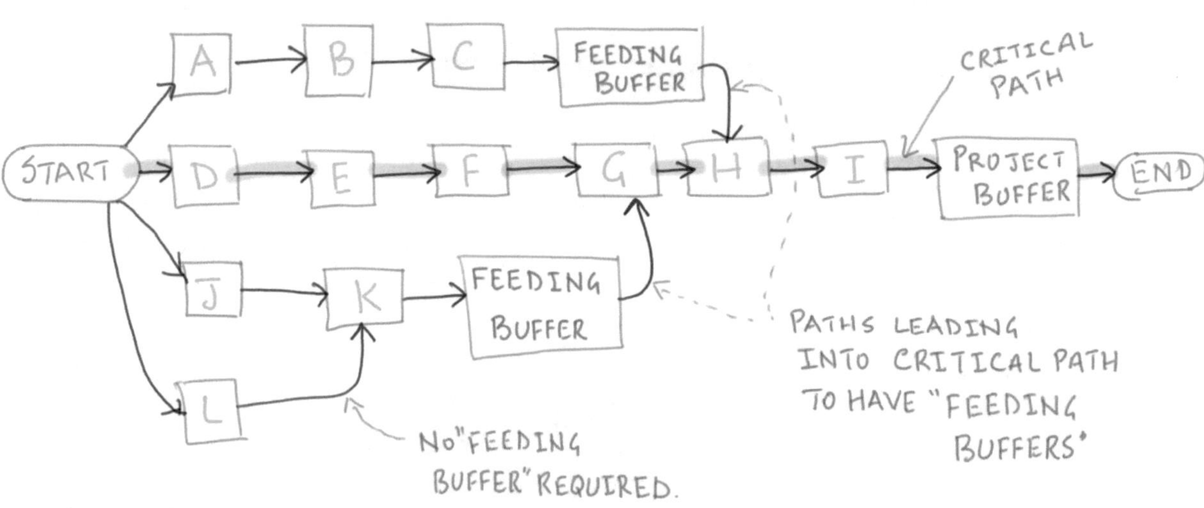

Resource Optimization Techniques are needed because while applying resources to the schedule and also trying to achieve the milestones some or all resources may get over-allocated. There could also be a situation where some resources are overbooked and some have a lot less work. In such a situation the Project manager must make an attempt at reducing such load imbalances.
There are basically two distinct kinds of Resource Optimization and any one of them could be used for optimization depending on the situation and constraints of the project.

RESOURCE OPTIMIZATION TECHNIQUES

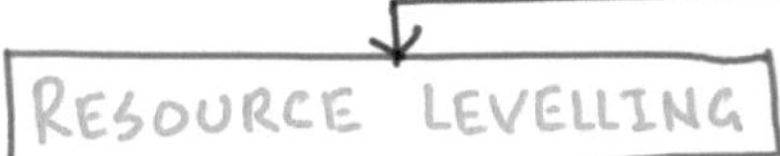

- → WORKING HOURS OF RESOURCES ARE FIXED.
- → MORE RESOURCES ARE PUT ON PROJECT IF AVAILABLE
- → IF NOT AVAILABLE, ACTIVITIES ARE DELAYED/ELONGATED TO ENSURE FIXED WORKING HOURS FOR RESOURCES.

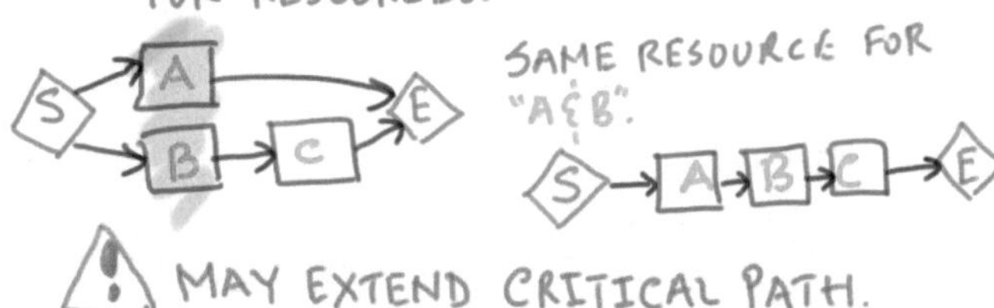

⚠ MAY EXTEND CRITICAL PATH.

RESOURCE SMOOTHING

- → DURATION MORE IMPORTANT THAN RESOURCE WORKING HOURS.
- → RESOURCES MAY WORK SOME AMOUNT OF EXTRA HOURS
- → EXTRA HOURS OF WORK SOMEWHAT EQUALLY DISTRIBUTED AMONG RESOURCES.

⚠ DOES NOT EXTEND CRITICAL PATH.
MAY REQUIRE OVERTIME.

If you have flexibility towards project duration or your organization has strict policies about the number of hours a resource can work, then the best option is to go for Resource Levelling, but it may increase/change your critical path. However, if the project constraints are such that milestones are non-negotiable then it makes more sense to opt for Resource Smoothing where the critical path is maintained but the optimization may not be total or very well defined. Some imbalances will always remain in Smoothing.

Data Analysis:
There are two techniques which are most common. One is "What-if Analysis". This technique is just as it sounds. The planners keep changing certain aspects of the schedule to see its effect on the overall schedule to uncover how the schedule would react under adverse or unexpected conditions to finally decide on the best "Settings" for the project at hand. Things like "What if we make all our resources work for 6 days in a week instead of 5 day week?" and then record, document and see how the project schedule reacts to the same. "What if we increase the working hours from 8 to 9 hrs.?", "What if we replace the existing resources with more efficient but high priced resources working for shorter durations?". "What if we overlap some activities to shorten the schedule?" and so on. However, in order to conduct any meaningful "What-if" analysis, the use of sophisticated scheduling software is imperative. "What-if" analysis is also used for risk events *e.g., "What if the work force goes on a strike during execution phase for 2 weeks?". "What if the supplier in China is banned from supplying due to possible government regulations?", "What if the price of raw material shoots up?" and so on.*
The other technique is "Simulation". Here probability and statistics is used to find the possibility of meeting the timelines or to find out different possible durations based on differing assumptions. This is usually done using complex mathematical models with "Data Spread" (upper limits and lower limits of assumptions) and sophisticated software engines like "Monte Carlo" is used for the same. This is usually done for mission-critical

projects "*e.g. A satellite Launch or a Cantilever bridge construction", but would be an over-kill for any average project.*

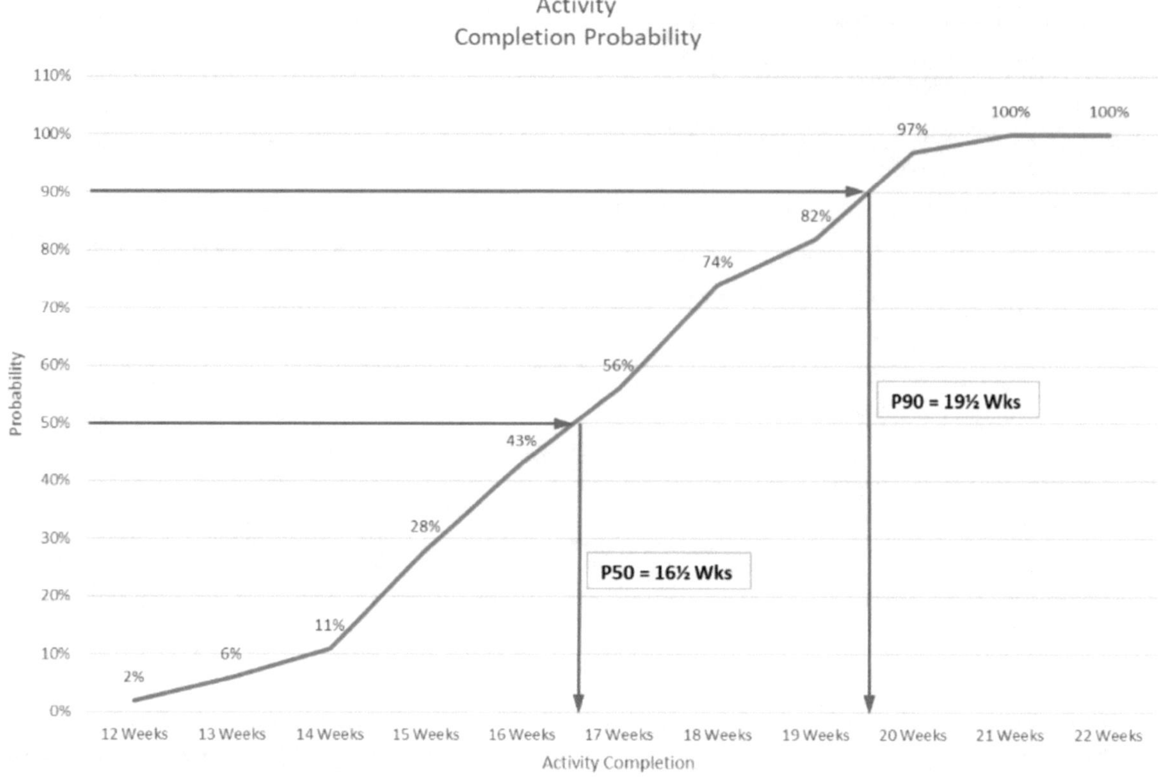

Monte Carlo has to be fed with a lot of permutation parameters such that the tool itself may generate 1,000s of combinations and show the overall chance of the completion of an activity or group of activities or the entire project, by a specific date. This tool, however, relies on very high quality and reliable historical data or "Intelligence" based data, therefore, if this data is not reliable or the intelligence data is arbitrary than the entire "Output" would be of no use. The challenge in using this application in the real world is that most organizations do not keep "honest" and "reliable" historical data.

When in a question Monte-Carlo is mentioned and one of the 4 options has either "Simulation" or "What-if" analysis than that is the right answers. This rule applies Vice-versa as well.

Leads and Lags (which have already been explained before) may need to be adjusted or re-looked at to ensure that the schedule is meeting the practical and targeted time constraints.

Schedule Compression may be needed to ensure that the "Ideal" project schedule becomes a "Realistic Schedule" that meets the timelines as enforced by the customer or the stakeholders. Specifically, in projects which are very sensitive to project timeline, there would be a need to compress the schedule. There are only two ways to compress a schedule without compromising on the Scope of the project. One is called Crashing and the other is called Fast-tracking. Crashing means that more resources are assigned to the critical path to shorten the overall duration of the project. Crashing will only work if it's done on the Critical path, for obvious reasons. However, this method may not always give you the desired results because human resource does not always give linear productivity. Human resources suffer from something known as the Law Of Diminishing Returns. Let us understand that with an example. Say there are 2 people working on an activity which will probably finish in 10 days. In order to make it finish earlier if we assign 2 more people (making the total 4 persons) it's not necessary that the duration would become 5. Human resources need time to get productive and hence though, the overall duration would be reduced it would not be linear. Therefore, in reality, the duration would reduce to say about 6 or 7 days. This means that we are paying more for resources and not getting the benefits in the same measure. This is basically the concept of Laws of Diminishing Returns. This does increase costs, oversight, and conflicts. Hence Crashing, though, is a common method applied by many project professionals, is not the best method and should be applied with a lot of caution.

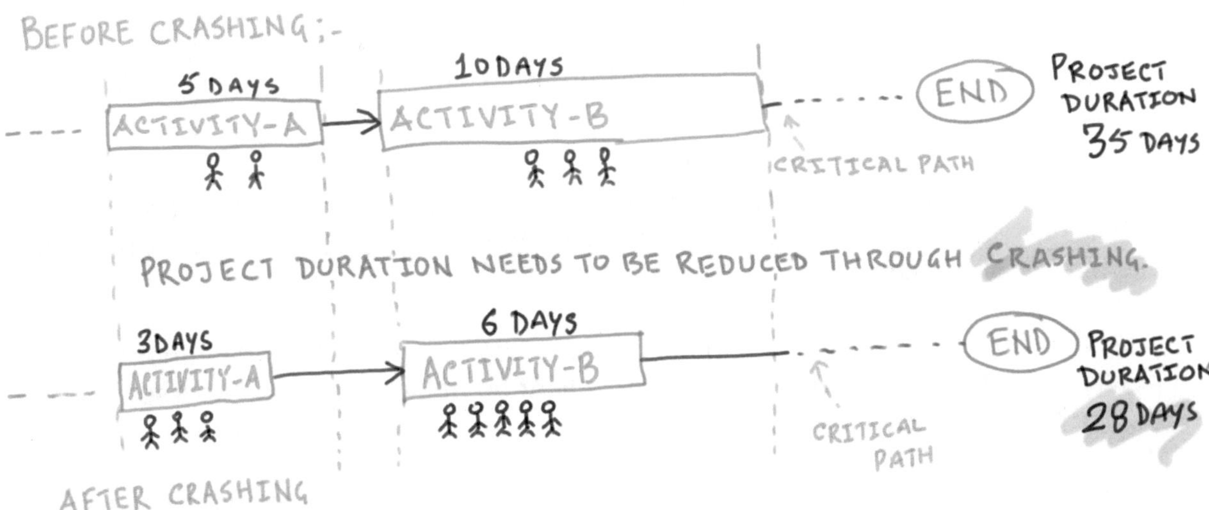

The other method of schedule compression is Fast-tracking. What it basically means is to look at the dependencies among activities which are on the critical path and try to alter them by looking at possibilities of making them overlap (Creating LEADS among critical path relationships). This usually does not increase the cost but may end up increasing risks due to overlapping of activities. *E.g., the designing of the software has to be complete before the construction of the same can start. However, the project planning team could look at starting some work or putting the construction platform and machinery in place before the design is approved just to save on time.* Now, this may not add to the cost but this does increase the risks. What if the design gets rejected?

Besides, there are a lot of activities which have a fixed dependency and cannot be altered.

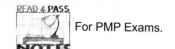

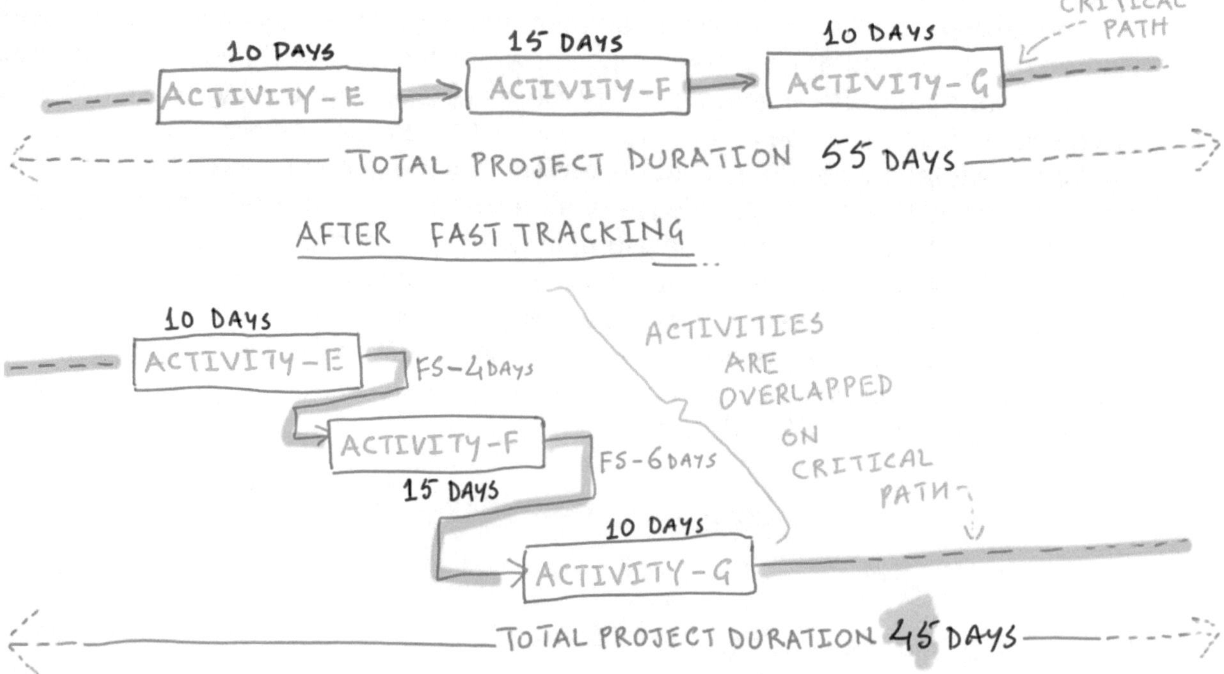

Hence the most practical rule has been to compress the schedule by first trying Fast-tracking on critical activities and in case the target of the compression is not obtained only then go for Crashing.

And to do all such analysis and compression and lead and lag adjustments as well as to calculate the critical path and determine float on activities, its best to use a **scheduling tool** to make it easier and practical.

Agile Release Planning, just as the name suggests, is a high-level and summary timeline of the various “Releases” that are planned in this project which is being done using one of the Agile Methodologies. In agile the deliverables are delivered using multiple Phases/cycles/ sprints. Hence this plan gives an overview of “When would each of the sprints start and end and in which sequence?”

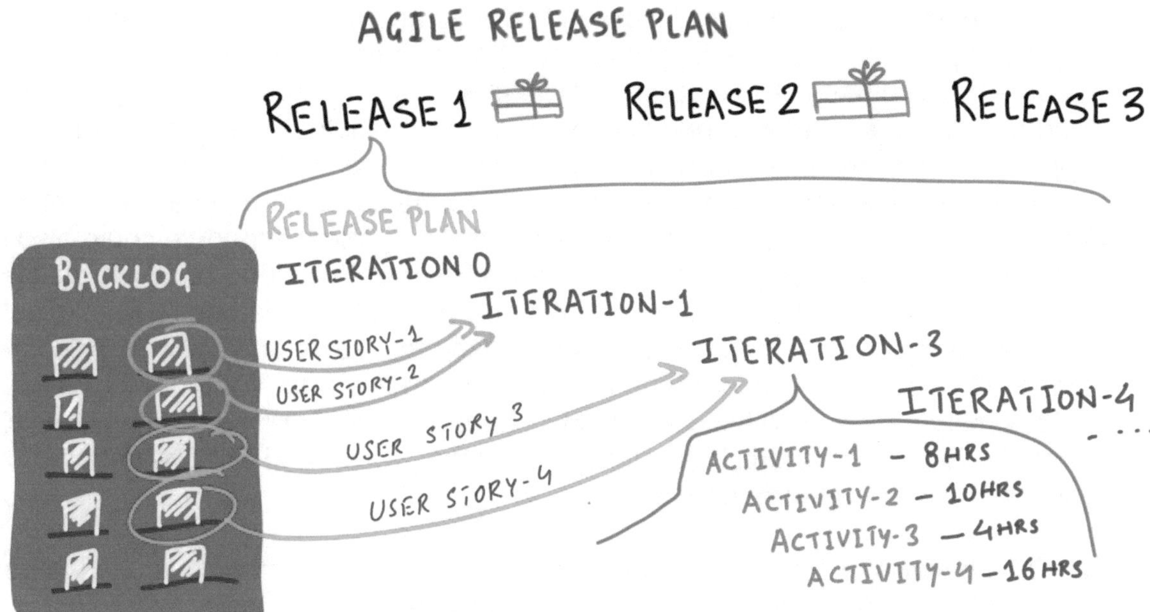

There are some terms that we must know from the point of view of Agile. This will help you understand agile a bit better (just in case you are not fully aware of it) and also understand where and how to use them. Agile is a methodology and NOT an alternate to Project Management. Agile is called so because it tends to "Show Results" earlier to the customer and is also suited for situations where the requirements are not stable and a lot of changes are expected during the lifecycle of the project.

Typically the whole Agile project is made up of "Releases". Each of the Releases provides a set of "Features" or "Abilities" that the customer can start using even before the entire project is over. *E.g., If the project is about agile deployment of internet banking system in a bank then the "Release – 1" could be about "Retail Banking", "Release – 2" could be about Home loan application, "Release – 3" could be about corporate banking and so on. Once Release 1 is delivered to the customer bank they can start the "Retail Banking" part of the internet banking and start doing business on it while the development is going on for "Release 2".* Now each of these Releases is made up of multiple "Iterations". Sometimes, in a "Release", the first Iteration could be called "Iteration Zero" to indicate that it's a planning iteration. All the features to be given out in the Release are broken down into "User Stories" (absolutely small level requirements/business rules) and it's decided how many user stories would be done in each of the iterations. As the iterations are being executed the customer could keep changing or revising user stories for the next set of iterations based on the outcome of the previous iterations. Once all the iterations in a release are successfully closed, it results in a "Release Delivered" to the customer.

9.13.2 Main Outcomes of the process Develop Schedule:

Schedule Baseline is the final approved schedule which would be used for comparing with actuals, during execution, to see if the project is on schedule or ahead or behind schedule. The only way to alter the Schedule Baseline (like any other baseline) is through a formal Change Control Management (something we will cover a bit later in this book).

Another main purpose of this process is to create an output called, **Project Schedule**. The final approved schedule is nothing but the Schedule Baseline. The schedule is a live document which needs to be updated systematically and regularly during the life of the project. There are various versions of the project schedule. Where there are multiple projects being undertaken under a single program there could be a "Master Schedule" which embeds the other schedules within it. The master schedule can be used to link two different schedules of the sub-projects under it. The project schedule could also be in a summary form where only the summary tasks are visible instead of all the tasks. The Project schedule could also be such that it only displays "Milestones". Such a schedule is called a Milestone Schedule and it's usually used for presenting the status/progress to the Clients, Customers or Senior Management as there is no use for them to get into unnecessary details. The typical Project Schedule is the Detailed Schedule which is normally used by the project manager to track the project and to have detailed discussions with his team members.

One of the views of the project schedule is the Network View which is used to assess the various kinds of dependencies among the activities.

MILESTONE CHART

TASK NAME	DURATION	GANTT - TIME LINE
GIFT STORE PROJECT	60 DAYS	
LOCATION	13 DAYS	
LEASE SIGNED	0 DAYS	◆ 8/18
RENOVATION	12 DAYS	
STORE RENOVATED	0 DAYS	◆ 9/9
DECORATION	15 DAYS	
STORE DECORATED	0 DAYS	◆ 9/27
INVENTORY	41 DAYS	
INVENTORY READY	0 DAYS	◆ 10/18

SUMMARY SCHEDULE

S.No	TASK NAME	DURATION	GANTT CHART - TIME LINE
1.	GIFT STORE PROJECT	60 DAYS	
2.	⊞ LOCATION	13 DAYS	
3.	⊞ RENOVATION	15 DAYS	
4.	⊞ DECORATION	12 DAYS	
5.	⊞ INVENTORY	41 DAYS	
6.	— — — — —	— -	— -
7.	— — — —	— -	
8.	— — — -	— -	

GANTT CHART

S.No.	TASK NAME	DURATION	GANTT CHART - TIME LINE
1.	GIFT STORE PROJECT	60 DAYS	
2.	⊟ LOCATION	13 DAYS	
3.	RESEARCH LOCATIONS	6 DAYS	
4.	VISIT LOCATIONS	2 DAYS	
5.	SELECT LOCATION	1 DAY	
6.	LEASE THE LOCATION	4 DAYS	8/18
7.	LEASE SIGNED	0 DAYS	
8.	⊟ RENOVATION	15 DAYS	
9.	CONTACT CONTRACTOR	5 DAYS	
10.	RELOCATE WALLS	8 DAYS	
11.	INSTALL WIRING	4 DAYS	9/9
12.	STORE RENOVATED	0 DAYS	
13.	⊟ DECORATION	—	
14.	— — — —	— -	—
15.	— — — —	— —	— — -

Schedule Model: is a representation of the plan for executing the project's activities including durations, dependencies, and other planning information, used to produce a project schedule along with other scheduling artefacts.
Project Schedule is a part of Schedule Model.

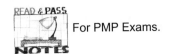

Project Calendars are the days and time periods on which project work would happen. *E.g., 5 day week for this project to be done in India. Or, Say for a project being done in*

Bahrain (an Islamic country that follows Hijri calendar system) the working days would be from Sunday to Thursday and the off days would be from Friday to Saturday. In tropical countries, the timings of the project may be such that there is no work to be done from 12 noon till 3 pm because of intense heat. It also lists down the non-working time and days as well as the different working time for different shifts available or project work, in case the project work has been planned to be done in shifts.

Please remember that a "Schedule Baseline" is part of the Project Management Plan and is not a live document. It is used for reference purposes. However the "Project Schedule" is a live document that regularly gets updated with what is actually going on in the project. Remember Schedule Variance = Schedule Baseline – Project Schedule (with latest actual information).

9.14 Ninja Drill – Planning - 2

In this Ninja Drill you will find the most important notes and pointers that are important from the point of PMP Exams and covers, Plan Schedule Management, Define Activities, Sequence Activities, Estimate Activity Resources, Estimate Activity Duration and Develop Schedule.

S. No.	Drill Points
1.	The main purpose of the process Define Scope is to help identify all possible activities for predictive projects or for the next iteration for the adaptive projects.
2.	The main Tools & Techniques of the process "Define Activities" are Decomposition and Rolling Wave Planning.
3.	The main outputs / outcomes / artefacts of the process "Define Activities" are: 1. List of activities 2. Attributes list 3. Milestone list
4.	Sequence Activities = Network Diagram = Activity On Node (AON) = Precedence Diagramming Method (PDM)
5.	Finish To Start [FS] is the most common kind of relationship among activities. Start To Finish [SF] is the least used kind of relationship among activities.
6.	Lag is a scheduled gap between two or more activities.
7.	Lead is a scheduled overlap between two or more activities.
8.	The main Tools & Techniques of the process "Estimate Activity Resources" are: 1. Analogous Estimating 2. Parametric Estimating 3. Single point estimating 4. Bottom-Up Estimating
9.	The main outcomes / outputs / artefacts for the process "Estimate Activity Resources" are: 1. Resource Requirements 2. Resource Breakdown Structure (RBS)
10.	Resource Breakdown Structure (RBS) is a hierarchical depiction of the category and kinds of resources needed for the project
11.	The earlier in the project lifecycle the Estimates are done the lesser accuracy they would have. While, the later the estimates are made the more accurate they are.
12.	The average range of accuracy of different levels of estimation are: 1. Rough / Order Of Magnitude – Range -25% to +75% 2. Analogous / Parametric Estimating - Range - 10% to +25% 3. Bottom Up Estimating – Range -5% to +10%
13.	The main Tools & Techniques of the process "Estimate Activity Durations" are: 1. Affinity Grouping 2. Analogous Estimating 3. Function Point 4. Multipoint Estimating 5. Parametric Estimating 6. Relative Estimating 7. Single Point Estimating 8. Story Point 9. Wideband Delphi
14.	T-Shirt Sizing is an example of "Affinity Grouping".
15.	Analogous Estimating is when the Duration of activities from a similar historical project is used to estimate the current project.
16.	Function Point Estimating is an estimate of the amount of business functionality in an information system. Function points are used to calculate a functional size measurement (FSM) of a software system.
17.	Multipoint Estimating = Three Point Estimating = Beta Distribution

18.	Parametric estimating uses an algorithm to calculate cost or duration based on historical data and project parameters.
19.	Single-point estimating involves using data to calculate a single value that reflects a best-guess estimate.
20.	Story Point estimating involves project team members assigning abstract, but relative, points of effort required to implement a user story.
21.	Wideband Delphi is a variation of the Delphi estimating method where subject matter experts complete multiple rounds of producing estimates individually, with a project team discussion after each round, until a consensus is achieved. (Can be Anonymous as well).
22.	Examples of Single Point Estimates are 1) Function Point 2) Bottom Up 3) Expert Input
23.	Examples of Historical Estimates are: 1) Analogous Estimates 2) Parametric Estimates
24.	Examples of Relative Estimates are: 1) Simple – Moderate – Complex 2) T-Shirt Sizing 3) Story Points
25.	Examples of 3 point or multipoint estimates: 1) 3 Point Estimating 2) Simple Average
26.	Examples of Consensus Based Estimating: 1) Wide-Band Delphi 2) Planning Poker
27.	The main outcome / output / artefact of the process “Estimate Activity Duration” is Duration Estimates.
28.	The main Tools & Techniques of the process “Develop Schedule” are: 1. Critical Path Method 2. Schedule Compression 3. Agile Release Planning
29.	The longest path in a schedule is called the “Critical Path”.
30.	Activities on critical path have “0” float / slack. When the float is negative on critical path activities, it means that the project is running behind schedule.
31.	Float = Slack = Total Float = The amount of time an activity can be delayed without delaying the project.
32.	Free Float is the amount of time an activity can be delayed without delaying the subsequent activity or activities.
33.	Sometimes in exams you may come across term called “Team Task Accountability”. This term is directly connected to Schedule / Gantt Chart. The best tool to develop “Team Task accountability” is a schedule with resources assigned to each of the tasks.
34.	While using “Forward Pass” the correct formula to find the value of EF is EF = (ES + Duration) – 1.
35.	While using the “Backward Pass” the correct formula to find the value of LS is LS = (LF – Duration) + 1.
36.	There are only two ways to compress a schedule and they are Fast-tracking and Crashing.
37.	Fast-tracking is making more tasks concurrent on critical path to reduce duration.
38.	Crashing is applying more resources to activities on critical path to reduce their duration.
39.	The main outputs / outcomes / artefacts of the process “Develop Schedule” are: 1) Schedule Baseline 2) Schedule Model 3) Project Calendars 4) Project Schedule
40.	Project Schedule is a part of Schedule Model.
	End Of Ninja Drill

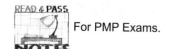

9.15 Planning For Cost And Budget (Plan Cost Management)

In these steps of planning a plan is made about how the cost would be estimated and budgeted in this project followed by the project team creating the estimate of the project or the next iteration and finally the management / sponsor approves a budget for the project / iteration. Though all the project processes and phases are interconnected, there is a stronger connection between Time Management Processes and Cost Management Processes. Questions like how many resources and kind of resources are being used for the project and for how long, are directly related to the cost of the project.
This is the planning stage where the Cost Baseline is established.

PROJECT COST MANAGEMENT
TIME
COST
SCOPE
COST BASELINE IS CREATED IN
THIS PLANNING STAGE.

Before we start understanding the internals of this Knowledge Area, it is important to understand basic terms like Price, Cost Estimate, Budget, and Actual Cost. Even though they sound straight forward, they are routinely misunderstood. Hence, I am just clearing the air to ensure that you too understand it correctly.
Price of the project is what you get from the customer for the product of the project or service. Once a Project Manager is assigned a project the Project Manager would want to **estimate** as to how much would it cost the organization in completing the project? This estimation can be based on various techniques to make it more realistic. When the estimates are provided to the sponsor or the management, they may make alterations to it (add or subtract) and provide a **Budget** to the Project Manager. Therefore the budget is nothing but an **Approved Estimate**. **Actual Cost** is what is actually incurred by the end of the project or at the end of any reporting period or project phase. In general, the Budget is supposed to be less than the price to keep a profit margin and the regular tracking is done to ensure that the actual costs are within the budget.

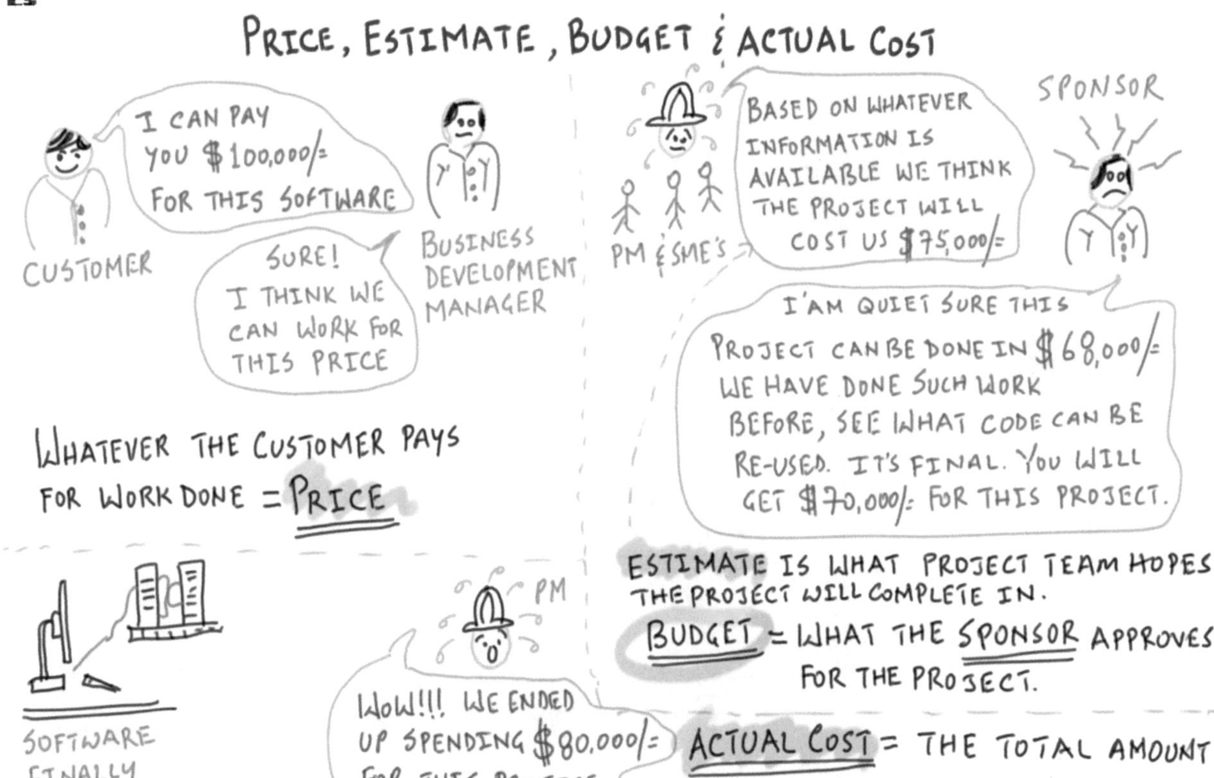

However, budget being always less than the price is not a standard rule. Depending on the kind of the project the price may be less than the budget or the budget may be more than the cost estimate or the actual cost may be much higher than anticipated. Say, you are a civil contractor and you wish to enter government project domain and you have never done such projects before. To be able to get in, you might have to use excessively low pricing even though you know that the actual cost may be much higher than what you are charging. But you are doing this only to get in and build experience. Hence this is where you would have purposely kept the price lower than budget and at the end when you see the total actual cost it would give you insights as to what all is involved in a Government project and how to estimate or bid for them in future.

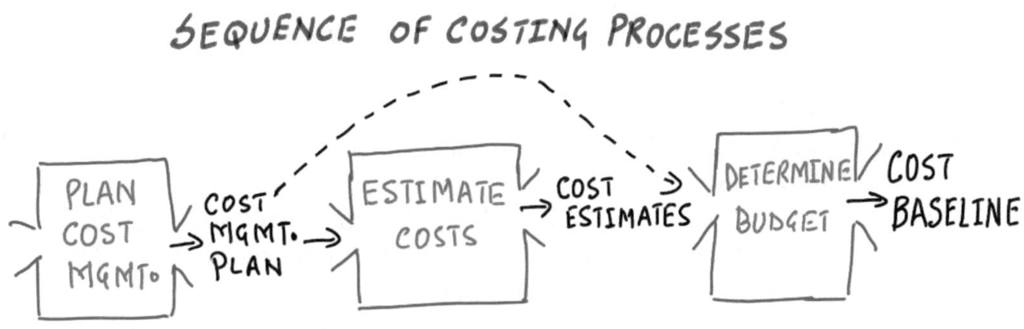

Another element of Project Cost Management is the occasional use of the concept of Life Cycle Costing. Lifecycle Costing is taking into account not only the cost of the project but also what the product of the project would cost to the client, post-handover, through maintenance, running costs, overheads and upkeep. Some projects may require a focus on the Lifecycle costing while some projects may not.

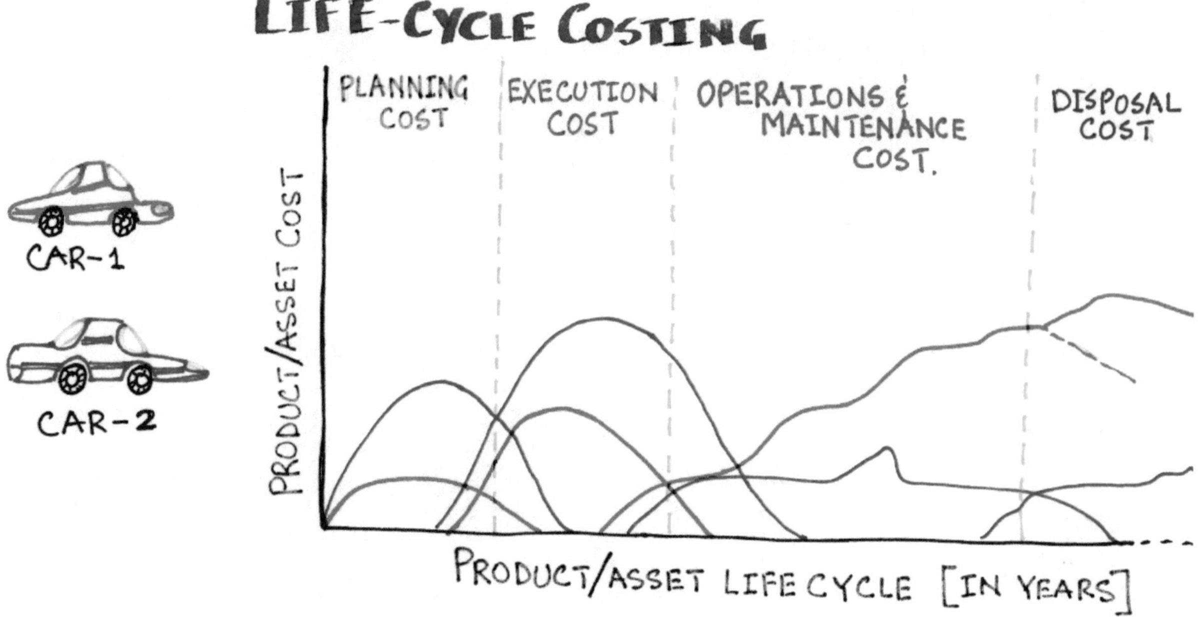

It is quite evident that the blue car has a higher cost to make but its total Lifecycle cost is way less than that of the red car which is cheaper to buy but significantly expensive to maintain and run. Quality comes at a cost and hence all the amount of money that is spent on achieving and or maintaining quality in a project is called the "Cost of Quality (COQ)".

At this time it's also important that the scope of "Cost Management" is understood. The cost management is about the management and tracking of costs only until the project ends. It does not include the "Financial and cost management" once the product of the project becomes operational. The financial earnings from the operations part have nothing to do with Project Cost Management of the project.

I know, I know, you may get this feeling …. Just a paragraph back this book was saying that costing a project should include "Lifecycle Costing" and now it is saying that the "Project Cost Management" has a scope only for the "Project Part" of the product and not the operations part. Well, let me try to explain this dilemma better. When the parents spend a lifetime bringing up their child and instilling values in the child which will last the child a lifetime, but their scope of work ends once the child leaves the parents' house and strikes out into the world on his own. The decisions made by the parents about the kind of education, value system, guidance were all based not only on the immediate future or till the time the child moves out but it was based on the lifetime of the child. Similarly in cost management, though the cost incurred on the project may take into consideration the "Lifecycle cost" of the project but the moment the project is handed over to the operations the scope of work of the project cost management is over. This would have nothing to do with the actual profits or losses earned from this product during its operations. Comprandi? ("Did you understand?" in Italian with Godfather accent)

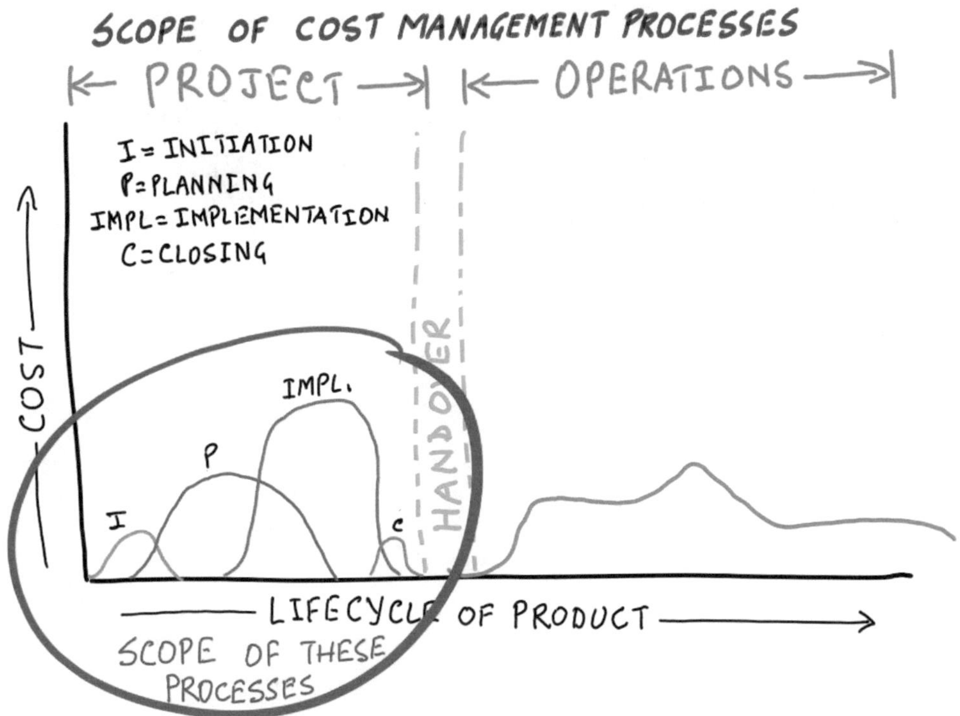

9.16 Developing Cost Management Plan

I am sure you can see a pattern here. "Look before Leaping". There is a mini (subsidiary) plan for every aspect of the project. The subsidiary plans are now increasingly called project plan components. It's these mini plans that come together to form the complete and comprehensive "Project Management Plan". The aim of this process is to produce a practical and effective Cost Management Plan which could be used for cost management within the project at hand. This process establishes the procedure, granularity, currency, thresholds etc. connected to the estimating, budgeting and controlling of the costs in the project. The more detailed and granular the cost management plan the more practical it becomes.

At this point it is important not to forget that when the methodology that is being used is Adaptive (Iterative, Incremental or Agile) then the project management plan would not be so detailed. There would be an overall rough plan without too much granularity while there would be a more detailed plan for each of the iteration that is going to be executed next. From the point of view of the PMP exams you need to keep this kind of mental flexibility to quickly shift between Predictive and Adaptive methodologies.

9.17 Estimate Costs

This is the process where the total project cost is estimated. This is where the project manager and the project management team and some stakeholders come together to estimate, as realistically as possible, based on the information available, as to how much the project would cost till completion. An attempt is also made at this time to breakdown the estimates to a more granular level (say phase level or even activity level).

Many organizations get this part of management rather incorrectly. They tend to forget that the “Estimates” are just that, estimates, and not a commitment. Estimates are made under the conditions and information known at a specific point of time and there is always a degree of variance from what would happen actually. The trick is to identify all possible elements of the project and then try to estimate at the most granular level as possible to become as close to reality as possible. However sometimes there are time constraints and sometimes, not everything about the project is known upfront. In such cases, estimates are done in a more superficial manner and would tend to have a higher degree of variance. In fact, there is a chart of variances that can be referred to for allowable degree of variance from reality based on the kind of estimate done.

KINDS OF COST ESTIMATE

S.NO.	KIND OF COST ESTIMATE	ACCURACY	WHEN USED?
1	ROUGH/ORDER OF MAGNITUDE/BALL-PARK	-25% to +75%	PRESALES, VERY EARLY IN THE PROJECT.
2.	BUDGET ESTIMATE	-10% to +25%	EARLY PLANNING PROCESSES BUT WITH MORE INFOR-MATION.
3.	BOTTUM-UP ESTIMATE OR DERIVATIVE OR DEFINITIVE OR DETERMINISTIC	-5% to +10%	LATER IN PLANNING WHEN ALMOST ALL INFORMATION IS AVAILABLE. WBS IS USED HERE.

When the costs are estimated they are estimated based on various elements of costs applicable to the project at hand. There are 4 kinds of cost elements. The Cost Element Types could be "Variable Cost or Fixed Cost" or "Direct Cost or Indirect Cost". Variable Cost is a cost element type that varies based on the usage of the resource. *E.g., Fuel, Cement, Labor, Steel etc., therefore, the more quantity or numbers that are utilized the more the cost would be and vice versa. Basically, such cost elements affect the cost on "rate basis".* Fixed Cost, on the other hand, is a cost element type which is independent of the "rate of use". It's a fixed cost element that would be added to your project cost no matter how much you use it or even when not used at all. *E.g., An office rented for project work, Contractor hired for serving coffee and doughnuts at the project site on a fixed price model, Bus rented for a year for staff transportation.*
The Direct cost is a cost element that is charged only and only to a specific project. *E.g., Road roller machine hired only for the road construction project, IT Professionals assigned to a specific project, Food organized for staff staying back late at night because of a specific project.* Basically, all costs that are only charged to a specific project and not any other project. Indirect cost is a cost element that is not charged to a specific project but apportioned over all projects and other work going on within the organization. *E.g., Office Electricity, Office Cafeteria contractors fees, Climate control in the office building and so on.*

What needs to be understood that each cost estimable element would be one of the following 4 kinds viz., "Direct and variable" or "Direct and Fixed" or "Indirect and variable" or "Indirect and Fixed".

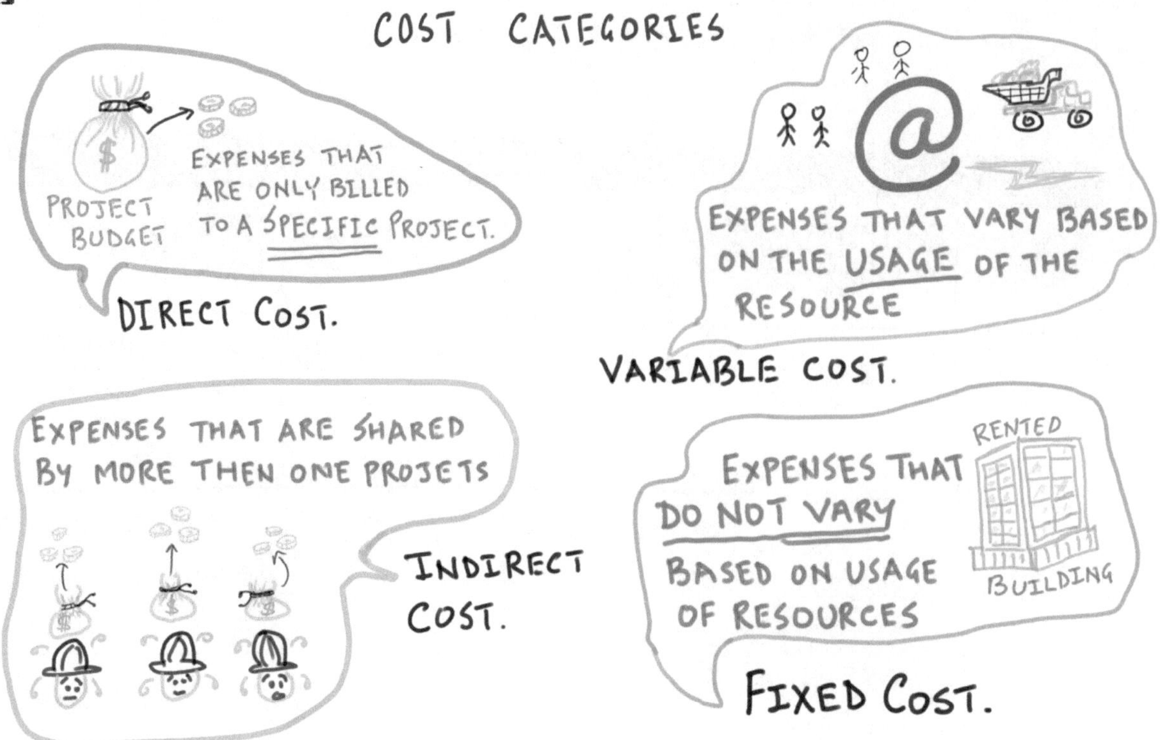

E.g., A building taken on rent for the entire office is an example of "Indirect – Fixed Cost"; All the electricity bill of the organization becomes "Indirect – Variable Cost"; All the material used for a specific project becomes "Direct – Variable Cost"; And the Road Roller leased for a specific project of road construction is "Direct – Fixed Cost".

Again, it is important to keep in mind that the estimation is done for each of the iterations separately in adaptive methodologies.

9.17.1 Tools and Techniques for Estimating Costs

1. Analogous Estimating
2. Parametric Estimating
3. Bottom-Up Estimating
4. Three-Point Estimating
5. Commercial Databases

Let us go through each of them.

Analogous Estimating basically means when the historical data of the similar past project is used to estimate the current project (something we discussed during ***ESTIMATE ACTIVITY DURATION*** process). It is creating an Analogy between a past similar project with the current one. This is usually done when much details are not available about the current project or there is not enough time to find out all the details of the project for a detailed estimation.
Though this method works very well while estimating duration and resources for a project, it is a bit tricky when applied to estimating Costs. In this method, the duration and resources and kinds and quantity of the resources are found out based on the previous

similar projects but the cost is calculated based on the current rates and NOT the old rates in historical records.

Analogous estimating is a kind of "Top Down" estimating where an attempt is made to estimate the project without getting into too many details.

Parametric Estimating is also a "Top Down" estimating method, where a standard formula with certain predetermined deliverables is used to estimate the cost of the project. This is quite prevalent in the Civil and Infrastructure and certain streams of oil and gas exploration projects. Here the past data has been analyzed and converted into formulas and these formulas need to be fed certain variables which give the overall size and complexity of the project to generate the cost estimates.
I hope you remember the illustration on analogous estimates in the process *ESTIMATE ACTIVITY DURATIONS*. It's exactly the same here except, here it is for estimating "Cost" instead of "Duration".
If the data analysis has been done properly in creating the standard formulas then the estimation done through this method is much more accurate than the Analogous Estimating method. This is the kind of estimating that is used by some "Civil Engineering" or "Piping and Plumbing" professionals who can give you a quote within minutes when you tell them the "Square Meters and numbers of floors of the house to be constructed" or the "total length of the piping that needs to be done" and so on.

Bottom-Up Estimating is the most detailed method of estimation. This method takes more resources and time (compared to Top Down estimating methods) but is the most accurate method of estimating. This is done by first breaking down the project into the most granular form (best when WBS is used) and then estimating each of the smallest elements at the lowest levels (which is easier to do at such granular levels) and then aggregating them all the way up to the total project level to determine the project cost estimate. Hence the name "Bottom-Up" estimating.

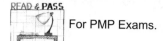

Bottom-Up estimating is also called by 3 other names (all starting with the letter "D" hence 3D) **D**eterministic, **D**erivative and **D**efinitive.

Before we go any further it's important to step back and look at the various estimating methods and their classification. It would be easier to understand this classification now as you already know what each of the terms means.

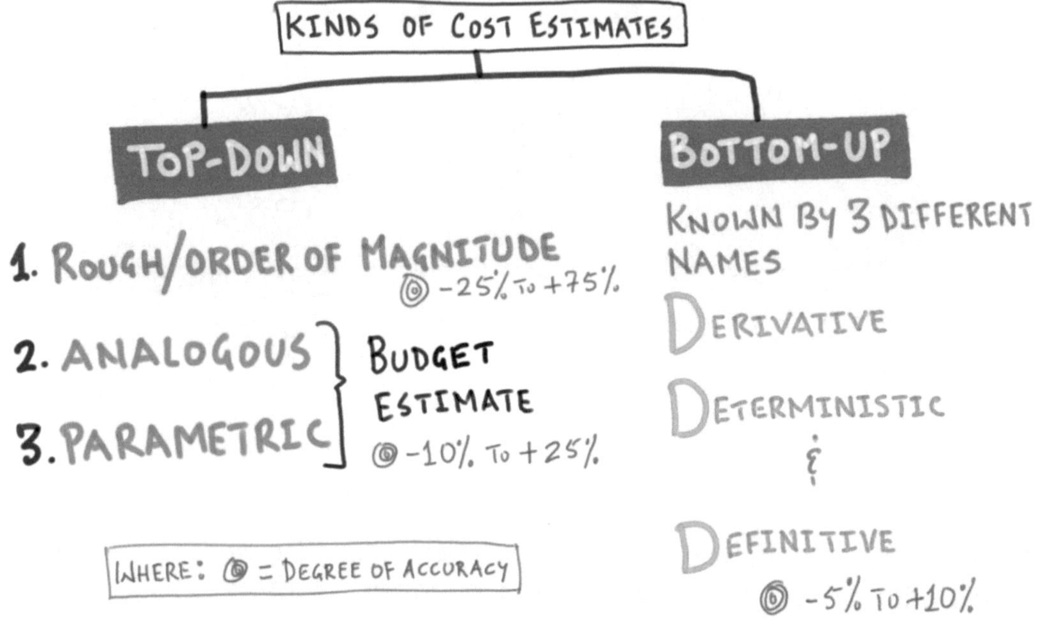

Three Point Estimating (also known as Multipoint Estimating) is not really an estimating technique in itself. It is a technique that is used for reducing the risk associated with obtaining data from people. This is the reason why Three Point Estimating does not feature in the chart above.

Just because Three Point Estimating uses formulas does not make it a Parametric Estimate.

Earlier we understood the functioning of the Three Point estimating technique in the process "*ESTIMATE ACTIVITY DURATIONS*". There we used it for Durations (Time) but here it is used for Cost Estimation. Nothing else changes. It applies exactly in the same way and in the same fashion. I hope you remember Three Point Estimating. If not please go back to the process "*ESTIMATE ACTIVITY DURATION*" earlier in this book.

Commercial Database: Well established and age old industries, like civil construction, road construction, public infrastructure, power sector etc. have something called the commercial database. These databases are a fast look-up table to check the cost for the kind of work and the dimensions and the materials proposed to be used in the project. Yes it is just as simple as that. These are either available on purchase from authorised publishers or are available through industry associations.

COMMERCIAL DATABASE

CIVIL & INFRASTRUCTURE TABLE INDIA (2022-23)

ID. NO.	DESCRIPTION	UNIT OF MEASURE	PROD. RATE	COST (RS)
1.	CONCRETE [PLUM]	CU.M	5 CUM/hr	2,400/CUM
2.	RUBBLE STONE	CUM	3 CUM/hr	2,850/CUM
3.	4 INCH BRICK	SQM	10 SQM/hr	680/SQM

ID. NO.	HUMAN RESOURCE	MEASURE	BASE PRICE	TAX
420	BRICK MASON	HOUR	Rs 120/=	Rs 10/=
611	CEMENT MASON	HOUR	Rs 190/=	Rs 21/=

Alternatives Analysis is used to look at the various alternatives involved in the project (*E.g., using machines vs laborers, outsourcing work vs making it in-house, using value engineering or not etc.,*) and then to decide which would be the most cost effective for the project at hand. Each alternative involved in the project would have some costs and hence estimating and comparing them becomes an important tool of this process.

Reserve Analysis is the study of how much extra money is required, over and above the normal project costs, to tide over identified risks (Known – Unknowns). This reserve may be in the form of a percentage of the total project estimated cost (not a recommended method because then it would mean that proper risk identification and management has not been done) or it could be for specific elements and activities of the project. In this process, the reserve amount is the suggested amount of reserve which is pending approval to be added to the Project Budget.

During this time the management may also like to find out how much of a management reserve that they would like to keep for the project at hand. The Management Reserve is over and above the reserve discussed above. Management Reserve is for the Unidentified Risks (Unknown – Unknowns).

Cost of Quality is the amount of money that would be spent on first achieving the stated quality standards and then maintaining them. Every organization has to spend some money on Cost of Quality (COQ) and if this amount is not added to the project estimate then by default the estimate would be understated. Money spent on rework, reviews, testing, and audits form part of the Costs Of Quality. COQ is discussed in details in the knowledge area Quality Management. The best way to estimate this amount is to look at the past percentage of money actually spent on COQ activities vis-à-vis the actual total cost of the project. Project specific needs and standards of quality to be achieved and assumptions around the same could also be used for estimating for COQ.

9.17.2 Main Outcome of the process Estimate Costs:

Cost Estimates are the numerical cost estimates (in a specific currency) for the project. Now this estimate could be at the entire project level or broken down to project phases or summary level or it could be as detailed as all the way till individual activity level. Smarter estimates also allow for cost inflations for longer duration projects and also includes Contingency reserves.

Basis of Estimates are the assumptions, current knowledge, constraints or any other information on which the estimates have been based upon.

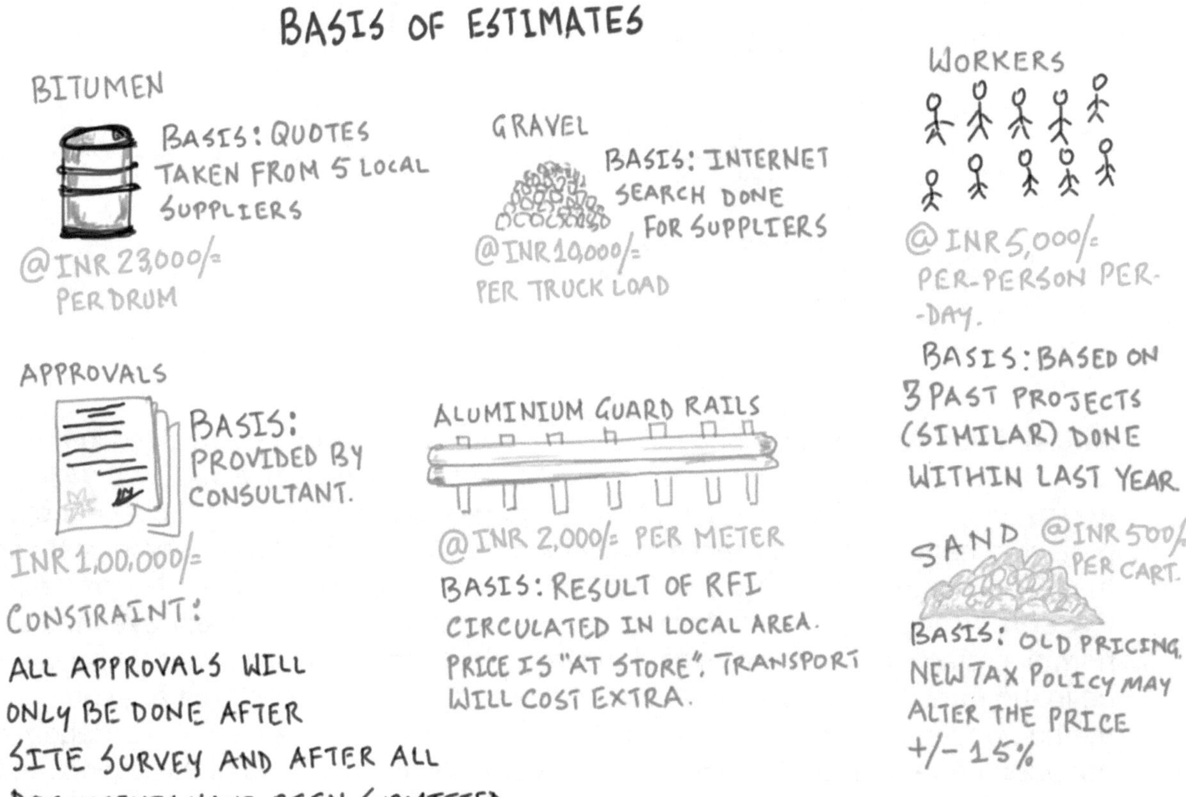

Documenting the basis of estimates along with the estimates puts into perspective exactly how the estimates were developed. It also puts a safety margin on the estimates because if the basis of estimates changes so should the estimates.

And due to the new findings during the course of this process certain **project documents** may get **updated** like project schedule, resources calendars, and risk register.

9.18 Determine Budget (Fixing The Budget)

Once the project cost estimation has been prepared, it is presented to the sponsor (and the senior management) who would then conduct sanity check, look at their strategy for this project and assign a Budget for the project. The Budget is nothing but the estimate which is approved by the management and from this point on this Budget would be the reference point for the cost tracking of the project.

There is a difference between the Project Budget and the Cost Baseline. This difference is important to be understood. When a budget is released it's not released as a lump sum for the entire project. It is apportioned as per the work packages or phases or project summary activities. If all the budget for the work packages is added up it would add up to the total amount of money apportioned (budgeted) for the project work. However, some Contingency Reserve is kept for the identified risks over and above the amount for the project work. These two add up to be what is called the "Project Cost Baseline". Just because identified risks have been provided for does not mean that those are the only risk that is applicable to the project. There are a lot of unidentified risks that may affect the project. Hence the management may (this is completely optional based on how important this project is for the strategy of the organization) keep an arbitrary amount as an additional reserve, called Management Reserve, for Unidentified Risks. Once the amount for the project and the contingency reserve amount and the amount for Management reserve are all added up it becomes the "Total Project Budget".

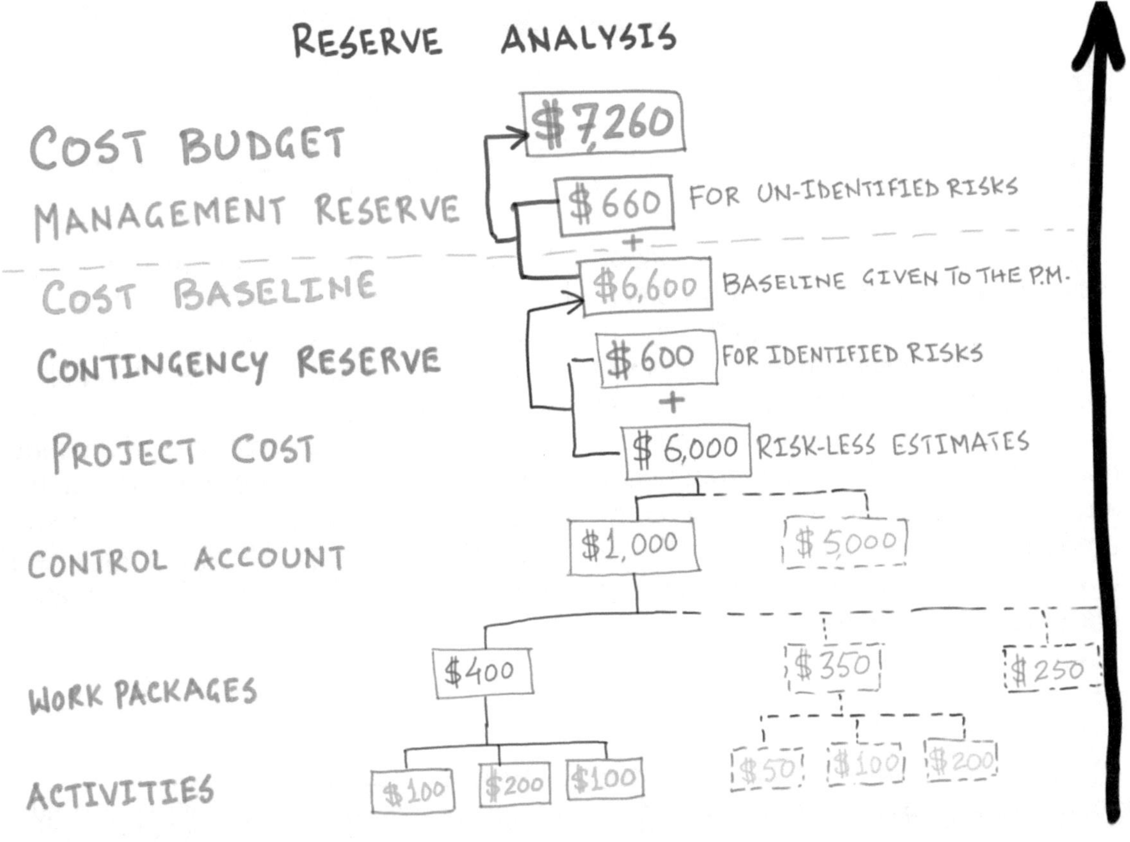

Remember:
Cost Budget = Cost Baseline + Management Reserve
Or
Cost Baseline = Cost Budget – Management Reserve
Or
Cost Baseline = Project Estimate + Contingency Reserve
Or
Project Estimate = Cost Budget – Management Reserve – Contingency Reserve

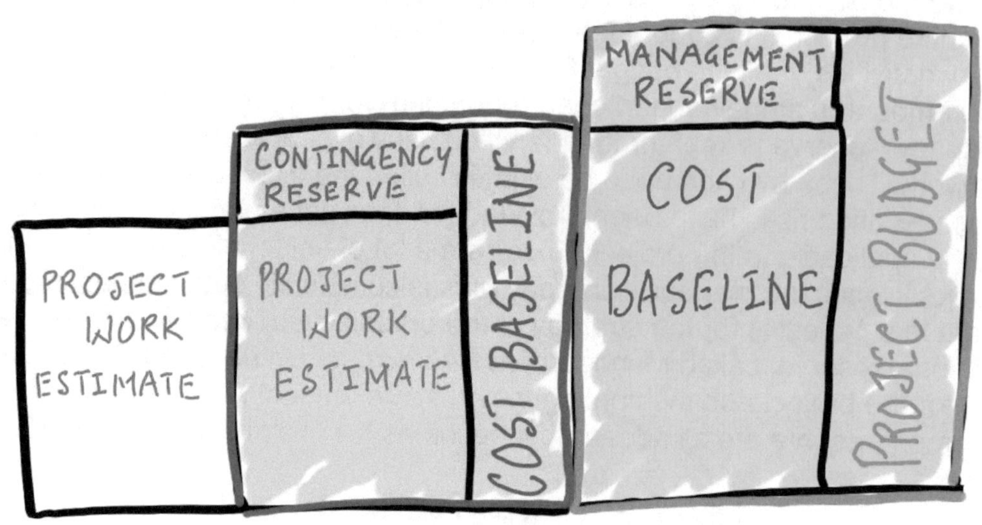

PROJECT ESTIMATE + CONTINGENCY RESERVE = COST BASELINE
COST BASELINE + MANAGEMENT RESERVE = PROJECT BUDGET

There is a proper formula and procedure to calculate the amount of the Contingency Reserve and that is something we would do in the Knowledge Area Risk Management. However, when it comes to Management Reserve there is no procedure or mechanism to calculate the specific amount to be kept aside. Why? That's because since unidentified risks are called so because no one can think of them (the moment you think of something as an example it is identified hence no one can really give an example of unidentified risks) and hence the exact amount cannot be calculated. Some organizations try to keep say 10% of the total project cost as the management reserve while some just keep an amount arbitrarily (or an amount that they can afford to keep). Hence, please remember that there is no way to specifically calculate the amount of money to be kept aside for Management Reserve.

9.18.1 *Main Tools & Techniques of Determine Budget*

Cost Aggregation is the way the budgeted amounts, at the work package levels, are rolled up to the Cost Account level and how the Cost Account Level amounts are rolled (added up / aggregated) all the way up to the total project level.

Data Analysis (mainly **Reserve Analysis)** is about the amount to be set aside for Contingency reserve and the amount to be kept aside in the Management Reserve. The management may even decide not to keep any Management reserve whatsoever.

Historical Information Review technique is used for bringing about a sanity check on the cost estimates submitted. The data from historical projects may be used as benchmarks or a reference point for validating the current estimates. Some matured industries like Civil and Infrastructure tend to formulate parameters for such validations. *E.g., Our existing profitability per square meters is USD100.00. Hence a budget that reduces such profitability must be questioned or revisited*.

This process, viz., ***DETERMINE BUDGET,*** is visited multiple times during the lifecycle of the project to see how much of the budgeted fund is remaining and how much has been utilized. This act of ascertaining expended versus remaining fund is called **Funding Limit Reconciliations.**

It is common for large projects to obtain external sources of funds. In which case the budget would have to include the specific times in the lifecycle of the project that the external sources would provide **financing** to the project.

9.18.2 Main Artefacts of Determine Budget

Cost Baseline is the budgeted amount for each of the phases of the project plus the contingency reserve for the project activities/elements. This serves as the reference point to compare with during the lifecycle of the project while conducting project tracking. Costs actually expended can be compared for each phase with what was supposed to be spent in that phase, as per the cost baseline.
This trend of proposed phase wise spending is generally shown in an “S” curve. This curve when plotted over time tends to have a gently sloping curve which resembles the letter “S” hence the name.

COST BASELINE "S" CURVE

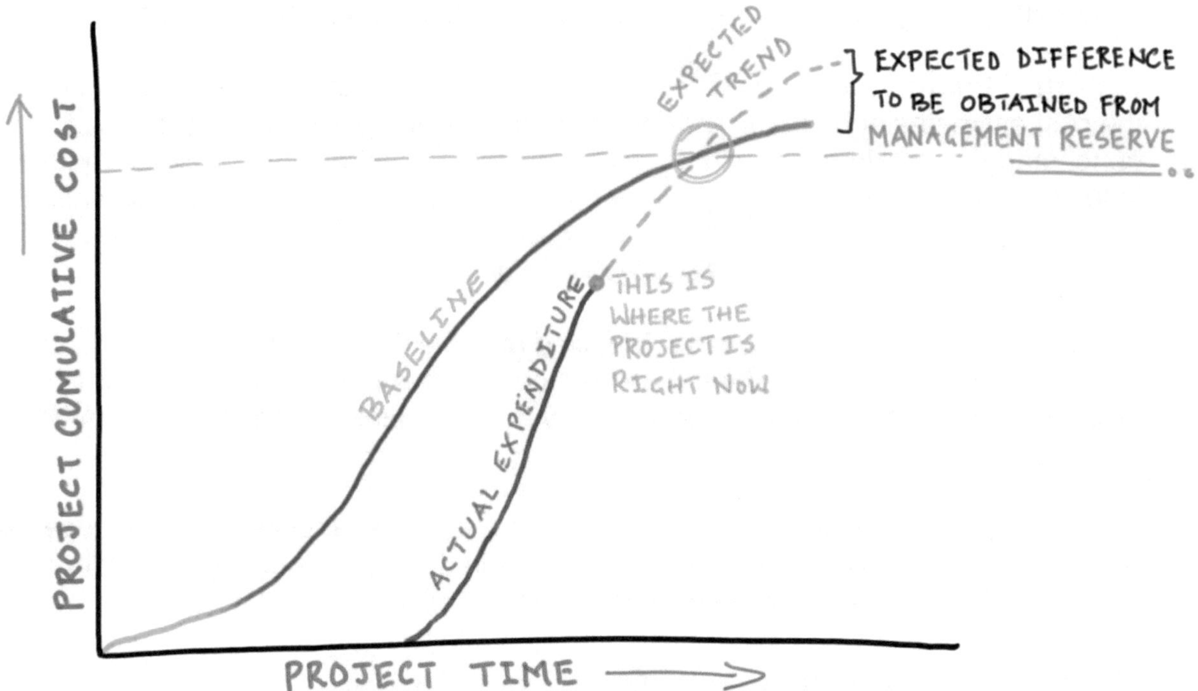

It's important to see that the output is "Cost Baseline" and not "Project Budget" as most of the time it's not a good idea to let the project management team know about the existence and quantum of Management Reserve. Remember the age-old project management saying "Work always expands to fill the time and money allotted for it."

Project Funding Requirements are periodic funding requirements of the project based on the project phases or milestones or the reporting periods. *E.g., By 1st of May USD 1,000,000.00 would be given to the project team. Or once Planning is completed a sum of USD200,000.00 would be required for Requirements and then for Designing USD 150,000.00 would be required and so on.* The funding period decided by the project organization has to be consistent, once decided.

Because of the insights generated due to this process, certain **project documents** may get **updated**.

9.19 Planning For Quality (Plan Quality Management)

Let us first understand the term quality itself.
As per PMI and other Quality Institutes including "Total Quality Management" (TQM) the definition of "Quality" = "The degree to which a set of inherent characteristics fulfill requirements". What it means is, that the "Inherent Characteristics" of the product or service fulfills the "Requirements". Put in other words, it's the "Requirements" that define the quality. Hence, the importance of the discipline of "Requirements Elicitation".

To understand the term Quality better and to be able to practically implement it and test and track it in the project, the term Quality is best described as under: -

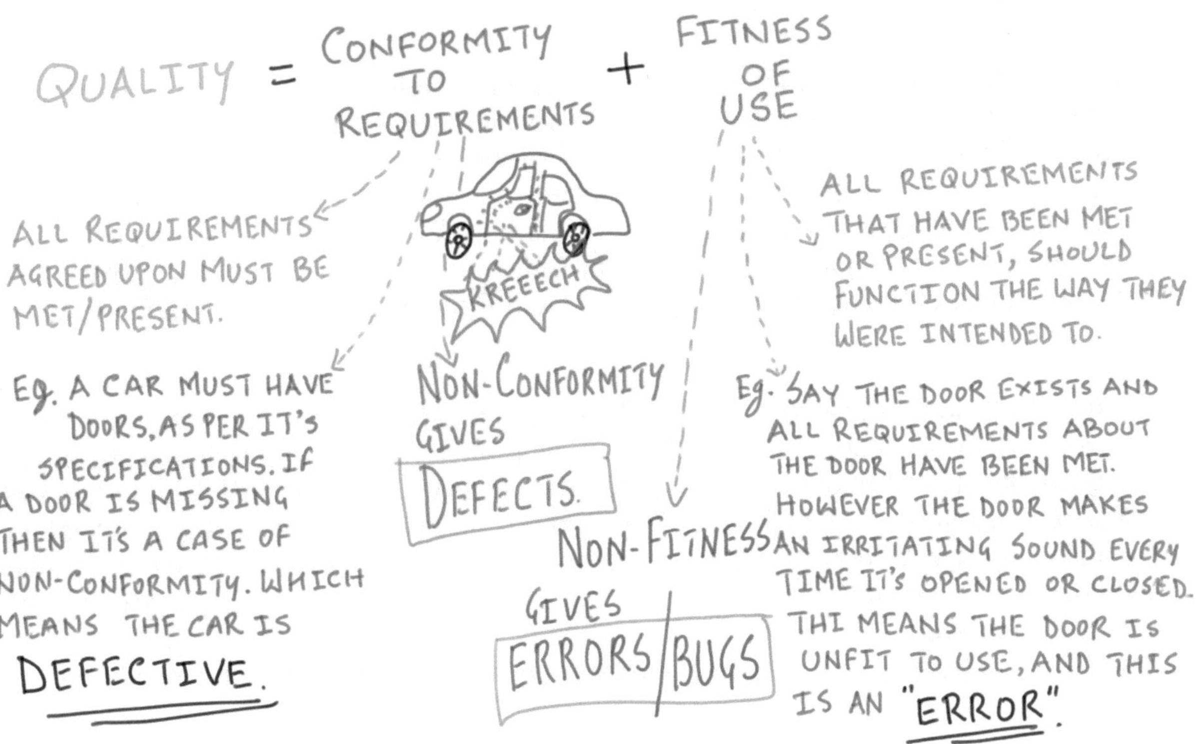

"Conformity To Requirements" means that whatever that has been written in the requirements, must be delivered in the product of the project. The absence of any stated requirements means the product is defective. It's as simple as that. However just because the requirements have been met does not mean that the Quality has been achieved. There is one more condition to be satisfied and that is the "Requirements should be fit to use" in the product. This can be best explained with an example. Let us say, you wish to buy a sports car. You go to a car dealer and a car meets your specifications and fancy. You go through the manuals about the features it has to offer and its specifications. You now inspect the car and find that one of its "Headlights" is missing. Now, it's clearly mentioned in its manual and brochures that it has two headlights. In such a condition would you buy the car? The answer is, a resounding, NO!!! This is because the car does not have all the "Requirements" as mentioned in its manual. This makes the car "Defective". Let us change this scenario a bit. Let us say that you wish to buy a sports car and you like a car at the car dealers place, you inspect it and find that it has all the requirements as mentioned. You go ahead and buy it. You drive around your new car and in a few days, you get some rains. Some rain water seeps into the headlight and because of the heat of the lamp, it fogs the inside of the headlight. What would you call this? Is this a defect? If in the manual it was written that the "Headlights" are leak proof and seepage proof then this would mean that this is a defect. However, if there is no mention of any such statement then this is a "Fitness Of Use" issue. You would not "Reject the car" because of this. You will, however, want the car dealer / Car

Company to "Fix this problem". Non-conformity to "Fitness of use" gives you Error (also called Bugs in IT and Telecom sectors).
This brings out another thing into focus, which is that "Non conformity to requirements" is more dangerous than "Non conformity to fitness of use".
That is the reason why all authentic Quality institutes and Gurus talk about "Zero Defects" and not "Zero Errors".

Did you notice that there are no words like "Customer Delight", "Customer Value Added offerings", "Customer extras used at all while defining and discussing "Quality". Hard as it may sound, these words are superfluous at best and should never ever be used. The only term is "Customer Satisfaction" which essentially means, least defects and acceptable numbers of errors/bugs. In fact terms like "Customers Value-Added Offerings and Customer Extras" fall into the category of "Gold Plating" which means giving something extra to the customer outside of the scope of the project. Gold Plating is considered ***bad*** in Project Management.

Difference between "Grade" and "Quality" must be clearly understood. A lot of people confuse Quality with Grade. I do a very interesting exercise during traditional classroom training on Quality or Project Management. I simply ask a question. "Which car has better Quality, Rolls Royce's Silver Ghost or Tata Nano (one of the cheapest and smallest cars in the world)". Always, without fail, 90% of the participants choose Rolls Royce to be a higher quality car. That's when I tell them that my question itself was wrong and these two cars cannot be compared.
These two cars belong to a completely different grade. Quality cannot be compared across grades.

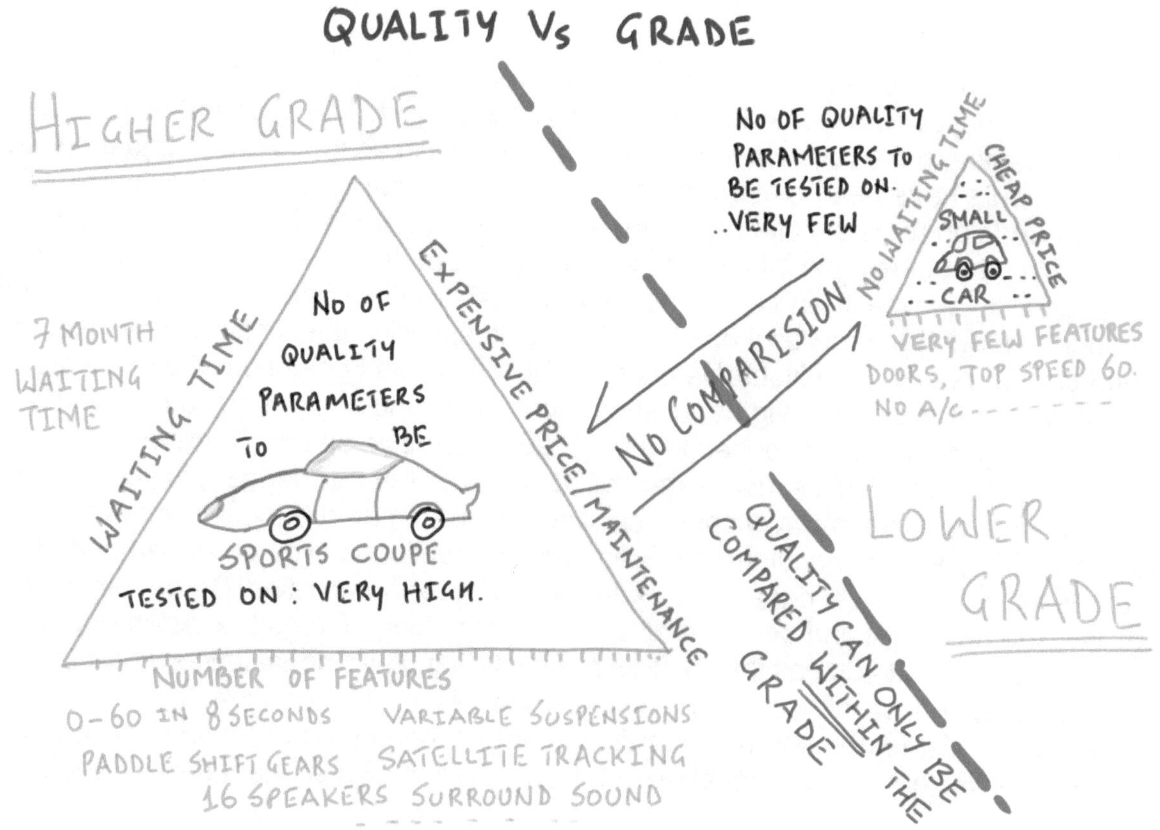

There is another set of terms that need explanation viz., Precision and Accuracy. Precision and Accuracy do not mean the same thing. Let me take the AirGun target shooting example. "Which of the shooters has better accuracy?"

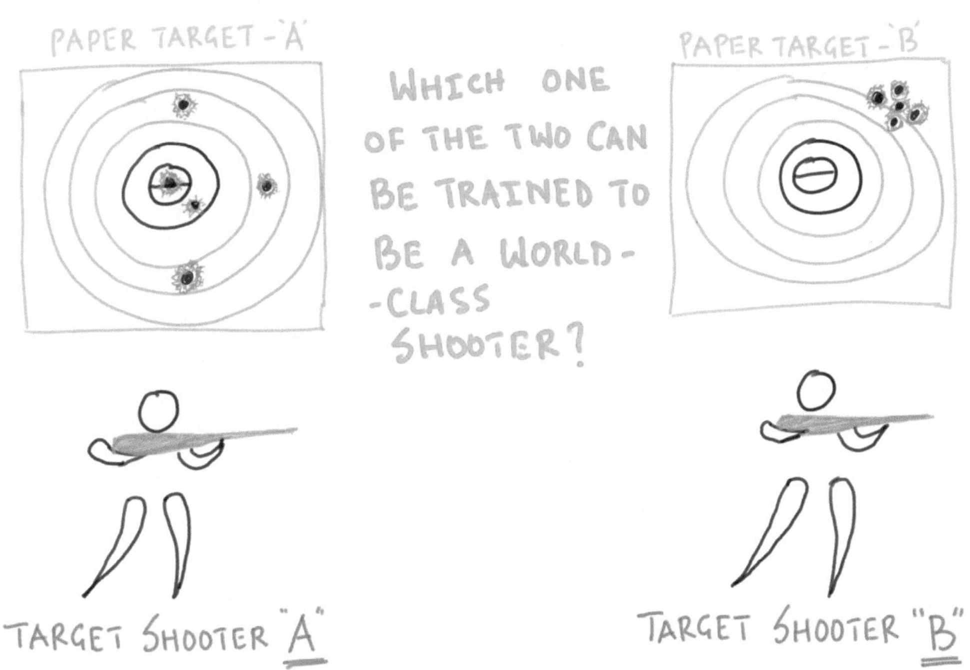

Shooter for Target A is more accurate as he got some shots closer to the bull's eye. However if I was to ask you, "Which shooter is better?" You will be confused. This is tough. What if I tell you Shooter for Target B is a lot better as he is "Consistent / Precise" even though he is consistently wrong, would you agree? Shooter for Target A is not precise and he cannot be even trained further, as his weakness is not known. The Shooter for Target B can be taught to shoot in the bull's eye and then he would be consistently accurate. This is why for a Quality process to be worthwhile it should be Consistent/precise before it can be accurate. Remember, when it comes to Quality, like most things in life, precision first accuracy later. Oh yes! You want to know "What is Excellence then?" Well Excellence is when you get those "Air Gun" shots "consistently on the bullseye". Excellence is when you are consistently accurate (or your process is consistently accurate). Excellence is exactly what "six-sigma intends to achieve.

Quality is about continuous improvement. The Quality processes themselves should be geared up for continuous improvement. I hope you remember that we talked about PDCA (Plan – Do – Check – Act) during our discussion about the 5 process groups and the fact that it's a "Cycle of continuous improvement".
"Kaizen" a Japanese continuous improvement philosophy proposes "little – little" improvement almost on a daily basis thus amounting to a huge improvement by the end of the year. Being little improvements on a daily basis does not cost much to the organization and not much of change in work style and processes is required in Kaizen. However, when it

comes to "Six Sigma", a US-based continuous improvement method, it does not talk about little-little improvements. It talks about 6 month's investment in research and analysis to look for quantum improvement. Though this is not done daily, but say twice a year, each improvement is very big and needs change in processes and working style and needs serious investment and commitment. However, if you look at both Kaizen and Six Sigma you will notice, despite the difference in approach, by the end of the year both styles would give you more or less same level of total improvement.

From the exams point of view, you should know the important benchmarks from six sigma.

SIX SIGMA BENCHMARKS

6σ

+/- 1 SIGMA = 68.26%
+/- 2 SIGMA = 95.46%
+/- 3 SIGMA = 99.73%
+/- 6 SIGMA = 99.99%

ACCURACY LEVEL

THERE ARE LEVELS 4 & 5 AS WELL BUT NEVER PRACTICALLY USED.

COMMIT THIS TABLE TO MEMORY

Another term that is important in Quality Circles (specifically in the Manufacturing and tooling industry) is "Just In Time (JIT)" inventory method. This was invented by Toyota (just like almost everything in Modern Quality principles) when they were looking at ways for reducing money blocked in tons of inventory. They decided to free up the locked up capital by filling the inventory bins with only the material that would be needed on a single day. At night they would be filled by the supplier for the next day's work, instead of piling up tons of inventory. This freed up a lot of capital. But there was a side effect. The "First Time Quality" of the assembly line workers improved. Let us take an example. If you were an assembly line worker who had to screw 500 bolts on to the wheels of the car every day and you had over 10,000 bolts in the inventory bin. You would be a bit careless. You may do more misalignments, thread slips or wrong side bolting, as you know that a few wasted material is not a problem for you. On the other hand when suddenly you find that you have to put 500 bolts and you have exactly 500 bolts in your bin that day (because of JIT). You would be extremely careful with each and every bolt. This improves first time quality. And this is why JIT finds a reference in Quality Procedures even though it's an Inventory method. Remember in JIT the inventory = 0. JIT means not keeping any inventory, only enough material in the bin for use in a day or a shift. However, JIT also requires intense and high level of management oversight.

The entire focus of practical quality is “Prevention over Inspection”. Preventive Quality Management is when the processes are made in such a way that the work itself is done in a way that assures / guarantees meeting quality requirements once it is tested or inspected. Inspection based quality management (the older western style of management) where the product would be built up without any preventive measures but when ready, thoroughly inspected for any flaws or lack of quality requirements. Again it was Toyota which propounded the theory of “Prevention over Inspection” and is now a mainstream philosophy globally. They realized that if you wait for testing of the products at the end and if the product is rejected, the amount of money lost was huge as the product was completely built up. Hence they came out with “Preventive Measures” during the making of the product itself which would ensure that when it’s tested finally, nothing gets rejected (or at least the numbers of rejections come down drastically). This, obviously, brought in tremendous savings and motivation among workers and robustness to engineering process as well.

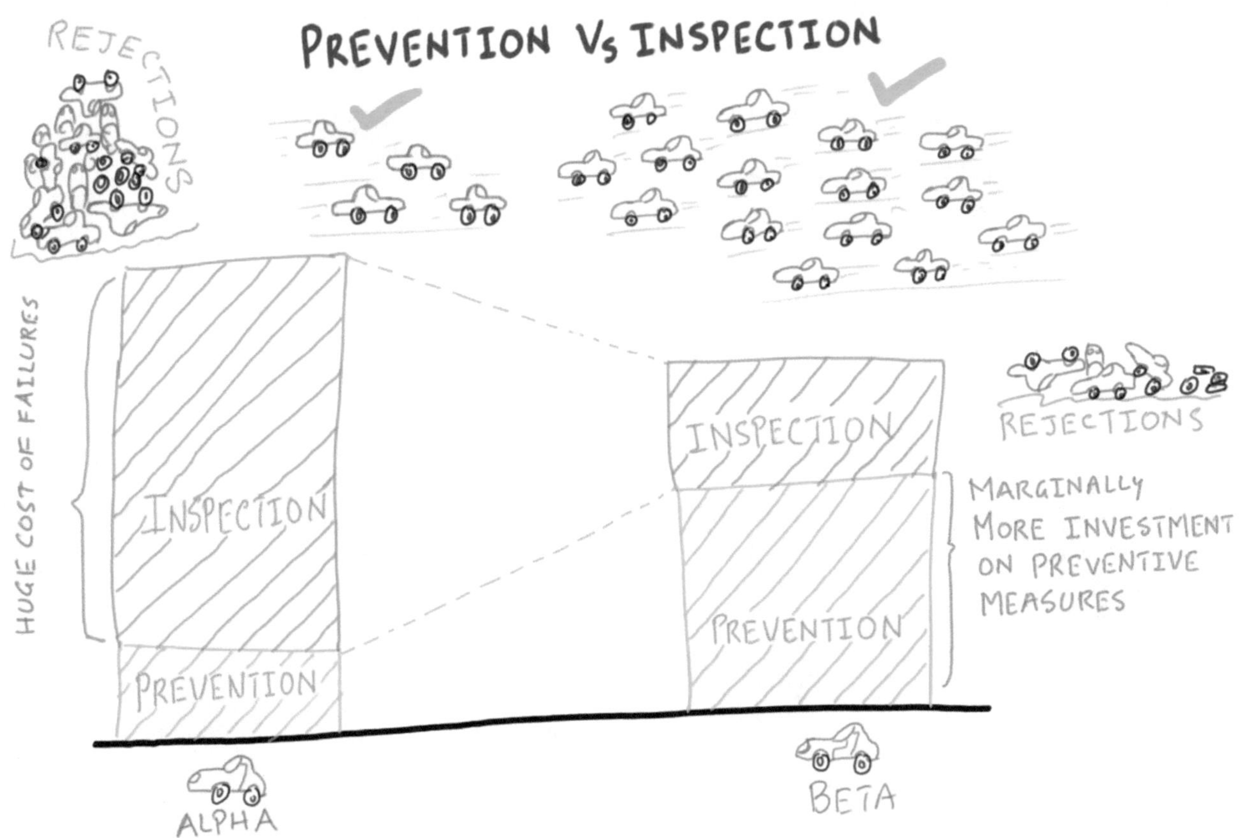

One of the examples you can see in this world is how automotive companies are cutting corners in a bid to reduce prices and outsourcing to cheap suppliers with suspicious quality processes, but end up paying a huge price when they have to end up recalling thousands (and in some cases hundreds of thousands) of cars.
Prevention is better than inspection.

The exams also pays homage to the greats of Quality Management viz., Edward Deming, Joseph Moses Juran, Philip B. Crosby, Genichi Taguchi, and Kaoru Ishikawa. Every once in a while you may get questions about who did what.
This should help you with those questions.

DONS OF QUALITY

EDWARD DEMING

CREATED:

STATISTICAL SAMPLING

RULE OF 85%

JOSEPH MOSES JURAN

TALKED ABOUT:

1. COST OF QUALITY [COQ]
2. QUALITY IMPROVEMENT
3. PLANNING & CONTROL OF QUALITY
4. FITNESS OF USE

PHILIP B. CROSBY

TALKED ABOUT:

1. CONFORMANCE TO REQUIREMENTS
2. PREVENTION OVER INSPECTION
3. ZER0 DEFECTS
4. COST OF NON-CONFORMANCE

GENICHI TAGUCHI

CREATED:

1. DESIGN OF EXPERIMENTS [DOE]
2. "QUALITY IS DESIGNED IN NOT INSPECTED IN."

KAORU ISHIKAWA or Dr. ISHIKAWA

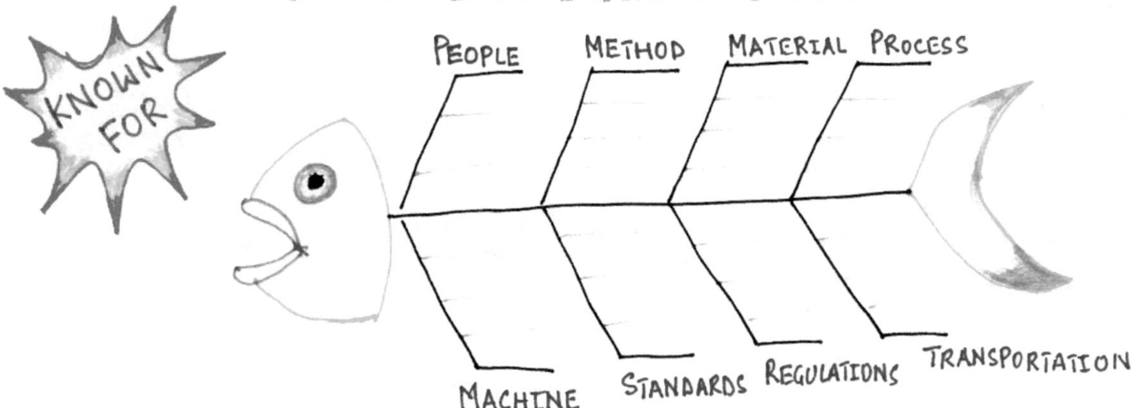

FISHBONE DIAGRAM

ALSO CALLED

CAUSE AND EFFECT DIAGRAM

ALSO CALLED

ISHIKAWA DIAGRAM

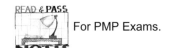

Of late (though rarely) questions about who invented Six Sigma also comes up. For this you must know that the inventor of Six Sigma was William B. Smith Jr. (popularly known as Bill Smith) when he was working in Motorola. Six Sigma is a registered mark of Motorola.

Different organizations work on different maturity levels of quality. As per the best schools on Quality (including TQM), there are five levels of "Quality Maturity" with associated cost of quality.

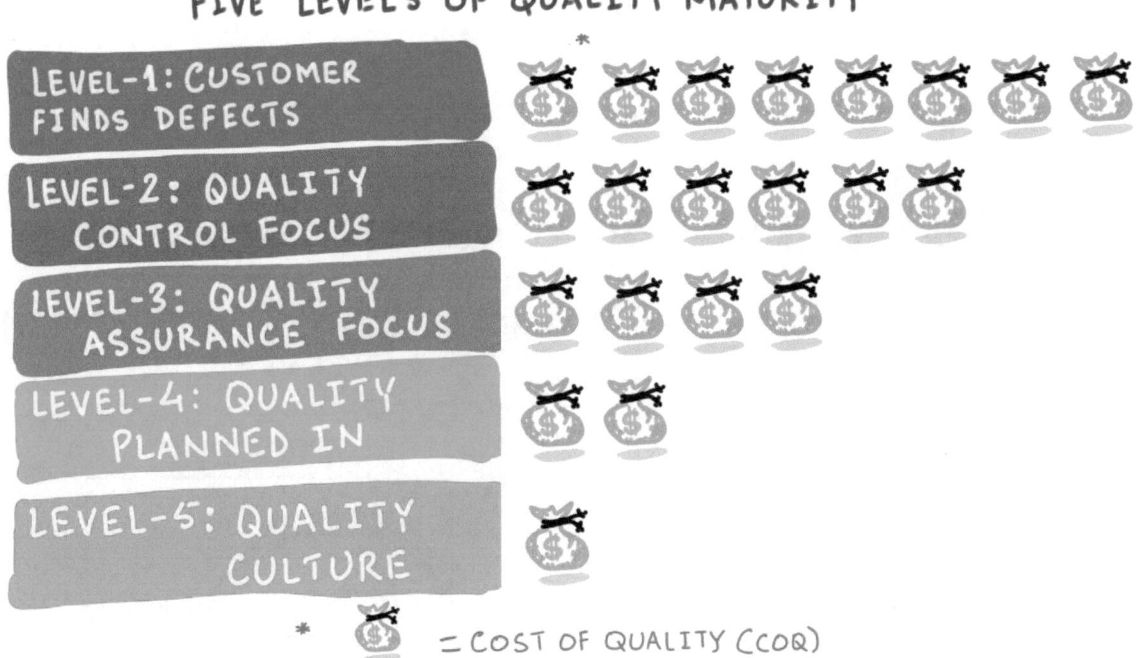

This process, *Plan Quality Management*, ensures that all the policies, processes, checklists and audit principles are in place before the project starts. This process also lists down the various Quality Matrices against which the actual performance would be measured. This process produces one of the 10 Subsidiary plans that make up the overall project management plan.

Planning for Quality in a project is largely aligned to the overall Quality Policy that has been put in place within the organization.

9.19.1 Main Tools & Techniques of Plan Quality Management:

Benchmarking: is done to ensure that the quality of the product of the project measures up to the output of the best in class project (either within the organization or within the industry). This benchmarking targets/parameters may not always have to come from other "best-in-class" projects or competitors, they can also come from industrial standards like Capability Maturity Model Integration (CMMI) or Six Sigma, as well.

It's best not to get confused between Benchmarks and Baselines. For all purposes they are the same viz., a reference point to compare your actual data with. However to differentiate between reference point for plans and reference point for Quality this differentiation of name has been made. When it comes to Project Management, a Baseline = Final Approved Plan just before execution for tracking the project; however a Benchmark = reference point for anything in quality to be compared against.

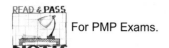

Cost Benefit Analysis is about ascertaining which Quality Tools or Processes would be the most cost-effective in this project. The attempt here is to undertake only those quality processes and tools and techniques which would give incremental benefits to the project without being too expensive to the project. This prevents organizations from becoming uneconomical while implementing quality in their projects. *E.g., An automated tool that checks for prospective defects and costs USD 50,000.00 and is expected to reduce the defect density in the final product by say 40% with an expected saving of (just saying) USD 500,000.00, is worth the investment and worth spending some time training the project team on this new tool.*

QUALITY: COST BENEFIT ANALYSIS

THIS IS EXACTLY WHAT SHOULD NOT BE HAPPENING.

AIM OF QUALITY IS "REDUCED REWORK", "HIGHER PRODUCTIVITY", "LOWER COSTS" & "INCREASED STAKEHOLDER SATISFACTION".

~:PRACTICAL QUALITY FOCUS INCREASES PROFITS":~

Cost of Quality (COQ) is the amount of money, material, resources and time (all translated into monetary cost) that would be required to first ensure that the product of the project meets all quality parameters and then the cost expended in rework, inspections, fixes and warranties etc. if the quality parameters are not fully met in the product of the project.

Simply put Cost of Quality = Cost on Prevention + Cost of Failure

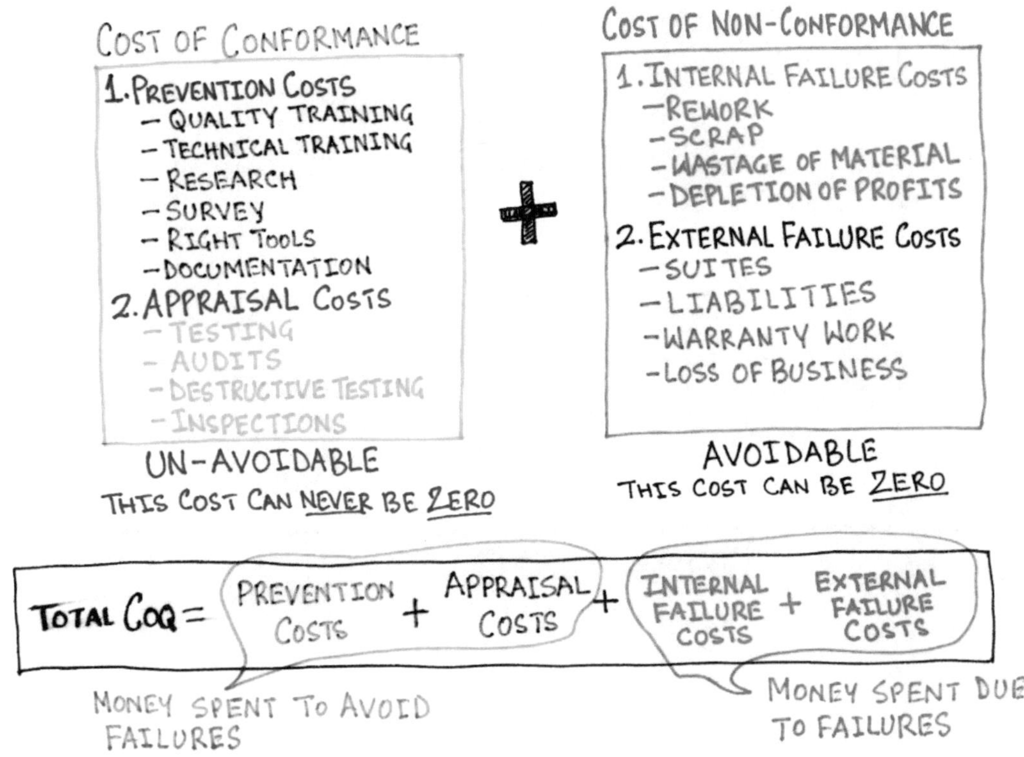

Review this illustration multiple times. It will help you solve several questions on Quality.
Some schools of thoughts have kept the average COQ of projects at 34% or more. It is estimated that the COQ of IT based projects is even higher, nearing 40% of the total project cost. This makes the COQ a very important thing to watch out for and something that can be worked upon to be reduced in a project.
The concept of “Prevention over Inspection” comes from this.

Japan propounded the concept of using Quality as a weapon when it came to winning markets for their products. While most organizations, in the 70s and 80s, focused on Inspection of products that were already produced, Japanese organizations marginally increased their investment on “Preventive quality measures”. The diagram shows the economics behind such a simple but effective moves. It took decades for the rest of the world to wake up to this simple and effective quality related move.

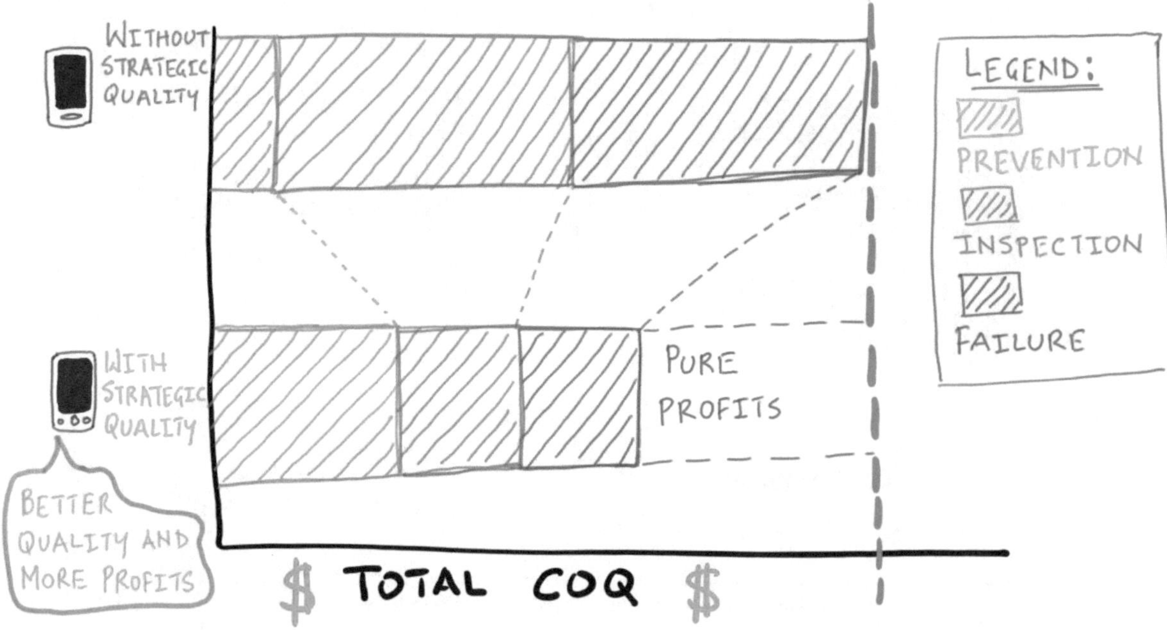

Test and Inspection Planning is about the kinds of testing and inspection that would be done and during which stages of the project using which kind of tools and resources.

Test And Inspection Planning and Logical Data Model are tool and technique of only one process viz., *PLAN QUALITY MANAGEMENT*.
Benchmarking And Mind Mapping are tools and techniques of three processes viz., *COLLECT REQUIREMENTS*, *PLAN QUALITY MANAGEMENT,* and *PLAN STAKEHOLDER ENGAGEMENT*.
Cost Of Quality is the tool and technique of only two processes viz., *ESTIMATE COSTS* and *PLAN QUALITY MANAGEMENT*.

9.19.2 Main Artefacts of Plan Quality Management:

This process has 4 outputs and they are Quality Management Plan, Quality Metrics, Project Management Plan Updates and Project Documents Updates.

Quality Management Plan contains the processes and the plans that would be used for this project. They are usually derived or cut out from the organizational quality policies. This plan is one of the 10 subsidiary plans of the overall project management plan and it could be rather detailed or general based on the kind and size and complexity of the project being undertaken.

QUALITY MANAGEMENT PLAN

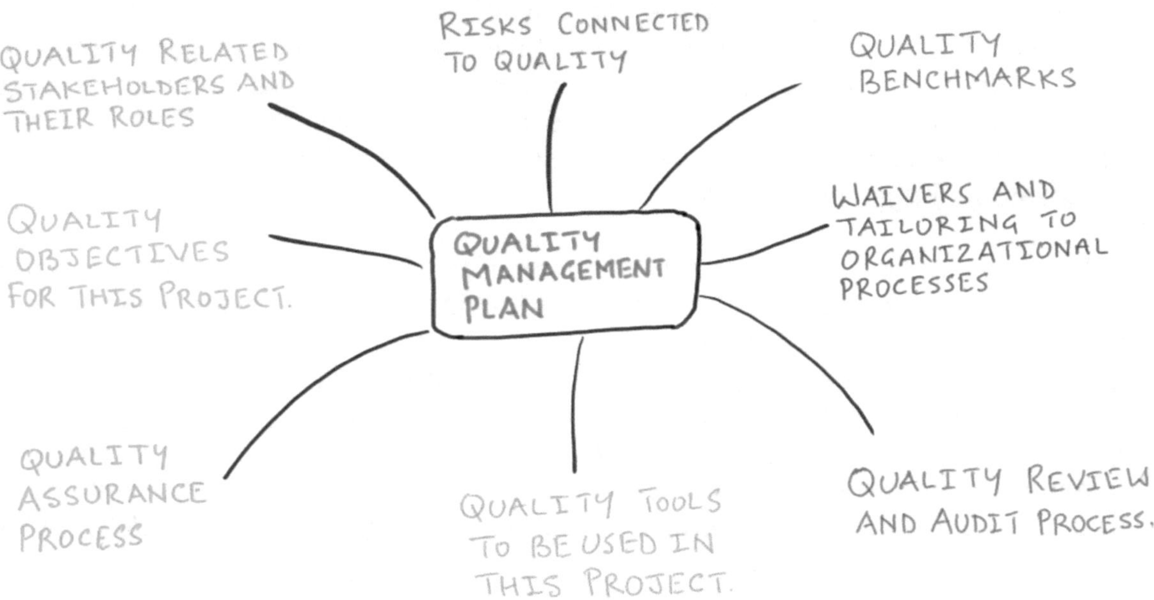

Quality Metrics contain the important heads under which values and measurements would be done to track the project in terms of Quality. This contains all the important things to be measured and reported during the lifecycle of the project as far as Quality is concerned. This metrics is used mostly in the Quality Assurance though it's filled in *CONTROL QUALITY* as well. It's called metrics as it contains the heads under which values are collected, benchmarks or targets of values being aimed for and some of them would also have tolerance levels to show the acceptable and unacceptable limits of variations.
Let us look at a Quality Matrices from a civil infrastructure project:

QUALITY MATRICS

S.NO.	PARAMETERS	PHASE-1	PHASE-2
1	AVERAGE CURING TIME PER PILLAR.	15 DAYS	
2.	DEFECTS PER 1,000 Sq.Mts	28	
3.	AVERAGE COST OF REWORK PER DEFECT.	¥70,000/-	
4.	AVERAGE NUMBER OF HOURS SPENT PER SITE INSPECTION	22 Hrs.	
⋮	⋮	⋮	⋮

9.20 Planning For Resources

This Knowledge Area is dedicated to the concepts of developing an effective team and dealing with team and other Human Resource challenges and issues faced in a project environment. So far our discussions have been rather scientific however, when it comes to Human Resource Management our discussions would be mostly around "Soft Skills". This entire knowledge area has to be understood more from Soft Skills aspects instead of straightforward management science.

The fact remains that the resources can be humans, machines, tools, equipment, material as well as animals (in some countries) but specific attention has to be paid to Human resources simply because of the fact that while mathematics and linear models can be applied for non-human resources, for humans a lot of variables come into picture. Humans have moods, education, background, habits, cultures, language, temperaments, beliefs, religion, perception, fear, expectations, attitude and race among scores of other things. This is why resource management is heavily focused around Human Resource management and therefore, most of the discussions around resources is about "Interpersonal Skills" or "Soft Skills".

Some of the soft skills needed while acquiring, building and maintaining a project team are: -

Before getting into the details of the processes you must get conversant with certain terms and their actual meanings. This would not only help in exams but also in the handling of real-world project teams.

Leadership is the ability to influence people without authority. **Managers** influence people with their authority. Leadership has many other meanings and almost everyone who ever writes a book on leadership tends to create their own meaning and perception, thus adding to the confusion. From the purposes of practicality and from exams point of view (and the original idea behind the concept of Leadership) there are two sides of a Project Manager (or for that matter any manger). One aspect is the Managerial-ship which is about how to use authority to influence people and the other is Leadership, which is about how to influence people without authority. Leadership would involve a lot more interpersonal skills like Neuro-Linguistic programming, Body Language, Cross-Cultural Understanding, Charismatic and Networking Skills. Let me share with you a simple example to showcase the practicality of this definition in your daily life. Let's say that as a Project Manager in a "Weak Matrix" you have been assigned some team members. Being a "Weak Matrix' you do not really have much authority over the project team. You write an email to one of the team members for some work. The team member being too busy with her operational work she does not reply or do the work. You send her repeated reminders to no avail. One day you get upset and send a nasty email to the person and her direct boss (the functional head) is kept in CC. Unfortunately this action would lead to even more resentment and work would suffer even more. The reason for this decaying situation is because you did not realize that you do not have authority over the person and hence using "authoritative behavior" would not work. Does this not sound familiar? Had you realized this upfront you would have used Networking, Personal Persuasion etc. (one of the leadership tools and techniques) to get the work done. Basically, you would have used Leadership abilities.

Influencing is the ability to coordinate and get others cooperation towards accomplishing certain goals. Now, these goals may be joint goals or your individual goals or organizational goals. Gone are the days when everyone just worked their own manual work. With organizational structures getting more complex and hierarchies getting flatter, as well as vertical, mangers, do not "Execute" all the work but need to get most of it done through others. The ability to get this done in a systematic and as dignified manner as possible is called the "Art of Influencing". This is applicable to both Leaders and Managers.

Political And Cultural Awareness is the knowledge of the existence of power centers within an organization or a function as well as the awareness that different people belonging to different cultures and they would need to be reached out to, differently, to get the same work done. Every organization or workplace would eventually have some power centers (and they are not always hierarchically driven) which have to be understood in order to get the work done for projects. This would mean that you understand that people would have different agenda (explicit or hidden) from that of your own. Another challenge with more global organizations is that employees would be from different cultural backgrounds. Hence a manager has to work towards creating a "Cross-Cultural Awareness" and use it as a gel that binds the team together. No longer can this be allowed to happen on their own. Jokes about other cultures or misunderstanding about other cultures can make a project team completely dysfunctional.

Trust Building is another big challenge that managers face in the growing complex organizations with cross-cultural teams. Without trust, it's difficult to build an effective and positive relationship with project stakeholders. The Trust Building has to be a deliberate effort by the project manager.

Coaching has to be provided to the team members during different phases of the project to empower them by enhancing their skills and competencies. Effective coaching results in increased overall performance as well as a positive environment of learning and working.

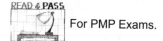

Coaching is also used for overcoming poor performance and help the team members address deficiencies in their skillset. Coaching should not be confused with counseling because, in Project Management counseling is about addressing "Won't do" issues with project staff, whereas Coaching is about addressing "Can't do" issues with project staff.

Project Management is globally going through a sea of new challenges when it comes to "Resources" and resource management.

- One of the challenges is the diverse kind of Resource Management Methods that exist around the management world today. Use of **Just-In-Time (JIT)** to pump up productivity, first-time quality and release working capital in the management bloodstream, is gaining popularity almost in every manufacturing and materials related industry. This methodology is mostly a part of operations but when projects are done in such organization the methodology is applied even there and this adds another layer of complication to the resource constraints on the project. There is another popular methodology in the infrastructure and manufacturing industries viz., "**Total Productive Maintenance (TPM)**". This is for the "Equipment" resources and not human resources. In industry, total productive maintenance (TPM) is a system of maintaining and improving the integrity of production and quality systems through the machines, equipment, processes, and employees that add business value to an organization. This is basically about keeping the equipment and machines in top working order with predictive maintenance (not reactive maintenance) to avoid any breakdowns and to keep the machines at optimum productivity while spending least amount of money on maintenance. Lean, Kaizen and Theory of Constraints (TOC) are some of the other resource related and resource connected methodologies and hence, while planning a project the PM must assess the different resource related methodologies in operations in the organization and see how to assimilate them within the project.
- **Emotional Intelligence (EI)** is gaining serious popularity around the world and for good reasons too. Let me explain what exactly Emotional Intelligence is. Let's say that you are involved in a project which is in execution and is painfully running behind schedule. This is one of those visible projects and the senior management is watching the project. One of the team members, whose work is especially running late, asks for a leave. You try to reason with him that it may not be a good idea at this time but for some reason the team member gets agitated and starts speaking loudly about the horrible working conditions, the way he has been treated, the kind of resources he has to put up with and that he has no time for personal life. Guess how you would react. Chances are that you would get agitated too and there is a high likelihood that you end up screaming your head off as well. This shows a lack of Emotional Intelligence. You and the team member may both be really good at work or intelligent, but none of that means anything without Emotional stability and equilibrium. Emotional Intelligence is to understand "Inbound" (your own emotional thresholds, push buttons, filters, irritant points etc.) as well as "Outbound" (empathy towards the others conditions, emotional temperatures of others, networking, relationship building, gauging conflicts) aspects of collective emotional environment and then handling one's own emotions and attempting to work with the emotions of others in a constructive fashion. Dealing with people is dealing with a wide range of emotions and those project managers who lack emotional intelligence do not tend to give good results. The project manager must also ensure and take steps to develop a very "Emotionally competent" team members as well.

- **Self-organizing teams** are on the rise because of the complexities involved in projects because of size of the project and methodology (like agile or iterative). Self-Organizing teams are units that function on their own (within certain parameters) without central control or oversight. It is increasingly becoming difficult to manage teams that "follow orders" as the size and complexity of the teams increase within an ever-changing external environment. The project manager has to put specific effort in building and supporting self-organizing teams which can constantly adapt to the changing environment and challenges within the overall project objectives and values.
- The next big challenge is the concept of "**Virtual Teams**". Teams are geographically distributed and sometimes never see other team members in person. This creates alienation and misunderstandings among the teams thus reducing the overall productivity of the team in general. As the projects become more global, cross-cultural, cost sensitive and dependent on collaboration technology, they tend to suffer the disadvantages of lack of productivity, heightened levels of conflicts, lack of team spirit, silo working styles and lack of any joint accountability. The project manager must understand these limitations in advance and specifically work towards building up a virtual team that overcomes these limitations. Virtual teams have some serious advantages as well. They allow access to experts from different parts of the world, reduce overhead costs, reduce transport and travel costs, involve people with skills but limitations or disabilities, promotes "Work-from-home" culture and reduce carbon footprints. Some of the challenges of a Virtual Team are feeling of isolation among team members, susceptibility to misunderstandings, gaps in communications and knowledge, lack of project or team loyalty, lack of clear communications because of cultural differences and time zone differences and serious dip in overall productivity.

Ok time to get into the innards of the process, Plan Resource Management.

9.21 Plan Resource Management

This process produces one of the subsidiary plans that make up the overall Project Management Plan, called the **Resource Management Plan**. This process establishes the reporting relationship within the project (Project Organization), establishes the roles and responsibilities of different stakeholders of the project and the team members, establishes the staffing management plan (which kind of resources is needed and when, during the lifecycle of the project) and documents the process for hiring, acquiring and working with virtual teams.

It would be a mistake to assume that the term "Resources" only mean human resources (though most of the discussion in these processes is about dealing with human resources as they are the most difficult to work with). Resources can be "Work Resources" (meaning resources that work or put in an effort to get the work done in a project) or "Material/consumables" (meaning resources that get consumed during the course of the project or change shape). There is no "Effort" associated with Material.

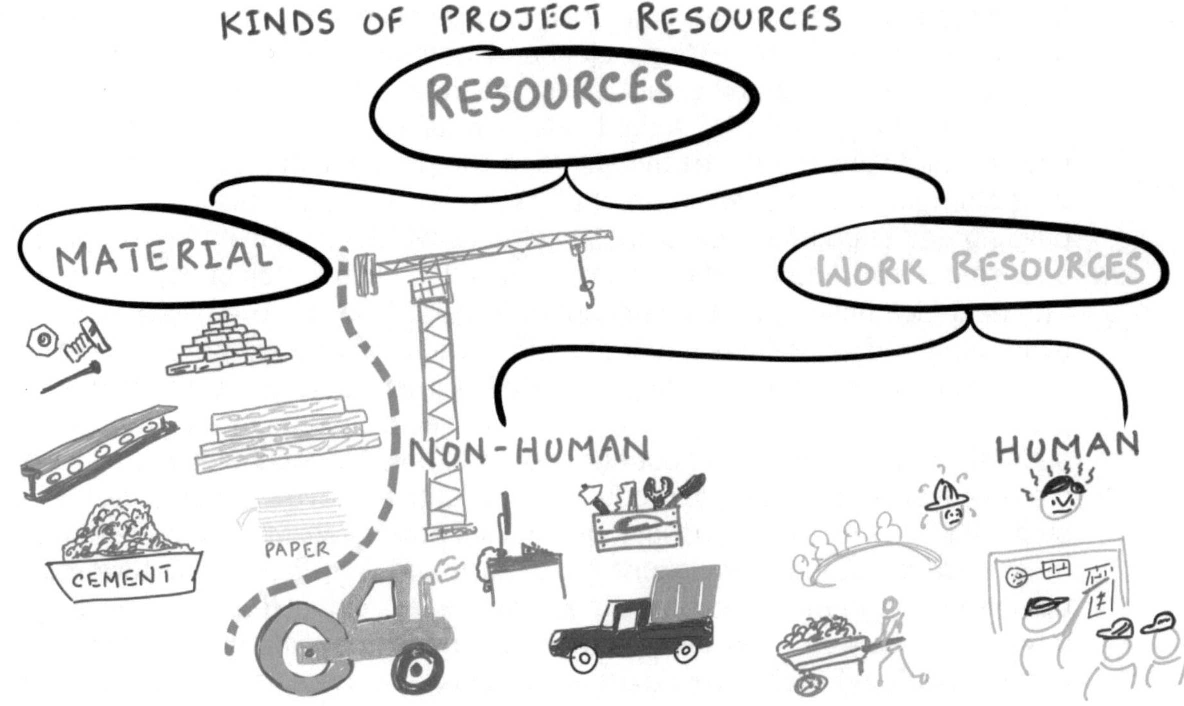

Remember that "Material" does not add to the "Effort" but only to the cost. However the "Work Resources" (both, Human or Non-Human) add to the cost as well as effort.

9.21.1 Tools and Techniques Of This Process: -

The most important tool & Technique for human resources is Motivation. Therefore it would make sense to talk about motivation a bit before getting into other techniques that implement or cater to motivation in one way or the other.

Motivation is essentially of two kinds. Intrinsic and Extrinsic.
Intrinsic motivating factors are the drivers that exist within the mind-set of a person. Intrinsic motivating factors are much longer lasting than Extrinsic motivating factors.
Extrinsic motivating factors are offered to a person subject to specific parameters. E.g., Awards, Citations, Salary Increments, Promotions, Perks etc.
Good leaders try to match Intrinsic motivating factors to a person by offering apt Extrinsic motivating factors.

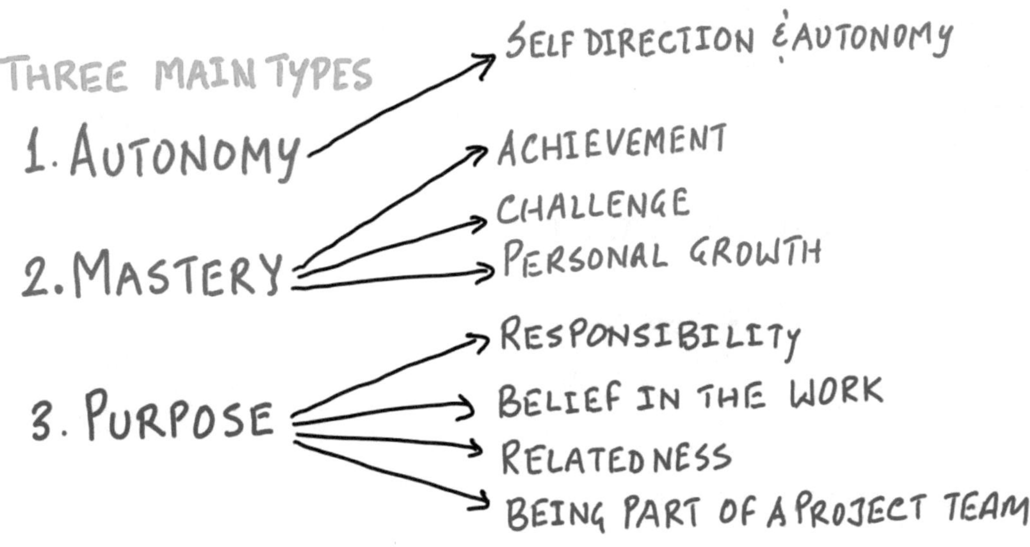

Resource Charts And Matrix

- **Hierarchical Charts** are used for showing the classification and position and relationships in a graphical top-down approach. The idea is to make the Roles and Responsibilities as granular and as clear as possible. There are some standard ways to clarify the roles and reporting structures. A visual organization structure shows the high-level reporting structure and is helpful in showcasing the overall project's reporting structure. An organization structure is also one of the most common techniques for showing the overall reporting structure. This is also called the "Organizational Breakdown Structure (OBS)".

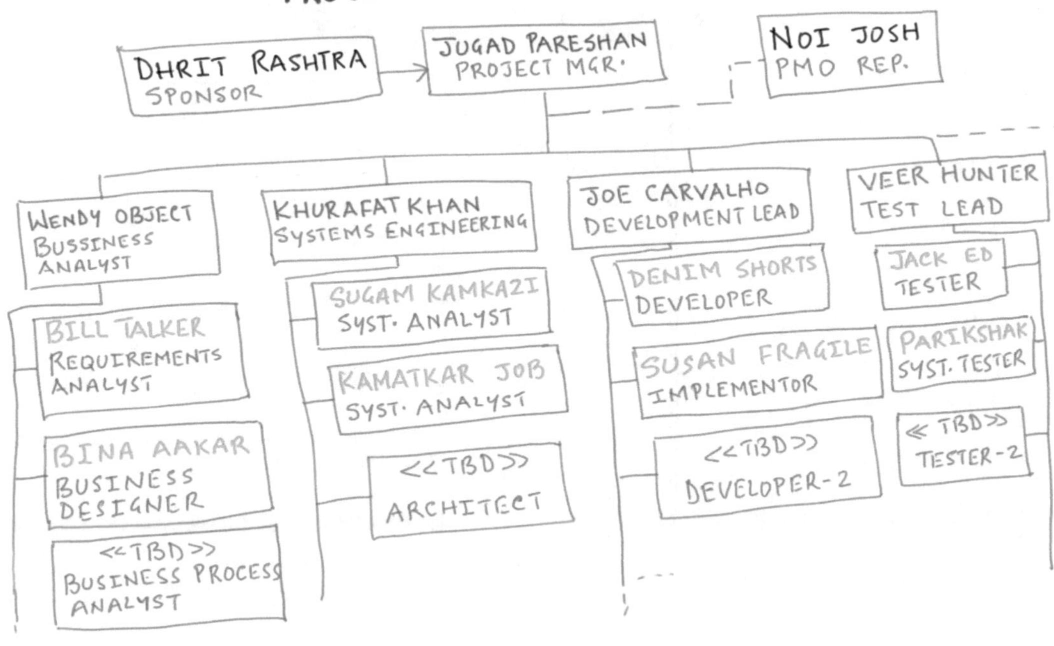

- **Responsibility Assignment Matrix (RAM)** is a more detailed way of documenting the roles and responsibility with high level of clarity. This is basically a matrix structure that shows work packages or tasks on one side and the responsibility of the resources/stakeholders vis-à-vis the work package next to it. The RAM can be high level where resources may not be mentioned specifically by name but by function or department. RAM can also be very detailed level where individual activities may be mentioned with specific names of resources/stakeholders listed.

RESPONSIBILITY ASSIGNMENT MATRIX

DELIVERABLE WBS CODE	TITLE (PEOPLE →)	PROJECT MANAGER	TEAM LEADER	HEAD OF DEPT.	SPONSOR	PURCHASING
1.1.1	QUESTIONNAIRE DESIGN	A	S A	P		
1.1.2	RESPONDENTS		P			
1.1.3	PRE-TEST		P	S		
1.1.4	FINAL QUESTIONNAIRE DECK	A	P	A	A	

P = PRIMARY RESPONSIBILITY S = SECONDARY RESPONSIBILITY
A = APPROVAL

A variation of RAM called, RACI Chart (Responsible, Accountable, Consult and Inform) is more widely used in manufacturing and infrastructure industries. Another kind of RACI chart is the RASI chart where "S" stands for "Support".

RACI CHART

TASKS	PERSONS / STAKEHOLDERS				
	BAAZIGAR	HUE ME	P.K. SWAY	KAMATKAR	B. SWINDLE
DEVELOP COURSE OUTLINE	A	R	I	C	I
SELECT IMAGES		A	C		R
DEVELOP CONTENT	A	C	R	I	I
DESIGN PARTICIPANT ACTIVITIES		A	R	I	
DEVELOP ASSESSMENT	I	A	R		
SCHEDULE PILOT	A	R	I		

R = RESPONSIBLE A = ACCOUNTABLE C = CONSULT I = INFORM

- **Text Oriented Formats** are the most basic kinds where the stakeholder's and team member's responsibilities and reporting hierarchy is written in a detailed descriptive manner.

Organizational Theory helps the Project Manager make use of, and provide for, some established organizational motivation theories in their project. In a project, the challenge is to get the teams together and get into performance mode as soon as possible to achieve the objective, and once that is done the project team gets disbanded. Depending on the kind of organization structure and its internal HR policies the Project Manager would use one or more of these Organizational theories in his Project's Human Resources Management Plan.

Once in a while, there are some questions asked about some of the most popular organizational theories. Therefor the important organizational theories have been mentioned here and it's worth understanding them.

Maslow's Hierarchy Of Needs is by far the most popular motivational and behavior theory that applies to almost every kind of organization. Maslow came out with the "Psychology of Motivation and Human Behavior" and termed it the Hierarchy of Needs. Motivation of people is determined by the "Current Needs" of the person. This "Need" itself changes over a period of time and therefore "what motivates him" also changes. As the person grows in career and maturity his needs shift upwards, from the most basic to the most mature, and hence a good manager must try and see the people making up the team in terms of which "Hierarchy of needs" that person belongs to and accordingly motivate the person or groups of persons. Maslow states that even when you have to get all the people to do the same thing you need to be motivated each of them differently. Hence to be able to practically motivate his team and establish the most appropriate HR policies in the Project a Project Manager must clearly understand Maslow's Hierarchy of Needs.

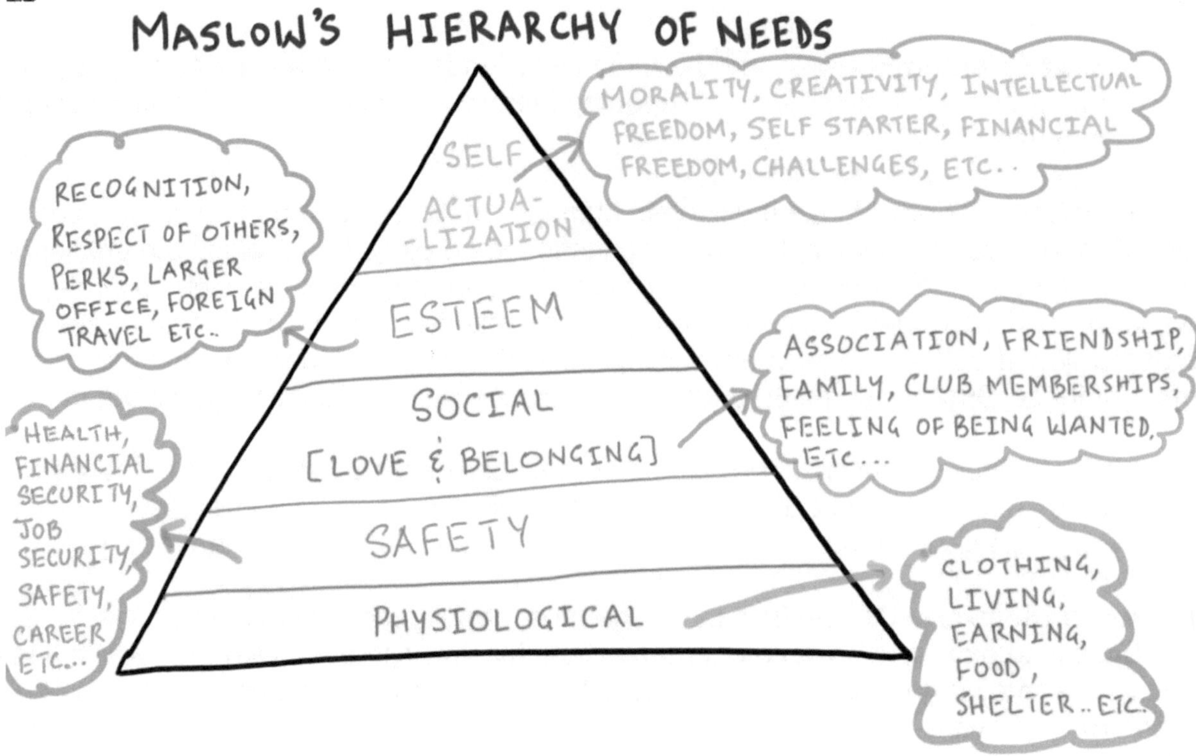

The Physiological Level constitutes basic needs like food, air, water, a roof over head etc. However in today's professional world, this does not exactly have to be Food, Air and water. Today this basic need is to focus on "Money". Hence to motivate a person at this level only monitory benefits would help.

Once the Physiological Needs are satisfied the human needs shift to the next level viz., the Safety level where the need for security and safety take precedence as a motivating factor. In today's world, this translates into an assurance of a "Secured Job" and a "Promising Career". Hence to motivate a person at this level giving Job security, making someone a permanent employee, providing health and family insurances etc. works wonders.

Post Safety Needs comes Social Needs (love and belonging). At this level, a person is more concerned about the feeling of belongingness both at the office and at home. To motivate person at this level giving memberships to specific organizational clubs, associations, making them guest speakers, giving recognition in public goes a long way.

Next is the Esteem Level. By the time a person reaches this level, he wants to let people know that he has arrived in life. Certificates of recognition and contribution, larger office, chauffer driven car, paid holidays and such other perks would be the motivating factors for the persons at this level.

And lastly, at the Self Actualization level, this is where the person wants to fulfill all his dreams and gets all the motivation he needs from within. The other needs do not really affect him. At this level, the project manager cannot really motivate the person but try and mentor such a person to give the best he can.

Another popular organizational theory is called the **Herzberg theory of Hygiene**. His theory was mostly a continuation of Maslow's theory of needs based motivation but continued to explain that there is a difference between "Motivating Factors" and "Hygiene Factors". He explained that a hygiene factor is something that is taken for granted by an employee and it's something which if present, does not provide any motivation, but which, if not present, would actually demotivate the employee. Let us take an example. Say you were hired into a company and you are given a desk and a chair with a filing cabinet and a laptop for work. Now, these things are taken for granted by you and expect from the organization so that you can work. These are not the things that will make you motivated as they are the bare necessities for work itself. However if for a few days these items are not assigned to you how would you really feel. Highly demotivated and disoriented. Hence these items are just Hygiene factors. On the other hand, if your boss gets you nominated for a very important training which will enhance your skills, does that not motivate you or is this something that you take for granted? For sure this will motivate you. Hence, improving your skills becomes a "Motivating Factor". Let us look at some Hygiene Factors and Motivating factors.

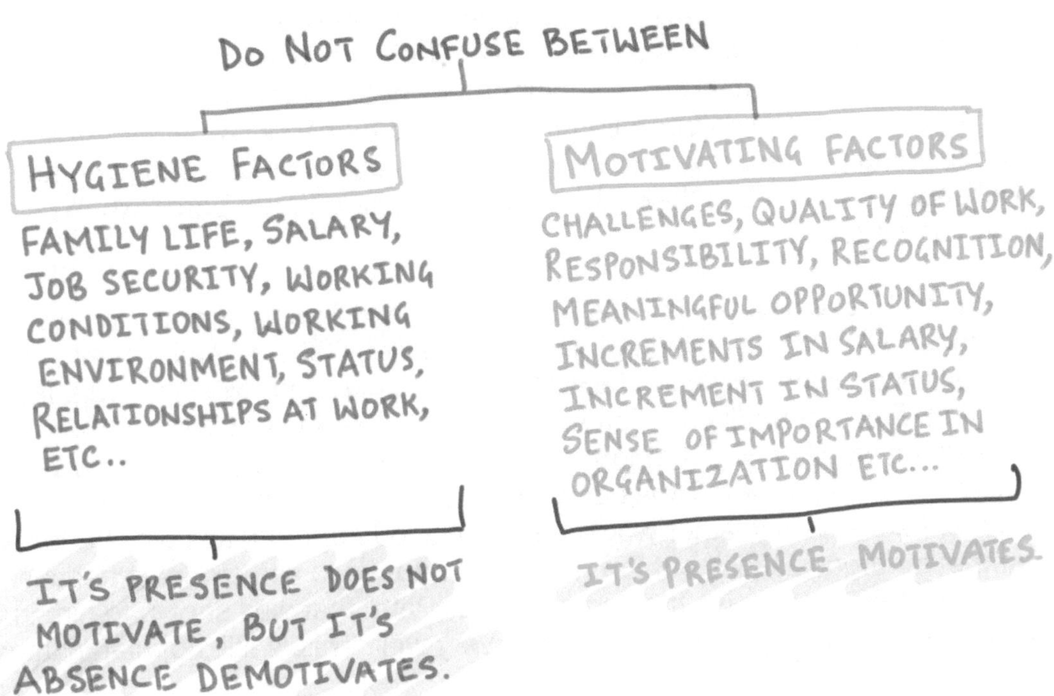

HERZBERG'S THEORY OF MOTIVATION
DO NOT CONFUSE BETWEEN
HYGIENE FACTORS
FAMILY LIFE, SALARY, JOB SECURITY, WORKING CONDITIONS, WORKING ENVIRONMENT, STATUS, RELATIONSHIPS AT WORK, ETC..
IT'S PRESENCE DOES NOT MOTIVATE, BUT IT'S ABSENCE DEMOTIVATES.
MOTIVATING FACTORS
CHALLENGES, QUALITY OF WORK, RESPONSIBILITY, RECOGNITION, MEANINGFUL OPPORTUNITY, INCREMENTS IN SALARY, INCREMENT IN STATUS, SENSE OF IMPORTANCE IN ORGANIZATION ETC...
IT'S PRESENCE MOTIVATES.

The whole purpose of Herzberg's theory is that one must differentiate between Hygiene and Motivating factors so that realistic motivating factors could be focused on while making a Human Resource Plan for the project.

There is a Management / Leadership theory that talks about the style of Management and it's called the "**Theory X and Theory Y**" of Management / Leadership.

"Theory X" style assumes that the people are unambitious, unmotivated, do not like to work and need constant monitoring. This management style calls for Micro Management and putting pressure on people to get the work done. This management style does not foster trust. The Managers / Leaders of this style follow the "Carrot and Stick" (Rewards and Punishments) approach to managing people. The line of authority is very straightforward in such management styles without much feedback. This management/leadership style does not promote innovation and people end up doing similar work all through.

"Theory Y" style assumes that the people are ambitious, trustworthy, like to work hard and like to be given opportunities to excel. Theory Y assumes that people become better when challenged with tougher and more challenging work. This style does not really put pressure on people through constant monitoring and control. There is hardly any Micro Management here.

While on the face of it, it seems that Theory Y is better than Theory X style, in reality, both of their advantages and challenges. Theory X is very good for work that needs "Consistency" and following a set path, like Assembly line, Construction work, Airport Control Towers, Shipping, Oil, and Gas pumping. However, Theory Y is very good for work that needs Innovation, anything that needs a fresh outlook and a new way of working.
If you look closely and remember the differences between a Project and Operations you will find that Theory X is more suited for Operations and Theory Y is more suited for Projects. Some organizations also classify their employees based on their working mindset as X employees (who can do operational work, need monitoring and control and need clear orders for executing work, not open to innovation etc.) and Y employees (who are open for challenges, can work on their own once given a target, get bored when given similar work again and again)..

Ouchi's Theory of Z (and no it's not connected to Theory X and Y above) is essentially a Japanese Theory of motivating a person by giving lifelong employment in the organization. This is still a major motivating factor in many eastern and western organizations. After taking early retirement from the Air Force, my father worked for 33 yrs., in a single organization and rose all the way to one of the top few officers of the organization. In my 20 yrs., of working for others I changed 7 jobs. Times do change and so does the theories that apply to motivating factors. I am sure my father would have got good opportunities with better pay from other competitor organizations but the reason he refused to join others is because he was not sure if those others would give the same "Career Path" that was shown to him in the organization where he worked. In his times it worked very well. This is still popular in Japan and some European companies.
Oh, by the way, this theory is called "Z" because it talks about employment until the "End of the career" of a person.

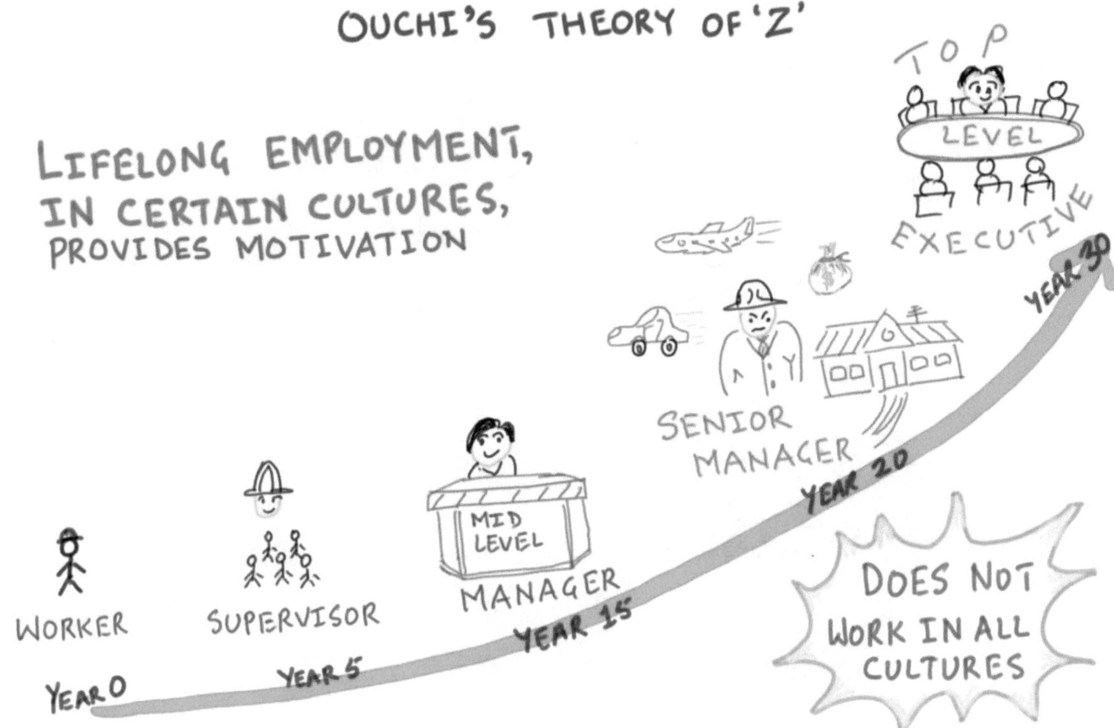

Vroom's Expectancy Theory: Predicts that employees in an organization will be motivated when they believe (or are convinced) that putting in more effort will yield better job performance; better job performance will lead to organizational rewards, such as an increase in salary or benefits; and these predicted organizational rewards are valued by the employee in question. Vroom's theory assumes that behavior results from conscious choices among alternatives whose purpose it is to maximize pleasure and to minimize pain.

McClelland' Motivational Needs Theory: Quite like Maslow's hierarchy of needs theory, McClelland states that people generally tend of have one or more of three distinctive needs. They are Need for Power, Need for Affiliation and Need for Achievement. A manager must ascertain the combination of needs that belong to a team member and motivate accordingly.

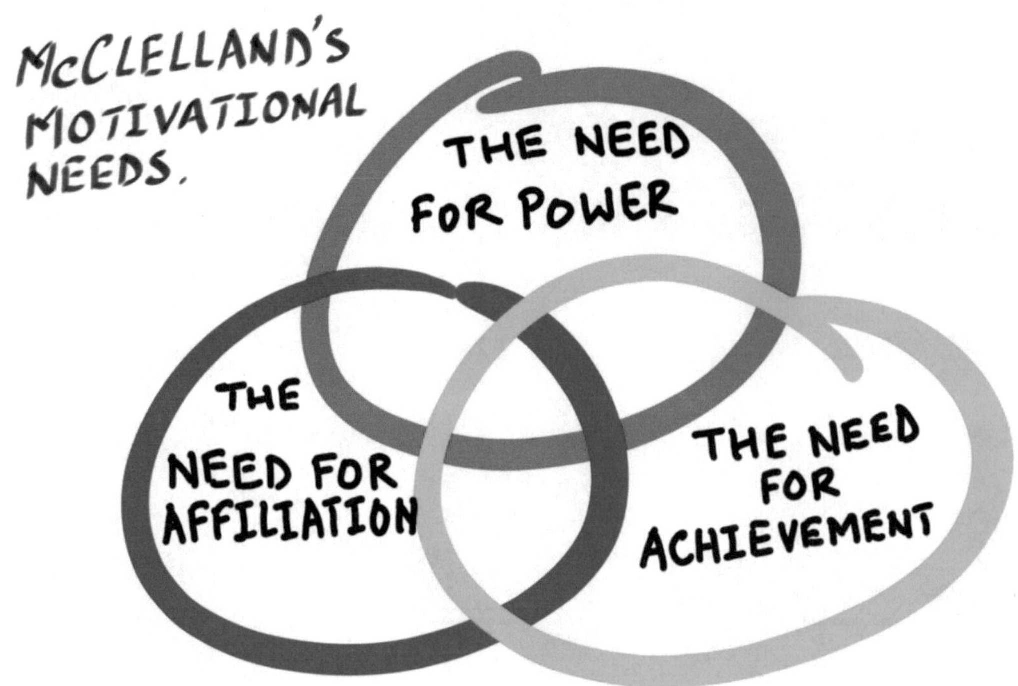

Skill Based Appraisals: While planning for the resources for a specific project, sometimes certain skill based appraisals would also need to be done to ascertain the apt fitment of the resource in question to the work in the project. E.g., If I was to manage a project for an offshore drilling platform in the middle of North Atlantic Ocean, I would need to get the resources who possess certain kind of mindset, certain kind of health criteria, certain kind of resilience, certain kind of technical skills that the project requires and also from attitude point of view I would need those resources who like to follow orders instead of trying be a cowboy. Offshore oil drilling platform is not a place for getting into a problem because the guys did not follow the safety protocol. There is just no scope for that. Though I took the example of an offshore oil drilling platform, the fact is every project has some specific skill and attitude requirements and hence the resource plan may even provide for certain specific kinds of skill appraisals that everyone must get through before becoming a team member in the said project. Some of the examples of such appraisals are:

1) Attitudinal Survey
2) Specific Assessments
3) Structured Interviews
4) Ability Tests
5) Focus Groups

9.21.2 Artefacts from this process: -

This process has 2 main outputs and they are Resource Management Plan and Team Charter.

Resource Management Plan contains, in details, as to how and by when would the project staff be assigned, managed and eventually released. One of the more important components of the Resource Management Plan is the “Plan for the Human Resources” or the “H R Management Plan”.

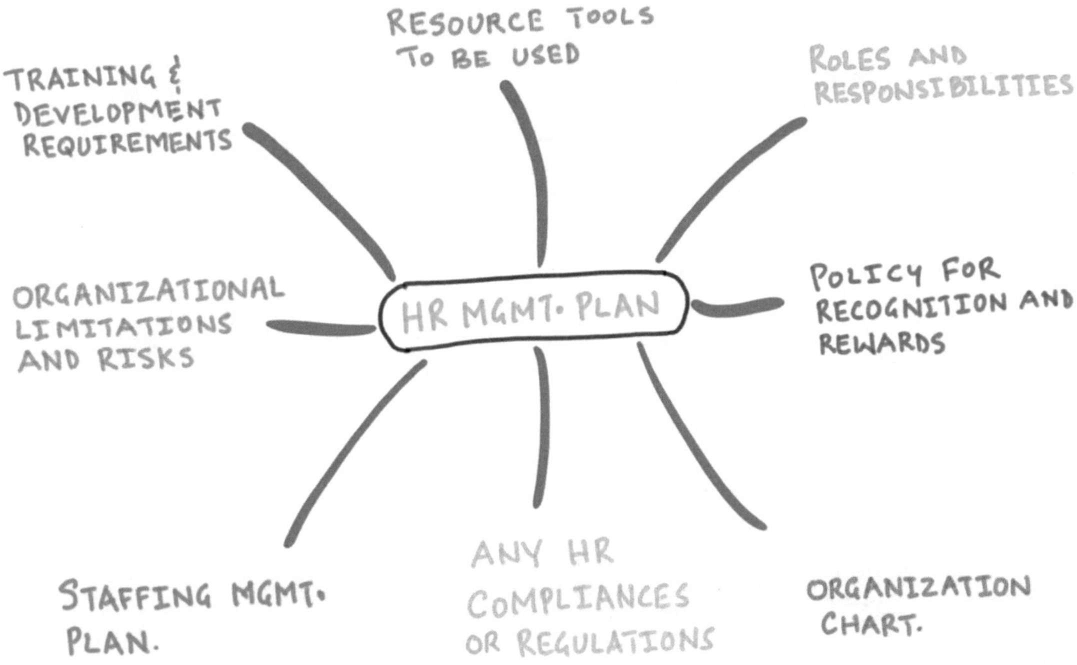

One of the elements of Resource Management Plan is the “Staffing Management Plan”. This plan shows the “Calendar Duration” as to when and how many and which kind of staff would be assigned to the project and when, how many and which kind of staff would be released from the project. This helps in proactive planning with resource managers. (Staffing management plan is also called Project Team Resource Management in various organizations as well in some of the questions in the exams).

In some organizations, this staffing management plan is documented as a matrix

STAFFING MANAGEMENT PLAN

RESOURCE NAMES	SEP.	OCT.	NOV.	DEC.	JAN.
PROJECT MANAGER	176 Hr	176 Hr	152 Hr	176 Hr	160 Hr
SYSTEM ANALYST-1	64 Hr	127 Hr	152 Hr		8 Hr.
SYSTEM ANALYST-2	64 Hr	23.5 Hr	152 Hr		8 Hr
PROGRAMMER-1	8 Hr	175 Hr	144 Hr		
PROGRAMMER-2	8 Hr	130 Hr	144 Hr		
TEST LEAD	88 Hr	210 Hr	56 Hr	103 Hr	112 Hr
TESTER		50 Hr	144 Hr	180 Hr	80 Hr
TECHNICAL WRITER	8 Hr		20 Hr		8 Hr
SENIOR ANALYST-1	180 Hr	150 Hr	23.5 Hr	176 Hr	140 Hr
SENIOR ANALYST-2	32 Hr	156 Hr			40 Hr
IMPLEMENTATION PLANNER	8 Hr	96 Hr	72 Hr		24 Hr

whereas in some organizations the staffing management plan is shown as a Histogram.

RESOURCE HISTOGRAM

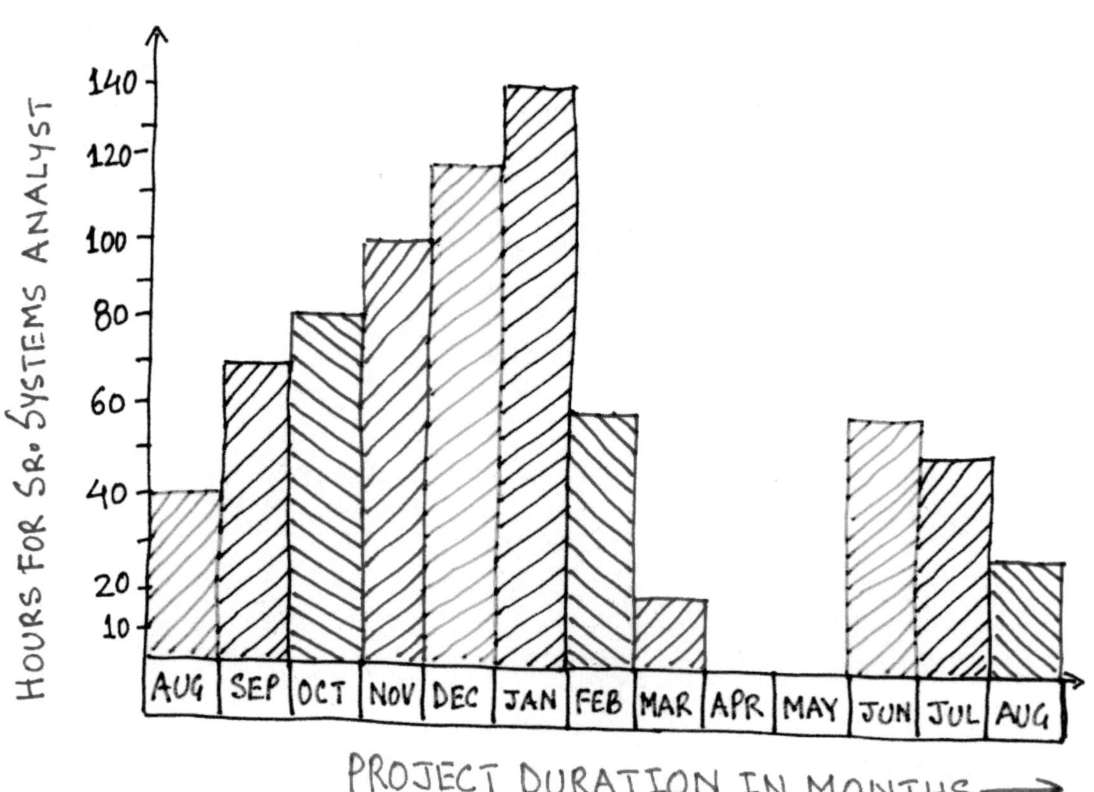

Team Charter is a document that establishes team values, ground rules, acceptable behavior, and team objectives to ensure team collaboration while at the same time reducing the chances of misunderstanding. Such a document is made in a group setting to ensure that every team member buys into this charter. This charter is even more important when the team is cross-cultural or Virtual, where there is a much higher chance of misunderstandings and confusions.

Team charter must be created by the team and agreed to by each and every team member. No exception. Project managers may help and guide the team to create an effective team charter but the actual content and the agreement to it has to be team effort.

One of the important elements of Team Charter is **Ground Rules**. Even though ground rules are a component in Team Charter, it is important to discuss them separately here for the simple reason that specific questions show up in PMP Exams on this topic. Ground Rules are essentially the “Do’s and Don’ts” or Code of Conduct for the team members vis-à-vis the project team. What are the acceptable practices and what are unacceptable practices, are clearly laid down in the ground rules. Since it is a portion of the overall Team Charter, Ground Rules must be created among the team members with their express inputs and consensus. The ground rules must also be accepted by and agreed to by each and every team member. There cannot be any exception. All team members must agree to it. Now in order for the team members to agree to every aspect of the ground rules the project manager must create an environment of trust. Without trust ground rules would just become a piece of paper that is not adhered to be the team members. Trust is crucial ingredient.

If in exams you get scenarios where they state that the team is facing a lot of confusions and conflicts. People are speaking over each other, or team members are not sure why different people are following different rules, in such cases the correct option would be to relook at or refer to the ground rules. Any confusion regarding do's and don'ts are nothing but the absence of ground rules or adherence to ground rules.

The ground rules affect the future behavior of the team members:

- By getting the entire team on the same page about behaviour
- Encourages collaboration among cross functional teams
- Reduces conflicts
- Encourages participation and inclusion
- Reduces confusion
- Faster resolution of conflicts
- Less supervision and interference by the project manager or leader

With more and more teams, organizations and industries relying on virtual team structure to get the work done, it only makes sense that the resource management plan must also contain plans around virtual team technology and collaboration techniques to be used during the project. Most common tools are:

- Shared Task Boards (like Kanban) to promote visibility
- Dedicated video conference line for enhanced collaboration
- Chat boards and shared messages for impromptu communication
- Knowledge repositories for sharing documents
- More opportunity for "face-to-face" discussions

It is always a great idea to include a co-located meeting among all team members at least once during the entire project lifecycle if the project is being done virtually. However this would be subject to the availability of the budget. Spending some money on getting all the team members together goes a long way in cementing bonds among diverse team members and the money spent on co-located meeting gets more than compensated by the productivity among the virtual team members during the project. If you plan to have a co-located meeting with all your team members, the best time to do that is during the Kick-off meeting. Kick-Off meeting is done immediately once the planning is completed and just before execution. This will not only create bonding but also ensure that all the team members are on the same page as far as the project is concerned.

The entire purpose of establishing a Team Charter (including the Ground Rules) is to help create a positive "Team Norm" in the shortest possible time. A "Norm" is the set of accepted behavior among the team members that are automatically followed as a given. Let me give you an example to fully comprehend the concept of Norm. When I was a child, at my parent's home my mother had established a clear rule that there would be no consumption of Non-Vegetarian food within the house. I and my father were both fond of non-vegetarian food but we could not eat it home. We had to get ourselves invited to our friends place or eat out at a restaurant but never at home. In the beginning, like any over confident child, I vehemently opposed this rule but my mother did not budge and always explained her side of logic. Over time we stopped resisting and internalized the rule. Now that my mother is no more with us we continue to do the same. We simply cannot comprehend the concept of eating non-vegetarian at home. My wife has internalized this rule as well and so has my daughter. This is the "Norm" at our home. This is how cultures and civilizations are created over time. However when it comes to Project, we do not have the luxury of time and hence we have to get the team to themselves enforce the rules in such a manner that it turns into the “Team Norm” at the shortest possible time.

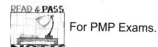

9.22 Ninja Drill – Planning - 3

In this Ninja Drill you will find the most important notes and pointers that are important from the point of PMP Exams and covers, Plan Cost Management, Estimate Costs, Determine Budget, Plan Quality Management and Plan Resources.

S. No.	Drill Points
1.	Cost Management Plan is the output of the process Plan Cost Management.
2.	Direct Costs are those expenses that are billed only to your project. Indirect Costs are expenses that are apportioned across all projects and operations within the organizations. Indirect Costs = Overheads.
3.	Variable Costs are those that vary in amounts based on the amount of usage or consumption. While Fixed Costs are those that do not vary based on usage or consumption.
4.	The main Tools & Techniques of the process "Estimate Costs" are: 1. Analogous Estimating 2. Parametric Estimating 3. Bottom-Up Estimating 4. Three –Point Estimating and 5. Commercial Database
5.	Commercial Database is the presence of databases specific to industries that include standardized cost estimating data and industry risk study information which could be readily used for estimating costs and / or schedule for a project.
6.	While estimating costs the following should also be taken into considerations: • Cost of Quality (COQ) • Reserves (Contingency and Management) • Alternative Analysis
7.	Cost Of Quality = [Prevention Cost + Appraisal Cost] + [Internal Failure + External Failure]
8.	The main output / outcome / artefact of the process "Estimate Costs" is Cost Estimations.
9.	Budget = Approved Project Estimate.
10.	Reserves are kept for risks. There two kinds of Reserves viz., 1. Contingency Reserve (for Identified Risks) and 2. Management Reserve (for Unidentified Risks).
11.	Project Estimate + Contingency Reserve = Cost Baseline Cost Baseline + Management Reserve = Project Cost Budget Project Cost Budget – Management Reserve – Contingency Reserve = Project Estimate
12.	S-Curve shows the cost cumulative curve to show patterns or trends of actual expenditure in a project against the baseline budget.
13.	The main outcome / output / artefact of the process "Determine Budget" are: 1. Cost Baseline 2. Management Reserve
14.	Quality is the degree to which a set of inherent characteristics of a product, service, or result fulfils the requirements.
15.	Quality = Conformity To Requirements + Fitness Of Use
16.	Defect = Non-Conformity to Requirements and Errors or Bugs = Non-Fitness for use.
17.	You cannot compare quality of products / services across Grades.
18.	TQM = Total Quality Management (The First Institute of Quality in the world) and provided PDCA.
19.	PDCA = Plan-Do-Check-Act = Cycle of Continuous Improvement. PDSA = Plan-Do-Study-Act = Cycle of continuous improvement for processes.
20.	Six Sigma Benchmarks are:

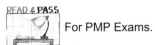

	• +/- 1 Sigma provides accuracy level of 68.26% • +/- 2 Sigma provides accuracy level of 95.46% • +/- 3 Sigma provides accuracy level of 99.73% • +/- 6 Sigma provides accuracy level of 99.99%
21.	At Six Sigma level the defects are only 3.4 Defects Per Million Opportunities (DPMO).
22.	Having a low grade is not a problem as it is part of the requirements but having a low quality is a problem.
23.	Lean = Waste minimization
24.	Kaizan = Change For Better, a Japanese philosophy of continuous improvement. This improvement suggestions are usually done by the labour, staff, employees themselves.
25.	Providing anything extra to the customer outside of the scope with the intent of delighting the customer but done without any approval from anyone, is called Gold Plating.
26.	The main Tools & Techniques of the process "Plan Quality Management" are: 1. Cost Benefit Analysis 2. Checklist 3. Cost Of Quality
27.	The main outputs / outcomes / artefacts of the process "Plan Quality Management" are: 1. Quality Metric 2. Quality Management Plan
28.	Project Team is a group of individuals who help the project manager conduct project work to meet the project objectives.
29.	Project Management Team is a subset of the Project Team.
30.	Tools & Techniques of the process "Plan Resource Management" are: 1. Responsibility Assignment Matrix (RAM) / Responsible, Accountable, Consulted and Informed (RACI) Charts 2. Organizational Theories on Motivation
31.	RAM = Responsibility Assignment Matrix RACI = Responsible, Accountable, Consulted and Informed RAM = RACI (also called RASI where "S" stands for Support)
32.	Extrinsic motivating factors are offered to a person subject to specific parameters. E.g., Awards, Citations, Salary Increments, Promotions, Perks etc.
33.	Intrinsic motivating factors are the drivers that exist within the mind-set of a person.
34.	Three types of Intrinsic Motivating factors: 1. Autonomy 2. Mastery 3. Purpose
35.	Physiological Needs are the lowest while Self Actualization are the highest needs on the Maslow's Hierarchy of Needs.
36.	As per Herzberg, Hygiene factors are those factors, presence of which does not motivate a person but its absence demotivates a person.
37.	Mc Gregor's "Theory X" style assumes that people are unambitious, unmotivated, do not like to work and need constant monitoring. This management style calls for Micro Management and putting pressure on people to get the work done.
38.	Mc Gregor's "Theory Y" style assumes that people are ambitious, trustworthy, like to work hard and like to be given opportunities to excel. Theory Y assumes that people become better when challenged with tougher and more challenging work.
39.	The three elements of Mc Clelland's motivation theory are The Need for Power, The Need for Affiliation and The Need for Achievement.
40.	Some of the Skill Appraisal tools are: • Attitudinal Survey • Specific Assessments • Structured Interviews • Ability Tests

	• Focus Groups
41.	The Team Charter is a document that establishes the team values, agreements and operating guidelines for the team.
42.	Things included in the charter could be: - 1. Team's Shared Values 2. Communication Guidelines 3. Decision-making criteria 4. Conflict Resolution Process 5. Meeting Guidelines 6. Team Agreements 7. Ground Rules
43.	Team Charter must be made by the team. The Ground Rules must be accepted by each and everyone in the team.
44.	Ground Rules are supposed to set a Clear Code of Conduct for the Team Members regarding working together as a Team.
45.	Project Manager must create an environment of TRUST so that the Team adhere to Ground Rules
46.	Common collaboration tools in Virtual Teams are: - • Shared Task Boards (like Kanban) to promote visibility • Dedicated and continuous video conference line for enhanced collaboration (also called Fishbowl) • Knowledge repositories for sharing documents • Opportunity for face-to-face discussions
47.	The expected behaviour of the team is called the Team Norm.
48.	The main outputs / outcomes / artefacts of the process "Plan Resource Management" is • Resource Management Plan (includes) • RACI / RAM • Team Charter • Ground Rules • List Of Physical Resources
End Of Ninja Drill	

9.23 Planning For Procurement (Plan Procurement Management)

This Knowledge Area is dedicated to the project outsourcing either in total or in parts. The moment a decision is taken by an organization to outsource a project (or just a part thereof) the processes of this Knowledge Area become applicable.
Let us look at the perspective first when it comes to Procurement Management.

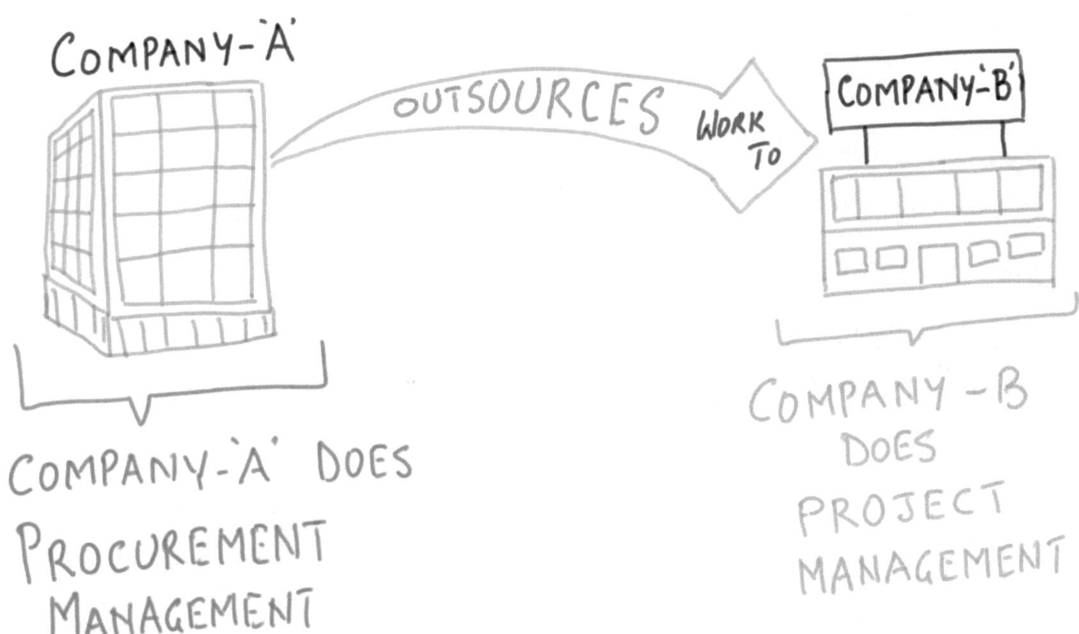

Outsourcing is done through the use of legal documents like Agreements / Contracts, therefore a lot of legalities come into picture while outsourcing the project. Hence, Procurement Management is replete with a lot of legal terminologies.

When something is outsourced it's not necessary that one project would only have one outsource. A single project from the buyer side may spawn a number of outsourcing. And each of the outsourcing would be treated as a separate contract and hence, a separate "Procurement".

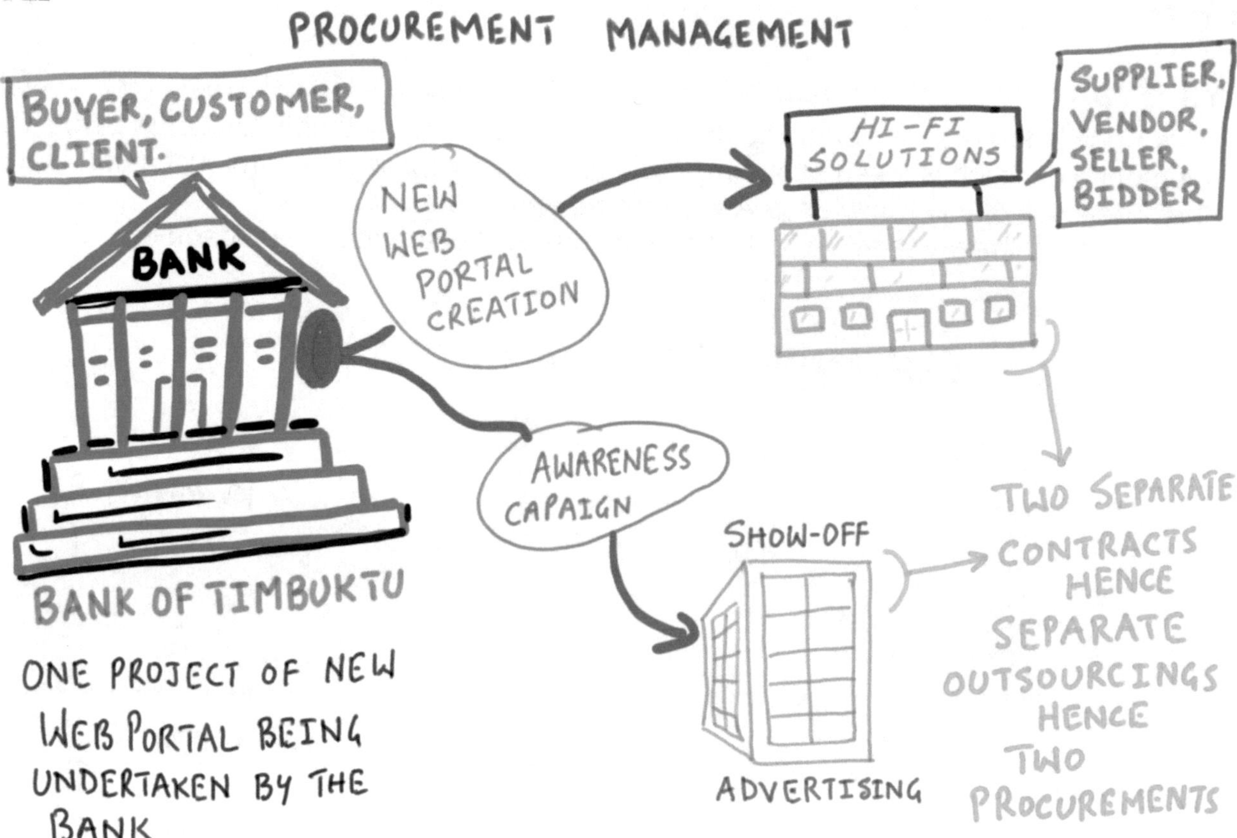

There can be a lot of depth in outsourcing as well. A buyer can outsource a project to sellers who in turn could outsource work to other sellers and so on. In several countries, including India, a limit has been placed on the level of depth that procurement arrangements can be allowed to create.

PROCUREMENT DEPTH

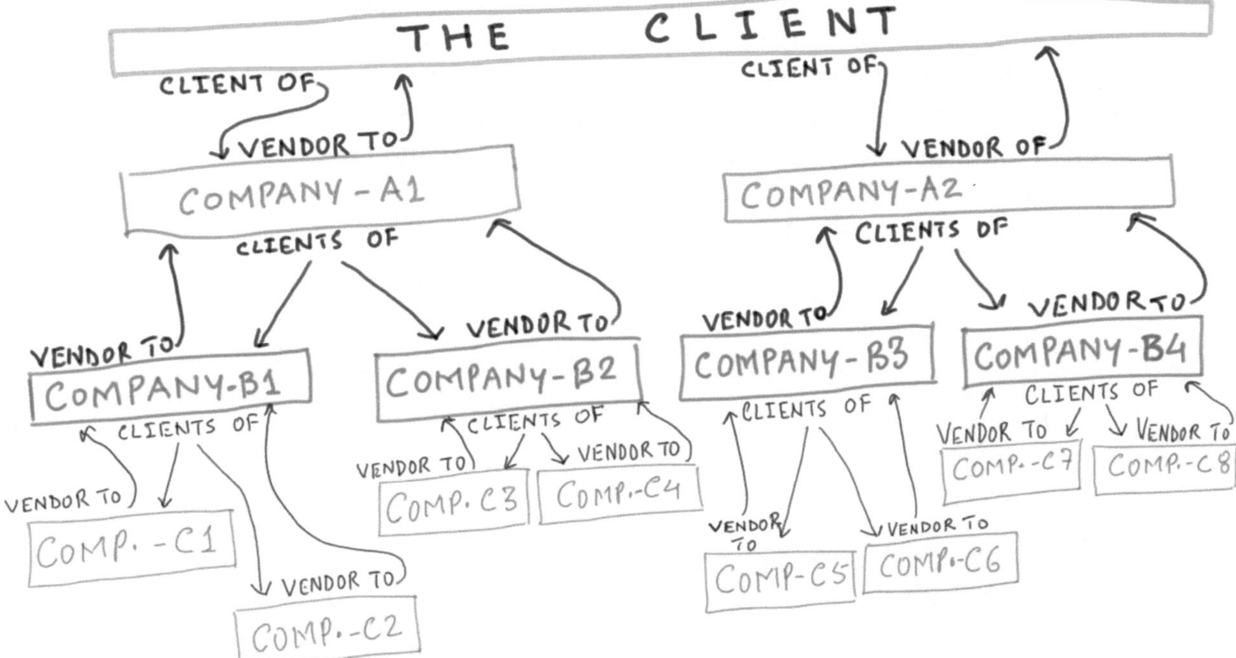

It is important to note that when it comes to procurements, the Project Team takes a secondary place vis-à-vis the Procurement / Legal team.
A lot of people ask me as to why does Procurement have so much legality? The reason is that there is corruption in the world but procurement situations have historically, generated the maximum corruption cases in the world. Hence the law has to try and prevent such corruption cases which makes this Knowledge Area full of legality. Besides when Agreements and Contracts are involved the Mercantile Law and the Law of Contracts come into picture anyway.

There is a lot of new development taking place in the field of procurement. Tremendous advances have been made in the management science of Supply Chain Management for streamlining the supply of material and equipment. Use of software in supply chain management has allowed shortening the time gap between order and receipt of the material or equipment. Procurement Management has started using a lot of technology. In high-end defense projects the Ministry Of Defense has started taking live camera feeds from the shop-floor of the vendor. Civil Construction and Infrastructure projects have started using RFID and Internet of Things (IoT) to track the shipment of the material and equipment better.
With the maturity in Procurement Management, organizations have started doing more rigorous risk management and ensuring that the terms of the contract clearly take care of some of the risks. Globalization has allowed organizations to get suppliers from any part of the world which has ushered in the International law into its fold.
In more technology intensive and complex projects and programs, before finalizing a vendor, buyers try out more than one suppliers for a short period of time (for consideration) to see which one is better and more reliable before going ahead with a full-blown signing of the contract with any one of them. This is called “Trial Agreements”.

PLAN PROCUREMENT MANAGEMENT is the process where the decision to outsource is made. The moment any outsourcing is considered, a "Make or Buy" decision is undertaken. If the decision is to "Make" than no other process of procurement is undertaken. However if the decision to "Buy" is made, then the processes of Procurement actually start.
There are many reasons why a decision of "Buy" could be made.

REASONS TO BUY
TO OVERCOME TECHNICAL RISKS
FOR OBTAINING BEST QUALITY SERVICES
WHEN THE ORGANIZATION RUNS SHORT OF SPECIFIC RESOURCES.
FREEING INTERNAL RESOURCES FOR OTHER PURPOSES.
IMPROVING ORGANIZATIONAL FOCUS AREA
TO GET THOSE THINGS DONE WHICH ARE NOT PART OF YOUR CORE COMPETENCE.
TO ACCESS GLOBAL KNOWLEDGE BASE.
FOR SHARING AN OPPORTUNITY
FOR COST BENEFITS
TO HELP EXPAND TO NEW MARKET AREAS.
FOR TEMPORARY ENGAGEMENTS THAT DOES NOT WARRANT CAPITAL INVESTMENT BY BUYING ORGANIZATION.
TO HELP DISMANTLE UN-PROFITABLE OR TIME CONSUMING FUNCTIONS.
BECAUSE OF BEING A PROJECTIZED ORGANIZATION.

What is basically done in this process?

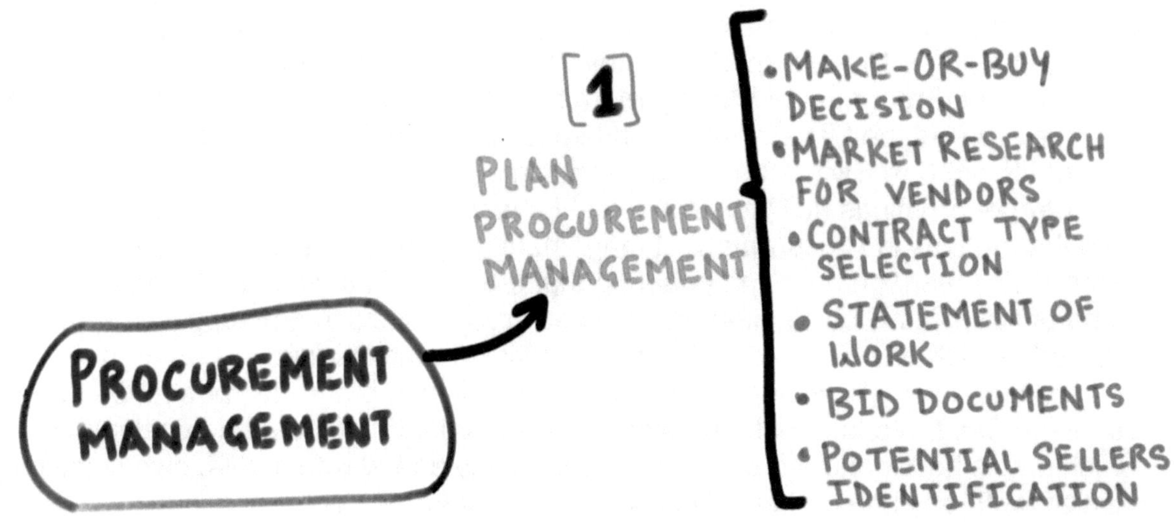
PROCUREMENT MANAGEMENT
[1]
PLAN PROCUREMENT MANAGEMENT
• MAKE-OR-BUY DECISION
• MARKET RESEARCH FOR VENDORS
• CONTRACT TYPE SELECTION
• STATEMENT OF WORK
• BID DOCUMENTS
• POTENTIAL SELLERS IDENTIFICATION

Many organizations, which have offices in multiple geographical locations, tend to have "Centralized Procurement Department", which essentially means that only one Procurement team located in the Head Office would handle all procurements irrespective of the country or geographical location where the procurement is being done.

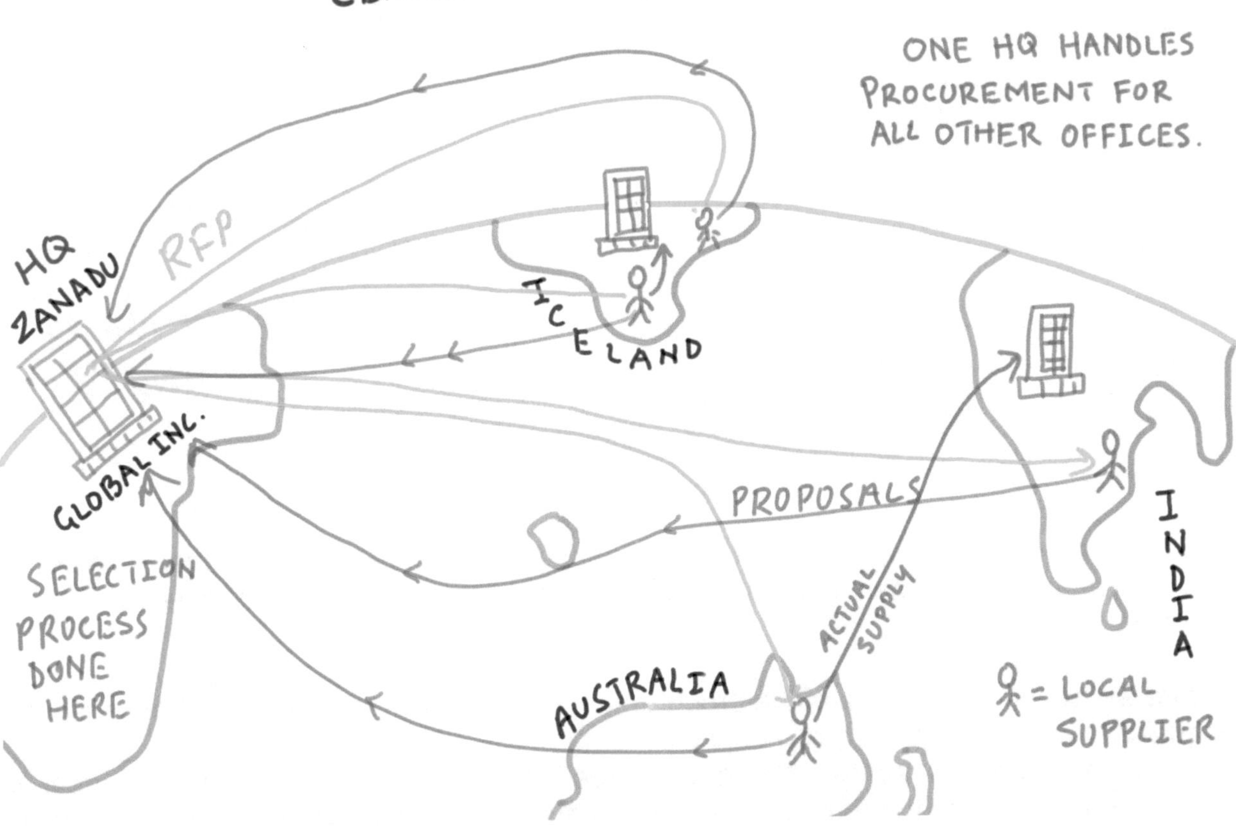

At the same time, there are a lot of organizations which have "Decentralized Procurement Departments" which essentially means that each of the local offices would have their own procurement departments to handle the procurements for those offices.

There are advantages and disadvantages to both types. Whatever the situation is the office structure of the procurement department plays a very important part in Procurement Planning.

Before we get into the details of the procurement planning it would make a lot of sense to get acquainted with some procurement specific terms:

1) **Contract and Agreement**: In reality there is a big difference between a Contract and an Agreement. Agreement is any understanding between two or more parties of legal age which has been agreed to legally through a legal instrument. Agreement is a very wide term. Contract, on the other hand, is any agreement that has a commercial transaction or exchange of money or money's worth in return for goods, services or action. Therefore a contract is a sub-set of agreements. From PMP exams point of view you can freely use both the terms interchangeably. PMP does not differentiate between the two.
2) **Request For Proposal [RFP]**: When the buying organization reaches out to bidders and wants to invite them to submit their proposals regarding some work that the buying organization wants to outsource, the buying organization first creates a comprehensive document which contains details about the work that needs to be done, by when it would have to be done, terms of the contract and more details about the work in the form of "Statement Of Work (SOW). Remember the RFP is sent out to the bidders by the organization that wants to outsource some work.
3) **Proposal**: Once the bidders have received the RFP from the buyer organization, the bidders take some time to understand the requirements, conduct business case and benefits management exercises to understand if this project is worth bidding for. If they find that it is worth bidding for, the bidder would then create a formal document that clearly lays down all details, approach, suitability, technical information and the commercials and submit it with the buying organization. This document that is

submitted by the bidders with the buying organization, is called Proposal. It is in response to a RFP.

4) **Statement Of Work [SOW]**: One of the biggest components of RFP is the SOW. This can be issued as a separate document or it could be included in the main document of the RFP itself. This document contains all the requirements as well as the scope of the work to be outsourced.
5) **Request For Quote [RFQ]**: RFP is issued by the outsourcing organization when that organization wishes to outsource some customized work or service. However when it comes to procurement of readymade articles or services, instead of an RFP, a RFQ is used. Unlike RFP, there are no SOW or other technical or service level details in RFQ. This is because RFQ is about procuring readymade articles or services and only needs to focus on the "Quote" / price of the product or service.
6) **Bid Documents**: These are a combination of documents (depending on the kind of procurement) that consists of all documents and forms that are sent out to the bidders for inviting proposals or quotes.
7) **Request For Information [RFI]**: Let us say that you want to outsource some work or procure a kind of equipment which is not easily available. You are not even sure if there are organizations in your geographical area which can handle your procurement requirements. Therefore, what you will do is create a document that contains the overall description of what you want and distribute it to as many bidders as possible with the intent to know if there are bidders in your area which can handle this work. This is what is called and RFI. This document does not invite anyone to send a proposal or a quote. If there are some bidders that respond to your RFI then you can empanel them and when you actually prepare the RFP or RFQ you can then send to these very bidders.
8) **Prequalified Bidders**: Indian Air Force (IAF), like any other major organization, regularly outsources a lot of work. However, since it is a defense organization it has a more detailed security protocol and regulations that every single bidder has to qualify before even the RFP can be issued to it. Just imagine if IAF has to run this security protocol selection process for each of the group of vendors that respond to each of the bid documents, you can imagine the colossal amount of work that would get added. Not to mention the immense delay in the entire procurement process. Therefore, what IAF does, it reaches out to bidders who would like to get security-prequalification with them. I got myself through that for all Project Management and Program Management services. There are a few others as well on IAF prequalification list which offer similar services as I do. IAF has done this with all kinds of work that they usually or routinely outsource. This way they have a list of pre-qualified bidders. The moment the procurement department gets a new request for outsourcing, they simply look at the list of prequalified bidders that can do that work and send out the bid documents to them. Rest what follows is the routine procurement process. It is not only with IAF, other organizations that outsource a lot and has some common protocol that all bidders must qualify, they usually have a prequalified list of bidders.
9) **Empaneled Vendors:** A lot of people (and unfortunately some books as well) tend to think that Empaneled Vendors are the same as Prequalified Bidders. This is incorrect. Let us take an example to explain this and also highlight the difference between empaneled vendors and prequalified bidders. Philips Healthcare specializes in commissioning CT Scanners as well as MRI's, among other things, at some of the top hospitals and diagnostic centers all over the world. Most of their commissioning involves creation of a radioactive waves protection partitions. This work is always

outsourced. This creation of a partition of radiations shields is a rather specialized work. Hence what Philips has done is instead of going through the entire procurement process each time there is a new commissioning project, they have hired and on boarded several organizations which specialize in this work. Even the compensation rates have been fixed with them for the next couple of years. This allows such amazing flexibility and professionalism in work that when Philips gets a new project, they simply reach out to anyone of the available "Empaneled Vendors" and request to get involved in the project. They are more or less an extended team of Philips. I guess now you can see the huge difference between the concepts of Qualified Bidders and Empaneled Vendors. By the way, another thing you must know is that bidders are those to whom bid documents have been sent to, while a Vendor is a selected Bidder.

I guess this is good enough information to begin going through the nitty-gritty of the process.

9.23.1 Main Tools and Techniques of this process: -

Expert Judgment could be procurement managers, supply chain professionals, legal experts, purchase specialists, SME's, project managers with similar past experience in procurement and even external consultants who excel at such procurements. They are the ones who suggest the kind of contract which is best suited for the kind work that needs to be outsourced, specific kinds of terms to be included in the contract as well as the overall process to be used in the procurement process.
Let us try and spend some time to understand the kinds of contracts that are important from the point of projects related procurement. There are literally 100s of different kinds of contracts but from the Projects point of view, there are just 4 kinds.

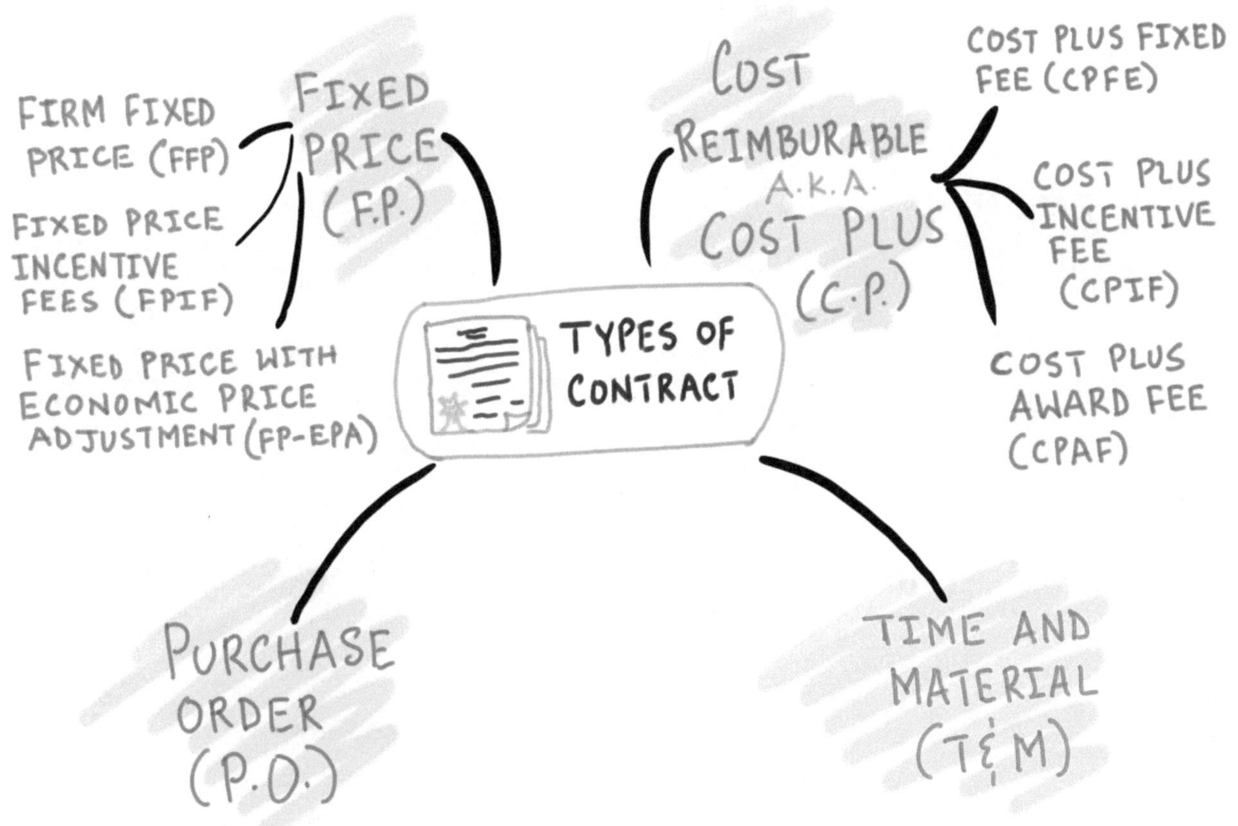

Let us start with the "**Purchase Order**". The most important thing to note about PO is that it is used only for purchasing "Off the Shelf Ready Made" articles. PO is not used for anything which needs fresh creation (like a new building or a software or a new medical formulation) but is used for "Ready Made" articles like Soap, Pens, Pads, Pencils, Standard Electrical Equipment, Laptops, Sand, Cement, Electrical Panels, Air Conditioners, Standard model generators etc. Since there is no customization involved there is no need for the Procuring Organization to issue a "Request For Proposal" (RFP) as there is no need to explain the specifications of the articles to be bought. All the procuring organization has to do is to let the bidders know the specific article/equipment sought, quantity and the time within which the delivery has to be made. This kind of document is called the "Request For Quotation" (RFQ). In reply to the RFQ floated by the procuring organization the bidders have to send back a "Quotation". For selection purposes there are no technical performance measurements, just the cheapest quote is selected. The PO is issued by the Procuring Organization to the selected vendor and has to be accepted by both of them.

When an RFQ is issued it means that the contract is a onetime purchase. Later on if the organization has to buy the exact same article or service they would have to go through the entire bidding process all over again.

PURCHASE ORDER (P.O.)

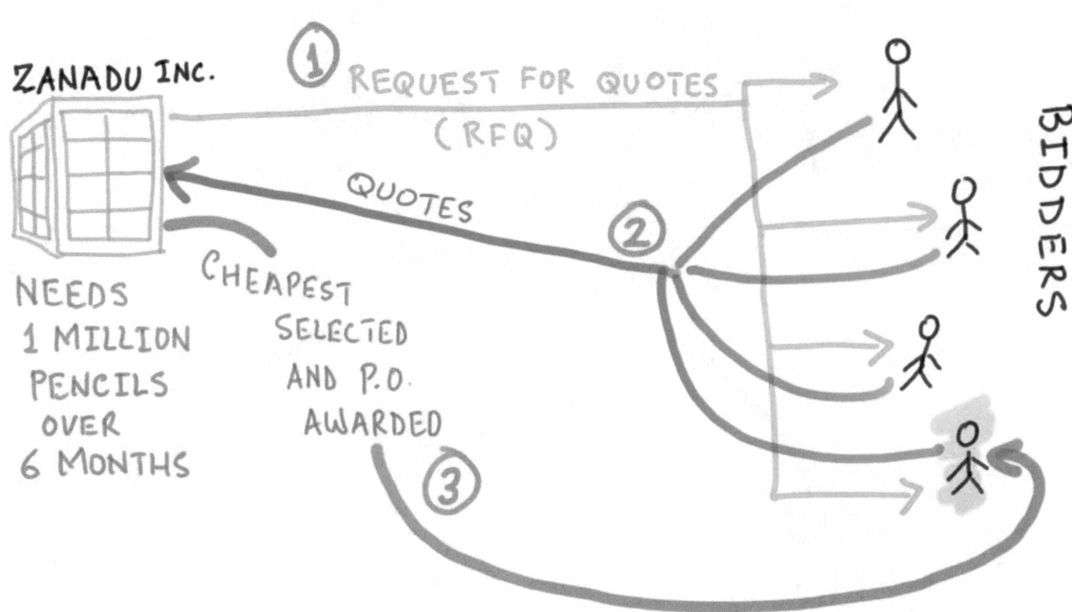

PO is also used for "Rate Contract". A Rate Contract is a running contract where a "Per Unit" price is agreed upon with the vendor and then different quantities of that material or equipment or services are procured at different times on the agreed upon rate. This kind of PO is established only when the quantity of equipment or material is not known in advance. Hence, in this case, the Procuring Organization issues a "Request For Bid" asking for the cheapest "Unit Price" of the material/equipment/service in question. The bidders respond through "Bids" and the cheapest is usually chosen and a PO is signed with the selected vendor for providing material/equipment/ services on the agreed upon rate in different quantities and frequencies over a given period. From exams point of view the RFB is not at all popular but then it's a related subject and as a good Project Manager you must know it.

Ok, so we are done with the PO.

Now on to the next Contract type, the **Fixed Price Contract**.
A fixed price contract takes the longest time to agree on compared to all the other kinds of contracts. Let us first understand why it's called a "Fixed Price" and why it's different from PO Contract. (A lot of people get confused between FP and PO contracts and end up using them interchangeably)
Let me give you an elaborate example to explain the concept of Fixed Price contract. Let us say your organization needs a "Financial Software for its Finance and Accounting Department". The organization tried to see if the standard Financial Software created by some companies would suit your needs but realized that it was not so. The only option now left would be to get a software "Custom-made" for your organization. For this, you would have to provide all the requirements to the bidders who in turn would give a demonstration of their technical competency as well as the price for the same. Since this is going to be a

customized software there would not be a price reference available in the market, and that is the reason why you would invite proposals from more than one bidders. Once the proposals from all the bidders are received you would conduct the "Technical" competency eligibility first. This would help eliminate some of the bidders. Only then would you look at the commercials/price quoted for the software by the bidders who passed the Technical Eligibility. Once the final bidder is selected a contract would be signed between your organization and the selected bidder where the bidder agrees to charge a price for the software to be constructed and delivered. The moment this contract is signed the price is now "Fixed". This means that if the vendor had not understood all the requirements completely, it's his fault and he would have to complete the contract whether he makes a profit or a loss. He is legally bound to fulfill this contract. This is why it's called a Fixed Price Contract but as you can see this kind of contract is only for "Custom made" work and not for Off The Shelf / readymade articles. This kind of contract requires a detailed RFP and the reply is in the form of a proposal and the finally selected vendor then enters into a Fixed Price Contract with the Procuring Organization.

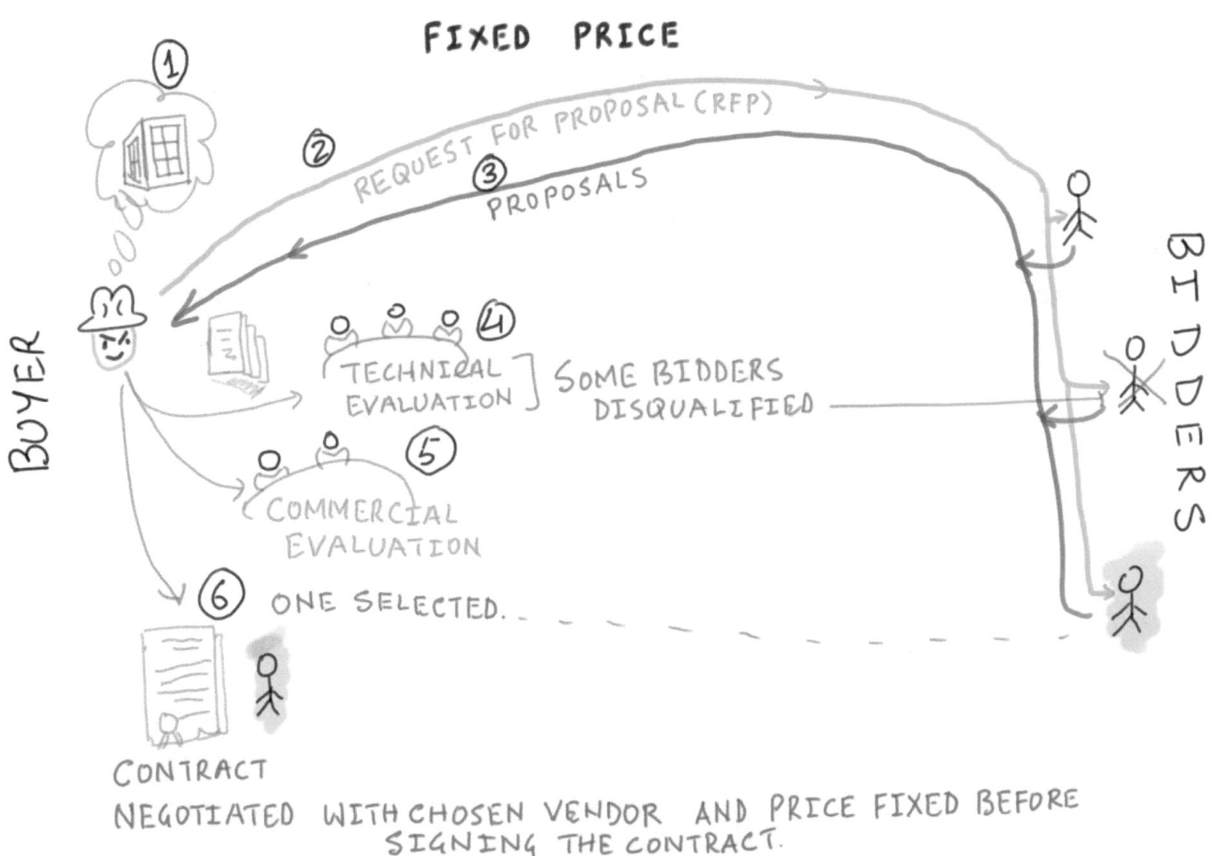

If you look at the way the FP contracts are set up they are quite risky for the vendors while there is absolutely negligible cost risks to the buyer. The concept of "Point of Total Assumption" may afflict the vendor and this is where instead of making some profits the vendor may end up making terrible losses. "The Point of Total Assumption" is when a vendor ends up using the entire price of the FFP contract and has still not been able to complete the project as per the contract. This point where the money spent by the vendor equals that of the total fees payable to him as per the FFP contract, is called the "Point Of Total

Assumption". Because from this point onwards, since the work is still not completed, the vendor has to "assume" all the costs till completion.

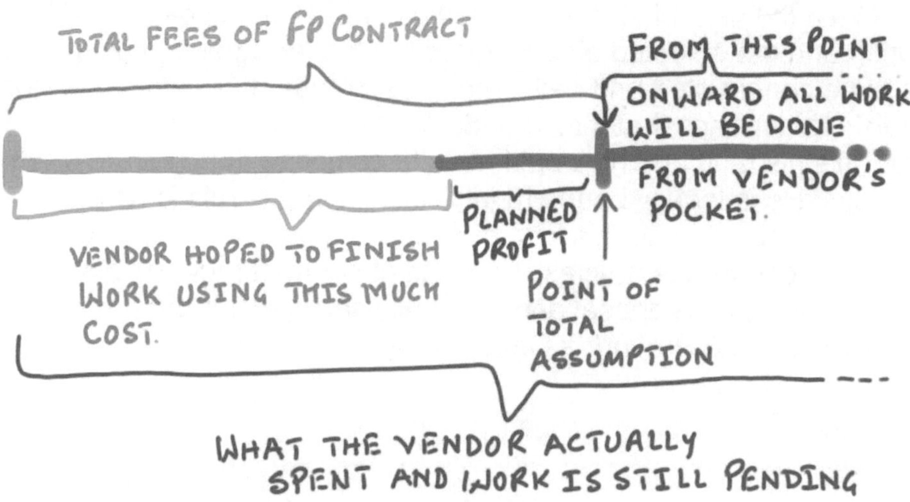

This is the reason why most buyers insist on an FP contract and that's why the vendors take some time to ensure that nothing is missed before they agree to the terms of an FP contract. Missing something at the contracting stage may lead to a serious budget overruns later during project execution, something which the buyer would not pay for. However, if there is a "Change of Scope" suggested by the buyer then the contract would go into a Change process and a new price would be agreed upon.

There are some variants of the FP contract.

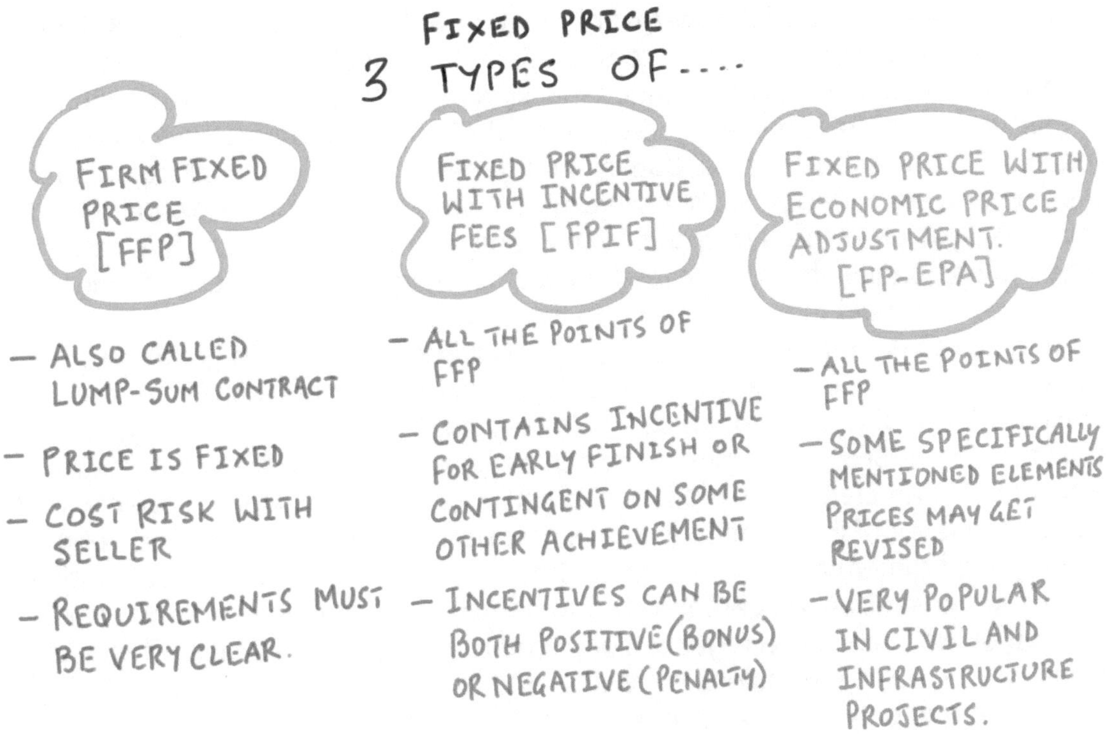

FIXED PRICE
3 TYPES OF....

FIRM FIXED PRICE [FFP]

- ALSO CALLED LUMP-SUM CONTRACT
- PRICE IS FIXED
- COST RISK WITH SELLER
- REQUIREMENTS MUST BE VERY CLEAR.

FIXED PRICE WITH INCENTIVE FEES [FPIF]

- ALL THE POINTS OF FFP
- CONTAINS INCENTIVE FOR EARLY FINISH OR CONTINGENT ON SOME OTHER ACHIEVEMENT
- INCENTIVES CAN BE BOTH POSITIVE (BONUS) OR NEGATIVE (PENALTY)

FIXED PRICE WITH ECONOMIC PRICE ADJUSTMENT. [FP-EPA]

- ALL THE POINTS OF FFP
- SOME SPECIFICALLY MENTIONED ELEMENTS PRICES MAY GET REVISED
- VERY POPULAR IN CIVIL AND INFRASTRUCTURE PROJECTS.

One is a Firm Fixed Price (FFP) which was just explained above. Another one is Fixed Price with Incentive Fees (FPIF) where an incentive is added to the contract for say, early finish of the project or related to performance etc. Hence an Incentive would be paid, provided the conditions of incentive are met, over and above the agreed upon Fixed Price. The third and the last variant of the FP contract is the Fixed Price with Economic Price Adjustment (FP-EPA). Say you are a vendor who has got a contract for building a hospital building for a large healthcare chain. This building would take 2 yrs. to build. However, you know that at the time you bid for this contract the price of Steel, cement, and sand were less compared to what they are today while you are actually building the hospital. You suddenly realize that being a Fixed Price Contract this excess cost would have to be borne by you due to no fault of yours. In such cases, this variant of FP comes in handy as it allows the vendor to state certain kinds of material and resources specifically in the contract so that if their prices change the FP contract would be automatically altered to allow for such price variation. However, the price variation would be allowed only for the material that has been clearly mentioned in the contract. The price variation allowable in the contract would depend on a listed “Price Index” for reference.

Ok, now we are done with the FP.

The third kind of contract is called the “**Time and Material**” contract. Now there is a reason why it’s called so. This is a very old form or contract and comes from European Villages during the early 17th Century when “Thatching” or “Laying” the roof of a house/hut was considered technical and was to be done in a way such that it keeps the snow and the melted snow water out during winters. It needed a specific technique which was known to few. These roof makers offered their services to others at a price and they came with their own material and tools. This usually was an hourly rate as they were not sure how big or small the house would be. This hourly rate not only covered their labor, transportation, tools, and material, it also covered the margin of profit as well. This then continued during the settlement days in Americas and settlers needed barn constructors and handymen to help them construct things and over centuries this kind of contract became very popular. In recent times this kind of contract earned certain amount of notoriety during the Y2K days. Scores of companies like power companies, banks, insurance companies and billing companies whose main systems were coded in "Cobol" where the year was written in 2 digits instead of 4, each of their "date" lines had to be changed from 2 digit year to 4 digit year. This could not be done by the companies themselves as they did not have the technical staff adept at coding to do the same. Nor could they give the code to vendors on an FP contract to update the code, for security reasons. Hence, the only way this could be done was to get Software Engineers from Software companies to work at these organizations within their offices and under their supervision. The Software companies would only negotiate a contract about the daily/weekly/monthly rate for each of the engineers and this rate would not only contain the salary portions but also an element of profit for the software company. Here suddenly the tables of risks turned in favor of the Vendor. The risk now belonged to the buyer and not the vendor. This is still used rather popularly wherever the buyer wants to retain control of the project and just needs some specialized persons for augmenting their staff to get some specific work done. Most of the Projectised organizations tend to get their technical staff on such contracts. This kind of contract is the fastest in creation and this is because not much of requirements are discussed and only the rates are negotiated and agreed upon.

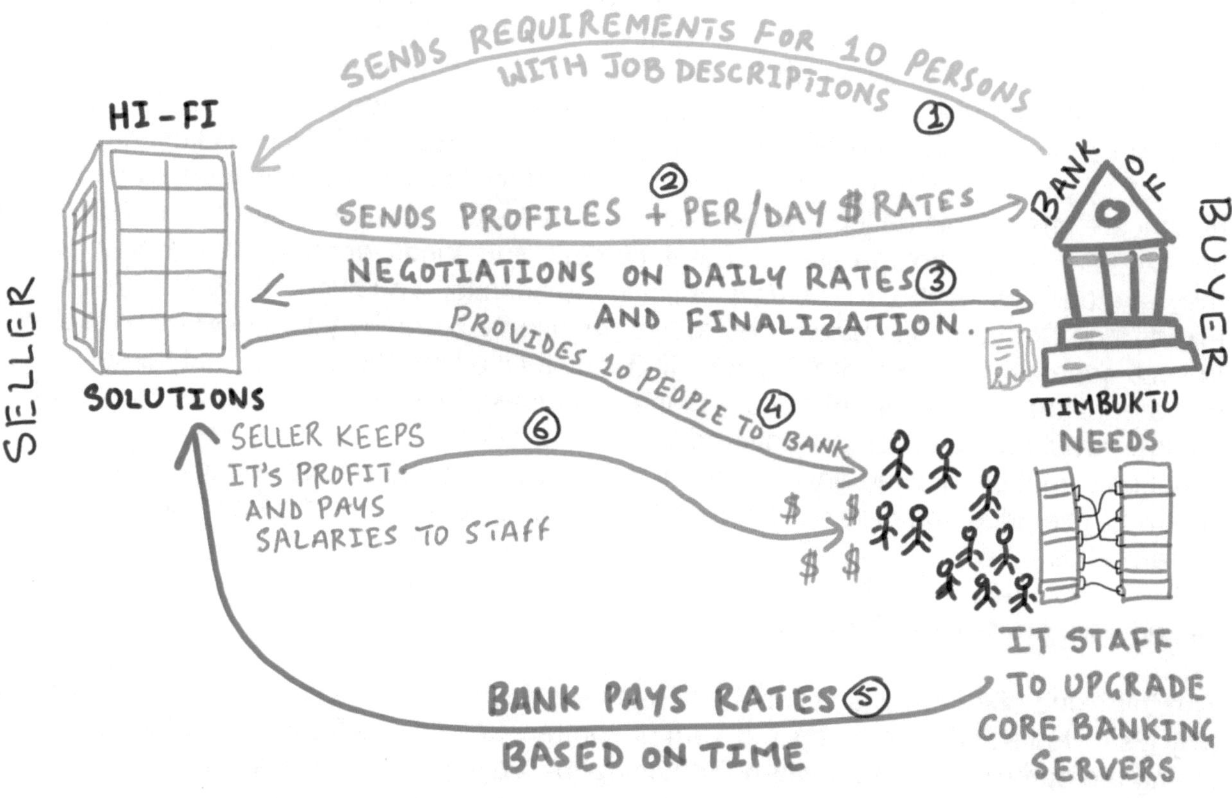

T&M contracts can also have some "Time Period" limitations as well to prevent excessive billing. In some of the long term, T&M contracts the daily rates may also have an "Escalation Clause" due to increase in the expertize of the staff or the overall general inflation.

There is a variant of T&M that has gained a lot of popularity in management world and consequently in PMP Exams. This variant contract type of T&M, called "Indefinite Delivery, Indefinite Quantity" (IDIQ), which is used mostly for Agile Projects. This is basically meant for hiring people for project work, just like the regular T&M but this type has the additional criteria of upper budgetary limit. Meaning the customer will keep paying the fees of the services rendered till the upper limit of the contract has not been reached. These contracts are for a fixed duration as well. Hence in such contracts either if the work is completed, or the duration is reached or the budget ceiling of the contract has been reached, the contract is closed. Again, this is most popular with Agile projects. E.g., I am hiring 10 software developers for an agile project for 10 months maximum duration at a cost of USD 1,000/- per 40 hrs week per developer. I have kept an upper limit of USD 600,000/- for this entire project. Hence the contract would be closed due to any of the following reasons:

- Work completed before time and before reaching the budgetary limit.
- 10 months duration reached.
- USD 600,000/- budgetary limit reached.
- Or the project is terminated.

Ok, so we are done with the T&M (and IDIQ as well).

Now let us talk about the 4th and the last kind of contract for Project world viz., the Cost Reimbursable contract. This is a rather special kind of contract and has to be understood well.

Cost Reimbursable (also known as Cost Plus) Contracts is where a buyer pays specific and agreed upon actual cost/expenses incurred by the Vendor for the duration of the work being done to produce the deliverable of the contract and once the vendor actually delivers work successfully and duly accepted by the buyer then the buyer pays a "Fees" (that is mentioned in the contract) which works as a profit to the Vendor. This kind of contract can be used for any kind of work but its best used for "Research and Development" work which is being outsourced a lot these days. The US defense used this form of contracting to get companies like Lockheed, Douglas, Northrop and McDonnell Douglas to develop advanced weaponry and aircraft for US Armed Forces. Today this kind of contract is still popular in Defense sector but it is also gaining tremendous popularity among the pharmaceutical research organizations who now outsource their R&D work to Projectised vendors. Let say your organization is a leading pharmaceutical company and you want to contract a promising "Pharmaceutical Research" firm to create a new formulation for a specific ailment. You know that in an R&D kind of projects there is no guarantee there would be any results after years of research. However, the vendor would need some finance during the course of research period. You know that you cannot use PO (as it's not a readymade product) or FP (as the requirements are not at all clear) or T&M (as the hourly rate would even contain an element of profit even though there is no guarantee that there would be any result whatsoever). The only contract type that could be used is "Cost reimbursable" where your organization and the vendor enter into a contract for a specific period (say 2 yrs.) during which you will pay them a certain amount only for certain agreed upon expenses on production of bills and evidence just to help the vendor sustain their research. If the vendor is able to make the required formulation to your expectation then you will pay a fee (say USD 2 Million) which would be the profit of the Vendor. However, if the vendor is unable to find anything then you will simply close the contract and no fees would be paid. The vendor has only got the expenses. This is a high-risk contract for both the parties but most of the cost risk lies with the Buyer.

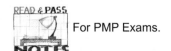

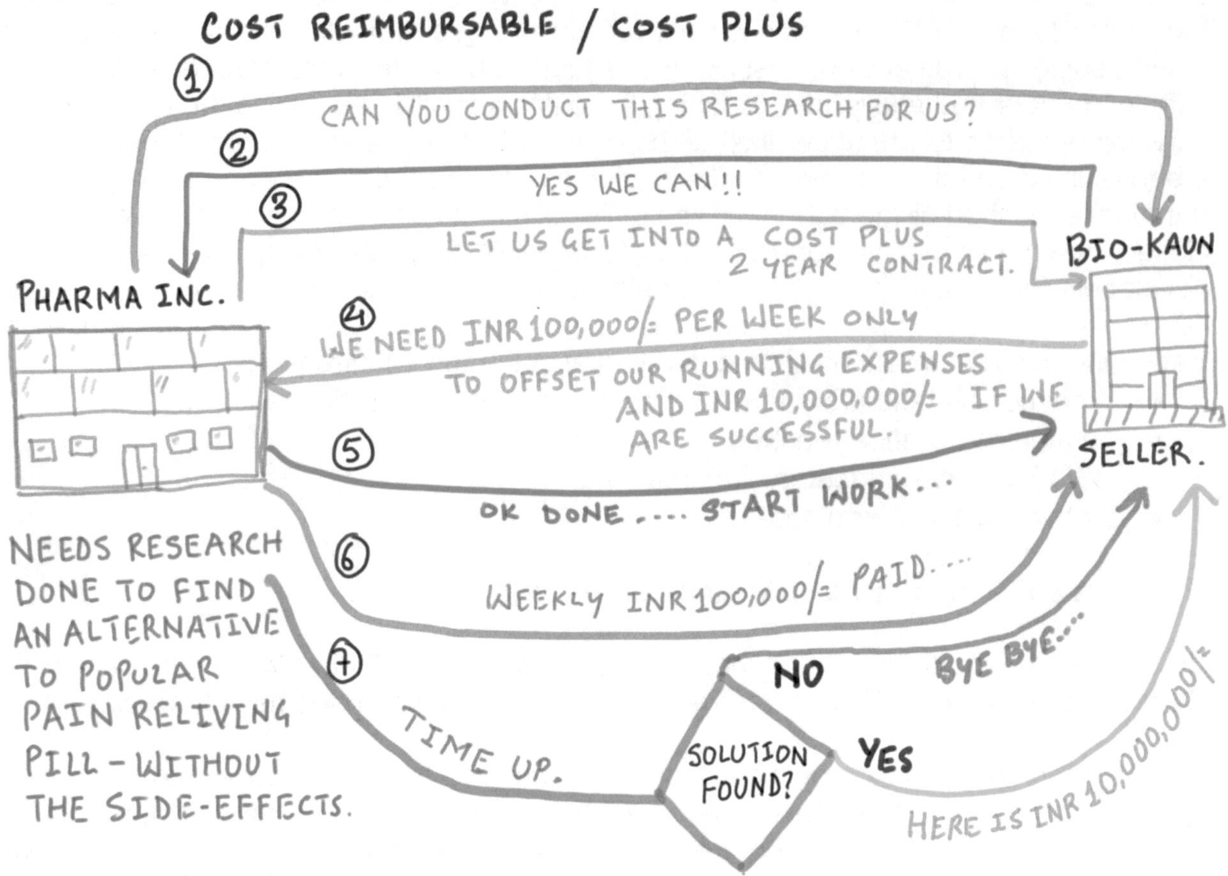

This contract type has three sub-types.

The Cost Plus Fixed Fees (CPFF) is explained in the very example that was discussed above. Cost Plus Incentive Fees (CPIF) addresses the concern the buyer has in a CPFF contract that a vendor may keep on taking the cost reimbursements and spend a lot of time on the research and development. Here in CPIF contract a "Target" expenses is fixed. While the buyer keeps paying for the allowable reimbursements on regular basis and the fixed fees is also given if and when the vendor provides the deliverables, but over and above that a certain ratio of additional profits incentives are provided to the Buyer for finishing the deliverables earlier. Let us say your organization got into a contract with a vendor. You may fix a target price of USD 1 Million of expenses. You have stated in the contract that if the expenses actually spent by the vendor is less than USD 1 Million you and vendor would share the balance in the ratio of say 80% to Buyer and 20% to vendor. However, the contract would also state that if the amount actually spent is more than the USD1 Million than the additional amount would be shared by the Buyer and vendor would be, say 60% and 40% where now the vendor has to share the excessive cost to the extent of 40%. This kind of cost reimbursable contract tends to discourage buyers from spending more on expenses and at the same time, there is a clear incentive to finish faster and cheaper.

Cost Plus Award Fees (CPAF) is mostly used in defense contracts and that too mostly in US. One of the best examples was the way Joint Strike Fighter Program was developed. This is the program that produced the famed F22 Raptor. This contract type was provided to two companies Boeing and Lockheed Martin for the development of a revolutionary new fighter that could play multiple roles as well as have vertical take-off and hover features, like Sea Harrier of UK. The contract was such that only nominal expenses were being paid for the research and development of a JSF, to each of the companies. The idea was that once the prototype JSF was built by each of the companies there would be competitive tryouts and the one that has better overall performance would be awarded the follow up contract of hundreds of JSF to be operationally built and supplied to the defense forces and this was where the companies would end up making money. As you can see this kind of award further ups the scale of risks. Here the risks are more with the Seller. The Award does not have to be an "Order of volumes" as in the case above. The award could also be '"Monetary Bonus or Incentive" which would be based on the performance parameters. More awards for more performance parameters being delivered. Usually, in this kind of contract, there are no "Penalties".

Market Research would be used to understand the availability, capability, capacity, and cost of possible bidders. For specialized outsourcing market research would also involve ascertaining if suppliers exist locally to supply such specialized material/equipment etc. Market research could be as basic as an internet search or as specific as hiring a consultant/research agency to spearhead this research for you.

Make-or-buy Analysis is undertaken to decide whether to buy (procure) or not to buy. **"Make Or Buy" Analysis** is done to figure out the feasibility as well as the "Cost and Benefit" analysis of outsourcing work to a third party. There are many reasons why an organization may or may not want to outsource work to a third party.

REASONS FOR NOT OUTSOURCING
FOR SAFEGUARDING PROPRIETORY INFORMATION
COMPLEX REGULATIONS PERTAINING TO OUTSOURCING.
BECAUSE OF LANGUAGE AND CULTURAL ISSUES
BECAUSE OUTSOURCED WORK MAY NOT BE DONE EFFICIENTLY
MULTIPLE TAXATION LAWS DUE TO MULTIPLE COUNTRIES.
TO RETAIN CONTROL OVER WORK AND QUALITY
FOREIGN RELATIONS NOT CONDUCIVE
TO AVOID SUPERVISION AND AUDITS
TO UTILIZE IDLE PLANT OR WORK FORCE
TO TRAIN OWN WORKFORCE

REASONS TO BUY
TO OVERCOME TECHNICAL RISKS
FOR OBTAINING BEST QUALITY SERVICES
WHEN THE ORGANIZATION RUNS SHORT OF SPECIFIC RESOURCES.
IMPROVING ORGANIZATIONAL FOCUS AREA
TO GET THOSE THINGS DONE WHICH ARE NOT PART OF YOUR CORE COMPETENCE.
FREEING INTERNAL RESOURCES FOR OTHER PURPOSES.
TO ACCESS GLOBAL KNOWLEDGE BASE.
FOR SHARING AN OPPORTUNITY
FOR COST BENEFITS
TO HELP EXPAND TO NEW MARKET AREAS.
FOR TEMPORARY ENGAGEMENTS THAT DOES NOT WARRANT CAPITAL INVESTMENT BY BUYING ORGANIZATION.
TO HELP DISMANTLE UN-PROFITABLE OR TIME CONSUMING FUNCTIONS.
BECAUSE OF BEING A PROJECTIZED ORGANIZATION.

There should be some specific reasons and economic justification for outsourcing and that is exactly why this technique of “Make or Buy” Analysis should be done before an outsourcing decision is made. If the decision is to “Make” than the Procurement stops right at this point. There is nothing done further as far as Procurement Processes are concerned. However, if the decision is to “Buy” then all the processes of the Knowledge Area Procurements Management would be undertaken in a proper sequence.

EXAMS
SPECIAL

Though seemingly not popular of late, there is a numerical question that shows up on this topic in the exams. A situation would be provided where say equipment is needed for some project work. And you are trying to decide whether to buy that equipment or to get it on rent/lease. If the equipment is rented that it costs you Euro. 500.00 Per day and on the other hand, if you purchased it, it would cost you Euro. 80,000.00 and a running cost of Euro. 100.00 Per day. This is not a difficult choice to make since you would like to know how many days is this equipment needed on this project. Say you need it for 10 months.

The best way to solve such questions is to make an algebraic expression out of it. X being the no. of days when whether you buy or lease the amount spent would be the same.

LET x BE NUMBER OF DAYS

$$\therefore 500x = 80{,}000 + 100x$$

$$\therefore 500x - 100x = 80{,}000$$

$$\therefore 400x = 80{,}000$$

$$\therefore x = \frac{80{,}000}{400}$$

$$\therefore x = 200$$

HENCE ON 200th DAY COST OF LEASING AND BUYING WOULD BE THE SAME..

Now that you know that on the 200th day whether you buy or lease the cost would be the same. However, since you need it for 10 months which amounts to more than 200 days, hence it makes sense to buy it. If you needed to use it for say 5 months (less than 200 days) it would have made more sense to just lease it.

In the real world, however, there are many more factors like core business, appointment of a new personnel for the equipment, customs laws, and accounting principles as well as depreciation policies etc., would be considered before taking a "Make or Buy" decision.

Source Selection Criteria lays down the parameters, process, and steps to screen multiple bidders to finally select one bidder. To prevent this process from becoming biased, arbitrary or ineffective in the selection of a vendor, a complete set of "criteria for selection" is decided and agreed upon at the planning stage. The rigor of the selection process must match the complexity of the project. This technique helps answer questions like, "What are the criteria on which we will select the vendors?" "What would be the pre-selection criteria or elimination criteria to prevent irrelevant bidders to even apply?" "How many qualifying rounds would be held?" "Would the price be the sole criteria or would it be in combination of Quality, Experience, and References as well?" "Which of the selection criteria is of the highest priority for us?" "What tools (like panel interview or murder board or weighted averages) would be used for finalizing selection of the vendor?"

9.23.2 Main Outcome of this process: -

Procurement Management Plan is one of the subsidiary plans / components that make up the overall Project Management Plan. This plan states exactly how the procurement would be done in this project. How the RFP would be distributed, how the proposals would be screened for eligibility, stakeholders to be involved in the procurement process, what would be the contract types and contract terms, scope of work to be outsourced, how the claims would be settled, how the work of the vendor be audited from time to time and how the procurement would be closed. This is a plan that governs all aspect of the procurement process. It also lays down how the scope of procurement would be changed.

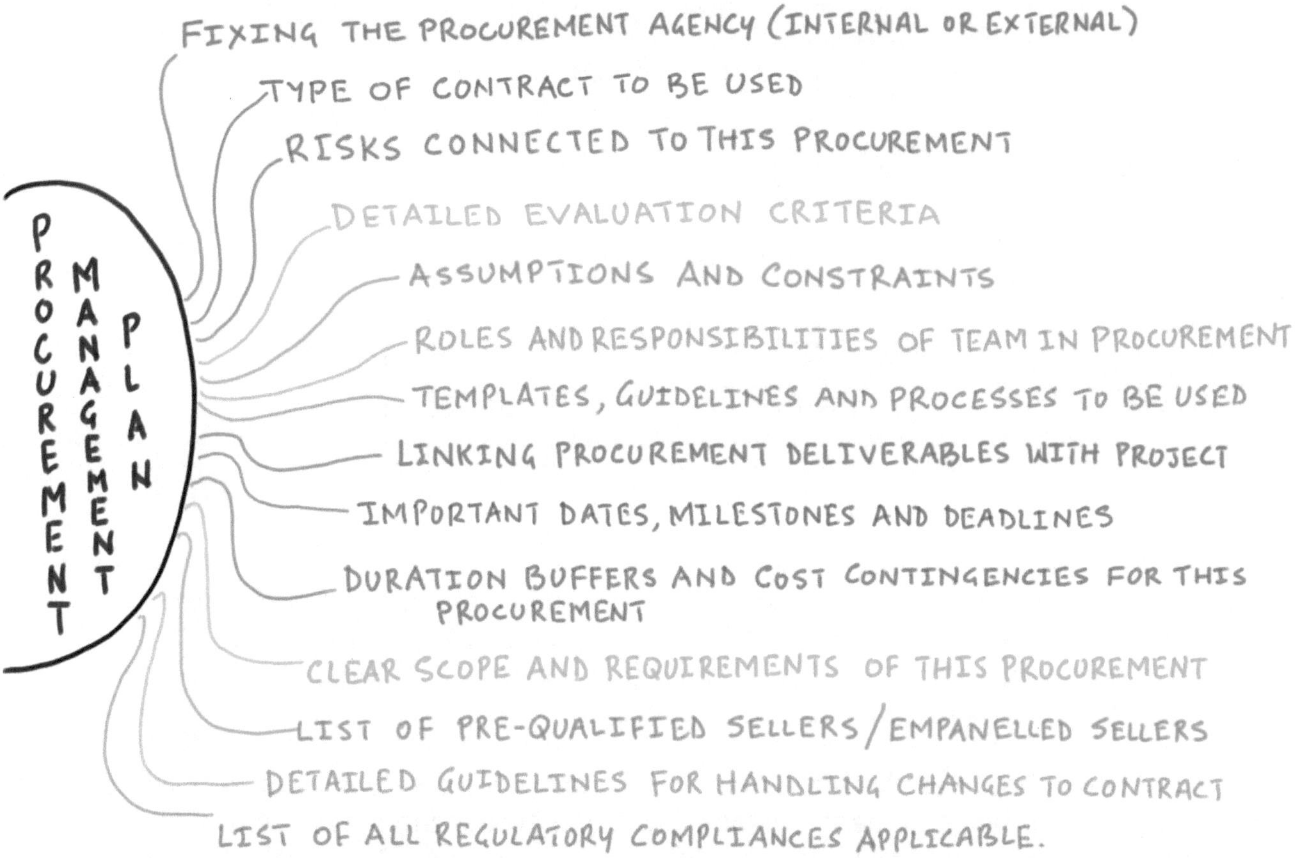

PROCUREMENT MANAGEMENT PLAN

- FIXING THE PROCUREMENT AGENCY (INTERNAL OR EXTERNAL)
- TYPE OF CONTRACT TO BE USED
- RISKS CONNECTED TO THIS PROCUREMENT
- DETAILED EVALUATION CRITERIA
- ASSUMPTIONS AND CONSTRAINTS
- ROLES AND RESPONSIBILITIES OF TEAM IN PROCUREMENT
- TEMPLATES, GUIDELINES AND PROCESSES TO BE USED
- LINKING PROCUREMENT DELIVERABLES WITH PROJECT
- IMPORTANT DATES, MILESTONES AND DEADLINES
- DURATION BUFFERS AND COST CONTINGENCIES FOR THIS PROCUREMENT
- CLEAR SCOPE AND REQUIREMENTS OF THIS PROCUREMENT
- LIST OF PRE-QUALIFIED SELLERS/EMPANELLED SELLERS
- DETAILED GUIDELINES FOR HANDLING CHANGES TO CONTRACT
- LIST OF ALL REGULATORY COMPLIANCES APPLICABLE.

Only one such plan is needed irrespective of the number of procurements that need to be done in this project.

Procurement Management Strategy; this is usually a part of the Procurement Management Plan itself, but it is shown separately from the Procurement Plan to showcase its relative importance. This is at a higher level than the plan. The plan must be based on the procurement strategy. Procurement Strategy is about understanding what kind of Contract would be best suited for this procurement, the delivery methodology or even development methodology to be used by the vendor and why, phases in which to make the payments to the vendor, and generally the overall phases of the contract. I guess an example would make it clear for you. *E.g., In one of the projects, we decided to go for inviting bidders only from foreign countries, because within the country there were many vendors who were common even to our competitors. The project being very secretive we had to go for this strategy even when we knew that the overall cost of procurement would be nearly twice the amount we would have paid locally. The plan was made in accordance to this strategy, the contract clearly mentioned disclosure of the client list of all bidders and so on. This gave us the necessary anonymity and the project was a grand success and took the competitors by surprise.*

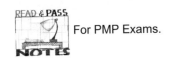

Bid Documents (also called Procurement Documents) are the set of documents that would be needed from beginning to end of procurement (or procurements) in this project. This output contains the entire set of procurement documents that would be needed across the lifecycle of this procurement.

Procurement Statement Of Work (Procurement SOW) contains the scope of work and the details of the work that needs to be outsourced. The way it should be written that the bidders would be able to understand exactly what is needed from them and they should be able to determine if they can do the work or not and if they can then there should be sufficient details in the SOW to help them estimate the cost and present a price to the buyer. SOW has to be made by the buyer's technical and legal team. Some organizations and some industries have a standard format for writing a SOW so that no relevant information is missed. SOW, later on, becomes the part of Request for Proposal (RFP) document.
It is important to note that for every service or item or material that is to be procured through a separate procurement process, there should be a separate SOW. Remember in some organizations SOW is also called Terms of Reference (TOR).

Source Selection Criteria (though this would also be part of the Procurement Documents discussed above but it's being discussed separately due to its relative importance) is the collection of all the parameters on which the bidder's proposals / Bids / Quotes would be compared before finally selecting the vendor. This set of criteria when used correctly and in a transparent manner should end up helping you select the best vendor for the job in the given circumstances.

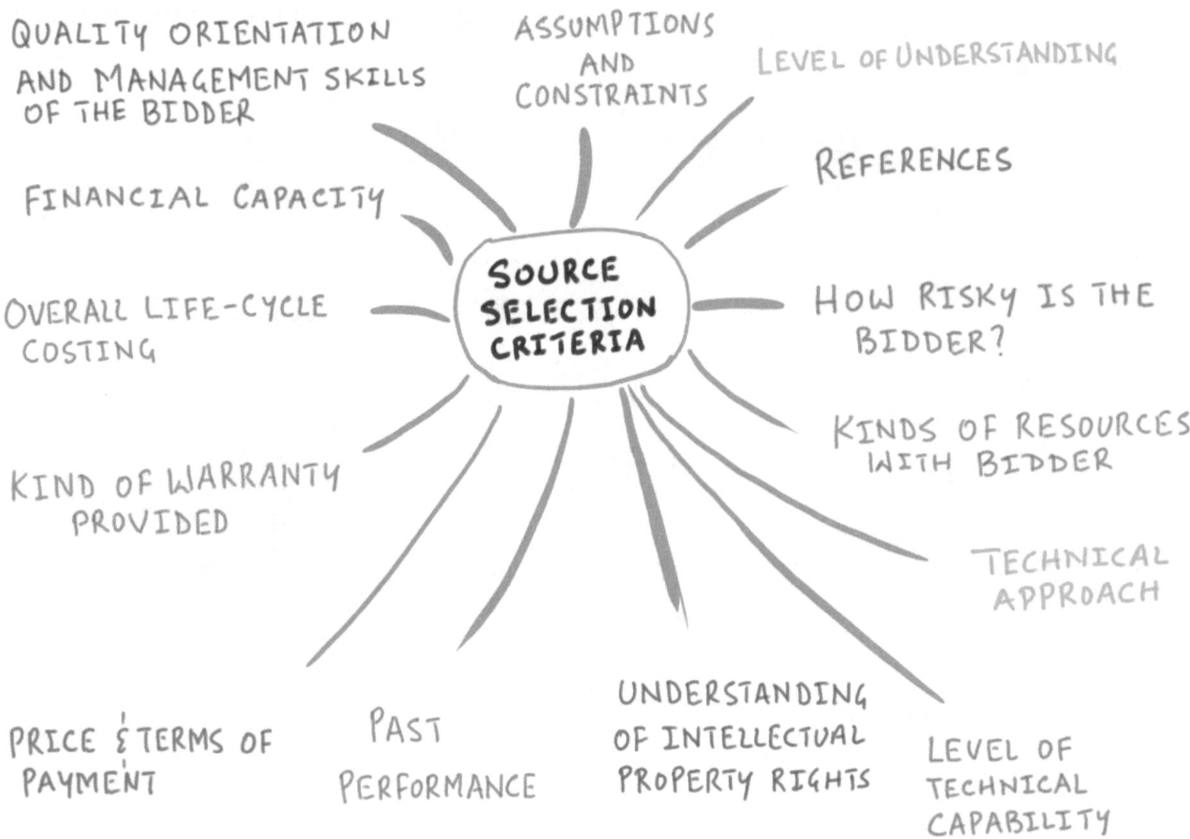

Since this is the process where it is decided to either “Make or Buy” hence the **Make or Buy Decision** is one of the outputs of this process. This decision must contain the reason and justification for the same. The risks associated as well as the assumptions taken for the decision should be clearly stated here.

Independent Cost Estimates is now getting more common than ever. This can be best explained through a real example. Long time back I was hired by Konkan Railways (probably one of the most efficient railway companies in the world, next only to the ones in Japan Rail. Those who know this company would gladly agree.) to look at the requirements for a very comprehensive “Anti-Collision Device” to be created as a prototype and understand its “Sizing” using Full Function Points (a method of finding the size of a proposed embedded system) and then used general productivity to estimate the total cost of the prototype. This was used by the Konkan Railways as a benchmark for assessing the bidders. This helped them get hold of a vendor that not only had a realistic cost estimate but also understood the application requirements very well as the sizing also must have been near to what I had calculated. Sometimes this is done for transparency and mostly it is done when the organization itself is unable to have any reference point on which to compare the bidders on.

9.24 Plan Stakeholder Engagement

This is the process where the "Stakeholder Register" is obtained from the previous process viz., ***Identify Stakeholders*** and strategies of dealing or working with or involving each of those stakeholders is made. *E.g., Let us say there is a High Power – Low-Interest stakeholder whose involvement could help your project a lot but he is not really interested in the outcome of the project. Hence plans like talking to him on regular intervals to showcase the importance of this project overall such that he helps with this project or getting some of his time officially allocated to the Project Schedule for requirements or some other important meeting where his inputs could help a lot and this could be done through your sponsor of the project.*

Basically in this process detailed and stakeholder-specific "Interpersonal Strategies" are developed to either enhance the utilization of the "Power / Influence / Impact" of the stakeholder on the project or to understand the level and kind of interest that a stakeholder has in the outcome of the project or both.
"Different strokes for different people", as the saying goes.
Planning here is ultimately aimed at improving relationships (or even not allowing the relationships to deteriorate further) with the various stakeholders and not just communicating with them.

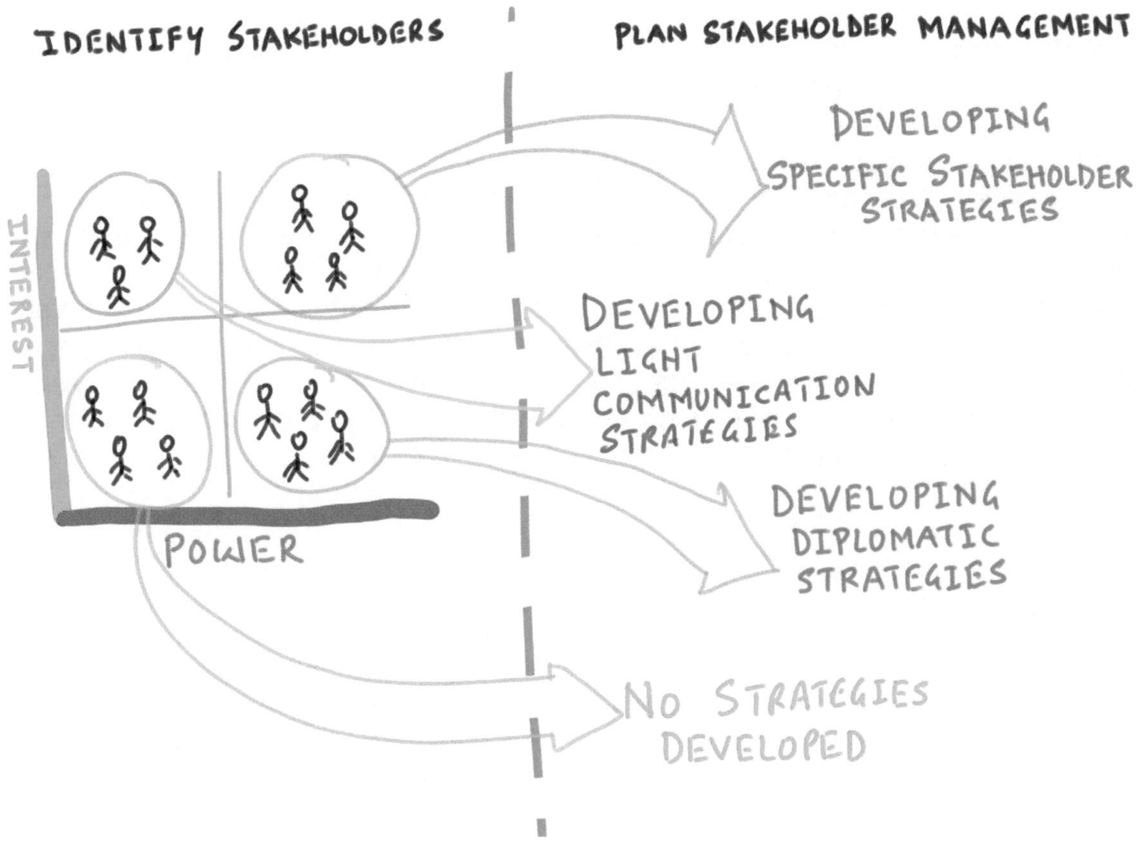

Let us get into the nitty-gritty of this process.

9.24.1 Main Tools and techniques of this process: -

Benchmarking would help you understand how the best organizations or the best of class projects handle their stakeholders. You could use those practices as a benchmark to help draw your own project's strategy of stakeholder engagement.

Tools like **Assumptions and constraints analysis** and **Root Cause Analysis** of stakeholder behavior may help you tailor or custom fit your engagement plan. *E.g., In one of the Government projects, we were hired to create a complete workflow system for them. This is during mid 1990s when there were still a lot of apprehensions about computers and software. The ground level staff were thwarting all our attempts at getting the requirements. This continued for so long that it threatened to delay the project. We spent some time together within the team and literally brainstormed the "root cause" of why the ground level staff were so uncooperative. We realized, that they feared that these "Computers" would replace them and they will be redundant. I know you may find this funny but it was similar to the fear mongering right now about Artificial Intelligence and how it could take away your jobs.* Having understood that we called them for a meeting and showed them case studies of other companies where no one was replaced, instead, their work became simpler and less strenuous. This basic alteration in our engagement with them changed everything and we ended up finishing the project a bit before time.

Mind Mapping could be used for representing what kind or combination of interpersonal techniques to use with which stakeholder.

Stakeholder Engagement Assessment Matrix
Representation Techniques are used to understand the gap between the current engagement level of the key stakeholders and other high priority stakeholders versus the required engagement levels. When the stakeholder analysis is done then the placement of the stakeholders is done based on the capability and influence etc., of the stakeholder. However, in reality, there could be many reasons, like bias, jealousy, hidden agenda, conflict of career goals, unawareness and so on, which would create this gap. Various methods could be used to make plans for filling this gap. The current engagement levels and the required engagement levels could be put into a matrix form.

STAKEHOLDER ANALYTICAL TECHNIQUES

STAKEHOLDERS	UNAWARE	RESISTANT	NEUTRAL	SUPPORTIVE	LEADING
KAMINO MOTO		C	D		
ARJUN SANSKAR				C	D
SALE DAKARO		C		D	
COOK POO		C	D		
PANARAT SUWARNA BHOOMI	C				D
JACK SWINDLE	C		D		

C = CURRENT LEVEL OF ENGAGEMENT   D = DESIRED LEVEL OF ENGAGEMENT

This kind of matrix helps create a strategy to deal with specific stakeholders. For example. From the illustration above, Kamino Moto is currently a Resistant stakeholder. He is resisting this project because of his own hidden agenda and perception. I do not see much support from him so I just make a strategy that is enough to make him less resistant. Something like convincing him that this project does not affect him at all. Thus making his desired state as Neutral. But on the other hand, there is a stakeholder by the name of Panarat Suwarnabhoomi who is simply unaware of this project. And I know that being a function head from where I will obtain the most resources for the project, I will spend a lot of time with her to get her buy-in in this project. My attempt would be to make her one of the Leading Stakeholders in this project so that she not only helps me but also shoulders some of my responsibilities in this project.

In some of my own projects (which I learned from one of the top brains in project management while working on several projects) I used to create an “Influence Chart” over and above the matrix discussed earlier. There were times when I would get some “Toxic” stakeholders or those stakeholders with whom my relations have deteriorated, for whatever reasons. I used to make a chart of who can I count on (could be anyone) to get the work done through the “Difficult” stakeholders. Who can pressurize or influence whom? Basically, I used to make a power-map of the stakeholders. This is taking stakeholder management to next level which borders on “Politics”.

At this point, you must know the difference between “Influencing” and “Manipulating”. Influencing is “using politics” and other interpersonal skills at your disposal, with stakeholders for the benefit of the project/organization. Manipulation, on the other hand, is use of "politics" and other interpersonal skills at your disposal for personal befits over and above those of the project/organization.

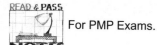

9.24.2 *Main Outcome from this process: -*

Stakeholder Engagement Plan contains all the strategy for each and every priority stakeholder to help engage the stakeholders or deal with them or develop relationships with them.
The strategy connected to influencing them along with the strategy of moving stakeholders from one state to another based on the "Stakeholder Engagement Assessment Matrix".
It's important to know that this is one plan that should not be shared widely as it may have a wrong effect on some of the stakeholders. This is usually kept as a black-book strategy for self and not widely distributed.

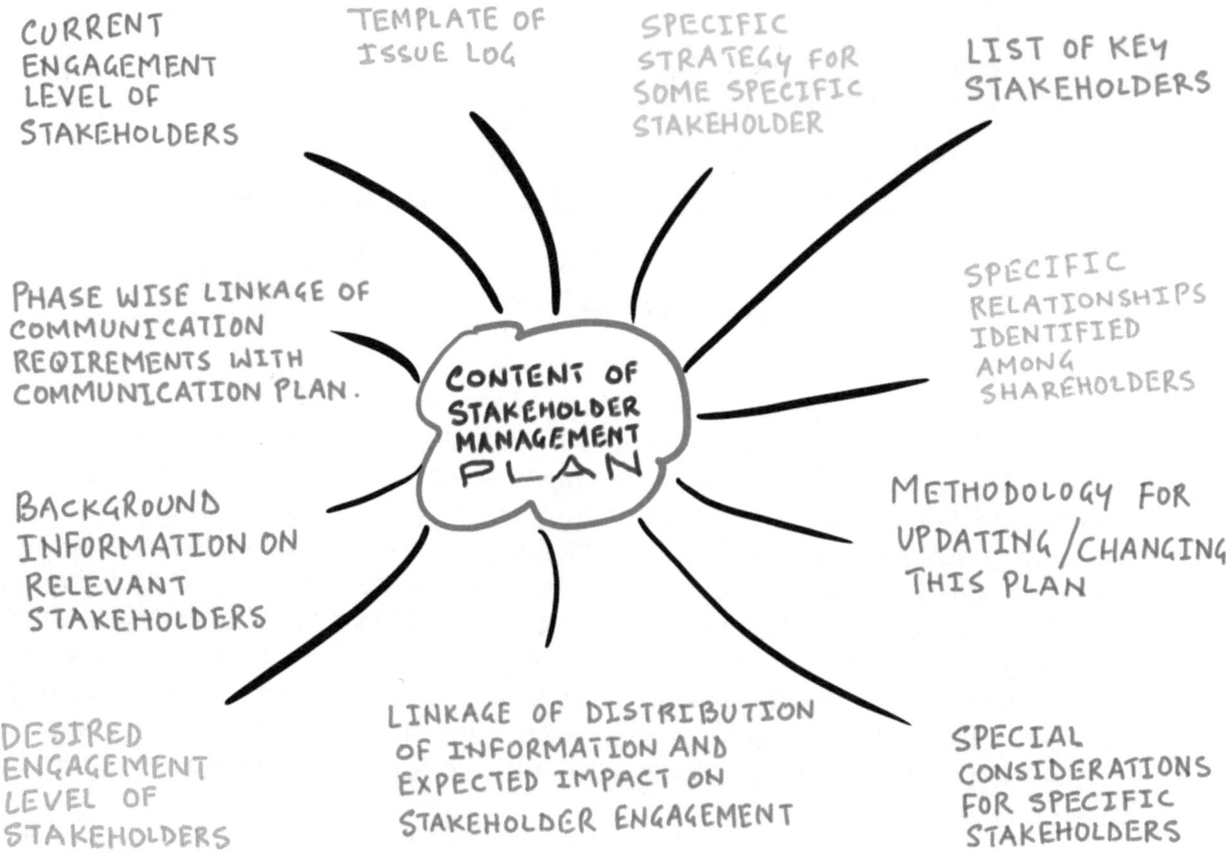

And yes, this is one of the subsidiary plans (planning components) that make up the project management plan.

9.25 Plan Communications Management

Communications to a project is like the “circulation system” to the human body. The circulation does not have to be the same in all parts of the body but they need to keep on going for the body to survive. Any blockage in circulation can lead to serious issues. It’s the same with Communications in project management. It’s actually the lifeblood of projects.

Let us understand what does the term “communications”, actually means.
Communication is the process of transferring information from one person to another / from one place to another in such a way that the intended meaning is not lost.
This means that communication is ***not just speaking***. To communicate, is not only to send a message but also to ensure that the message is understood by the receiver in the same manner as it was originally intended.

Communication is challenging because, when you send a message to someone, that message passes through “Noise” before being assimilated by that someone. Question is what this “Noise” is.

It’s not just the surrounding ambient sounds or the static noise on the phone lines (I was shocked to read in one of the most popular PMP® Preparation books in the world, stating that Noise is just the static on the phone lines and the ambient sounds in office place.) but more importantly it’s the “Noise” in the head of the receiver. These noises like Cultural Differences, Personal Bias, Lack of Trust, the difference in Management Language, the difference in education, the difference in outlook, the difference in priority etc., can change the meaning of the message in the minds of the receiver. Hence, to ensure that the receiver has understood the message well and in the same original intention, the originator of the message must take a feedback of the understanding of the message from the receiver and continue this “To-and from” messaging till the receiver understands the message as it was intended to by the originator of the message. This is what is called “Communication”.

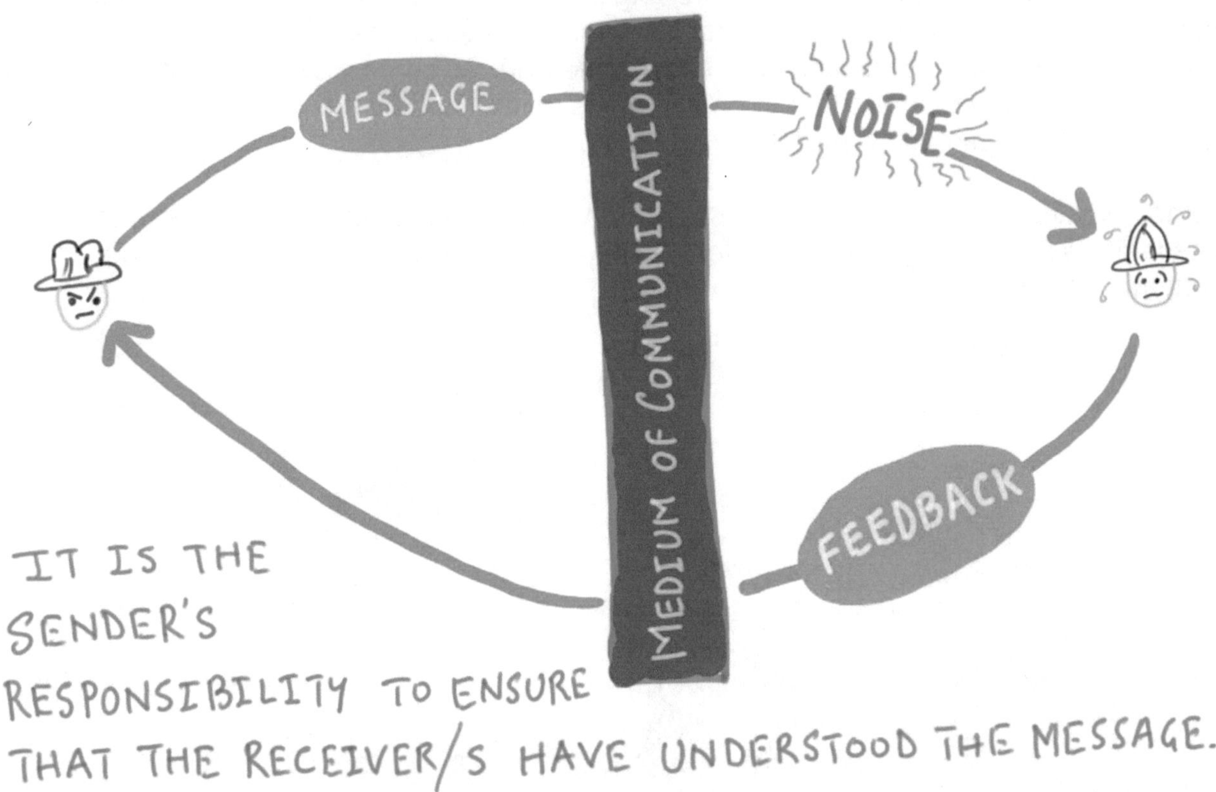
THE "SENDER - RECEIVER" MODEL
MESSAGE
MEDIUM OF COMMUNICATION
NOISE
FEEDBACK
IT IS THE SENDER'S RESPONSIBILITY TO ENSURE THAT THE RECEIVER/S HAVE UNDERSTOOD THE MESSAGE.

This Communication model may look inconsequential until you play the childhood game called “Chinese Whispers” (also called “Telephone” in most Arabic speaking countries). Here a group of people sits in a row and one person at one end of the row speaks an entire sentence into the ears of the person seated next to him, such that no one else can hear what is being said. This person, then, speaks the same sentence into the ears of the person seated next to him and so on. When the last person in the row is asked to recite the sentence aloud, the sentence would be significantly different from the original one. Now, how did this happen even when words were spoken directly into the ears of the person thus canceling any other ambient sounds? This is one of the hardest hitting examples of the presence of “Noise”. Now you can understand why stories change as they get passed from one person to another, why people act differently even when the email you drafted was crystal clear, why one conference call leads to 5 more calls to clarify confusions and why people react differently to the same set of instructions.

Communication is very important and the ability to communicate clearly is critical to the success of the project and hence it goes without saying that “Communicating” is one of the most important skills or leadership skill of a project manager.

It is assumed that almost the entire time (90%) of the Project Manager is spent communicating. This is not farfetched at all because well-drafted plans are one of the best communication tools as well.

There are several mechanisms by which information can be exchanged.

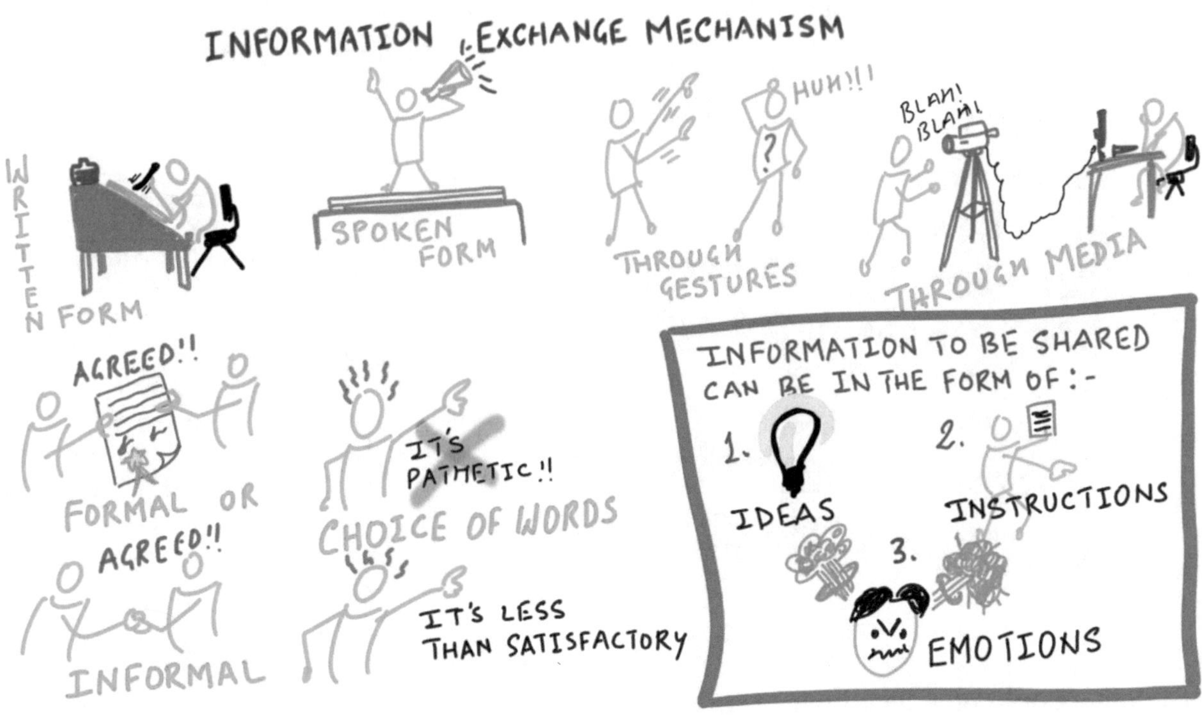

Communication has some barriers as well.

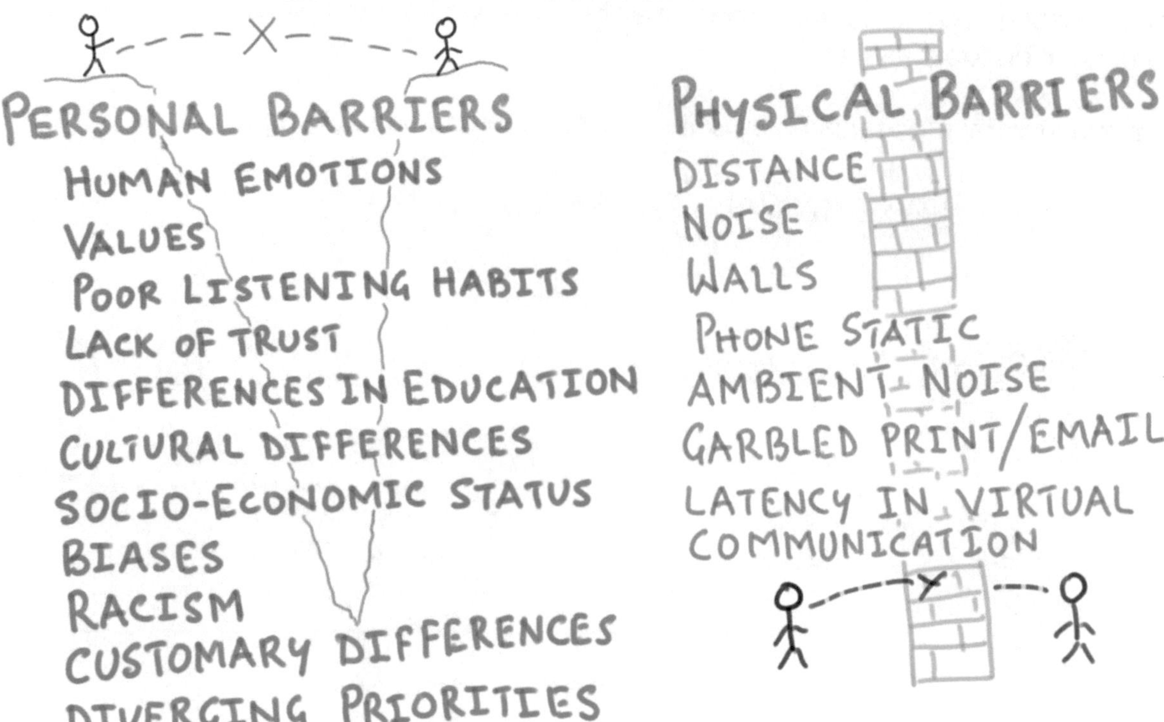

BARRIERS TO COMMUNICATION
PERSONAL BARRIERS
HUMAN EMOTIONS
VALUES
POOR LISTENING HABITS
LACK OF TRUST
DIFFERENCES IN EDUCATION
CULTURAL DIFFERENCES
SOCIO-ECONOMIC STATUS
BIASES
RACISM
CUSTOMARY DIFFERENCES
DIVERGING PRIORITIES
PHYSICAL BARRIERS
DISTANCE
NOISE
WALLS
PHONE STATIC
AMBIENT NOISE
GARBLED PRINT/EMAIL
LATENCY IN VIRTUAL COMMUNICATION

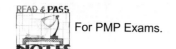

Effective communication builds a bridge between diverse stakeholders who may have different cultural and organizational backgrounds as well as different levels of expertise, perspectives, expectations, and interests.

Communications have several dimensions, some of them are:

- **Internal**: This is about communication with stakeholders within the organization or within the legal identity of the organization. (e.g., communicating with sponsors, team members, functional heads, resource managers, quality assurance departments etc.)
- **External**: This is about communications with stakeholders outside the legal limits/identity of the organization. (e.g., communicating with regulatory bodies, vendors, advertising agencies, consultants etc.)
- **Formal**: This is about communication that has a formal and evidentiary aspect to it. Such communications are used for directing the direction of the project and to be used as reference points and evidence. (e.g., contracts, memorandum of understandings (MOU), project charter, planning documents, agenda for the meeting, action items from the meeting etc.)
- **Informal**: This kind of communication is usually built for fact-finding, problem-solving, relationship building and for building trust. (e.g., unplanned discussions, coffee machine discussions, email, memo, social media, chats etc.) It is important to note here that “Emails” are still considered informal communication.
- **Upward**: This is about communicating with stakeholders who have higher powers or are higher in decision making or higher in roles and responsibilities. (e.g., Vice

President, Board of Directors, Departmental Head (if you are in a weak matrix kind of organization), sponsor etc.)

- **Downward**: This is about communicating with stakeholders who have lesser powers, roles or responsibilities or decision making authority than you. (e.g., Team members, vendors, trainees etc.)
- **Horizontal**: This is about communicating with peers in the organization. (e.g., Other project managers in the organization, quality assurance groups, testing and maintenance groups etc.)
- **Written**: This is communicating by writing. (e.g., Project reports, project charter, planning documents, emails, agenda etc.)
- **Oral**: Communication verbal mechanism is called Oral Communication. (e.g., Presentation, interviews, meetings, casual conversations, daily scrum etc.)
- **In-person**: This is about communicating with stakeholders in the same physical location and in person. This means that the sender and receiver of the communication are in the same physical location while communicating. (e.g., In-person meetings, on-location training, in-room presentation etc.)
- **Virtual**: This is about communication with stakeholders who are not in the same geographical location as you. This results in relying on "distance communication" tools to communicate and get your points across. (e.g., having a meeting with stakeholders distributed in multiple countries using any of the web-presence tool, chatting, emails, teleconferences etc.)

The reason why different dimensions have to be understood is that different dimensions may require a different approach and also ascertain which kind of information should be shared or discussed using which dimension. Each dimension of communication come with their own challenges and trade-offs.

I am sure you can see that communication may fall into multiple dimensions at any given time. E.g., an email is a written, informal and virtual communication whereas, an in-person status review meeting is a formal, in-person, oral communication.

A summarised way to look at the various "Types Of Communications" with some examples of each will not only help you with understanding this aspect of communication management thoroughly but will also help you react accurately to various PMP Questions on this topic.

TYPES OF COMMUNICATION

TYPE	FORMAL	INFORMAL
VERBAL	• PRESENTATIONS • PROJECT REVIEWS • BRIEFINGS • PRODUCT DEMOS • BRAIN STORMING	• CONVERSATIONS • CASUAL DISCUSSIONS • DISCUSSIONS BY WALKING ABOUT • AD-HOC DISCUSSIONS
WRITTEN	• PROGRESS REPORTS • PROJECT DOCUMENTS • BUSINESS CASE • ALL OTHER PLANS • ALL DOCUMENTED ARTEFACTS • PROCESSES & CHECKLIST • APPROVALS • AUDIT & COMPLIANCE REPORT • MINUTES OF THE MEETING	• BRIEF NOTES • EMAIL • INSTANT MESSAGING/TEXTING • SOCIAL MEDIA • MEMO

Communications are the lifeblood of the project and hence a lot of importance is given to it by PMI.
As per PMBOK® guide, there are 5Cs of written communications.

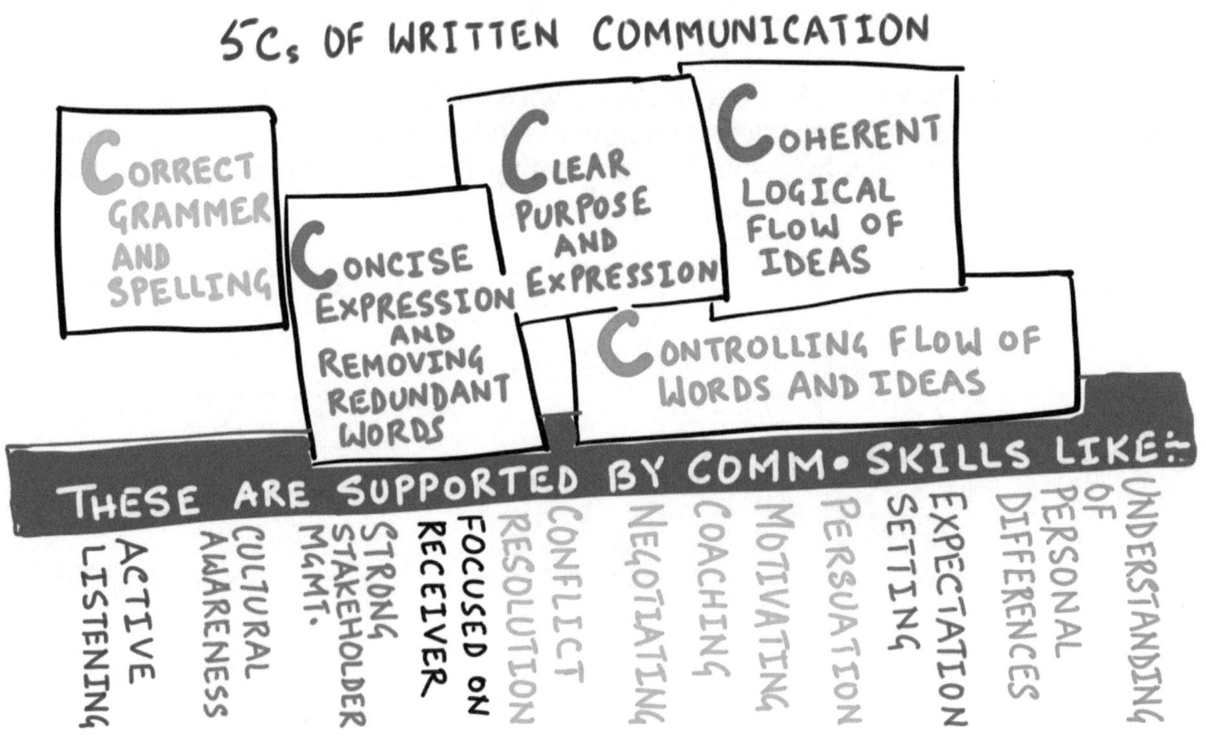

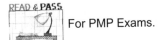

Some of the new challenges to the world of project communications are:

- Extensive use of Virtual Teams. Virtual Teams, though very cost effective and harnesses the expertise of people irrespective of the boundaries, is challenging for clear and precise communication. However, as more and more projects and services move to Virtual Platform the project managers must arm themselves with the ability to communicate effectively in a virtual team setting.
- Social Computing or simply said, Social Media has drastically changed the concept of "Accepted method of networking and building relationships". Since communication is the primary mechanism for networking and building relationships, project managers must be adept at communicating through social media as well for building networks and relationships.
- With the advent of tremendous development in the field of technology and platforms for communicating the project managers have a plethora of multifaceted approach to communications. Based on the needs of the project the project manager must choose an array of communication platforms, mediums, and technologies that would be best suited for clear communications in the project.

Though, at first, it may seem too much and purely academic to "Plan" communications but think about the numbers of "CC to all" emails that you have to deal with. The number of times you have to send the same information in multiple formats to different people, sometimes wondering "Do they even need this information?" The number of times you are pulled into irrelevant meetings and the number of times you call people to meetings only to realize that some of the invitees were probably not even needed there. You will realize, thus, that planning for communications is not such a bad idea.

Rumors are nothing but unplanned communications. Which means when you do not plan communications you are responsible for rumors. Now, how do rumors get created? Let us look at some basic mathematics. (Seriously).

Let us say you have a team of 5 people viz., A, B, C, D and E. Now A can talk to B and B can talk to A. Hence that is one channel of communication. Now, how many channels of communication would be there in this team of 5 persons?

CHANNELS OF COMMUNICATION

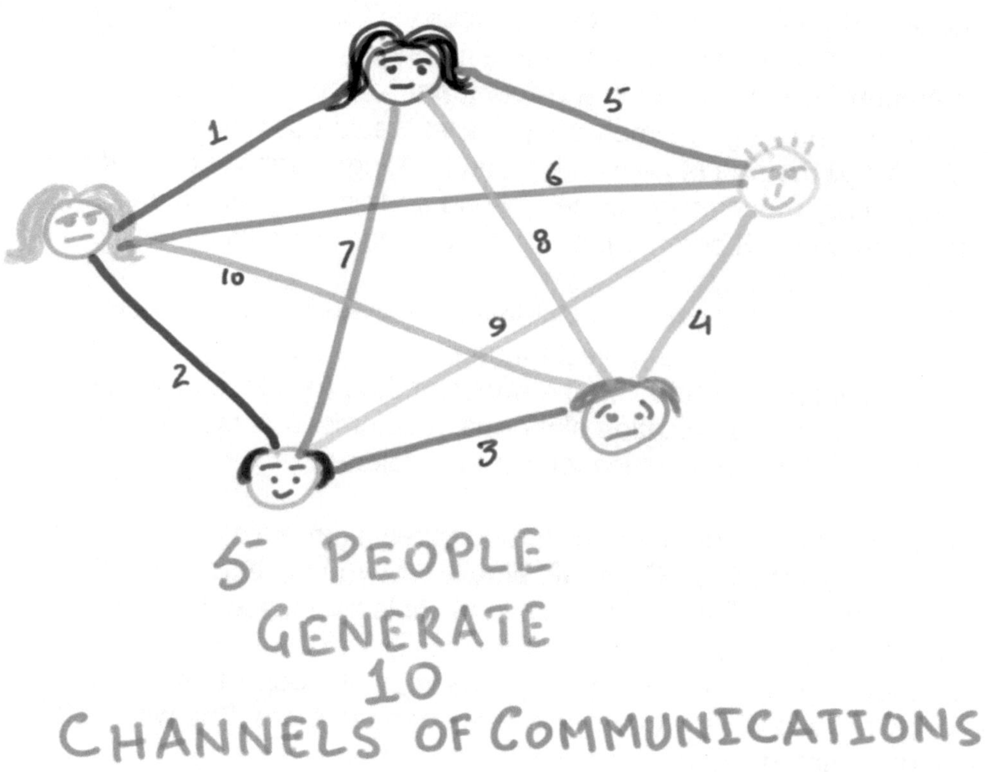

If no planning is done and the official channels of communication are not defined than people would use any channel available to them to get and give information. This is what generates rumors and the number of unnecessary emails/cc emails and the number of unnecessary meetings with unnecessary numbers of people.
The formula to find all the possible channels of communication is as under:

CALCULATING CHANNELS OF COMMUNICATIONS

ARE YOU KIDDING ME???

FORMULA = $\frac{n(n-1)}{2}$ (WHERE n = NUMBER OF PEOPLE)

S.NO.	NO. OF PEOPLE	CHANNELS OF COMMUNICATION
1.	10	45
2.	50	1,225
3.	100	4,950
4.	150	11,175
5.	200	19,900
6.	300	44,850
7.	500	124,750
8.	1,000	499,500

EXAMS SPECIAL

In exams, you would probably find one or more questions on this calculation. Let me give you a question that I have created and see if you can quickly answer this.

Question: You are a project manager with 5 people working under you and after some time 2 more persons join your team. By how much your channels of communication have increased?

It basically means that you have to calculate **n(n-1)/2** formula twice (once before the addition of 2 new members and once again after the addition of the 2 new members) and find the difference. Take some time to calculate on your own before looking at the solution given here.

The answer is 13.

The trick is to understand if in the question "was the Project Manager included in the count of the team members". If not, then add the Project Manager in the count. In the above question, it's clear that he was not included hence the total size of the team is 6 and not 5.

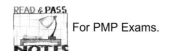

$$\text{FORMULA} = \frac{n(n-1)}{2}$$

∴ FOR 6 PERSONS

$$\frac{6(6-1)}{2} = \frac{30}{2} = 15$$

∴ FOR 8 PERSONS

$$\frac{8(8-1)}{2} = \frac{56}{2} = 28$$

DIFFERENCE

$$28 - 15 = 13$$

∴ THE CHANNELS OF COMMUNICATIONS HAVE INCREASED BY 13

Once "Stakeholder Identification" is done and the stakeholders have been prioritized, the communication planning can be done to understand who needs what kind of information in what format in what frequency and what would be the mode of information exchange. Things that need to be considered while planning for communication are:

ELEMENTS FOR COMMUNICATION PLANNING

- WHO ARE THE PRIORITY STAKEHOLDERS?
- WHO NEEDS WHAT INFORMATION?
- WHAT IS THE FREQUENCY IN WHICH INFORMATION IS NEEDED?
- WHERE WOULD THE INFORMATION BE STORED?
- WHAT WOULD BE THE FORMAT IN WHICH INFORMATION WILL BE SENT?
- WHAT METHOD AND WHICH TECHNOLOGY WOULD BE USED?
- WHAT WOULD BE THE LANGUAGES USED?
- WHAT CULTURAL DIFFERENCES TO BE KEPT IN MIND?
- NO.S OF CHANNELS OF COMMUNICATIONS?

9.25.1 Main Tools and Techniques of this process: -

Communications Requirements Analysis uses the Input "Stakeholder Register" to analyze which stakeholder needs what kind of information and in which format as well as the frequency (periodicity) of the transmission of that information. This analysis also understands which kind of information, if not transmitted to specific stakeholders, would lead to project failure. The channels of communication have also to be understood to understand the complexity involved in communication in this project. Various sources of information could be: -

- Organizational charts, roles, designations and hierarchies
- Project roles and the stakeholder's roles in the project
- Functions, departments, specialties and organizations involved in the project
- Development approach
- Geographical distribution of team members
- Languages and cultures the team spreads across
- Overall organization structure
- Internal information needs
- External information needs
- Stakeholder needs to be documented in the stakeholder register

There are a lot of different kinds of **Communication Technology** to choose from in a project.

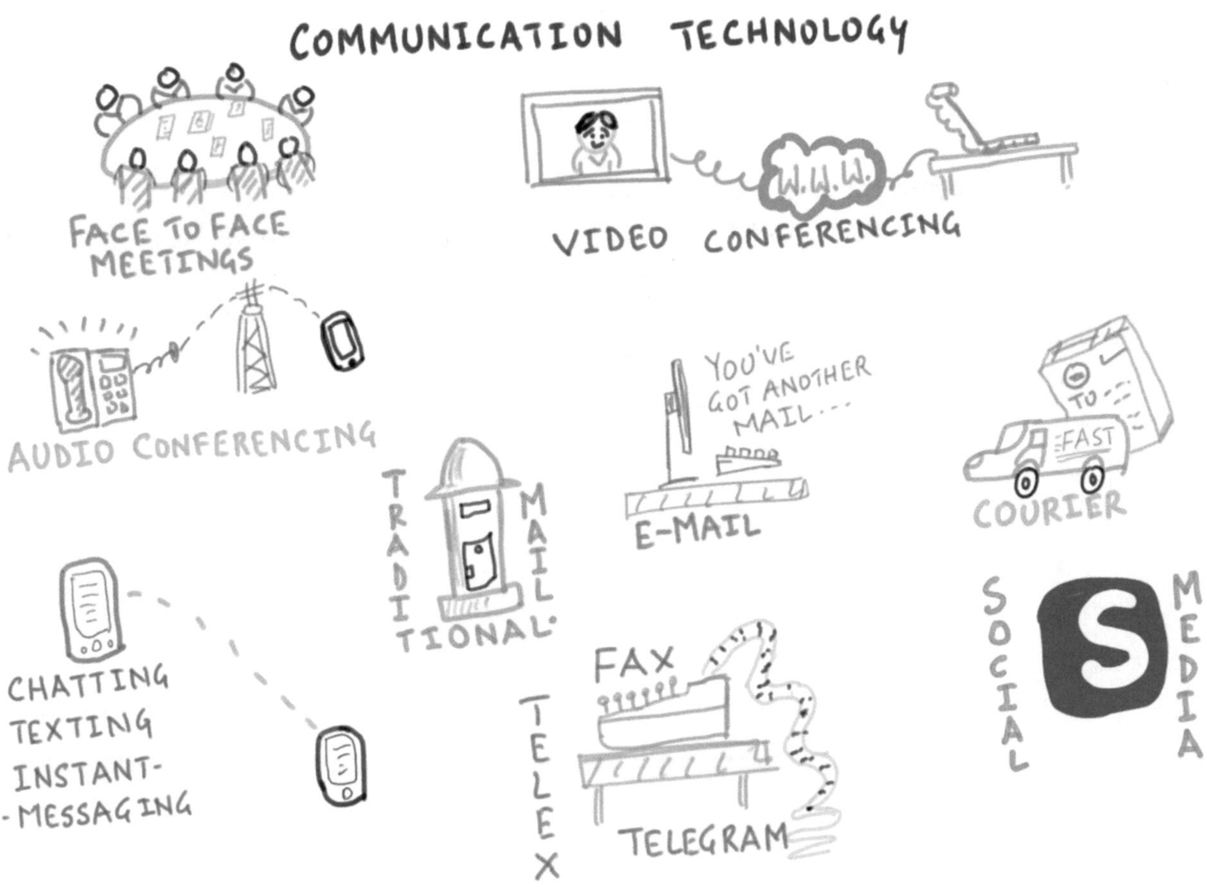

The choice of the set of Communication Technologies used in a project would depend on various factors.

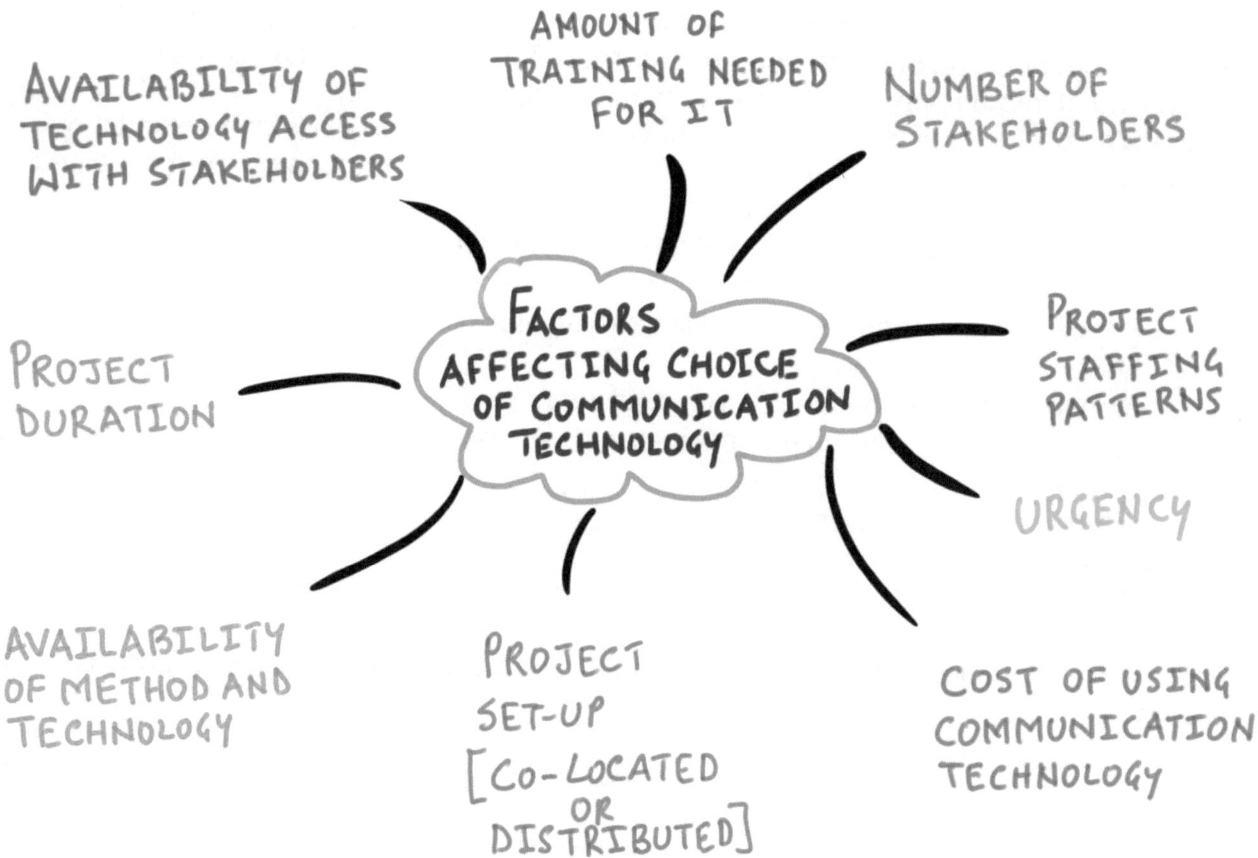

Various kinds of **Communication Model** may be used in a project depending on the needs and specific circumstances however, the most popular one is the "Sender Receiver Model" explained earlier at the start of this Knowledge Area.
This sender-receiver model becomes slightly different when this model is applied in "Cross-Cultural" scenario.

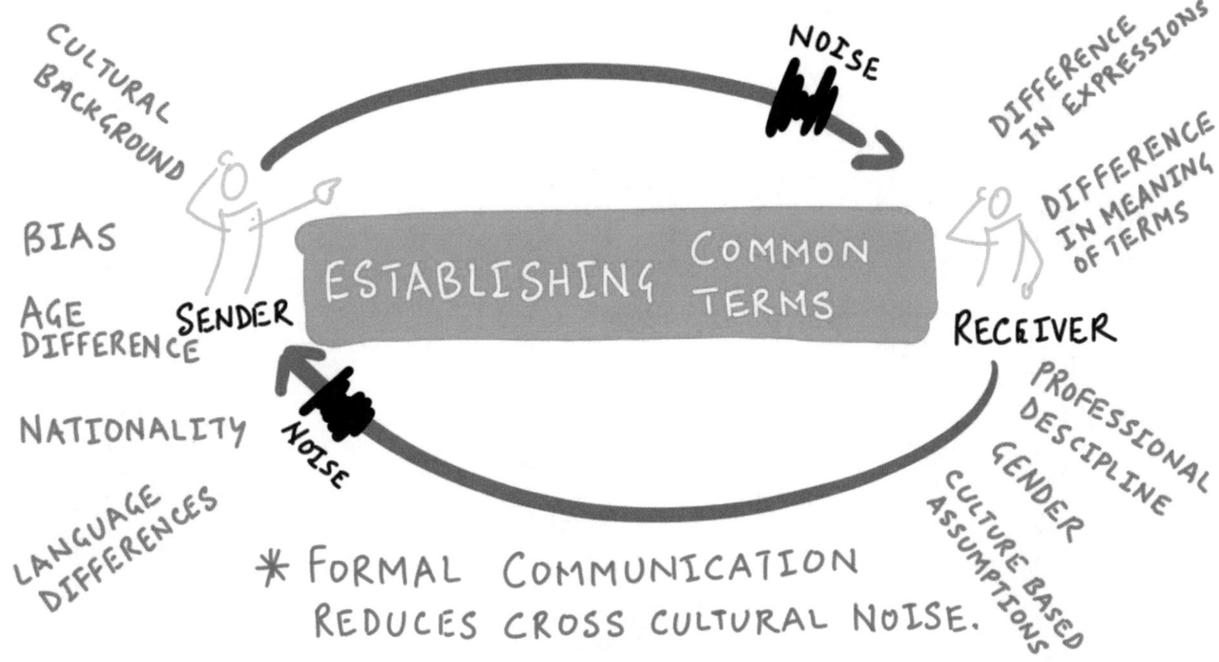

There are many other communication models like Shannon and Weaver Model, Schramm Model, Constructionist Model and Liner Model (among a lot more) but for exams point of view, you only need to understand the "Sender Receiver" model.

There are a variety of **Communication Methods** that could be used in a Project depending on the specific situations in a project. Communication method is

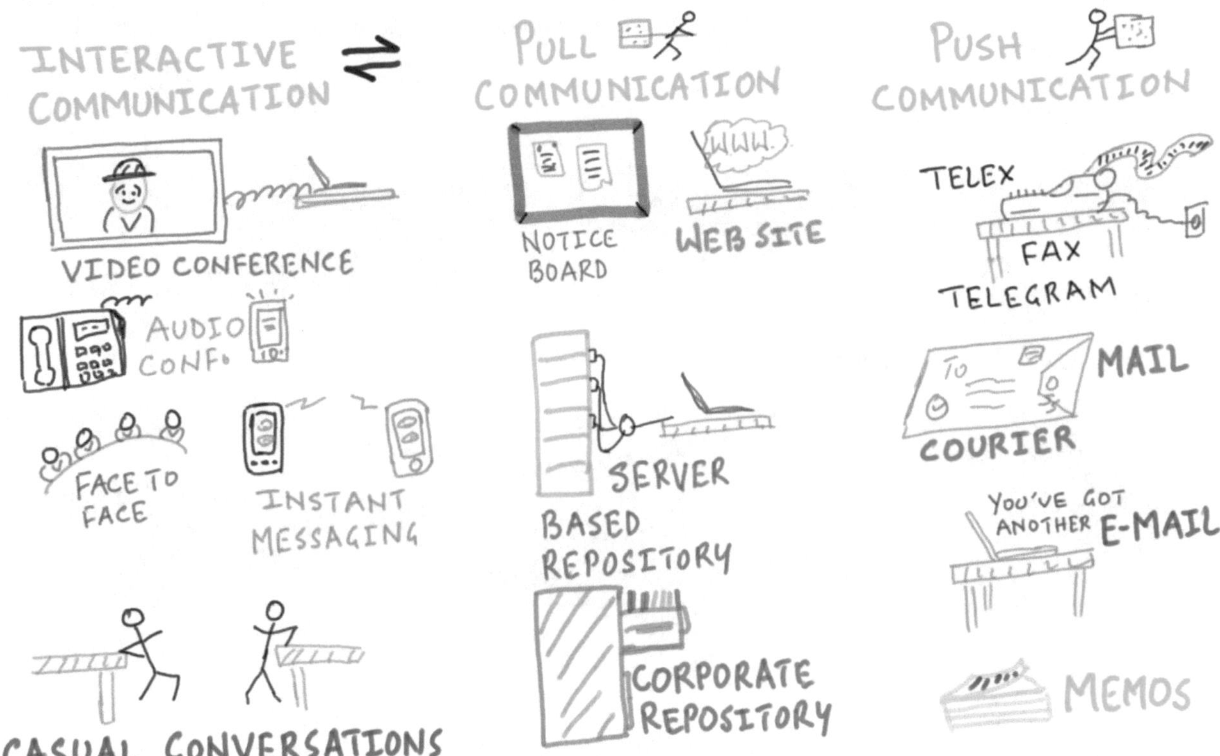

There are three main kinds of communication methods viz., Interactive Communication, Pull Communication, and Push Communication. Interactive communication is when two or more participants have a real-time interaction of exchanging, understanding and clarifying messages and information. This is by far the best method in reducing noise. Examples are face-to-face communication, video conferencing, audio conference, meetings, instant messages, casual conversations etc. Pull Communication is where the information seeker searches for and retrieves information that may have been kept by someone at a different period of time. Basically, a Pull Communication method keeps the onus of receiving communication, on the receiver. Examples of this method of communication are Notice boards, websites, virtual repositories kept on servers, physical files kept in a library or a file cabinet, white papers published etc. Push Communications are the method of communication where the sender decides when the receiver would see/get the information. Examples for Push communications are Memos, telex, telegrams, e-Mails, snail mails, Couriers etc.

Meetings are needed among the project management team members and some stakeholders to ascertain the communication needs, decide on the communication methods and communication technologies for the project at hand. As a part of the communication methods, there are 5 different **Approaches To Communications** and they are: -

- ***Interpersonal Communication***: One-on-one communications which could be face to face or virtual.
- ***Small Group Communication***: Meetings and workshops and focus groups within small groups of say 4 to 10 persons.

- ***Public Communications***: Where a single person addresses a large group and results in limited feedback.
- ***Mass Communications***: Where there is hardly any interaction between the sender and the receiver. Here a person or a group of persons simply send a message (using mass reach technology or medium) to a large group of people in general.
- ***Social Media Networking***: Where established and trusted social media platforms are used for reaching out to people and communicating with them.

Interpersonal And Team Skills

- **Communication Styles Assessment** is about trying to understand the communication styles that are appreciated by the targeted stakeholders so that you could communicate with them in the manner that those stakeholders are comfortable with. Overlooking this can be quite dangerous when it comes to critical stakeholders or unsupportive and neutral stakeholders. When I was in a rather difficult project in Japan, I needed the inputs of the Managing Director of the Bank on an urgent matter. Despite multiple emails, he did not reply. I was getting desperate so I walked up to his cabin (a very bold and reckless thing in Japan to walk into your boss's cabin without an appointment) and requested his inputs. He was shocked at my brash behavior but also understood my desperation. He told me that he received over 1,000 emails a day and there was no way he could answer all of them. So he has his secretary do the email screening on some predefined parameters. He went on to tell me that if there was something really urgent that he needed my attention on, I was to email him and then take a printout of that email and hand it to his secretary. Next time I had an urgency I did exactly that and got a reply within 2 hrs. This works.
  Communication Styles Assessment also takes into account the communication styles of individuals. There are several kinds of assessments in the industry that professionals use to understand exactly what kind of communication style do they have or to ascertain what kind of communication styles do some of the important stakeholders have, and then communicate with them taking their style into considerations. Let me take an example. Let us say you are dealing with a stakeholder who has a "Expressive" communication style. Which means that this stakeholder likes to use more words and description to communicate his thoughts or ideas, makes use of gesturing to aid to his communications, creates facial expressions and also uses assertive and responsive behavior. Once you know this communication style of the stakeholder, you will use similar communication style (even if you have a different communication style) to communicate important matter to this stakeholder. The PMP Exams does not ask any question on specific communication styles.
- **Political Awareness** helps the project manager to make a realistic and practical communication plan rather than an idealistic communication plan, which would not work. Every organization has power centers (because of roles or because of personal influencing abilities) and these power centers must be taken into account while organizing a communication plan. The project manager must also look at different modes of communication-based on the fact "which stakeholder wields how much power".
- **Cultural Awareness** is one of the biggest sources of conflicts and misunderstandings in cross border projects. Using one's own culture as a benchmark to judge (consciously or subconsciously) other cultures is fraught with danger and mistrust.

Cultural Awareness and Cultural Sensitivity goes a long way and hence they must be taken into considerations while creating a communication plan that spans cross-cultural teams. In certain cultures sending "to the point," messages are considered a very serious insult. While in another culture a "to the point" message is considered a sign of focus and professionalism.

Stakeholder Engagement Matrix can be used to show the gaps between what is the current position of the stakeholder vis-à-vis your project and what position you want them to be on. The communication plan must contain the "Strategy of communicating and reaching out to the stakeholder" to help take the targeted stakeholder from the current position to the desired position. You will get to know this matrix a lot better in the knowledge area Stakeholder Management.

Communications Requirements Analysis, Communication Models and Communications Requirements Analysis are Tools & Techniques that are unique to this process.

9.25.2 *Main Outcome from this process: -*

The **Communications Management Plan** is one of the subsidiary plans (project plan component) that make up the overall Project Management Plan. This plan should be formal and documented for mid-sized and larger projects where the channels of communication are many. Formal or Informal, there must always be a Communications Management Plan. Some of the common elements of the Communications Management Plan would include:

- Communication needs of stakeholders
- All the methods and technologies that would be used for communication
- What information would be sent in which format and in what frequency and to whom?
- Who would be responsible to send out which kind of information?
- Stakeholder groups and their individual priorities vis-à-vis project information and frequency
- How the communication would be recorded and stored and how they would be retrieved or referenced.
- Escalation and various approval processes
- Glossary and definitions of technical terms and acronyms being used
- Change process for altering or updating the communication plan itself.

This is not an exhaustive list but if a communication plan has these elements, it would be a matured and effective communication plan.

Communications Management Plan becomes input to 7 other processes. Important among them are ***MANAGE COMMUNICATIONS***, ***PLAN STAKEHOLDER ENGAGEMENT*** and ***MONITOR STAKEHOLDER ENGAGEMENT***.

9.26 Ninja Drill – Planning - 4

In this Ninja Drill you will find the most important notes and pointers that are important from the point of PMP Exams and covers, Plan Procurement Management, Plan Stakeholder Engagement and Plan Communications Management.

S. No.	Drill Points
1.	Procurement is seen from the perspective of the buyer.
2.	Every outsourcing from a project will each be treated as a separate Procurement.
3.	SOW = Statement Of Work, a document that tries to list in as much details as possible about what is needed by the customer through outsourcing.
4.	In procurements the purchase, procurement or legal team has more importance than the project team.
5.	Kinds of contracts are: 1) Purchase Order 2) Fixed Price 3) Time & Material and 4) Cost Reimbursable / Cost Plus
6.	Fixed Price Contracts are of 3 kinds: 1) Firm Fixed Price (FPIF) 2) Fixed Price with Incentive Fees (FPIF) 3) Fixed Price with Economic Price Adjustment (FP – EPA)
7.	Time & Material contracts are of two kinds: 1) Standard T&M 2) Indefinite Delivery and Indefinite Quantity (IDIQ)
8.	Cost Plus / Cost reimbursable contracts are of 3 kinds: 1) Cost Plus Fixed Fee (CPFF) 2) Cost Plus Incentive Fees (CPIF) 3) Cost Plus Award Fees (CPAF)
9.	Purchase Order (PO) is only created for the procurement of Ready Made articles or services.
10.	Fixed Price is the most common kind of contract when customizable work has to be outsourced.
11.	Customer creates a detailed document called Request for Proposal (RFP).
12.	The price is fixed the moment the FP contract is signed.
13.	Point Of Total Assumption the point at which the seller assumes the costs. In a fixed-price contract, this is the point where the costs have become so large that the seller basically runs out of money from the contract and has to start paying the costs of the remaining project themselves.
14.	In FP Contracts, the entire cost risk is with the Vendor.
15.	A selected "Bidder" is called a "Vendor".
16.	Time & Material [T&M] contracts are least risky for the vendors. They may entail some risk for the buyer.
17.	T&M is mostly used for augmenting staff on a temporary basis.
18.	The customer retains control of the project during T&M contract
19.	In T&M contract the overall scope is generally clear but the duration and quantity may not be known upfront.
20.	Indefinite delivery indefinite quantity (IDIQ). This contract provides for an indefinite quantity of goods or services, with a stated lower and upper limit, and within a fixed time period. These contracts can be used for architectural, engineering, or information technology engagements.
21.	The most important difference between T&M and IDIQ is the presence of upper and lower ceilings in IDIQ but not in T&M.
22.	IDIQ and T&M are both Rate based contracts
23.	Cost Plus contracts are often used when the project scope is not well defined or is subject to frequent change.
24.	Cost Plus / Cost Reimbursable category of contracts are risky for both the parties. However it is most risky for the Buyer.
25.	T&M Contract is the best when the client wants the work to begin right away.
26.	Cost Reimbursable is best when you want to buy expertise in determining what needs to be done.

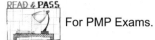

27.	FP is the best when the buyer knows exactly what needs to be done
28.	T&M is the best contract when the services of a person is needed to augment the existing staff
29.	FP is the best contract when the buyer wants the work done but he does not want the hassle of going through the invoices and auditing them
30.	FP is the best when buyer does not want to have cost risk
31.	Buyer has the most cost risk in which kinds of contracts. Cost Reimbursable.
32.	IDIQ is the best when you wish to have an agile project with an upper ceiling of expenditure.
33.	Source Selection Criteria is the detailed selection criteria that would be used for selecting the apt vendor.
34.	Independent Cost Estimates are usually done by a consultant external to the buyer's organization and it is used as a benchmark to select the prospective sellers.
35.	The main output / outcome / artefacts of the process "Plan Procurement Management" are: 1. Procurement Management Plan 2. Bid documents 3. Source selection criteria 4. Contract type
36.	Main Tools & Technique of the process "Plan Stakeholder Engagement" is Engagement Assessment Matrix.
37.	The five possible engagement levels of the stakeholders are: 1. Unaware 2. Neutral 3. Resistant 4. Supportive 5. Leading
38.	In general stakeholders with: 1. High Power – High Interest need to be managed closely 2. High Power – Low Interest need to be kept satisfied 3. Low Power – High Interest need to be kept informed 4. Low Power – Low Interest need to be monitored lightly
39.	The main output / outcome / artefact of the process "Plan Stakeholder Engagement" are: • Stakeholder engagement plan and • Updated stakeholder register
40.	The best way to check the productive working relationship of a stakeholder with a project is by observing if the stakeholder is continually engaged with the project or not. If the stakeholder is continually engaged in the project then it means they have a productive working relationship with the project.
41.	If the stakeholders are constantly requesting for changes in significant numbers, in a project than it would mean that those stakeholders are not aligned to or not aware of the project objectives.
42.	Surveys, interviews, and focus groups are also effective ways to determine if stakeholders are satisfied and supportive or if they oppose the project and its deliverables.
43.	A review of the project issue register and risk register can identify challenges associated with individual stakeholders.
44.	Mood Charts could be utilized during the project lifecycle to gauge the engagement as well as satisfaction level of the stakeholders vis-à-vis the project.
45.	Communications is to transfer the message to the receiver(s) in such a way that the receiver understands the message the way it was originally intended by the originator.
46.	Email is an "Informal – Written" type of communication.
47.	Main Tools & Techniques of the process "Plan Communications" 1. Communications Requirements Analysis 2. Communication Technology 3. Communication Models 4. Communication Methods 5. Political Awareness 6. Cultural Awareness

48.	Communication requirements analysis mainly involves the ascertainment of the channels of communication within the team / stakeholders.
49.	N (N-1) / 2 is the formula for finding the numbers of channels of communications. N stands for number of people in your team / number of stakeholders.
50.	Any question on this formula in the PMP® Exams has only one trick, see if the PM has been included in the number of team members, if not add 1 to arrive at the correct value of N.
51.	General factors that affect the choice of communication technology for the project: • Urgency for information • Availability and reliability of the technology • Ease of use of technology • Length of the project and cost/benefit of the technology • Project environment • Sensitivity and confidentiality of the information • Number of people who would use the technology
52.	Communication model is also called the "Sender – Receiver" Model.
53.	The three methods of communication are "Interactive", "Pull" and "Push Communications".
54.	Live and instant sharing of information among two or more people, using any kind of medium, is called Interactive Method of Communication.
55.	Pull method of communication is when the sender of the message puts up the message or information at a location (physical or virtual) and relies on the interest and choice of the intended receivers to seek and go through the information or message.
56.	Push method of communication is when the sender of the message or information sends the message or information to the specific address (physical, virtual or digital) of the intended receiver forcing the receiver to go through the message or information.

End Of Ninja Drill

9.27 Risk Management Planning (Plan Risk Management)

The term "Risk" is one of the most misunderstood and often misused terms in Project Management. Very few professionals truly understand the concepts and justification for Risk Management, though everyone speaks about it. This is also the topic which has been explained wrongly in almost all the famous books written on PMP. One of the reasons that prompted me to write this book.

Here, we will understand it in a way that is not only practical but also help you ace the exams without a sweat. Suggest that you go through this section again must you feel the need for it.

First thing to do is to have crystal clarity on certain terms viz., Risk, Issue, Gain, Opportunity, and Threats. There are some other terms as well which are important in risk management but we will take them up as we go along.

Risk is any **uncertain** event that has an **impact** on the project. Which means we could also state the Risk as

RISK = UNCERTAINTY X IMPACT

In order for something to be a risk, the event has to be not only uncertain (meaning, it has not happened yet and may or may not happen in future) it also has to have an Impact to the project in terms of cost, resources, schedule, morale or in any substantive manner. This Impact may be positive to the project or negative. I know some of you would not be able to digest the last statement about Risk being Positive or Negative. This part is hard to digest because even in some universities and some trusted web resources (like Wikipedia) Risk is suggested to be only "Negative" in nature. However, I would request you to understand this topic (just like every other topic in exams) only from this book.
Let us look at the positive and negative aspects of Risks in a simple way.

In the above illustration, you can see there are two distinct cases. In the first case, we can see a cute little cat *(I hope it looks like a cat)* on a table next to an expensive bottle of wine. There is a chance that the bottle of wine may fall. This may or may not happen. But if it does happen it will affect you negatively. Till the bottle is on the table it's a risk (Negative risk or threat) as it may or may not happen. But if it does fall and break apart and spill all over, it would then cease to be a risk and be called a Problem or an issue, because it is not uncertain anymore; it has happened and the damage is done.

In the second case, there is an apple tree laden with ripe and juicy apples. Wind is blowing and there is a chance that if the wind pics up some apples may fall which would allow you to enjoy them. But since this is uncertain and affect you positively, if they happen, it's a case of a Positive risk or Opportunity. However, if the apples do fall then it's no longer uncertain and are called Benefits, Gains or Windfall.

To understand the true meaning of the term Negative and Positive Risks let us take a simple example. Let us say that in your project you need to import some machinery (from, say Europe). This would mean that your countries currency exchange rate against Euro would be important. Now if your country's exchange rate is stronger (meaning you have to spend less of your currency for each of Euro) than it's a positive risk and you would want your currency to be stronger against Euro. This is an example of Positive Risk. You might be thinking that this could go the other way as well, meaning the currency could become weaker against Euro. And if that happens then you suffer losses because now you have to shell out more of your currency for each Euro. This would be a good example of a Negative Risk. This example also brings a very important point to light and that is, “Risk” in its self is neither Positive nor Negative. The way it would impact “your” project would decide if the “Risk” is negative or positive. The same “Risk” event may affect different projects differently depending on how it “Impacts” those projects individually. Let us take some extreme examples to get this point across. Say there is a chance that there would be an earthquake due to a fault line passing through Timbuctoo. Now, this would be surely a “Negative” risk for the projects and residents in Timbuctoo however for the construction and civil infrastructure companies it would be an opportunity for a chance to reconstruct and redevelop damaged areas. Hence no matter what uncertain event you look at, you will find that while it would affect some people negatively, it would affect some people positively if the event actually happens.

Just in case you are one of those who does not like the term “Risk” to also denote a Positive Impact then you can use alternate terms viz., Threat (to mean Negative Risk) and Opportunity (to mean Positive Risk).

Therefore:
Risk = Uncertainty X Impact.

The mathematics needed for measuring “Uncertainty” is “Probability” hence the Risk statement can be rewritten as

RISK = PROBABILITY X IMPACT

The question we must ask is why exactly we should spend time on Risk Management. Risk Management has some costs and needs resources for the same. Let us take the example of the wine bottle on the table. If no one had identified the situation as a “Threat / Negative Risk” than the bottle would have fallen and money would have been wasted not only on the wine bottle but for cleaning the floor and the carpet. However, since someone identified it as a risk the bottle was removed from the table and kept at a more secure place the risk was significantly reduced. This simple action saved a lot of money and effort. Issues cost a lot. Many professionals call it “Fire-fighting” when they just keep jumping from one issue to another and soon it’s called a “Chaotic” situation. Just imagine how much money and resources are wasted on taking care of issues/problems (Negative risks which have already occurred), not to mention the levels of stress. The main purpose of Risk Management is to reduce chaos, reduce costs spent on fire-fighting and therefore reduce stress. Risk Management also identifies Opportunities and try to make them happen, which are otherwise never even thought of, while being too busy jumping from one “Fire-Fighting” to another.

Risks may be Project Specific or General to the organization. This distinction is needed to ensure that the project manager and the project team is not wasting their time on General Organizational Risks but working on only Project Specific Risks. Question is how do you actually differentiate between the two.
I have developed a simple yet effective way to filter out the two.

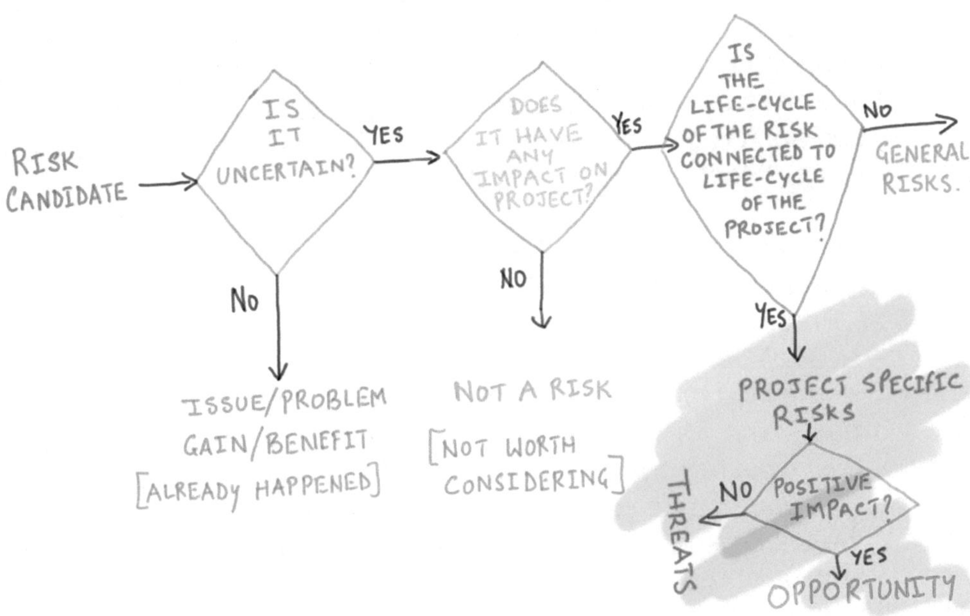

Risks that do not affect your project alone are called "General Risks" and they would have to be handled by the organization through their general insurance or other organization-wide responses. *E.g., High-tech companies having an organization-wide security policies and access control to prevent any kind of "Tech Theft" or "Industrial espionage" is an example of General Risk being handled at the organizational level. Individual projects within the organization do not have to individually provide for such risks.*
However, at the same time, it's very important to know that "What is general and what is project specific risks", changes from situation to situation. *E.g., An infrastructure company is executing a huge dam project in a rural area in Pakistan. On site of the project there are risks of theft and terrorist attacks hence these would not be treated as "General Risk" (as that is the only project going on there) instead it would be treated as a "Project Specific Risks" and the necessary response would have to be created by the project team for the same.*

From a practical point of view, you must remember that the risk event may occur because of multiple causes and each risk event may have more than one consequences. Consequences = what would happen if the risk event (positive or negative) actually happens. One risk may have more than one consequences.

While identifying risks, it's common for the project managers and the project teams to concentrate on event-based risks. (If this happens....some consequences will happen). These are important and they are called "Event-Based Risks". However, an attempt should also be made at identifying "Non-Event Based Risks". There are two kinds of Non-Event based risks and they are Variability and Ambiguity Risks. Variability risks are those that are based on the project environment and other variables that may affect the project. *E.g., Fluctuation in the currency exchange rate, more or less rains during the time of dam construction, changes in customs fees making the imports more expensive or cheaper, numbers of defects and errors found during actual testing which would have a direct effect on the duration for fixing and consequential regression testing.* These are all variables and can vary from giving a positive impact to giving a negative impact. Such risks are called

"Variability Risks". They need to be identified but the response to them would not be the same as those for "Event-Based Risks". Variability risks typically result in a potential spread of possible values for some parameter relating to a planned event or activity, covering outcomes that are both higher and lower than expected. This presents a problem if we try to manage variability risks using the standard risk process. How can a range of possible outcomes be represented by a single "risk event"? This is exactly what is handled using "Simulation" through "Monte-Carlo Analysis".

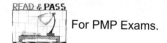

Ambiguity Risk, just as it sounds, are the risks that get created due to incomplete knowledge connected to certain aspects of the project. *E.g., When we had taken up a project to create the world's first "Predictive Fraud Detection System" code-named "Sniffers" which was supposed to look at all banking transactions in real time and predict suspect cases which may result into some kind of financial fraud (much before the fraud actually occurs). There are so many areas which we did not know to even frame the rules. There was too much ambiguity. For this, we hired some of the best banking brains and persons from "Financial Crimes Division" to understand some aspect of it.* We basically used research, suggestions by experts and brainstorming to convert ambiguity into some semblance of "Events". Another way to handle Ambiguity Risks is to change the mode of development methodology from "Waterfall" to more exploratory like Agile, Spiral or Iterative.

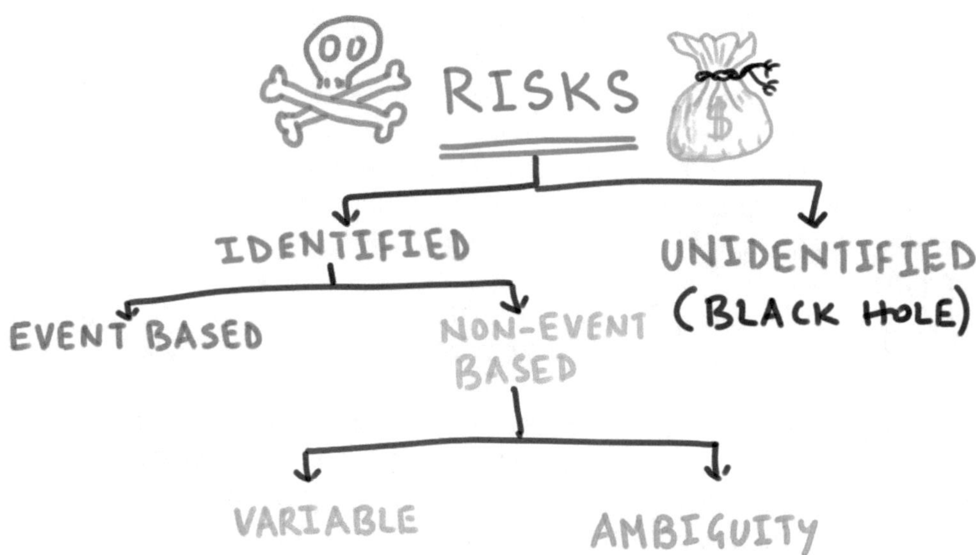

Just because you have identified some risks, they are not the **only** risks that affect your project. Identified Risks are just the ones you could "foresee". No one can really give an example of "Unidentified Risks" because the moment anyone utters a risk, it becomes Identified risks. Even if you take examples of what happened in the past or lessons learned, they too become Identified Risks, going forward. Unidentified Risks are a big "Black Hole" that may directly manifest themselves as "Issues or Gains".

BEING RISK SMART

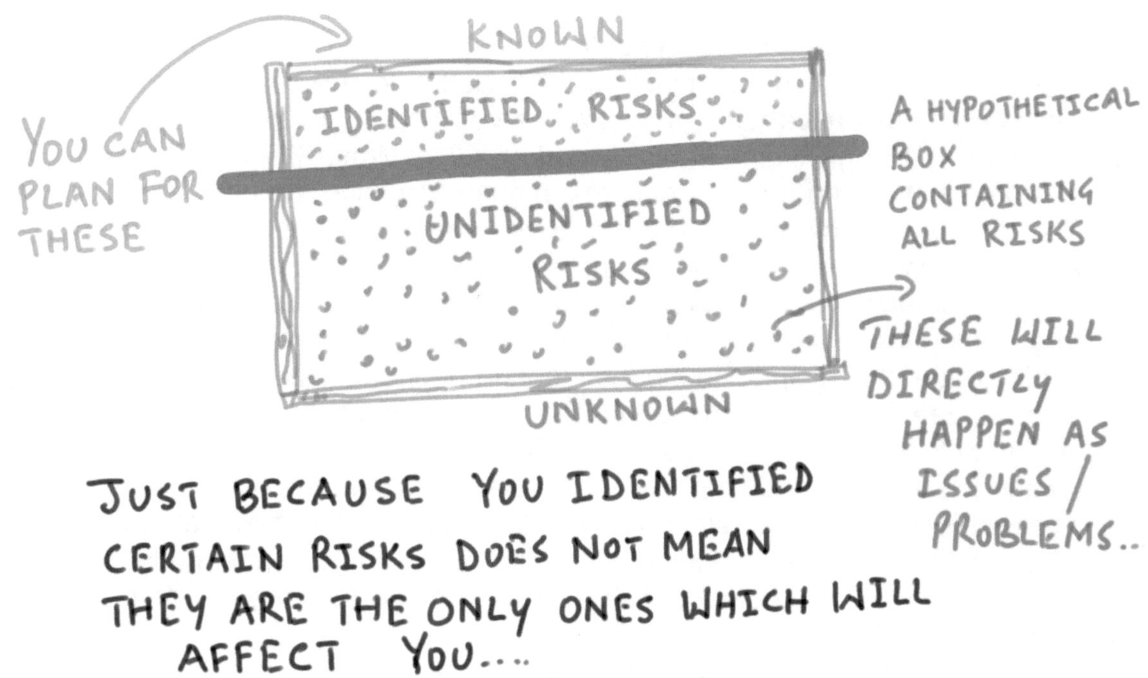
KNOWN
IDENTIFIED RISKS
UNIDENTIFIED RISKS
UNKNOWN
YOU CAN PLAN FOR THESE
A HYPOTHETICAL BOX CONTAINING ALL RISKS
THESE WILL DIRECTLY HAPPEN AS ISSUES / PROBLEMS..
JUST BECAUSE YOU IDENTIFIED CERTAIN RISKS DOES NOT MEAN THEY ARE THE ONLY ONES WHICH WILL AFFECT YOU....

The only way to reduce the numbers of unidentified risks, over time, is to go crazy identifying risks. The more you identify risks the lesser the unidentified risks would be.

Sometimes in organizations you may end up meeting an old-school guy like me or my father (as well as in PMP Exams questions on this topics) who will use different terms for risks and issues. To understand them remember the following:

Known – Known = Issue, Problem or Gain or Benefit.
Known – Unknown = Identified Risks
Unknown – Unknown = Unidentified Risks.

Project Resilience is how well a project is able to handle risks that come its way without getting thrown off track. The better the risk management the better the project resilience. I will simply give a real world example that would not only make it easy for you to understand this practically but also be able to handle questions on it. One first time movie director (name withheld) who had very limited resources and money at his disposal wanted to make a detective thriller in the most beautiful hills of India. He had signed up some good actors and that had used up most of his budget. So he spent a month only doing risk management by having some kind of back up or response for every kind of risks that he could dream up. He chose to go to the hill station during the off-season to obtain discounts but the snow build up would create havoc. He had broken the entire shooting schedule into segments like "If there is too much snow which are the indoor scenes that I need to shoot", "if so and so falls ill which parts of the script can I shoot till he gets better", "How many simultaneous shoots do I have to do to ensure that the project finishes in time and would the cost of the extra camera and cameramen be offset by reduced time" and so on and on. He was so well prepared by the time shooting started that though some of the risks actually did happen (one of the main actors fell seriously ill, once there was a landslide and one of his cameras got lost in snowfall) and yet he finished the entire movie under budget and before time. This is exactly what "project resilience" means. I am sure you will never forget this one.

One last thing to know about risks before we get into absolute details of this Knowledge Area, it's the Risk Attitude. This is one of those things which has been badly explained in most of the books on exams. To understand this better, let's take my example. I am an adrenalin junkie. I love adventure sports (Yep! Even Today). I have done Base-jumping, Bungee Jumping, Hang Gliding, Mountaineering, White Water Rafting, Trekking, Free Falling, Waterfall Jumping and so on. I have a huge "Appetite" for risk. This makes me a "Risk Taker". I have many friends who are "Risk Averse" as they have a very low "Appetite" for risks. When I got married my wife made some clear rules about Adventure Sports. I was not to go to Nepal anymore for white water rafting as the rivers are really dangerous there and there are regular reports of people dying there. I cannot dive over the waterfall ever again. I can trek and participate in mountaineering provided I go in a group of friends with a guide. No Bungee Jumping. I can do parasailing but only over water bodies. I guess you guys get the drift. Now what you see here is that I still have a very high "Appetite" for risks but now due to my family and other responsibilities I have some "Measurable Tolerance". This is called "Risk Tolerance". Now I have a daughter who has taken after me and loves adventure sports. For her, I have instructions like "She can go on mountaineering and mountain treks only up to a height of 5,000 meters as well as not go up an incline more than 60 degrees in angle". This is what is called "Risk Threshold".
Since there are different kinds of people in any organization it's important that Project Tolerances and Thresholds are clearly listed so that people's own "Risk Appetite" do not affect the way project is run. Organizations must clearly mention Project Risk Tolerances and Project Thresholds. Risk Tolerance is the measurable amount of risk that is acceptable. Risk Threshold is the measurable point beyond which the risk becomes unacceptable. Risk Attitude is basically a combination of Risk Appetite, Risk Tolerance and Risk Threshold.

Like everything else in Project Management, a bit of planning is done before anything else. This process produces one of the 10 subsidiary plans that make up the overall project management plan. This one focuses on planning for the stakeholders to be involved in risk management, laying down of the tolerances and the thresholds, templates, and matrices to be used in risk management, sources for identifying risks and so on. This has to start as early in the project as possible.

9.27.1 Main Tools and Techniques of this process: -

Expert Judgment could be all the people/stakeholders who could help with practical planning for risks in this project. They could be the Sponsor, Senior Management, Financial Professionals, Subject Matter Experts, Domain Experts, Consultants, Industry specialists, Experienced Team Members, PMO and anyone else who could contribute to this process.

Stakeholder Analysis is done to understand the key stakeholders who can influence risk management in the project as well as to help understand the "Tolerance Levels" of the stakeholders towards risks.

9.27.2 Main Outputs from this process: -

Risk Management Plan is one of the subsidiary plans that make up the overall Project Management Plan.

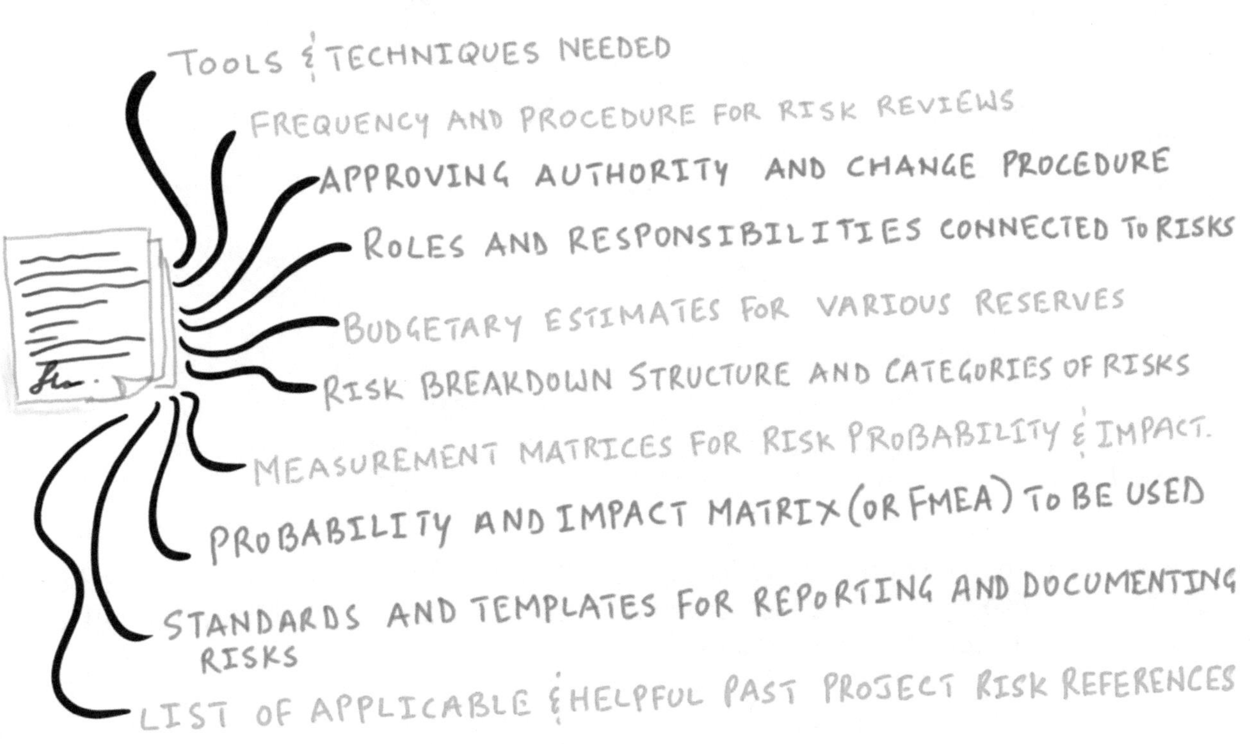

Risk categories are not individual risks but eventually help in identifying individual risks. Risk Categories are the major "Buckets" which could be used for identifying specific kinds of risks. *E.g., Financial Risks, Legal Risks, Sourcing Risks, Regulatory Risks, External Risks and so on.* Later on while identifying risks each of these "Buckets / Categories" of risks would be picked up to find all possible risks under it before moving on to the next risk Category. Works similar to the WBS. In fact once Risk Categories are identified it's usually shown in a Hierarchical Structure and is called the "Risk Breakdown Structure".

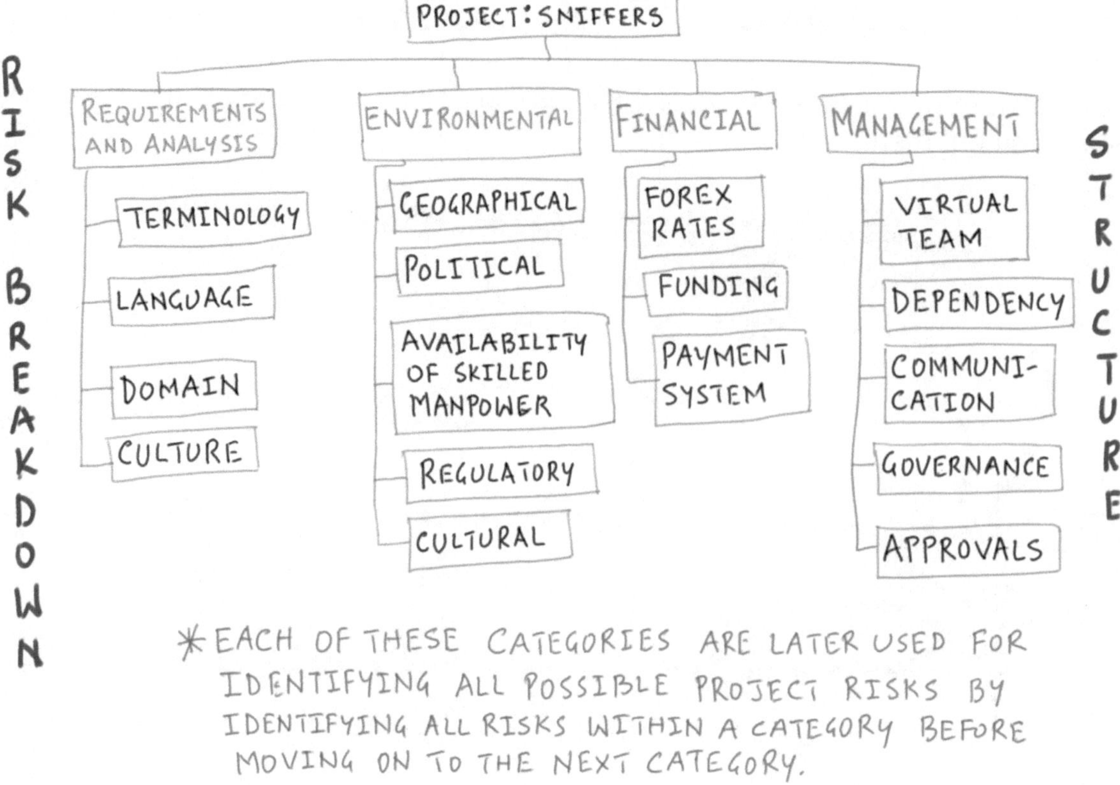

As part of this plan, a comprehensive listing (usually in the form of a matrix) needs to be created to state exactly what is a high probability and what is low probability and what is high impact and what is considered a low impact.

RISK PROBABILITY & IMPACT

SCALE	PROB.	+/- IMPACT ON PROJECT		
		TIME	COST	QUALITY
VERY LOW	1-10%	<= 1 WEEK	<€ 1,000/-	MINOR IMPACT
LOW	11-30%	1-4 WEEKS	€1K-5K	MINOR IMPACT ON FUNCTIONALITY
MEDIUM	31-50%	1-3 MONTHS	€5K-10K	SOME IMPACT ON KEY AREAS
HIGH	51-70%	3-6 MONTHS	€10K-20K	SIGNIFICANT IMPACT.
VERY HIGH	>70%	>6 MONTHS	€ >20K	SERIOUS IMPACT ON OVERALL FUNCTIONALITY

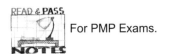

9.28 Identify Risks

The whole purpose of this process is to identify as many risks as possible along with their consequences and duly classified into Negative Risks / Threats or Positive Risks / Opportunities.
Risk Management is only as good as this process. The numbers or risks and their granularity (how detailed the risk is) defines the quality and practicality of the rest of Risk Management. In projects, it is important to identify as many risks as early in the life of the project, as possible. This is because the better prepared you are up front the lesser number of surprises you would get in projects and the more prepared you would be. However it's also important to know, irrespective of the number of risks that have been identified at the beginning of the project, this process has to be repeated earnestly at various stages across the lifecycle of the project.

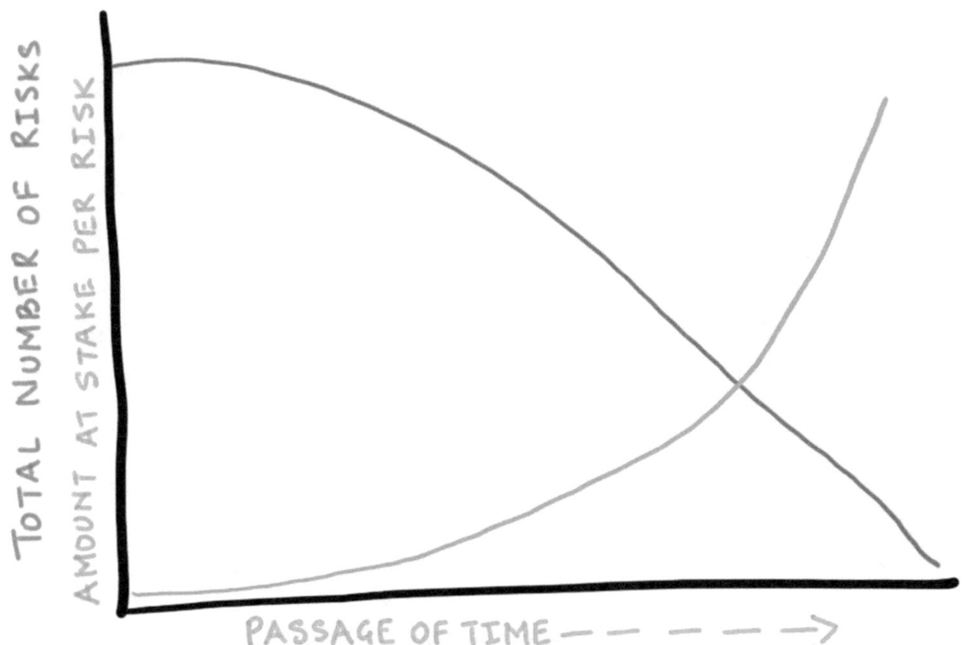

Progressive elaboration happens during the project and therefore as we progress into the project the number of risks become lesser but, since some work has already happened, even if one of those risk occurs, the impact of that risk would be huge. This means that over the lifecycle of the project the risks would change along with their priority and even new ones may get identified as well.
Though it is not always possible that every stakeholder of the project can be involved in Risk Identification but the idea is to involve as many as practically possible because, different people have a different take, expertize and view of the project. This tends to ensure that you have a good collection of risks.

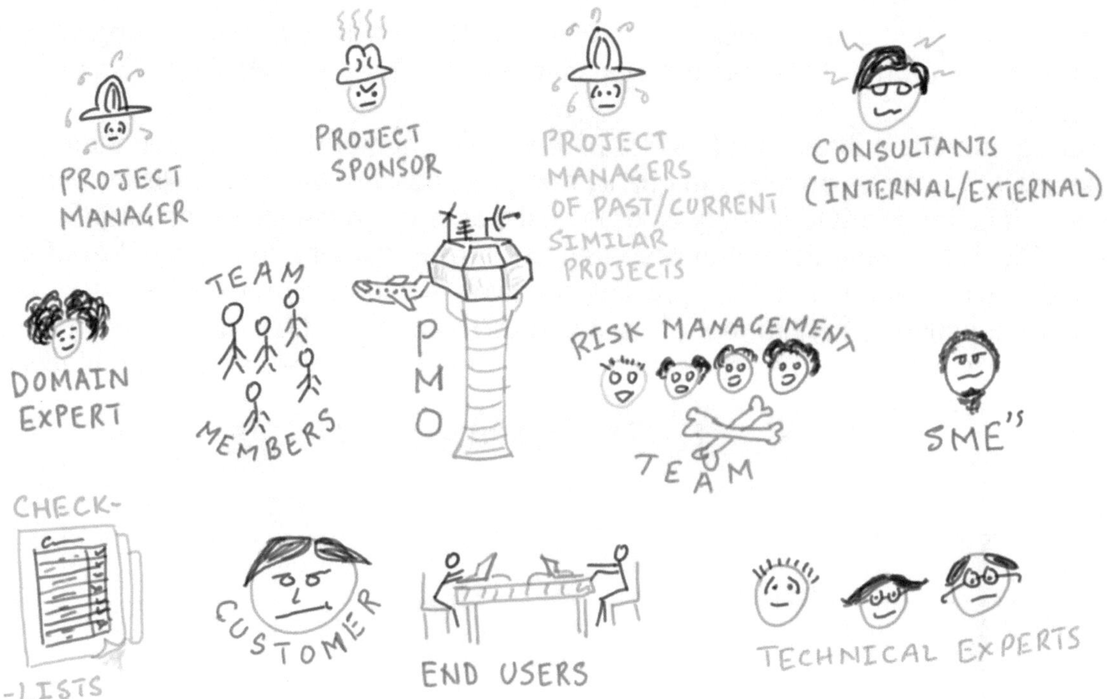

During this process, each of the “Risk Categories” is taken individually and all possible risks (opportunities and threats) are identified under that category before moving on to the next Risk Category.

Let us get into the details of this process.

9.28.1 Main Tools and Techniques of this process: -

Brainstorming is one of the ways to get expert judgments and other stakeholders to list as many risks as possible. Brainstorming could be a silent one or a traditional one. Whatever the case may be, the idea is to find as many risks (both threats and opportunities) with their consequences, as possible.

Checklists are used by many organizations for helping the stakeholders to come out with as many project related risks as possible. Most of the matured organizations use their historical data and experience to make a “Categorized” list of risks that are usually applicable to projects within that organization. This categorized list of risks can be converted to a structured checklist which could be used by the project manager of a new project to see how many of the risks mentioned in the checklist are applicable to his project. These checklists prevent the project manager from missing out on some risks. However, checklists are a good starting point and not an end in themselves. The quality of the checklists would also depend on how recently it has been revisited and updated.

Interviews could be done (face to face or virtually) with subject matter experts (SMEs), Risk Managers, Consultants with expertise in risk management, project managers of

similar past projects, technical persons and so on. In some projects, confidentiality would have to be maintained for the participants to such interviews. *E.g., Setting up of a Nuclear Power Plant is fraught with risks and most of the risks can be collected from the best nuclear scientists in the world and for that you have to ensure their identities are not known while they help identify all possible risks connected to your project.*
Remember! The Anonymous way to conduct the interview method and to gain consensus from the participating stakeholders, is called "Delphi" technique. In Delphi method, none of the participating stakeholders ever come to know who the other participants were.

Root Cause Analysis can be used to find the underlying causes and reasons which could give rise to "potential" problems or gains. These potential problems or gains are nothing but risks.

Assumptions And Constraint Analysis are a technique of validating the assumptions and constraints which are being taken for granted. Basically, this technique uses the assumptions taken for this project as listed in the document "Assumption Log" and from other project documents and plans and then looks for evidence, data, reasoning, and basis for such assumptions and constraints. The assumptions and constraints for which no evidence, data, reasoning or basis is found, become risks. Sometimes removal of a constraint may result in an opportunity as well, although at a cost.

Strengths, Weaknesses, Opportunities and Threats (SWOT) Analysis is a technique that helps in differentiating "Weaknesses" from "Negative Risks / Threats" and "Strengths" from "Positive Risks / Opportunities". Many times while identifying risks, strengths (which are facts) are mistakenly identified as Risks and same is the case with Weaknesses. This diagramming technique creates 4 separate boxes where Strengths, Weaknesses, Opportunities, and Threats are listed separately. The strengths and weaknesses are identified and listed first. Then the "Opportunities" resulting due to strengths are listed along with the "Threats" resulting from "Weaknesses". SWOT Analysis helps identify "Organizational and Project Internal Risks".

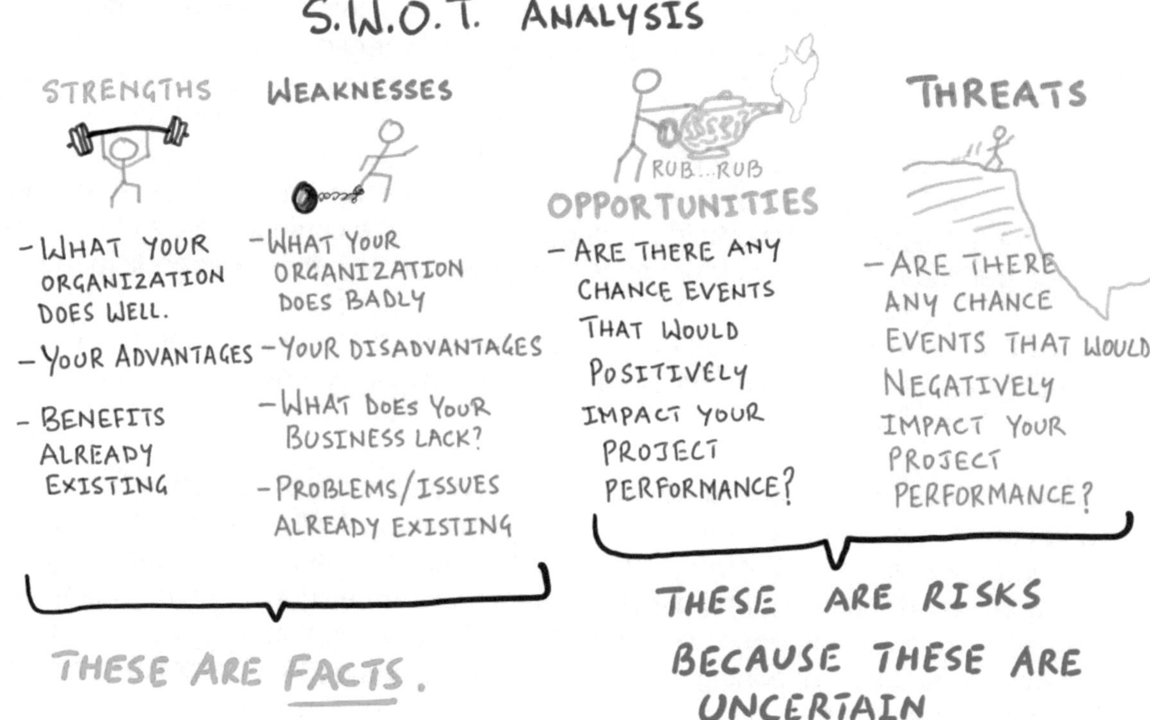

Document Analysis of current project documents and documents of past similar projects help identify risks. More than one "Critical Path" would make the project risky, non-availability of any QA checklists would generate some quality related risks, historical data of average "defect density" would help identify risks connected to our quality abilities and final inspection. Even constraints mentioned in certain documents may help in identifying related risks.

Prompt Lists are the common industry-wide or organization-wide list of categories that must be used (to begin with) to identify risks. This is done to ensure that no area of the project is missed out. In the real world when people get together to identify risks, they tend to go too deep into some areas of the project while completely missing or ignoring many other areas. Having a prompt list ensures that discussions are "prompted" for all the areas of the project. There are some standard prompt lists like "4 M's" which stands for "Man, Machine, Material, Method", or VUCA (Volatility, Uncertainty, Complexity and Ambiguity), or PESTLE (Political, Economic, Social, Technological, Legal and Environmental) or TECOP (Technical, Environmental, Commercial, Operational and Political) or there could be just a list of categories without these fancy acronyms like Resources, Technical, Administration, Management, Legal, Quality, Financial, Sub-contractor, Communication, Knowledge and information, Approval, Political, Commercial and, Environmental. If during planning for risks you had already created a comprehensive RBS, you may not need to use prompt lists. This is used when no categories had been identified earlier. These days another new Prompt List has been coined which is BANI (Brittle, Anxious, Non-linear and Incomprehensible). BANI may or may not show up in exams because this was coined chiefly around Covid uncertainty during 2020 and 2021.

9.28.2 *Main Outcomes from this process: -*

The **Risk Register** is basically the output of most of the Risk Management Processes but the content of the Risk Register changes from Processes to Process. (In other risks processes it would become part of the "Project Documents Updates"). Here in this process the Risk Register is created the very first time and contains all the identified risks along with their consequences. Some organizations (and this is a very good practice) assign a unique ID to each of the risks identified. The risk has to be properly worded such that the reader does not have to ask for any further explanation nor should the reader be confused.

A well-formed Risk Register would list the risk and the various consequences for each of the risks. The risks should also be clearly marked or segregated as Threat or an Opportunity. Risks could also be connected to some specific phases of the project and hence some indication of how "Urgent" they are (how soon in the project lifecycle they may occur) should also be marked. Though this is not a very popular method and does not amount to much before prioritizing the risks, some "Initial Responses" (what would be done towards) to the risks can also be documented in the Risk Register.

RISK REGISTER

S.No.	RISK EXPLANATION	CATEGORY	CONSEQUENCES	PROB.	IMPACT	RATING	RESPONSE	TRIGGER	OWNER	CURRENT STATUS	ADDITIONAL NOTES

Risk Report is a summarized document listing the most important, though high level, aspects of the project risks. This document keeps getting matured through the different processes of risk management and become output of all the other risk processes but as part of the "Project Documents Updates", just like Risk Register. As an output of this process, this report would contain things like

- Total numbers or risks identified
- Total numbers of Negative Risks (Threats) and total numbers of Positive Risks (Opportunities)
- List of categories or sources that have the highest numbers of risks.
- List of persons who participated in the risk identification process.

And obviously, due to the new learnings from this process, some of the project documents may get updated.

9.29 Perform Qualitative Risk Analysis (Risk Prioritization)

In the previous process, we have identified all the possible risks that would be applicable to the project at hand. In a perfect world, we should be able to take care of each and every risk identified and have a pertinent response for the same. However, in the real world no project has an "Open Budget" and "Unlimited Resources" hence, it's just not possible to respond to each and every identified risk. The best and most practical alternative is to first prioritize the risks and then respond to the highest priority (critical) risks. This act of prioritizing the risks is done in this process viz., Qualitative Risk Analysis. Once the "Critical Risks" are prioritized the responses are created only for those "Critical Risks". This is the standard and most effective method for handling risks.

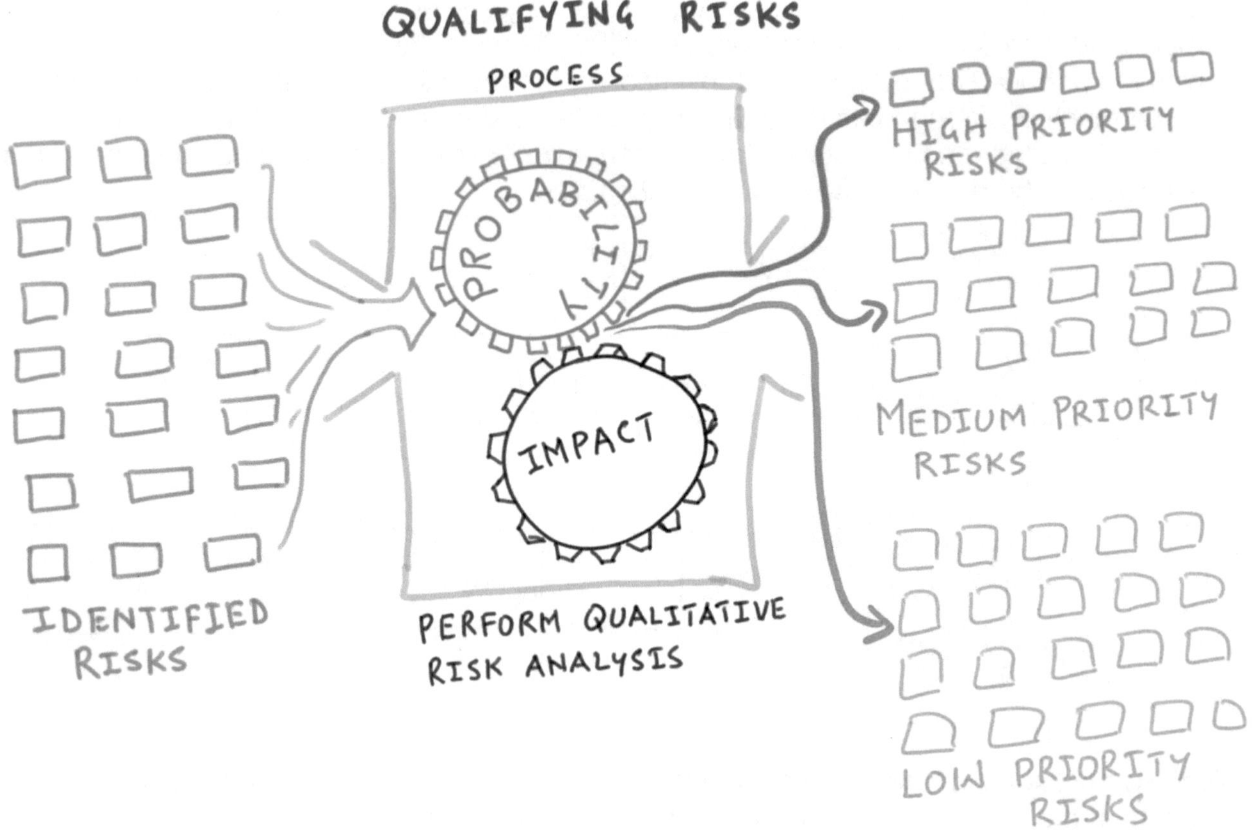

Let us get into the details of this process.

9.29.1 Main Tools and Techniques of this process: -

Techniques like **Brainstorming** and **Interview** would be used to find out the probability and impact of each of the risks. This would be instrumental in mapping the same on to a "Probability and Impact Matrix". This could be done in open forum or as a Delphi technique. This should be done in such a way so that there is no "Groupthink" or any kind of "overpowering bias".

Risk Data Quality Assessment is a conscious attempt at finding out the validity and authenticity of the data on which the risks have been prioritized. What it basically means is

that, instead of taking the supplied data by the various stakeholders about Risks at face value, an attempt should be made to look for some evidence, the basis of data, the source of data, justification of suggestion etc., before using that data for prioritizing risks.
Please understand that the rigor with which you would conduct the risk management process would also depend upon the Risk Tolerance of the organization. If the organization is a Start-Up the level of rigor on risk management would be low because almost everything they do is rife with risk anyway. Hence by doing risk management, they are only trying to minimize the no. of risks facing them. On the other hand, if the organization is a well-established one with a widely known brand name, they would tend to be risk averse and hence the level of risk management rigor would be a lot higher.

The Technique of **Risk Probability and Impact Assessment** is conducted using the tool of **Probability and Impact Matrix**. Taking the list of the risks from the Risk Register, for each risk the probability and its impact is ascertained with the help of stakeholders and consultants. The impact could be on scope, time, cost, quality or any other aspect of the project. One risk may have multiple impacts on the project. Once the probability and impact of each of the risks have been ascertained they would then be individually mapped onto the Probability and Impact Matrix for prioritization.
A Probability and Impact Matrix is a grid with Impact on one side and Probability on one side.

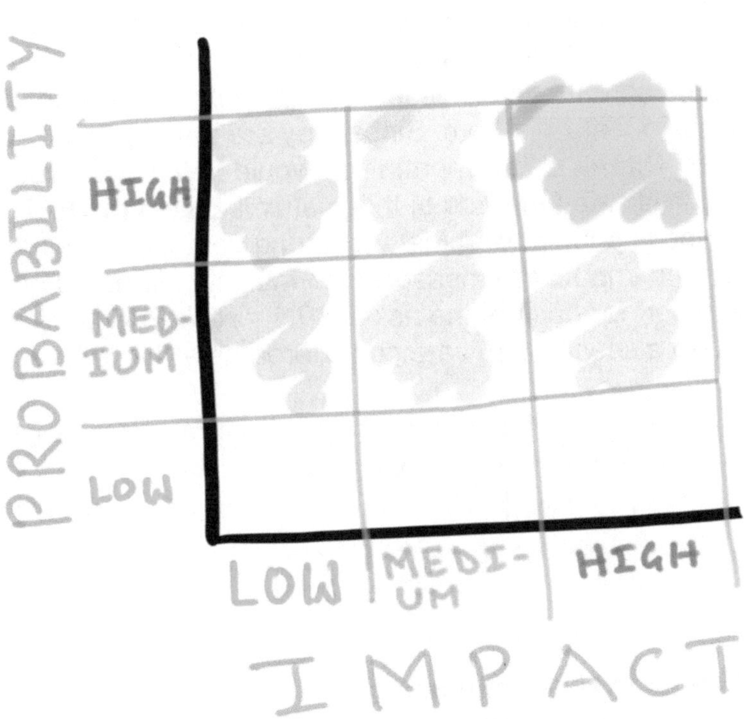

Some organizations prefer to have a more numerical level in the Probability and Impact Matrix which provides a little more granularity.

PROB. AND IMPACT MATRIX

PROBABILITY →					
5	5	10	15	20	25
4	4	8	12	16	20
3	3	6	9	12	15
2	2	4	6	8	10
1	1	2	3	4	5
	1	2	3	4	5

IMPACT →

The organizations may decide on the "numbers" and they mean, for risk qualification purposes as shown above. In this matrix, the prioritized section is usually marked as red. It is important to note here that distinction does not have to be made between "Threats" and "Opportunities" while prioritizing them. Since they are being prioritized it really does not make a difference as both Threats and opportunities would both have Probability and Impact ratings. A more sophisticated method of this matrix is called the Failure Modes and Effects Analysis (FMEA) and is popular with Manufacturing vertical as well as Six Sigma Projects. In FMEA, probability and Impact are measured on multiple elements of the project. This results into a "Priority Number" for each of the risks (RPN = Risk Priority Number). Once this is done, all risks above a specific RPN are considered as a "High Priority / Critical" risks.

A lot of people feel that when Numbers and ratings are used for prioritizing the risks they are **quantitatively analyzing** the risks. This is not true. No matter how you are prioritizing the risks (using numbers or otherwise) you are in Qualitative Risk Analysis.

Assessment Of Other Risk Parameters

Impact and Probability are by far the most common and widely used parameters (and in most projects, the only parameter) for prioritizing risks but there are several other parameters as well which could be used, over and above, the Impact and Probability parameters, based on the different situations in different projects. Let us go through them: -

- **Urgency** does not mean how soon the risk would occur in the lifecycle of the project. That is what “proximity” is. Urgency is the speed with which the response of that risk has to be applied. Basically, urgency is the speed with which you would have to do something about the risk. The sooner you are expected to do something about the risk the more urgent it is. In several companies, this parameter is used over and above the prioritized risks (using Impact – probability matrix) to understand which of the prioritized risks have to be acted upon immediately and those risks become even more critical.
- **Proximity** is “how soon the risk is going to occur?” The sooner in the project lifecycle, it is going to occur the higher is its proximity. In several organizations, a moderate priority risk with higher proximity is more critical than a higher priority risk with low proximity (meaning which is going to occur later in the project).
- **Dormancy** is “How soon do we feel/discover the impact of the risk once it would occur?” Some companies even call it the “latency of risk”. This is an important parameter in infrastructure, disaster recovery, mass good movers and civil projects. From among the high priority risks (using Impact – probability) those risks for which the impact would be felt or discovered after a lot of time, become even more critical. This is because once those risks occur no quick action would be possible as the very knowledge, that the risk has occurred, would dawn on you much later. Hence for such risks, stringent responses are made so that they do not even occur. I guess an example would be in order.
  *When the South African government was implementing its prestigious “Gautrain” (pronounced “g**H**owTrain”) from Johannesburg to Pretoria they had to build a track on areas which were not on proper bedrock but dolomite rocks. Dolomites are fragile and result in “Sink Holes”. Now just imagine if a fast train filled with passengers and traveling at 160km/hour is engulfed by a sinkhole. It’s almost impossible to detect when and where a sinkhole would be created. Therefore they realized that there would not be any kind of early warning sign for this that could be used for stopping trains, they created an artificial bedrock by laying down foundations of wide pavement like concrete on which the tracks would be laid so that the weight would be distributed and sinkholes would not get created.*
- **Manageability** means how easily the risk owner would or the project team be able to apply the risk response or be able to handle the impact of the risk. Needless to say the “The Lower the manageability, the higher the criticality of the risk” and vice – versa.
- **Controllability** is the degree to which the project team or the project owner can control the outcome of the project. Obviously, the criticality of the risk is inversely proportional to the controllability of the risk.
- **Detectability** is the ease with which it would be known that the risk is about to happen. The higher the detectability the higher the risk.
- **Connectivity** is when one risk is connected to a few other risks. The more the number of risks that are linked to a single risk the higher its connectivity and therefore the higher its criticality. A higher connectivity risk may end up triggering a lot of other risks.
- **Strategic Impact** is “does the risk has such an impact that it would affect the overall strategy of the organization?” This strategic impact could be positive or negative. *E.g., Long time back when I was working in Japan for a Bank (being the vendor IT Program Manager) and the bank’s chairman gave us a new project called “Sniffers” where we had to build an engine that would detect “possible*

frauds and money laundering cases" even before they actually occur. Since nothing like this was ever built by anyone ever in the world, I took it as a negative risk. But my companies MD saw it as a great opportunity to fulfill his companies "Strategy". His company's strategy was to become the largest provider of banking software in the world. He told me that since such a solution does not exist in the world this is one of the best opportunity for him to gain a strategic advantage. He later spent even more money to ensure the success of that project and which he later converted into a product.

- **Propinquity** is a term that means "very close to the heart of someone". Therefore in certain cases, some of the stakeholders say that some risks are very close to their thinking and therefore those risks would be a high priority. *E.g., One of the political leaders of the country, who is sponsoring the project of a rural hospital, says that the risk of project is very close to his heart as he may face the effect of it in the elections that are very close too. So, even though you did not feel that the risk of delay is high you will still treat this risk as a high priority as this risk is closer to the heart of an important stakeholder.*

Interpersonal And Team Skills, particularly **Facilitation skills** are needed to ensure that everyone participates, there is no bias and that there is no "group think" and at the same time, there is a conducive environment for all to offer their contribution in an honest and focused manner.

Risk Categorization is an attempt to categorize or group risks based on certain parameters or characteristics. One of the most common categorizations is to group all the "High Priority" risks together so that one would not have to search through the risk register to find them. If they are spread all across, chances of missing one or two become higher. Another way to group the risks is based on the Risk Categories in RBS (Risk Breakdown Structure). This way all risks are grouped as per the Categories and it's easy to find risks and sort through them. Within the categories, the risks are further grouped as per the priority. This would also help to understand which Categories tend to have the highest numbers or critical risks. Risks could also be categorized and grouped as per the "Departments / Functions" it affects. This is usually done in a "Weak Matrix" kind of organization. The whole purpose of categorizing risks is to make it easy to find specific risks as well as to be able to create "Responses" for a whole category of Risks. Of late there is an increasing trend where the risks are categorized based on the "Phase" of the project they are related to. This not only shows which phases of the project need more attention (the phases which have more number of high priority risks) it also helps decide which risks need attention earlier than others.

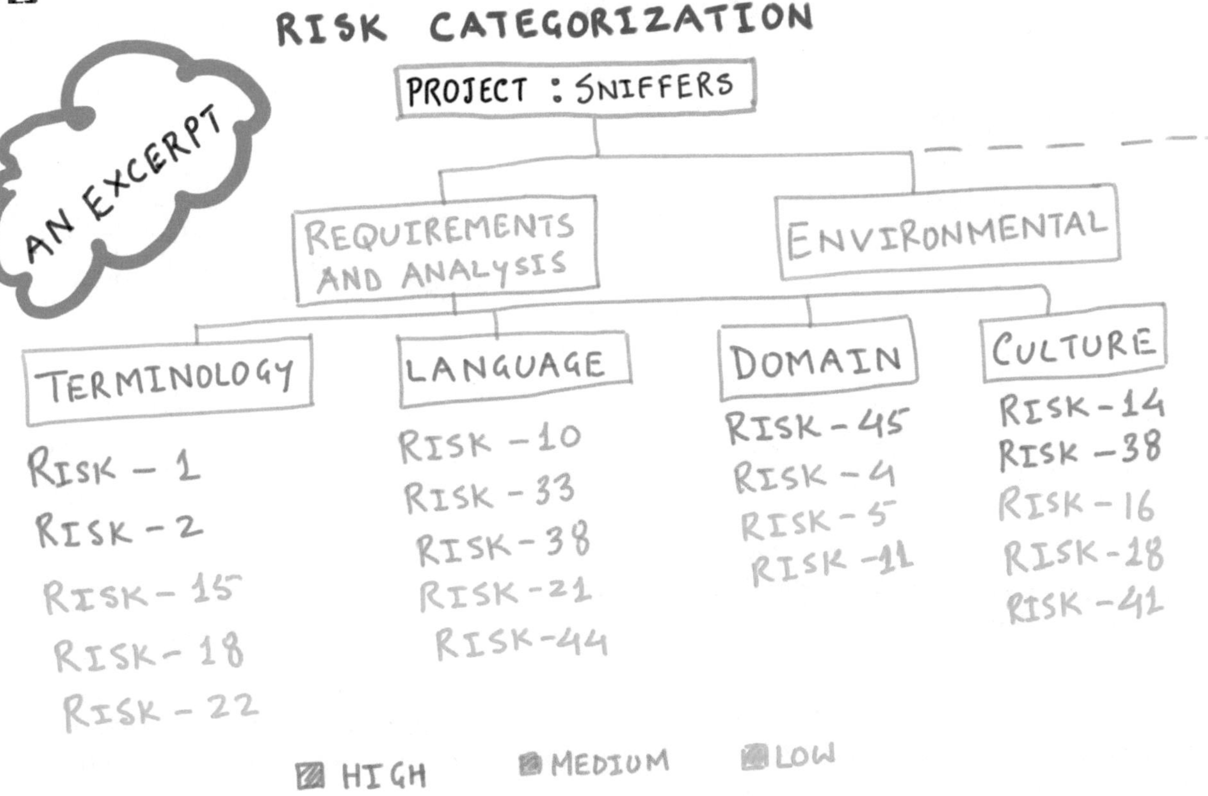

9.29.2 *Main Outcome from this process: -*

This process has only one output and it is **Project Documents Updates**.

Project Documents consists or many project documents but among them, the two that always get updated are the Risk Register and the Risk Report. Now Risk Register and Risk Report were the output of the previous process viz., *IDENTIFY RISKS* but once it is created in a project for the first time, it becomes the part of the "Project Documents" and hence the output here in this process is "Project Documents Updates" where the Risk Register gets updated with new and revised information.

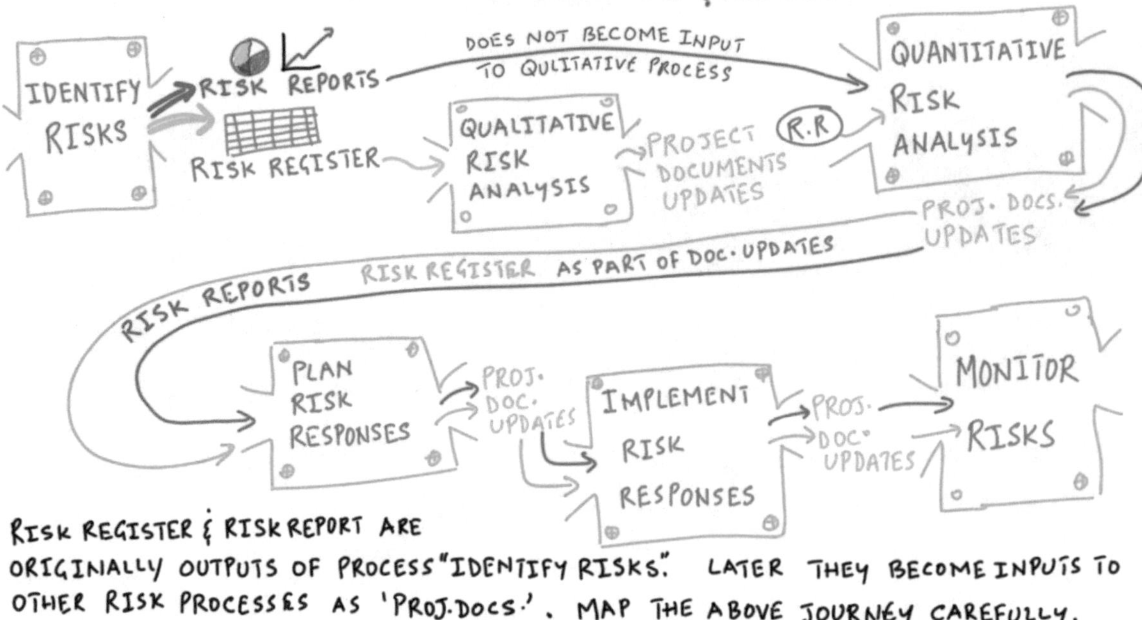

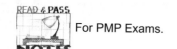

The Risk Register is updated with the High Priority risk ratings in the decided risk categorization. Some reasons are also mentioned why certain risks are high priority. If the Risk Urgency Assessments have been done then the "Urgency Rating" of the risks are also updated in the Risk Register.
This is exactly what is the journey and life of the document Risk Report as well.

Before we end this process there is something rather important that you should know, not only from the real world project point of view but also from a certification point of view. Once you have used the Probability and Impact Matrix for prioritizing the risks you also come to know the overall risk rating/ranking of the project. It would answer the question "How risky is your project?" The more the percentage of identified risks show up in the "Critical Risk" area of the prioritization matrix the riskier your project becomes in general. Say, if 40% to 50% of all the risks you identified are high priority risks, it simply means that the project, in general, is very risky or the overall risk ranking of the project is very high.

9.30 Perform Quantitative Risk Analysis (Optional Process)

Quantitative Risk Analysis always happens after the Qualitative Process. Qualitative Risk Analysis prioritizes the risks and Quantitative Risk Analysis uses quantitative and other modeling techniques to further analyze the risks to understand how exactly the risk is going to impact the project. It's also important to know that in almost all the projects, when Risk Management is done, the process of Qualitative Risk Analysis would be done. The Quantitative Risk Analysis may or may not be done. It would be the prerogative of the project manager to conduct this process in the project or not. It is generally seen that this process is usually done in larger and more complex projects.
So, what is really done in this process?
In this process further analysis and investigation is done on the "high priority" risks, something that was ascertained in the previous process viz., *QUALITATIVE RISK ANALYSIS*.
In this process, it's also decided as to how much money should be set aside as Contingency Reserve or for schedule in terms of Buffers. During the Cost Management processes, we

realized that some extra money has to be kept aside for identified risks which are called the "Contingency Reserve". It is in this process that the Contingency reserve amount is calculated.

Keeping this in mind let us get into the nitty-gritty of this process.

9.30.1 Tools and Techniques of this process: -

Interview: Traditional interview methods or Delphi methods could be used to get inputs from experts, consultants, key stakeholders, technical persons or SME's regarding quantifying risks. Either only one specific person may be interviewed for finding financial impacts of certain category of risks or more than one person could be interviewed for the same. Obtaining data from one singular expert does not involve any science at all, however, if the data is being obtained from multiple persons than several techniques are available.

- One is Consensus, where all the persons being interviewed talk to each other and more or less arrive a specific number. This consensus could be achieved through brainstorming, virtual meetings or face to face meetings or it could also be done anonymously (The Delphi Technique).
- Second is using Three Point Estimate. Here only three persons are approached for each risk and they are asked to state their best estimate of financial impact of the high priority risk. Once the three data points are obtained the standard formula of
-

$$D = \frac{P + 4M + O}{6}$$

WHERE:
P = PESSIMISTIC
M = MOST LIKELY/MIDDLE VALUE
O = OPTIMISTIC
D = DURATION

would be used to arrive at the final estimate.
Third is using Cause and Effect Analysis to analyze various areas where the risk might have an impact. This is done until a very granular level is achieved. Later each of the granular level impacts is calculated and added up to the total Impact. Sometimes Root Cause Analysis is also conducted.

Representation of Uncertainty is the mathematical distribution of uncertainty using one or more of probability theorem. The possible probability distribution of risks is calculated based on multiple inputs to represent "all possible cases of outcomes" of the risk. This is used for prioritization. This is the mathematical model that usually becomes the input for "Monte Carlo Simulation".
It is not very common to use this model in projects. This is used in projects that involve large infrastructure projects or mission-critical projects that have a lot of variables of risks. *E.g., What is the uncertainty of winds higher than 120 Km/hrs over the harbor where this new suspension bridge is being made? Historical data would be collected and run against all possible weather situations in that area, to understand if the bridge needs more*

strengthening to prevent it from oscillating out of control due to high-velocity wind. The cost and time for understanding such mathematical models are justified in this case.

One of the ways this is done is by making the "Threat Profile". This is usually a colour coded graph where only the critical threats (high priority) are listed and tracked over the life cycle of the project. The trend that should be seen in a well-managed project would be the overall reduction of the consequences as well as the probability of these threats as the project progresses.
Threat Profile shows how the "Negative Risks" are behaving over a period of time in the project.

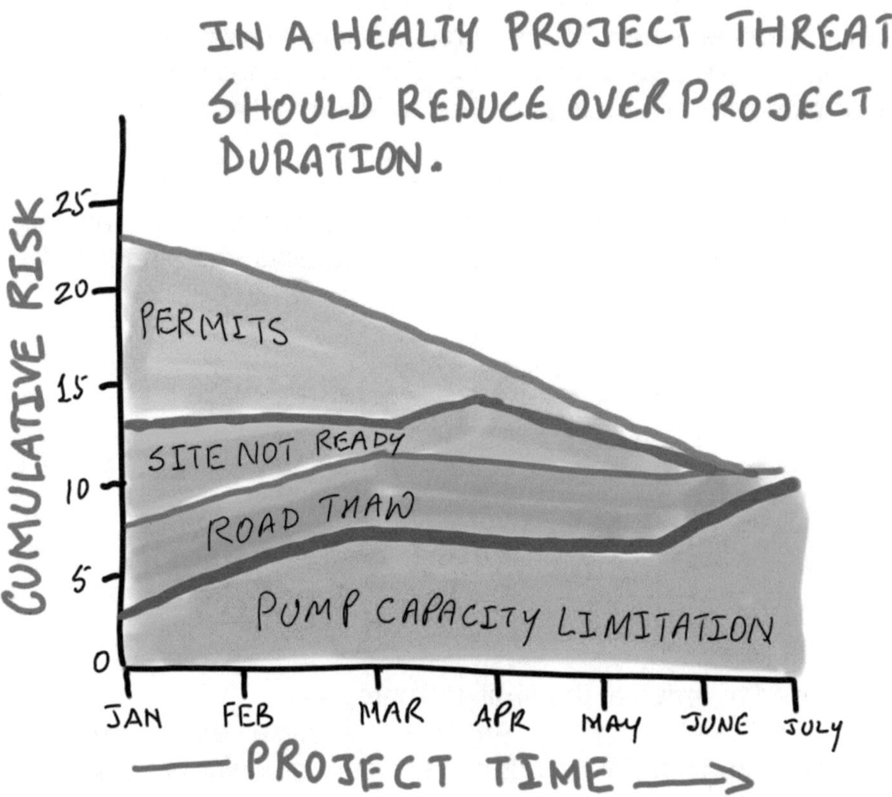

Simulation is a mathematical model that uses multiple parameters for impact and the probability distribution of a risk to show all possible outcomes in different situations. Simulation is done using a tool called "Monte Carlo Analysis". This is usually not done manually as the effort would be way too much to get any material benefit from this exercise. This is usually done through a tool called "Monte Carlo Technique / Method / Analysis / Engine". In principle, Monte Carlo methods can be used to solve any problem having a probabilistic interpretation and simulating Risks is just one of the applications of Monte Carlo. Some of you would wonder why this technique is named after a city in Europe. Monte Carlo simulations are named after the gambling hot spot in Monaco, since chance and random outcomes are central to the modeling technique, much as they are to games like roulette, dice and slot machines.

MONTE CARLO SIMULATION RESULTS

S.NO.	SELECTED PREMIUM	EXPECTED PROFIT	STANDARD DEVIATION	WORST CASE/ BEST CASE PROFITS
1.	$ 50/-	$ 1,430,807/-	$ 1,816,279/-	$ (4,018,031/-)
2.	$ 60/-	$ 3,267,329/-	$ 1,570,115/-	$ (1,443,017/-)
3.	$ 70/-	$ 6,024,908/-	$ 1,990,28/-	$ 354,069/=
4.	$ 80/-	$ 8,497,356/-	$ 1,631,740/-	$ 3,602,134/=
5.	$ 90/-	$ 11,472,155	$ 1,002,633/=	$ 8,464,256/=
6.	$ 100/-	$ 13,489,612/-	$ 1,482,734/-	$ 9,041,408/=

MONTE CARLO SIMULATION OF INSURANCE PREMIUM RANGING FROM $50/= ANNUALLY TO $100/= ANNUALLY ACROSS VARIOUS STATISTICAL PERMUTATION AND COMBINATIONS.

Remember Monte Carlo = “What-if” analysis as well as “Simulation”.

Sensitivity Analysis of risks shows us which of the high priority risks are more sensitive than the others. This sensitivity would mean exactly how “Sensitive” a Risk is to even the slightest changes in any factors affecting the risk. This is an attempt to find out, from among the high-priority risks which risks are more out of control. One of the best ways to find the more sensitive risks are the ones that would have a “domino effects” on the other project risks. This means searching for those risks that would trigger other risks if it happens.

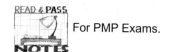

In a more academic sector, the Sensitivity Analysis is part of Simulation work. In such simulation what is done is that some factors affecting the risks are identified and measured. Once they are identified, the values of these factors are hypothetically changed, one at a time, to see which of the high priority risk reacts to it more than others. *E.g., If in a six sigma project one of the risks is "People resisting to change" and one of the factors that could affect it (positively or negatively) is the "Peoples effort towards Six Sigma effort being rewarded/compensated.*" Now as the compensation and the rewards are increased the less resistance there is to change. In fact, just by instituting a reward alone will dissolve resistance to a large extent. On the other hand, not having any rewards would create the most "Stonewall" resistance. If we check the effect of this factor on other high priority risks and find that "People Resisting to Change" is most highly affected due to this factor compared to others, then this risk is more "Sensitive" to "Establishment of rewards and compensation for Six Sigma efforts".

As you can see this would be done for each of the factors of the risks and some risks would be more sensitive to certain factors than others. This kind of simulation is done in projects which is very complex and has a lot of money at stake. Use of these tools in a mid-sized project is overkill and the effort expended on this would not be worth the returns.

If you are good at the Chart wizard of Microsoft Excel you will find that for such "Sensitivity Analysis" there is a graph called "Tornado Diagram". In this diagram, the ***risks*** are shown on the "Y" axis and ***the range of change*** is shown on "X" axis. The risk that has the largest range is shown as a bar at the top of the graph followed by the risk that has the second largest range and so on. This graph is supposed to be drawn for each of the factors that have been identified.

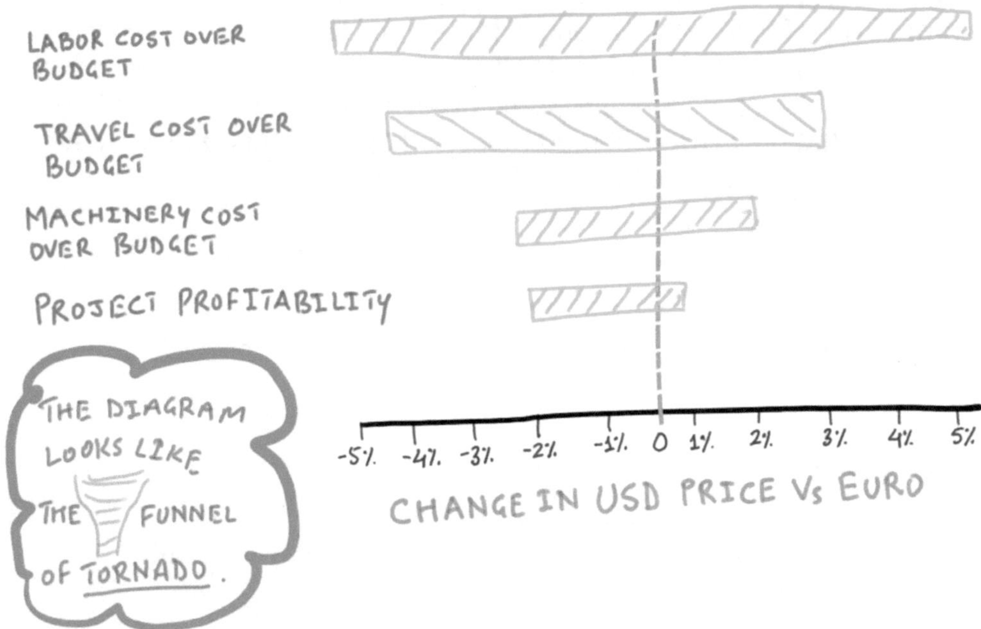

Creating the Tornado Diagram may be a bit daunting but reading it is not difficult. The largest bar in the tornado diagram is basically the most sensitive risk to the factor in question. I guess by looking at the "Tornado" diagram you would know why it's called so. It actually looks like the funnel of a tornado.

If in the exams it is asked, "How to measure the sensitivity of a risk?", simply select, "by using tornado diagram".

Decision Tree Analysis. Before we get into the details of the decision tree analysis there is another concept that you must know and that is EMV. There is a technique that is used for finding out the amount that should be set aside as contingency reserve and it's called "**Expected Monitory Value (EMV)**". Let us take an example. If you had a high priority risk that had a probability of 60% and a financial impact of USD10,000.00. How much should be set aside for the "Contingency Reserve" for this risk? You may think that well if the risk actually occurs than full impact amount would be expended viz., USD 10,000.00. While someone may say that only USD6,000.00 must be kept in Contingency Reserve as the probability is 60%. Let us see what is the EMV Formula.

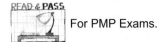

EXPECTED MONITARY VALUE [EMV]

FORMULA : EMV = PROBILITY X $IMPACT

EXAMPLES :-

S.NO.	RISK NAME	PROBABILITY	IMPACT($)	EMV ($)
1	RISK-1	60%	1,000/-	600/-
2	RISK-2	80%	100/-	80/-
3	RISK-3	70%	2,000/-	1,400/-
4	RISK-4	65%	500/-	325/-
5	RISK-5	90%	1,200/-	1,080/-

This may seem odd to you, knowing well that if a risk occurs the full quantum of the risk would happen, so it seems EMV is creating an insufficient contingency reserve. This is not true as there are other risks whose EMV would be calculated and added to the Contingency Reserve and if some risks actually happen then money from this reserve would be used to meet them. Not all the risks are going to happen and hence this is a good way to make a Contingency Reserve. This is exactly how the Insurance companies take seemingly fewer amounts of "Fees" annually but insures your cars for a sizeable amount. Not all cars would meet with mishaps.

CONTINGENCY RESERVE THROUGH EMV.

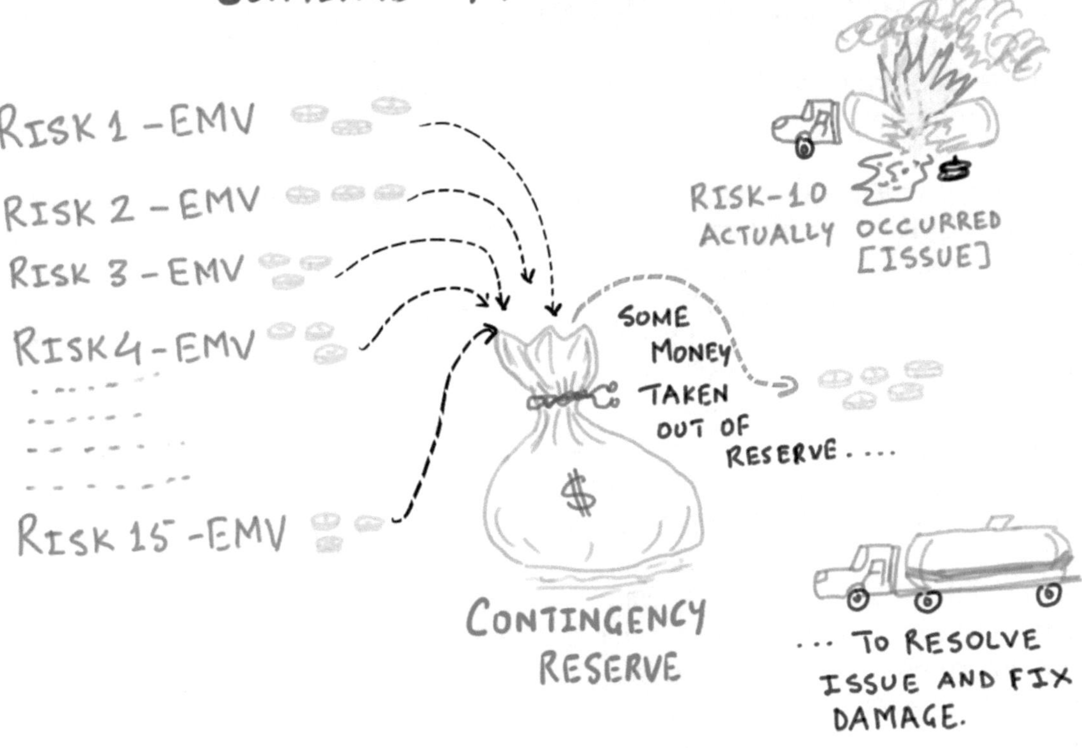

So far we have looked at the calculation of EMV assuming that the risks would all be "Threats". How do we calculate the EMV or "Opportunities" and how do we add it to the contingency reserve? The EMV is calculated in exactly the same way as shown before. However, the EMV amount of an Opportunity is actually reduced from the contingency reserve as this is the amount that is expected to come in and not go out.

CONTINGENCY RESERVE CALCULATION

THREAT-1 EMV = $200/=	CONTINGENCY RESERVE = $200/=
+	
THREAT-2 EMV = $500/=	CONTINGENCY RESERVE = $700/=
+	
THREAT-3 EMV = $1,000/-	CONTINGENCY RESERVE = $1,700/=
−	
OPPORTUNITY-1 EMV = $600/=	CONTINGENCY RESERVE = $1,100/=
+	
THREAT-4 EMV = $800/-	CONTINGENCY RESERVE = $1,900/=
−	
OPPORTUNITY-2 EMV = 1,000/-	CONTINGENCY RESERVE = $900/=

CONTINGENCY $900/= RESERVE

In the real world, different cultures and different countries and different organizations calculate the EMV of Opportunities differently. In most of the European and Asia Pacific regions, the Contingency reserve is made only for Threats. While in many other countries like some Middle Eastern countries and many companies in US, they balance out the contingency reserve by including both, EMV for Threats and EMV for Opportunities.

Sometimes in exams you may get a question which asks you to calculate the EMV in the provided scenario. In the scenario they may end up providing details about an opportunity as well as about a threat. In which case you have to calculate the EMV of opportunity separately and that of Threat separately and then to arrive at the NET EMV you have to deduct the EMV of THREAT from the EMV of OPPORTUNITY. Let me provide one such example. What is the EMV of a 70% Chance of a $200,000/- Profit and a 30% Chance of a $300,000/- loss?
In this case you will see that the EMV of Opportunity is $140,000/- while the EMV of Threat is $90,000/-. Using the rule that I have mentioned above, about deducting EMV of Threat form EMV of Opportunity: $140,000 - $90,000 = **$50,000**. And that is the correct answer.

Connected to the EMV there is a decision making technique called the "**Decision Tree Diagram**". The purpose of this diagram is to help choose between multiple risky options, each with future cost implications so that the combination of "Cost and Risk" (EMV) is lowest. This can be best explained with an example.
Let us say your organization has got a contract from a client. They are paying well for the project but they are very sensitive about time. They have put a penalty clause in the contract that would charge you USD1,000.00 for every day of delay. Now you are going to outsource a portion of the project to a third party. You have asked your procurement department to suggest the vendors who can do this kind of work and what would their estimate be. The procurement department comes back with the following options with some background information about the prospective vendors.
One – Vendor Alpha. Asking for USD110,000.00 for the work. However, in the past Alpha has delayed in 50% of the contracts. His worst delay was as much as 90 Days.
Two – Vendor Beta. Asking for USD 140,000.00 for the work. However, in the past Beta has delayed in 10% of the contracts and his worst case delay had been as much as 30 Days.
The idea here is to go for the least risky one that also takes care of cost-effectiveness as well.
Let us solve this using Decision Tree Diagram. The first step is to plot all that we know.

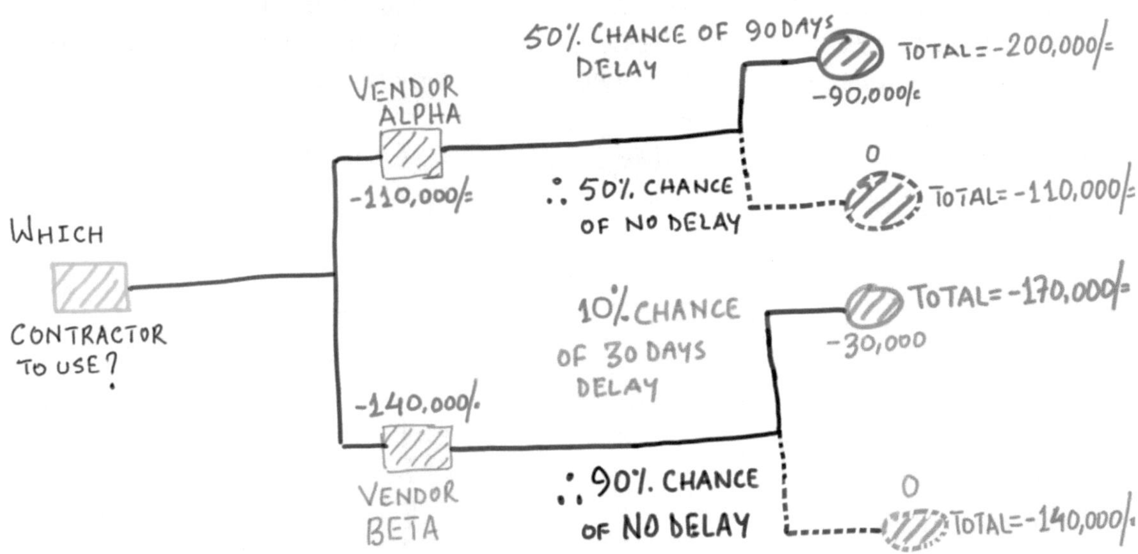

Once we plot the alternatives in the decision tree diagram, we need to calculate the EMV of each of the alternatives.

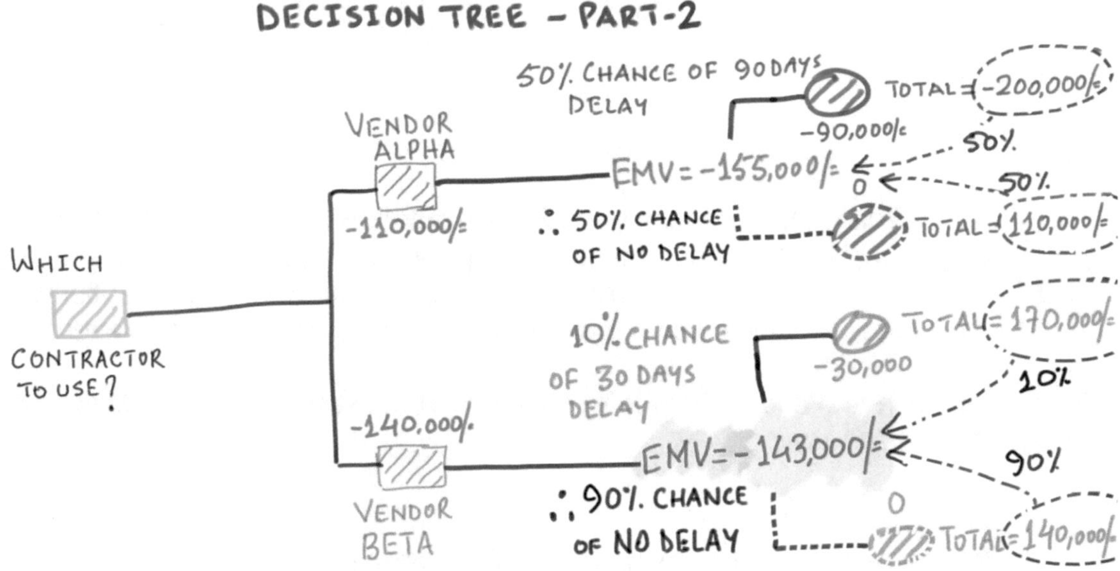

Influence Diagram An influence diagram (ID) (also called a relevance diagram, decision diagram or a decision network) is a compact graphical and mathematical representation of a decision situation. Influence Diagram shows, just as it sounds like, influences between various elements. Decisions are usually shown using Squares, Actions are usually shown using ellipses (also called Uncertainty node as this is where the risks are), Arrows represent "what influences what" and the Value or Result is usually shown using a diamond. There are many other varieties of ID but the style shown below is by far the most common one.

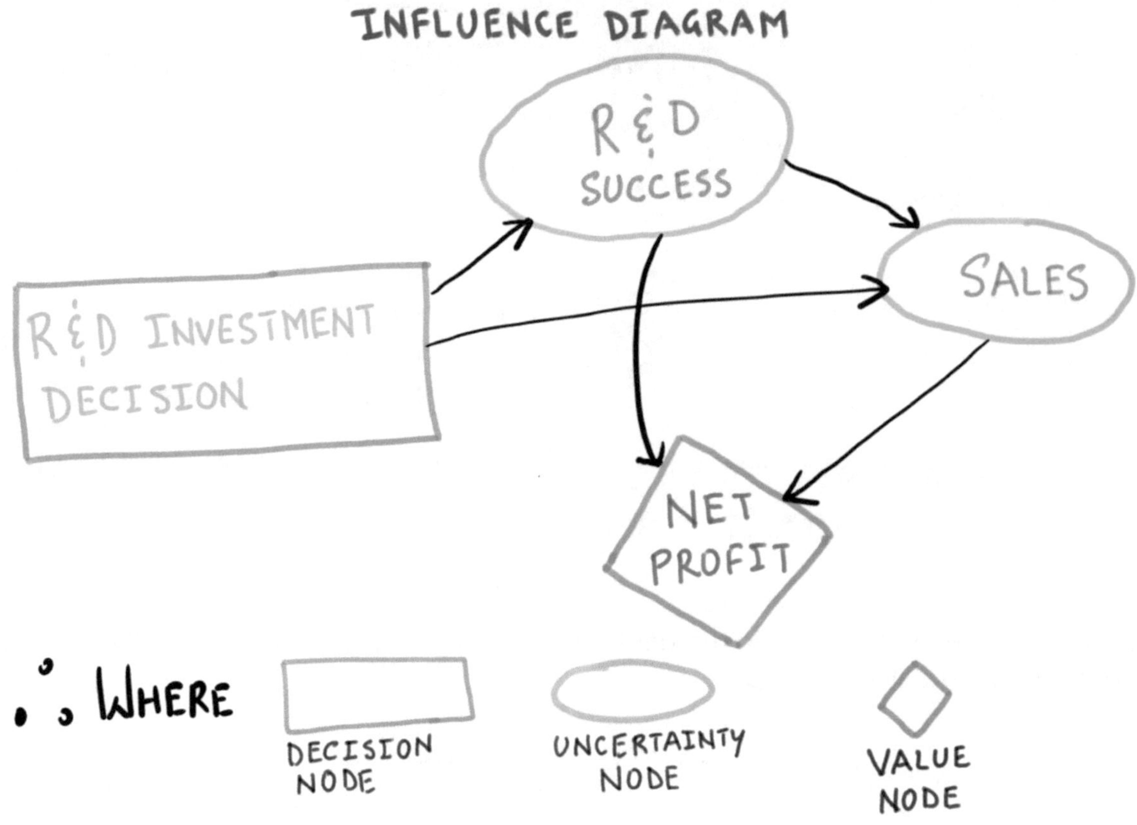

The tools and techniques Representation Of Uncertainty, Sensitivity Analysis, Decision Tree and Influence Diagram are all unique to this process. You will not find them in any other process. This means if in a question you see any of these terms it would mean that the questions scenario is about Quantitative Risk Analysis.

Simulations is a tool and technique to only two processes viz., ***Develop Schedule*** and ***Perform Quantitative Risk Analysis***.

9.30.2 Main Outcome from this process: -

This process has only one output and it's the "Project Documents Updates".

In this process again the main document in the "**Project Documents Updates**" is the Risk Register and Risk Report. In this process, the Sensitive Risks are identified from among the high-priority risks and the Risks probability and impact could be changed from qualitative to more quantitative terms. The Risk Register may get updated with the overall probability of achieving the project objectives given the time and budget constraints and yes the Budget is also updated with the "Contingency" reserve.

9.31 Plan Risk Responses

Remember the example, earlier, about the wine bottle kept at the edge of the table with the risk that it might fall and break. Having identified the risk you may decide to shift the bottle to a safer place. This act of "Shifting the bottle" is called a "Response" to a Risk.
This process is all about how to plan a proper response to risks. Since the response to the risks would depend on whether they are a Threat or an Opportunity, the responses would be broadly classified into two viz., responses for Threats and responses for opportunities. These responses are only for the High-priority risks and none other.

This process cannot be undertaken until at least, Qualitative Risk Analysis has been done. Theoretically speaking this process is to be done till even the Quantitative Risk Analysis is also done but in reality, Quantitative analysis is not done in each and every project.

Each of the responses may entail some cost and resources and may also take some time. Before implementing any of the responses it would be prudent to see the impact of executing the response on cost, time and Quality as well as other aspects like resources, risks, communication, and procurement too. There have been times when certain responses that seemed like a great idea could not be implemented because of the humongous cost and time involved.

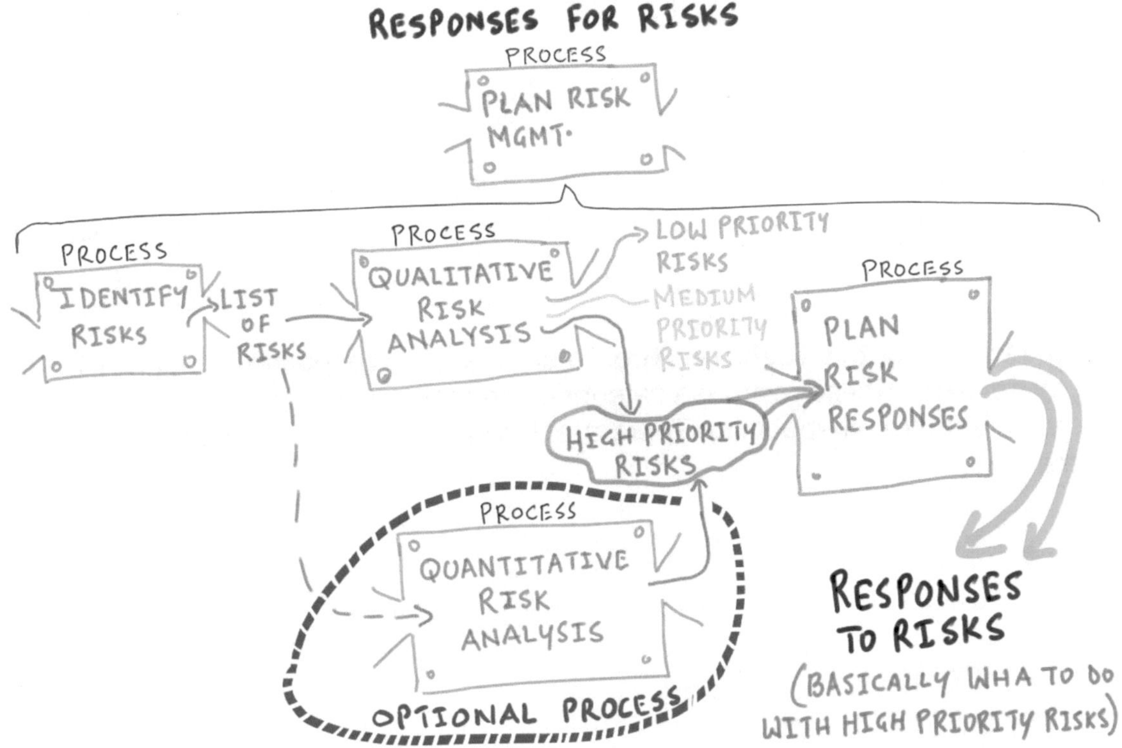

9.31.1 Main Tools and Techniques of this process: -

Interviews and **Brainstorming** would be used to get the most out of the Expert Judgment. The Project Manager would also have to use Interpersonal and Team Skills like Facilitation skills to get the experts to focus on the project risk responses and give honest and unbiased suggestions and recommendations.

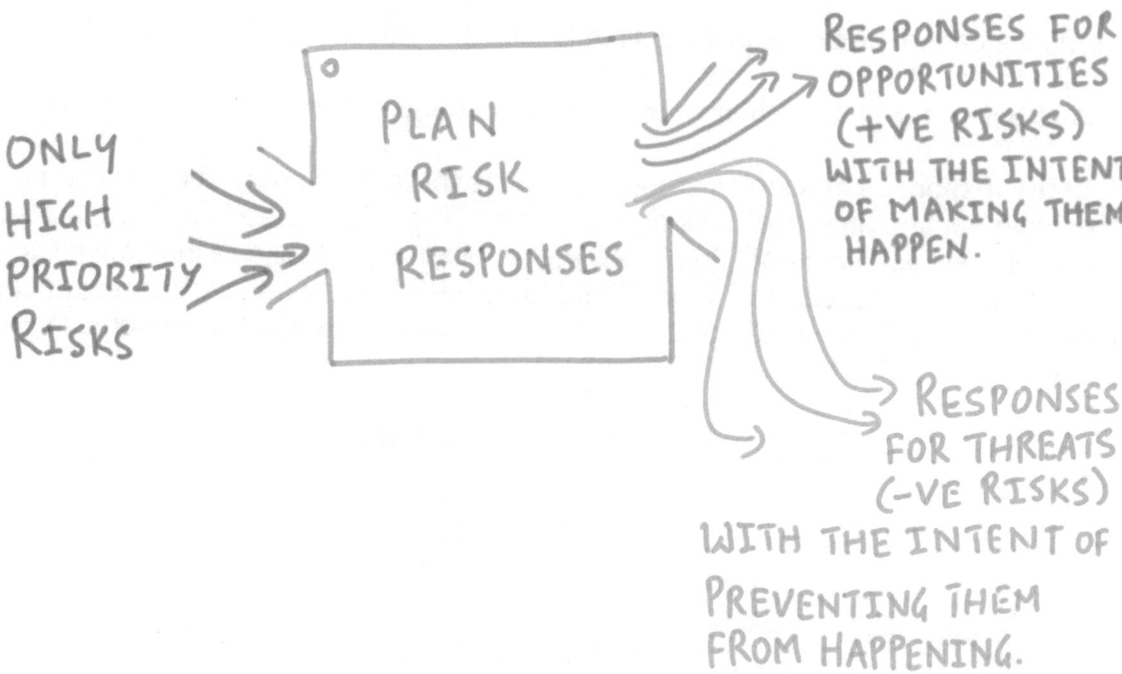
TWO KINDS OF RESPONSES
ONLY HIGH PRIORITY RISKS
PLAN RISK RESPONSES
RESPONSES FOR OPPORTUNITIES (+VE RISKS) WITH THE INTENT OF MAKING THEM HAPPEN.
RESPONSES FOR THREATS (-VE RISKS) WITH THE INTENT OF PREVENTING THEM FROM HAPPENING.

Strategies for Negative Risks or Threats are standard response categories for Threats. All of the responses in these response categories concentrate on “preventing” these Negative Risks or Threats from happening. There are five strategies for responding to Threats and they are

RISK RESPONSE STRATEGIES FOR THREATS

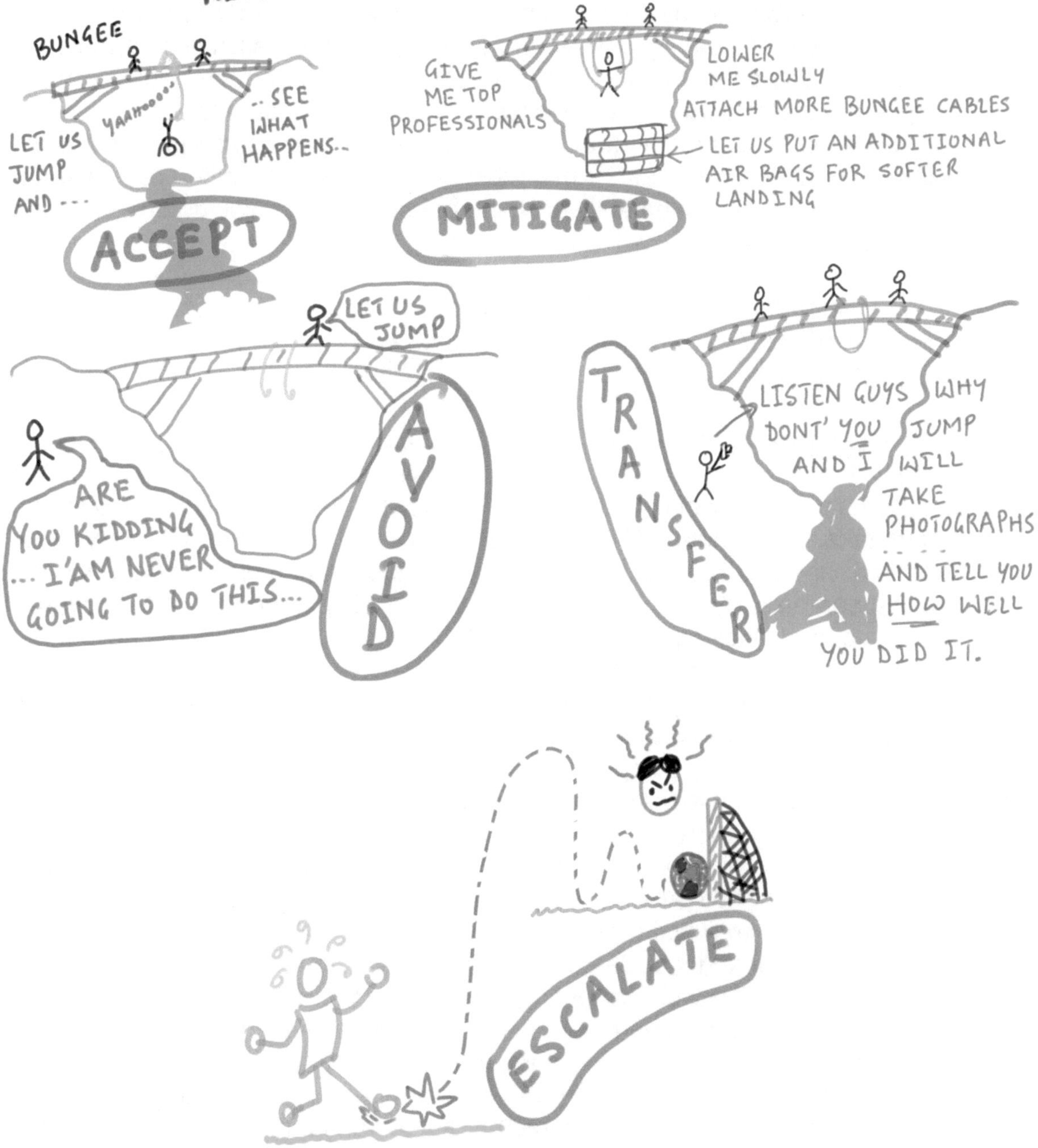

BUNGEE
LET US JUMP AND ...
YAAHOOOO
.. SEE WHAT HAPPENS..
ACCEPT

GIVE ME TOP PROFESSIONALS
LOWER ME SLOWLY
ATTACH MORE BUNGEE CABLES
LET US PUT AN ADDITIONAL AIR BAGS FOR SOFTER LANDING
MITIGATE

LET US JUMP
ARE YOU KIDDING ... I'AM NEVER GOING TO DO THIS...
AVOID

LISTEN GUYS WHY DONT' YOU JUMP AND I WILL TAKE PHOTOGRAPHS ..... AND TELL YOU HOW WELL YOU DID IT.
TRANSFER

ESCALATE

- **Accept:** Accepting a Negative Risk / Threat is done when even though the team is aware that the risk is a high priority risk but as of now they do not have any response. They cannot think of anything that can be done about it. And once they decide to go ahead with the project despite the threat they can do nothing about, is called "Accepting The Risk". Acceptance of risk is also done when there is a response but the cost of the response is so high that it becomes meaningless to use that response and therefore a decision is taken to just go with the flow by accepting the risk. There are two ways this acceptance is done. One is **Active** and one is **Passive** acceptance. Passive Acceptance simply means that no conscious action would be taken whatsoever with the hope that the risk just does not materialize. *E.g., Your organization is using a lot of imported machinery for your current project. Which*

means that your costing may get adversely affected due to changes in custom rules.
There is a suggestion by the ministry of finance about the possibility of increasing taxes and customs duties to write-off some of the fiscal deficit. The project has already started and you cannot really do much about it as the contracts with the machinery suppliers are also done. This is a case of "Passive Acceptance".
Active Acceptance, on the other hand, is about creating a backup plan (commonly referred to as "Backup Plan" or the "Plan B") which is not really a response that prevents the risk but is the answer to the question "What would you do if the accepted risk actually happens?".
E.g., Continuing with the same example earlier, if you decide to make a contingency reserve or let the management know about this possibility of increase and get their buy-in for releasing some money from Management reserve, if this event actually occurs, then this would be a case of Active Acceptance.

- **Mitigate:** Mitigating a negative risk/threat simply means "Reducing" it. Since risk priority is made up of probability and impact, the only way to reduce risk is to either reduce its probability of occurrence or reduce its impact, or a combination of both.
  Let us take an example. Let us say that in your IT project your "Chief System Architect" has told you that he is looking for a job as he has been very upset due to the last appraisal. You have ascertained that this is a serious threat (probability is high as he is already looking out for a job and the impact is very high as he is the chief architect in your project, a lot is dependent on him) hence you would like to try and mitigate it. You could try and convince the Sponsor to offer the architect a "Mid-term" bonus so that it reduces the probability of the Chief Systems Architect leaving the organization. Let's say that your sponsor does not like the idea as it may create a precedence where everyone tries to arm-twist the organization. Now that you realize that you cannot reduce the probability, you could reduce the impact by taking on board another architect who "Shadows" the Chief Systems Architect such that the impact of the Chief Architect's exit from the project, would not be high.
  It is important to note that most mitigation responses would have a cost element associated with it and a trade-off analysis must be done at this stage to ascertain if the cost of "Mitigation" is worth investing in vis-à-vis the cost incurred in allowing the risk to happen. May I remind you that Impact and Probability are not the only parameters on which the risks are prioritized, they are the most popular. In case the risks have been prioritized using some other set of parameters, the term Mitigation would reducing the risk on all those parameters such that the risk itself becomes lower priority.

- **Transfer:** When the risk response involves a third party it's called a Transfer. One of the most common forms of "Transfers" are the outsourcing as a response to a negative risk. Let us take an example. You are in a project that involves the import of a lot of heavy machinery from foreign countries. This would involve liaising with some regulatory bodies like Customs. You know that your organization does not have any good experience in such matters. And because of this, you have marked it as a high priority risk. You are suggested that the entire work of liaising should be given to a third party which is rather famous for such work. If you actually do outsource this work to a third party than you have responded to the risk by "Transferring" the risk.
  However realistically speaking, a transfer is not really a complete transfer. It just means giving the ownership of responding to the risk to someone else at a cost or

kind. The accountability of the success of the response is still yours. Another form of Transfer is taking an insurance. For most high capital investment infrastructure projects, there is a tradition of obtaining insurance (say for Calamity, Injury or death to labor and so on). You will notice three things when it comes to transferring. One it comes at a cost, Two it involves a contract/agreement and Three, because of the response a new risk may get generated (taking the same example stated above, what if the third party, though very good with this kind of work, are very busy and may delay your work and incidentally your project). When the response to a risk produces another risk, that new risk is called the "***Secondary Risk***". The secondary risk has to be analyzed from the point of view of probability and Impact and at times there has to be a response plan even for the secondary risk as well. Sometimes the secondary risk may be so high that you may not want to go ahead with that response at all. Remember, when it comes to projects, it's all about trade-offs.

- **Avoid:** This response is usually misunderstood by most people and unfortunately the explanation of this is given wrongly in most books dedicated to PMP® exams. Avoid simply means not doing the work that involves a threat / negative risk. Many organizations may decide not to take on a risky project to protect its brand image. Canceling a project entirely for avoiding risk is called "Total Avoidance". However many times an attempt is made by the project team to re-negotiate the scope so as to remove the part which the project team finds risky. This is what is generally called a partial avoidance. However, if you decide to outsource a risky part to a third party, it does not become avoidance, it becomes Transfer. Avoidance of risk can also be done by changing some crucial aspect of the project. *E.g., While building a huge signature bridge (called Thanh Tri) in Hanoi, Vietnam the program managers were facing a really daunting risk of the super heavy pillars of this mammoth suspension compressed concrete bridge, sinking on the sides of the river because of the lack of stable bedrock for the pillars to rest on. They scouted for site that had better bedrock foundation and actually shifted the construction site accordingly. This way they eliminated the entire risk of "Pillars Sinking into the ground due to pressure and absence of bedrock". However this was done at an enormous extra expenses. And this brings to light the fact that "Avoid" as a response, may also cost the project.*

- **Escalate**: Sometimes the act of responding to certain risk may be outside the authority level of the Project Manager and in this case, the Project Manager would simply escalate it to the Sponsor or to the specific person that the project manager thinks is the right person to handle this problem. Usually, this happens in the Programs and larger projects. Escalation is also done when the risk encountered is more of a general risk and not a project risk. *E.g., While planning for constructing roads through farm country where people own a lot of agricultural and farmlands, the project manager finds a very critical risk that the farmers would not allow the government to acquire land on compensation for building the road. The Project Manager knows that this is part of the Legal Department of the Government and not the Public Works Division. He escalates the risk to the competent authority in the Legal Department to respond to the risk and help him obtain the necessary land as per the designated map for road construction.*

Strategies for Positive Risks and Opportunities are a combination of responses for high priority opportunities identified in the project. There are only 4 possible responses to an opportunity and they are

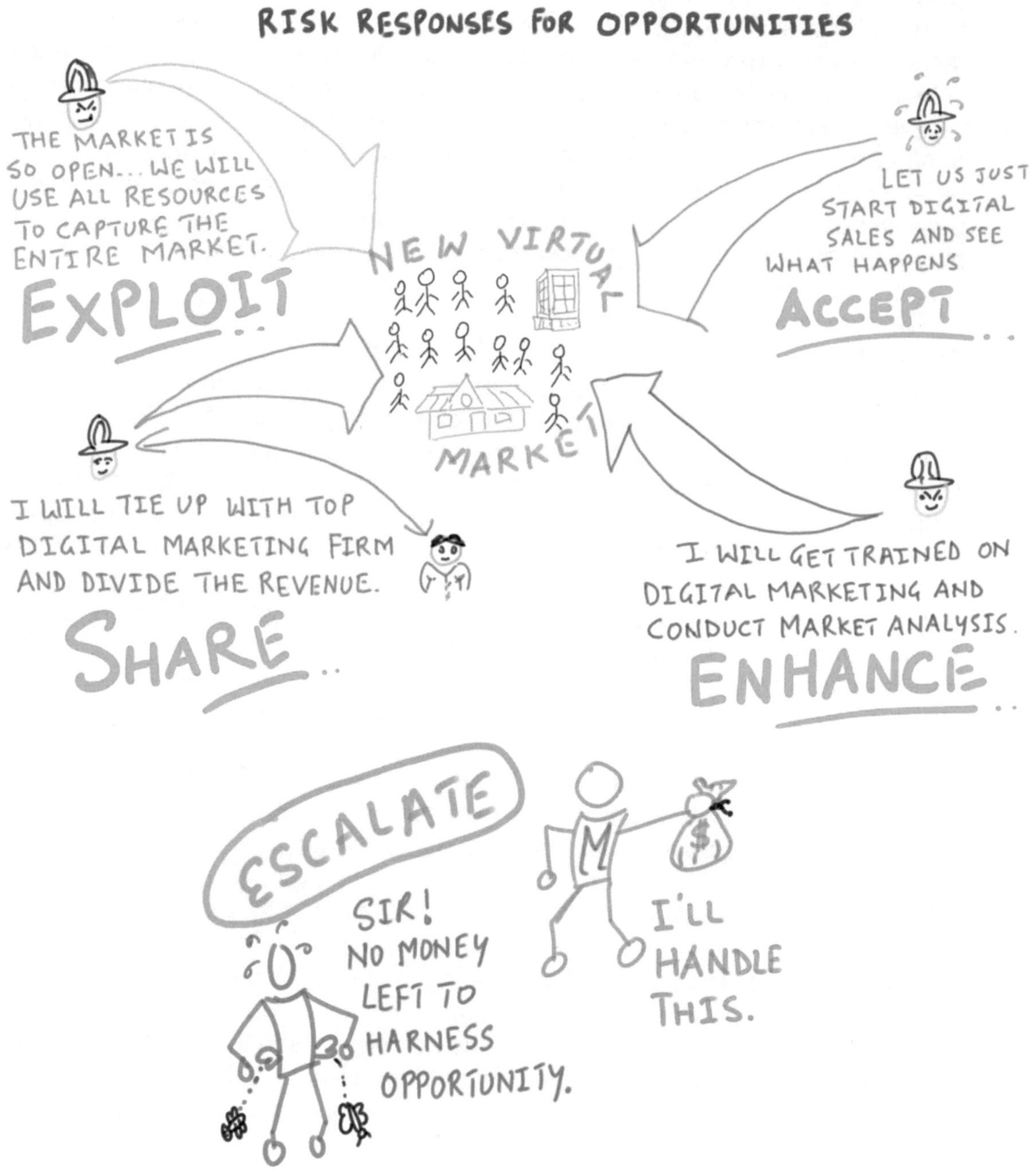

RISK RESPONSES FOR OPPORTUNITIES

THE MARKET IS SO OPEN... WE WILL USE ALL RESOURCES TO CAPTURE THE ENTIRE MARKET.
EXPLOIT..

NEW VIRTUAL MARKET

LET US JUST START DIGITAL SALES AND SEE WHAT HAPPENS
ACCEPT..

I WILL TIE UP WITH TOP DIGITAL MARKETING FIRM AND DIVIDE THE REVENUE.
SHARE..

I WILL GET TRAINED ON DIGITAL MARKETING AND CONDUCT MARKET ANALYSIS.
ENHANCE..

ESCALATE
SIR! NO MONEY LEFT TO HARNESS OPPORTUNITY.
M
I'LL HANDLE THIS.

Let us understand each of them individually.

- **Accept:** Here too it has exactly the same meaning. The project team may be aware that there are High Priority positive risks/opportunities but they may not have any response whatsoever and just hope that the opportunity in question actually materializes. This is basically being ready to receive the gains and benefits from the materialization of the opportunities without really doing something about it. This is also done when the cost of responding to the opportunity is not feasible. Again for this, there could be Active and Passive acceptance. Practically however, it's only passive acceptance for opportunities that is usually done by the organizations.

- **Enhance:** This is just the opposite of "Mitigate". Here the project team looks at ways to either increase the probability or the impact of the opportunity. This response would usually involve some costs and hence a trade-off analysis has to be made. *E.g., When faced with a challenge of serious competition from very large well-known organizations who were also bidding for a Defence project, while ours was a rather small organization, we decided to hire some Ex-Army officers to help us draft the proposal. The language of the proposal was in the terminology and format which the Army was using and this resulted in our organization scoring the highest in technical portion of the evaluation process. Needless to say that we won that contract and went on to win many more.* This is what enhance looks like. It had a cost element attached. However, we decided that this cost was justifiable for the kind of contract we would end up getting if we were successful. This simple investment drastically increased our chances probability wise.

- **Share:** Share is just the opposite of "Transfer". Whereas in "Transfer" a tie-up is done with a third party to get rid of a Threat. When it comes to Share, it means tying up with a third party to ensure that the opportunity is maximized. Joint Ventures, Mergers, and Acquisitions are the most prominent way for "Sharing" an opportunity. *E.g., Lockheed and Martin Corporations were always competing with each other for the defense contracts and they both had some specialties and serious weaknesses. Due to their competition, there were other players coming into the scene. In 1995 both these companies decide to merge to undertake a very large Defence project, something that neither of them could have fulfiledl individually. Since then they have maintained the merger and have gone on to become the largest defense contractor in the world.*

- **Exploit:** This method is usually confused with "Enhance" as they seem rather similar. However, exploit basically means maximizing not just the chances of a specific opportunity but also to be able to create more. The purview of this is much wider than a specific opportunity or a project. *E.g., In one of the projects, I was involved in, a Bank had asked us to make an analytical engine that would look at the patterns of transactions across various channels of banking and predict any kind of fraud or wrongdoing or simply mark them as suspect transactions, if it seemed that something was about to go wrong. We had never done such a project ever. As a dutiful project manager, I raised it as a serious risk and looked at options of buying some similar kinds of components from the market place. At this point, the CEO of the organization walked into my cabin and told me that this is a very big opportunity. He asked me to look at it as an opportunity which is much wider than this specific project. He made me realize that if this was an opportunity with one bank than I am sure other banks need it too and no one is really addressing it. So let us not just focus on one project and let us put our efforts into making a product out of this and then not only fulfill this current contract but also corner this entire market. Let us* ***Exploit*** *this opportunity. This was a great decision as this product turned out to be a world record holder as far as Banking Industry applications/solutions were concerned.*

- **Escalate:** An opportunity may be escalated to someone else for finding the response when the project manager finds it is outside his authority to respond to that risk. This could also happen when the Project Manager finds that the risk is of a general nature and not project specific. *E.g., While working for a "Sniffers" project (for detecting money laundering cases and fraudulent cases before they actually occurred) my team came across a lot of instances where "Accounts Reconciliation" was not happening when "banking handoffs were happening" from one system to another. This was raising a lot of manpower bills for manually co-relating the systems and their outputs. We saw this as a tremendous opportunity for my organization to establish several "Reconciliation System" which was already a product in our organization. I passed on (read that "Escalated") this opportunity to the Global Product Head of "Reconciliation Engine" to take this up and also provided the interfaces that we required for input into our sniffer's system.*

Contingent Response Strategies
For most of the risks, the responses have to start as soon as possible. However, there are some risks for which the responses are not be started until there is an early warning sign that the risk is about to occur. For such risks "Triggers" (or early warning signs) are earmarked and the risk owner would then wait till the "Trigger" is activated before the response is executed. *E.g., While constructing large dams (I have been inside the tube, where propeller is placed for the rushing water to propel it for generating electricity, of the largest dam built in North Africa, called the Kehinji Dam on River Niger in Nigeria, which had a very elaborate warning and contingency plan system) the flow of the rivers has to be diverted just like a traffic diversion. The flow of the river is diverted to circumvent the location of the dam and then reconnect with the original path of the river, further down steam. During torrential downpours and the "doldrums", the river rises quite a bit in Nigera. There are danger marks kept at the point of river where the diversion occurs and are monitored. When the danger mark is reached, knowing that the temporary diversion would not be able to handle the water volume and may flood the area around and even seep into the city, they used to open the diversion from the other side of the dam construction site as well, effectively making the dam an island for a period of time. Once the volume subsided they would close the "contingency diversion" and then it's business as usual. The opening of the redundant stream's gate is contingent to the water level warning sign.*

Strategies For Overall Project Risk
Overall project risks are those risks that affect the entire project in general and not just portions of it. Exactly the same responses are done as above, based on the fact if it was a Negative Risk or a Positive Risk.

While you have understood the responses for Threats and Opportunities there are a few other things that must be made clear before we go on to the next "Tools and Techniques" of this process.

Residual Risk: This is the amount of risk impact that still remains even after the response is applied to it. *E.g., Use of Airbags in passenger vehicles to prevent serious injuries during automotive accidents. However, the use of Airbags has not completely eliminated injuries though, the severity of those injuries has definitely gone down. The possibility of minor injuries inflicted on the vehicle occupants despite the deployment of airbags, is what is* *called, a residual risk.* Most of the time the term Residual Risks are associated with Threats/ Negative Risks.

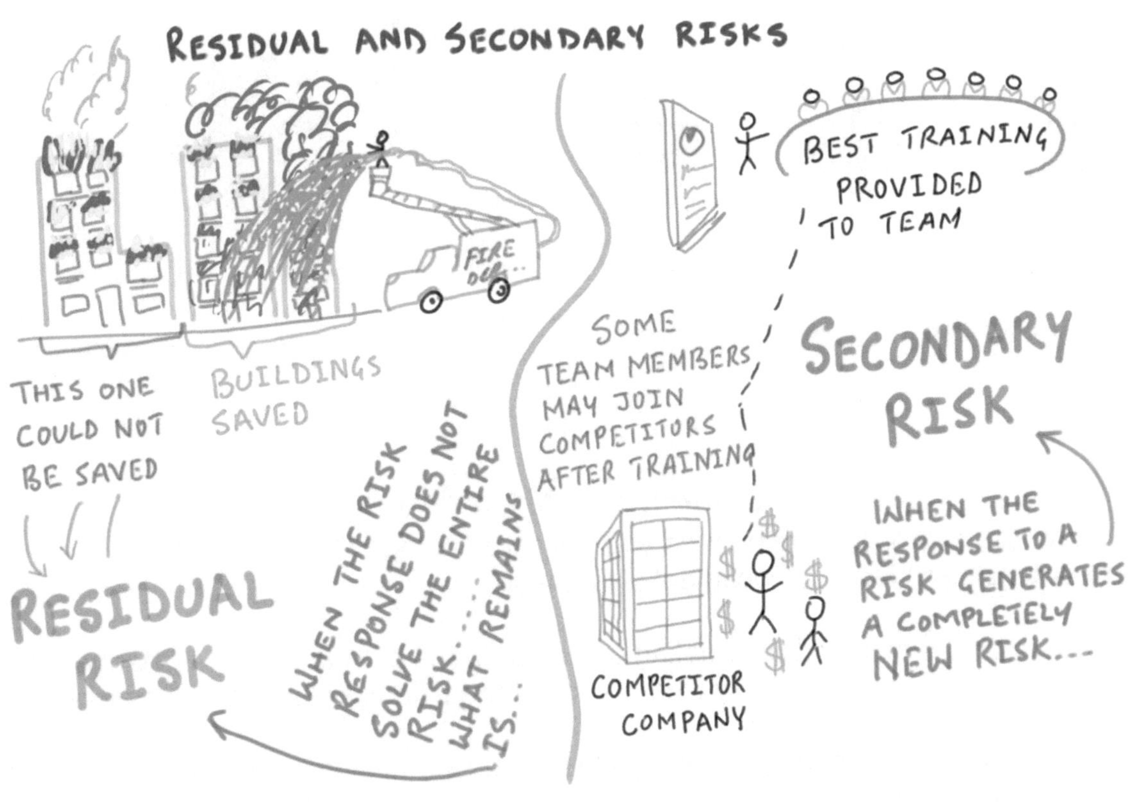

Simply Put; **Residual Risk = Risk Impact – Risk Responses**
In Rare situations the Risk Responses my overshadow the Risk Impact and a gain may happen as a result. *E.g., A person whose property is under insurance catches fire and the person ends up getting more insurance compensation than the sum of all the losses he suffered due to fire.*

Secondary Risk: This is the generation/identification of a brand new risk as a direct result of a response to a risk. This secondary risk must also be analyzed to see its priority level.

Risk Trigger: A Trigger is an early warning sign that an identified risk is about to happen. This is treated as an early warning sign which is used as a sign for starting the "Response" for that risk. Some risks have to be worked on from the very start of the project while there are lot of risks which need a trigger. Risks that have a trigger, their Responses are applied only when the trigger is activated. Triggers are applicable only for contingent response strategy.
E.g., There could be a risk that the Cost of a project may get over budget. The trigger has been placed for this risk as "Accumulated Costs till reporting period over budget by 10% of the budget for all tasks completed till the reporting period". The moment such a condition occurs then it would be that the Trigger of the risk has been activated and the response for the same has to be now applied.

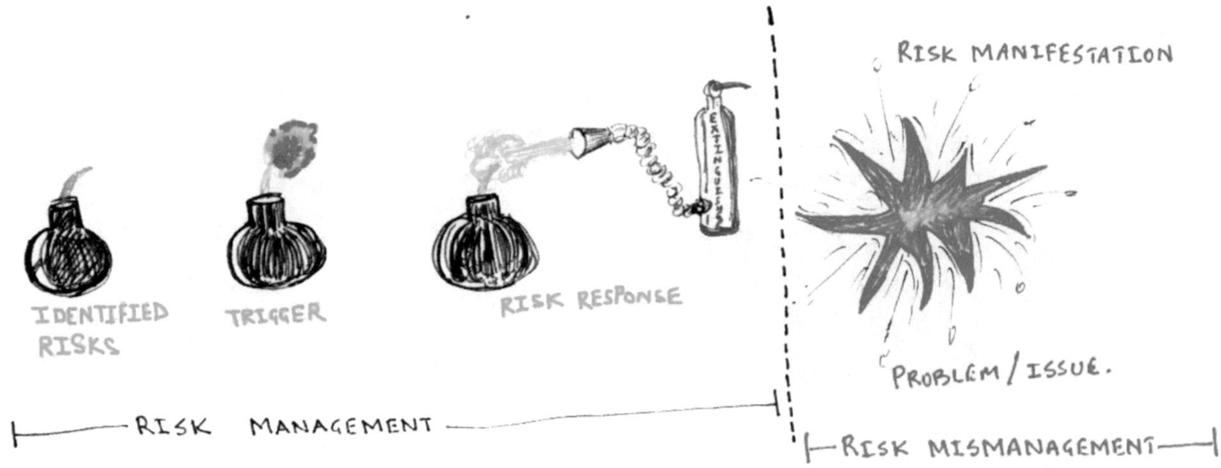

9.31.2 Main Outcome from this process: -

This process has only three outputs and they are Change Requests, Project Management Plan Updates and Project Documents Updates.

Some responses may end up creating a change in the plan and hence Change Request is an output here. And we all know where each of the Change Requests goes to. CCB in ICC.

Because of the responses generated in this process and since these responses may add to costs, scope and or schedule there is a high likelihood that various elements of the **Project Management Plan** may get **updated**. One of the first things to get updated would be the WBS with "Responses". Basically, anything in the plan or the baselines that get affected by the responses would need to be updated.

The other important **documents** updated would be Risk Register, with responses for the risks and the owners for the risks, and Risk Reports, showcasing the latest situation of project risk and risk management.

9.32 Compiling The Project Management Plan (Develop Project Management Plan)

This process provides the complete Project Management Plan. The Project Management Plan is also the document which contains the Baseline. We also know that there are 24 processes that are present in the Process Group "Planning". This process, *DEVELOP PROJECT MANAGEMENT PLAN*, is the 24th process (the very last process) in the process group Planning.

The Project Management Plan contains how the project would be executed, controlled and closed. This ensures that everything about what is going to happen in the project is placed in one single document so that everyone knows which document to refer to for the project at hand.

What you must remember that actually what this process does is it takes the output of various other planning processes (almost all the other planning processes) and compiles them into one well-arranged document and this document becomes the Project Management

Plan. Hence it's quite obvious that this process does not do anything new of its own, it is one of those "Umbrella Processes" that was mentioned earlier in this knowledge area.

While "Project Management Plan" is being developed the first time it may go through several iterations before getting finalized. The finalization process is usually (or rather should be) a formal process with formal approval. This finalized version of the Project Management Plan is what gets baselined. After this, any changes to this plan (specifically the three baseline elements viz., Scope, Cost and Time) have to go through a formal "Change Management" process.

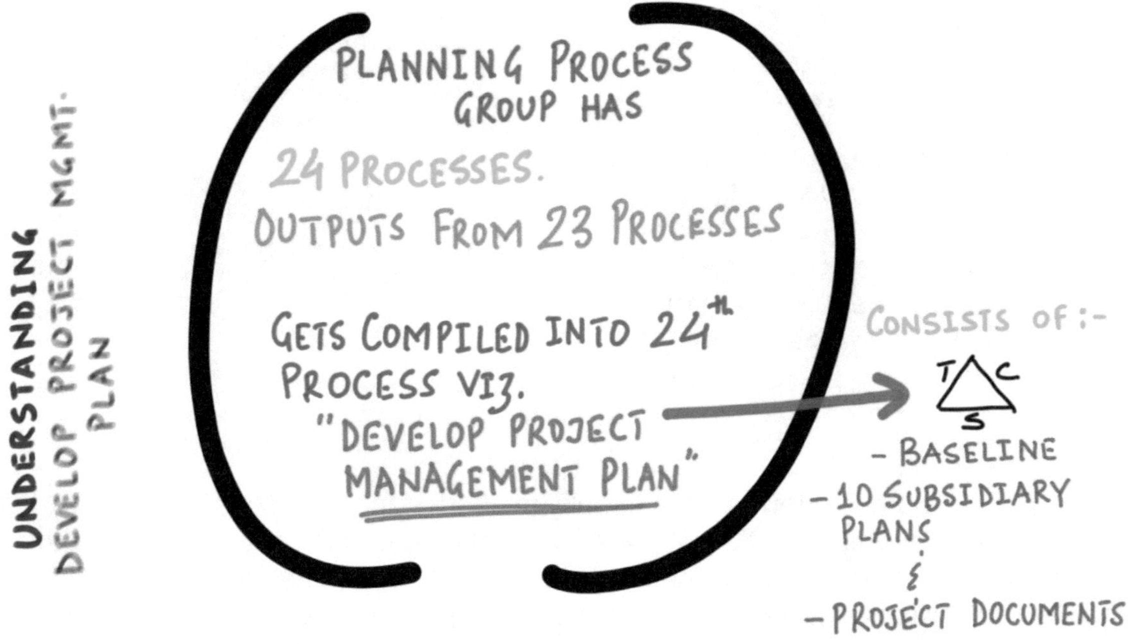

Let us look at the interiors of this process:

9.32.1 Main Tools and Techniques of the process:

Expert Judgment could be the project manager himself, PMO, Consultants and other planning experts who could help create a practical, granular, reliable, maintainable and realistic project plan. Decisions on tailoring or altering certain processes, templates, choosing development lifecycle, level of configuration management and documentation etc., are taken during this process by the expert judgment.

9.32.2 Main Outcome of the process:

The process *DEVELOP PROJECT MANAGEMENT PLAN* has only **one output and it is the "Project Management Plan"**.
A well balanced and practical project management plan must have the following:-

OVERALL CONTENTS OF THE PROJECT MANAGEMENT PLAN

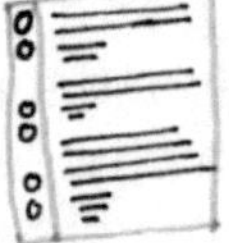

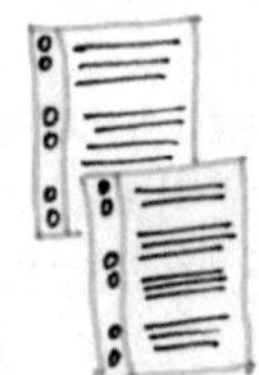

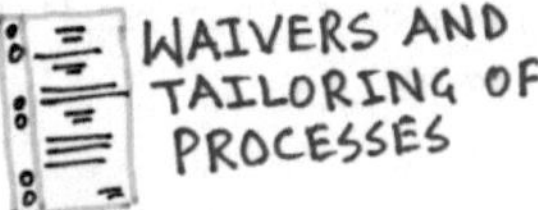

PROJECT DOCUMENTS

STATEMENT OF WORK [SOW]
ISSUE LOG
CHANGE LOG
RISK REGISTER
STAKEHOLDER REGISTER
ACTIVITY LIST
CHANGE REQUESTS
QUALITY CHECKLISTS
QUALITY METRICS
SELLER PROPOSALS
PROJECT CHARTER
PROJECT CALENDARS

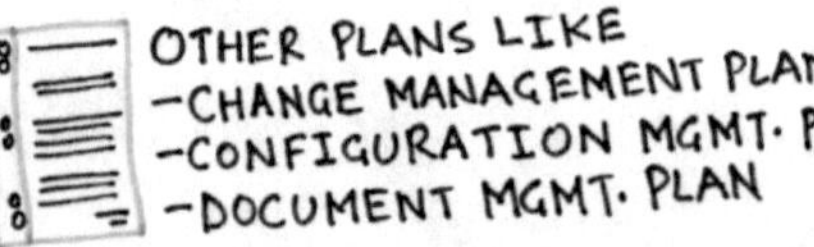

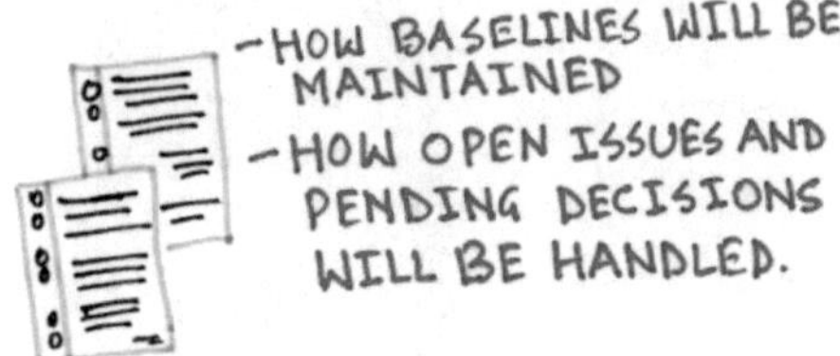

-HOW BASELINES WILL BE
MAINTAINED
-HOW OPEN ISSUES AND
PENDING DECISIONS
WILL BE HANDLED.

There is a term that is usually misunderstood which is called “Kick Off Meeting”. Most organizations use this term differently and hence the confusion. As per the exams as well as the authentic meaning of the term “Kick Off Meeting” is when the detailed planning is done, the team members and the affected stakeholders and cross-functional teams are informed of what is expected of them and what kind of work is in store for them and is also used as a forum for expectation setting among the team members. This meeting is held immediately after the Project Management Plan is approved and just before any work is done in Execution. Kick off Meeting, so to say, is the very last step in Planning.

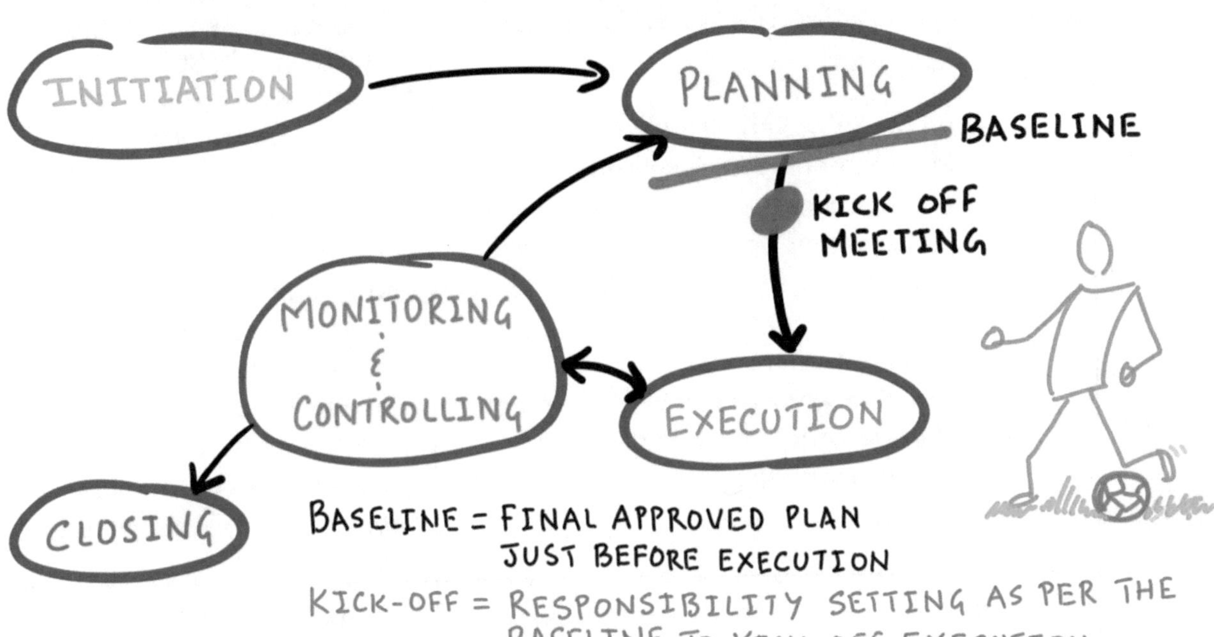

The Project Management Plan is made up of Project Plans and Project documents. The time is ideal for us to know the difference between Plans and Project Documents. Seems a lot of people do get confused between the two since, technically speaking, plans are documents too. Hence, it's important to know the difference between these two kinds of documents viz., ***Plans*** and ***Project Documents***. Plans tell us how to conduct the project or a part of it. Plans show us "which is the best way to handle various elements of the project, given the constraints and situational considerations". Project Documents, on the other hand, are repositories of information pertaining to various aspects of the project. These documents are more dynamic than the plans as some or the other kind of information is being put into these project documents. These project documents help in following the plans or even help us understand if the plans are effective or not. Project documents are updated without any approvals but any plan would need approvals for any changes. Ok! Let us take examples of project plans and project documents.

S. No.	Plans	Documents
1	**All the Subsidiary Plans Viz., Scope Management Plan, Requirements Management Plan, Schedule Management Plan, Cost Management Plan, Quality Management Plan, Resource Management Plan, Communications Management Plan, Risk Management Plan, Procurement Management Plan and Stakeholder Management Plan.**	**Change Logs, Issue logs, Stakeholder Register, Risk Register, Project Schedule, Requirements Documentation, Work Performance Data, Work Performance Information, Work Performance Reports, Procurement Documents, Proposals, Statement of Work, Schedule Data, Milestones Report, Forecasts, Change requests, Basis of Estimates etc.** ***I am sure you get the picture now.***
2	**All the baselines viz., Scope Baseline (WBS, WBS Dictionary and Project Scope Statement), Time Baseline and Cost Baseline.**	***Additional Plans: -*** ***Change Management Plan, Configuration Management Plan, Performance Measurement Baseline, Testing Plan, Project Lifecycle Description and Development Approach (Project Methodology)***

Though most of the plans are created in different processes, this process too makes a few plans. Some of these are:

Configuration Management Plan: Configuration Management Plan is the "Plan" to name, number and control the configuration of the product of the project.
A product is made up of various "Components" or "Artefacts" or "Modules" or "Configurable Items". Changes may happen to certain Artefacts. How the relevant documentation, processes, other artefacts that get affected by the changes in one artefact, need to be labelled, maintained, documented, controlled and approved etc. is detailed out in this plan called "Configuration Management Plan".

Change Management Plan: States exactly how any change would be implemented or rejected within this project. It is one of the components of Project Management Plan.

- This plan provides answers to the following questions:
- What will be called a "Change" in this project.
- The stakeholders who can propose a change
- Steps for evaluating the impact analysis of a proposed change
- Steps for evaluating whether to approve the change or reject it
- What documents need to be amended and updated due to the approved or rejected change requests?

- How the entire change process would be monitored to ensure that the process has been done satisfactorily.

Test Plan / Testing Plan: This document describes deliverables that will be tested, tests that will be conducted, and the processes that will be used in testing. It forms the basis for formally testing the components and deliverables. It will also contain the stakeholders that would be part of the Testing as well as the Roles and Responsibility vis-à-vis the Testing. Tools and machinery that would be used for testing are also mentioned here along with an indicative timeline for the testing activities.

9.33 Ninja Drill – Planning - 5

In this Ninja Drill you will find the most important notes and pointers that are important from the point of PMP Exams and covers, Plan Risk Management, Identify Risks, Qualitative Risk Analysis, Quantitative Risk Analysis and Develop Project Management Plan.

S. No.	Drill Points
1.	The general sequence of Risk Management process are: 1) Plan Risk Management 2) Identify Risks 3) Qualitative Risk Analysis 4) Quantitative Risk Analysis (Optional Process) 5) Plan Risk Responses
2.	Risk = Any uncertain event that has an impact on the project. The impact may be positive or negative.
3.	Risks with possible negative impact are called Negative Risks or **Threats** Risks with possible positive impact are called Positive Risks or **Opportunities**
4.	A threat that has already occurred is called Issue or Problem. An opportunity that has already occurred is called Benefit, Gain or Windfall
5.	One has to do "Workaround" for dealing with issues.
6.	Risk Threshold = Measurable scales of tolerance. Above a certain "Threshold" of negative risk, it would not be taken. Below a certain "Threshold" the negative risk would be taken.
7.	Known – Known = Issues / Problems / Gains / Benefits Known – Unknown = Identified Risks (Threats / Opportunities) Unknown – Unknown = Unidentified Risks
8.	Project Resilience: Building flexibility and backups in the project to even counter / withstand the Unidentified Risks as and when they actually occur.
9.	The main output / outcome / artefact of the process "Plan Risk Management" are: • Risk Management Plan • Risk Breakdown Structure
10.	Risk Breakdown Structure (RBS) is basically a hierarchical representation of potential sources of risks. These are also called the overall categories of risks.
11.	The main Tools & Techniques of the process "Identify Risks" are: • Brainstorming • Checklists • Interviews • Root Cause Analysis • Assumption And Constraint Analysis • SWOT Analysis • Prompt Lists
12.	SWOT = Strength, Weaknesses, Opportunities and Strength.
13.	Prompt Lists are the common industry-wide or organization-wide list of categories that must be used (to begin with) to identify risks. This is done to ensure that no area of the project is missed out.
14.	VUCA = Volatility, Uncertainty, Complexity and Ambiguity
15.	PESTLE = Political, Economical, Social, Technical, Legal and Environmental
16.	BANI = Brittle, Anxious, Non-linear and Incomprehensible
17.	Conceptual ambiguity—the lack of effective understanding—occurs when people use similar terms or arguments in different ways.
18.	Situational ambiguity surfaces when more than one outcome is possible.
19.	Complexity exists when there are many interconnected influences that behave and interact in diverse ways.
20.	The main output / outcome / artefact of the process "Identify Risks" is Risk Register.

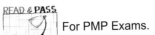

21.	"Qualitative Risk Analysis", where the risks are prioritized and "Quantitative Risk Analysis", where the Risk is further analyzed.
22.	"Quantitative Risk Analysis" is an optional process.
23.	The most popular method for prioritizing the risks is by using the Probability & Impact Matrix.
24.	Failure Modes and Effects Analysis [FMEA] is used for prioritizing only the threats.
25.	FMEA generates a Risk Priority Number [RPN] where the larger the number the higher the risk priority.
26.	Threat Profile shows how the Negative Risks are behaving over a period of time in the project.
27.	Proximity is "how soon the risk is going to occur in the lifecycle of the project vis-à-vis where you are on the project?"
28.	Urgency is the speed with which the response of that risk has to be applied.
29.	Connectivity is when one risk is connected to a few other risks.
30.	Propinquity is a term that means "very close to the heart of someone important". Risks due to propinquity will always be considered "Critical Risks" / High priority risks.
31.	Tornado Diagram is used for measuring and representing the overall sensitivity of risks.
32.	Simulation: Software is used to simulate various permutations and combinations of variables that affect the Candidate Risk which helps in showing Trends in Possible Outcome to help focus our efforts.
33.	Simulation = Monte Carlo Analysis
34.	Expected Monitory Value (EMV) = Probability X Financial Impact of risk.
35.	Always deduct EMV of possible Losses from EMV of possible Profits to arrive at the correct Net EMV.
36.	Decision Tree Analysis = The purpose of this diagram is to help choose between multiple risky options, each with future cost implications, so that the combination of Cost and Risk (EMV) is lowest.
37.	Influence Diagram (ID) (Also called Relevance Diagram) shows, just as it sounds like, influences between various elements.
38.	Main Tools & Techniques of the process, Plan Risk Responses are: 1. Strategies For Threats 2. Strategies For Opportunities 3. Contingent Response Strategies
39.	Risk Responses for Threats are: 1) Accept 2) Mitigate 3) Transfer 4) Avoid and 5) Escalate
40.	Risk Responses for Opportunities are: 1) Accept 2) Enhance 3) Share 4) Exploit and 5) Escalate.
41.	Outsourcing and Insurance are the only two ways to transfer risks.
42.	Contingent Response Strategies = Some response strategies (for Opportunities as well as for Threats) need to be based on the happening of some other event. They are based (Contingent) on an early warning sign or some event, hence the name. These events are usually called "Triggers".
43.	Residual Risk = Risk Impact – Risk Responses
44.	Secondary Risk: When the response to a risk produces another risk.
45.	The main output / outcome / artefact of the process "Plan Risk Responses" is Risk Response Plan.
46.	Risk Response Plan is made up of: 1. Reponses For Threats 2. Responses For Opportunities 3. Risk Owners
47.	Change Management Plan States exactly how any change would be implemented or rejected within this project. One of the Subsidiary Plans.

48.	Test Plan / Testing Plan describes deliverables that will be tested, tests that will be conducted, and the processes that will be used in testing. • It forms the basis for formally testing the components and deliverables. • It will also contain the stakeholders that would be part of the Testing as well as the Roles and Responsibility vis-à-vis the Testing. • Tools and machinery that would be used for testing are also mentioned here along with an indicative timeline for the testing activities.
49.	A Plan cannot be updated or changed without proper approvals while the Documents can be constantly updated throughout the lifecycle of the project without any approval.
50.	The immediately next thing that is done after the plan is approved, is to hold a Kick-Off meeting to let all the connected stakeholders know what is the plan, what is expected of them, creating a buy-in for the project among them and to obtain their commitments.
End Of Ninja Drill	

10 Project Implementation

This is the stage / phase which is essentially the combination of Execution and Monitoring & Controlling. This implementation phase is applicable to every single methodology and not just predictive. In Agile once the iteration planning is done the rest of the iteration is nothing but Implementation, essentially the combination of Execution and Monitoring & Controlling. The only difference is that in Predictive the implementation is done only once and that too for the entire project.

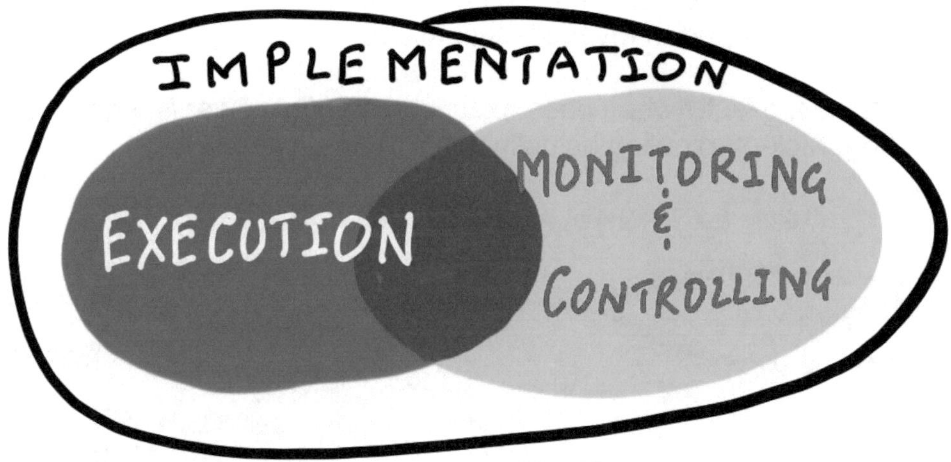

If I were to ask you, what is the first thing to be done just after planning that will start the implementation in a project? What would you answer?

The correct answer would be the “Kick-Off Meeting”.

Kick-Off meeting is applicable to all methodologies. For larger Iterations in Agile, Incremental and Iterative methodologies, having a “Kick-off” before implementation of that iteration is always a great idea.

The main purpose of the Kick-off meeting is to ensure that all the team members as well as the stakeholders involved in execution understand exactly what needs to be done, understand the vision, understand what is really expected of them, get appraised of the plan and the baselines and also to get to know the other team members and stakeholders involved in the project. Kick-off meeting is not only applicable to co-located teams. It is equally applicable to virtual teams. In one of my global projects where the team was spread over 11 countries across 3 continents and 7 languages where the project involved a large automotive product global launch, I got a special budget sanctioned done for 43 team members to fly down to India (the project HQ was in India) for the kick-off meeting. The planning was done earlier and we thought that we will gain two major wins by getting the entire supervisory team for a kick-off meeting in co-located manner. One was to ensure that everyone understands what is expected of them and how the team will function and basically the do’s and don’ts of the project collaboration. But the second reason was to get the geographically and culturally diverse team to get to know each other and develop a bond. See, I have participated in umpteen numbers of virtual team based projects to understand that when people connect only through virtual platform there is a larger degree of lack of

understanding about each other. And this lack of understanding affects the bonding and hence the day to day work. The mutual accountability lacks and it creates hiccups in smooth flow of information and development of trust. I realized that the "Kick-off" meeting is the best time to get all the virtual team members together. The cost of doing this is far compensated by enhanced project performance for the entire duration of the project. There were times, when I could not get the budget to organize this, in which case, I would organize multiple meetings among the virtual teams using high-end video conferencing to get a near collocated feel of the meeting. Several of these meetings would be for just general chit chat and getting to know each other better.
I was surprised to see that even the questions in PMP exams support this concept that I have used for the better part of my professional life.

Now the question is, exactly when does execution start? Answer is, immediately after the Kick-off meeting. Kick-off meeting actually Kicks off the execution.

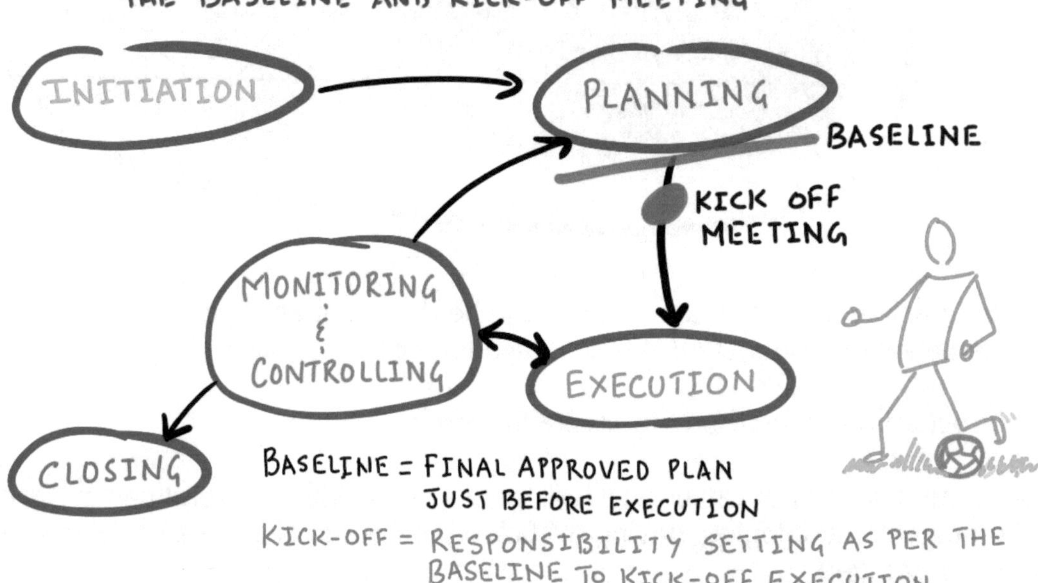

Ok, time for us to get into the processes involved in Implementation. Though Execution and Monitoring & Controlling processes are more or less intertwined and happen in tandem, for better understanding and structure, I have first explained the "Execution" processes and only then all the "Monitoring & Controlling" processes.

10.1 Acquire Resources:

Acquire Resources is the very first process in execution. *Acquire resources* is nothing but the execution of the "Resource Management Plan" and this is where the team members, facilities, tools, materials and equipment needed to complete the project work, are obtained. As and when the need for the specific resources and material is supposed to arise in the project, in conformance to the resource plan, the actual resources and material are assigned to the project. This is the process where the project manager gets hold of his project team and the other resources and material needed to execute the project.
I am sure from your experience you know that resources are not so easy to come by irrespective of the fact that the resources are internal or from external sources. Hence the

project manager must use the best of influencing and negotiation skills to obtain as close to what could be, an ideal set of resources.

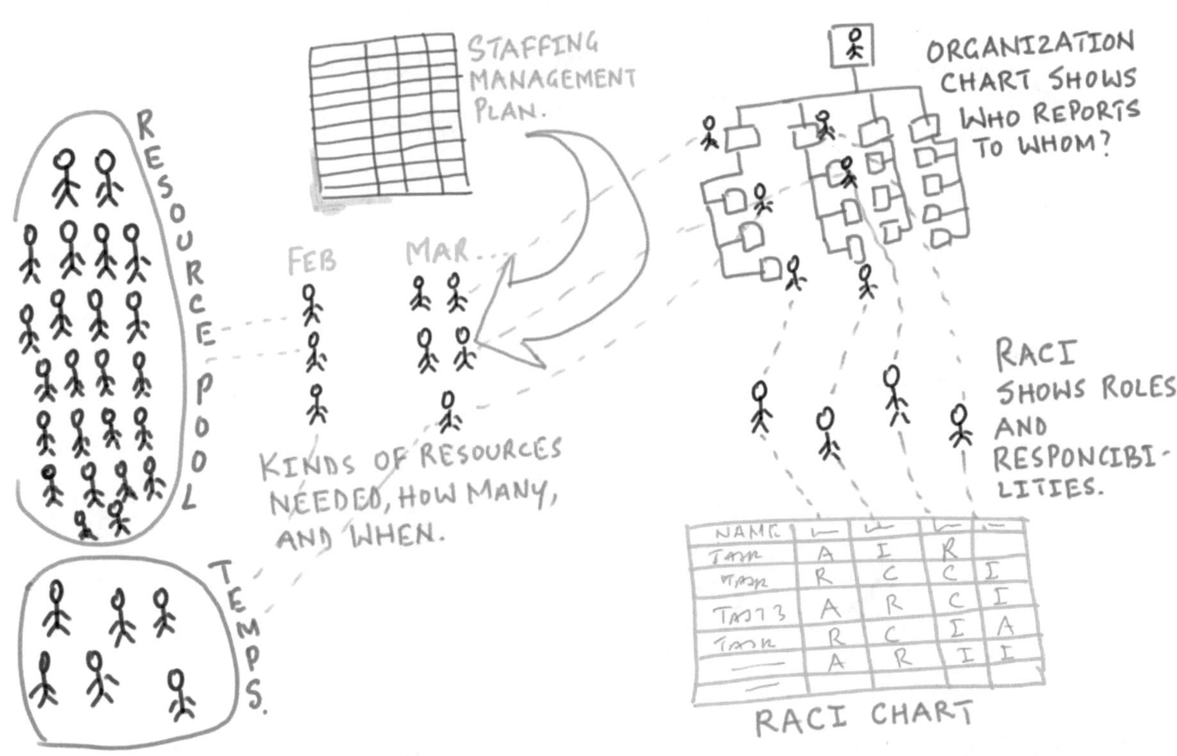

10.1.1 Main Tools and Techniques of this process: -

Multicriteria Decision Analysis: When staff is selected for a project it's not always a very straightforward decision making. Multiple criteria are looked at before a decision is made. This is called Multi-Criteria Decision Analysis. Multiple criteria may be selected upon which resources may be scored to evaluate if they should work on the project or not. Besides, these criteria themselves may be prioritized (weighted) among themselves to swing the selection even more towards project specifics.
Here is a list of the most common criteria used in Multi-criteria decision analysis.

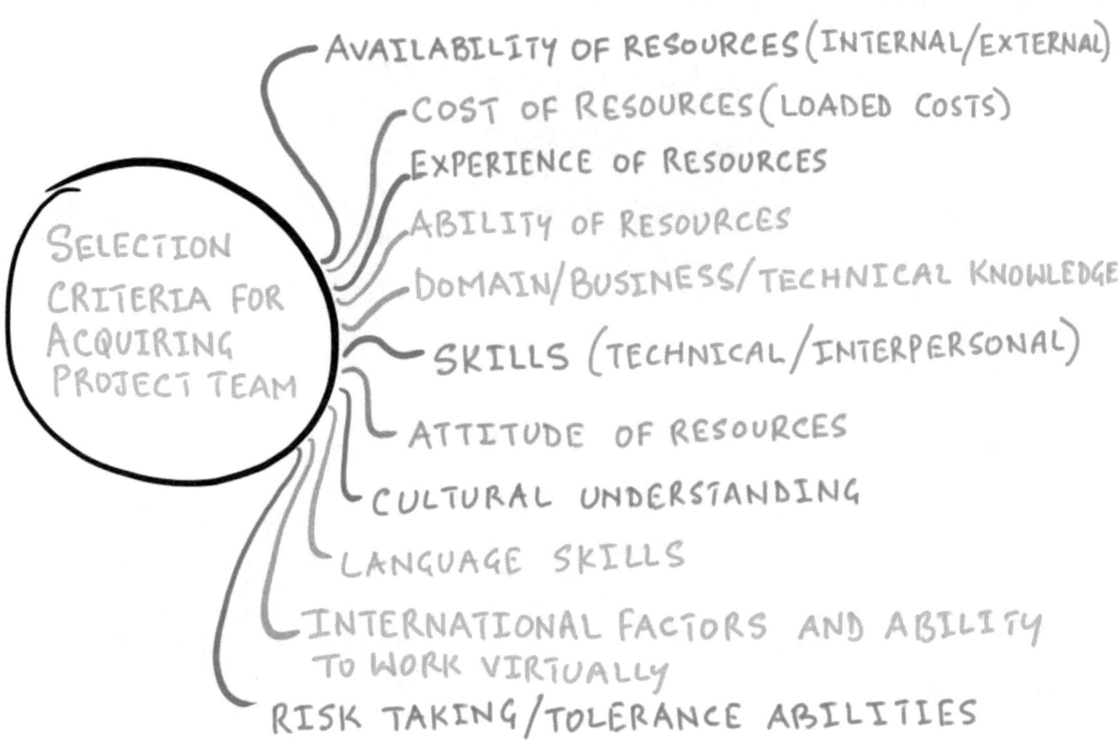

Resource Selection: There is a concept of resource types since the last decade, which is now increasing in popularity because of the general rise in the overall complexity of the project. Generally the human resource types are, I, T, Pi and Comb shaped.

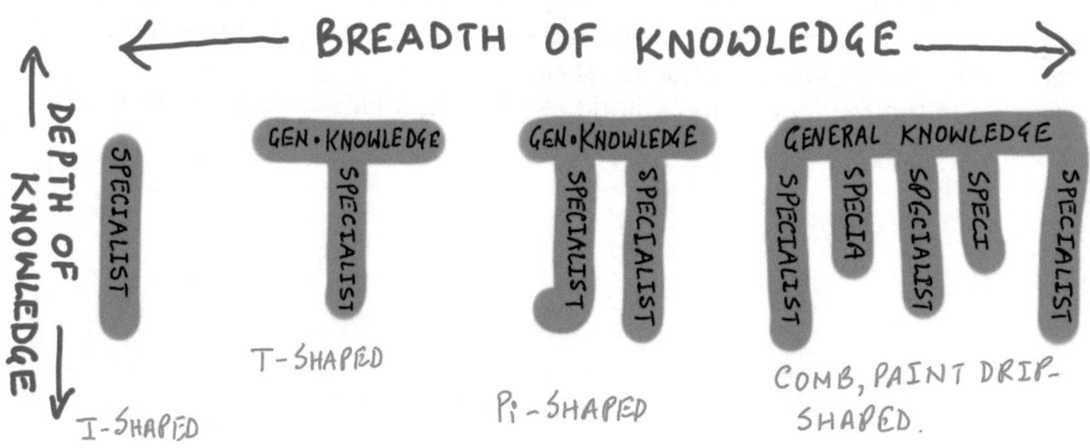

"I" shaped resource is a person with one deep skill but does not know anything about the other skills needed in the project. Such skill shapes are most suitable for operational work and in certain kinds of predictive project. Instead of giving a very technical example that may align to a specific industry, allow me to provide an example that all of you can relate with. Let us say that I know how to drive a tractor. I know everything about driving a tractor. I can drive it on any terrain. I can drive all makes and kinds of tractors and extremely well versed with the various accessories that come with it. I can even repair a tractor. But that is all I know. I have one deep skill about tractors. But I have no clue about trucks, Cars, Jeeps, scooters and pickup vans. And I will never drive them or use them. In such a case I would be an "I" Shaped skill resource. I will do extremely well in a project where the requirements are well known or in operational work where the resources need to be super specialised in specific kind of work. I guess you can see the advantages as well as the disadvantages of such a resource.

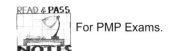

"T" shaped resource is a person with one deep skill and some general and overview idea of the other skills needed in the project. Such resources are more popular in Predictive and Iterative methodologies. Taking the previous example. What if I had a deep skill in Tractors, just as stated above, but I do know something about driving a car, pickup truck and a SUV. I will not be as confident driving them as I would be while driving a tractor, but if the situation truly needs someone to drive a car I could lend my services. I guess you can see where I am going with this. Just transpose these simplistic examples on to the kind of skills required in your organizations or your project and you will be able to relate to it easily.

"Pi" shaped resources are those resources that have two deep skills and a general idea about the other skills required for the project. Such resources are needed in Incremental and Agile projects. Such resources can be made to switch skills based on team compositions and iteration requirements. Just in case you do not remember your science symbols, Pi symbol looks like this "**π**". This is a symbol that I got from the MS Word Symbol directory. It is not a perfect depiction of Pi but I guess this will do. Can you notice two verticals connected at the top by one horizontal line?. Taking the same example, let us say I have two deep skills. Tractors and Trucks. At the same time I do have some basic experience and idea about driving cars, SUVs and bikes. During a tough situation where a car driver or a SUV driver or even a bike rider is needed and there is no one else that can do it, I can come forward to offer my services. Though not absolutely adept at cars and SUVs, I can keep the work moving. You can see why certain seasonal farmers would prefer me. On the same salary I can drive the tractors during framing season, drive the truck during harvesting and selling season and driver cars and SUV during off farming season. This flexibility comes in handy in those kind of work where some changes are expected.

The "Comb Shaped" (also called "Paint Drip" and "Broken Comb") resources are those who have multiple skills with differing depth of knowledge in them, along with an overview of other skills that are needed for the project. These resources are in highest demand in Agile projects for the simple reason that such resources would be flexible enough to undertake a wide variety of roles in the project team thus eliminating the need for on-boarding different resources for different iterations. This allows the same team to bond better and continue through the entire length of the Agile project. Such resources also command a much higher pay package, and understandably so. As you can see how a paint drip or a broken comb looks like. Let us say I am very good at Tractors and I can even repair them, I

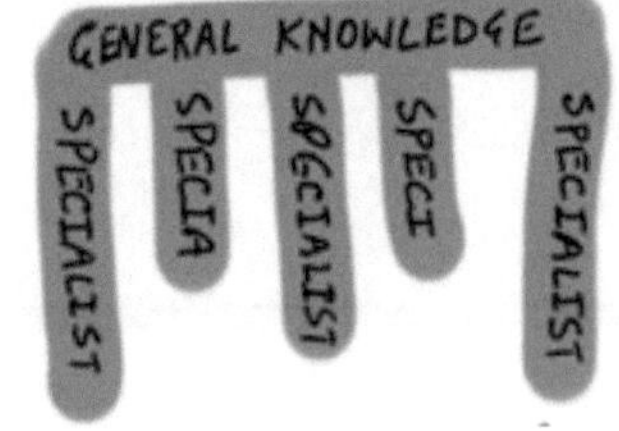

am also an exceptional driver of trucks and have a good amount of experience but I do not know how to repair them. I can drive the Cars of all makes and with all different kinds of transmissions but I cannot do off-roading in SUVs though I can drive them rather well in normal conditions. I can barely drive bikes but have driven them in the past. I also know a thing or two about earth moving machines but have better experience with cranes. You can see that I have varying degrees of expertise in different skills and general idea about a few other skills. This is what is a called a resource skill type of Comb or paint drip or broken comb. I guess it is quite obvious to you now that such resources would be important in those situations where changes are a constant phenomenon. There you go, now you know all about resource types.

Negotiations: If you have worked as a Project Manager for a few projects you would have seen that you rarely ever get the resources with the exact qualifications and competencies that you required in the project. This would mean that you would have to do a lot of "**negotiations**" with the sponsors, functional heads, senior management, Human Resource Managers, vendors, contractors, and PMO. Negotiation is an interpersonal technique that is needed to obtain a good mix of resources in the project. Good resources are always in demand from other projects and organizational work hence a win-win situation has to be developed by the project manager to get resources as near to the targeted capability as possible.

This is also a good time to know that Negotiations are different from Bargaining. Negotiations make both the parties feel that they have "won" something in this understanding/agreement; hence the phrase "**Win-Win**" for Negotiations. Bargain, on the other hand, is more like "**Win-Lose**" where one party wins (or tries to win) at the expense of the other. Such agreements do not tend to last long as the losing party tries to wriggle out, as soon as possible, from this exploitative situation. Compromise means both parties letting go of something to meet midway and hence, compromise is also called "**Lose-Lose**".

NEGOTIATION, COMPROMISE & BARGAINING

Pre-Assignment: There are times that a project is obtained only because some specific people can do that kind of work, or it could be that some specific resources may have been promised to the customer and the customer wants those resources to be part of the project. This is called **Pre-Assignment**. Pre-Assignment is not an ideal situation as it makes the project "Person Specific" and thereby making the project very risky. Just imagine what happens to a project if the "Pre-Assigned" resource decides to leave the organization. However, this practice is quite common in smaller and midsized projects, hence it finds mention in PMBOK® Guide.

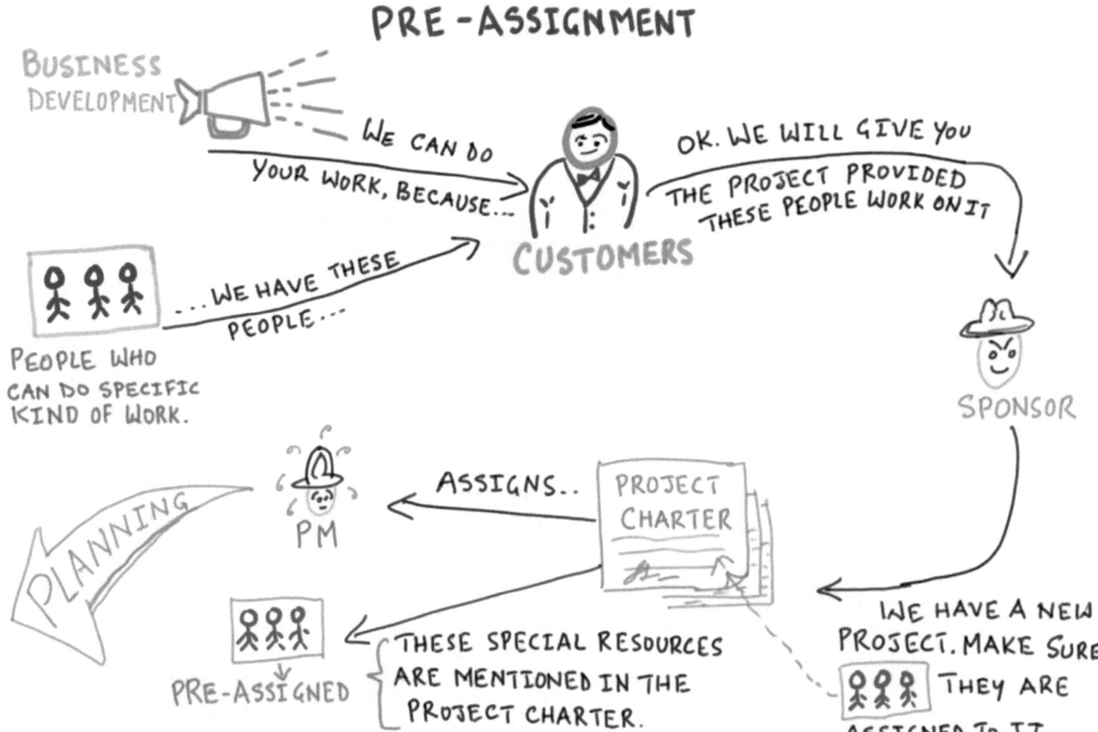

Whenever resources are pre-assigned to the project their names and roles must be mentioned in the Project Charter itself, this ensures that the project, which has these resources pre-assigned to it, has the first right on these resources irrespective of where they are currently working.

Virtual Team: There are many kinds of projects which do not need all the resources to be physically present at a specific location together to get the project work done. The work can be done by people from different geographical locations and teaming up over the communication and collaboration tools (like Web Presence, Emails, Video Conferencing, and Teleconferencing) and such a ***team*** is called "**Virtual Team**". These days most of the Software and Information Technology Projects are being done using Virtual Teams. Such teams have their own challenges and advantages. They save a lot of costs, can have flexible hours, can work from home and utilize the geographical "Time Difference" to extend one day and in some cases work for almost 24 hrs., without having to pay for any overtime.

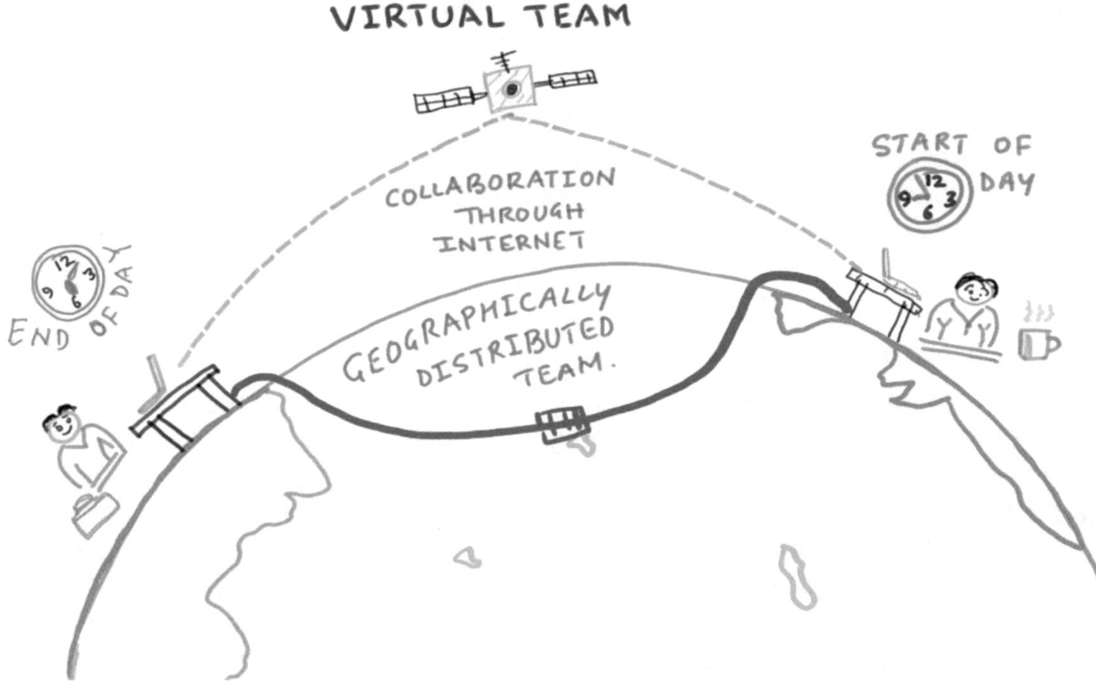

However, Virtual Teams generally take longer to complete work as there are difficulties to create performing teams within a virtual setups. Cultural differences and lack of "*Sense of belonging*" also throw up a lot of quality related and commitment related issues in projects that use virtual teams. Keeping in mind how the travel costs are rising and the fact that many organizations have become global, the importance of Virtual Teams is on the rise and there is a need for the Project Managers, project professionals, and team members who are adept at working within Virtual Teams.
Virtual teams concept also helps get persons with certain mobility challenges, disabilities as well as those who wish to work from home, involved in the project.

Pre-assignment is a tool and technique which is unique to this process (meaning it cannot be found in any of the other processes).
Virtual Teams is a tool and technique of only two processes viz., ***ACQUIRE RESOURCES*** (this one) and ***DEVELOP TEAM***.

10.1.2 Main Outcome from this process: -

Physical Resource Assignments contain the list, price, rate and other technical details of all the resources duly assigned to the various activities of the project at different times across the lifecycle of the project. This documents the "actual resources" that were assigned and not the planned ones. This document could be used later for understanding if there were differences between the planned assignments versus actual assignments and if that lead to any substantial project outcome.

Project Team Assignments keeps a record of the actual persons assigned to the project with their roles and responsibilities and their contact details and even organization charts.

Resource Calendars contain the working days, shifts, timings, percentage allocation and other such details about the resources assigned to the project.

Resource Calendars are first time output of the process "***ACQUIRE RESOURCES***". Resource Calendars do get updated as part of the Project Documents Updates in the processes ***CONTROL SCHEDULE***, ***DEVELOP TEAM*** and ***CONDUCT PROCUREMENTS***.

10.2 Develop Project Team (Develop Team)

Once the project has acquired the staff, the Project Manager has to work with the group of people to convert them into a "Team". If you go by the basic definition of team it says, "A group of people coming together to work towards a common objective." This definition is the most popular one but it is just half-truth. There are umpteen case studies from the real world projects and sports world which point out clearly that this definition is not complete. One of the most prominent examples was the Soccer (Football – for non-US based sportspersons) world cup 2014 where one of the most powerful teams consisting of players, each one world famous, got defeated by a football team that did not have such great names individually but collectively they were invincible. Now both the teams had "come together for a common objective" viz., to take the soccer world cup. It came to light that during the play while the famous team started playing in a disconnected manner because each of them had their own styles however, the other team played with such "Coordination" that even when individually each of the team members were not as talented as their counterparts in the famous team, as a team they became invincible and took home the world cup. There are many other such stories about amazing work done as a "Team" in almost all parts of the world and almost all kinds of domain, industry, defense, and sports.

When a group of people becomes a team they portray "Synergy Effect". Synergy is when two or more things, people, animals, substances etc., come together to create an output which is more than the sum of the outputs of the individuals.

Synergy is just the opposite of the "Law of Diminishing Returns".
A successful team usually shows the following characteristics.

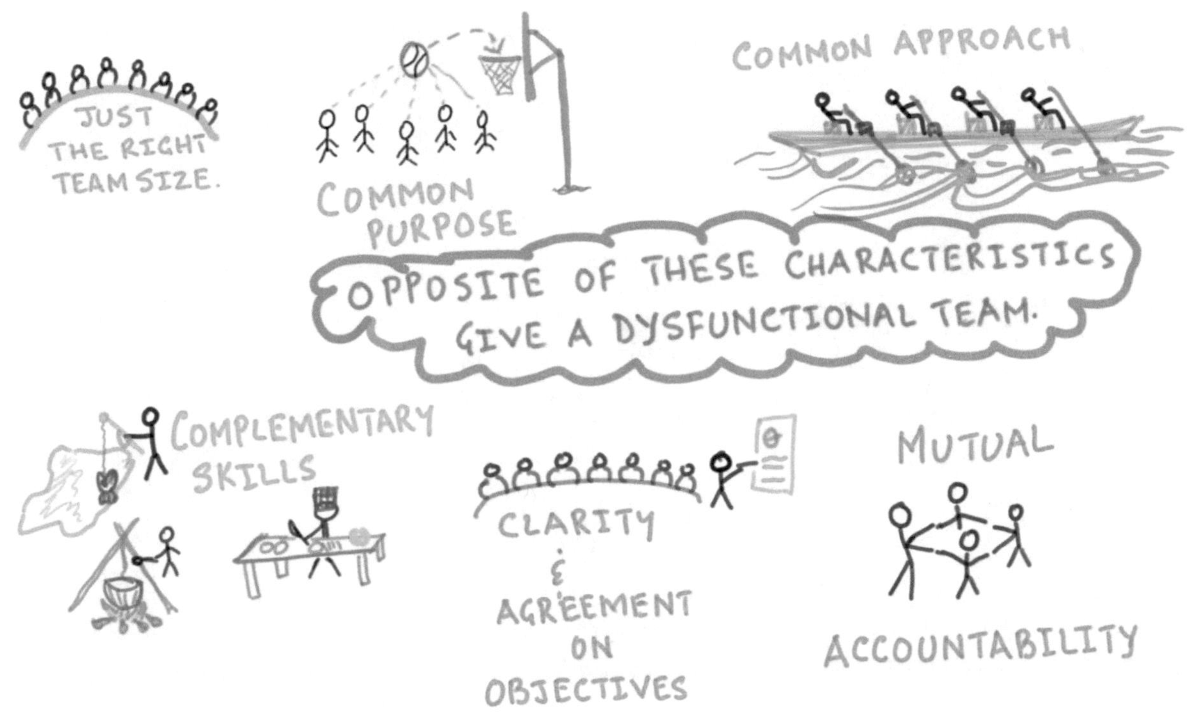

Team Building does not happen automatically. This is a deliberate exercise and hence there is a full process dedicated just for this. The Project Manager has to build the team through observation, communication, creating clear roles and responsibilities, leadership, motivation, coaching and mentoring and ensuring that the team has the right technical skills. Once a team is formed the result is higher performance, lesser supervision, less micro-management, lesser conflicts, higher motivation, higher ownership towards work and much lower quality issues. Building a team assumes a more complex and challenging situation as the project staff has to be developed into a "Team" in a very limited period as the project itself is temporary.

The PMBOK Guide states the following as the characteristics of a "High Performing Team":

1) Using Open And Effective Communication
2) Shared understanding
3) Shared Ownership
4) Trust
5) Collaboration
6) Adaptability
7) Resilience
8) Empowerment
9) Recognition

In today's world the concept of "Cultural Diversity" has also to be addressed as more and more teams are formed with cross-cultural professionals.

There are some serious hurdles to team building and they are: -

I am a movie buff and watch a lot of movies including Hollywood movies. One movie, a sequel of "Captain America", explained the concept of ***team*** very well. When Captain America's boss scolded him for a failed mission by saying, "You had the best, most talented and gifted team on the face of the earth and yet you failed"; Captain America replied, "There has to be ***Trust*** among the team members to get results… else we are just a bunch of guys shooting guns". (The exact dialogues may not match this word by word but then you get the picture; Right!).

Let us now get into the details of this process.

10.2.1 Main Tools and Techniques of this process: -

Co-Location means putting all the team members physically together. The physical proximity itself generates good relationships. Colocation facilitates communication and communication facilitates a great team building. However, it's not always possible in certain kinds of Industries like IT and Telecom where there is increasingly higher reliance on Virtual Teams. Hence, in the case of virtual teams, more virtual meetings and virtual team building exercises have to be conducted to build a team. Co-location should ideally be done across the lifecycle of the project, however if that is not possible then it could be done temporarily during the most crucial stages of the project and if even that cannot be done then at least a common meeting room / common room/association room should be earmarked for the team members to gather there and interact with each other. Co-located teams have the added advantage of "Osmotic" communication. Osmotic communication is a very intuitive way of communicating where one can ascertain reaction to a situation or ascertain whether someone likes what you said or not just by looking at their reactions. Let me give you an example. At your home (since you and your family are co-located) let us say you wish to order out. You look up from your desk and ask your spouse if it is ok to order Chinese. While you spouse says ok but the expression on your spouse's face indicate, "Again Chinese, is that all you can order", and you immediately say hey, how about Indian food for a change. And you notice the smile on your spouse's face and realize that you have done the right thing. Do you notice that the spouse did not say much and yet you could know instinctively what would work and what would not. This is called osmotic communication. Transport this concept to your workplace and you will remember that this happens there too if you and your team is co-located. And this is basically the biggest challenge when you work virtually. It is hard to experience osmotic communication which so essential in team bonding.

In exams, the term Colocation is sometimes referred to as "Tight Matrix" or "War room". Do not confuse the term "Tight Matrix" with the 3 kinds of Matrix organizational structures. If you see the term "War Room" or "Tight Matrix" in the exams it simply means "Co-located team".

Virtual Teams, despite having great advantages, suffers a lot from the point of view of team building and building trust among the team members as they are geographically distributed and may never ever get to meet each other. The project manager has to ensure that there are more "Get to know each other" meetings during the early phases of the project where they just spend time trying to understand each other before the real work starts. This helps in building some trust and appreciation for the other members and would significantly reduce the misunderstandings and conflicts during the later stages of the project. In one of the companies, I got the entire team together for a week (physically in one location) for detailed planning and kick off meeting. This worked so amazingly for the project that lasted 1 year that we hardly had any people issues. It was well worth the cost of getting them together. However, in larger teams, this is just not a viable option. Virtual teams with cultural differences need a bit more work from the project managers. He has to ensure that all of them develop and subscribe to a common language and terms.

In one of the projects I conducted a day long training (virtual) for some of the common terms in project management and their meaning. This was done to ensure that every one of us would be on the same page and spoke the same management language. Everyone knows that the best conversation and relationships are built around water-coolers, coffee stations, pantries etc. something that is not possible in the virtual world. What I did is that I created a Limited Group on Facebook for them to interact with the clear instructions that the FB group would not be used for any kind of project related discussions. This too worked amazingly well to build bonding and trust.

Communication Technology (this topic would be discussed in more details later in this book in another process) is crucial for communications and storing of information as well as retrieval of information at appropriate times. There is an unnecessary reliance on email for this. This is a bad idea. For co-located teams sending out too many emails is not a good idea. Use of shared portals and drives and storage spaces are a lot better than just emails for Virtual teams. Instead of everyone having different versions of the same documents with them locally it's best that all of them access the same version of the document from a virtually shared portal or a virtual drive. Communication Technology comes at a cost, therefore wherever possible, for virtual teams, get hold of Video Conferencing. Chats are a lot better for clearing up misunderstandings which may have cropped up due to emails and teleconferences.

Conflict Management is something the project managers have to be very swift and adept at, to help in team building. The fastest way to disintegrate a team is to let conflicts run amok. This topic would be discussed in more details in the process ***MANAGE TEAM***.

Influencing has to be used by the project manager and the project leaders to get the team to agree on team charter, rules of engagement and to obtain consensus on the technical aspects of the project, to build trust and understanding.

Negotiation would have to be done to achieve agreements towards expectations. Negotiations with the team help the team feel that they too get something out of the project as well. Remember, negotiation is a "Win-Win" situation.

Team Building is one of the topics that is not really well understood by most project professionals around the world. So what is essentially a "Team Building Activity"? A team-building activity is about putting the team members together, outside of their official roles, in such a way such that they would have to interact with each other in a sub-conscious as well as consciously informal manner, thus getting to know each other in way that would prevent them to have unhealthy conflicts, on the one hand and bring synergy, on the other hand, when they all come back to their official roles. Let me show you the practical power of this by reciting a situation I faced long time back in my career. I was heading a team of over 45 professionals ranging from 25 yrs. olds to 38 yrs. old in Japan for a very ambitious banking project. This was the first time any major IT team from my country had gone to Japan. Since this project was speeded up we had hired people specifically for the project. This meant that most of the team members did not know anything about each other. Soon the horrors of reality started dawning on me. My team members would fight over living quarters, daily allowances, language problems, food issues, process issues, trust issues and just about every other issue you can think of. There came a time when 90% of my time was spent on solving personal issues of the team members. One day my boss just called me to show how unhappy he was of my progress and how this project was important for the organization. He was sympathetic to my problem and he suggested that I should take my entire team on a day-long outing to Kamakura (a religious and tourist place near Tokyo). I was not sure about this but he convinced me to do this. I got the team together, broke this news to the team with the rule that everyone has to come for the trip or no one would go. On that eventful day, fantastic things happened. Young guys helped the families of the older guys, people with linguistic skills took leadership roles to interact with railway officials to buy tickets and read the maps etc., some got interesting snacks and people joked about it. Someone sang and others joined in. By the time we got back everyone had a nickname, knew what food others liked, had already made plans of watching a movie together, young bachelors had already got invites from family units for dinners etc., and from that moment on the team went on to do wonders with hardly any personal conflicts. Even the profession-related conflicts remained civil and healthy and most of the basic issues were handled within the team. I guess you can see how terrific the output of this one day "Team Building Activity" was.
Since then, having understood the sheer power of team building, I have engaged in team building exercises from a 10-minute stand-up discussions and bonhomie (which costed nothing) to 5 days outdoor rafting, camping and paintball sessions (that cost us close to a USD100,000/-).

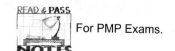

Every team building exercise does not have to be expensive and outdoors. However, while conducting team-building activity it is very important to also know "when" to do the same. Team building activities done too soon or too late would not cut it. Besides, one needs to truly understand what is happening to the team at any point of time to decide exactly when to conduct "Team-Building Activities". For this Bruce Tuckman has developed the 5 identifiable stages of team development and it's called the Tuckman's Ladder.

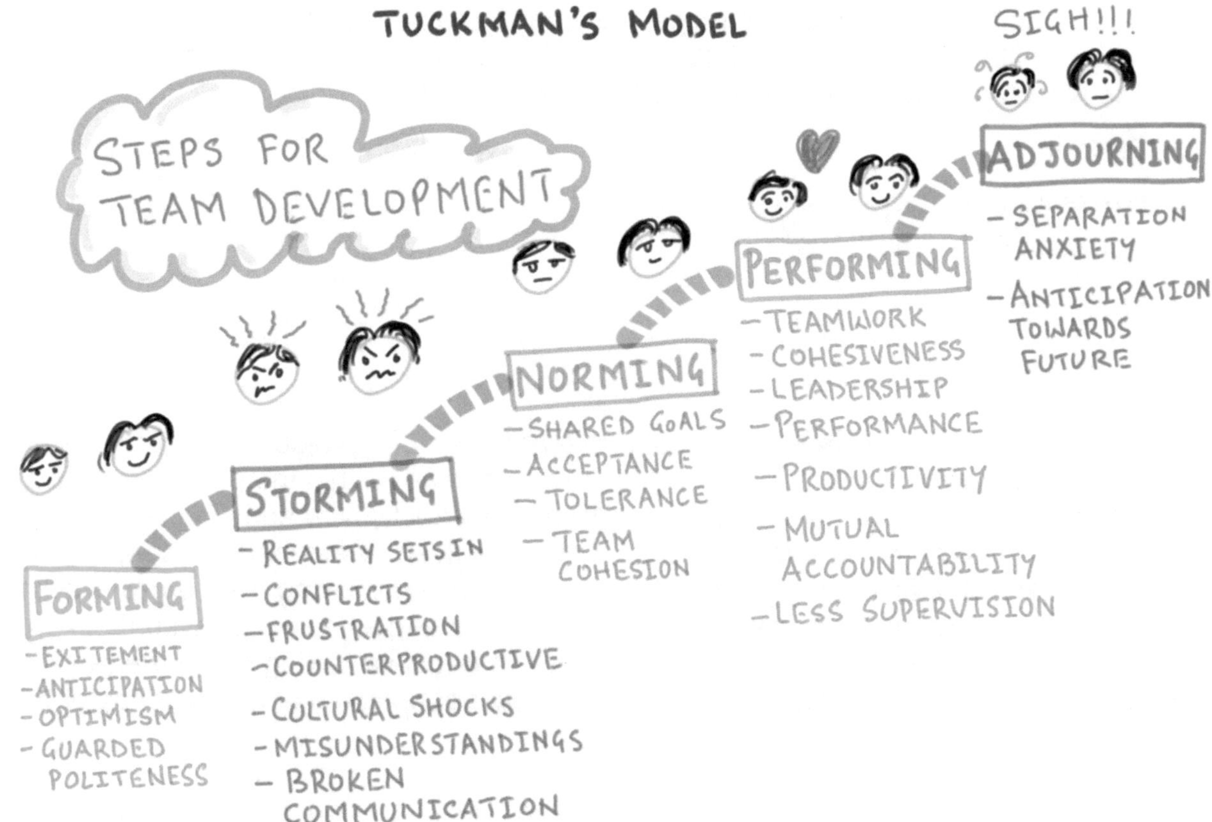

It's not necessary that in each and every case the team would follow these steps. There are times when the team may get stuck in a stage or completely skip a stage altogether.
The best time to conduct "Team-Building Activities" is during ***storming*** as it helps people get over storming and into the "Norming" phase.

It is important to note here that once a team has reached the performing stage and then some changes are made to the team composition, the team will roll back to the Storming stage. Sometimes in questions in PMP Exams, while such a change in team is discussed but the option of "Storming" is not provided among the choices. In that case look for "Forming" and if you find it, then that is the correct answer.

Ground Rules help in avoiding conflicts and unprofessional situations at the workplace. By clearly stating what kinds of behavior is acceptable and what is not, what kind of language is acceptable and what is not, what kinds of jokes are acceptable and what is not, what kind of cultural discussions are not acceptable and so on, the biggest triggers for conflicts are removed. Ground rules could be established by the project manager but it's best when the team themselves establish certain ground rules. Remember ground rules are part of the Team Charter. Ground rules must be created with inputs from team members and each and every team member must accept it without even a single exception.

Key Performance Indicators (KPIs) help the team to achieve the performance that would be measured in the form of metrics. Performance can be achieved if there is a targeted efficiency or performance that needs to be achieved. It helps the team get focused and work

together. Qualitative statements may get misinterpreted hence KPIs being measurable and usually quantitative in nature tends to get the team work towards a common target.
For the KPIs to be effective they need to be SMART.

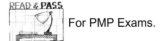

- **S**pecific
- **M**easurable
- **A**chievable
- **R**elevant
- **T**ime-bound

Recognition and Rewards is the most important power of a project manager. This is the most powerful way to showcase what is desirable behavior within the project organization. The Human Resource Management Plan documents exactly how and when the rewards and recognition would be given. What rewards should be given, would be dependent on the various organizational theories so that the specific person receiving the reward is actually satisfied. It is crucial that the process of giving rewards and selecting a person for rewards must be clear and transparent so that no one gets a negative feeling about the reward process and question the reward itself. Rewards cannot be given at the expense of breaking up the team.

Sometimes there are questions on the various powers of a project manager. Questions from this are getting increasingly rare but they may still show up. The following are the various powers of a Project Manager.

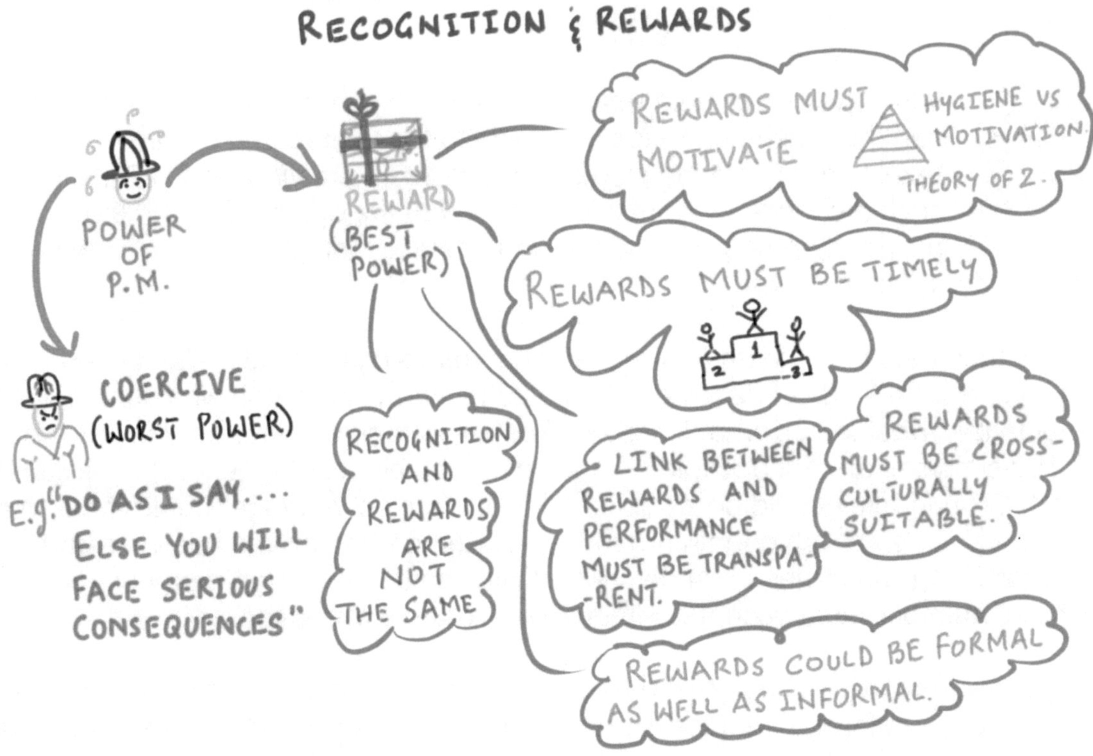

What you need to know is that the "Best" power of the project is "Power To Reward" the team members. However if in the question instead of "Best" the situation shows that it is a new team or the project manager is new to the team than the "First" power to be used by the Project Manager is the "Formal Power". The worst power of a project manager is the "Coercive Power".

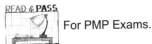

Training is needed to ensure that the project staff is technically competent and complement each other as well. Since the team has to work on the deliverables of the project, even the team that gels very well together may find the going tough if they are not technically competent or complementing each other when it comes to technical work. Hence "Training" is a very important tool for team development. A skills analysis can be done to identify the skill gaps among the team. Once the skill gaps are known, trainings could be organized and scheduled to meet those specific gaps. This might require budget change considerations if such trainings are not available at the organizational level. Once the trainings have been identified and scheduled, the team members who are supposed to undertake specific trainings are identified and duly informed. It is a better idea to follow up with the team members a few times before the training date to ensure that most of the identified team members, if not all, get trained. Now a days training are done in several formats. External or Internal trainer could conduct an offline traditional classroom training. Trainings could be done live online or on demand using recorded videos. Whatever the case may be, the effectiveness of the training must be obtained using a feedback and post training assessments. Of late this topic is fairly popular in PMP Exams.

Interpersonal Skills: needed by the Project Manager during this process can be summarized as under

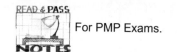

Virtual Team Development: Geographically distributed teams are called Virtual teams. They are just the opposite of co-located teams. Virtual teams has a lot of benefits. Some of them can be listed as under:

1) People can work from home.
2) Inclusion of physically challenged or differently abled in the work stream
3) Reduction in transportation costs
4) Reduction in office overheads
5) Access to talent from anywhere in the world
6) Creation of diverse team
7) Offers flexibility of working time to the employees

However Virtual Teams tend to have some challenges as well. Some of them can be listed as under:

1) Harder to create Team Bonding and Identity
2) Technology based Communication and Information Sharing is not intuitive
3) Harder to track performance of individuals
4) Logistical challenges
5) Lack of Non-Verbal communication
6) Harder to measure engagement levels
7) Indifference and lack of trust
8) Lack of Osmotic communications
9) Meeting among team members only for work making bonding difficult.
10) Marked reduction in overall productivity due to above reasons.

Ideally the best situation is to have the teams co-located. In fact Agile Alliance always talks about ensuring that the Agile teams are co-located. However with the way the world is shaping up, how the global borders are getting blurred, global pandemic and the need to harvest the benefits mentioned earlier, more and more projects are being done virtually. Which essentially means that more and more projects would be faced with the challenge of developing the team virtually.
Over time, some best practices have been identified for speeding up team building over virtual platform. (These points are also very crucial in answering several PMP Questions on this topic. And of late, a large number of questions show up in PMP Exams on this topic.)

1) *Co-located Kick-Off Meeting:* This is something that I have discussed earlier in this book. I have done this trick several times and I also suggest organizations where I am consulting on Agile adoption. Let me elaborate this point from another angle. I am sure this has happened to you as well. When you have been talking to someone on phone for some time and you have not met them ever, you unknowingly make a mental picture about that persons personality. However when you finally get to meet that person face to face, you end up saying, “I imagined you quite differently in my mind.” This happens quite a bit. Now imagine when the entire team is virtually connected, just imagine the amount and combinations of perceptions that get crated by each other. And this comes in the way of healthy bonding and consequently the quality and effectiveness of work. To overcome this phenomenon, one of the best things to do is to get the team together for a co-located meeting and team building, at least once during the entire lifecycle of the project. The best time for this is for the Project “Kick-off” meeting. For the Agile teams this is best during the Vision and

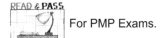

Roadmap workshop. This helps the team to bond and get to know the "real" each other and hence once they go back and continue working virtually, they work as though they are still co-located and lot less number of misunderstandings happen. This co-located meeting is however subject to availability of Budget. When there is a budgetary constraint then the next best thing to do for this virtual team is to organize multiple video conferences with the team members to help them get to know each other as well as they can. The earlier this is done in the lifecycle of the project the better it is. Hence the best time is just after the initial planning and before execution when the entire team has been on-boarded.

2) *Set Expectations Upfront:* This seems kind of an obvious thing to do but is very rarely done. Letting every team member know what is expected of them, both in terms of work and in terms of behavior, goes a long way in getting the virtual team to work better together. Clarity of information and expectation setting seems to go a long way in ensuring proper coordination among the team members.
3) *Define Ground Rules:* Just like in co-located meetings, establishment of Team Charter with Ground Rules go a long way in ensuring that team members abide by the code of conduct. This alone ensures that needless conflicts and misunderstandings do not occur among the team members. If the virtual teams are in different time zones it would make a lot of difference if the ground rules also contain provisions about cultural acceptance and keeping the others time-zone (and therefore the working time) in mind while interacting and working. This helps create a sense of belonging and trust among the team members.
4) *Send Time Limits For Responding:* I am sure this has happened to you. You sent out an email to a virtual team member about something you need information on. The other team member does not reply. After waiting for half a day you get a bit agitated and call the person up with the intention of letting the person know the importance of the email. However when you call him you realize that all this time the person was compiling all the relevant information for you. And this makes you feel a bit guilty about doubting the intentions of that other team member all this time. The solution in this situation is, "Responding" even when the work is not done yet. This keeps the other team members from "Guessing" and "Imagining" reasons for delay. If, within the team, it was decided that every query must be responded to within one hour, it would make a huge difference. If the work is not completed within the hour then a response can be sent saying "we are still working on it and will get back to you in next 30 minutes".
5) *Water*-Cooler *Chit Chat*: In a co-located team the team members are interacting for a lot of *other things than just work. Which is not so in virtual teams. They end up meeting and interacting only for work and nothing else. This generates a sense of being* "Cut-off" from the team. It is a really powerful feeling that affects the team member in more ways than one. I myself had noticed this way back in the early 2000s and ensured that virtual teams interact on several occasions other than just work. We celebrated birthdays online where people sang birthday songs together from 8 different countries and 5 different time zones. These things make a huge difference in bonding. A deliberate efforts must be made by the project manager or the facilitator to ensure that the team interacts for general chit chat as well. This is how I came to know that in Japan this general chit chat is called "Pecha Kucha" (pronounced PaychaKcha).
6) *Team Building Activities* : Virtual teams too need team building activities for precisely the same reason as that for a Co-located team. However the team building activities

would be different. Some of the common team building activities that deliver great result are “2 truths and a lie” (where every team member shares three things about themselves and the rest of the team has to guess which of those 3 things is a lie) and “Introduce another team member”. There are a few other more creative games that need some individual set up but the point is whatever activity you do, you must ensure that team building activities are done several times through the entire lifecycle of the project.

Diversity And Inclusion: World is made of diverse cultures, languages, food preferences and appearances. This is precisely what is beautiful about this world. However certain cultures tend to refer to their own culture, language, religion and skin pigmentation to be a global baseline and then, knowingly or unknowingly, generate biases against those who are at variance from their baseline. In its more advanced form it is called racism. With more and more teams getting cross cultural any kind of biases about other cultures can disintegrate the project team. Hence, one of the important tools in building a cross cultural team is creating awareness and acceptance for other cultures. This can be done through Diversity trainings as well. Inclusion is about ensuring that team members from any culture, gender (yes certain cultures have institutional gender bias), religion, skin pigmentation, food preferences, physical challenges etc. they all have an equal say in the team. The team is empowered to make decisions collectively as well as it becomes a psychologically safe environment to work in. Even if it means making certain specific considerations to specific team members, so be it. Some of the deliberate actions that can be taken by the project manager to ensure inclusion are:

1) “Team Language” to overcome differences in languages which will also overcome the habit of “Common Language” team members to form “Sub-Groups” within the larger teams thus creating communication issues.
2) Promoting acceptance and tolerance towards everyone.
3) Create an environment that takes advantage of the diversity. Diversity is actually a powerful thing because it allows you to solve problems in multiple ways.
4) Opportunity to learn other’s culture thus becoming a more responsible global and professional citizen.
5) Raise Trust and Cohesiveness among team members through collaborative exercise and team building activities.
6) Promoting collaborative culture among the team.
7) Promoting respectful and inclusive team culture.

Leadership In Team Building: There are some important leadership models that are used at several places within the project lifecycle. However, they are more popularly used during the team development process and therefore I am taking this excuse to discuss these models at this place. I will try my best to explain these models to you as best as I can so that you have a proper and practical understanding.

1) ***The OSCAR Model***: It is quite obvious that OSCAR is an acronym. I will soon come to the full form of the acronym. What you should know, before that, is the fact that this model is amazing for helping anyone create a detailed plan for their personal or professional targets. This is something I have used a lot during coaching. Even today when I talk to my daughter about some of the things that she wants to do, I use the OSCAR model to help her put that idea into a plan and the best part is that she feels empowered because most of the work is done by her. I only ask leading and general

questions in the form of OSCAR model. There is sequence in which the questions must be asked. And it is this sequence that this acronym translates into.

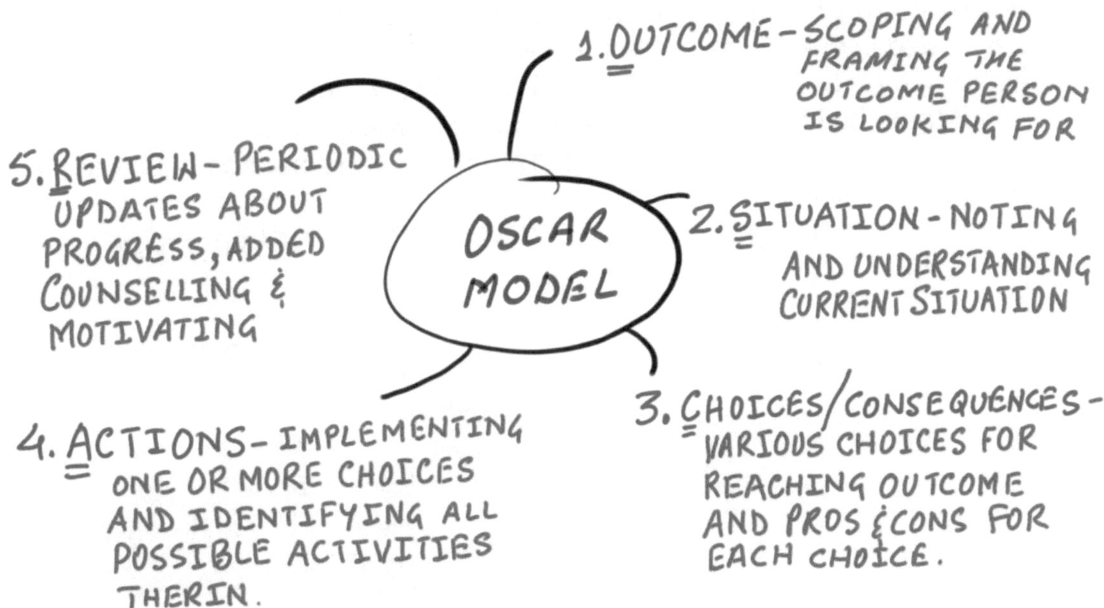

The first set of questions should be around OUTCOME. These questions are asked to help the team member (or the person you are coaching) to frame a finite, specific and measurable outcome that they are looking for. Sometimes people just have a general idea of what they want, something that needs to be scoped out clearly and precisely by asking questions to the person making that person think in details. Besides, talking about Outcomes also helps set a very positive tone to the entire discussion. Once the coach is satisfied that the outcome has been sufficiently detailed out, the coach will then start asking questions around the current situation. This allows the person coached to see the gap between where they are right now versus where they want to be. Here again, questions are asked till the current Situation is very well laid down along with its pros and cons. Once that is done, then questions are asked around the third point viz., Choices / Consequences. Coach must ask a lot of questions to ensure that the person coached identifies as many choices or paths that would close the gap identified due to the previous two questions. Again, this is repeated till the pros and cons of each of the possible choices are listed. Once that is done, another series of questions would need to be asked to help the person coached to prioritize and finally select one or two choices that the person being coached would eventually execute. Once that is done and finalized, the coach then starts asking questions around the detailed action plan against the choices that were prioritized during the previous question. This stage is called Action. At this place the questions are asked to ensure that nothing is left out. I use WBS with my coached to ensure that every detailed bit of action items are identified and nothing is left out. I even work with them to make a general sequence in which these action items would be taken for best results. All of this is done by asking more and more detailed questions. Review is the continuity part where the coach has periodical review with the coached to ascertain if all the necessary actions were indeed being taken, what has been the progress so far, solve any impediments or challenges faced etc. This review phase continues till completion or achievement of the OUTCOME that this all started with. In PMP exams the questions would not show up in as much details but then as I told you that this book is to not only help you ace PMP exams but also help you become practically effective. Try this, it really works. This is one of my favorite tools for coaching.

2) ***Drexler/Sibbet Team Performance Model***: This is basically a model to get the team developed in specific steps that would ensure that the team starts performing appropriately or as targeted. This is basically a 7 step process. The first 4 steps are about team building while the steps from 5 to 7 are about performance and sustainability of team performance. The steps are rather self-explanatory. Let me jot them down as under:

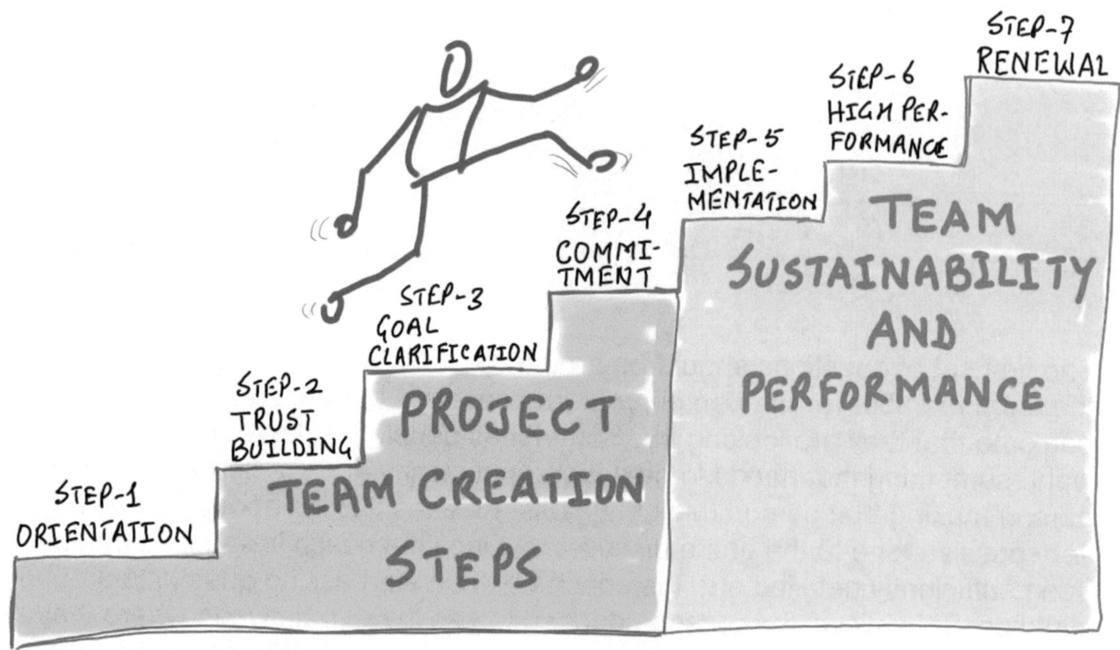

3) ***Situational Leadership/***: Though it is called "leadership", it is more of a managing styles based on different kinds of situations involving different kinds of team members you may be dealing with. Basically what this model lays down is that a manger or a leader cannot delegate work to all the team members in the same manner. This is because team members are different. This model goes on to state 4 different kinds of team members. These 4 combinations are created from the permutation and combinations of two characteristics viz., Competence and Commitment (towards work / project). It is rather obvious that if you have some team members who are Highly Committed as well as possess High Competence you will simply Delegate the work to them. You do not need to support them nor do you need to follow up with them nor do you have to tell them exactly how to do the work. The diagram below summarizes the concept of situational leadership appropriately. The details of this were discussed earlier in this book as well. If you need to refresh go back to the Framework chapter and you will find it towards the end.

SITUATIONAL LEADERSHIP

MODERATE COMPETENCE VARIABLE COMMITMENT SUPPORTING S3	SOME COMPETENCE LOW COMMITMENT S2 COACHING
DELEGATING S4 HIGH COMPETENCE HIGH COMMITMEN-	S1 DIRECTING LOW COMPETENCE HIGH COMMITMENT

SUPPORTIVE BEHAVIOR →

DIRECTIVE BEHAVIOR →

Individual And Team Assessments are done at two levels, one, at an individual level (by using assessments like Attitudinal survey and structured interviews) and two, at the entire team levels (like team strengths, patented team analysis like Belbin assessments etc.,). This is done to find the areas of strengths and weaknesses, both at individual levels and team levels, so that the same could be provided for and addressed. Knowing the gap between what is expected from a team member versus what he actually has helped decide the kind of training and coaching the team members have to be given. Even changing the roles of the team members to suit their attitude and strengths would also have a very high effect on the overall team building. *E.g., If I know that my teams general weakness is that they are all very creative but not very detailed in finding faults with their work as well as desk checking, I will spend some time training them on basic testing techniques as well as ensuring that they all have a detailed set of "Checklists" to prevent issues and errors while they work.*

Co-location, Team Building (from the group of Interpersonal And Team Skills), Recognition and Rewards, Training and Individual and Team Assessments are the tool and technique of only one process viz., ***Develop Team***.
Virtual Team is the tool and technique of only two processes and they are ***Acquire Resources*** and ***Develop Team***.

10.2.2 Main Outputs from this process: -

Team Performance Assessments help the project manager understand the actual effectiveness and performance of the team vis-à-vis the project work. All the training, team development activities and other interpersonal initiatives done should eventually raise the performance of the team. Some organizations use Earned Value Management to understand the cost and schedule efficiency of the team. Sometimes such Performance Assessments are done through independent consultants to find not only technical and skill related gaps but also find soft-skill gaps and other demand-based skill gaps like "Virtual Team Expertise". To be able to understand if there has actually been an improvement in "Team Performance" there have to be some matrix that is recorded and analyzed for the same. Some of these could be

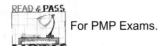

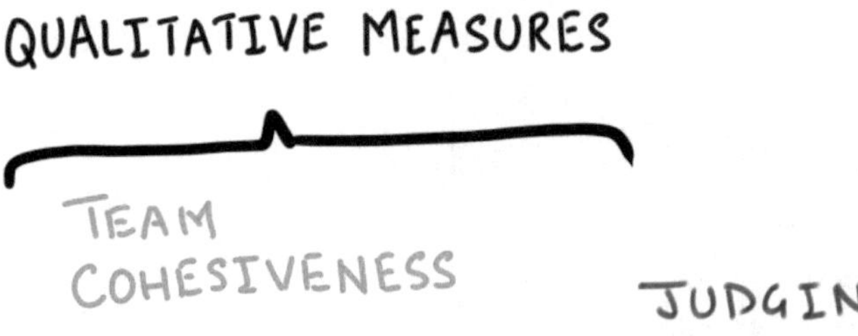

The main output of this process, “Team Performance Assessments”, becomes input to only one process viz., ***Manage Team***.

10.3 Manage Project Team

The whole purpose of “Developing a Team” was to get the project team to perform. Higher performance would ensure better quality, better timekeeping and better utilization of budget. A high-performance team is the best guarantee for meeting the project objectives. However, just like you need to press the accelerator to get your car running at a specific speed, does not mean that you will let go of the accelerator once you reach that speed. You would not press so hard on the accelerator either. You would just keep an eye on the speedometer and keep adjusting the pressure on the accelerator to maintain the required speed. Similarly, you need to keep watching the performance, conflicts and other signs in your team that predicts disharmony in the team so that you could handle the team issues quickly and keep the team performing. This, in effect, is the crux of what happens during this process.

The Project Manager needs interpersonal skills to keep the team focused on performance and project work. The most important interpersonal skills are the skill to handle Conflicts effectively and decisively.

There is a very close relationship between the processes “Develop Project Team” and this process “Manage Project Team”. Develop Project Team is almost a continuous process and the performance of them would trigger the Manage Project Team. The process Manage Project Team is triggered to keep the “Team performing and developed as a team”.

The “Team Performance Assessments” bring to light the individual and team related slippages and weaknesses and therefore the project manager may apply targeted solutions to the same.

It is important to note here that when it comes to PMP Exams, most of the questions from this process would be around conflicts, reasons for conflicts, stages of conflicts, conflict resolution techniques and emotional intelligence.

Let us get into the details of this process.

10.3.1 Main Tools and Techniques of this process: -

Conflict Management is the most important technique in this process. To ensure that the project team keeps on performing the project manager must use appropriate conflict management technique to resolve conflicts and issues swiftly and decisively.
The term "Conflict" has a lot of meanings based on context where it is applied. However, from the Projects point of view, conflict is any difference of opinion or clash which is negatively affecting project work. The project manager must not get involved in every difference of opinion. There are some golden rules that help in real world "Conflict Handling" as well as for answering questions in the exams, and they are: -

- Conflicts are natural and are actually good when in control.
- Conflict is a team issue and should not be seen as an individual issue (unless it is due to lack of Personal Integrity).
- Openness always helps in conflict resolution.
- It's better to focus on the issue, not people or their personalities.
- It's also better to focus on the present and the future but not the past. Past is a dead issue.
- The earlier you resolve a conflict the better it is.

When we talk about "The earlier you resolve a conflict…" we must know that there are some stages of conflicts. These stages are from nascent stage of a conflict to its aftermath stage. Hence, a good manager and a leader would try and resolve a conflict in as early a stage as possible to minimize the damage to the team and the project environment.
Let us first have a look at the stages of conflict.

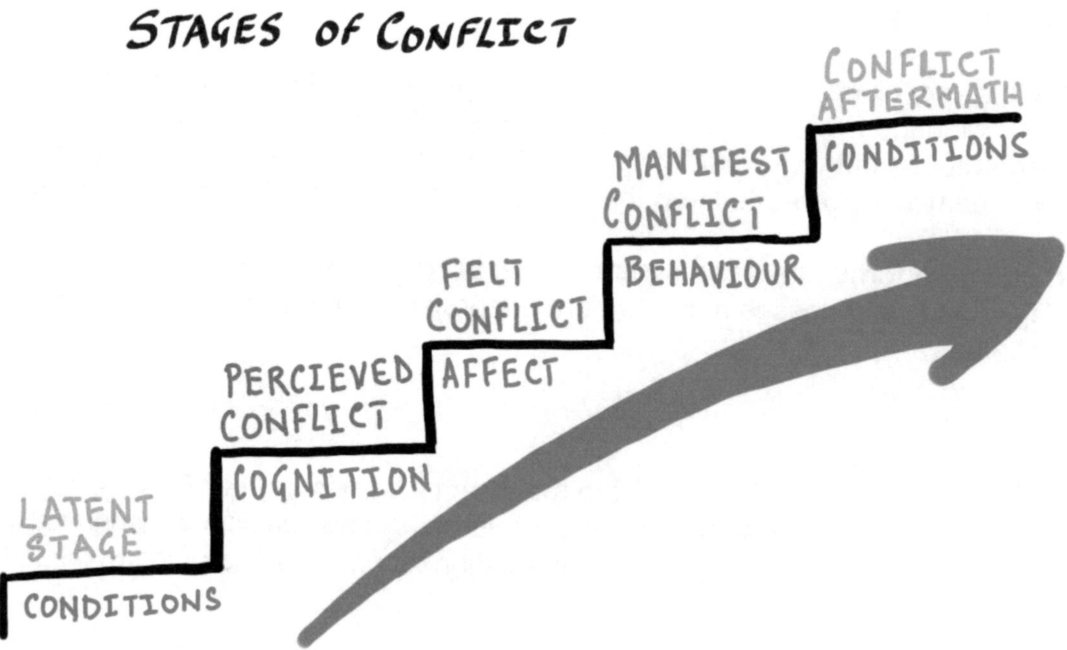

These five stages can be lightly explained as under:

1) **Latent Stage**: Participants not yet aware of conflict.
2) **Perceived Stage**: Participants aware a conflict exists.
3) **Felt Stage**: Stress and **anxiety**.

4) **Manifest**: Conflict is open and can be observed.
5) **Aftermath**: Outcome of conflict, resolution or dissolution.

Once a conflict occurs, a project manager has to use just the right technique for "Conflict Resolution" given the situation. The choice of the conflict management technique would depend on the importance of the conflict vis-à-vis the project work, project lifecycle during which the conflict happens, amount of time available for conflict resolution and whether the conflict resolution would have a short term or long term effect on the project.
There are various kinds of conflict handling techniques.

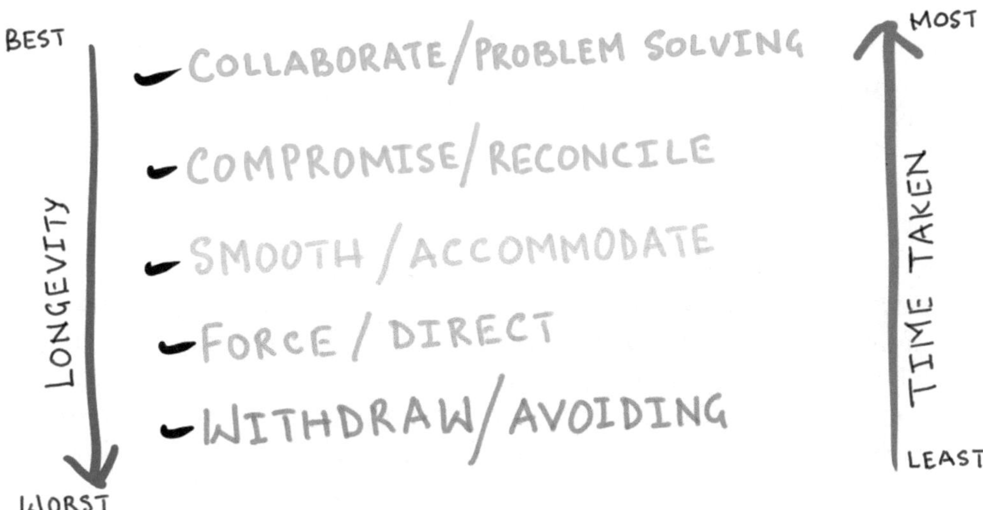

The term "Longevity" means, the amount of time the solution would be effective or simply, how long would the solution last. You can see that as the resolution methodology gets easier, they require less time to implement but suffer from reduced longevity of effectiveness. As a project manager, you have to balance the longevity with the time taken for conflict resolution.
It is also important to know the top reasons for conflicts in a project environment.

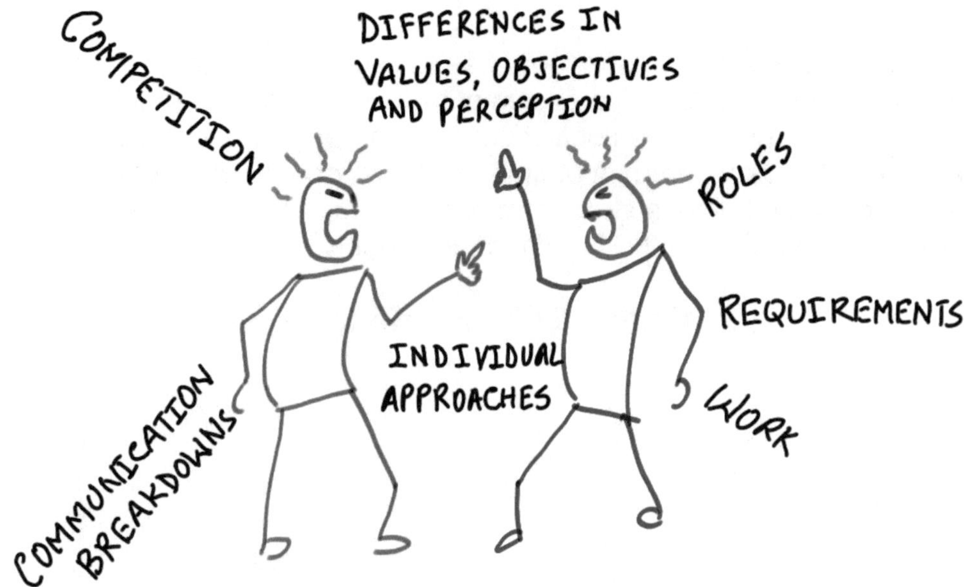

Let us look into these individual conflict resolution techniques:

1. ***Collaborate / Problem Solving***. This method means getting to the root cause of the conflict. This would mean that the project manager would have to sit with all the conflicting parties together and dig into the real reason why this conflict has happened. This takes a lot of time and patience of the project manager but when the root-cause is identified then the conflict resolution is such that no other conflict would arise between the parties during the lifecycle of the project. Project Manager could get the conflicting parties to start a dialogue under his supervision (without actually participating) and asking them to collaborate on the solution that would work with both. This is the method that is used by the United Nations to solve problems between two warring nations. *E.g., One of the technical teams is constantly submitting their deliverables late and this is leading to a lot of conflicts and confusions between the Team Leader, Project Leader, Technical heads and the technical teams. If the project manager calls all of these parties to a meeting to understand their individual issues and challenges to find a common solution that everyone would be able to appreciate, then this would be an example of conflict resolution using "Collaboration / Problem Solving".* This method is the most powerful method but takes a very long time. Hence it's best done during the earlier stages of the project when it would be worth spending this kind of time for conflict resolution.

2. ***Compromise / Reconcile*** method of conflict resolution is about finding a middle ground between the conflicting parties such that all parties stand to lose something or give up something to reach a middle ground of agreement. Something that all of them can live with. *E.g., A serious conflict of a vendor consistently providing late deliverables and the customer pressing for the contracted penalty could also be resolved by both taking the middle ground by giving up something, like, while the vendor agrees to some extra amount of work (not in contract) the customer giving up his right to claim penalty. This way*

the vendor does not get blacklisted and the customer gives up his claim for a heavy penalty. This method is also called "Lose – Lose" as both parties stand to lose something for an agreement or a conflict resolution. This method is adopted when there is less time for a detailed conflict resolution. Also one must understand that "Compromise" is done for mending deteriorating relationships.

3. ***Smoothing / Accommodating*** is more of a slanted way of conflict resolution technique where usually one party to conflict is reasoned with to give up their claims, positions etc., and continue as usual, for the overall harmony and benefit of the project. This is usually done by getting the party to focus on the "Common positions" rather than differences. *E.g., One of the sole suppliers in a highly technical project has seriously defaulted on a delivery. The customer is using the contracted provisions for compensations and penalty which the supplier is steadfastly refusing to pay. Since the supplier is very crucial to the project's success and there are no other suppliers that can do this work, the project manager may convince the customer's procurement department not to press with the compensation for the overall success of this project and to let this default pass.* This is not really a conflict resolution technique but more of an "Accommodating" technique and is not always a good solution. This should be only done when there is hardly any time or when you are stuck in such a way that giving a free pass to one party is the only way going forward.

4. ***Force / Directing*** is a method where the project manager uses his authority and position to get the conflicting parties to set aside their issues and concentrate on work. This is not the kind of conflict resolution technique that you should apply all the time unless you are in the Army. In any armed forces, this is the standard way for solving minor conflicts among army personnel. This method of conflict resolution should only be applied during fighting mode or towards the end of the project where any other method of conflict resolution is either not practical time wise or practical effort wise. *E.g., The project is about to close and right now the project is being handed over to the operations team. One of the project team members has objected to some of the remarks of one of the members from the operations team. As a project manager, you lightly reprimand both the team members and curtly ask them to focus on their work and nothing else.* This method is definitely crude but is needed at some crucial points.

5. ***Withdrawal/avoiding*** is when the project manager looks away from a conflict situation or postpones the resolution or hopes that someone else would resolve it. This is the worst that a project manager can do if the conflict affects his own project. The only time a project manager should avoid or withdraw from a conflict is when the conflict is in the jurisdiction of another project manager. Basically here the project manager does not do anything. This is one of the fastest ways to lose respect and trust from among the project team. At times this resolution technique is required to be adopted when the conflict is among those stakeholders that really do not affect your project and you do not have the time to attend to them or when you are in such a tight situation that if you get distracted by a conflict you may end up having a larger problem to deal with.

Decision Making. The project manager would have to use various decision-making techniques (like voting or cluster voting or unanimity or majority) to get the team to agree on certain points that affect team before going forward in the project. *E.g., In a team, which is made up of cross-cultural team members, have been having some serious issues connected to their beliefs and religion. While the majority of the team members love to have pork (being their main diet) the other group has been having serious reservations and conflicts because in their religion pork is not permitted. Food being served in a canteen on site it was getting increasingly difficult for the team to eat together and these differences were creating distrust and even active animosity at the workplace. The project manager worked with the team to take a decision that from that moment no pork would be served during meals so that all the team members could eat together and there are no religious tensions.* It was hard for the majority group to let go but when they saw how serious the topic is for the other group they decided to go along with the decision. This later resulted in amazing team spirit and trust and reliance on each other. Decision making is difficult but is necessary to move forward.

Group decision making almost always follows a "Divergence – Convergence" pattern. Which means that initially several members of the group will be poles apart initially and through discussions and facilitations they will move towards convergence and finally consensus. Group decision making works best when everyone in the group gets a chance to be heard or contribute. Apart from the group decision making techniques discussed above, there are a few more that need some mention:

1) "*Fist of Five*" Technique. (Something that we have already discussed earlier during planning processes).
2) *Roman Voting*: This voting style is based on how a gladiator's fate used to be decided in Roma, by the audiences present in the arena / colosseum towards the end. The voting involved giving a "Thumbs Up" or "Thumbs Down". If more thumbs up were given the gladiator in question would live to engage in another fight. But if there were more thumbs down, the gladiator would be fed to lions and disposed of. Fortunately in today's world things are not that violent but this voting style has stuck on and it is commonly used in quick group decision making.
3) *Dot Voting*: This is almost exactly like the 100 points prioritization / voting method that we covered earlier during the process collect requirements. Instead of points, each participant in the group gets certain numbers of sticky dots. Each group member may then spread these dots across several choices. They may stick more dots on specific choices and less on other choices and none on the choices that do not appeal to them. This way, once every one has stuck their dots across the choices, the numbers of dots are counted on each of the choices and the one with the most dots is taken as the group decision.

4) *Wide-Band Delphi*: This is something that has already been discussed in the process *Collect Requirements*. Basically, this method can be used for any group decision making and obtain consensus through various rounds of discussions.

Emotional Intelligence is of significant importance when the project manager and project leaders have to handle conflicts or to help the team make a serious decision. EI is not only about emotional equilibrium of the self but also about understanding the emotional condition of the others so that tact and diplomacy could be used to reduce tensions and make the team focus on the project activities. One of the ways to understand the emotional state of others is called “Observation and Conversation”. **Observation / Conversation** is a relatively new technique for managers to pre-empt people issues. It basically states that the managers must physically go around striking up informal conversations with project team members and generally see what they are up to and what is bothering them. By observing the body language of the team members it becomes clear how motivated the team really is and if there are signs of team conflicts. This method of management has now been formalized through “Management By Walking Around (MBWA)” and is being taught as a specialization in Management Schools. One does not get to “Know” their team by sitting in the manager’s cubicle and looking at impersonal reports. It’s been seen that Managers who informally interact with team members and generally observe their team tend to pre-empt issues and solve problems much faster than traditional managers. In virtual teams this can be done by having a conversational “one-on-ones” with each of the team members using video conferencing.

Emotional intelligence involves the following components:

- Personal (Self) Side
  - Self-Awareness
  - Self-Regulation
  - Motivation
- Interpersonal Side
  - Social Skills
  - Empathy

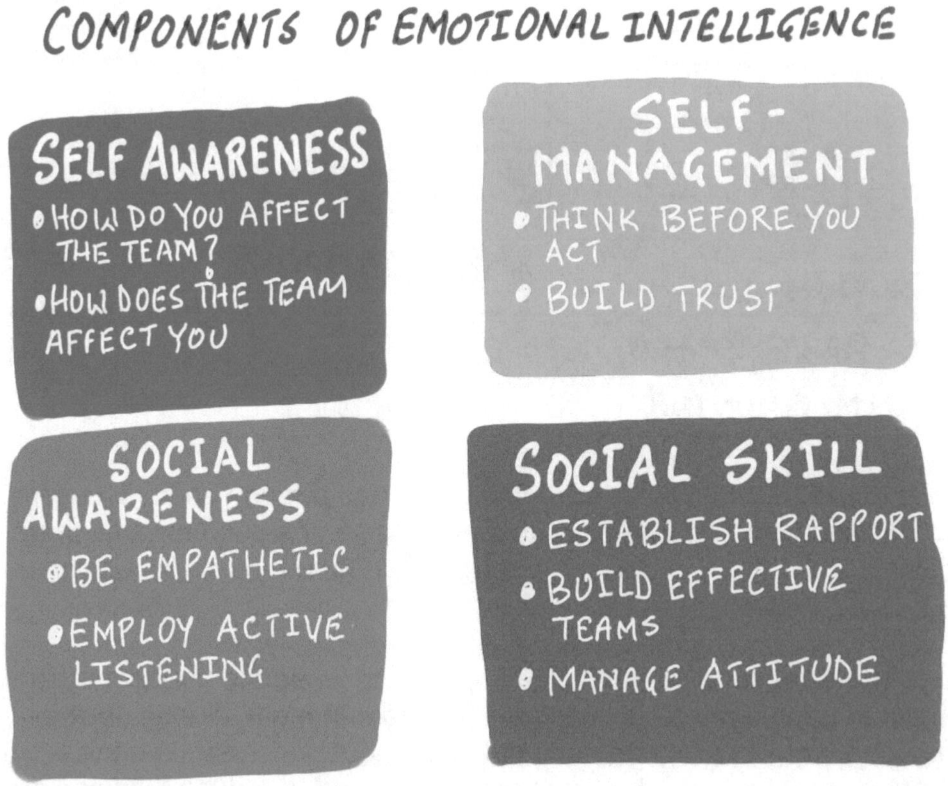

COMPONENTS OF EMOTIONAL INTELLIGENCE

SELF AWARENESS
- HOW DO YOU AFFECT THE TEAM?
- HOW DOES THE TEAM AFFECT YOU

SELF-MANAGEMENT
- THINK BEFORE YOU ACT
- BUILD TRUST

SOCIAL AWARENESS
- BE EMPATHETIC
- EMPLOY ACTIVE LISTENING

SOCIAL SKILL
- ESTABLISH RAPPORT
- BUILD EFFECTIVE TEAMS
- MANAGE ATTITUDE

Personality Profile Assessment: There are a lot of assessments in the management world which are used for assessing the overall personality of the individual team members to ascertain their personality type and therefore, consequently the pros & cons applicable to their personality. These kinds of assessments help others understand each other better. It also drives home, in a rather scientific manner that we are all different and it is ok to be different. These assessments help us understand the following:

1. The personality type of the individual team members
2. The dominant (higher number) of specific personality types in a team
3. The personality types that are missing from the team
4. Which person is more suited for which kind of work.
5. The overall strengths and weaknesses of the entire team based on the personality type mix that is making up the team.
6. Helps people understand their own personality as well as their own communication perferences

There are lot of personality profile assessments. I am listing a few here just so that you could find more about them if you are interested. However from the point of view of the PMP Exams the only one that you need to focus on is MBTI and it is covered in sufficient details later within this section.

1) Theory Of Psychological Types
2) Myers-Briggs Type Indicator (MBTI)
3) DiSC Model
4) True Colors Methodology
5) Social Style Model
6) Whole Brain Thinking
7) Belbin Theory (This is my personal favorite when it comes to team composition).

Ok then, let us now talk about Myers-Briggs Type Indicator (MBTI) assessment. Isabel Briggs Myer and her mother Katherine Briggs developed this assessment tool, hence the name. MBTI focuses on 4 pairs (8 types) of personality types. Each pair basically states opposing personality types from the point of view of comparison. Let us have a look at these 4 Pairs (8 basic personality types): [Questions to show up on PMP exams on these 8 basic types].

1) Extraverted Vs Introverted
    a. Extraverted
        i. Outward
        ii. Action oriented
        iii. Enjoy frequent social interaction
        iv. Feel energized after spending time with people
    b. Introverted
        i. Inward turning
        ii. Think through situations on their own
        iii. Social interactions few but very deep
        iv. Feel energized by spending time alone
2) Sensing Vs Intuition
    a. Sensing
        i. Decision making based on facts and observations
        ii. Rely on their own senses
        iii. More reality oriented
        iv. Love hands-on experience (if possible)
    b. Intuition
        i. Decision making is based on their gut feel
        ii. Rely on observable patterns
        iii. Focus more on possibilities
        iv. Abstract thinking manner
3) Thinking Vs Feeling
    a. Thinking
        i. Facts and data oriented
        ii. Facts and data over emotions
        iii. More consistent in their decision making style
        iv. Logical and Impersonal
    b. Feeling
        i. Emotions over facts and data
        ii. More focused on their feelings towards a situation

            iii. Focus on people while making a decision
4) Judging Vs Perceiving
    a. Judging
        i. Prefer structure
        ii. Firm decision
    b. Perceiving
        i. Open
        ii. Flexible
        iii. Adaptable

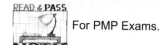

What MBTI has gone on to do is that it has provided a specific key letter to each of these 8 basic personality types. Let me show that to you as under:

1) Extraverted [E]
2) Introverted [I]
3) Sensing [S]
4) Intuition [N]
5) Thinking [T]
6) Feeling [F]
7) Judging [J]
8) Perceiving [P]

Let us look at a few questions the answers to which would help us ascertain the personality types.

1. How do you operate in meetings?
    a. Do you like to talk things through? If Yes! Then you are Extraverted [E]
    b. Or do you prefer time to think things through? If Yes! Then you are Introverted [I]
2. What is your preferred working environment?
    a. Do you like a busy and lively environment with opportunities for interaction? If Yes! You are Extraverted [E]
    b. Or you prefer quiet space for reflection and concentration? If Yes! You are Introverted [I]
3. How do you recharge at the end of the day?
    a. Re-energizing by doing something active? If Yes! You are Extraverted [E]
    b. Or you do that by having time to wind down and think things through? If Yes! You are Introverted [I]
4. What kind of hobbies do you enjoy?
    a. Hobbies that involve action and allow you to meet others? If yes! You are Extraverted [E]
    b. Or you love the ones that encourage reflection and allow concentration? If yes! You are Introverted [I]
5. What kind of instructions work well for you?
    a. Do you prefer step by step, realistic instructions that are clear and accurate? If yes! You are Sensing type [S]
    b. Or do you prefer to be given the overall purpose and work it out for yourself? If yes! You are Intuition based [N]
6. How do you approach learning something new?
    a. You like to try things out and experience, focusing on learning that has a practical application? If yes! You are Sensing type [S]

   b. Or rather explore how learning fits with other ideas and explore imaginatively? If yes! You are Intuition based [N]
7. What information do you need when buying something?
   a. The facts, specification and details to see if it will meet your needs? If yes! You are Sensing type [S]
   b. Or an overview and imagine how the product will work for you, a vision of the future and how you will use it? If yes! You are Intuition based [N]
8. How do you go about making decisions?
   a. Do you step out of the situation to decide objectively, using impersonal criteria? If yes! You are Thinking type [T]
   b. Or do you step into the situation to weigh things up and take into account personal circumstance? If yes! You are Feeling type [F]
9. How do you like to be recognized/appreciated?
   a. For a job well done at the end of a task? If yes! You are Thinking type [T]
   b. Or for personal contribution and to be valued throughout the project? If Yes! You are Feeling type [F]
10. How would you help someone with a problem?
   a. By fixing the problem, by looking at practicalities and focusing on tasks? If yes! You are Thinking type [T]
   b. Or by supporting someone, seeing how they feel about the situation and focusing on relationships? If yes! You are Feeling type [F]
11. What is your approach to deadlines?
   a. Do you work in a step by step approach to complete a task, being frustrated by last minute pressure or change? If yes! You are Judging type [J]
   b. Or do you prefer to work in an emergent, flexible way feeling energized by last minute pressure? If yes! You are Perceiving type P]
12. At what point do you come to closure on a decision?
   a. You prefer to decide sooner rather than later so you have the decision made and you can plan accordingly? If yes! You are Judging type [J]
   b. Or rather keep your options open as long as possible so you aren't tied down by a decision? If yes! You are Perceiving type [P]
13. When do you work and when do you play?
   a. Tend not to feel comfortable playing whilst there is work to be done, see play as a reward for finishing work? If yes! You are Judging type [J]
   b. Or play without the outstanding work interfering with your enjoyment, seeing life as too short not to take the opportunity to play? If yes! You are Perceiving type [P]

You may be wondering why I went about sharing so many questions to help you better understand the base personality types. Well, for one, it is really powerful way of ascertaining people and their personality and thereby becoming more accepting of them as an individual, and second, some of these may show up in the PMP exams as scenarios (or something on similar lines).

People are complex and hence their personality is a combination of some of these 8 basic personalities with one basic type being dominant. In MBTI there are 16 such combinations and each of these combinations are made up of some of the "Key Alphabets" provided in the list above. The very first alphabet of any of the 16 personality types indicate the dominant basic personality type. To be able to relate to each of these personality types MBTI has provided a "label" that best defines that personality type. (You do not have to worry too much about these 16 personality types from the point of exams. They do not show up in PMP Exams. If at all there are questions in PMP exams on MBTI they limit it to just the 8 basic types). Let us have a look at these 16 types.

1. **ISTJ** - The Inspector
2. **ISTP** - The Crafter
3. **ISFJ** - The Protector
4. **ISFP** - The Artist
5. **INFJ** - The Advocate
6. **INFP** - The Mediator
7. **INTJ** - The Architect
8. **INTP** - The Thinker
9. **ESTP** - The Persuader
10. **ESTJ** - The Director
11. **ESFP** - The Performer
12. **ESFJ** - The Caregiver
13. **ENFP** - The Champion
14. **ENFJ** - The Giver
15. **ENTP** - The Debater
16. **ENTJ** - The Commander

All right now you know some details about the MBTI. Exactly how the individual personality is found out about a specific person is what the MBTI assessment is all about. Interesting world, isn't it?

Critical Thinking: Critical thinking includes disciplined, rational, logical, evidence-based thinking. It requires an open mind and the ability to analyze objectively. Critical thinking, especially when applied to discovery, can include conceptual imagination, insight, and intuition. It can also include reflective thinking and metacognition (thinking about thinking and being aware of one's awareness).

Critical thinking is applied to all aspects of project work and is particularly used more during "Problem Solving" or "Creating an alternative solution".

Critical thinking reduces assumption taking and knee-jerk reaction.

Influencing can be done with or without authority. The technique of influencing people without authority would have to be used by the project managers as there are times that the project managers may not have a direct line of authority on some team members, specifically in a matrix and weak matrix kind of organizations.

Leadership skills would need to be exercised by the project manager and the project leader, to inspire the team. There are various kinds of leadership skills that the project manager may use.

Let us understand each of these leadership styles. (Only covering the ones not covered earlier in this book).

1) Laissez-Faire: This style of leadership is all about letting people be. Letting them chart their own course. Laissez Fair literally translates into “Allow To Do”. It is a French term and I can never pronounce it right. Originally it was a term coined to describe a principle that meant that the government should not interfere with how people would like to do business. However this concept is now adopted into leadership aspects of management world. In most cases, when this is applied to management world, it

results in chaotic conditions. This leadership / management style can only work in the most mature of all team members who have complete idea of what is expected of them.

2) Transactional Leadership: This kind of leadership only works in short term associations or for operational work and is mostly related to the outcome that is expected. Which means there is transaction of something like, "I will give you something you want if you give me what I want". Let us say, you are working with a team. They are supposed to meet certain targets. You may find that they are slipping a bit and hence you offer them a trip to Andaman's (one of the most beautiful Island resorts in the world) if they meet or exceed the target. This kind of leadership does not always involve something in kind. As a leader you can also give recognition. I will give another example of this. Since I travel a lot, I find myself talking to the check-in counter officers for most airlines. I have developed a habit to always talk and find a few details about the person behind the counter. I try to take their names correctly and also try and find out where they are from. Just doing this gives them the kind of recognition and respect that they usually never ever get from anyone else. They tend to remember the one person who was interested in them. Now guess who do they help if they find a luggage a bit overweight or accommodate a special request for specific seats. And when they have to upgrade anyone, who do they have in mind. I hope this clarifies.
3) Dictatorial: Also known as Autocratic style, this leadership / management style basically does not take any input from anyone else in the team and simply lays down what others have to do. This is usually done in mission critical work or projects (like special ops. Conducted by armed forces or emergency protocol execution). This leadership style is also used when the team consists of people with low relevant skills.
4) Interactional: This kind of leadership involves certain amount of interaction with the team. Using various influencing skills to converse and engage with the team to finally get them to act in the direction proposed by the leader / manager. Networking, casual conversations, Neuro Linguistic Programming (NLP) as well as Charisma could be used for this. This is something you would like to use when you have to influence a group of people in a meeting to move in a particular direction.
5) Transformational: This leadership is about transforming the abilities and thinking patterns of the person being mentored. This is usually done one to one and not one to many. This leadership is chiefly used while mentoring someone. It has a long gestation period and the mentor must have the patience to stick with the team member till they see targeted transformation. At any point of time have around 30 persons I am mentoring for long term. In one extreme case an engineer who had a severely emotion linked stammering issue can now speak clearly, lucidly and for hours without getting any episode of stammering. But this could be achieved in 3 yrs time. In one case a middle level manager has become a country head. And there are some other examples. One of the finest example of this is the parents, who spend a sizeable part of their life transforming a child through patient value system inculcating and helping choose the right paths.
6) Charismatic: This kind of leadership style is about influencing others by using their appearance, body language, energy they exude, the way the speak, the way they carry themselves, the way they approach a problem or work etc. One of the finest examples is how the "Officers" in an Army are groomed to become "Influencing" officers. The regular army men just look up to them. To be able to achieve this kind of aura around them these army officers spend a lot of time developing these abilities.

Another example of Charismatic leaders are the scores of Actors and Models who, because of their Charisma, can influence you to buy stuff that they suggest trough a video or print advertisement. Charisma can also come from excelling at their respective field. N Sridharan (Metro Man and the award winning program and project manager) carried this “all knowing “charisma with him.

10.3.2 Main Outcome from this process: -

The most important outcome of this process is the “Continued Team Performance”. If this process has been applied successfully the team will keep on performing.

The other outcome from this process is the Issue Log. We will discuss the Issue Log in details later in this book, when we reach the process ***MANAGE COMMUNICATIONS***.

10.4 Ninja Drill – Implementation - 1

In this Ninja Drill you will find the most important notes and pointers that are important from the point of PMP Exams and covers, Acquire Resources, Develop Team and Manage Team. These are the three processes which account for over 70% of all interpersonal questions that show up in PMP Exams.

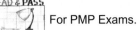

S. No.	Drill Points
1.	Remember just before the start of implementation and immediately following the conclusion of the planning a Kick-Off meeting is held for expectation setting and ensuring that everyone knows the plan as well as what is expected of them.
2.	In Agile, Kick-Off Meeting could be conducted immediately after iteration planning and just before work starts on that Iteration.
3.	The main Tools & Techniques of the process "Acquire Resources" are: 1) Multicriteria Decision Analysis 2) Negotiations 3) Virtual Teams 4) Skill Types / Skill Shapes
4.	Multicriteria Decision Analysis is basically the selection criteria for acquiring project team members.
5.	Negotiations are "Win-Win" agreements.
6.	Whenever you find a question talking about that there are some resources that are important to you in the project but are not easily available from the resource managers / functional heads, your perfect solution would be to Negotiate with them.
7.	Virtual Teams are teams that constitute of people who would not be meeting face to face but over technology based communication systems.
8.	"I" Shaped person is someone who has deep specialization in only one skill.
9.	"T" Shaped person is someone who has one deep specialization and broad understanding of other skills required in the project.
10.	"Pi" shaped person is someone who has two deep specializations and broad general knowledge about other required skills for the project.
11.	"Comb" [Paint Drip] shaped person is someone who has several deep specializations and also general knowledge about other required skills needed for the project.
12.	The main outputs / outcomes / artefacts of the process "Acquire Resources" are: 1. Physical Resources Assignment and 2. Project Team Assignments
13.	The common characteristics of a High Performance team are: 1. Using Open And Effective Communication 2. Shared understanding 3. Shared Ownership 4. Trust 5. Collaboration 6. Adaptability 7. Resilience 8. Empowerment 9. Recognition
14.	Project Manager serves as a Visionary Leader by articulating Vision, Values and Mission of the project to 1. Inspire team 2. Keeps them focused 3. Develop a sense of pride 4. Foster collaboration among team members 5. Keep team aligned to end user and customer outcomes 6. Help challenge the "Status Quo"
15.	The entire objective of Team Development is to obtain effectiveness in project work, efficiency and performance.
16.	Key Performance Indicators (KPIs) are set to link Team Performance with Project Vision and Objectives.

17.	KPIs need to be SMART Specific Measurable Achievable Relevant Time-bound
18.	Building trust among the team is crucial for team development.
19.	Presence of Team Charter created by the team themselves aids in Team Development process.
20.	Ground rules prevent a lot of unnecessary and frivolous conflicts.
21.	If there are a lot of unnecessary conflicts among the team members then the best way to reduce conflicts is to create Ground Rules.
22.	Empowering a team has a lot of positive effects in Team Development and team bonding.
23.	Empowerment means delegating some local decision making powers to the team members themselves.
24.	It is the project manager's duty to ensure that the team does not engage in belittling any culture, race, skin pigmentation, religion or language.
25.	The project manager must correct any behaviour of the team members that goes against the principles of Diversity and also ensure that the team goes through Diversity training.
26.	Inclusiveness means gender equality.
27.	Important points on Diversity and Inclusion: • Team Language to overcome differences in languages and the habit of "Common Language" team members to form "Sub-Groups" creating communication issues. • Acceptance and Tolerance • Create an environment that takes advantage of the diversity • Opportunity to learn other's culture • Raise Trust and Cohesiveness • Promoting collaborative culture • Respectful and inclusive team culture
28.	Common challenges in a Virtual Team: • Harder to create Team Bonding and Identity • Technology based Communication and Information Sharing lacking personal touch • Harder to track performance of individuals • Logistical challenges • Lack of or limited Non-Verbal communication • Harder to measure engagement levels • Indifference and lack of trust

29.	Some tactics for building effective Virtual Team:
	• Recognize the fact that virtual team building is different and more difficult then co-located team
	• Focus on collaboration and team norms over tools
	• Use face-to-face (by travel or video conferencing) whenever possible
	• Set expectations upfront
	• Define ground rules for interactions and inclusiveness
	• Provide constant feedback and reinforcement
	• Set time-limits for responding to each other
	• Separate time for general chit-chat (Virtual watercooler environment)
	• Provide opportunities to meet up in person (when possible)
	• Search for and provide opportunities for "Team Building"
	  ○ 2 truths and a lie
	  ○ Introducing other team member

30.	The five steps of Tuckman's Ladder are: 1) Forming 2) Storming 3) Norming 4) Performing 5) Adjourning
31.	Once a team has reached the performance stage and at that time a new team member is introduced or is replaced with someone existing in the team then the entire Team will fall back to the Storming step and they would have to be guided back ultimately into performing step.
32.	The best power of a project manager is Reward.
33.	If the project manager is new to the organization or is new to the team, then the best power for the project manager to start with is Formal.
34.	The power that gets attached to you because of your articles, your fan following and your generally accepted expertise on certain aspects is called Referent.
35.	The worst power of a PM is Coercive
36.	The various training options available to the team are: • Virtual Instructor Lead Training • Self-paced e-learning • Document review • Pairing And Mentoring
37.	The project manager or the organization must publish a training calendar and provide reminders to the team members about the availability of the training to ensure that the trainings are duly utilized for skill improvement.
38.	After the training some sort of post training evaluation must be done to ascertain the effectiveness of the training
39.	Team Assessments are conducted to essentially uncover problems and shortcomings within teams.
40.	OSCAR Model: This model is used by the leaders to help a team member plan and ultimately achieve a personal target or goal.
41.	OSCAR = Outcome, Situation, Choices / Consequences, Actions and Review.
42.	Drexler / Sibbet Model: This is a seven step Team Performance model. Using this model a Project Manager or leader may first create the team and then later sustain or manage it.
43.	Critical thinking includes disciplined, rational, logical, evidence-based thinking. It requires an open mind and the ability to analyse objectively.
44.	In Situational Leadership Delegating is done to the team members who are high on competence as well as high on commitment.
45.	In Situational Leadership Directing is done for the team members with Low Competence and High Commitment.
46.	In Situational Leadership Coaching is done for the team members with average commitment and average competence.
47.	In Situational Leadership Supporting is done for the team members with High Competence and Average Commitment.
48.	Laissez Faire: Here the leader allows the team to do what they want. Basically allowing the team to make their own decisions and establish their own goals, also referred to as taking a hands-off style.
49.	Laissez Faire leadership style usually ends up creating chaos within the team.
50.	Transactional Leadership: This kind of leadership is required when routine work has to be delegated to the team members. Mostly utilized in operational situations. This leadership style is completely goal and target focused.
51.	Servant Leader: This leadership style demonstrates commitment to serve and put other people first; focuses on other people's growth, learning, development, autonomy, and well-being; concentrates on relationships, community and collaboration; leadership is secondary and emerges after service
52.	Transformational: This leadership style focuses on inspiring the team member to transform their personality and / or skills into a better more improved version of themselves.
53.	Charismatic: This leadership styles uses the leaders energy, the way they carry themselves, their body language and their confidence to influence others.
54.	Interactional: An interactional leader is a hybrid of transformational and transactional leaders, yet with even more charisma.

55.	The main output / outcome / artefact from the process "Develop Team" is Team Performance Assessments.
56.	The main Tools & Techniques of the process "Manage Team" are: 1. Decision making 2. Emotional Intelligence 3. Conflict Management 4. Personality Profile Assessments
57.	The main components of Emotional Intelligence are: • Personal (Self) Side o Self-Awareness o Self-Regulation o Motivation • Interpersonal Side o Social Skills o Empathy
58.	Conflict Management is the application of one or more strategies for dealing with disagreements that may be detrimental to team performance.
59.	Conflicts are natural and forces the need to look for, as well as to weigh, alternatives.
60.	While resolving conflicts the focus should be on the issue and not on the individuals.
61.	Ineffective or non-existence conflict management may give rise to animosity, destructive behaviour, poor performance and reduced productivity.
62.	Common Causes of Conflict: 1. Competition 2. Differences in values, objectives and perception 3. Disagreements about role requirements, work activities and individual approaches 4. Communication breakdowns
63.	The five stages of conflict are: 1) Latent 2) Perceived 3) Felt 4) Manifest 5) Aftermath
64.	Conflict management and resolution techniques form Best to worst: 1) Collaborate / Problem Solving 2) Compromise / Reconcile 3) Smooth / Accommodate 4) Force / Direct 5) Withdraw / Avoiding
65.	Project Manager's / Leaders expected behavior during conflict resolution: • Keep communications open and respectful • Focus on issues, not the people • Focus on the present and the future, not the past • Search for alternatives together
66.	Personality refers to the individual differences in characteristic patterns of thinking, feeling, and behaving.
67.	The most popular personality assessment tool in exams is MBTI. This is a tool which is frequently used to help individuals understand their own communication preference and how they interact with others.
68.	The four pair categories in MBTI are [total of 8 basic personality types] 1. Introversion/extraversion, 2. Sensing/intuition, 3. Thinking/feeling, 4. Judging/perceiving.
69.	Influencing is the ability to coordinate and get others cooperation towards accomplishing certain goals.

70.	Political and Cultural Awareness is the knowledge of the existence of power centers within an organization or a function as well as the awareness that different people belonging to different cultures and they would need to be reached out to, differently, to get the same work done.
71.	Your team has Shared Ownership when all project team members know the vision and objectives. The project team owns the deliverables and outcomes of the project.
72.	Your team is a High Performing team if they trust each other and collaborate. The project team adapts to changing situations and is resilient in the face of challenges. The project team feels empowered and empowers and recognizes members of the project team.
73.	The amount of material used, scrap discarded, and amount of rework indicate that resources are being used efficiently or not.
74.	The Main output / outcome / artefact from the process "Manage Team" is Issue Log.
End Of Ninja Drill	

10.5 Manage Communications:

This process is about executing the Communications Management Plan and taking care of the "Ad Hoc" requests for project information by stakeholders.
During this process, the Project Manager and the Project Management Team has to use more of Leadership techniques to ensure that the execution of the Communications Management Plan is effective.

A variety of communication skills are needed during this process.

COMMUNICATION SKILLS

- CULTURAL CONSIDERATIONS
- INTELLIGENCE
- KNOWLEDGE BASE
- BODY LANGUAGE
- EMOTIONAL QUOTIENT
- SEMANTICS
- LANGUAGE SKILLS
- CHOICE OF WORDS

- EMOTIONAL STATUS
- AUTHORITY/POSITION
- FOCUS ON OBJECTIVE
- CHOICE OF METHOD AND TECHNOLOGY
- PERCEIVED CREDIBILITY
- CONTEXT AND REFERENCE
- DIRECT/INDIRECT COMMUNICATION

While communicating one must keep in mind the percentage of communication that is transmitted.

COMMUNICATION SURPRISE

SURPRISE SURPRISE

WORDS ACCOUNT FOR 7% OF MESSAGE

TONALITY ACCOUNTS FOR 38% OF MESSAGE

BODY LANGUAGE ACCOUNTS FOR 55% OF MESSAGE.

100%

This should explain why the first choice should be to have a face to face communication. If that is not possible one must try to talk on phone and only when that too is not possible, go for emails. Basically the more important the discussion the higher should the sum of the percentages, preferably 100%, should be. It is important to note for your scientific brain that this percentage distribution has been done only for the English language and none of the other more scientific languages like Hindi (and all its derivatives including other native languages of India), Japanese or Chinese (I am sure there are more such scientific languages in this amazing world but I know of only these three as of now).

10.5.1 Main Tools and Techniques of this process: -

Communication Technology and Communication Methods: discussed earlier during the process *PLAN COMMUNICATIONS MANAGEMENT*.

Communication Skills (there are 4 elements in this group and all the four are used in this process). This group contains some essential communication skills that the project managers or the responsible project team member must possess or use to communicate effectively.

- **Communication Competence** is a combination of clarity of purpose of the communication, leadership behavior, alertness towards relationships and "What to say to whom, when and under what circumstances to obtain what kind of effect".
- **Feedback** is essential to any kind of interactive communication. Feedback is what helps assess if the communication was a success or not. Feedback also helps in revisiting the method, technology, and style of communication, if need be.
- **Nonverbal communication** is important as it accounts for 93% of the total communication (38% for tonality and 55% of body language) and hence the project

managers must use tonality, gestures, expressions and standing style to emphasize the verbal communication. When on a telephonic conversation the receiver is getting only 45% of the communication (words 7% and Tonality 38%) and hence modulation of voice, gaps in words, pitch and volume must be in line with the message being communicated.

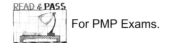

- **Presentations** are a very important form of communications. There are various kinds of presentations (from slide-based to casual conversation based, from speech based to document walkthrough based etc.) and the project manager must use the most appropriate form of presentation based on the situation, needs of the stakeholders and the end effect/reaction that the project manager wants after the presentation.

Project Management Information System (PMIS) is a general term for a system (automated or manual or a combination of both) which facilitates the storage, organization, and retrieval of Information. There are a variety of tools/systems for this from Cloud-based, server-based to traditional filing based corporate libraries. In some organizations, this now also includes the social media platforms as well.

Project Reporting is all about collecting the project reports on the health and other aspects of the project and transmitting to as per the Communication Management Plan to the apt stakeholders. Different stakeholders and groups of stakeholders usually need different levels of project information.

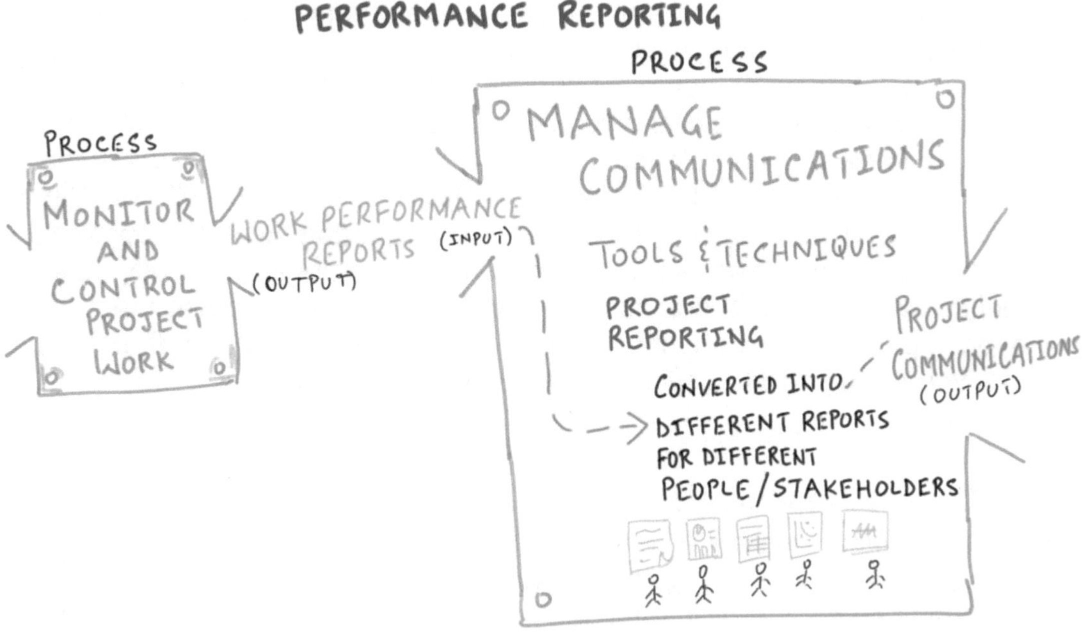

Interpersonal And Team Skills like Active Listening, Conflict Management, Cultural Awareness, Meeting Management, Networking, and Political Awareness would be needed to actually execute the communication plan as per the required strategy mentioned in the "***Plan Stakeholder Engagement***".

The tool and technique "Project Reporting" is unique to this process viz., ***MANAGE COMMUNICATIONS***.
The group of tools and techniques called "Communication Skills" is a tools and technique in only two processes and they are ***MANAGE COMMUNICATIONS*** and ***MANAGE STAKEHOLDER ENGAGEMENT***.

Active Listening, though part of Interpersonal and Team Skills, is important enough to be discussed separately and in greater details. Active Listening is one of the most important communication skills and yet the most underrated by most managers and leaders. I have discussed this with example a bit later in this book when we talk about stakeholders. However at this point let us talk about the various kinds of Active Listening. There are two main purpose of active listening. One is making the speaker comfortable that they are actually being heard and two, the listener fully comprehends exactly what is being spoken about before the listener begins to speak.

1) *Reflecting*: this involves repeating gist of what is being spoken about to confirm to the speaker that you are listening and understanding as well as trying to confirm their understanding.
2) *Attending / Attentive*: this involves providing non-verbal cues and signs to the speaker that you are in fact listening and understanding them. This is usually done by placing both hands on your lap (if sitting in front of the speaker without a table in between) or table, leaning forward, doing nothing else and maintaining eye contact.
3) *Following*: this involves giving verbal and non-verbal cues (often together) to let the speaker know that the listener is following and understanding everything that is being said. Asking open ended questions like, "Then what happened?" or "Can you tell me more about ……" etc., help the listener to understand the entire context around what is being spoken or narrated. Nodding head at appropriate intervals makes the speaker feel that the listener is following them and in fact understanding them. If on phone or even in person, "Yes, oh, or aha" could also be used to ensure that the speaker know that you are trying to follow them and understand them.

10.5.2 Main Outcome from this process: -

Project Communications are a collection of all the project information, reports, emails etc., which are being transmitted as per the Communication Management Plan as well as those which are due to some ad-hoc information requested by some key stakeholders and not covered in any other communication so far.

This output, Project Communications, becomes input to four other processes and they are ***DIRECT AND MANAGE PROJECT WORK***, ***CLOSE PROJECT OR PHASE***, ***MONITOR COMMUNICATIONS,*** and ***MONITOR STAKEHOLDER ENGAGEMENT***

And because of the findings and learnings from this process the **Project Management Plans** (like Communications Management Plan and/or Stakeholder Management Plan), **Project**

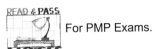

Documents (like Issue Logs, Stakeholder Register) and **Organizational Process Assets** (like Time Sheets, Communication Templates, and Organizational Records) may need to be updated.

10.6 Manage Quality: -

The whole idea of this process is to execute and audit the processes, during execution, in such a way that the things are done right the first time while doing it. It's an execution thing. *MANAGE QUALITY* is an entire process that is dedicated to "Preventive Quality Measures". While the final inspections and testing would be done in Quality Control, the execution would be done in such a way using such processes and checklists and duly audited to ensure compliance to processes, that when the product is checked nothing gets rejected. *MANAGE QUALITY* is a way of execution that "Assures" that once the product is delivered it would meet all its Quality Requirements.

A lot of people find this part hard to grasp and still think it's nothing but Quality Control and involves testing and inspections. Let me give you one of the simplest examples to show you the profound importance of this process.

Let us say, one day a guy walked into his home and finds his wife in the kitchen cutting some vegetables in a hurried fashion. She tells him that he needs to go out for some grocery shopping urgently as her parents (His In-Laws) are coming over for dinner. The guy is suddenly thrown into top gear and he is all action now. While she is reciting the things that need to be bought he goes about changing his clothes, getting his car keys, getting some bags and all the while making mental notes of what his wife is telling him to fetch. He gets into his car and he decides to go to the best place for grocery. He enters the grocery store, buys some stuff that he could remember, and calls his wife to confirm some of the other things she said. He buys more stuff and gets into his car to go to another grocery shop where they have a higher grade of some of the stuff that he wants to buy. But then he calls his wife again asking about the quantity, shape, size, brand etc. This time she loses her temper "Why can't you remember things and don't keep calling I am busy too". The poor fellow moves from one store to another, he takes more time and all this while the stress is building up. When he finally reaches home and keeps the bags on the kitchen counter, his wife does the Quality Control, she finds so many things wrong that she feels as though all this time has been wasted. He got a different brand of butter or too less quantity of spring onions, or he got larger carrots instead of baby prewashed carrots and there were some things he completely forgot. See he worked hard, actually much harder than he should have, he took stress, and zigzagged from one store to another and it hurts him when she points out so many mistakes with his hard work. Sounds familiar. These things happen in the professional world as well. Ok! Let us conduct this scenario again and this time using the "*MANAGE QUALITY*" way. This guy walks into his home, his wife tells him the things he needs to get urgently. He quietly gets hold of a paper pad and a pencil. As she tells him what to get he asks her questions like "which brand?", "how much quantity?" and such other specific questions. She may not appreciate his questioning as this appears to be taking too much time. However, he patiently ignores her impatience and irritation and continues to coolly make a comprehensive list. Once he has noted things down, he gets into his car and he already has a mental map of the exact sequence of stores he would go to. He checks if he is carrying the discount cards for the stores he is going to. He goes from one store to another in the sequence decided, he does not get distracted by other sales and offerings on display and buys only the stuff he needs to get as per the list. During all this time he does not call back home, he does not take stress and he ends up getting home faster. Wife does the Quality Control again and finds hardly any mistakes. Both styles of working involved work but the latter was the "Quality" way. I think this gives you a clear picture of what exactly is "*MANAGE QUALITY*".

I know some of you may call this "Quality Assurance" and you would not be entirely wrong. The only difference is that "Quality Assurance" is an organization wide initiative that is responsible for creating processes, checklists, tools and techniques, templates and collect important quality matrices so that they can be used by the "*MANAGE QUALITY*" process for each of the projects. Simply said, Quality Assurance is Organization Wide while *MANAGE QUALITY* is for a specific project.

The project manager and the project team may use some of the services of "Quality Assurance" department to execute some of the *MANAGE QUALITY* work. If the project itself lacks some of the quality-related expertize, professionals from the Quality Assurance department may be called upon for help.

MANAGE QUALITY is the concept of "Doing it right the first time itself" and therefore this is for the entire project team and not just for the quality professionals.

MANAGE QUALITY

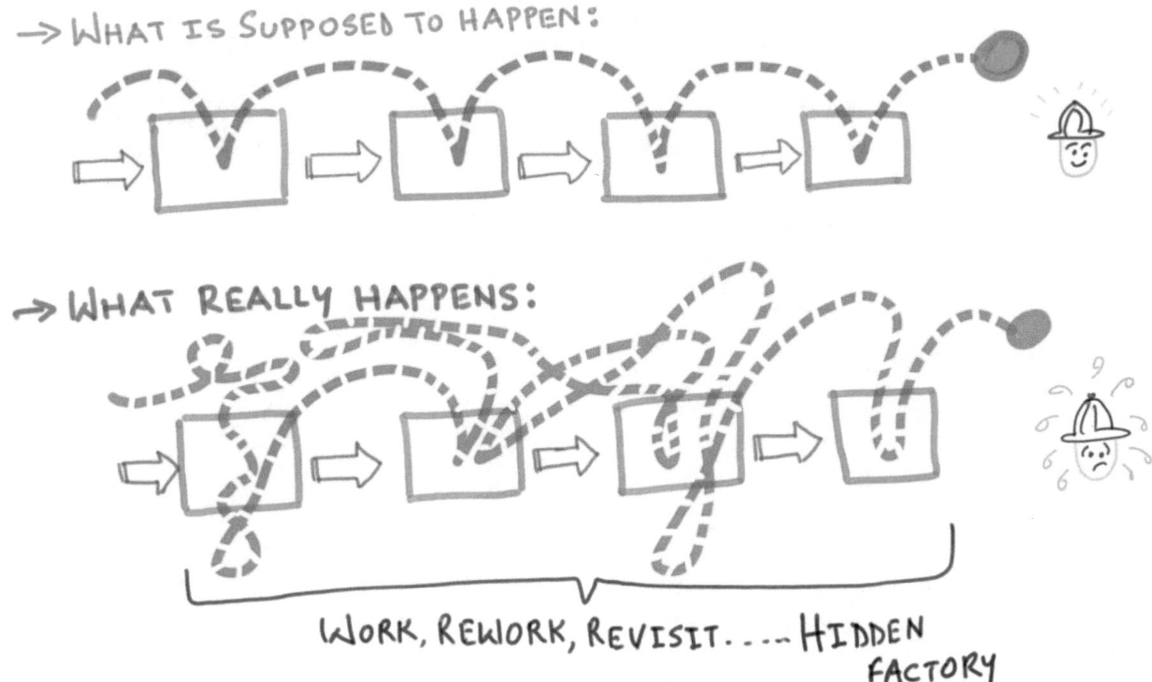

At this time it's very important to understand the relationship between *MANAGE QUALITY* and *CONTROL QUALITY*. *MANAGE QUALITY* is an execution thing to assure that the product meets all quality requirements. The inspection and testing are done in the process of *CONTROL QUALITY*. The "Feedback" about the effectiveness of the process *MANAGE QUALITY* would be given by the *CONTROL QUALITY* process. Remember from the time we discussed the Process Groups / IPECC where it was mentioned that Controlling Processes work in tandem with the Execution processes and there is constant feedback from Controlling processes to Execution processes.

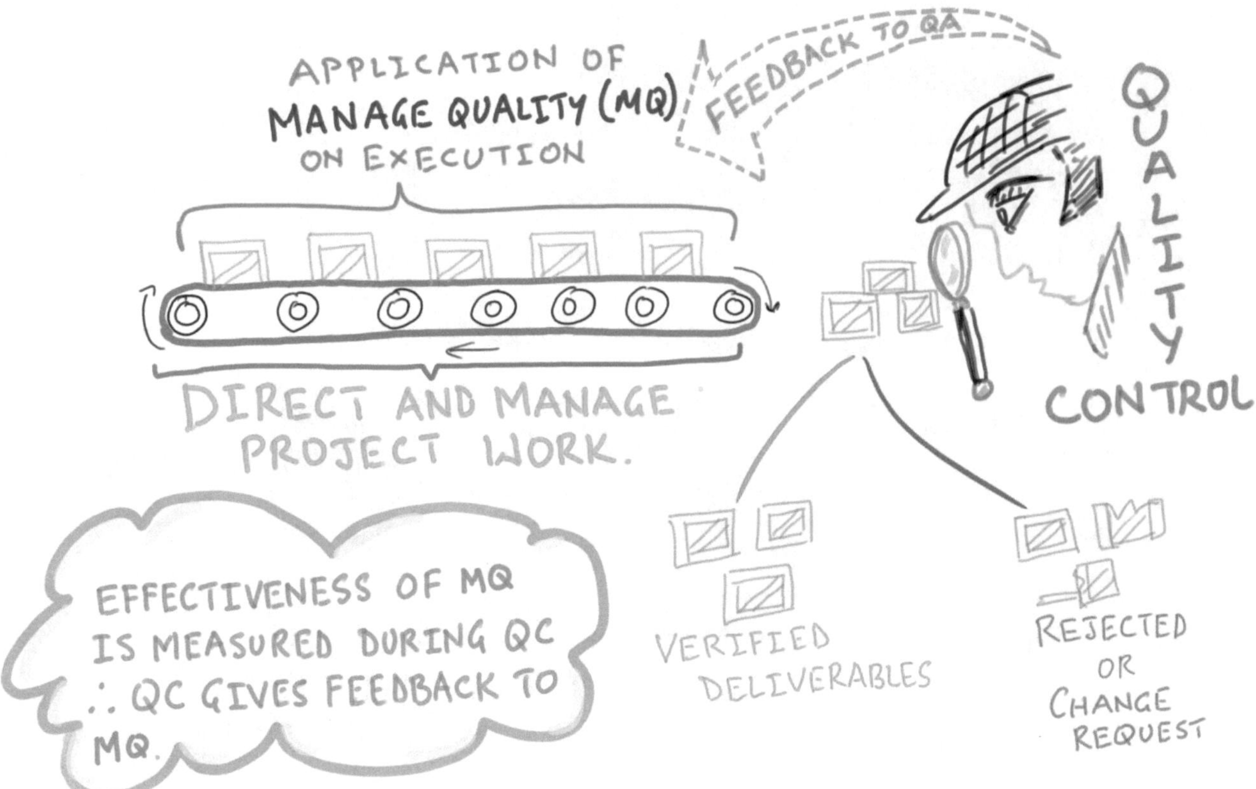

Let us now get into the details of this process.

10.6.1 Main Tools and Techniques of this process: -

Checklist is a document that is used during execution to either follow certain predetermined steps of execution or ensure that things are not missed during execution. This is one of the foremost tools in "prevention" of quality issues. For each of my training I have a comprehensive "Checklist" to ensure that I do not forget any of the training props or ideas or supporting documents right down to seating arrangements and signing of the feedback and attendance. Checklists are responsible for bringing about a lot of consistency in the work and assures that certain common "mistakes" (errors of commission as well as omissions) are prevented.

Quality Checklist					
Project:					Date:
	Verfification				
Quality Item	Yes	No	N/A	Date	Comments
Does the project have an approved quality management plan?					
Has the quality management plan been reviewed by all stakeholders?					
Do all stakeholders have access to the quality management plan?					
Is the quality management plan consistent with the rest of the overall project plan?					
Have product quality metrics been established, reviewed, and agreed upon?					
Have process quality metrics been established, reviewed, and agreed upon?					
Do all metrics support a quality standard which is acceptable to the customer?					
Do all metrics have agreed upon collection mechanisms?					
Do all metrics have an agreed upon collection frequency?					
Have quality metrics review meetings been scheduled throughout the project's duration?					
Are all metrics clear, measurable, controllable, and reportable?					
Is the project team familiar with the project's quality review process?					
Does the project have an appropriate number of resources assigned for quality assurance and control?					

Process Analysis identifies processes that may need some kind of improvement. Every single project that happens within an organization is also a very good opportunity to improve the quality processes while using them. The process improvement may be about creating a better measurement tool, making the process optimized towards a tighter benchmark, removing some wasteful and needless steps, adopting an industrial benchmark like six-sigma etc.

Root Cause Analysis (RCA) is a structured and step by step process of breaking down the problem/issue in such a way that the underlying root-cause for the problem/issue is identified. Once this underlying cause is removed the problem/issue is resolved. This prevents the team from making guesses about the cause and wasting time with causes that may not have a direct relationship with the problem at hand. **5 Whys** is one of the techniques of "Root Cause Analysis". The concept of 5 Whys is, a team looks at the issue or a problem and asks "Why did this happen?" From the answer received ask the next why on the answer itself "So why did this happen?" and so on. Usually, it is seen that by the time you reach the 5th why you would have reached the absolute "Root Cause" of the problem. It is not necessary that the root cause has to be found out only by the 5th "Why", sometimes the root cause is visible after 3rd or 4th why and sometimes it's visible after the 5th why.

Please remember not to confuse between Root Cause Analysis with Cause And Effect Analysis. Most of the people use Cause and Effect Analysis (also called Fishbone diagram or Ishikawa Diagram) and call it "Root Cause Analysis". These two are actually different in reality as well as in PMP® exams. Cause and effect is one of the tools for identifying the "Root Causes" of a problem but is not a Root Cause Analysis itself. This is the reason for Cause and Effect Analysis also to be called a "Why-Why" diagram. Cause and Effect Analysis is one of the "diagramming tools" to help with Root Cause Analysis. Yeah! Yeah! I know, too similar, but come on, you do not call a very good "Camera" as "Photography" do you? No! A good camera is a tool for "Photography". The quality of your photography would be resultant of how well you know how to use the camera. I guess you got it now. ☺

Affinity Diagram is a tool that has been discussed before and you are aware of it. I am repeating the image of affinity diagram here again to help you recollect.

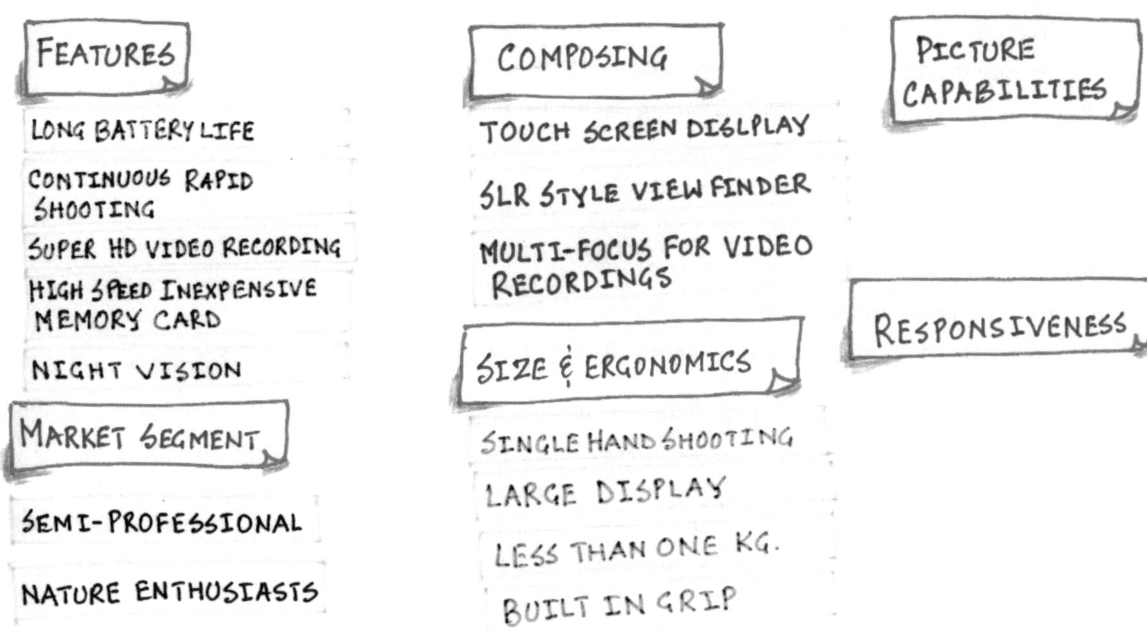

In this process, Affinity diagram can help organize potential causes of defects into groups with interrelations such that it would be easy to identify areas that would need most focus to prevent defects.

Cause-And-Effect Diagram is a very powerful diagram that was invented by Dr. Ishikawa and this diagram is known by three other names viz., Ishikawa Diagram, Fishbone Diagram (well it actually looks like a fishbone structure after you have consumed a river fish, something very popular in Japan. My apologies to the vegetarians and vegans but this was a name given by Japanese and I had no say in it.) and Why-Why diagram (because it can be used also for 5 Why analysis or Root Cause Analysis). The purpose of this diagram is to, first identify all possible major "Causes" of a problem and then further breakdown each of the "Major Causes" into "Sub Causes" and even "Sub – Sub Causes". Once all the major causes have been decomposed then voting, cluster voting or brainstorming is used for eliminating the "improbable causes". This would leave some of the sub-causes that just cannot be eliminated and that becomes the focus area. This diagram prevents the team from striking out in every direction to solve a problem and wasting time and resources, by focusing on the critical few. I have used this tool several times in projects and problem solving and find tremendous value in it. It would be worth your time to go through it in a bit of more details.
Let us go through the steps of making one with an example.
The first thing to be done is to clearly state the problem as shown below.

My first ever consulting in Bahrain (a small and rather beautiful pearl of an island in the Gulf region of Middle East) was for the US Navy. US Navy has one of the largest naval ports in Bahrain at a place called Juffair. I was to consult the “Supply Chain Management” group. Since I was a civilian and not even a US Citizen, there was no way the consulting would be done inside the military zone of Juffair, the US Navy guys rented a nice conference room in a hotel called Novatel built on some reclaimed area. Inside the conference room was a corner that always had a lot of stuff to munch on as well as a beautiful coffee machine. I usually do not drink coffee more than once a day (just after breakfast) but the coffee coming out of that machine was so aromatic that I too was consuming 2 to 3 cups during the 8 to 9 hrs we were in that room. As for the Americans, well they were drinking more coffee than water. I noticed that the coffee grounds that this machine was using was called “Arabica”. I loved it. However on the 4th day, when we entered the conference room we found that the coffee machine was replaced with a brand new shining coffee machine. It took us a bit of time for us to figure out what to press and where to press to get a small cup of coffee. It was an Italian espresso machine. I noticed that the rest of the ingredients, like the coffee grounds, were the same. However when we tried the coffee, we almost retched. It was horrible and had a sharp stench to it. I almost gaged and had to visit the washroom to rinse my mouth. Several of us had this issue. One of the participants, a very sharp young person, by the name of Debra (I still remember her name) made a satirical remark. “Perhaps Mr Veee Jaay (she could never get my name right) could use one of his fancy project management tricks to find why we are being served such horrible coffee”, she said. I suddenly realized that this was a great time to teach them the power of a great tool called cause and effect. The rest of the series of diagrams following, is what we did there and eventually narrowed down on the probable cause.

CAUSE AND EFFECT DIAGRAM

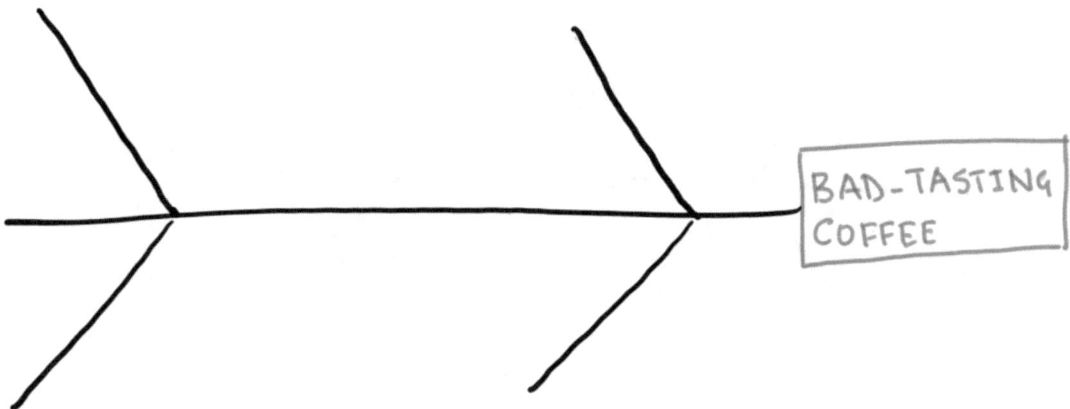

Once the problem is stated, an attempt is made to find all possible causes for this problem. This identification of the problems is done in a structured manner. First, all possible “Major Causes” are identified and listed around the problem line as shown below. In most cases, its best to start with 4 M's (Man / People, Machine, Material, and Method) and then extend the number of Major Causes based on the problem at hand.

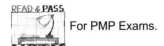

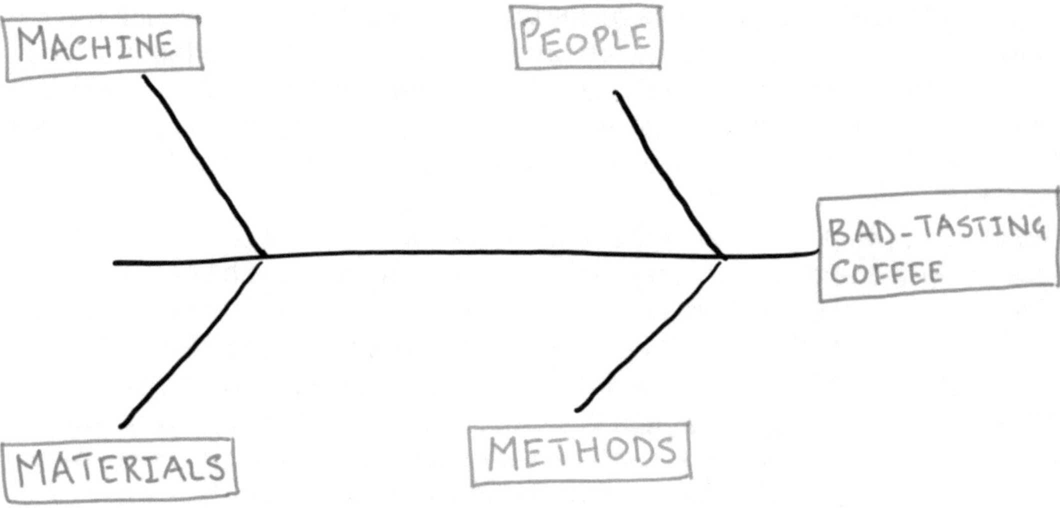

The Major Causes are broken down to the most granular levels possible and done in a structured manner, one Major Cause at a time. A Major Cause may be broken down into various sub-causes and each of these Sub-causes may be further broken down into sub-sub-causes.

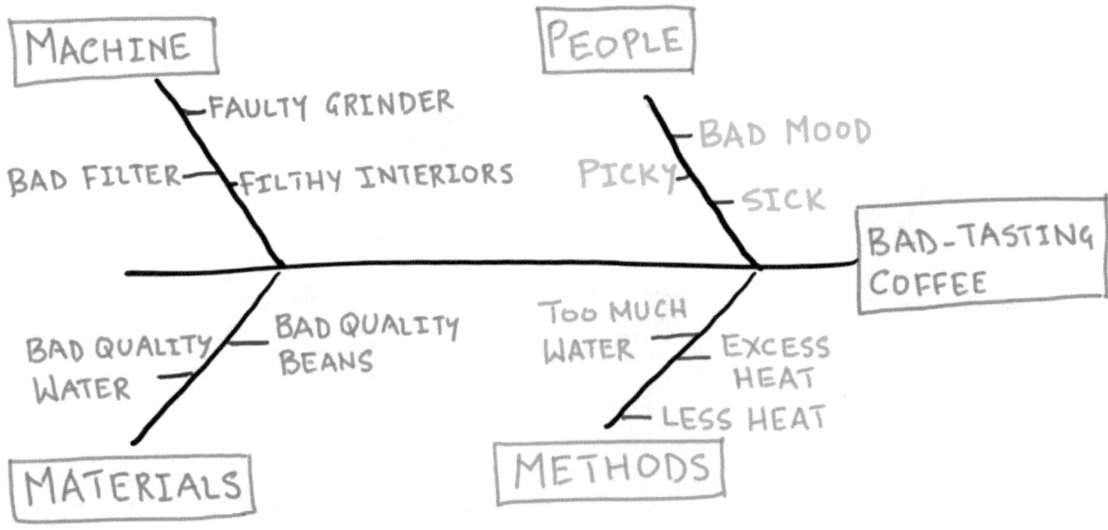

Once all causes are identified an attempt would be made to eliminate the "improbable causes" (causes that may not be responsible given the situation and surrounding information). Once all possible eliminations are done then the ones which cannot be eliminated have to be treated as suspect cases or suspect problem areas and these are to be worked upon to finally solve the problem.

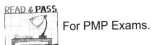

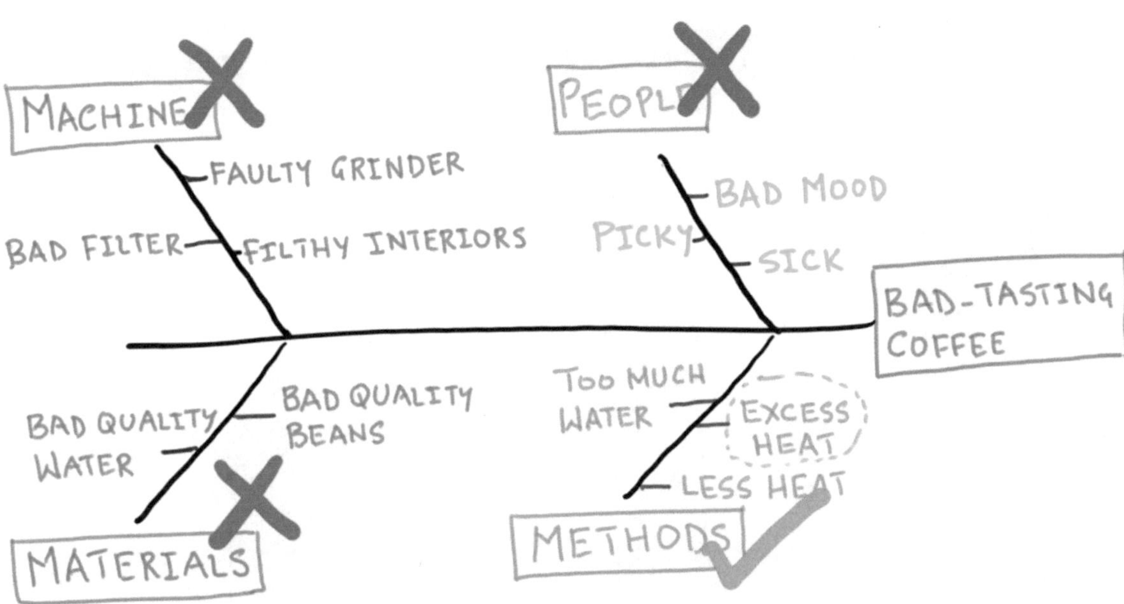

If you had read my problem statement well you would notice that this was not a case of bad mood, or picky people or people being sick, when we complained of bad coffee. Most of us had that experience and hence all the causes connected to "People" could not at all be the case. We eliminated that. Machine could be filthy, or there could have been a faulty grinder or it could be fitted with a bad filter. Though it is possible, the chances for that to happen in a brand new machine and that too implemented by a luxury hotel was rather improbable. Hence we just parked it for the time being. Since we had already noticed that the materials were all the same as were used in the previous machine, hence there was no way that materials could be the reason for bad tasking coffee. We eliminated that too. The only thing we did not know or confirm about was the method. Chances were that there was something wrong with the method of coffee preparation which was producing such horrible coffee. We all selected that as the main cause. However, since a complaint was made with the management, an engineer had come over to rectify the issue and when he finished we had asked him as to what was the issue. To which he replied that someone in the testing division of the hotel procurement group had tried to test the limit of its thermostat and had not brought it back to normal and therefore all coffee solution was being burnt inside. If this does not show case the amazing power of the tool, than what will?

This technique saves time and rework by making people focused on problem and understanding the problem before trying to solve it.
This tool is used for prospective and potential problems as well, during planning. This tool can be used for identifying risks as well. This tool is best used in a team setting.

Flowcharts, do we really have to talk about it? You have been making it since childhood. Here the flow chart (or activity diagram) can be used for documenting and representing all the steps that result in defects and errors, or it could be used to lay down the process with areas where more defects happen.

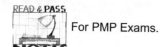

Histogram is one of the very first tools you would learn in "Statistical Graphs". This graph shows the frequencies of any reading. I guess an example would refresh your childhood memories of "Mathematics Classes" (did I hear some cold sighs!!?).

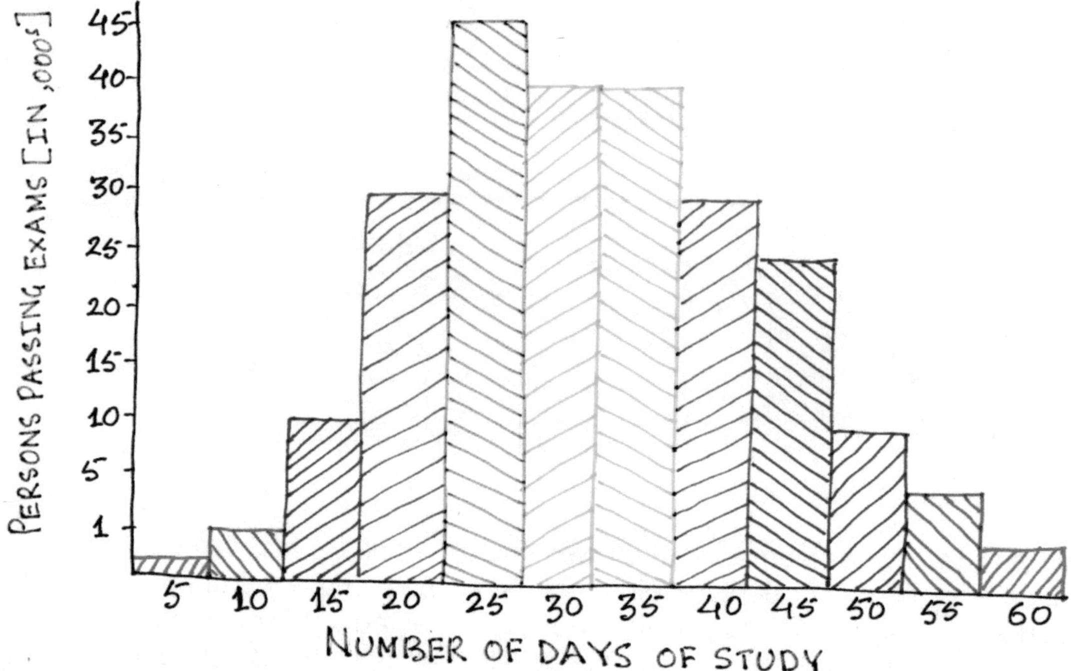

Matrix Diagrams is a tool that illustrates the critical relationships between or among two or more groups. It can be enhanced to show things like the strength of the relationship or the different aspects of the relationship.

MATRIX DIAGRAM
(FOR TEA)

CAUSE / EFFECT	TASTE	VOLUME	TEMPERATURE	COUNT
KETTLE FOR BOILING		○	○	6
ADDING WATER	△	○	◉	13
ADDING TEA	◉			9
ADDING SUGAR	○			3
ADDING MILK	◉	△	△	11
STIRRING	○			3
TOTALS	25	7	13	

LEGEND: △ = WEAK = 1
○ = MODERATE = 3
◉ = STRONG = 9

I hope you do remember that there are several types of matrix diagrams, something we have already discussed earlier. There are L Shaped, T Shaped, Y Shaped, Roof Shaped, C Shaped, and X Shaped Matrix Diagrams.

Scatter Diagrams is a graphical tool that tries to understand the correlation (or the lack of it) between two variables. E.g., Let us say that you feel that in your organization you are getting a lot of defects after the project is handed over to the customer. Right now you see that you only do 2 rounds of testing before handing over the product to the customer. You decide that you must have 4 rounds of testing before the handover. However, you would need to check if this move really reduced the latent defects. For this, you would have to plot a scatter diagram.

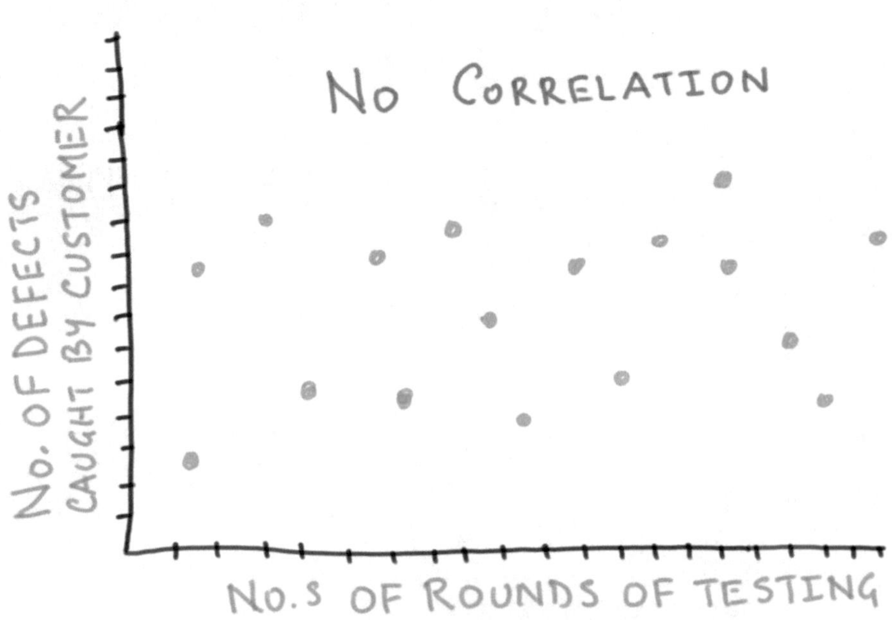

However, if you decide to increase the number of test cases while keeping the rounds of testing as two. You may find the following.

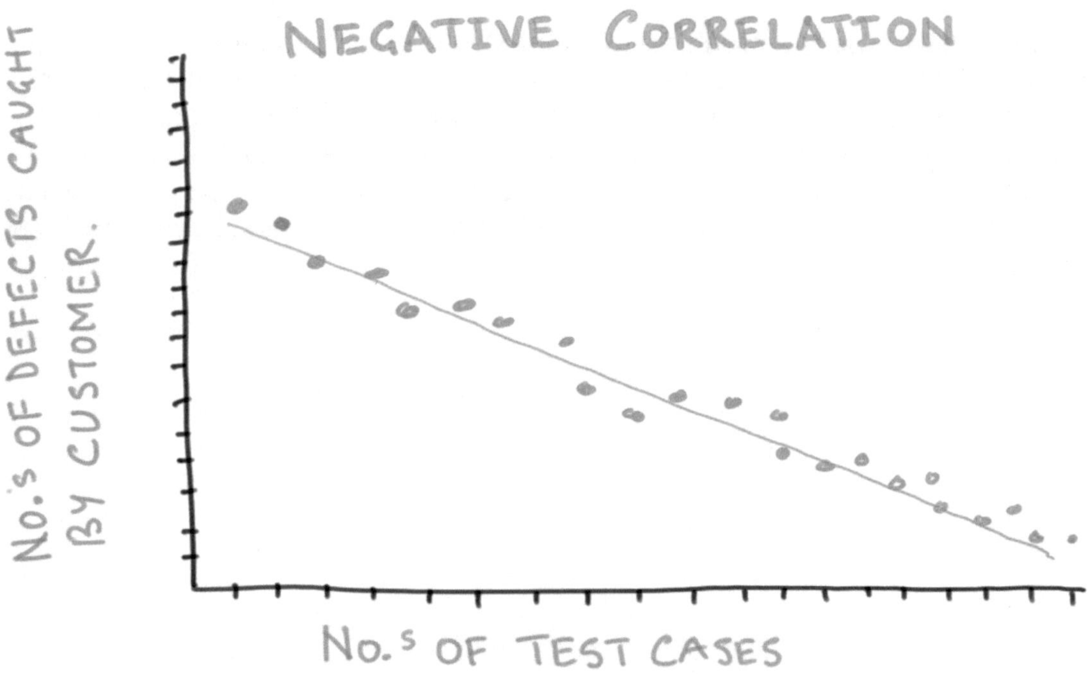

This shows a “Negative Correlation” something which you wanted to see in the first place. This shows that there is no correlation between increasing the no. of rounds of

testing to the number of defects, but there is a negative correlation between the number of test cases and the number of defects found by the customer.
The other possible outcomes from a scatter diagrams can be

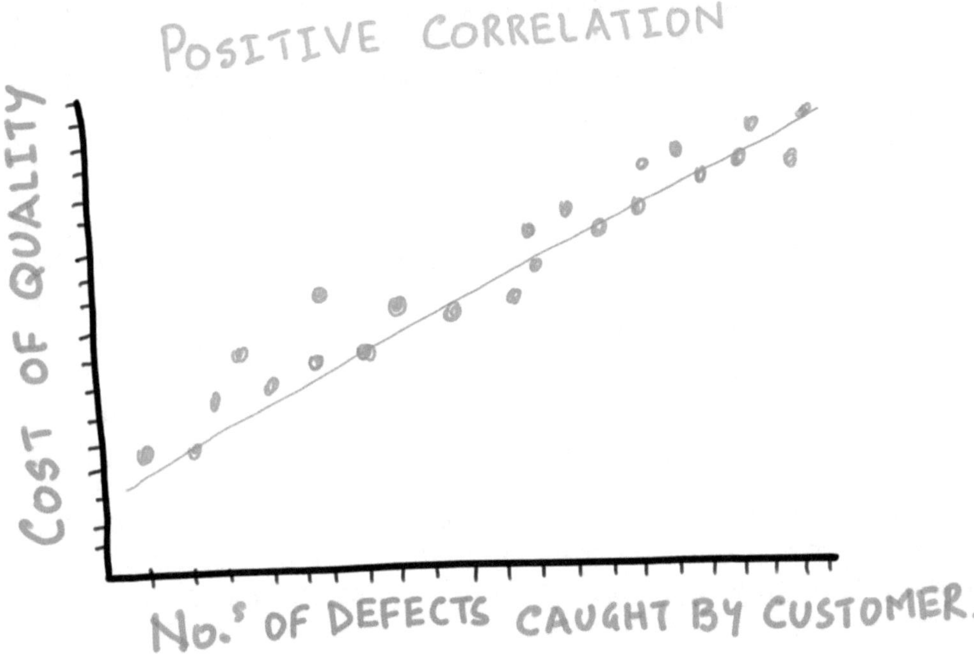

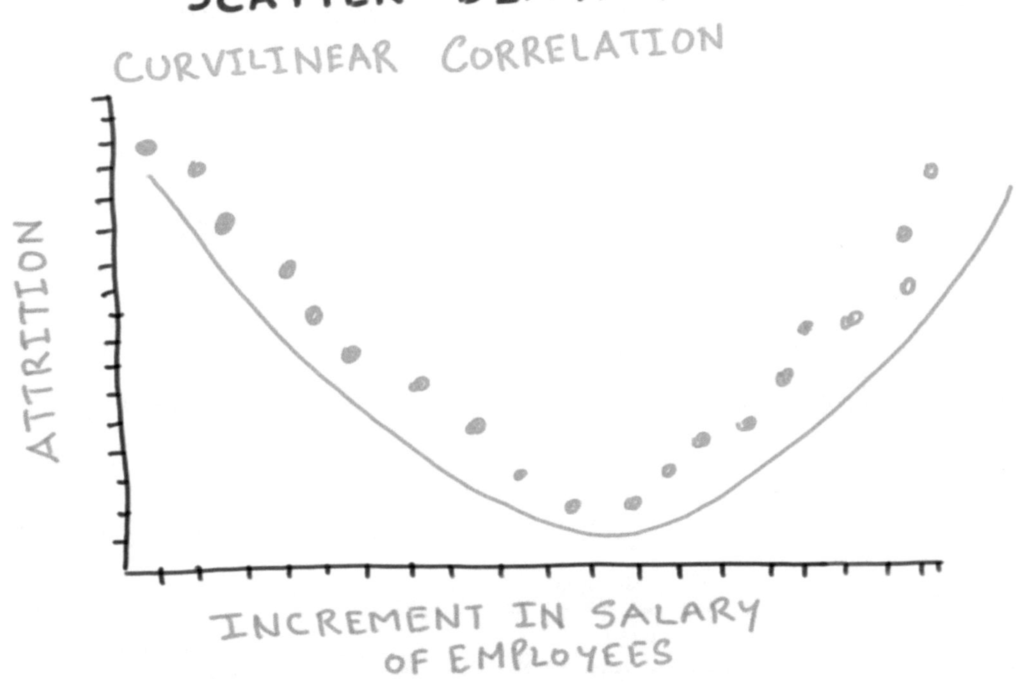

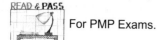

Audits also called "**Quality Audits**" are usually conducted by teams/agencies outside of the project team to independently assess the level of compliance with the Quality Assurance processes and checklists. These are usually done by external quality consultants, Quality Assurance Department representatives, internal audit teams, PMO and such. Audits are done to ensure compliance.

Design For X (also called Design for Excellence or simply DfX) is a mechanism by which some technical aspects of the product (which is the "x" factor of the product) which needs more focus than others and the entire designing of the product would be based on that. Ideally one would like to have all possible features in a product that is best in industry, in a specific product, but that is just not possible. Therefore specific aspects of the design may be focused on more than others to create a unique selling proposition for that product. Let us take an example. There is a company from one of the Scandinavian countries that makes furnitures. These furnitures are not really known for beauty and aesthetics and yet they sell the most in the world. Every single furniture set from this company is designed in such a way that it would be excessively easy to transport them to the buyer's place (mostly by the buyer themselves) in a disassembled state, and assembled by the buyers themselves without any technical help. This company's USP is great furniture which is value for money and is "assemble yourself". Which means that this company designs each of the furniture sets using Design For self-assembly, where self-assembly is that X which is the prominent factor of design. Hence when it comes to quality, the majority of the quality aspects, in this organization, would be around "Easy Storage", "Ease of assembly", "Ease of Disassembly", "Availability of all parts and tools in the box" and so on. Not so much on aesthetics or safety or durability.

Problem Solving is all about finding solutions for issues and problems or even potential issues and problems. This method could include Critical Thinking, Lateral Thinking and several other methods connected to constructive problem solving. Problem Solving usually has the following steps.

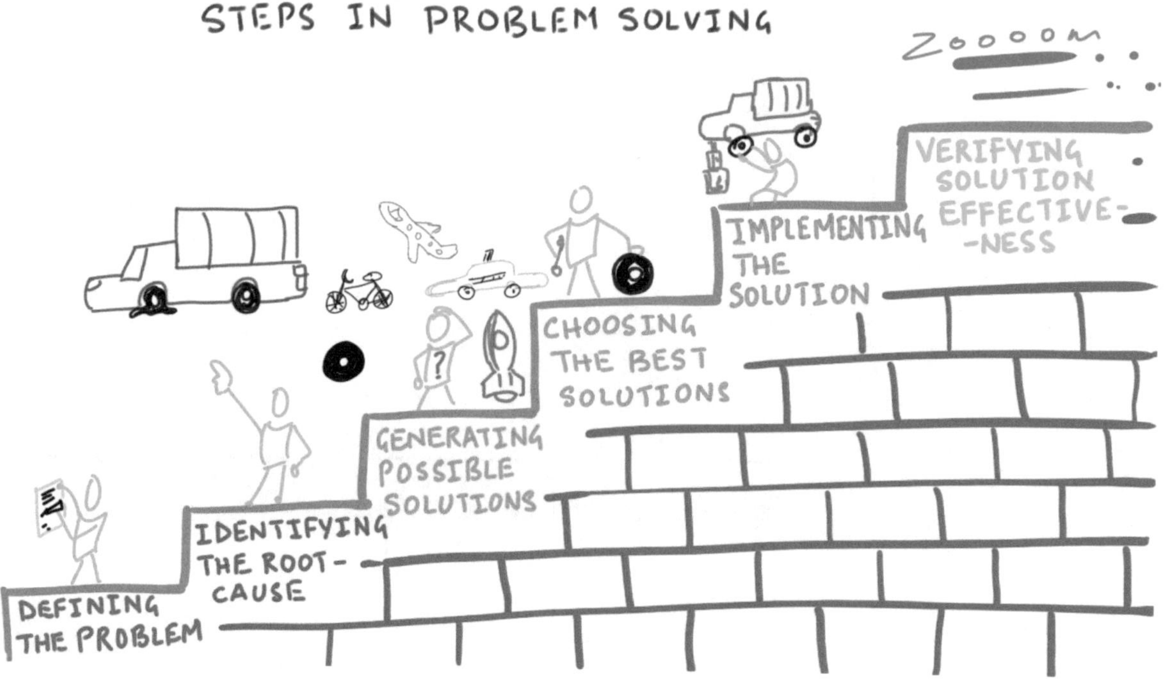

Quality Improvement Methods: There are standard methods like Lean, Six Sigma, PDCA and Kaizen, for improving quality processes.

10.6.2 Main Outcome from this process: -

Quality Reports are a general report on current "Quality Conditions" of the project. This is a report that basically shows quality issues reported, who reported those issues, their current status of resolution, actions taken, costs expended on quality related work and issues, some indicators of process benchmark breaches, recommendations for improvements, some important matrices dully filled in based on what was decided during quality planning, corrective or preventive actions taken etc. This becomes input to 5 other processes and they are *MONITOR AND CONTROL PROJECT WORK*, *CLOSE PROJECT OR PHASE*, *VALIDATE SCOPE*, *MANAGE COMMUNICATIONS,* and *CONTROL PROCUREMENTS*.

Test And Evaluation Documents are filled in checklists during execution, reviews conducted and important matrices collected during execution which needs to be submitted to the process "*CONTROL QUALITY*" before inspection and other tests and evaluations can be conducted in the process "*CONTROL QUALITY*". These are those documents that inform the *CONTROL QUALITY* process what all has been actually done in the execution for prevention. The level and intensity of testing and inspections would depend on this input in "*CONTROL QUALITY*".

Change Requests may need to be created if there are some corrective or preventive actions that need to be undertaken which in turn have alteration effect on one or more baseline elements. And all change requests become an input to the process Integrated Change Control. CCB in ICC.

10.7 Conduct Procurement Management: -

This process begins when the RFP or RFQ is being distributed to the prospective bidders and ends with the signing of the contract with the selected vendor. Remember all the "Procurement Documents" were made in the planning process discussed earlier viz., *PLAN PROCUREMENT MANAGEMENT*. This process, *CONDUCT PROCUREMENT MANAGEMENT,* is the execution of the Procurement Management Plan to select the best most relevant vendor for the work to be outsourced. This process starts when the procuring organization distributes or broadcasts a document called "Request For Proposal" (RFP) or "Request for Information" (RFI) or "Request for Bid / Quotation" (RFB/Q).
RFP is needed when the product / Work / Service needed is not available off the shelf and hence the bidders have to be explained in details what the requirements are what are the terms and conditions to be fulfilled if anyone chooses to work on the outsourced work. RFI is meant only to understand the capacity, capability, availability and other crucial details about the prospective bidders before the RFP could be issued to them. The information collected from replies to RFI about bidders could be used for pre-qualification. Pre-qualifications are some conditions and capability requirements that must be met by the prospective bidder even before they can send a proposal to the procuring organization in reply to the RFP. Pre-Qualifications like "Companies with less than 2,000 engineers need not apply", "Must have CMMI level certification", "Must be listed on the local stock exchange", "Must have

documented proof of having worked on some specific technologies" and so on. RFB / Q is sent out to the prospective bidders when the work/product/ service needed is "Off The Shelf" or "Ready Made" and for this, the bidders return "Bids / Quotations".

RFP is a comprehensive documentation and must have all the elements that must allow a Bidder to make a complete proposal along with a clear understanding of what they are getting into.

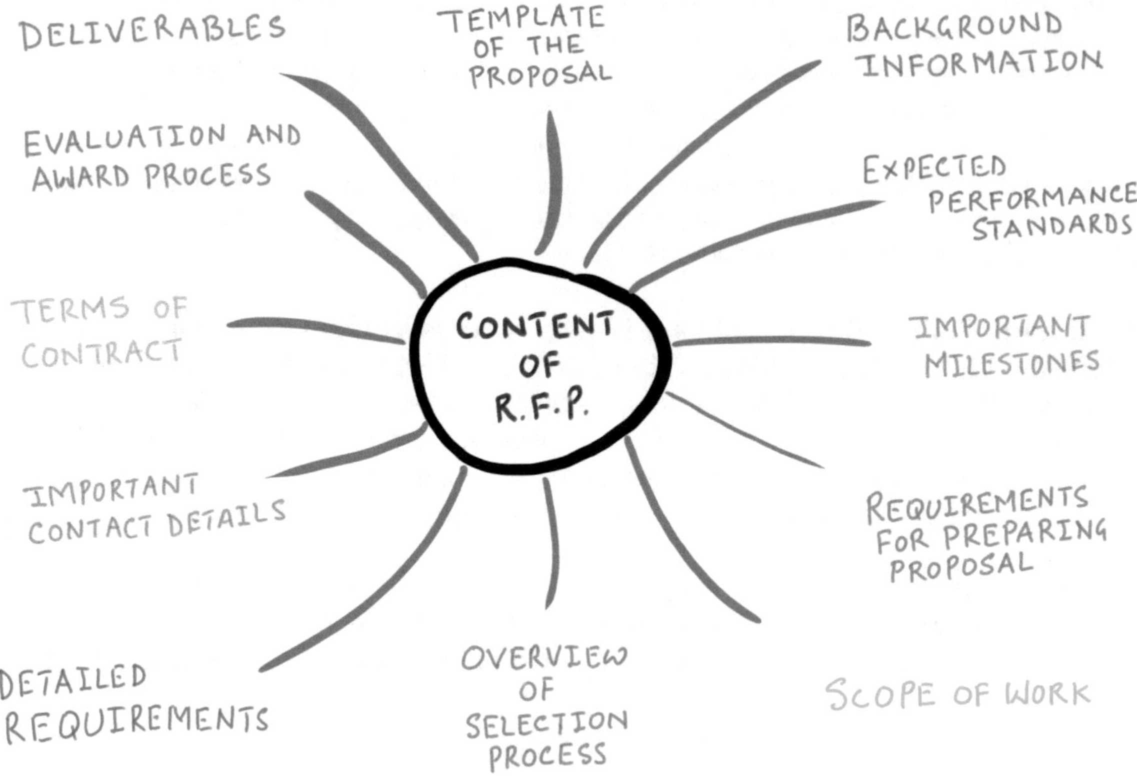

So, what is done in this process?

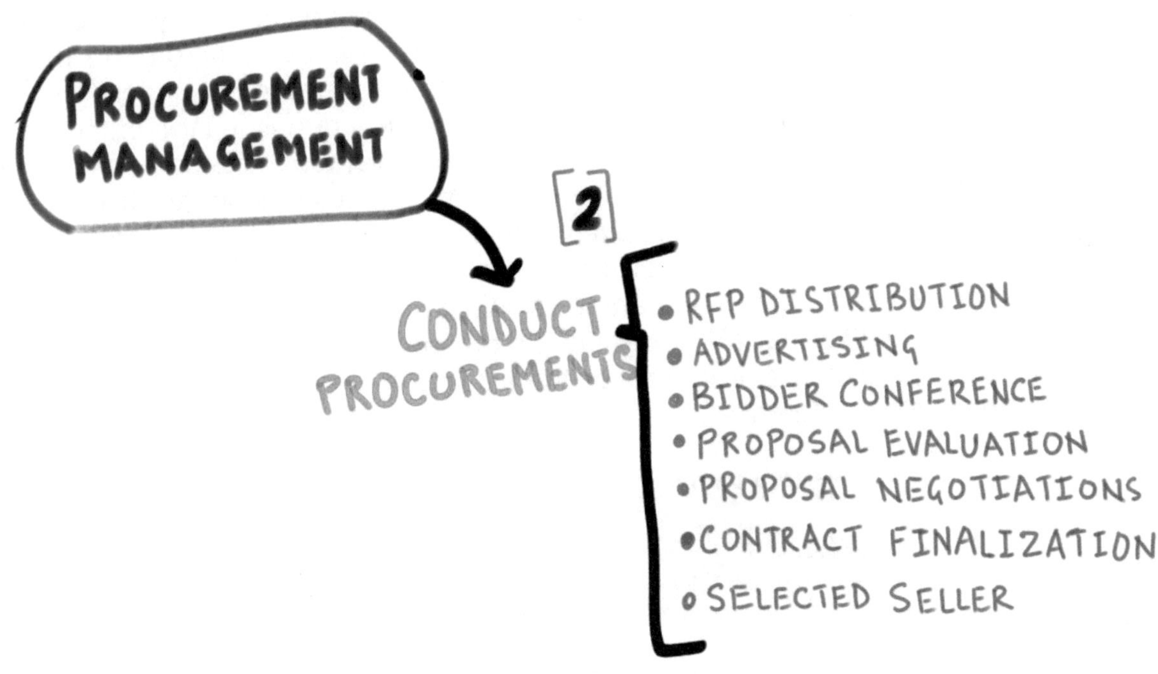

Let us get into the details of this process.

10.7.1 Main Tools and Techniques of this process: -

Expert Judgment for this process are legal advisors, supply chain experts, procurement department professionals, corporate lawyers and people adept at contracting. They can be from within the procuring organization or from outside the organization. Sometimes a panel of experts are made to evaluate the proposals which have some internal and some consultants.

In some kind of Industries and domain (like all major Government contracts) it's mandatory to give an **advertisement** in the newspaper or some specific gazette for a wider reach and equal opportunities. Some times when the organization is unable to find enough prospective bidders on their own it's better to advertise so that prospective bidders from other regions may also show interest in the work. Some countries and industries have running website where all the latest RFP's from those industries are posted and anyone could use it to show interest for bidding provided they meet the pre-qualification requirements.

When RFP is issued to the prospective bidders it's not necessary that they will understand everything very well from the RFP itself. They may have a few questions that might have a bearing on the way they would like to present the proposal or how to estimate for the proposal. If each of the prospective bidders reaches out to the Procuring organization with their questions the procurement department would be overworked with answering questions and most of them would be even repetitive. However, it's important for the procuring organization to ensure that all the bidders' questions are shared with every bidder along with answers to ensure that all of them are on the same page. The procuring organization does not want that some of the bidders quoted less just because they did not understand the work well. Hence, to bring transparency and to answer everyone's questions the procuring organizations organize "Q&A" sessions or "**Bidder Conferences**". Date, time and venue are given to all the prospective bidders (usually this information is stated in the RFP itself) and on that appointed date and time representatives from each of the bidders would attend the conference and ask questions and receive answers about the RFP. What is even better is that everyone hears the questions and answers asked by anyone else. The Bidder Conferences are held after the RFP is sent to the prospective bidders and much before the final date for submission of the proposals by the bidders. In complex RFPs there could be more than one Bidder Conferences.

BIDDER'S CONFERENCE
INDIVIDUAL QUESTIONS ON RFP....
BIDDERS
BUYER
BIDDERS
Q&A SESSIONS
I CANNOT ANSWER EVERY ONE'S QUESTIONS INDIVIDUALLY ... LET US CALL THEM ALL TOGETHER
ANSWERS TO QUESTIONS.
ADDENDUM TO RFP
AFTER THE CONFERENCE THE BUYER DOCUMENTS ALL QUESTIONS AND ANSWERS AND DISTRIBUTES TO ALL BIDDERS.

Proposal Evaluation Techniques are needed to ensure that the procuring organization ends up selecting the best and cheapest vendor from among those who submitted the proposal. There are many techniques for doing the same but all of them have one thing in common, they try to minimize the personal bias of stakeholders while selecting the most appropriate vendor. There are several popular methods to evaluate the proposals received. In large organizations and in complex work being outsourced the proposals have to be submitted in two parts one is the "Technical and Fitment" part and the other is the "Commercial" part. The technical part of the proposal is opened first (without looking at the Commercial part) to see how many proposals qualify the "Technical Evaluation". Some would get eliminated in this round. Once this is done, only then the "Commercial" part is opened and that too for only those proposals that passed the “Technical” round. And the cheapest among them is selected as the final vendor. This method ensures that the cheapest vendor is selected from among those who are technically qualified.

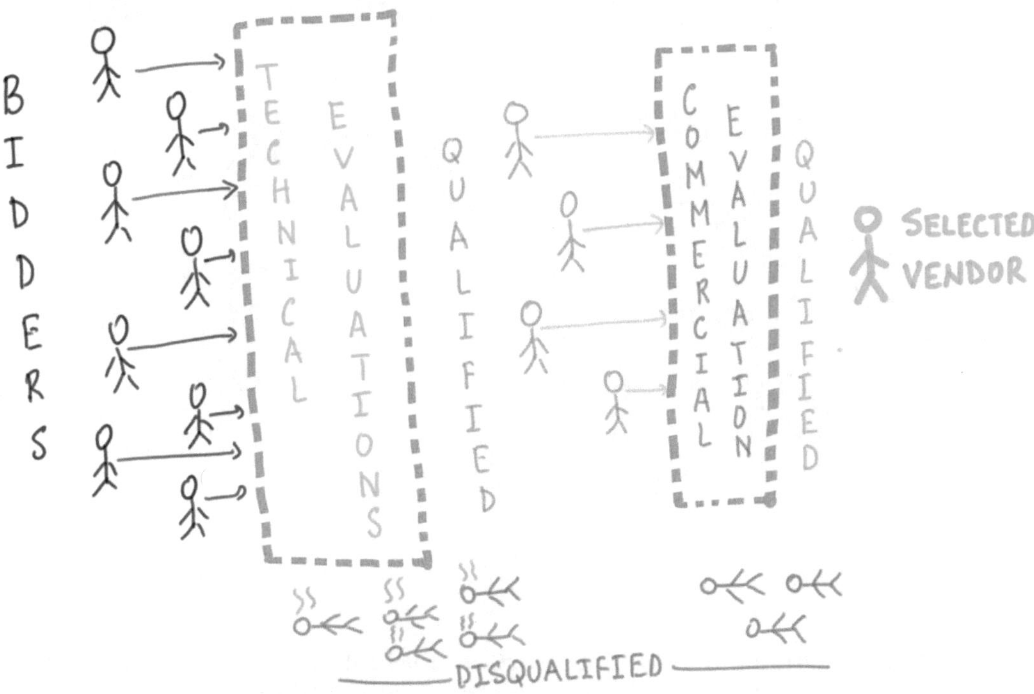

Another popular method is called the “Weighted Method” where each of the proposals is put into a matrix which has all the relevant criteria mentioned there. Most of the time those criteria are weighted, amongst themselves, to show which criteria is relatively more important than others. Now, when each of the proposals is entered in the matrix a rating is given to that proposal against each of the criteria. Once that is done than the ratings of the proposal on each of the criteria is multiplied with the “priority weight” of the criteria itself and then aggregated. Hence the proposals with the highest aggregate wins.

Some companies hire professional consultants to help with the selection process if they themselves are unable to lay down selection criteria.
In some “Mission Critical” procurement a Negative Selection method is used which is usually called the “Scrub-Down” or the “Murder Board” method. Here a panel of experts speaks only negative things about each of the proposals. No positives are spoken. This way, once all the proposals have gone through the murder board than the proposals with the “Least Negative” remarks get selected.
Some of the most common criteria used for evaluation of proposals are: -

Negotiations: Once the vendor is selected there is a round of intense negotiations on the terms of the contract just before signing the final contract. These set of negotiations are called "**Procurement Negotiations**". These negotiations can last a few hours to a few weeks and in some really large projects, a few months.
Negotiations at this time are usually on

There are 5 steps/stages in Negotiations and they are: -

1. Protocol setting *(to introduce all parties to the negotiations as well as to fix the scope of the negotiations)*
2. Probing *(to figure out exactly how much the other party can be pushed in a deal and exactly what is their limit beyond which they would not budge)*
3. Scratch bargaining *(giving and obtaining concessions to help move together to a point of agreement that is win-win for both)*
4. Closure *(finalizing the point of agreement)*
5. Agreement *(contracting the agreement)*

Remember that Negotiations are an attempt at creating a "Win-win" situation among two parties where both feel that there is something in the contract for them. One of the objectives of the negotiations is also to establish healthy working relationships with the other party, to network and also set expectations for the long run.

10.7.2 Main Outcome from this process: -

Selected Seller is one of the main outputs of this process and it states the specific vendor which has been selected for the procurement at hand.

Agreements (actually the finally negotiated and accepted Contracts) is also one of the main outputs of this process which states all the terms that have been agreed upon by both the parties and from this moment on it would become the guiding document for tracking progress and closing the work. This is the same agreement which becomes an input to the "Project

Charter" of the Vendor organization who is initiating the project at their end. An agreement for procurements is usually supposed to have the following elements

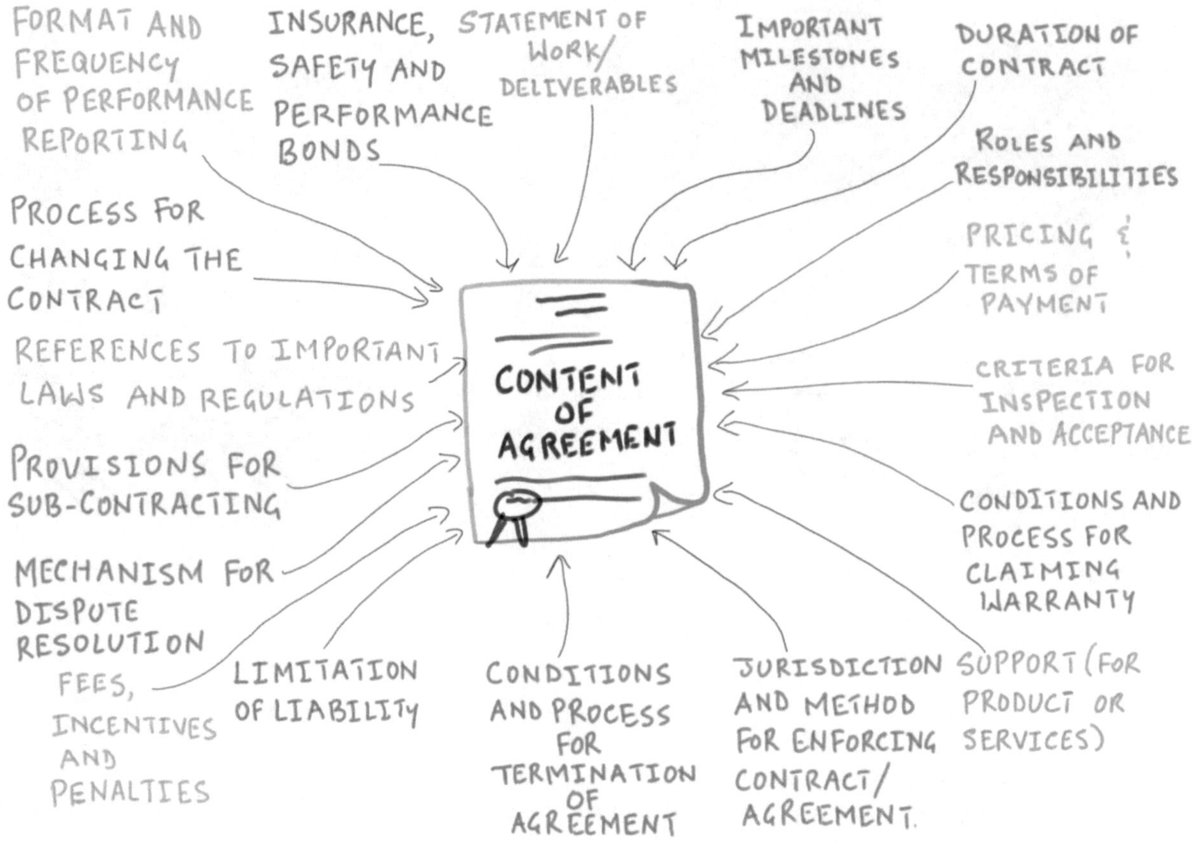

Some **Change Requests** may need to be issued due to new findings or due to negotiations during this process. All these change requests become input to only one process viz., Integrated Change Control. Remember CCB in ICC.

10.8 Direct And Manage Project Work (Create Deliverables)

This process is the "Umbrella Process" of all other processes of the process group "Execution". This is where all that is planned is executed as per the plan. This process covers all the other "Execution Processes" and hence it's called an Umbrella process.

Please note that the term "Umbrella Process" is not a PMBOK® or PMI term. It is a term being used in this book to describe certain processes and their overall bearing on the process group.

Basically, in this process, the Project Management Plan is executed and the deliverables are produced. This is where the deliverables of the project are created.

However different methodologies generate deliverables differently. Predictive and Iterative methodology provide the entire set of deliverables at one go at the very end of the project. On the other hand Incremental and Agile provide intermittent and usable deliverables.

Let us look into the interiors of this process: -

10.8.1 Tools and Techniques of this process:

Project Management Information System (PMIS) is an "information and work" allocation system that traverses the entire organization and is used for supporting all aspects of projects in an organization right from initiation to closing and generating dashboards for the senior management. This system is never a complete singular homogeneous software system but is made up of multiple interrelated systems and sub-systems which are usually a combination of Software-based, automated and manual paper-based systems. This is one of the main tools and techniques of this process as the PMIS is comprehensively used by all concerned stakeholders to convert a plan into deliverables.

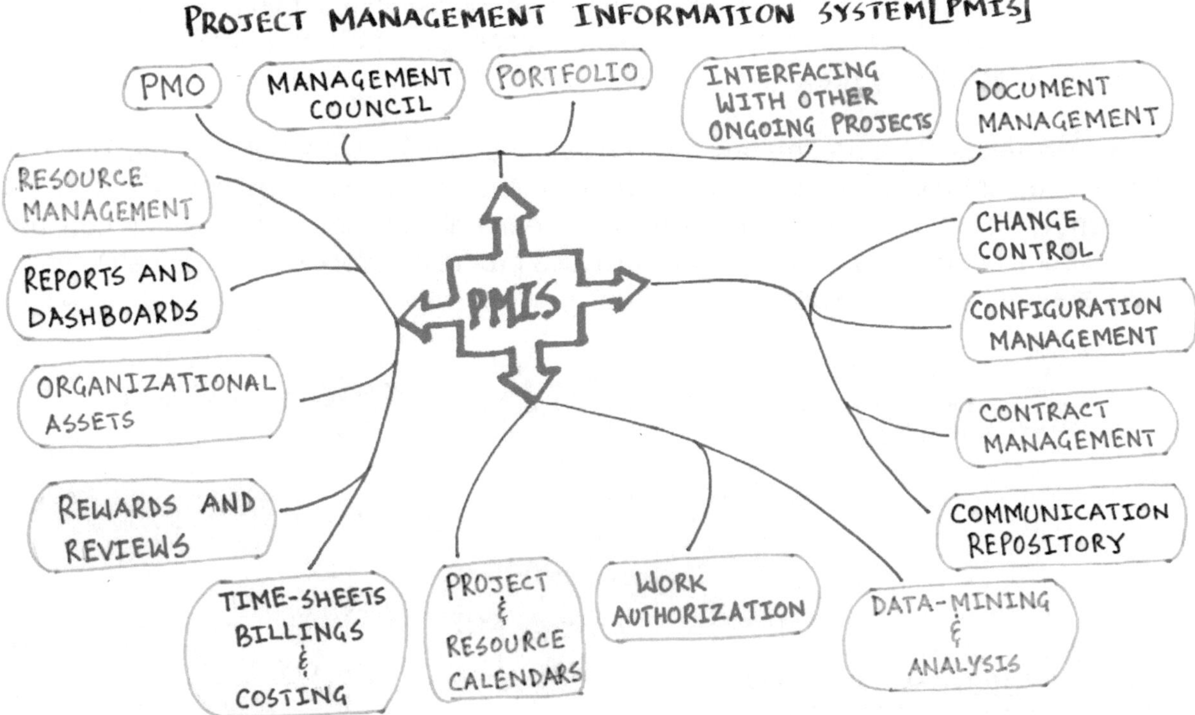

Meetings are needed among the various stakeholders to direct projects and to distribute work, solve problems, discuss issues and so on. Though Meetings is one of the Tools and Techniques of this process it does not mean that Meetings should be conducted indiscriminately. Meetings must be conducted only when the agenda has already been circulated before and only the concerned stakeholders are involved. Meetings are done best face to face. Virtual meetings need more preparation and organization to overcome the problems and drawbacks associated with virtual meetings.

Remember the golden rule "No Agenda = No Meetings". If in the question you are given a scenario where the agenda is not prepared or it's not ready than the best option would be to postpone the meeting.

10.8.2 Main Outcome from this process:

Deliverables are the main output of this process. These deliverables may be internal or external. Deliverables are typically tangible components or a capability of a project which can be verified and which helps achieve any aspect of the project. This deliverable may be just a document, completion of a phase, technical product, a service or the completion of the entire product of the project. Obviously, this is the most important output of this process.

It is important to note that all the deliverables from this process become input to only two processes and they are 1. *MANAGE PROJECT KNOWLEDGE* and 2. *CONTROL QUALITY*.

MBI and MVP: For agile projects the deliverables have to be in the form of Releases. And these releases must be either "Minimum Viable Product (MVP)" or "Minimum Business Increment (MBI)". We have already discussed the concept of MBI and MVP earlier, therefore you must be adept at it by now.

Work Performance Data are the raw data collected about the work being done. This data is used by some controlling processes to convert it into meaningful information and consequently, that information is converted into meaningful reports which can be consumed by the project stakeholders. However, this process produces Work Performance Data or just the raw data related to execution.

EXAMPLES OF WORK PERFORMANCE DATA

WORK PERFORMANCE DATA

- WORK COMPLETED
- START AND FINISH DATES OF SCHEDULED ACTIVITIES
- NUMBER OF CHANGE REQUESTS
- STATUS INFORMATION
- EXTENT TO WHICH QUALITY STANDARDS ARE MET
- COST INCURRED/BUDGET REMAINING
- RESOURCES UTILIZED
- NUMBER OF TEST CASES DONE
- NUMBER OF DEFECTS
- ACTUAL DURATION

This WPD or Work Performance Data becomes input to all the "Monitoring and Control" processes except "*MONITOR AND CONTROL PROJECT WORK*" and "*INTEGRATED CHANGE CONTROL*". I hope you remember that there are 12 processes in the process group "Monitoring and Controlling", therefore this output becomes input to 10 processes and they are all "monitoring and controlling" processes barring the two mentioned above.

Issue Log is a register where the Project Manager (or some of the team members) records all the disagreements, conflicts, differences of opinions and other such issues from the various stakeholders. These are documented in one place so that they can be individually tracked to closure. This also helps in prioritizing the issues, instead of just trying to solve each of the issues as and when they are reported. The resolutions are also written against the issues logged. Some issues remain open and hence are usually referred to as "Open Issues" during the time of the handover or moving from one phase to another. I learned to maintain a register similar to this in my projects as I realized that people report issues and raise objections etc., but if they are not recorded in one singular place they would be lost or forgotten and eventually be reminded or crop up during one of the most inopportune times and places. There were times I had to cut a sorry face in front of my superiors and even team members, several times, and that is how I realized the importance of using this document.

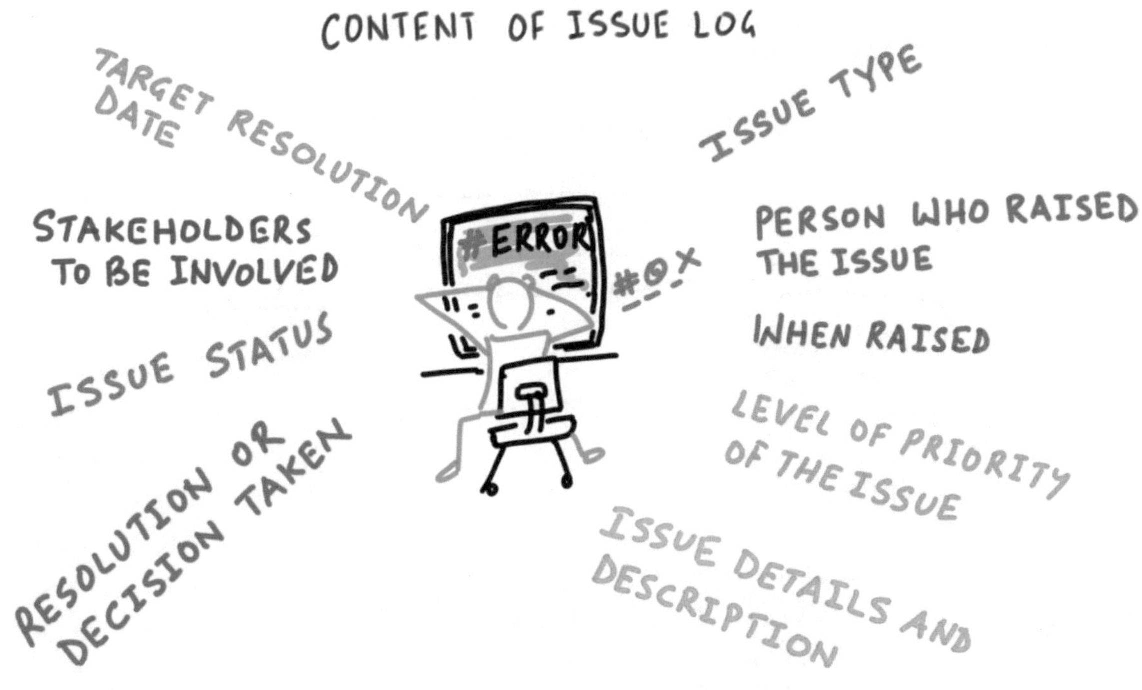

Change Requests are also generated if some new information or omissions or any other realization comes to light while executing the project. Now this change request may be for changing a baseline or any part of the plan, could be recommended preventive action or recommended corrective action or recommended defect repair. However, it is important to note that each and every of these ***change requests become input to*** one and only one process and that is "*Integrated Change Request*".

10.9 Manage Project Knowledge

Project Knowledge or Lessons Learned is the most important topic for any organization but practically the most understated and undervalued activity nevertheless.

Most organizations, being inept at Managing Knowledge, tend to make the same mistakes a thousand times over with different teams and at different times with no one getting any wiser by the day.
This process is dedicated to looking out for, collecting, documenting and disseminating project knowledge and lessons learned across the lifecycle of the project. Instead of waiting till the end of the project to collect and document "Lessons Learned" the process allows the project team to do the same across the lifecycle of the project. The intention of this process is not only to help the specific project but also the organization, in general, to translate the benefits to other projects at a later time.

Lessons Learned resides in the mind and experiences of the stakeholders (particularly the project team) in a project. These "Lessons" could be Explicit (very easy to document and explain with evidence in a cause and effect fashion and can be replicated by others in the same manner) or it could be Implicit (experience in the minds of the individuals which is very difficult to document and replicate as the documentation may not contain the contextual information connected to the lesson). This is the reason why "Lessons" should be stored in a story form that also shows the context, situation and what was going on in the mind of the person along with the political situation when the "experience" was gained which is now being documented as a lesson.

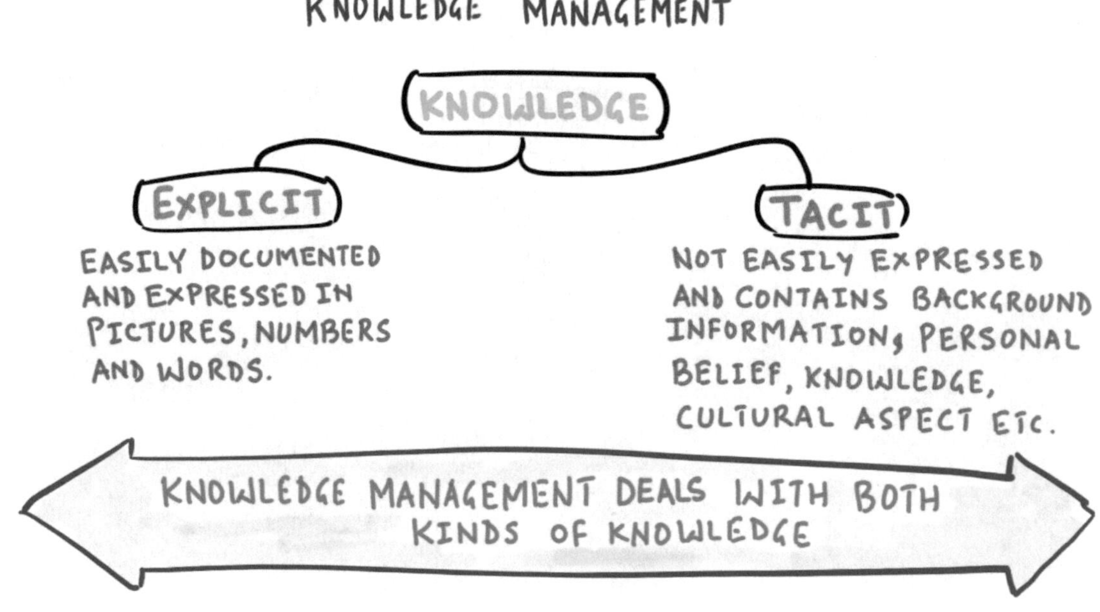

10.9.1 *Main Tools and Techniques of this process.*

Knowledge Management is a sum or combination of various tools and techniques that fall within this overall heading. Some of the commonly used Knowledge Management Tools are: -

Information Management is a sum or combination of tools (automated or manual) which help in documenting, storing, sorting and disseminating lessons learned or new knowledge. Information Management is what is used for storing and retrieving the lessons learned and new knowledge obtained from “Knowledge Management” sessions. Some organizations have rather sophisticated software and enterprise-wide tools for this and this truly helps in disseminating information amongst the entire width of the organization.

Interpersonal And Team Skills like Active Listening, Facilitation, Networking are needed along with Leadership and understanding of Political Awareness to help organize effective and practical Knowledge Management Sessions and to help obtain the lessons learned and to unearth new knowledge.

10.9.2 Main Outcome from this process.

Lessons Learned Register is an output of this process during the early stages of the project after that it becomes an input to various processes (as a part of Project Documents). Several processes have outputs as lessons learned (again as a part of Project Document updates) and all those Lessons Learned become an input to this process. It is recommended to conduct this process at the end of each phase. In this register lessons and new knowledge can be stored in more than one format and methods, like videos, audios, documents, pictures, stories, calculations and so on.
In agile projects, this is referred to as Retrospective. Retrospective is done, involving all team members who participated in the iteration, immediately after the review / demo of the deliverables in that iteration. Each iteration ends only after Retrospective. The following guidelines must be used for retrospective meetings:

- Team members to indicate “what went well” and “What could be improved” for the recently concluded iteration.
- Identify the reasons for improvements

- Improvements suggested by more team members assume higher priority
- Reiterate finalized improvement areas with the team
- Consensus or buy in from team on improvement plan
- Update requirements in product backlog (if necessary) after discussing with the Product Owner.
- Implement change from next iterations.

10.10 Ninja Drill – Implementation - 2

In this Ninja Drill you will find the most important notes and pointers that are important from the point of PMP Exams and covers, Manage Communications, Conduct Procurements, Manage Quality, Direct & Manage Project Work and Manage Knowledge.

S. No.	Drill Points
1.	Active Listening = It requires that the listener fully concentrate, understand, respond and then remember what is being said. This is opposed to reflective listening where the listener repeats back to the speaker what they have just heard, to confirm understanding of both parties.
2.	Active Listening - Reflecting: Repeating gist of message to clarify understanding / situation
3.	Active Listening - Attending: Non-Verbal signs to show that you are paying attention, like • Eye Contact • Leaning forward
4.	Active Listening - Following: Demonstrating understanding of message / situation through o Hand gestures o Nodding o Verbal affirmations like "Yes", "oh!" Etc. o Aske open ended questions
5.	Communication Competence = A combination of tailored communication skills that considers factors such as clarity of purpose in key messages, effective relationships, and information sharing, and leadership behaviors.
6.	In a verbal communication, Words account for 7%, Tonality (Para lingual) account for 38% and Body Language accounts for 55% of entire communication.
7.	Concept of Osmotic Communications: • Means of receiving information without direct communication by overhearing and through nonverbal cues. • Happens automatically in Co-located teams. • Among virtual teams this can be obtained through creation of "Fishbowl" experience. • This is very effective in resolving issues and problems either before they arise or the moment they arise.
8.	Osmotic communication is not possible in Virtual teams unless they use "Fishbowl" concept.
9.	Many ad hoc requests for information or misunderstandings might indicate that engagement and communication activities are not effective.
10.	Levels of complaints and issues can also be used to indicate satisfaction or dissatisfaction of the stakeholders.
11.	A Mood Chart can track the mood or reactions of a group of very important stakeholders by the project team. At the end of each day, project team members can use colors, numbers, or emoji to indicate individual stakeholder's frame of mind.
12.	The main Tools & Techniques of the process "Manage Quality" are: 1. Checklist 2. Root Cause Analysis / Fishbone Diagram 3. Audits 4. Design for X (DfX) 5. Problem Solving And Critical Thinking
13.	Checklists are the list of steps needed to be taken to do a particular thing. This is to ensure that nothing is missed and assures "First Time" Quality.
14.	Cause And Effect Diagram is also called Fishbone Diagram or Ishikawa Diagram.
15.	Audit or Quality Audit: It is done to check for compliance with the quality standards, prevention processes and the Quality Management Plan.
16.	Design for X [DfX] (also called Design for Excellence or simply DfX) is a mechanism by which some technical aspects of the product (which is the "x" factor of the product) which needs more focus than others and the entire designing of the product would be based on that.

17.	Steps In Problem Solving: 1) Defining the problem 2) Identifying the root cause 3) Generating possible solutions 4) Choosing the best solution 5) Implementing the solution 6) Verifying solution effectiveness
18.	The main outcome / output / artefact of the process "Manage Quality" are: • Filled Checklist • Test And Evaluation Process • Quality Report
19.	Quality Report is a project document that includes quality management issues, recommendations for corrective actions, and a summary of findings from quality processes and activities. It may include recommendations for process, project, and product improvements.
20.	The process "Conduct Procurements" starts the moment the buyer organization distributes the RFP / RFQ and this process ends the moment a vendor is selected and a contract is signed.
21.	The main Tools & Techniques of the process "Conduct Procurements" are: 1. RFP / RFQ / RFB Distribution / Advertising 2. Bidders Conference 3. Vendor Selection
22.	Bidders Conference is done between the time the RFP has been issued and the submission of the proposals by the bidders, for clearing the doubts and questions of the bidders.
23.	If a bidder approaches the buyers and obtains a clarification separately the buyer makes a copy of the question and answer and sends it to every one of the bidders.
24.	Vendor Selection is based on the Selection Criteria that was decided and documented in the Procurement Management Plan.
25.	"Single Source" arrangement is when the Buyers have a special relationship with a Vendor, maybe they are a preferred vendor. In such arrangements, the Buyer directly gives the contract to the preferred vendor without inviting any competitive bids from anyone else.
26.	"Sole Source" is a seller who is the only one in a geographical area to supply certain products or services. Here the buyer would not have any other option but to reach out to this sole source.
27.	The main outcome / output / artefact of the process "Conduct Procurements" are: • Selected Seller / Vendor • Signed Agreement / Contract
28.	The process Direct and Manage Project Work does three things: 1. Use Project Management Plan to Create Deliverables 2. Repair defects in Deliverables 3. As the project management plan changes, ensures that the changes are reflected in the project deliverables.
29.	Deliverable = Any unique and verifiable product, result or capability to perform a service, that is required to be produced to complete a process, phase or project.
30.	Feature are a group of functionality that could be banded together to deliver business value.
31.	In predictive development, little change in the initial requirements reflects understanding.
32.	In projects where requirements are evolving, a clear understanding of requirements may not take place until well into the project work.
33.	Project Knowledge = Explicit Knowledge + Tacit Knowledge
34.	In Agile projects knowledge management is done at the very end of each of the iterations and it is called Iteration Retrospective.

35.	Guidelines for conducting a Retrospective: • Team members to indicate "what went well" and "What could be improved" for the recently concluded iteration. • Identify the reasons for improvements • Improvements suggested by more team members assume higher priority • Reiterate finalized improvement areas with the team • Consensus or buy in from team on improvement plan • Update requirements in product backlog (if necessary) after discussing with the Product Owner. • Implement change from next iterations.
36.	We know that the retrospective / lessons learned / knowledge management is working well when the team status reports show fewer errors and rework with an increase in velocity.
37.	The main output / outcome / artefact of the process "Manage Project Knowledge" is Lessons Learned Register.

End Of Ninja Drill

10.11 Monitor Communications: -

Communication is the lifeblood of the organization, in general, and of the project, in particular. Communication Management Plan is created to ensure that just the right kind of information in the right format is sent to the right stakeholder in the right frequency to ensure the success of the project. However, during execution, when the plan is put to work some gaps may come to light. These gaps would need to be removed to ensure that the Communication Management is not only timely its practically effective as well.

One of the main indicators of an ineffective communication plan is complaints from project stakeholders about gaps in information. If there are too many ad-hoc meetings happening within the project environment that too means that the communication plan needs to be relooked at.

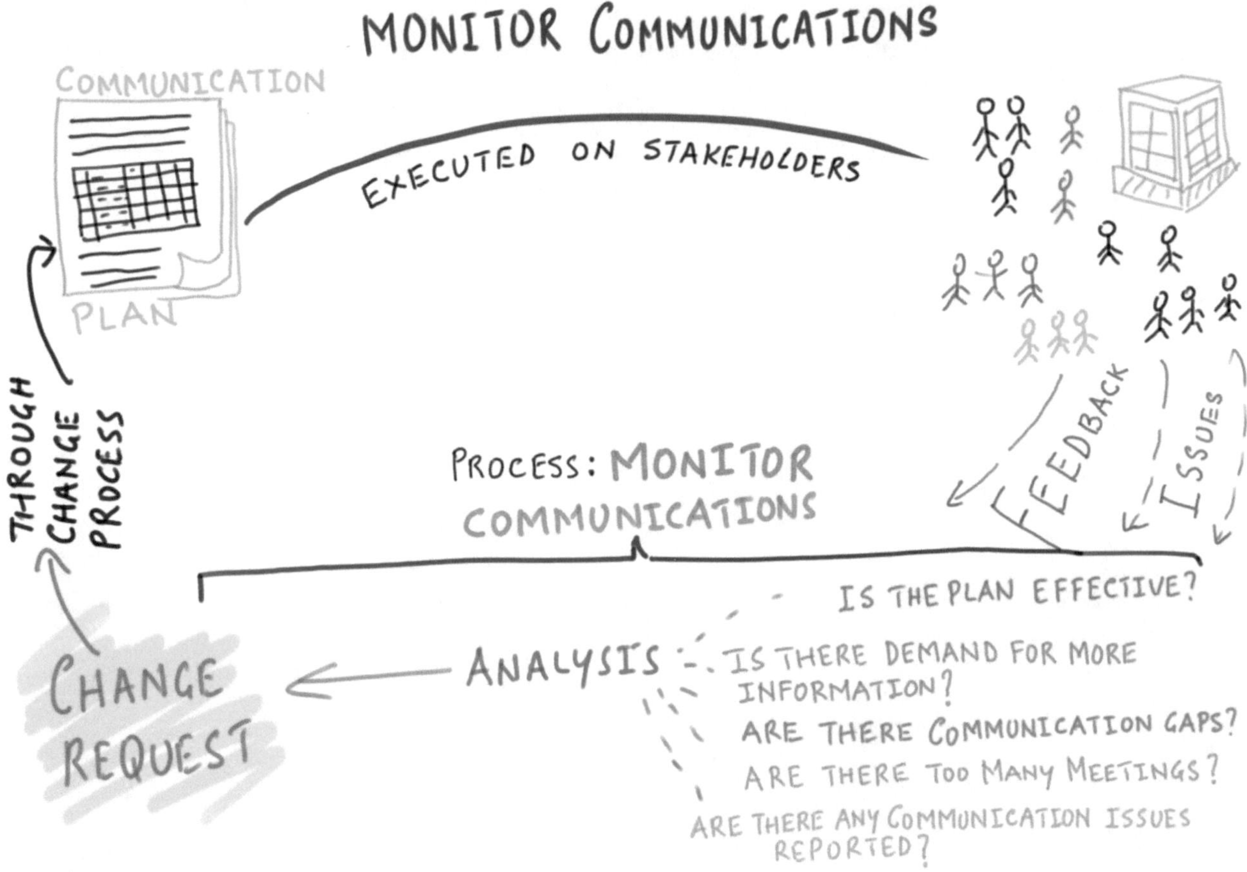

Let us now get into the details of this process.

10.11.1 Tools and Techniques of this process: -

Observation / Conversation is a relatively new technique for managers to pre-empt people issues. It basically states that the managers must physically go around striking up informal conversations with project team members and generally see what they are up to and what is bothering them. In virtual teams this can be somewhat replicated by conducting series of casual video based “one-on-one’s” with each and every team members individually. By observing the body language of the team members it becomes clear how motivated the team really is and if there are signs of team conflicts. This method of management has now been formalized though "Management By Walking Around (MBWA)" and is being taught as a specialization in Management Schools. One does not get to "Know" their team by sitting in the manager's cubicle and looking at impersonal reports. It's been seen that Managers who informally interact with team members and generally observe their team, tend to pre-empt issues and solve problems much faster than traditional managers.

10.11.2 Outputs / outcomes / artefacts of this process: -

Out of the 12 processes in the Process Group "Monitoring And Controlling", there are 10 Processes which has "**Work Performance Information**" is an output. All these Work Performance Information become Input to only one process, which is "Monitoring and Control Project Work". Here from this process, this output would contain information about Project Health, status, progress, and forecasted measurements.

Based on the outcome of this process there could be some changes in the project baselines thus generating **Change Request**. Remember CCB in ICC.

And it could be that due to the learnings from this process the **Project Management Plan,** some **Project Documents** and **Organizational Process Assets** may get updated.

10.12 Monitor Risks

The whole concept of the process "*MONITOR RISKS*" is to get smarter during the lifecycle of the project. This process helps ascertain if the project team did a good job of identifying, managing and responding to the risks.
Let us assume that this box contains all the possible risks that may happen to your project (Hypothetically speaking). Just because you and your team has identified some risks does not mean that they are the only risks applicable to your project. There would be many other risks that you cannot even think of, which are basically the Unidentified Risks.

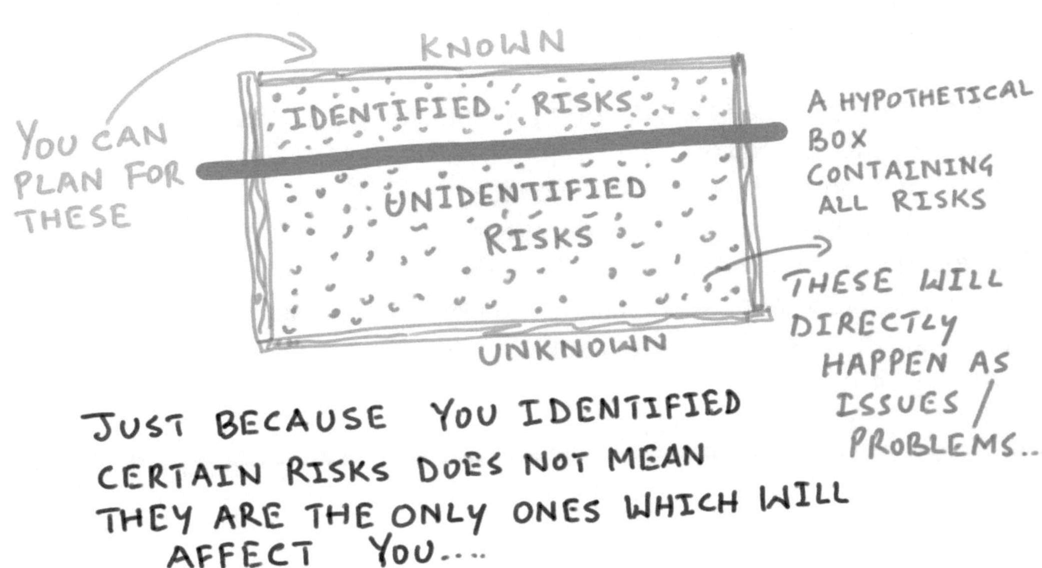
BEING RISK SMART
KNOWN
IDENTIFIED RISKS
YOU CAN PLAN FOR THESE
UNIDENTIFIED RISKS
A HYPOTHETICAL BOX CONTAINING ALL RISKS
THESE WILL DIRECTLY HAPPEN AS ISSUES / PROBLEMS..
UNKNOWN
JUST BECAUSE YOU IDENTIFIED CERTAIN RISKS DOES NOT MEAN THEY ARE THE ONLY ONES WHICH WILL AFFECT YOU...

Which means that for the risks that you have identified and hence prioritized, you may actually make some responses but for those risks that you have not been able to identify, if they happen they will manifest themselves directly as Issues or gains.

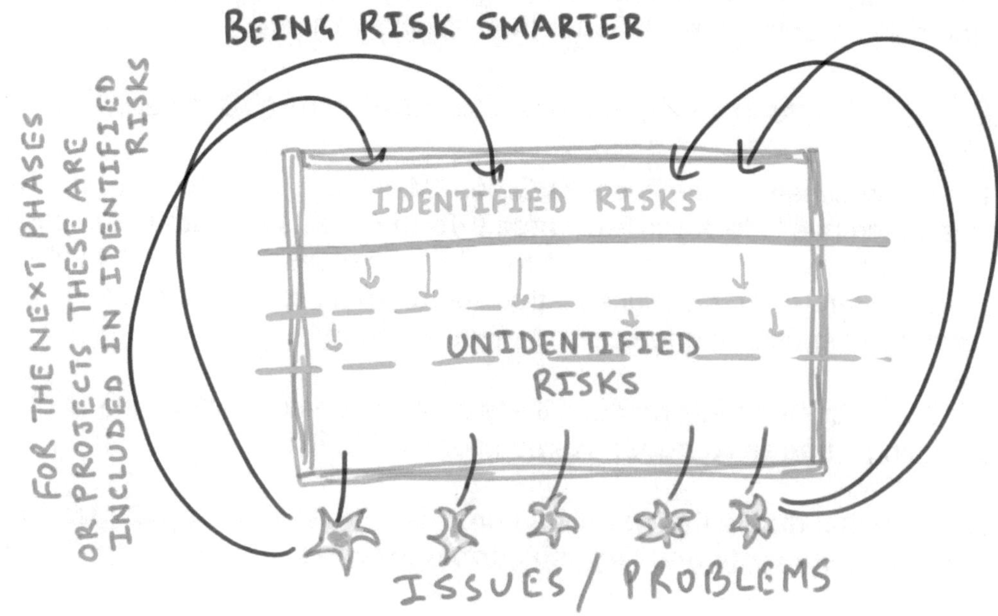

The question is, would you learn from this or not? *Monitor Risk* is a process that forces a project team not to make the same mistake again in the same project. Besides, even for the risks that you identified, it's not necessary that your responses would actually be effective. In this process, the project team gets a chance to see if they missed any risks, if the responses that they designed for the risk was correct or not and if there is a trend that is developing in the project for specific category or risks. Hence, over the lifecycle of the project the number of "Unidentified Risks" should become lesser and lesser as we progress into the project. Needless to say that it's not possible to wipe out each and every "Unidentified Risks". There is simply no technique to know all of them.

Summarizing the steps usually taken during *Monitor Risks* process:

- Frequently Monitor Risks
- New Risks identification and classification
- Identification of new risks due to changes in projects and changes in environment
- Assessing the effectiveness of the Risk Reponses
- Conduct Audits to ensure compliance to response plans
- Revisiting Reserves to ascertain sufficiency
- Updating PMIS
- Updating Lessons Learned Register
- Revisiting the Risk Management Plan or the Risk Response Plan if required
- Raising a change request if required

10.12.1 Main Tools and Techniques Of This Process: -

Technical Performance Analysis means comparing the "Current Technical Performance" with the "Planned Technical Performance". This comparison may show some variances. Once these variances are analyzed or broken down, the issues that led to such variances would come to light. This is like "reverse engineering" to figure out the issues that escaped us and affected the project. *E.g., In a software development project, as per plan, the Human Resource Portal should have been updated with all the realistic test data for unit and system testing. However, in actuals, the team had to upload the data and delete it and are now waiting for the test data. Working backwards (like 5 Why) it was revealed that the HR managers had sent the actual HR data (which violates all possible privacy policies of the organization) which was loaded up in the system by the team, thinking it was test data, and then the team was made to delete all traces of the data from the system by the HR department. Now the HR is creating test data which is realistic, for which the team is still waiting.*

Reserve Analysis is done during this process to see how much of the contingency reserves has already been utilized and can the rest of the pending projects be done in the remaining contingency reserve. If it is assessed that the rest of the project may not be able to be done in the remaining reserve than the project team may want to talk to sponsor to get some funds from "Management Reserves" if any.

Audits (or Risk Audits) help in two things, one, to ascertain if the risk responses and the risk plans are being actually followed by the project team and two, to ascertain if the risk responses are effective and actually generating the desired results. During audits it must be seen if certain risks even after being responded to, had residual risks and if so, to what extent.

10.12.2 Main Outcome from this process: -

Work Performance Information is an output of this process just like the nine other "Monitoring and Controlling" processes. This becomes an input to one and only one process viz., *MONITORING AND CONTROL PROJECT WORK*, where all the information from various controlling processes is compiled to generate a meaningful report for the key stakeholders who would be able to take project decisions based on those reports. This one here carries the "Risk" related information.

Change Requests may need to be issued if because of this process some serious preventive or corrective actions are to be taken which would affect the project baselines.

10.13 Control Schedule

Once the project is in "Execution" the monitoring and control processes compare the planned vs actuals to state the variances. One of the Monitoring and Controlling processes is *CONTROL SCHEDULE* which basically compares the "Actuals" with the Schedule Baseline and states the variances and other schedule related health pointers. Getting the project back on track to meet the project schedule and project schedule forecast are also within the scope of this process.

SCHEDULE CONTROL - REALITY CHECK

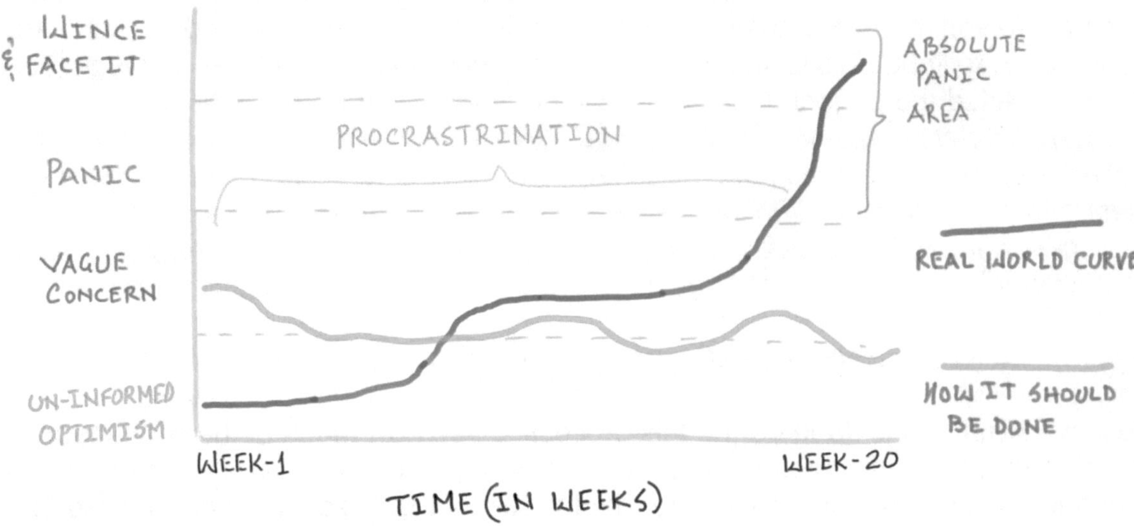

Some of the corrective actions and preventive suggestions would have to go through the Change Control Process (Through Integrated Change Control) hence one of the outputs of this process is “Change Requests”.

Some of the things that happen during this process are listed herein below to give you an idea about the scope of work of this process.

1. Project schedule gets updated with actual work and milestones achieved.
2. Project actuals are compared with the schedule baseline and variances are calculated.
3. Conducting stand-ups and retrospectives to capture lessons learned and new Knowledge identified and taking corrective actions if any. (Agile Methodology specific)
4. Backlog reprioritization. (Agile methodology specific)
5. Based on variances, forecasted end date of the project is calculated and compared with the baseline end date.
6. Based on the current and forecasted variances, corrective actions and preventive actions are devised.
7. Retrospectives are conducted and backlog is reprioritized or adjusted for remaining duration
8. Detailed performance analysis is conducted using techniques like Earned Value Management (this method would be discussed in the next knowledge area called Project Cost Management).
9. Compress the schedule to try and meet the baseline scheduled time.
10. Making and reporting using the burndown chart. A burndown chart is a graphical representation of work left to do versus time. The outstanding work (or backlog) is often on the vertical axis, with time along the horizontal. It is useful for predicting when all of the work will be completed. (Agile methodology specific)
11. If the changes and variances are so much that the original schedule baseline end date cannot be achieved, than a change request could be issued to alter the baseline.
12. Analytics can also be done during this process to see if there are some trends that need to be kept in mind and provided for. (*E.g., A specific supplier supplying the*

deliverables late, or there is a tendency of over 10% delay in each of the previous phases).

13. Issues that have affected the project schedule so far and the new risks that have been identified as far as the project schedule is concerned.
14. Sometimes the project schedule relationships among activities and the leads and lags may be adjusted as a corrective or a preventive measure and if that changes the schedule baseline than it has to be done through a Change Request.

This should give you a comprehensive idea of what kind of work is usually done in this process.
Now let us look into the inner workings of this process.

10.13.1 Main Tools and Techniques of this process: -

Earned Value Analysis is one of the foremost tools for controlling Schedule and Cost. This is the best way to find the health of your project at any given time. However, since Earned Value is used for not only measuring the health of the project from the point of view of Schedule but also from the point of view of cost, the entire concept of Earned Value Analysis is discussed in detail in the next process ***Control Costs***.

Red Amber Green (RAG) Charts: These are charts with summary or milestone entries in them instead of the entire detailed schedule. Based on the status of the project activities or milestones, in terms of schedule, the various activities, summary items or milestones would be color coded as Green (showing either the work on the summary task or milestone has not started or has started or even completed but it was done within the planned duration), Amber (meaning that the amber summary task or the milestone has already breached the early warning duration threshold and needs preventive action by stakeholders to bring it back on track) and Red (meaning that the warning or failure duration threshold has been breached on these summary activities or milestones and needs urgent attention by the decision making stakeholders without any further ado). In most cases, if sufficient attention is given when the summary task or milestone glows Amber, they would never reach critical condition of Red. When a summary task or milestone turns red, the only option then is to undertake Workaround.

Iteration Burndown chart is the tool that is used for schedule control in Agile Methodology. This chart tracks the work that remains to be completed in any given iteration. This chart also shows the “Forecasted” completion based on the current rate of work as against the planned line, thus helping calculate the “Forecasted Variance” as well.

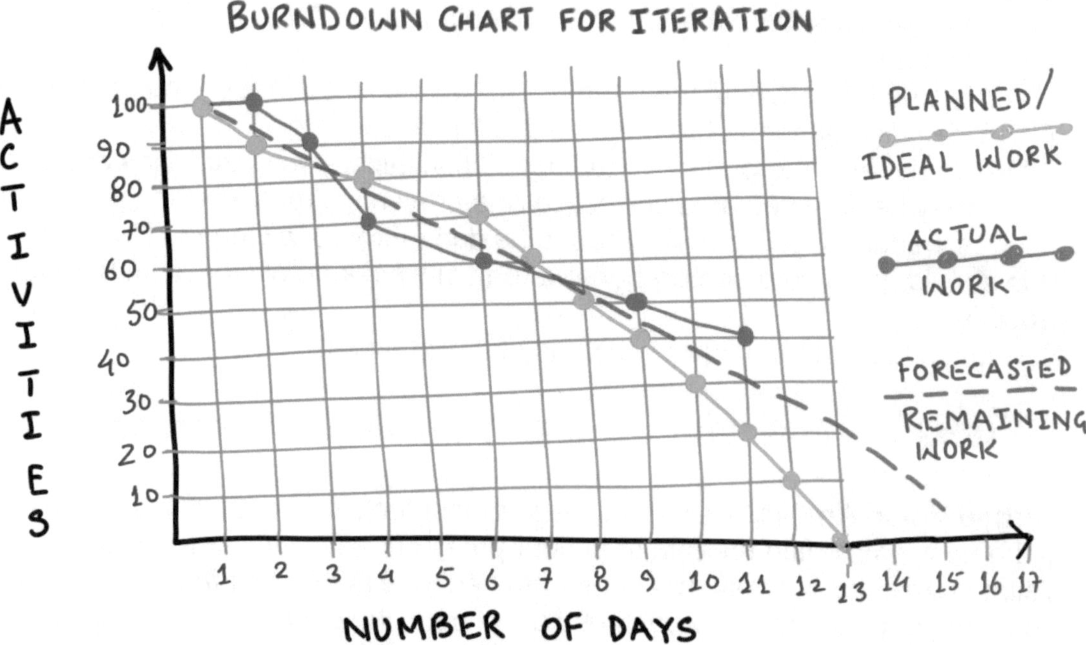

In a Burndown Chart if the "actual work line" is above the "Ideal work line", then it would mean that the iteration is running behind schedule. However, if the "actual work line" is below the "ideal work line" then it means that the iteration is ahead of schedule. Every time when a segment of the "actual work line" becomes parallel to "X" axis, it means that the team was idle or stuck in something that prevented work from progressing and this challenge must come up during the next days "Daily Stand Up" meeting.

Just like the "Burndown Chart" there is a chart which is called the "Burnup Chart". "BurnUp Chart" is literally the inverse of the Burndown chart. A burnup chart indicates the user stories or story points or work completed at any point of time. In a burnup chart, when the "actual work line" is above the "ideal work line" then it would mean that the iteration is ahead of schedule and vice versa.

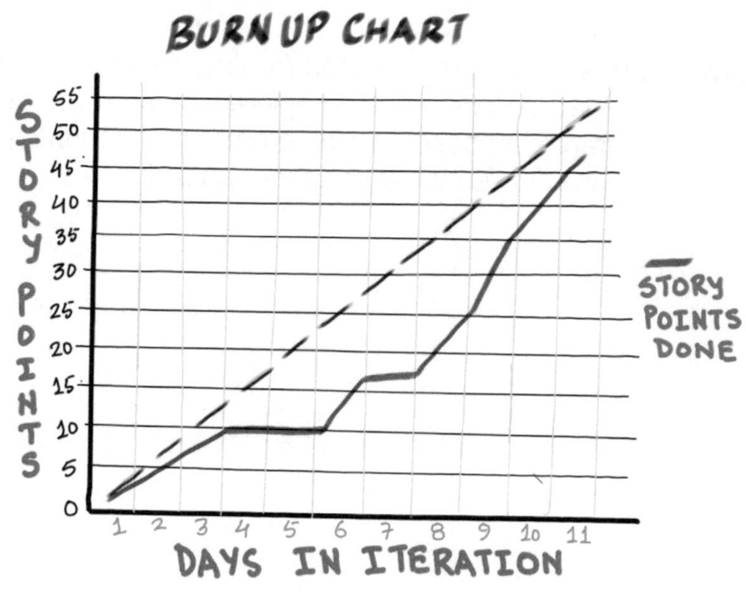

Some teams like to combine the two charts and create something that is called the "Combined Burn Chart". Apart from showing both burnup and burndown there is another element in this chart and that is the "Scope Line". Scope line shows the stability of the user stories / requirements during the life of the iteration. Ideally speaking the scope line should be a straight horizontal line indicating that no user story has been added or removed from the running iteration. However, many times user stories are removed or added within a running iteration, and when that happens, there will be an upsurge or down surge in the scope line indicating addition of user stories and removal, respectively. By including the scope line in the Combined burn chart it becomes a good reference point to check the inflection points in "Actual work line" with the scope line. In general, every time some user stories are added to an existing iteration the scope line will upsurge at that point. Consequently, this should reflect in the "Actual work line" as a temporary flat area, meaning the team accommodating the new user stories and hence the flat line.

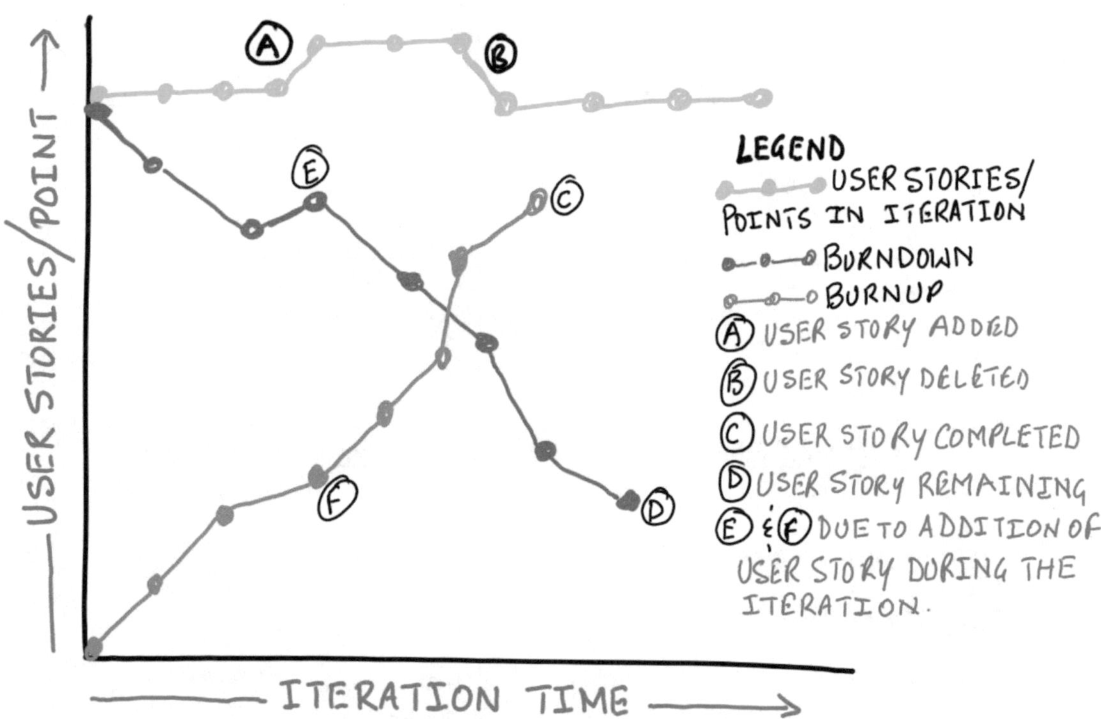

Along with these charts, efficiency measures like Velocity and Throughput also help us understand the progress within an iteration. They also help in forecasting the estimated finish date / period.

Performance Reviews is comparing the baseline with the actuals like activities to be completed as per baseline versus actually completed, baseline start dates of activities versus actual start dates of those activities, milestones to be achieved versus actually achieved, current rate of progress versus actual rate of progress, forecasts on schedule based on the variances calculated and the reasons for the same. In order to conduct fruitful analysis the progress and or delays on critical path may be investigated, investigation may be done on the amounts of floats utilized, techniques like Earned Value Management may be used to find status, progress, and forecasts (will be discussed in details in the very next process). Critical Chain may also be investigated to see how much of the project buffer has been utilized and how much is left and if the remaining buffers would suffice for the project and so on. The more numerical oriented the performance review is, the better and more effective it would be.

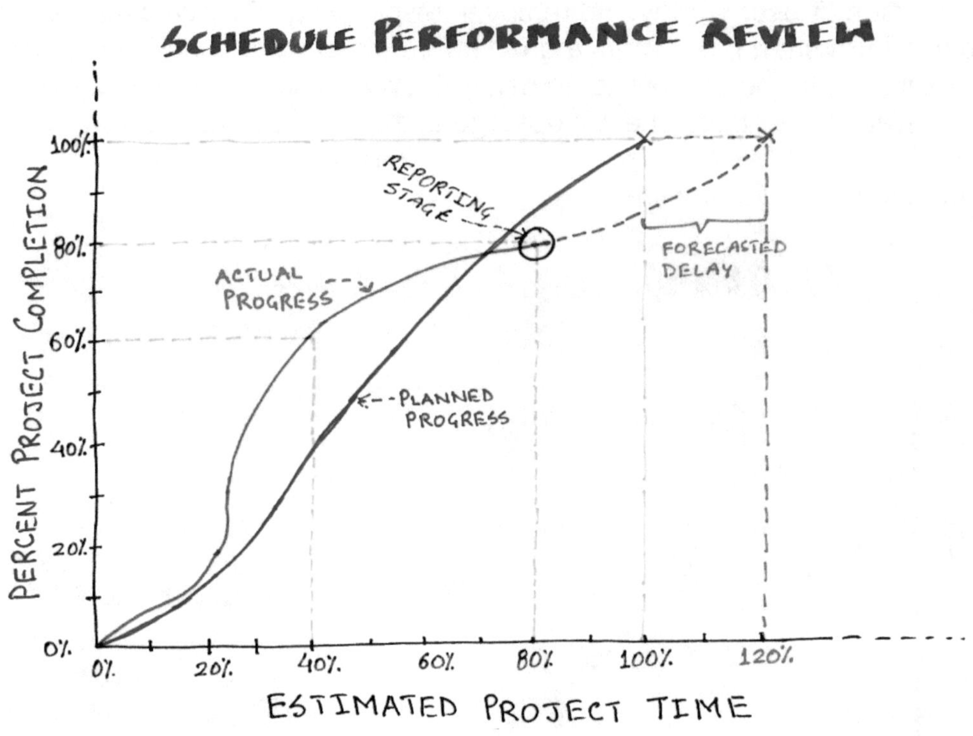

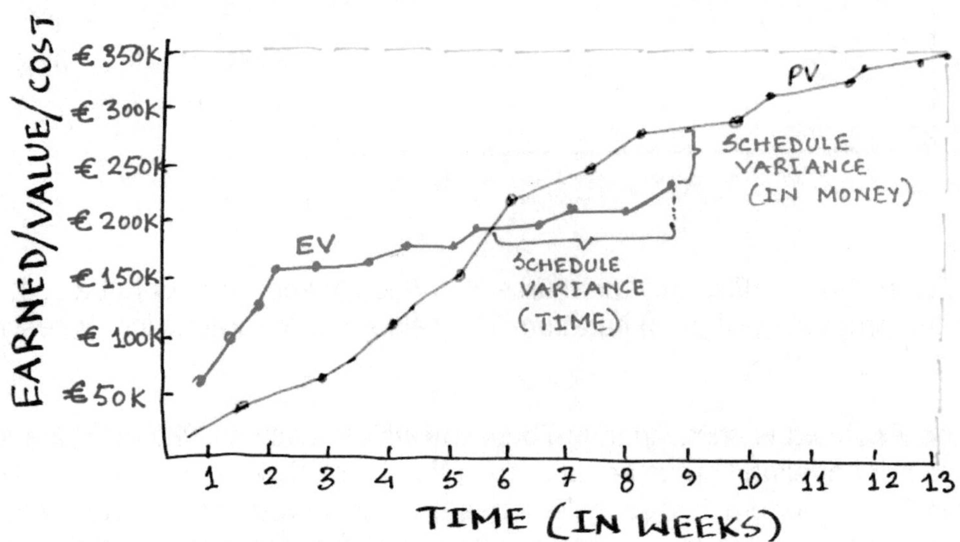

In the past, Bar Charts were used to show or ascertain "Actual versus Planned" variances in the schedule. This method of performance review is not very popular anymore however, some industries like manufacturing and infrastructure still use them. Do not worry about the "Earned Value Chart" you will understand it completely by the time you are done with the next process Viz., CONTROL COSTS.

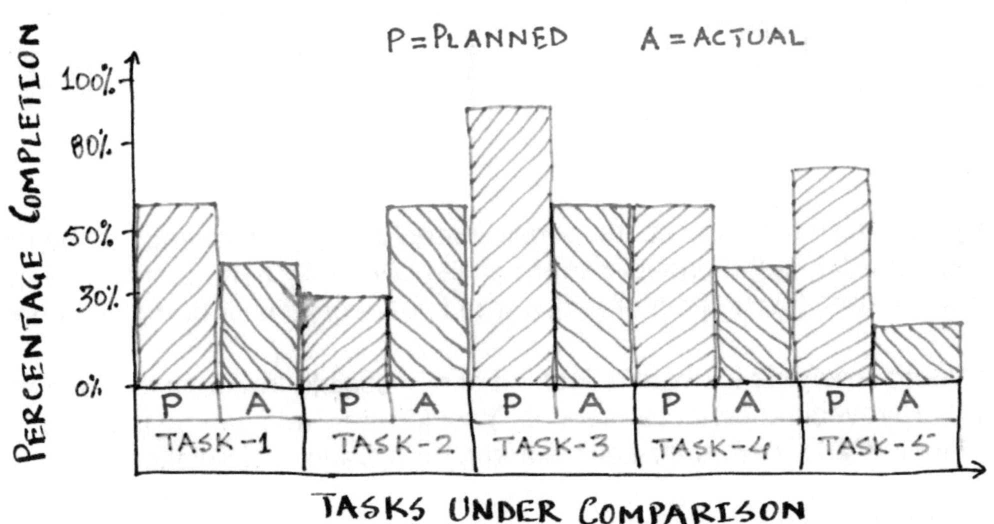

The only purpose of the BAR chart in Schedule Control is to observe schedule variances using visual indicators.

Kanban Chart: Hope you remember that while burndown / burnup charts are used for Iteration based agile (all iterations have the same duration) the Kanban charts are used by Flow based agile (iterations would have different durations). Kanban is also used for planning, but at the same time, the way it is made it also works very well for tracking the project. Cycle time and lead time are used to ascertain if the work is progressing as per plan or there is a variance.

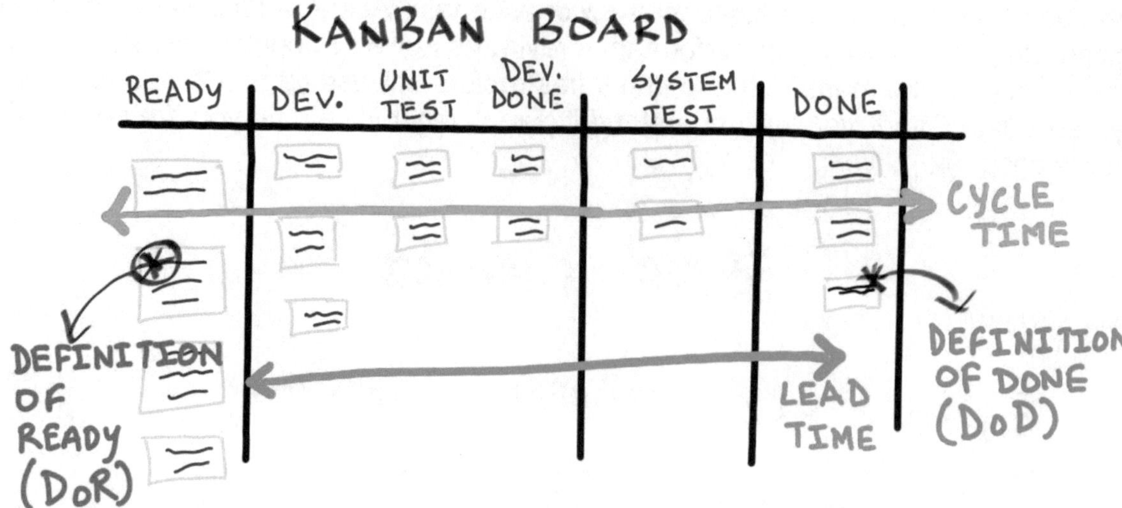

Trend Analysis is also used to see the general trend of the performance of the project. It answers questions like "Is the project performance continually deteriorating or improving?" This trend can be seen through bar charts, earned value graphs or burndown charts as well.

What-if Scenario Analysis is used for looking at all possible tradeoffs for each alternative for correcting or preventing project variances. Yes! Monte Carlo can be used for this. Remember Monte Carlo = What-if Analysis and Monte Carlo = Simulation.

Critical Path Method is used to study the effect of the variances on the Critical Path. If the critical path is affected than the "Schedule Compression" techniques would have to be adopted to bring the project back on track.

Project Management Information System (PMIS) would be used to collect data, send out reports, check resource calendars and resource allocations. Scheduling tools are part of this as well.

Based on the outcome of the Performance Reviews it might be needed to **optimize the resources** using any of the two techniques viz., Resource Levelling or Resource Smoothing.

Leads and Lags may need to be adjusted as understanding of the project improves or to bring the project back on track.

One of the known methods of getting the project schedule back on track in case of project delays is the **Schedule Compression Techniques** viz., Crashing or Fast-tracking.

10.13.2 Main Outcome from this process: -

Work Performance Information is an output of 10 out of 12 Monitoring and Controlling Processes and hence it is an output of this process as well. This contains the performance indicators in terms of earned value or percentages or overall comparative statements which would be used to produce intelligible and action-oriented reports. This is one of the main outcomes of this process. This output later becomes an input to the process "*Monitoring and Controlling Project Work*" where comprehensive project reports are developed. Work performance Information has very wide implications, however, since it is an output of this process "*Schedule Control*" it only contains performance information only from the point of view of Schedule.

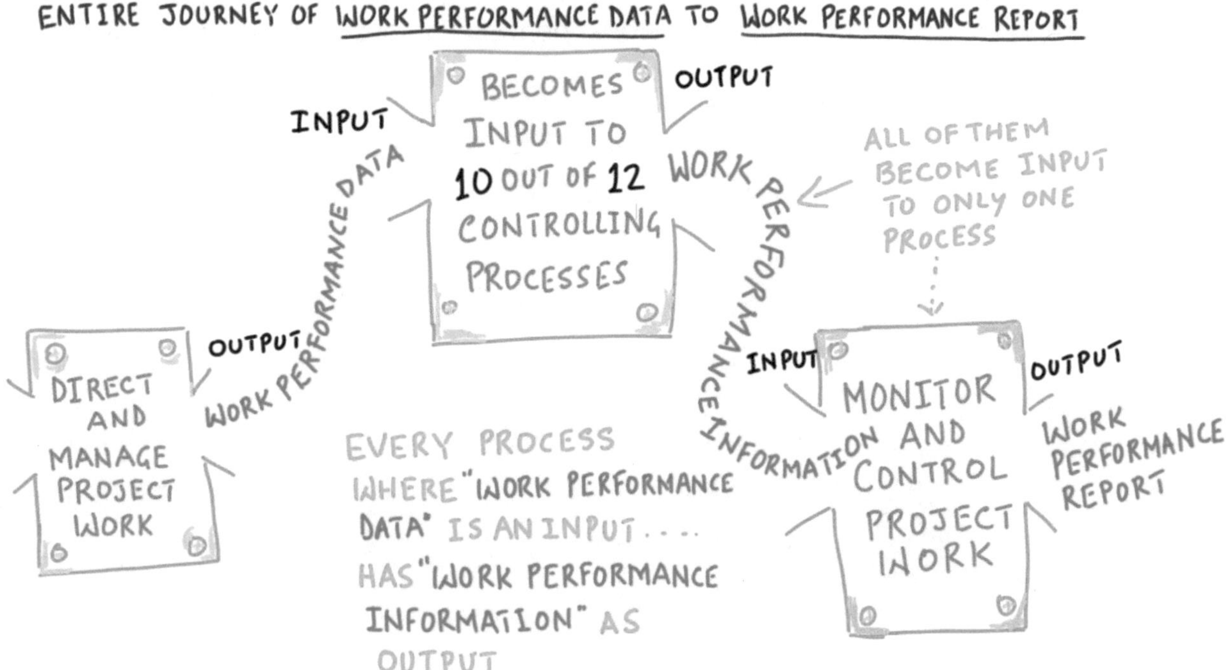

Schedule Forecasts are a future indicator of how the project would perform time wise based on the past rate of work and past schedule performance. Most of the time Earned Value Indicators are used for this kind of forecasting.

Change Requests have to be issued because of the corrective or preventive actions being taken to redress the schedule variances unearthed during this process. Attempts to alter the scope of the project or change in the baseline or changes in the overall schedule may need to be issued as a change request to be duly approved through a formal change approval process through the process "*INTEGRATED CHANGE CONTROL*". Remember, all Change Requests (which is an output of 24 processes) become input to one and only one process and that is *INTEGRATED CHANGE CONTROL*.

And because of the findings from this process and the actions taken during this process **Project Management Plans** (like Schedule Management Plans, Risk Management Plan, Cost Management Plan, and even the Schedule Baseline) may get updated. Some **Project Documents** (like Risk Register, Schedule, Resources Histogram or Staffing Management Plan etc.) may also get updated as an outcome of this process.

10.14 Control Costs

As the name suggests, this is the process where the actual costs and actual project spending is compared with the cost baseline to understand status, progress, and forecast of the project. This process is also used for managing Changes to the Cost Baseline.
Just tracking the project on cost alone would be meaningless until the actual work done / to be completed is also taken into account.
So what all happens in this process?

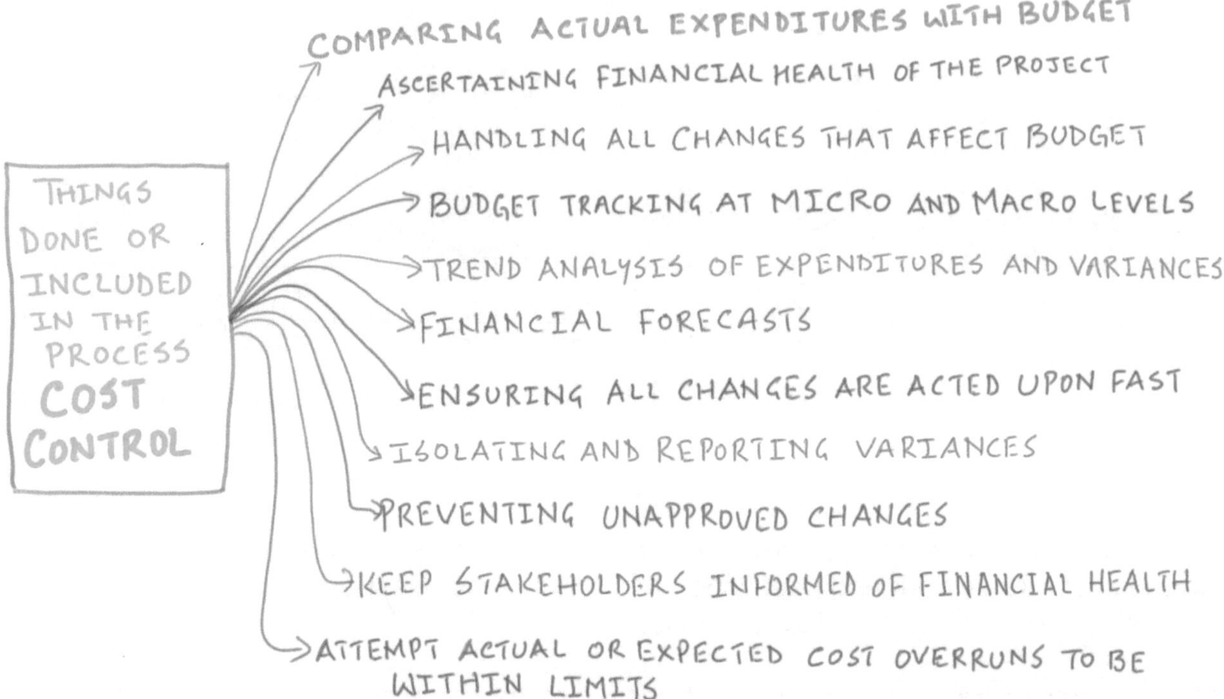
CONTROL COST - OVERVIEW
THINGS DONE OR INCLUDED IN THE PROCESS COST CONTROL
COMPARING ACTUAL EXPENDITURES WITH BUDGET
ASCERTAINING FINANCIAL HEALTH OF THE PROJECT
HANDLING ALL CHANGES THAT AFFECT BUDGET
BUDGET TRACKING AT MICRO AND MACRO LEVELS
TREND ANALYSIS OF EXPENDITURES AND VARIANCES
FINANCIAL FORECASTS
ENSURING ALL CHANGES ARE ACTED UPON FAST
ISOLATING AND REPORTING VARIANCES
PREVENTING UNAPPROVED CHANGES
KEEP STAKEHOLDERS INFORMED OF FINANCIAL HEALTH
ATTEMPT ACTUAL OR EXPECTED COST OVERRUNS TO BE WITHIN LIMITS

One of the best methods of tracking a project on Schedule and Cost is through a methodology called the Earned Value Analysis and Management. It's in this process that we will become well versed with the Earned Value Analysis and Management.

A surprisingly large numbers of organizations are unable to effectively monitor and control costs. Some of the common reasons why this happens is shown below:

Time to get into the details of this process.

10.14.1 Main Tools and Techniques of this Process: -

Let us first take care of the concept of **Earned Value Analysis, Variance Analysis, and Trend Analysis** together. This would take some time as the entire concept would be explained in practical and realistic terms. But first of all, if you are one of those who feel that EVM is hard and complex, please discard that feeling. It's one of the most powerful and amazing ways to track a project. But is it difficult? No!

What we need to know is that EVM not only helps tracks cost but also helps track schedule (Time). You may remember that in the earlier process *CONTROL SCHEDULE* it was mentioned that the tracking of schedule would be taken up along with tracking cost. And well here we are.

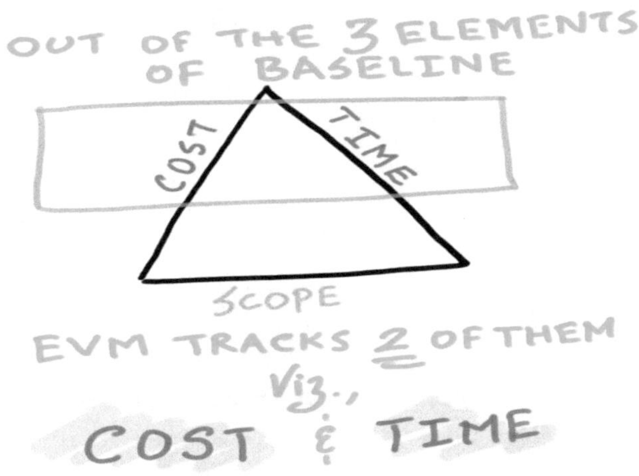

In order to properly ascertain the health of a project, three different reports are generated. One is **Status Report** (Which tells you where you are, in the project, as of now and what is the current condition of the project between the last reporting period and now), second is **Progress Report** (which shows the rate at which time and money are being utilized, from the beginning of the project till now) and the third is **Forecast** (which uses the progress reports to predict how much time and money would the project end up taking by the time it finishes). By being able to do this at every reporting cycle, corrective action or preventive action could be taken much earlier in the lifecycle of the project. Besides it may also let the project team know much earlier in the lifecycle of the project if at all it's worth continuing the project any further or not.

Let us take a simple example to show the overall mechanism of EVM and how practical it is to use this method.

Let us take an example where your boss is in the historic city of Taj Mahal, Agra, and you are in Delhi. The two cities are exactly 200 Kilometres apart (just saying). (*For the readers in USA, a KM is a Kilometre and it is what the rest of the world uses in measuring distances. In case you still have to think in miles, divide the KMs by 1.6 and you will get approximately the miles conversion.*) Your boss wants you to come over to Agra to meet a client who is supposed to fly out the same night. He wants you to give a technical presentation to the client before the client flies out, to help clinch the deal. Being 200 km., you commit that you would be there at Agra in 3 hrs time. So the target is 200Kms in 3 hrs. Now, assume that there is a restaurant called "The Midpoint Hotel" which happens to be exactly at 100 km mark from Delhi. Which means that you would take 1.5hrs to cover the 100 km to reach The midpoint Hotel and another 1.5 hrs from The Midpoint Hotel to Agra.

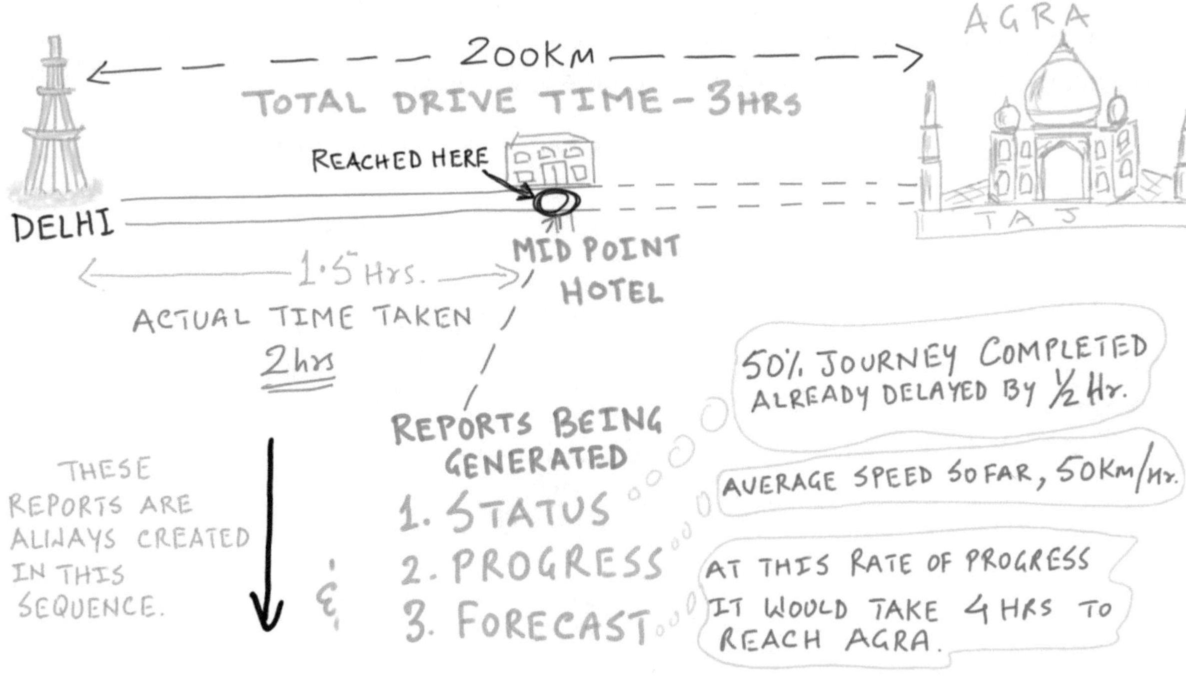

As you start for Agra you move at different speeds based on different traffic conditions and after some time you reach the "*The Midpoint hotel*". You have been driving for some time and now wish to drink some coffee and some snacks before embarking on the next leg of the journey. You look at your watch and you are surprised that you have taken 2hrs. You were supposed to take 1.5 hrs to reach The Midpoint hotel. This puts you behind by .5 hrs (half an hour). You decide to understand what the implications are, due to this delay, on the entire initiative. You will produce three reports viz., Status, Progress and Forecast Reports.

From the status report it's clear that you have completed 50% of the journey and you are already .5 hrs behind schedule.

Now you will calculate the Progress Report.
The progress report is calculated with the main purpose of forecasting. You have covered 100 kms in 2 hrs which means that your average speed, so far, has been 50Kms / hour. This is your progress report. Progress is always a fraction.

Now you will have to forecast your expected time of reaching Agra. You know the total distance is 200 kms and your average speed has been 50kms / hour. You realize that you will end up taking 4 hrs by the time you end up reaching Agra (Distance divided by average speed.) Which means, by the time you finish the journey, you would be delayed by 1 hr, while the current delay is .5 hrs.

Seeing this forecasted variance, you will find it prudent to make a call to your boss and explain the situation and how it affects your forecasted rest of the journey. If the Boss is ok with the delay, you will continue but if he says that the delay is so much that you would not get the time to present to the Client before he flies away, then it would make sense to turn back now and discontinue the initiative. This, in essence, is the power of EVM.
The idea to use this example was to showcase how simple and practical EVM is and when applied to a real-world project, it is not much different.
However, in this example, we used a single dimension of "Time" alone. In the real-world projects, we need to check the health using two dimensions viz., Cost and Time (schedule). To enable that and to abstract the complexity of calculations, EVM has 3 Variables, which would be used to calculate just about every formula from Status to Forecasting. However, one last thing you need to know about EVM is that everything in Earned Value is calculated in Money.

The three variables of EVM are: -

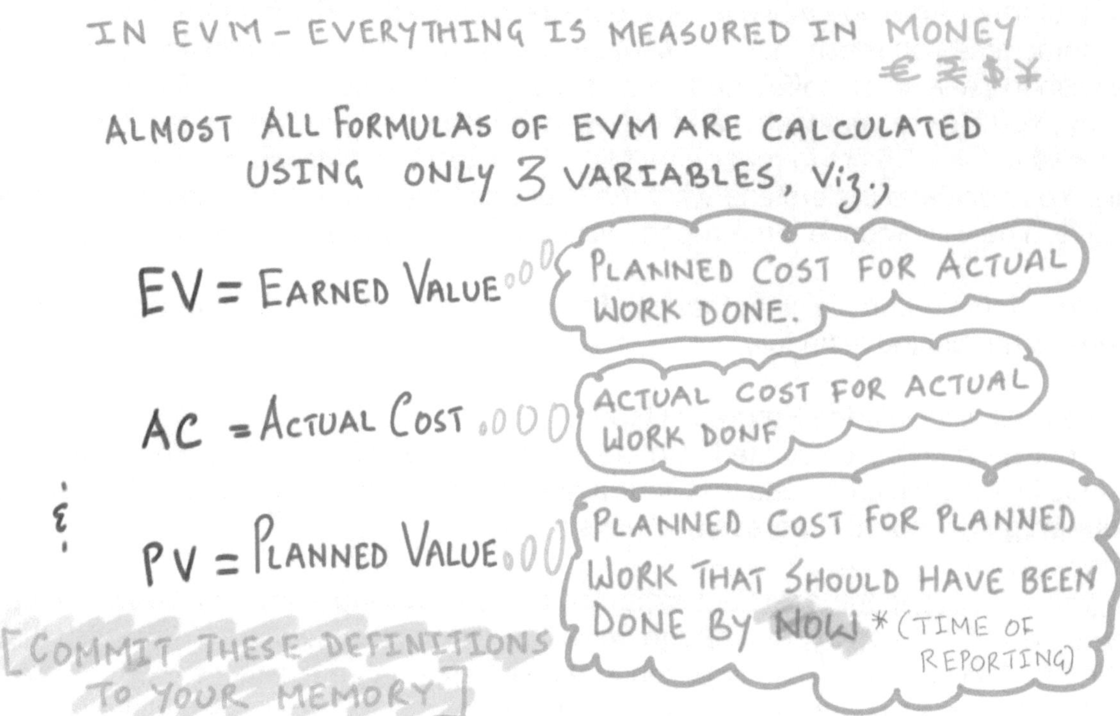

EVM - BASICS
IN EVM - EVERYTHING IS MEASURED IN MONEY
€ ₹ $ ¥
ALMOST ALL FORMULAS OF EVM ARE CALCULATED USING ONLY 3 VARIABLES, Viz.,
EV = EARNED VALUE
PLANNED COST FOR ACTUAL WORK DONE.
AC = ACTUAL COST
ACTUAL COST FOR ACTUAL WORK DONE
&
PV = PLANNED VALUE
PLANNED COST FOR PLANNED WORK THAT SHOULD HAVE BEEN DONE BY NOW * (TIME OF REPORTING)
[COMMIT THESE DEFINITIONS TO YOUR MEMORY]

The first thing to be done when trying to ascertain the health of the project is to find the correct values of these three variable EV, AC, and PV at that moment of time.
Let us take a simple project to understand the EVM completely.

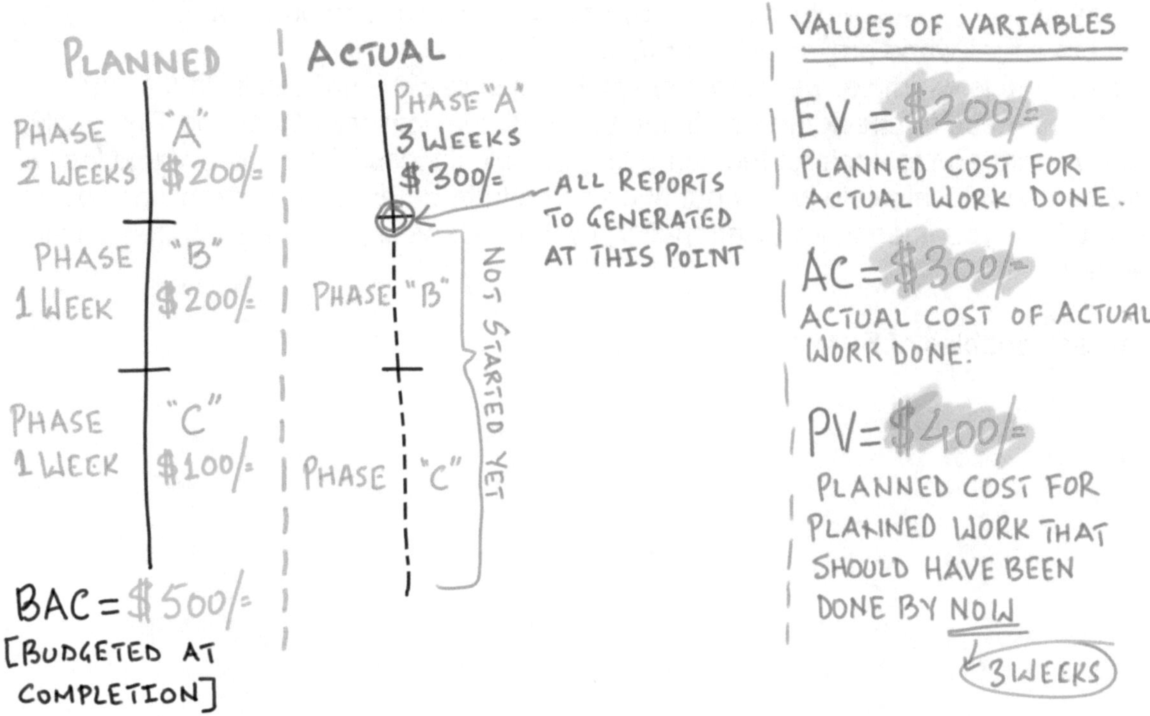

Looking at the example of the project let us first see what the value of each of the Variables is.

VALUES OF 3 VARIABLES

EV = $ 200/=

AC = $ 300/= &

PV = $ 400/=

Please revisit the definitions above multiple times to find out why the values of the 3 variables are so. Please do not move forward till you are in sync.

Now that we have the values of each of the EVM Variables, let us now start with ascertaining the health of this project.
Let us first start with the **Project Status**. This shows what the current condition of the project is. For this, we just need two formulas, one for Variance in Schedule and one for Variance in Cost.

EVM- STATUS REPORT

CV* = EV – AC

*CV IS COST VARIANCE

SV* = EV – PV

*SV IS SCHEDULE VARIANCE

To understand formula let us look at the definitions of the variables once again. CV = EV – AC. EV = Planned Cost for Actual Work Done whereas AC = Actual Cost for Actual Work done. Actual Work Done is common, hence Planned Cost vs actual cost for the actual work done states the Cost Variance.
SV = EV – PV. Where EV = Planned Cost For Actual Work Done whereas PV = Planned Cost For Planned Work That Should Have Been Done By Now. Planned Portion is common between the two. On the planned schedule, EV shows where we are as of now, whereas PV shows where we SHOULD have been by now. The difference between the two shows us the Schedule Variance. The logic is very simple and would give you tremendous confidence in Earned Value Management. If you did not get the logic of this, please go through it from the beginning of this topic again. Remember, understanding is more important than mugging up. Let us use the Status Review formulae on the project given here.

CALCULATING CV & SV

CONTINUING WITH THE SAME EXAMPLE.

VALUES OF 3 VARIABLES

EV = $200/=

AC = $300/= &

PV = $400/=

NOW: CV = EV - AC

∴ CV = 200 - 300

∴ CV = -100

AND: SV = EV - PV

∴ SV = 200 - 400

∴ SV = -200

The outputs of these formulas can help you conduct a root cause analysis about the problem afflicting your project. For a moment let us step outside this example. Let us say in one of the project status reports you got CV = 0 and SV = -200. You would say the problem is that the cost is exactly as per the budget but the schedule is behind / late. But that is just the symptoms. One needs to look at the reasons where the Cost Variance would be Zero while the Schedule Variance is negative. Under what circumstances can this happen.
One of the reasons why this can happen is because some activities (during the reporting period) started late but still took the same duration. This way the resources worked for the planned duration (cost remaining the same) but since these activities were started late, there is a Schedule Variance. Think of more reasons. Another reason could be that there were some unannounced holidays or non-working time in between the duration of some of the activities. This kept the cost extended the same while delaying the schedule. There are some more reasons and I will leave that to you to find out. This is the only method which can help a project manager diagnose the problem instead of just looking at the symptoms.

What do you think are the problems when in a status report you get CV = - 200 and SV = 0. The symptoms show that there are absolutely no variances in schedule but a sizeable variance in cost. If you try and diagnose the problems you will realize that one reason why this may happen is because “Crashing” is being done in the project to meet the timelines.

This increases the cost to meet the schedule. Another reason why this could have happened is because the price of the resources increased due to inflationary conditions. There are some more reasons and I will leave them to be found out by you. Do you see the amazing power of diagnosis that you could apply with EVM?

Now think of the underlying reasons for CV = -200 and SV = - 200 or when CV = 300 and SV = 300 and so on.

Coming back to this example (small case study) the CV = - 100 and SV = -200. This means that we are doing badly on both but we are doing more badly on Schedule. One of the reasons for such a symptom could be "Unproductive" resources as these resources are taking more time to get the work done thus creating variances on both the fronts. This kind of symptom may also mean that the planning by the project manager was unrealistically tight as well.

I guess now you can understand how powerful the earned value is and it can give such insights into the project without spending too much time in analysis.

Now, on to the Progress Report Calculations. The formulas for the progress reports are

EVM - PROGRESS REPORT | **INTERPRETATION.**

$*CPI = \frac{EV}{AC}$ PROVIDES RATE OF SPENDING MONEY

SUBSTITUTING VALUES FROM CASE STUDY

$CPI = \frac{200}{300} = \frac{2}{3}$ or 0.67

*CPI IS "COST PERFORMANCE INDEX"

IF CPI = 1 = AS PER BUDGET
CPI > 1 = UNDER BUDGET
[MEANS YOU ARE DOING BETTER THAN THE BUDGET]
CPI < 1 = OVER BUDGET
[MEANS YOU ARE DOING BADLY COMPARED TO THE BUDGET.]

$*SPI = \frac{EV}{PV}$ PROVIDES THE RATE OF UTILIZING TIME.

SUBSTITUTING VALUES FROM CASE STDUDY

$SPI = \frac{200}{400} = \frac{2}{4} = 0.50$

* SPI IS "SCHEDULE PERFORMANCE INDEX"

IF SPI = 1 = AS PER SCHEDULE
SPI > 1 = AHEAD OF SCHEDULE
[MEANS YOU ARE DOING BETTER THAN THE SCHEDULE]
SPI < 1 = BEHIND SCHEDULE
[MEANS YOU ARE NOT KEEPING UP WITH THE PLANNED SCHEDULE]

The whole purpose of calculating the progress values is to be able to calculate the Forecasts.

Moving on to the third report for project health assessment viz., Forecasting.

Forecasting has various formulas. The most prominent one is “Estimated At Completion” (EAC). EAC calculates the amount of money that would be spent on the entire project once it's completed. This is derived in multiple ways depending on the situation of the project at the time of reporting. Basically, it answers the question “If we keep this rate of spending and if this is the current situation of the project, how much would we end up spending on the project by the time it’s completed?”

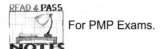

This is the most common and prominent forecasting formula.

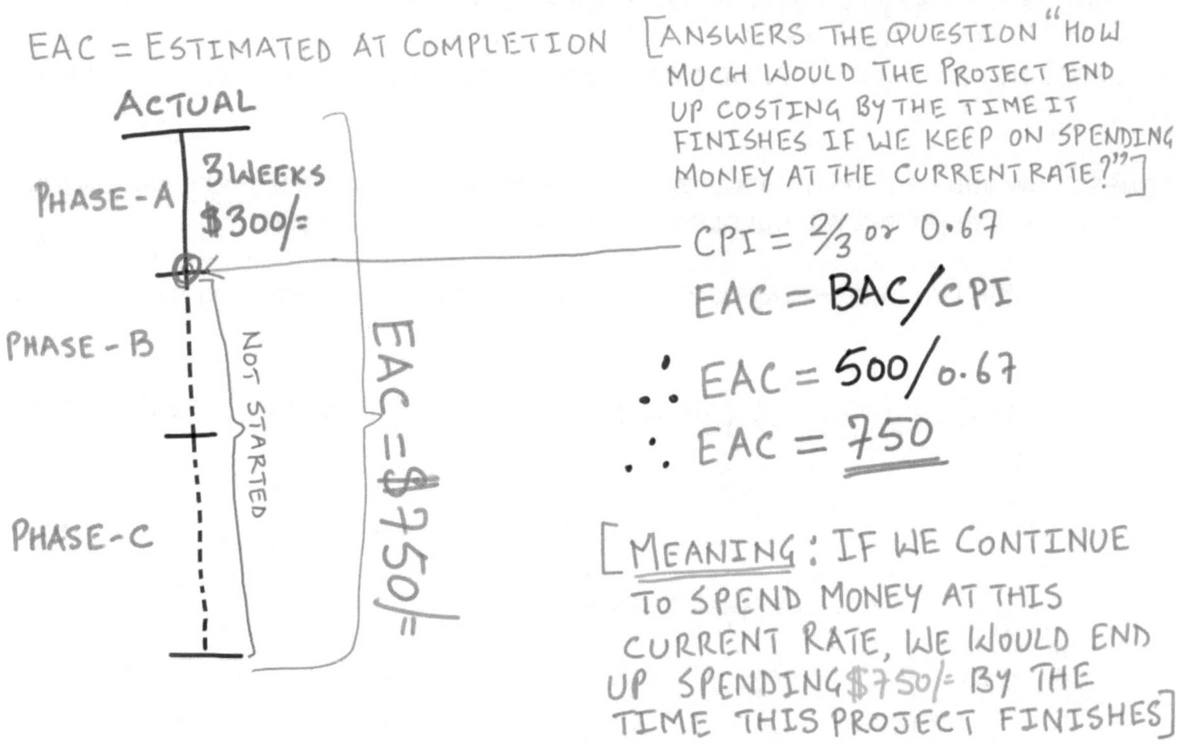

Once the EAC is calculated then it can be compared with the Total Planned Cost of the project or “Budgeted At Completion” (BAC) to find the forecasted variance. This is done by using the formula “Variance At Completion” (VAC).

EVM : VAC – CALCULATION

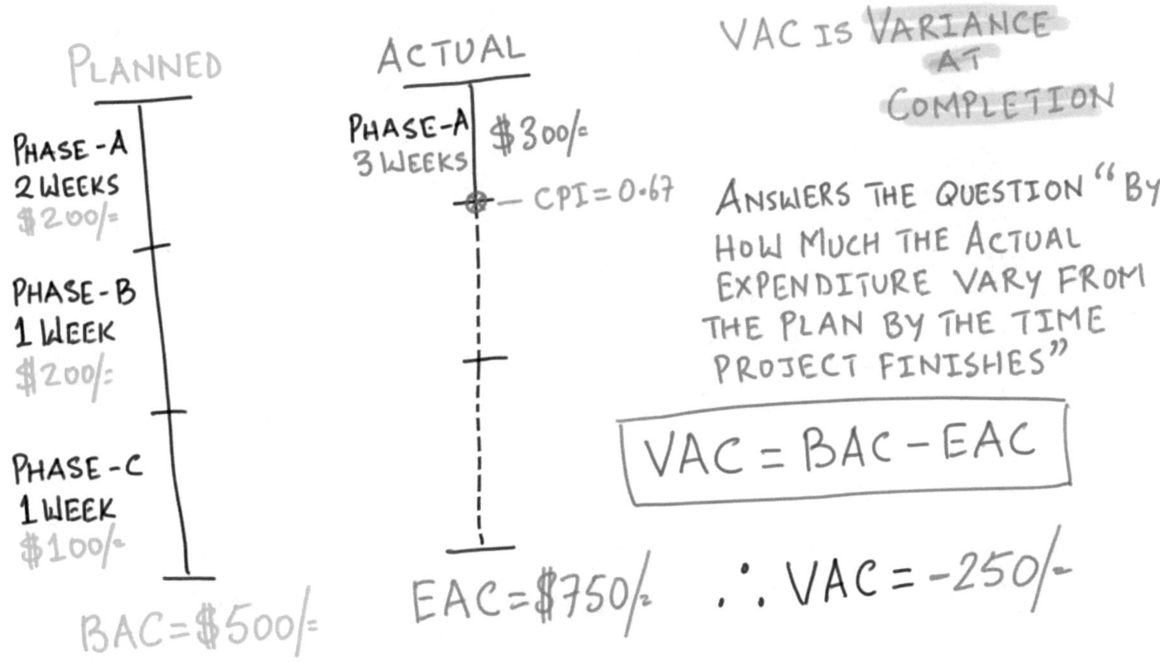
PLANNED
PHASE-A
2 WEEKS
$200/=
PHASE-B
1 WEEK
$200/=
PHASE-C
1 WEEK
$100/=
BAC=$500/=
ACTUAL
PHASE-A
3 WEEKS
$300/=
CPI=0.67
EAC=$750/=
VAC IS VARIANCE AT COMPLETION
ANSWERS THE QUESTION "BY HOW MUCH THE ACTUAL EXPENDITURE VARY FROM THE PLAN BY THE TIME PROJECT FINISHES"
VAC = BAC – EAC
∴ VAC = -250/-

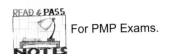

By default, the EAC gives "Cost" forecasting. We can also twist the EAC to calculate forecast on time/schedule basis. For this, we have to suffix it with small "t". Hence EACt would mean calculating the EAC based on time and not cost.

EVM: EAC_T & VAC_T

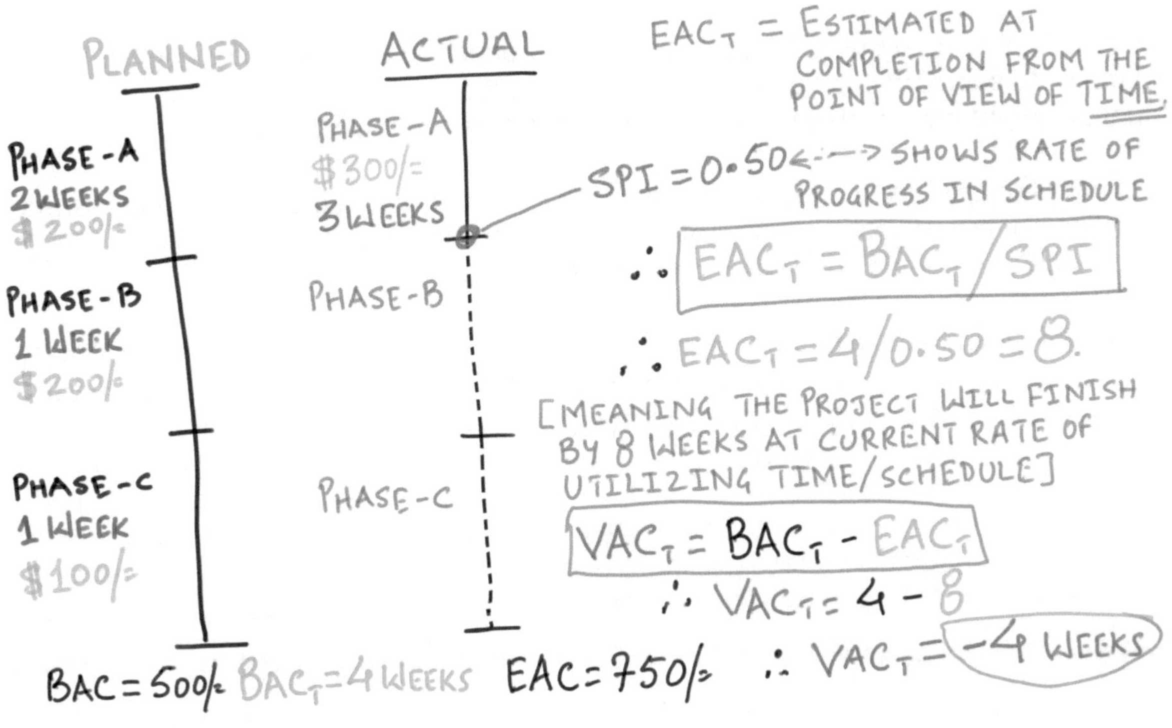
PLANNED
PHASE-A
2 WEEKS
$200/=
PHASE-B
1 WEEK
$200/=
PHASE-C
1 WEEK
$100/=
ACTUAL
PHASE-A
$300/=
3 WEEKS
PHASE-B
PHASE-C
EAC_T = ESTIMATED AT COMPLETION FROM THE POINT OF VIEW OF TIME.
SPI = 0.50 ← → SHOWS RATE OF PROGRESS IN SCHEDULE
∴ EAC_T = BAC_T / SPI
∴ EAC_T = 4/0.50 = 8.
[MEANING THE PROJECT WILL FINISH BY 8 WEEKS AT CURRENT RATE OF UTILIZING TIME/SCHEDULE]
VAC_T = BAC_T - EAC_T
∴ VAC_T = 4 - 8
BAC = 500/= BAC_T = 4 WEEKS EAC = 750/= ∴ VAC_T = -4 WEEKS

Forecasting has another formula and it's called "Estimated At Completion" (ETC).

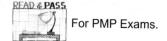

ETC answers the question, "How much would it cost to complete the rest of the project?" which means the part of the project that is not yet completed. EAC shows the forecast of the entire project including the part of the project which has already been completed.

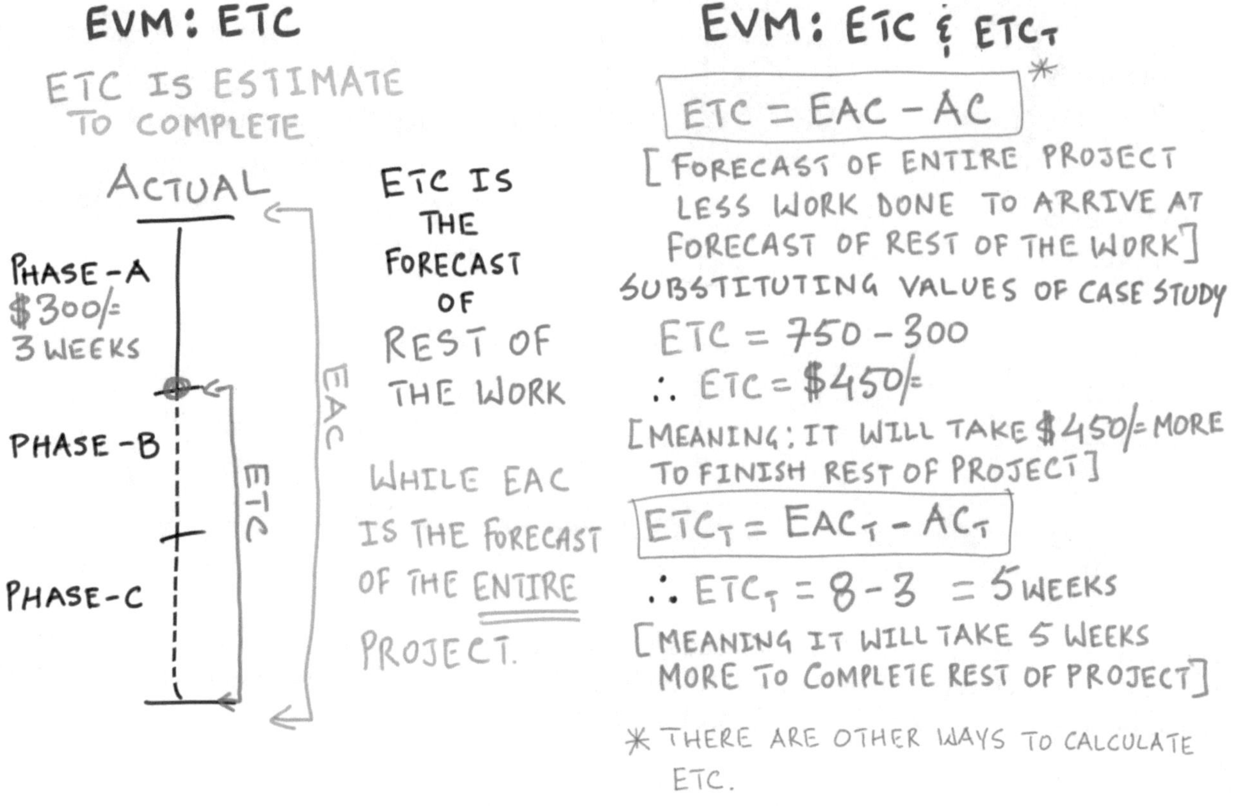

EVM: ETC
ETC IS ESTIMATE TO COMPLETE
ACTUAL
PHASE-A
$300/=
3 WEEKS
PHASE-B
PHASE-C
ETC
EAC
ETC IS THE FORECAST OF REST OF THE WORK
WHILE EAC IS THE FORECAST OF THE ENTIRE PROJECT.
EVM: ETC & ETCT
ETC = EAC - AC *
[FORECAST OF ENTIRE PROJECT LESS WORK DONE TO ARRIVE AT FORECAST OF REST OF THE WORK]
SUBSTITUTING VALUES OF CASE STUDY
ETC = 750 - 300
∴ ETC = $450/=
[MEANING: IT WILL TAKE $450/= MORE TO FINISH REST OF PROJECT]
ETCT = EACT - ACT
∴ ETCT = 8 - 3 = 5 WEEKS
[MEANING IT WILL TAKE 5 WEEKS MORE TO COMPLETE REST OF PROJECT]
* THERE ARE OTHER WAYS TO CALCULATE ETC.

It's important to note that ETC could be formula based or it could also mean "a fresh new estimate" (discarding the old one) done for the rest of the project. This would depend on the situation. Right now let us just calculate the same as per the formula.

I am sure that you have already started to think about the fact that based on different conditions of the project the way EAC is calculated should also be different.
Let us look at the various possible conditions individually.

You might face a situation in the project that either there is not much variance and you expect the project to continue at the same rate or there is a substantial variance but there is no solution available to you, hence your project would be forced to continue at the same rate. *E.g., Let us say during the status of the project you got hardly any variance, say CV = 0 and SV = -10 (or something similar with minor variance) hence this would mean that you would proceed as per the same speed as you are more or less on track. It could also happen that you may have a serious variance like CV = -300 and SV = - 200. You have identified that this is because of unskilled/low skilled team members working on the project and hence your project is suffering from serious productivity issues. However, your sponsor/management has clearly communicated to you that no other resources can be substituted nor hired from outside because of Human Resource Hiring ceiling being reached. In this case, despite the fact that you have a serious variance, since you do not have a solution, you will calculate the*

"Forecasted Completion" based on the previous speed. In both these cases, you will use the following formula for EAC.

$$EAC = BAC / CPI$$

Another situation could be that while conducting a health check you realize that the variances have been there because of a "Flawed and unrealistic" estimates during planning. Now that you are better aware of the situation you would have to make a "Fresh New Estimate" for the rest of the project work on which the work has yet not started. In this case, you cannot use the earlier CPI or SPI because the plan itself was incorrect. In such case, the formula of EAC would change. You cannot do anything about the money already spent viz., AC.

$$EAC = AC + ETC$$

A BRAND NEW ESTIMATE FOR REST OF THE WORK REMAINING

The third situation could be that the variances were because of an "Atypical" event (one-off event that rarely happen) because of something that happens rather rarely and is not expected to be repeated in the lifecycle of the project. *E.g., Delays in schedule due to Curfew in the city because of political unrest or Earthquake or Weather warnings and as such.* This means that such an event was a "One-off' event and is not likely to happen again during the rest of the project lifecycle. In such cases, realizing that the delay was because of reasons beyond your control and the fact that, had this event not occurred, you would have been on track, you will use the following formula: -

$$EAC = AC + (BAC - EV)$$

REST OF THE PLAN

Reserve Analysis is done at every phase end or at the end of every reporting period (along with earned value analysis) to see how much of the Contingency Reserves have been used up and how much of it is pending. Could the rest of the project be done with the remaining contingency reserve? If the contingency reserves are depleted then a case may be made to obtain some from Management Reserve. Decision may have to be made here to request or additional reserves or to discontinue the project without any additions to the reserve.

To-Complete Performance Index (TCPI) is the technique to understand the "Required Speed" at which the project has to be completed to meet the targeted EAC or BAC.

Taking the same case of "Delhi – Agra" road trip case. By the time "The midpoint" hotel was reached the delay was already .5 hrs (instead of 1.5 hrs, 2 hrs were taken) and the average speed so far had been 50Kms per hour. When you make a call to your boss from the Midway and tell him that you would be delayed, he may impress upon you the importance of reaching Agra as per the original commitment. You would like to calculate the "Required Speed" for the rest of the distance such that the original commitments are met. Target to be met for original commitment, despite the delay, is 100 km in the remaining 1 hr. Required Speed = 100 Kms per hour. You realize that since your current speed so far has been only 50 km per hour it's almost impossible to suddenly reach a required average speed of 100 km per hour. Let us say you communicated this situation to your boss that the required speed is impossible to be met given the circumstances. The boss may let you know that if you take 4 hrs (in total or another 2 hrs) to reach Agra, the prospective client would have already left for the airport. He also understands that you cannot reach as per the original commitment viz., 3 hrs. So he suggests you a new target of reaching there in 3.5 hrs (another 1.5 hrs for 100 kms). You calculate the required speed again and realize that it would require an average speed of 67 kms per hours to meet this new commitment. You also realize that increasing the average speed from 50 kms per hour to 67 kms per hour is a calculable risk and, more or less, manageable. Now for the rest of the journey, you would keep an eye out whether your current speed is as per the "Required Speed".
This is exactly how entire projects should be tracked based on the required average speed. This technique has two formulas. The first one helps you calculate the required (Speed of spending money) CPI to finish the project as per the original BAC. This calculation is shown as under.

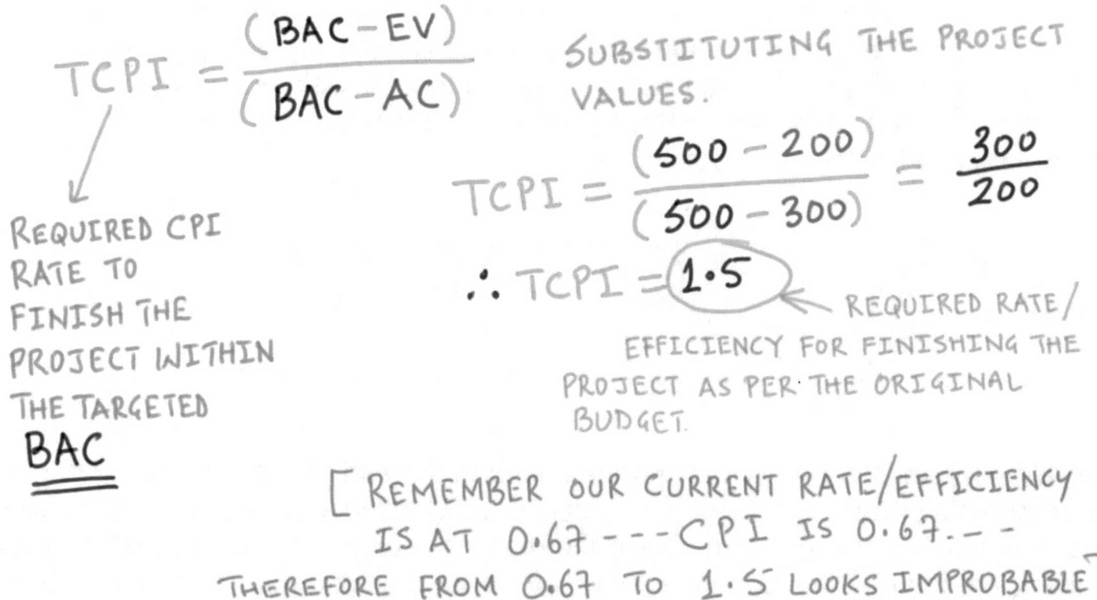

TO-COMPLETE PERFORMANCE INDEX - TCPI
TCPI = (BAC - EV) / (BAC - AC)
REQUIRED CPI RATE TO FINISH THE PROJECT WITHIN THE TARGETED BAC
SUBSTITUTING THE PROJECT VALUES.
TCPI = (500 - 200) / (500 - 300) = 300 / 200
∴ TCPI = 1.5
REQUIRED RATE/ EFFICIENCY FOR FINISHING THE PROJECT AS PER THE ORIGINAL BUDGET.
[REMEMBER OUR CURRENT RATE/EFFICIENCY IS AT 0.67 --- CPI IS 0.67. - -
THEREFORE FROM 0.67 TO 1.5 LOOKS IMPROBABLE]

The second formula is about calculating the required speed (asking speed) for the rest of the project based on a new (revised) target by the sponsor or the customer. This revised target may be called the EAC. This may happen because may times, the original BAC becomes unviable to be met. In which case the management may give a new target and this new target may be called the New EAC (basically a targeted EAC). Now you would like to know the Required CPI to meet the targeted EAC.

TO-COMPLETE PERFORMANCE INDEX - TCPI

THE MANAGEMENT MAY HAVE A NEW TARGET BUDGET AND THIS WILL BE REPRESENTED BY **EAC**

$$TCPI = \frac{(BAC - EV)}{(EAC - AC)}$$

THE NEW TARGETED BUDJET SAY $600/-

SUBSTITUTING THE VALUES

$$TCPI = \frac{(500 - 200)}{(600 - 300)} = \frac{300}{300} = 1$$

THIS MEANS THAT THE REQUIRED RATE/ EFFICIENCY TO FINISH THE PROJECT WITHIN $600 IS A CPI OF 1.

[CURRENT RATE IS 0.67, HENCE MOVING TO REQUIRED EFFICIENCY OF 1 LOOKS POSSIBLE]

Now, as you progress in your project and conduct regular health checks you will also constantly compare your "Actual CPI" with "Required CPI", among other things, to ascertain if you are in a position to meet the targets.

You will realize the following here:

1) Whenever your TCPI is higher than 1, the lesser likelihood that you project would finish within the BAC or the targeted EAC. A higher than 1 TCPI means that you would have to perform better than the budget consistently for the rest of the project.
2) Whenever your current CPI is greater than 1 the TCPI would be less than 1. Meaning your current speed of spending money on the project so far would help decide the TCPI (the asking speed) for the rest of the project.

These two statements are not only practical but they will also help you answer one or two questions correctly in the PMP Exams.

Just for review purposes, each and every variable and formula of EVM is being put up here in a tabulated way.

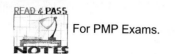

VARIABLE	DESCRIPTION
EV EARNED VALUE	PLANNED COST FOR ACTUAL WORK DONE
AC ACTUAL COST	ACTUAL COST FOR ACTUAL WORK DONE
PV PLANNED VALUE	PLANNED COST FOR PLANNED WORK THAT SHOULD HAVE BEEN DONE BY NOW

NAME	FORMULA	DESCRIPTION
COST VARIANCE [CV]	EV−AC	−VE VALUE MEANS OVER BUDGET
SCHEDULE VARIANCE [SV]	EV−PV	−VE VALUE MEANS BEHIND SCHEDULE
COST PERFORMANCE INDEX [CPI]	$\frac{EV}{AC}$	SHOWS EFFICIENCY OF SPENDING MONEY. LESS THAN 1 MEANS NOT EFFICIENT.
SCHEDULE PERFORMANCE INDEX [SPI]	$\frac{EV}{PV}$	SHOWS EFFICIENCY OF UTILIZING TIME. LESS THAN 1 MEANS NOT EFFICIENT.
ESTIMATED AT COMPLETION [EAC]	$\frac{BAC}{CPI}$	1. WHEN THERE IS NO SUBSTANTIAL DIFFERENCE AND WORK WILL PROCEED AS PER SAME CPI. 2. WHEN THERE IS SUBSTANTIAL DIFFERENCE, BUT NO SOLUTION EXISTS. PROJECT WILL PROGRESS AT SAME CPI.
	AC+ETC	WHEN THE ORIGINAL ESTIMATES WERE INCORRECT AND A COMPLETELY NEW ESTIMATES HAVE TO BE MADE FOR THE REST OF THE PROJECT.
	AC+(BAC−EV)	WHEN VARIANCE IS "ATYPICAL" REST OF PROJECT WOULD BE AS PER THE ORIGINAL PLAN.
ESTIMATE TO COMPLETION [ETC]	EAC−AC	HOW MUCH WOULD THE REMAINING PROJECT COST?
VARIANCE AT COMPLETION [VAC]	BAC−EAC	−VE VALUE MEANS OVER BUDGET BY THE TIME THE PROJECT COMPLETES.
TO-COMPLETE PERFORMANCE INDEX [TCPI]	$\frac{(BAC-EV)}{(BAC-AC)}$	EFFICIENCY REQUIRED TO MEET THE ORIGINAL BUDGET.
	$\frac{(BAC-EV)}{(EAC-AC)}$	EFFICIENCY REQUIRED TO MEET THE NEW TARGET "EAC".

There are times when examinees get confused about which formula to use between CV and CPI and between SV and SPI. The wordings of the questions seem misleading to some. Whenever the question asks about the speed of spending money, cost efficiency, Cost Index, Speed of utilizing money, Rate of cost expenditure on project you must use the formula CPI. Whereas if the question is asking about if you are under or over budget, or overspending or under spending or asks what is the cost variance, use the formula CV.

Similarly, if the question asks you about the rate of utilizing time, speed with which the schedule is being covered, rate of time utilization, rate of covering the schedule, rate of progress based on time/schedule, use the formula SPI. Whereas if the question asks you about being ahead or behind schedule, schedule variance, how far ahead or how far behind schedule, taking more time or less time, use the formula SV.

Measurement Pitfalls: This is not really a tools & techniques of this process, but rather an addendum to them. Whenever we measure something we need to be careful to ensure that we do not fall into some of the typical measurement pitfalls. Let us go through some of these pitfalls:

1) **Hawthorne Effect**: This effect is based on a research that was done at "Hawthorne General Electrical Plant" wherein they found that some aspects of people's behavior changes when they come to know about what is being observed about them and what kind of measurements and data are being collected about them. This effect is real and has to be understood keeping in mind that this may not always generate a conducive result. Hence, the kind of measurements that you are collecting will alter the behavior of the team members and employees, therefore the measurements must be devised keeping this phenomenon in mind.
   Let me provide couple of examples. I was consulting in one of the foremost Indian organizations where I was in their main office for 4 days. During lunch time my team and I would visit their amazing cafeteria with truly amazing and healthy food options. What I noticed that there was a large white board kept at the very entrance of the cafeteria that had two measurements written about the previous day. One, the amount of food wasted in Kgs, and two, the amount of paper tissues used in Kgs. Just these two had such an amazing subconscious effect that people were careful about the portion of food they were piling on their buffet trays. This was working so well that I found a reduction of over 10 kgs in food wastage and a reduction of just over 250gms of paper tissues consumption over a period of just 4 days. Yet another example that I should share with you is something I noticed in one of the lower maturity organizations that I had worked with a long time back. The management over there was keenly observing the duration an employee was spending in office. This created an environment of lethargy where employees just dragged their feet, took it easy, and hung around in the office late resulting in disastrous reduction in productivity and astronomical rise in overheads. Not something that the organization was hoping for.
   This effect would be alive and kicking within a project as well and hence all project measurements must be decided on keeping the behavioral aspects of people in mind.

2) **Vanity Metric:** These are those kind of measurements that give you a false sense of progress without diving into the real condition of the work. Statements like "80% of the project is completed" or "We have spent over 200,000 person hours in this initiative", have no meaning because it does not tell you if your project is on time, does it have any quality issue etc. Several project managers tend to hide behind such metrics to look good during management reviews, but later suffer the consequences for not

having collected meaningful metrics. This is also closely connected to **Misuse of Metrics**.

3) **Demoralizing Effect:** Let us say, your project has been delayed and consequently gone over budget. Your EVM indicators show that your team would have to finish the rest of the project at a TCPI of 1.8 to stay within the budget. Since their current CPI is way below 1, the team knows very well that this is not even achievable. And thus go about doing their work without any motivation or sense of pride. Measurements and metrics, if made beyond reach, have a tremendous demoralizing effect on people. Remember, your KPI's and Metrics must be SMART. Where "A" in SMRT stands for "achievable".

4) **Confirmation Bias:** Confirmation bias is the tendency to search for, interpret, favor, and recall information in a way that confirms or supports one's prior beliefs or values. This is very evident in news channels now a days. Each and every news channel is either in complete support of the current government or completely against it. Hence for any economic index, or any crime metrics or any such national metrics, both kinds of news channels contort the meaning of the measurements to forward their agenda. This same thing happens with organizational measurements and project metrics. This is the reason why Sponsors and Project Managers must maintain an unbiased mindset to truly understand the metrics and what they mean for the project or the organization, instead of jumping to pre-ordained conclusions.

5) **Correlation Vs Causation:** Closely related to the concept of Confirmation Bias, this pitfall is about making incorrect deductions or correlations from metrics. Let us say that your project is running behind schedule. And then you also note that project is over budget as well. This makes you to draw the collusion that the project is over budget because the project is delayed. Something which may not always be correct. What if you try to bring the project back on track, schedule wise, but you do not see any improvement in project budget indicators. Therefore metrics must be looked at in a manner to arrive at proper diagnosis instead of making informed and stereotypical correlations.

10.14.2 Main Outcome from this process: -

Work Performance Information contains the project health information that could be used by the management and the project managers to fully comprehend the project situation and formulate plans for future as well as communicate the same to the key stakeholders. Here the content would be mostly Earned Value Analysis and Trend Analysis calculations. All "Work Performance Information" become input to only one process and that is "*MONITOR AND CONTROL PROJECT WORK*".

Cost Forecasts tell the future expected condition of the project. How much money could be utilized by the time the project gets over? Things like EAC and ETC and VAC are calculated. Even TCPI could be calculated to show what is the asking rate of cost efficiency to finish the project in a given budget or financial target.

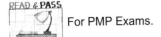

Because of the findings from this process some Corrective actions or Preventive actions may have an impact on the baseline. This would warrant the issue of a **Change Request**.

10.14.3 EVM Questions for a bit of practice.

1) EVM Question Basic
   You are managing a project with a BAC of $93,000, EV (BCWP) of $51,840, PV (BCWS) of $64,800, and AC (ACWP) of $43,200. What is the CPI?
   A. 1.5
   B. 0.8
   C. 1.2
   D. $9,000.00

2) EVM Question Basic
   You're working on a project that has an EV of $7362 and a PV (BCWS) of $8232. What's your SV?
   A. - $870.00
   B. $870.00
   C. .89
   D. Not enough information

3) You are working on a project with a PV of $56,733 and an SPI of 1.2. What's the Earned Value of your project?
   A. $68,079.60
   B. $47,277.50
   C. $68,733
   D. 0.72

4) You are working on a project with an SPI of .72 and a CPI of 1.1. Which of the following BEST describes your project?
   A. Your project is ahead of schedule and under budget.
   B. Your project is behind schedule and over budget.
   C. Your project is behind schedule and under budget.
   D. Your project is ahead of schedule and over budget

5) Your project has a BAC of $4,522 and is 13% complete. What is the earned value (EV)?
   A. $3,934.14
   B. There is not enough information to answer.
   C. $587.86
   D. $4,522.00

6) You are managing a project laying underwater fiber optic cable. The total cost of the project is $52 per meter, and the project is to lay 4 km of cable across a lake bed. It's scheduled to take 8 weeks to complete, with an equal amount of cable laid in each week. It's currently end of week 5, and your team has laid 1,800 meters of cable so far. What is the SPI of your project?
   A. 1.16
   B. 1.08
   C. 0.92
   D. 0.72

7) A project manager is working on a large construction project. His plan says that the project should end up costing $1.5 million, but he's concerned that he's not going come in under budget. He's spent $950,000 of the budget so far, and he calculates that he's 57% done with the work, and he doesn't think he can improve his CPI above 1.05. Which of the following BEST describes the current state of the project?
   A. The project is likely to come under budget.
   B. The project is likely to exceed its budget
   C. The project is right on target.
   D. There is no way to answer this question.

10.14.4 Answers to EVM Questions

1) Correct option is **C**. CPI = EV / AC; 51,840 / 43,200; 1.2
2) The correct option is **A**. SV = EV – PV ; 7,362 – 8,232 ; - 870. It is important to note that even the possible wrong answer is also given in case you switch the positions of EV and PV in the calculations. Hence you need to be thorough with your calculations.
3) Correct option is **A**. SPI = EV / PV. Therefore EV = SPI * PV; 1.2 * 56,733 = 68,079.60
4) The correct option is **C**. Less than 1 of SPI = Behind Schedule (Basically doing badly against the planned schedule) and greater than 1 of CPI = Under Budget (Doing better than the planned budget).
5) The correct option is **C**. Remember the original definition of EV. EV = Planned Cost for ACTUAL work done. The question shows that the actual work is 13% and the total planned cost (BAC) is $4,522.00. Therefore 13% of BAC = EV = 587.86.
6) The correct option is **D**. This is a much simpler question then what it appears to be. Let us only concentrate on the question asked. Question wants to know the value of SPI. SPI = EV / PV. Hence we only need to find two things viz., EV and PV. EV means "Planned cost for actual work done". Actual work done is 1,800 meters and the planned rate of $52 per meter amounts to EV of $93,600.00. Now on to PV. PV means "Planned cost for planned work that should have been done by now". As per the original plan, an equal amount of cable had to be laid over 8 weeks. Which means 4,000 meters were to be laid in 8 weeks hence, 500 meters were to be laid each week. In 5 weeks, the cable laid should have been 2,500 meters. Hence PV = $52 x 2,500 = 130,000. Now the SPI = 93,600 / 130,000 = 0.72.
7) The correct option is **B**. Since this question is asking about speed it means that the question is about TCPI. It's asking you whether or not a project is going to come in under budget, and that's what TCPI is for. Good thing you were given all of the values you need to calculate it! The Actual % Complete is 57%, the BAC is $1,500,000 and the AC is $950,000. You can calculate the EV = BAC x Actual % Complete = $1,500,000 x 57% = $855,000. So now you have everything you need to calculate

   TCPI = BAC - EV = ($1,500,000 - $855,000)

   BAC – AC = ($1,500,000 - $950,000)

   TCPI = 1.17

   Since the TCPI is greater than 1 hence it would mean that the project is likely to exceed its budget.

10.15 Ninja Drill – Implementation - 3

In this Ninja Drill you will find the most important notes and pointers that are important from the point of PMP Exams and covers, Monitor Communications, Monitor Risks, Control Schedule and Control Costs.

S. No.	Drill Points
1.	The main output / outcome of the process Monitor Communications is Issue Log.
2.	If stakeholders are constantly complaining of communication gap, not aware of certain information and / or not sure about the condition of the project, the Communication Plan must be revisited and corrected if found lacking.
3.	Overall steps in the process "Monitor Risks": • Frequently Monitor Risks • New Risks identification and classification • Identification of new risks due to changes in projects and changes in environment • Assessing the effectiveness of the Risk Reponses • Conduct Audits to ensure compliance to response plans • Revisiting Reserves to ascertain sufficiency • Updating Lessons Learned Register • Revisiting the Risk Management Plan or the Risk Response Plan if required • Raising a change request if required
4.	The main Tools & Techniques of the process "Control Schedule" are: • Earned Value Management • RAG Chart • Information Radiators / Burn Charts • Critical Path Method • Schedule Compression
5.	Burndown Chart (opposite of BurnUp Chart) shows the number of Story Points remaining in the iteration / sprint at any point of time. It also shows pattern up to the point which would help in forecast as well. This is similar to SPI of EVM.
6.	In a Burndown Chart when your actual progress is below the ideal / planned progress line than your iteration is ahead of schedule.
7.	In a Burnup Chart when your actual progress line is below the ideal / planned progress line than your iteration is behind schedule.
8.	For an overview of an iteration visually depicting "which User Story is in which stage of the Iteration", can be seen on the KanBan Chart.
9.	Combined Burn Chart shows how much work is remaining as well as how much work is completed. It also shows the stability of the user stories during the iteration.
10.	Milestone Charts are for reporting to senior management and customers.
11.	Bar Charts are used for displaying the overall progress and measure schedule variances in a project at any point of time. Traffic Light Charts can also be used for the same.
12.	Hawthorne effect: What you measure changes the behaviour of people. If you just measure time and volume people will just spend more time producing quantity which may have lower quality and not create any customer value or satisfaction.
13.	Demoralization: Excessively high targets will demoralize people.
14.	Misusing the metrics • Focusing on less important metrics rather than the metrics that matter most, • Focusing on performing well for the short-term measures at the expense of long-term metrics, and • Working on out-of-sequence activities that are easy to accomplish in order to improve performance indicators.
15.	Confirmation bias: We tend to see and derive what we want to'
16.	The main outcome / output / artefact from the process "Control Schedule" are: • Schedule Reports • Schedule Forecast

17.	The main Tools & Techniques of the process "Control Costs" are: • Earned Value Analysis • Variance Analysis • Reserve Analysis • To-Complete Performance Index
18.	To measure the health of a project, 3 reports are made and they are: 1. Status Report, 2. Progress Report and 3. Forecast.
19.	EV = Earned Value = Planned Cost for Actual Work Done.
20.	AC = Actual Cost = Actual Cost for Actual Work Done
21.	PV = Planned Value = Planned Cost for Planned Work that should have been done by NOW.
22.	Cost Variance [CV] = EV – AC
23.	Schedule Variance [SV] = EV – PV
24.	Cost Performance Index [CPI] = EV / AC
25.	Schedule Performance Index [SPI] = EV / PV
26.	EAC = BAC / CPI [To be used either when the project is more or less on schedule and hence you will continue the rest of the project as well in the same pace / rate, or when the project is behind schedule but you do not have any recourse or solution and hence you have to continue at the same pace irrespective.]
27.	EAC = AC + ETC [To be used when your earlier estimates were completely wrong and hence at this point of the project you have to calculate a fresh estimate for the rest of the project viz., ETC or Estimate To Completion].
28.	EAC = AC + (BAC – EV) [To be used when the delay is due to an atypical reason which is unlikely to happen again, hence the rest of the project would be continued as per the rest of the project plan. (BAC – EV provides the rest of the plan)]
29.	EAC provides the forecast for the entire project including the portion that has been completed, but ETC provides the estimate for the rest of the project from that point onwards.
30.	Variance At Completion [VAC] = BAC – EAC. (BAC = Budgeted At Completion or simply put the total planned cost)
31.	Cumulative expenditure done on project as compared to the cost baseline is shown in the form of S-Curve.
32.	To Complete Performance Index [TCPI] provides the "Required rate of CPI" to finish the rest of the project in order to finish within the provided budget (BAC) or an agreed upon target.
33.	TCPI for a Specific BAC = (BAC – EV) / (BAC – AC)
34.	TCPI for a new target or new EAC = (BAC – EV) / (EAC – AC)
35.	TCPI value of greater than 1 will make it difficult to finish the project in the given budget and most likely the project will finish over budget.
36.	TCPI value of less than 1 will make it easy to finish the project within the given budget and most likely the project will finish under budget or on budget.
37.	How do you know if your forecasting is reliable? Check your previous forecasts and see if they were more or less representing your current performance indicators. If they were close then the chances are that your forecasts for the future would be reliable as well.
38.	The main outcome / output / artefact of the process "Control Costs" are: 1. Cost performance report / Cost report 2. Cost Forecast
End Of Ninja Drill	

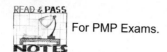

10.16 Control Quality

The main purpose of this process is to "Check / Inspect" if the quality requirements have been met in the product of the project before it's handed over for Scope Validation and final approval by the customer/client. *Control Quality* is inspection and testing based and the outcome would either result in Change Requests, Quality Control Measurements or Validated Deliverables which could then be handed over for Scope Validation.

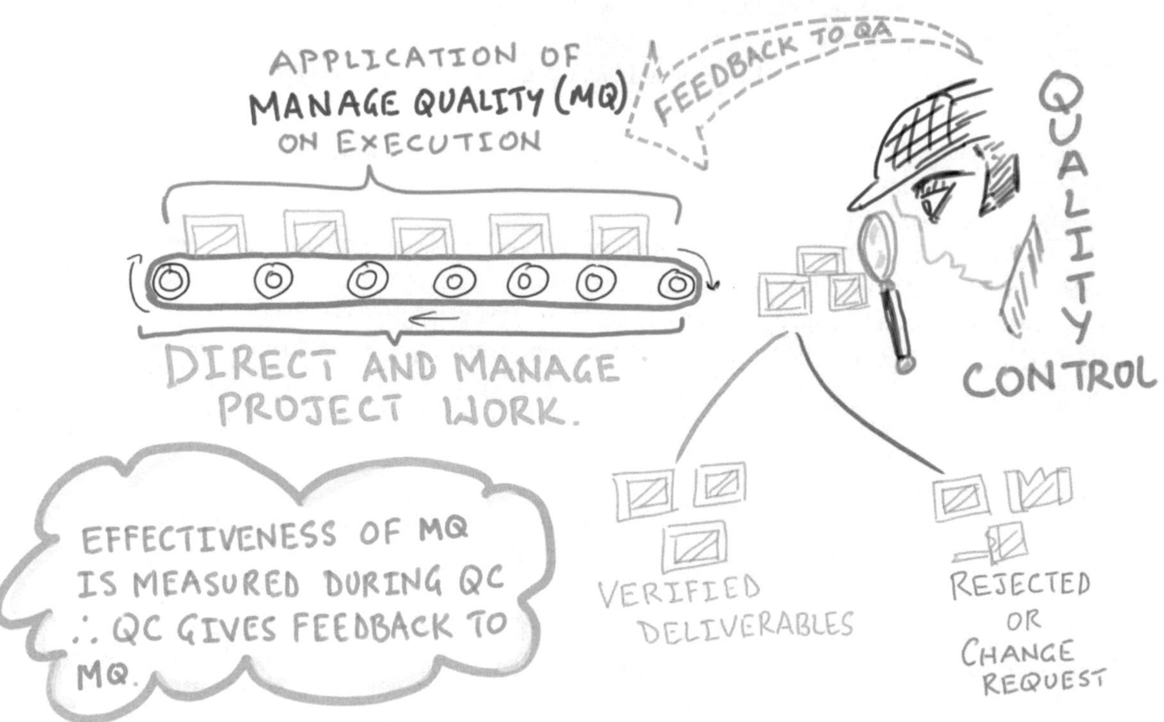

MANAGE QUALITY (MQ)
ON EXECUTION
FEEDBACK TO QA

IS MEASURED DURING QC
∴ QC GIVES FEEDBACK TO

Control Quality process is performed to measure the completeness, compliance, and fitness for use of a product. Control Quality cannot detect "Defects" or Non-Compliance to requirements and that's why "Scope Validation" is done after this process to ensure that all the requirements have been met.

10.16.1 Main Tools and Techniques of this Process: -

Checklist has already been explained earlier. In this process, it would be used to ensure that all the steps in Control Quality are indeed being taken so that there are no errors of omissions and commissions unearthed during inspections and testing.

Check sheets (also known as tally sheets) are used for collecting data in real time at the location where the data is generated. The data it captures can be quantitative or qualitative. When the information is quantitative the check sheet is called a tally sheet. This is supposed to be in a structured form so that when the data is recorded on to it, it could be used for predicting potential problems or gaps or it could be used as data supplement for "Causes of the problem", once the problem has been identified. The frequency of readings from this form may even help make a Pareto chart.

MOTOR ASSEMBLY-CHECK SHEET

NAME OF DATA COLLECTOR: JUGADU ERP
LOCATION: TIMBAKTU
DATA COLLECTION DATE: 28/JUNE/2017

DEFECT TYPES/ EVENT OCCURRENCE	DAYS						TOTAL
	MON.	TUE.	WED.	THU.	FRI.	SAT.	
SUPPLIED PARTS RUSTED	I	IIIII	III	III	IIIIII	IIIIIIII	26
MISALIGNED WELD	II				III		5
IMPROPER TEST PROCEDURE							0
WRONG PART ISSUED	II	I			IIIII		8
FILM ON PARTS							0
VOIDS IN CASTING			IIIII			II	7
INCORRECT DIMENSIONS					II		2
ADHISIVE FAILURE	I			I		II	4
TOTAL	6	6	8	4	16	12	

My father, who was a "turnkey project manager" for Paper Plants, had put up plants in various parts of the world. When he was putting up the plant for the government of Nigeria (the biggest in whole of Arica at that point of time) I used to accompany him to his office. I used to love those 100-ton rollers and giant furnaces digesting wood to pulp. The first thing my father used to do was to get hold of these "Check sheets" (They were called Record sheets during those days) from production, from inspectors and the production quality control departments and used to draw his conclusions about what quality issues were being faced. Like, in one instance people were not able to understand why the 200 tons lot at night was too brittle even when the mix in the boiler was perfect, he managed to see the co-relation between brittle paper and the temperature fluctuations in steam-heated primary 100-ton rollers. On inspections, it was revealed that one of the valves in the steam inlet was broken thus heating the rollers more than was needed which was slightly "Cooking the paper" to higher levels of crispiness. I thought I would tell you something I understood back when I was a kid in 1977 and still remember the power and use of these Check sheets. These check sheets could also be used for documenting the errors and defects unearthed during inspection.

Statistical Sampling: Statistical Sampling is used since it may be too expensive and it may take too long to test/inspect every line of code, or box of soap, or batch of cell phones or truckload of cotton. In such cases, it's just not possible to do so. What is done instead is to take samples from different batches and tested/inspected thoroughly and the results from that test/inspection are projected to the entire batch/production. This may not give absolutely accurate results but it's accepted in most places and organizations. *E.g., Your organization is producing 1 million boxes of pencils every day and you wish to know how many of them do* *not have the standard strength before breaking. Would you apply this "Strength Test" to each and every pencil. That would make the whole process too expensive and may drive the cost of the pencil too high and at the same time reduce productivity. You would rather pick up 1,000 boxes from different days and times and test them and apply the results to the rest of the production and take actions accordingly.*

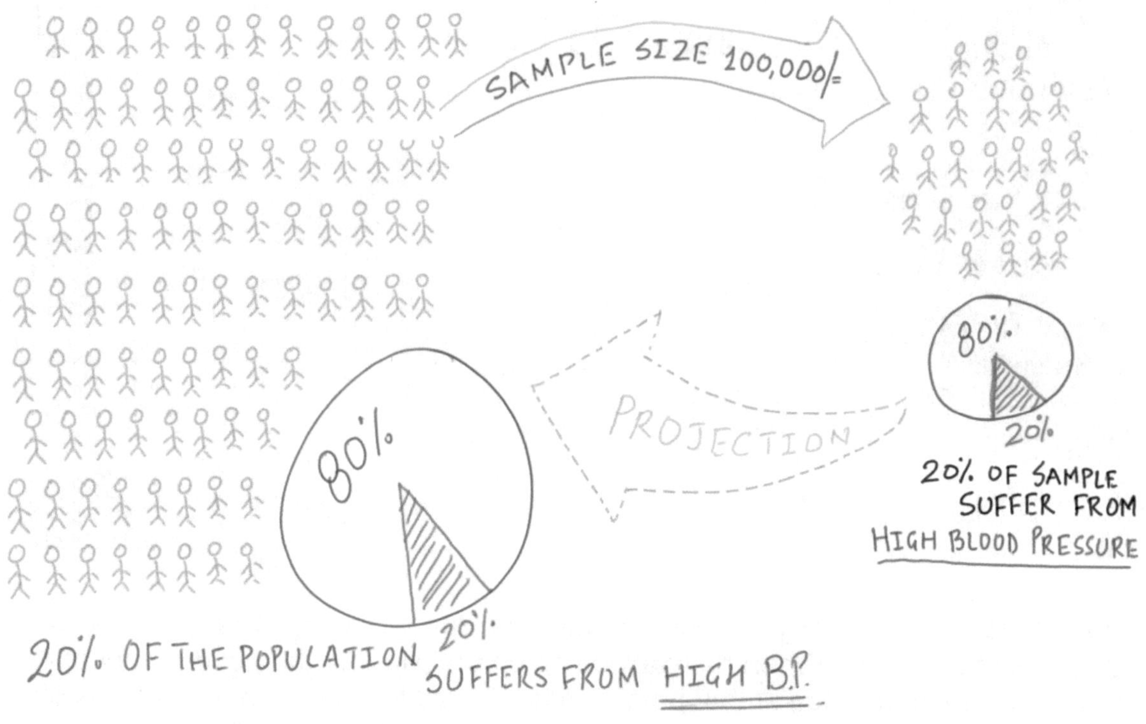

Performance Reviews is basically the observations based on the comparison between the quality benchmarks and quality metrics as stated in the Quality Management Plan and the actual results of testing, inspections, and reviews.

Root Cause Analysis (RCA) just as explained earlier, but here it is used for quality problems and issues which have already happened and unearthed during testing, inspections, and reviews.

Inspection is the actual physical examination of work product to determine if they conform to the documented standards and specifications. Inspections are post facto, which means that the deliverables have to be ready before inspections can be done. (In some organizations they can be called Testing, Inspection Review, Reviews, peer reviews, inspection audits or just audits and even walkthroughs.)

Inspection is a tool and technique of only three processes and they are *VALIDATE SCOPE*, *CONTROL QUALITY*, and *CONTROL PROCUREMENTS*.

Testing / Product Evaluations is done to find defects and errors (bugs) in the product or service. Different application area would need different kinds of testing. IT organizations have something called Unit Testing, Integration Testing, System Testing and User Acceptance Testing, Black box testing and white box testing while in the Infrastructure industries Strength test, stress test, load test, sink-ratio test, load bearing, and vibration test etc.

I guess all of us know what is testing but some of us may have a question as to what is the difference between testing and inspection. Inspection is a wider term which involves testing as well. Inspection is more to do with "conformity to requirements, or designs or specifications" while Testing is about validating specific aspects of inspection. *E.g., You are a project manager working on an infrastructure project of building a road bridge over a river. The government inspector would come and inspect if the design and width of the columns are as per the approved specifications, the width of the bridge is as documented and the material mix is as per the specifications and regulations. However his inspection would not be completed till he does some tests like "Stress Test or load test" on some of the pillars by getting 10% more weight (then specifications) on few of the targeted pillars, or test the consistency of the pillar material by drilling a hole into a pillar and taking a sample of the concrete mix to see it has the right consistency.* Once the physical inspection, as well as the tests, are done the Inspector may be satisfied to give the go-ahead to the rest of the work. I hope this has made the concept clear. I was quite disturbed to see wrong answers in some of the popular websites which people have begun to take for granted in terms of authenticity.

Cause And Effect Diagram is something you already know well. However, you need to know that in this process it is used for finding the causes of the Quality Issues, Errors or Defects that have already happened.

Control Charts are one of my favorite quality tools because they are the only tools that help in measuring the health of a process. The first thing to understand about a Control Chart is that it is the tool to assess the health of a "process" and not a specific project. Control Charts are used to understand whether or not a process is stable. Readings from various projects are taken for a specific process and plotted on this chart and based on the trends shown in the plotting of the data the health of the process is ascertained.
Let us look at the various elements of a Control Chart.

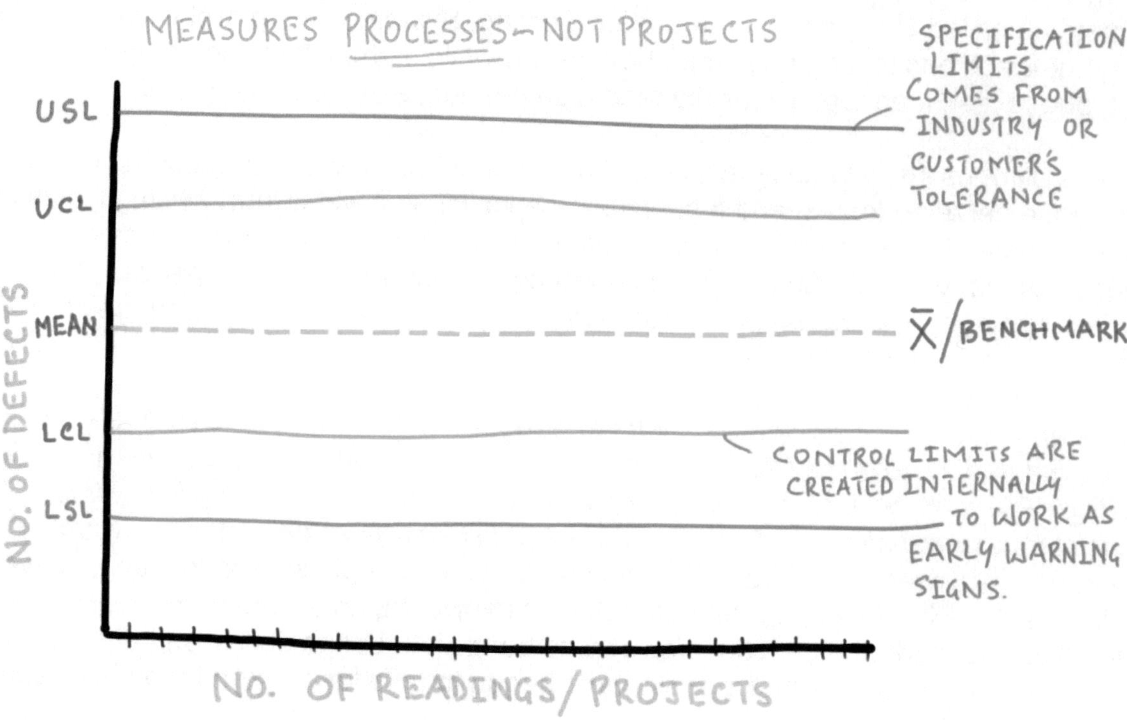

When readings are plotted on to the control charts various trends and observations can be made. Let us take these trends one by one to understand them better.
Some readings would result in data points coming alternatively on either side of the mean.

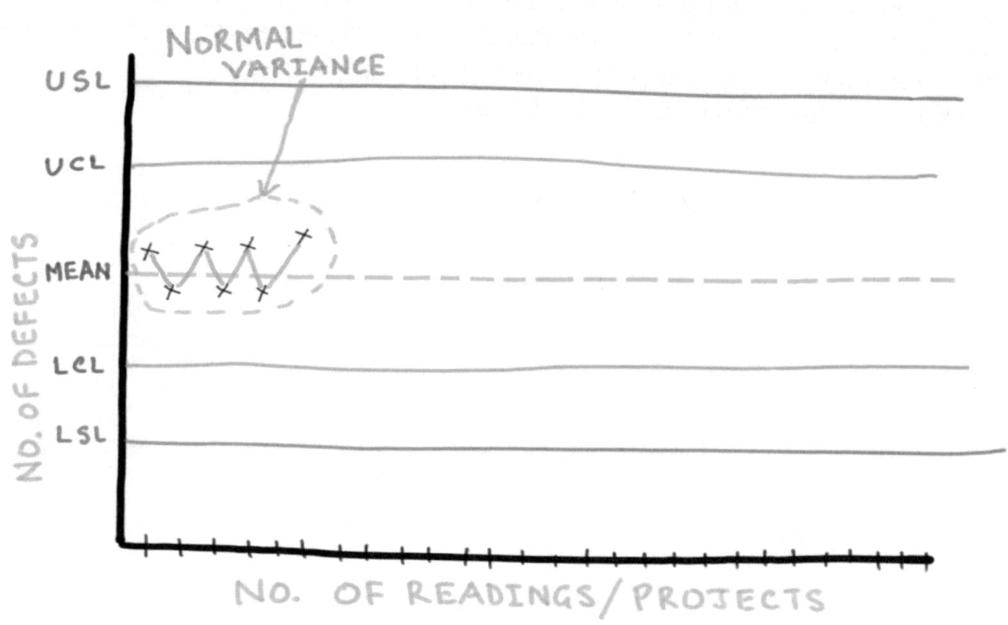

Irrespective of what it looks like it's a healthy trend. This is exactly what a healthy process looks like. These alternative data points are called "Normal Variance" and one cannot really find the reasons for this variation. *E.g., You are supposed to be reporting to your office sharp at 9:00 am. However your real-time recordings would be more like 8:55 am, 9:10 am, 8:53 am, 9:07 am and so on. You would not know the reason why you are 5 minutes early or 7 minutes late.* This is called normal variance and is healthy.
When readings show a continuous trend, either above or below the mean, it violates the "Rule of 7" and hence, it's termed as a suspect case and warrants investigation.

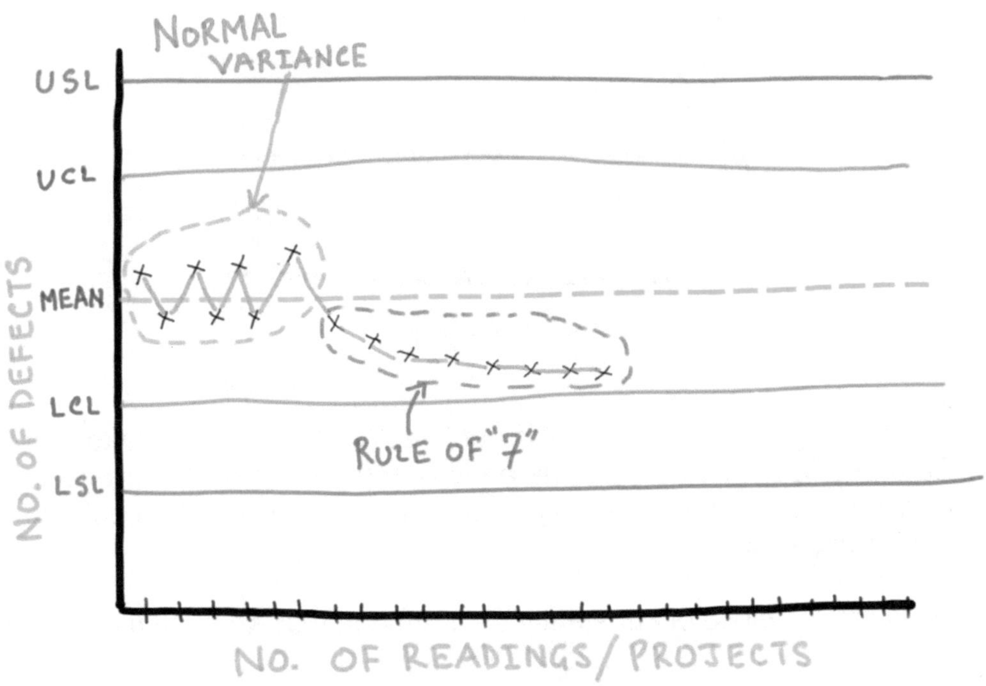

A "Rule of 7" occurs when 7 or more consecutive data points get plotted either above the mean or below it. This shows that there is some kind of skewness or "pulling" factor in the process that is making the process lean in one direction. This always needs a thorough investigation. Usually the "Rule of 7" is an early warning sign of something about to go wrong.

When any one or more data points breach the Upper control Limits or Lower control limits than the process is termed out of control and warrants immediate corrective action. Since these control limits have been created as an early warning signs in relation to the Specification Limits, no real damage has occurred but you would still need to bring them within the control bands fast.

CONTROL CHARTS

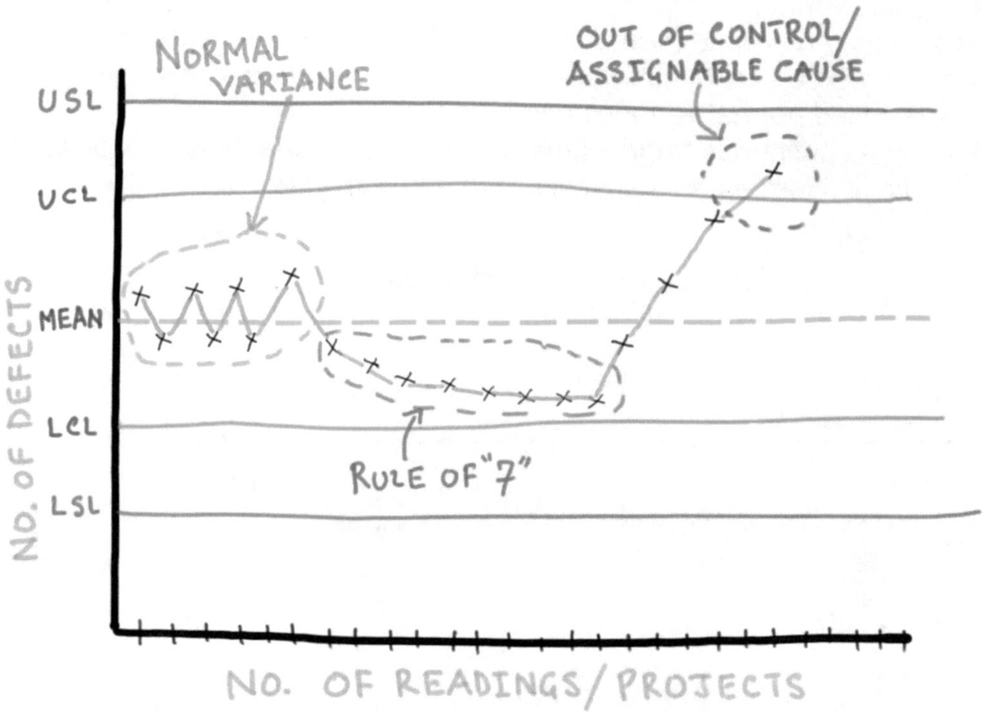

Even when the data points go out of control all is not lost. You have time to take corrective actions as the UCL and LCL are nothing but the early warning signs of Upper Specification and Lower Specification Limits, respectively. All is lost when we allow a data point to go outside of the specification limits.

When the data points are too close or constantly on the mean that would usually mean data manipulation.

CONTROL CHARTS

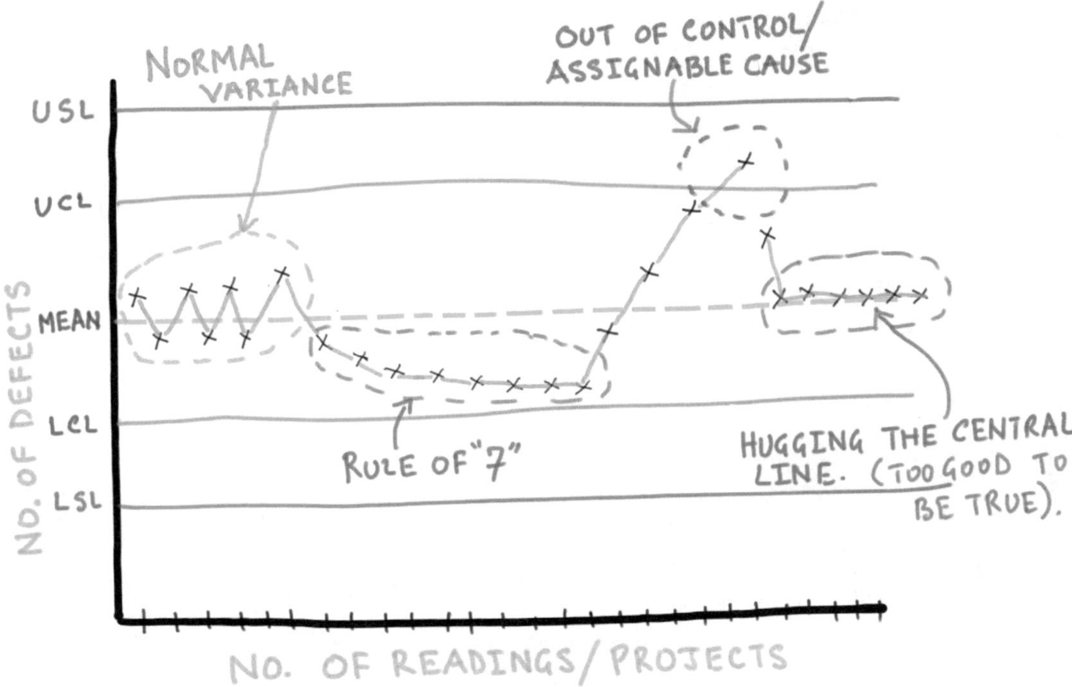

If in the exams you get a question stating a scenario where 7 or more data points show up on any one side of the mean it would mean Rule of 7. However, at times, you may not find the answer option of "Rule of 7" if that happens then go for the answer option "Out of control".

Histograms are something that you are already very well aware of. In this process, it can be used to show the frequency of errors reported against the specific artifacts, or by the sources of errors. This usually shows which artifacts or phases or sources are more error-prone.

Pareto Charts These are vertical bar diagrams showing frequencies of occurrences of a specific event or issue or problem. Once all the frequencies are noted down and plotted into bar diagrams (histograms) the 80/20 principle is applied on to it for prioritization purposes. This diagram helps understand where to apply the limited resources for maximum benefits. Just to remind you that 80/20 principle is a prioritization principle where the focus should be on those 20% things that would generate a benefit of 80%. These percentages do not have to be taken literally. This rule simply means that one must focus on the fewer elements that give the biggest benefits instead of trying to solve everything.

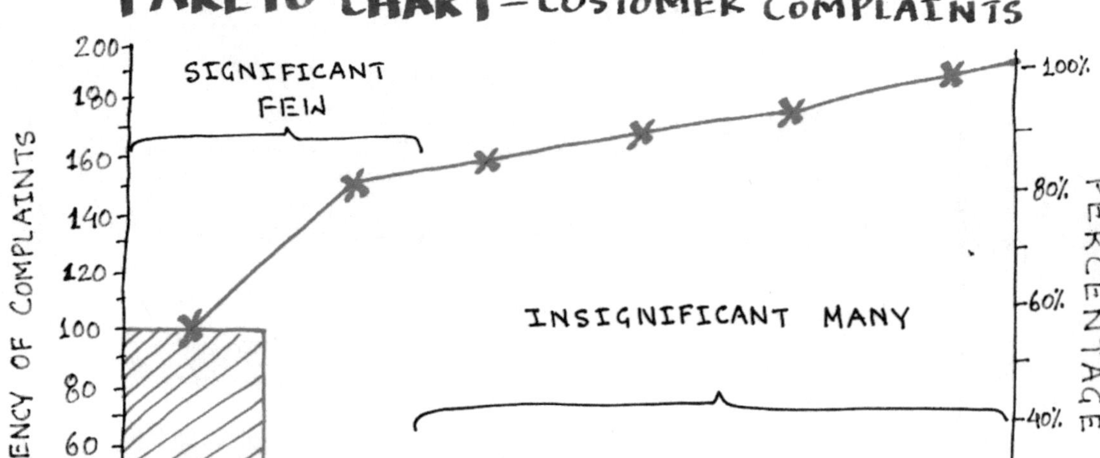

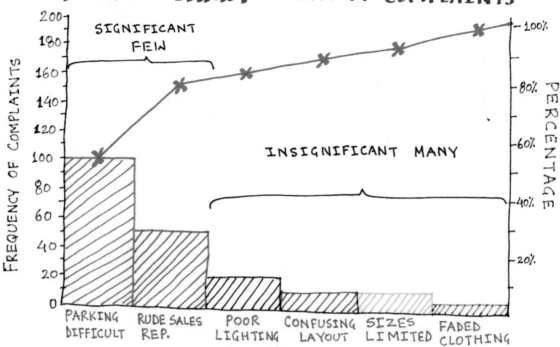

Process Decision Program Charts (PDPC) is a technique designed to help prepare contingency plans. The emphasis of the PDPC is to identify the consequential impact of failure on activity plans and create appropriate contingency plans to limit risks.

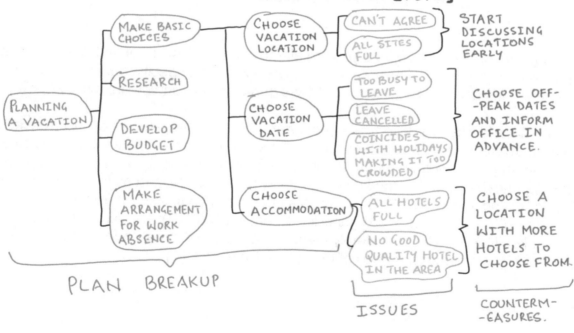

PROCESS DECISION PROGRAM CHART [PDPC]

PLANNING A VACATION
MAKE BASIC CHOICES
RESEARCH
DEVELOP BUDGET
MAKE ARRANGEMENT FOR WORK ABSENCE
CHOOSE VACATION LOCATION
CAN'T AGREE
ALL SITES FULL
START DISCUSSING LOCATIONS EARLY
CHOOSE VACATION DATE
TOO BUSY TO LEAVE
LEAVE CANCELLED
COINCIDES WITH HOLIDAYS MAKING IT TOO CROWDED
CHOOSE OFF-PEAK DATES AND INFORM OFFICE IN ADVANCE.
CHOOSE ACCOMMODATION
ALL HOTELS FULL
NO GOOD QUALITY HOTEL IN THE AREA
CHOOSE A LOCATION WITH MORE HOTELS TO CHOOSE FROM.
PLAN BREAKUP
ISSUES
COUNTERMEASURES.

Scatter Diagrams is something you are already aware of. Here the scatter diagram may be used to understand if the corrective actions / preventive actions undertaken have some effect in reduction of errors (or any specific effect that was wanted). If there is no correlation of the corrective action to that of the effect then it only means that the corrective action is not working.

And yes **Meetings** would have to be held for daily stand-ups to see the quality condition of the sprint (in an agile project) or to understand the various corrective measures that can be used in the project, or for reviewing the approved change requests to the project or for retrospective meetings (for agile projects).

10.16.2 Main Outcome from this process: -

Quality Control Measurements contain the results of the *CONTROL QUALITY* Process and they are sent to only one process viz., *MANAGE QUALITY*.

Verified Deliverables are the deliverables which have been approved/passed by this process as they contain the necessary quality requirements. These Verified Deliverables would be sent to the process *VALIDATE SCOPE* to ensure if the deliverables meet the documented scope.

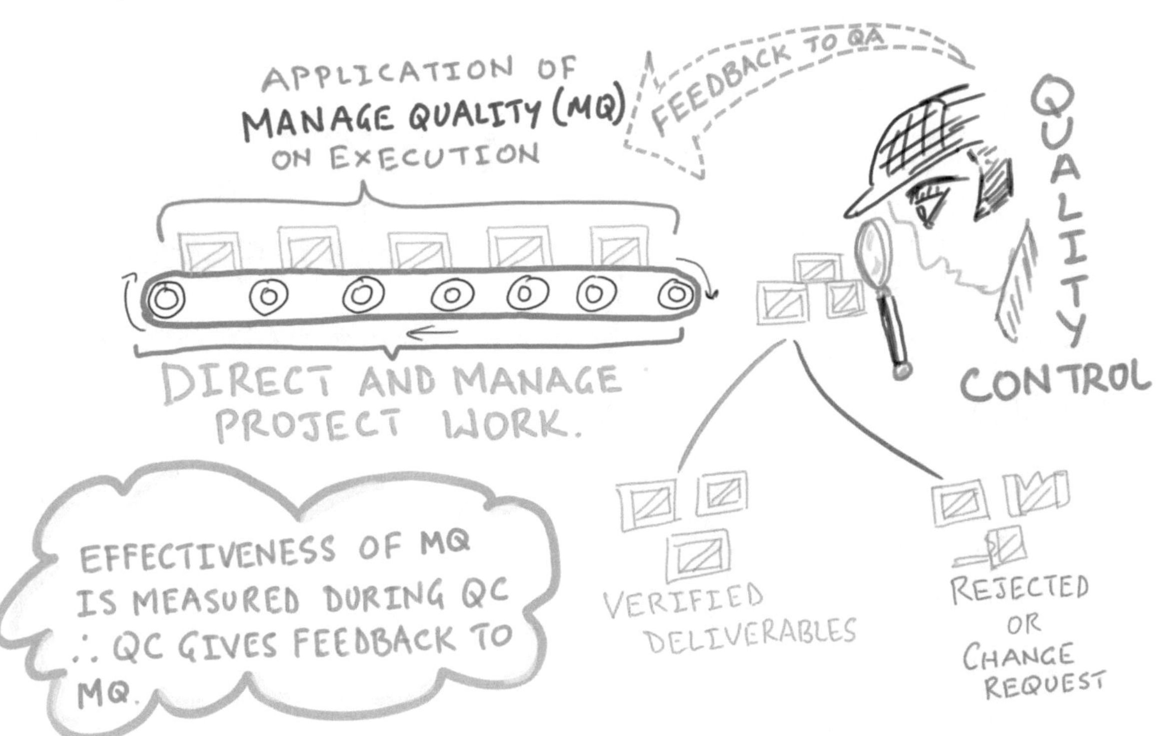

Work Performance Information is information about various aspects of the project that needs to be taken into account during Monitoring and Controlling before taking any decision. Work Performance Information from this process contains information about the overall results of the *Control Quality* process on the deliverables of the project. Work Performance Information becomes the input to one and only one process Viz., *Monitor And Control Project Work*.

10.17 Control Procurements: -

When the contract is signed between the buyer and the selected vendor it becomes procurement for the buyer but becomes a project for the vendor. This process is about the consistent monitoring and controlling done by the buyer on the vendor to track the project as well as to ensure that the vendor is adhering to the terms of the contract. The agreement/contract signed by the two parties becomes the reference document to track the project. There could be some changes to the scope or any other baseline of the outsourced project which would need not only the usual change management but also "Contract Change Management" as the contract is a legal binding document. Usually, there are some provisions in the contract for settling any claims and disputes arising during procurement execution. This process also handles any kind of arbitration, claims or any kind of disputes that may arise on the behest of any of the parties to the contract.

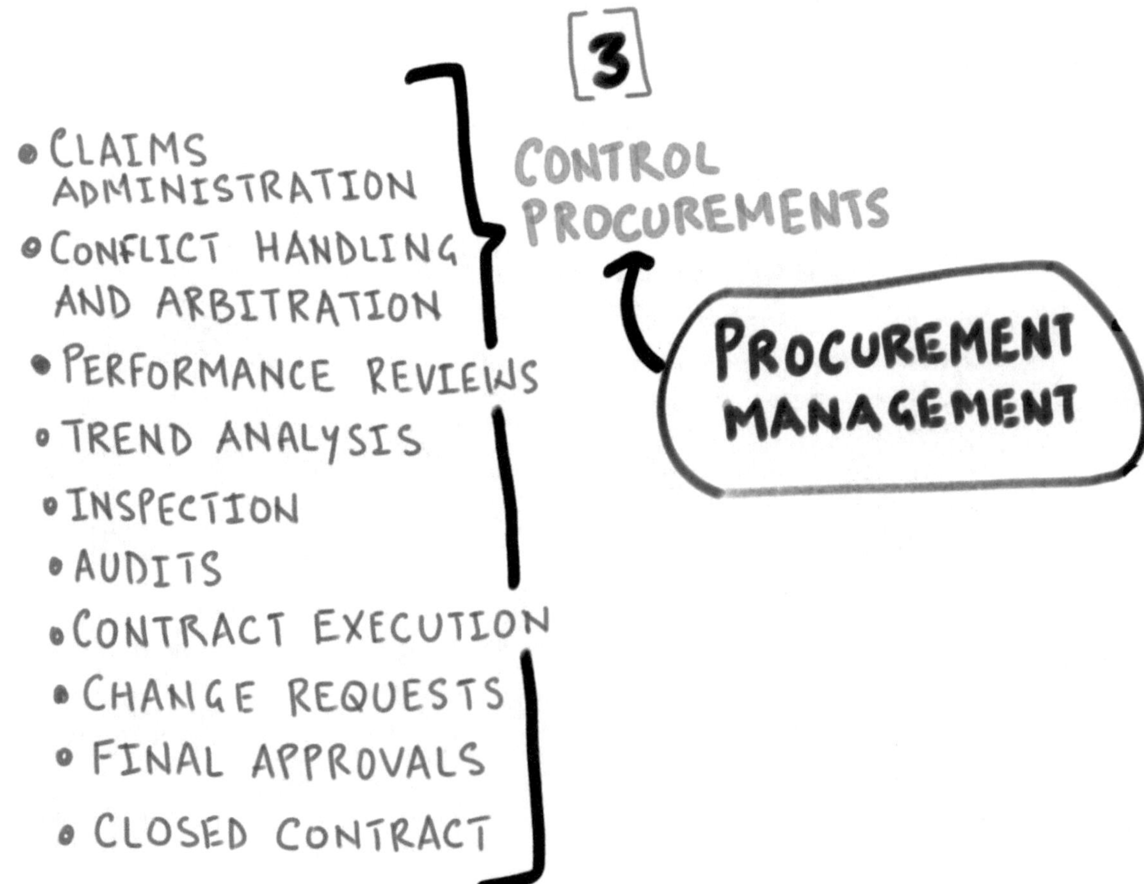

This process is also connected to payments as well. Agreements/contracts contain the payment terms based on the completion of certain amount of work.

This means that the buyer would like to ensure that required work is actually completed before the payment for the same is made.
During this process, both parties have to maintain all documents and notes and emails and faxes connected to the contract. Contract being a legal document, all supporting documents would need to be legally stored and referenced from time to time as the procurement work progresses. Needless to say here that each and every term of the contract has to be provided for.

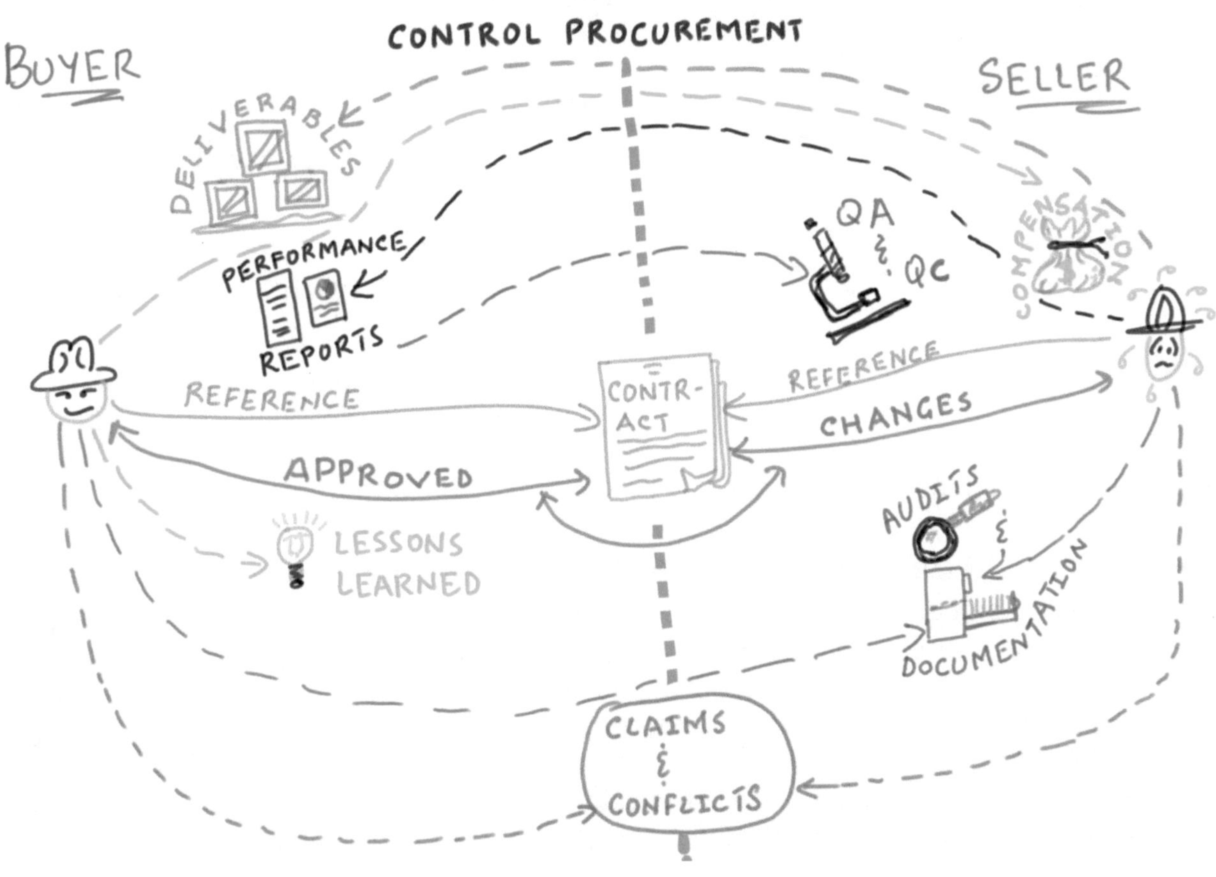

This is also the process where the procurement journey comes to an end. This process of "*Control Procurements*" is done for each of the procurements individually to close them. The terms of the contract are used for the closure of the procurement. Sometimes the procurement closes because of "Termination". In case of termination, since the work is not completed and the vendor needs to be compensated for the amount of work done (even if it's not complete), a negotiated settlement has to be done for the same.

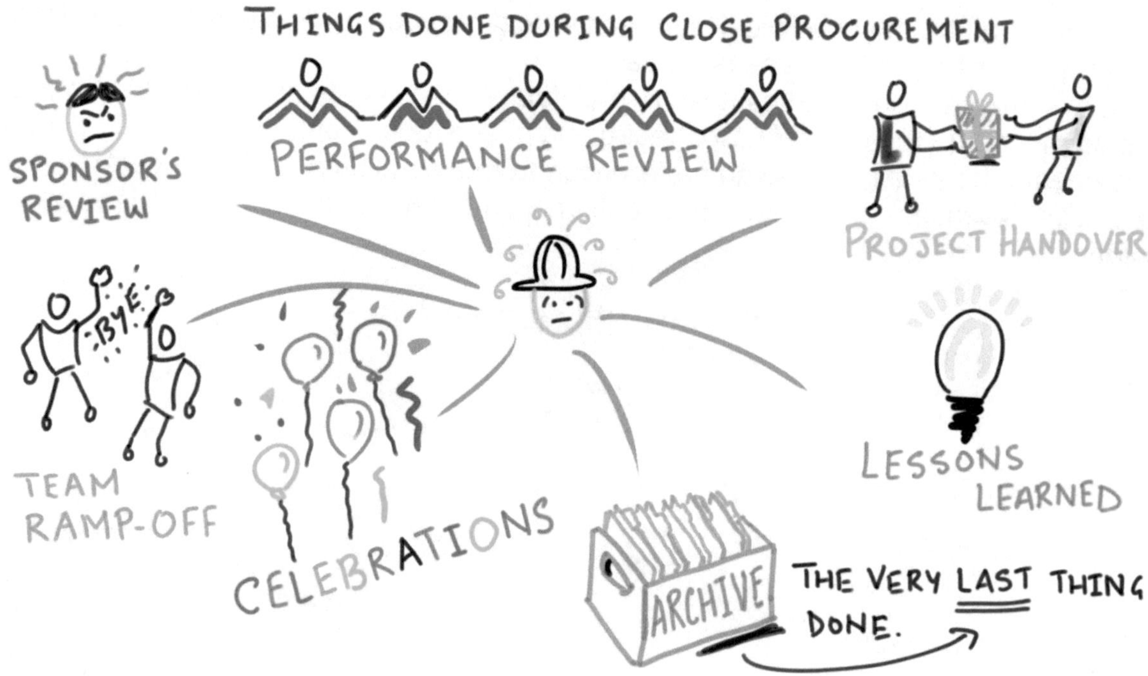

Let us now get into the details of this process.

10.17.1 Main Tools and techniques of this process: -

Sometimes in a procurement situation, the vendor may end up incurring expenses which were outside the purview of the contract and in such cases the vendor may raise a claim which would go under review and negotiations before the same is settled by the buyer. This is basically called the **Claims Administration**. In most matured contracts the procedure for handling claims is clearly provided which need to be followed judiciously. However, in absence of any such terms in contract, the claims could be settled through Negotiations, Arbitration or even through the local judiciary system. There are many reasons why the claims may get generated.

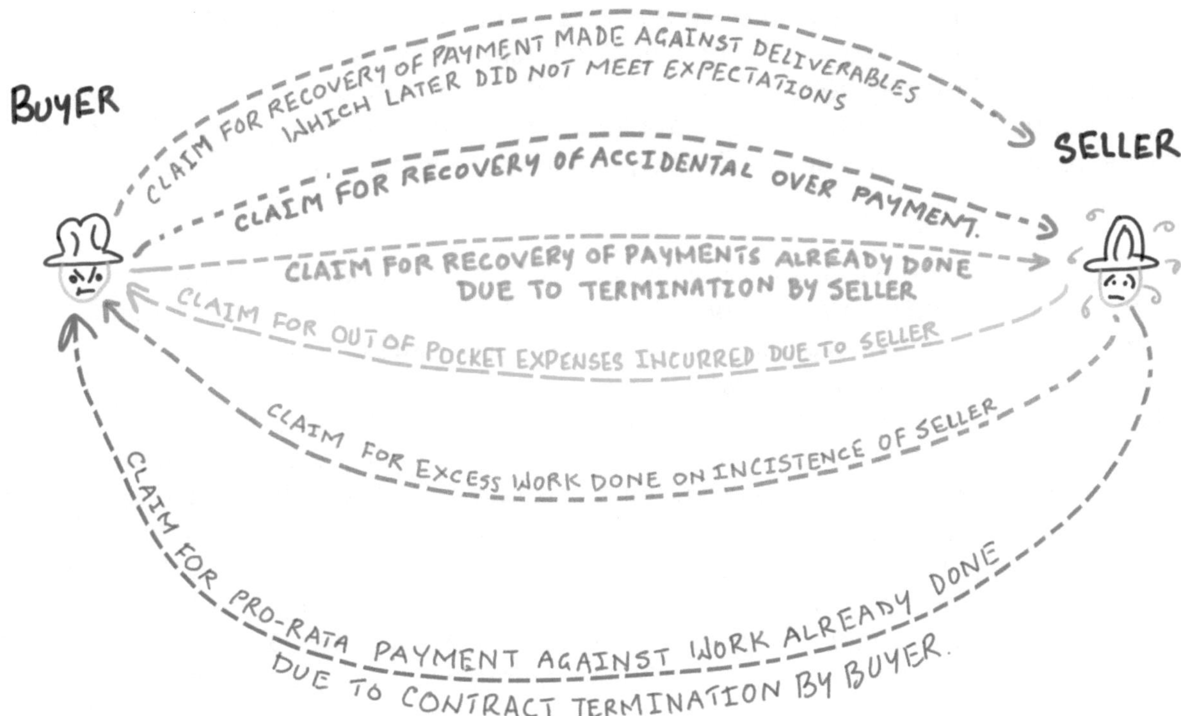

Performance Reviews: The main purpose of the **Procurement Performance Reviews** is to review the work done by the Vendor so far and make an informed decision about course correction for future work or not. Results from such reviews may also end in termination of the contract. Such reviews may be based on the reports periodically sent by the vendor or it could be supplemented with audits done by the buyer on the vendor work and then comparing the results with the vendor progress reports so far. Sometimes “Trust” issues also come into knowledge and the situation would have to be addressed accordingly. These reviews are inherently of two kinds viz., One – Technical Reviews (done by the technical or project team from the buyer to understand how the work is progressing as per the SOW or the specifications or the requirements documents) and Two – Legal Reviews (done by purchase or legal professionals to see how well the terms of the contract are being adhered to and if the vendor is using some gaps in the contract to their advantage).

Earned Value Analysis is by far the most objective and accurate method of understanding the health of the project. EVA could be used to understand how well the vendor is progressing in the project and if forecasts are such that vendor can finish the work in the given time and price.

Trend Analysis can help understand what would be the situation of the project by the time it ends, if it continues to spend money and time at the current rate. Trend Analysis would also help show if there are areas (say Quality of the deliverables) that are consistently going wrong in the procurement and by knowing this the buyer can work with vendor to re-plan such that the negative trends do not show up later in the procurement again.

Inspection and **Audits** is a regular feature of any procurement control and hence this is a technique by which the buyer comes to know exactly what is happening on the outsourced project. These techniques feed into the previous "Tools and Technique" of Procurement Performance Reviews. Usually, the details of the Inspections and Audits are given in the contract itself or they may be agreed upon separately in a formal manner. The buyer may hire an external consultant to do the same for them, for lending transparency to the exercise, and reduce bias. The contract usually states as to who will bear the cost for such Inspections and Audits.

At this point of time there are some additional points that we need to discuss.
In exams you may find some questions connected to ethics and professional conduct while talking about procurement situation. This is so because, most of the global corruption tends to happen around "procurement" practices.

1) ***Gifts***: Gifts are something people exchange in the course of personal and professional relationships. However the main question is, at what point of time does a Gift become a Bribe? The answer for this is surprisingly simple and straightforward. Usually, every professional organization has a policy regarding giving and receiving gifts. This policy mentions the amount worth of gift that the employee can receive as well as the amount worth of gift it can give to others. Any gift that is higher than the stated amount (giving or receiving) is automatically deemed as a bribe. When giving gifts it is important to also check with the intended receiver, their policy about gifts to ensure that you are not violating the policies of that receiver organization. There are many organizations where employees are not allowed to receive any gifts whatsoever. In which case any gift received (irrespective of the amount) is deemed a bribe.
2) ***Conflict of Interest:*** A conflict of interest occurs when an employee places his or her interest over and above that of their organizations'. Suppose you are in a position to select a vendor. You ask one of your cousins to bid for the procurement because you are in the position to select. Here you are using this opportunity to make a personal / family gain instead of getting the best vendor for the organization. This is an example of conflict of interest. There is another aspect of conflict of interest. Let us say you are in a position to select a vendor. Unknown to you, your cousin also bids for the proposal, like any other bidder. This situation is also called "Position of conflict of interest". When you become aware of your cousin having submitted a bid, you need to inform your manager immediately. After that follow the guidance of the manager. In fact, when it comes to conflict of interest, yours or someone else's, you need to inform the manager about this. If your manger is in a conflict of interest position, you need to go over his head and inform your manager's manager.
3) ***Being Honest and Fair:*** As a project manager you are supposed to maintain professionalism at all times. This includes being honest and fair. This is one of the 4 values of Project Management as well. Even if you make a mistake, you must own it and admit to it and inform the affected / connected stakeholders immediately and work towards correcting it. Let us say that one of your vendors have forgotten to invoice you for a legitimate work she has done, it is your duty to remind her of the same. You are not expected to show any kind of bias towards or against anyone. You are supposed to treat everyone fairly and equally.
4) ***Discrimination:*** As a project manager you will watch out for any kind of discriminatory behavior shown by any stakeholder and will take it upon himself to discourage such behavior and also ensure those stakeholders go through a diversity training. If your vendor tells you that they cannot work under one of your team members because of

gender, ethnicity, race or skin pigmentation you will give them a chance to eject such behavior failing which you will not work with the vendor anymore. When it comes to "Discrimination" there should be a zero tolerance policy.

10.17.2 *Main Outcome from this process: -*

Closed Procurements is an administrative order that closes all aspects of the procurement and even the unique id attached to this contract is nullified. No expenses or resources can be assigned to this procurement anymore and all contracts connected to this procurement is considered completed or simply closed and not in use. This may look like an insignificant statement but its real-world implications are huge as every trace of this specific Procurement has to be wiped from any live project tool like PMIS systems or any kind of live projects directories etc. This involves that every single stakeholder is informed of this closure. It must be seen that when a procurement closes it's not necessary that the project, of which this procurement was a part, also closes. Project closure is a different ballgame.

At times there are questions about the correct sequence of procurement closure. I have listed the same below to ensure that you get such questions right.

Step – 1 Procurement audits to ensure that all the content of the contracts has been met.
Step – 2 Performance evaluation or testing or verification by the vendor at their end.
Step – 3 Performance evaluation and audits and validation by the buyer.
Step – 4. Formal acceptance, negotiated settlements and handover
Step – 5. Lessons learned and procurement documents archival.

Work Performance Information contains all the key dashboards and points that would help the project and other key stakeholders make informed decisions. Remember "Work Performance Information" is an output of 10 of the 12 Monitoring and Controlling Processes and they all become inputs to one and only one process viz., "*MONITOR AND CONTROL PROJECT WORK*". In this process, this output contains key information about the condition of the outsourced work with forecasted situation as well. Here it also contains the degree of adherence to the terms of contract as well.

10.18 Control Scope

Towards the end of the project, the customer compares the final deliverables with the requirements document and approves it if satisfied. That process of final approval by customers is called "*VALIDATE SCOPE*". However, if the final deliverables are not accepted after validation then it would be very expensive and the whole work would have to be done all over again. Any smart project manager would not wait all the way till the end to find out if the deliverables are as per requirements and specifications or not. He will institute regular control points, while the project is being executed, to ensure that the project is going in the right direction and that all the requirements are actually being adhered to. This preventive process is called *CONTROL SCOPE*.

There are two purposes of *CONTROL SCOPE*. One is to ensure that the product of the project is as per the requirements and specification documents and two, to handle the scope change requests that may crop up during the life of the project work.

An experienced project manager also uses this process to check for any "Gold Plating" or "Scope Creep". The term Gold Plating has been discussed earlier. However, Scope Creep happens when any change request is directly implemented without going through the formal change control process. This is a very common phenomenon and must be guarded against. Basically, any unapproved implementation of change is a "Scope Creep". Needless to say, Gold Plating, may lead to Scope Creep.

Time to look into the interior of this process.

10.18.1 Main Tools and Techniques of this process:-

Variance Analysis is conducted to see just how much the scope of the work done so far, and how far is it different from what it should have been. Whether the variance can be corrected without making any changes to the plan or does the plan have to be changed for bringing the variance under control. Most of this variance is done using the "Work Performance Data" which is received as input in this process from the Execution process "*DIRECT AND MANAGE EXECUTION*". Based on the outcome of this, change requests may be raised from this process.

The tools and technique of "Variance Analysis" is a tools and technique of only 5 processes and they are *MONITOR AND CONTROL PROJECT WORK*, *CONTROL SCOPE*, *CONTROL SCHEDULE*, *CONTROL COSTS* (the control processes of the three baselines) and *CLOSE PROJECT OR PHASE*

10.18.2 Main Outcome from this process: -

Work Performance Information contains the variance information which can be used for making appropriate decisions. It could also contain forecasted information about the scope of the project which could prompt the project manager to take early preventive/corrective actions.

I hope you can recall that Work Performance Information becomes output of 10 processes and they are all Control Processes. Basically, this becomes output of all the controlling processes except the processes *Integrated Change Control* and *MONITOR AND CONTROL PROJECT WORK*. (There are 12 processes in process group Control). All these Work Performance Information from these 10 of the control processes becomes input to one and only one process viz., *MONITOR AND CONTROL PROJECT WORK*.

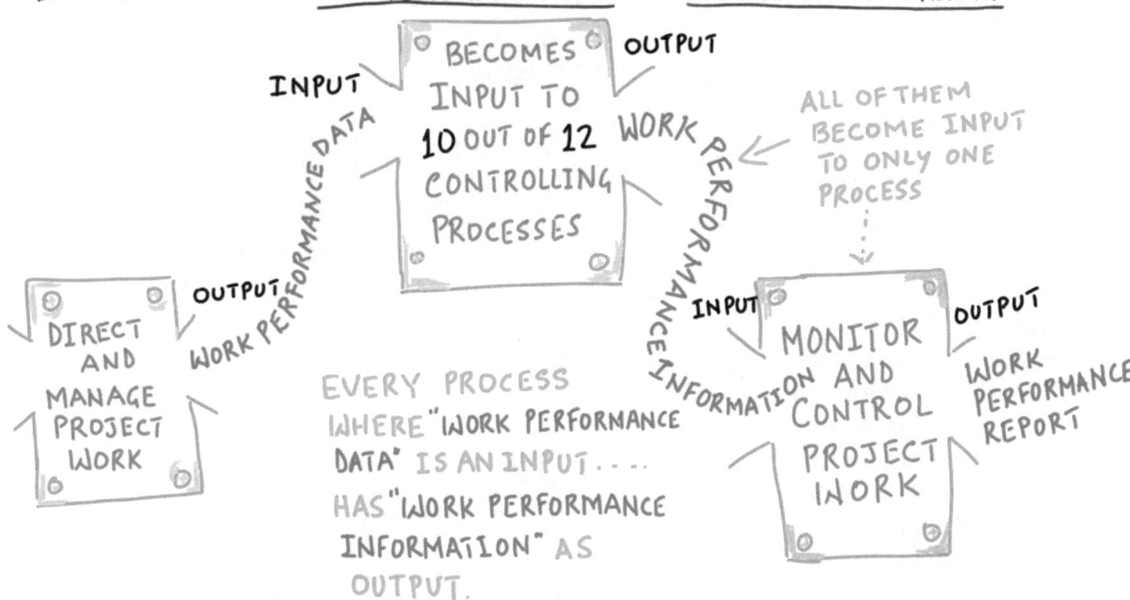

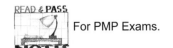

Due to the results of the Variance Analysis done during this process, it may come to light that some re-planning would have to be done to bring the project back on track, scope wise. For this, one or more **Change Requests** would have to be released and hence this becomes one of the possible outputs of this process. Remember that all the Change Requests become input to only one process called Integrated Change Control (ICC). These change requests could be Recommended Defect Repairs, Recommended Corrective Actions or Recommended Preventive Actions.

Project Management Plan and Project Documents may get updated due to the result of this process. Plans like Scope Management Plan, Scope Baseline any other baseline elements, cost management plan may get updated while projects documents like Project Scope statement, Requirements Documentation, Traceability Matrix, Risk Registers etc., may need to get updated. Some lessons may also be learned (new way of requirements testing or additions to checklists etc.) which would be updated in the document 'Lessons Learned".

10.19 Ninja Drill – Implementation - 4

In this Ninja Drill you will find the most important notes and pointers that are important from the point of PMP Exams and covers Control Quality, Control Procurement and Control Scope.

S. No.	Drill Points
1.	Control Quality process is also known as the Verification process.
2.	In Control Quality deliverables are checked against the Quality Requirements and Quality Metrics.
3.	In Control Quality ddecision is made whether Deliverables will be passed as "Verified" or not.
4.	Quality Control process produces the Quality Report that states the current status of "Quality" as well as suggestions for improvements or modifications of quality processes if needed.
5.	The main Tools & Techniques of the process "Control Quality" are: 1. Check sheets 2. Statistical Sampling 3. Inspection 4. Control Charts 5. Histogram 6. Scatter Diagrams
6.	Check sheet (not the same as checklist) is a format that documents / notes instances of defects and errors unearthed during testing. This can be used for analysis and decision making after the testing. Also called "Tally Sheet".
7.	Statistical Sampling is done because testing or inspecting the entire population is too time taking and very expensive.
8.	Inspection Is a "Post-Facto" analysis to see if something / deliverable conforms to rules or targeted matrices or not.
9.	Control Charts are used to measure the health of the process.
10.	It is difficult to find the reasons for Normal Variance in a Control Chart. Normal Variance is healthy.
11.	When 7 or more data points show up on any one side of the mean, it's called the "Rule of 7" and warrants an investigation.
12.	Hugging the central line or data continuously falling on the Benchmark is suspicious and hence the authenticity of the data must be ascertained.
13.	Histogram is a bar chart that shows the graphical representation of numerical data.
14.	Pareto Chart / Pareto Diagram is a histogram that applies the Pareto principle of 80/20 principle thus ascertaining the critical few defects, bugs, inconsistencies etc., that need to be tackled first.
15.	Scatter Diagrams represent the "Co-efficient of Correlation" between two quality variables.
16.	The main outcome / output / artefact of the process "Control Quality" are: 1. Verified Deliverables 2. Quality Report
17.	The primary reference document during the process "Control Procurements" is the contract.
18.	Contract closure on termination: • Early Termination is a special case of contract closure • Early termination can result from a mutual agreement • Early termination can result from a default of one of the parties • In such cases the rights of the parties are contained in the specific provisions of the contract • Degree of completion is ascertained and the buyer than pays the amount for the completed work • Settlement is done through negotiations
19.	Steps for closing a contract based on successful completion: 1. Step – 1 Procurement audits to ensure that all the content of the contracts has been met. 2. Step – 2 Performance evaluation or testing or verification by the vendor at their end. 3. Step – 3 Performance evaluation and audits and validation by the buyer. 4. Step – 4 Formal acceptance, negotiated settlements and handover 5. Step – 5 Lessons learned and procurement documents archival.

20.	The amount worth of gift that you can receive is mentioned in your organizational rules. If you accept any gift that is worth higher the allowable limit, it is considered a bribe. In those organizations where no gift is allowable then receiving any gift no matter how small, is still considered a bribe.
21.	Conflict of Interest: when a person is in a position to derive personal benefit due to her official position at the expense of the organization she is serving. Just being in a position of conflict of interest needs to be reported to appropriate authority. If you notice someone else in a position of conflict of interest you need to report on her to the appropriate authority.
22.	Discrimination: Zero tolerance is to be had for anyone who is discriminating against genders, races, religion, nationality and language.
23.	Ethical Behavior: Even if the vendor forgets to charge the fees for his work done it is your duty to inform him immediately. If you have made a mistake you will own it immediately and transparently.
24.	Words in a contract have more value than the corresponding numeric figures.
25.	A procurement audit demonstrates that appropriate processes utilized were sufficient for the procurement and that the contractor is performing to plan.
26.	The main output / outcome / artefact of the process "Control Procurements" are: • Terminated Contract • Progress Reports / Audit Reports • Completed Contract
27.	Scope control assures all requested changes and recommended corrective actions are processed through the project Integrated Change Control process.
28.	Project scope control is also used to manage the actual changes when they occur and is integrated with the other control processes.
29.	Control Scope is also responsible to actively discourage and prevent "Scope Creep" or even "Gold Plating".
30.	Scope Creep = Uncontrolled changes that impact project scope. Incrementally, may surprise the project team with budget, schedule, resource impacts
31.	Gold Plating is one kind of Scope Creep. Gold Plating is when one or more team members add features or specifications, otherwise not mentioned in requirements document, with the aim of delighting the customer and without obtaining any approval from the customer as well.

End Of Ninja Drill

10.20 Integrated Change Control

Out of 49 processes that make up the project management there are 24 processes that have "Change Request" as output. All those "Change Requests" become input to one and only one process and that is "Integrated Change Control". This process is responsible for approving or rejecting or parking the "Change Requests" that have been raised. That's all this process does. Accepts Change Requests and approves or rejects it. This process is the "Change Control Center" of project management.

Every project needs a group of stakeholders who can decide if a change request should be approved or not. Such a group is usually titled "Change Control Board (CCB)". CCB is governed by the provisions of the process of Integrated Change Control (ICC).

Always remember this line "CCB in ICC". Which means, whichever question you come across that talks about "Change Request approval" you need to remember it's done by CCB and the applicable process is ICC.

Any of the stakeholders can raise a "Change Request" and each and every of those change requests have to go through the process Integrated Change Control. There could be some emergency procedures for a certain category of changes where every single step may not be followed for implementing or rejecting a change request.

Sometimes "Change Requests" are known by different names like "Recommended Corrective Action", "Recommended Preventive Action", "Recommended Defect Repair", "Suggested Improvement" and so on. Notice the words "Recommended" and "Suggested" which signify that they have not been approved yet which essentially means that they are inputs to the process ICC. Remember that a "Change Request" becomes a "Change" only once it's approved by the CCB in ICC. Hence a "Recommended Preventive Action" once approved would be called a "Preventive Action" and so on.

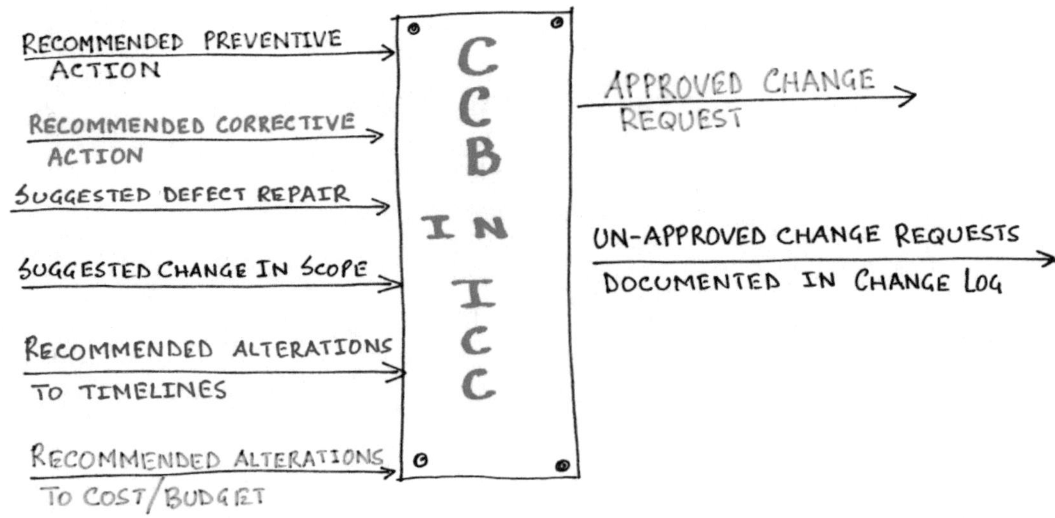

Before we get into the details of this process, let us understand some basic concepts. There are two levels of change. Organizational Change and Project Level Change. Organizational change means a change that affect a larger part of the organization. Examples of such a change are Change in business, change in product mix, change in organizational strategy, change in portfolio mix, adopting an enterprise wide management system or tool, organizational restructuring or adopting a new global standard. Organizational changes last a longer time and may end up creating a lot of project level changes. On the other hand, in a project level change, the change is limited to the boundaries of the project itself. A project level change alters one or more elements of the project's tripe constraint. Most of PMP focus is on project level change. However once in a while you may find some basic question about the organizational change. Everything about Organizational Change has been discussed earlier towards the end of Project Framework. You may want to revisit that section before proceeding. In this process we are only going to focus on the Project Level Change because that is precisely the purpose of the process ***INTEGRATED CHANGE CONTROL***.

Some of the reasons for change in a project are:

1) Inaccurate Initial Estimates
2) Specification Changes
3) New Regulations
4) Missed Requirements
5) Unidentified Stakeholders
6) Changes In Business Environment

One thing should be made clear that though the CCB has the authority to approve or reject change requests, it's ultimately the responsibility of the Project Manager to ensure that every Change Request goes through the proper change request process.
Some larger and complex projects may even have "Emergency Based Change Request Process" which may less time taking and without all the detailed steps as the normal Change Management Process. In such emergency process usually one or two persons represent the entire CCB and take a call on change request. This is also called the "Autocratic Change Process". Remember an autocratic change management process is only applied for emergency change requests. Some projects may even have provisions for different "Categories of change requests (based on Size, complexity, who initiates it etc.)" following different change management processes.

The concept of Change Control is very closely related to Configuration Management. Configuration Management System goes hand in hand with the Integrated Change Control Process. Configuration Management System is about ensuring that the physical or virtual product artifacts and all supporting technical and management documents are duly changed and version controlled along with each and every "Change" that is effected using the ***INTEGRATED CHANGE CONTROL*** Process.

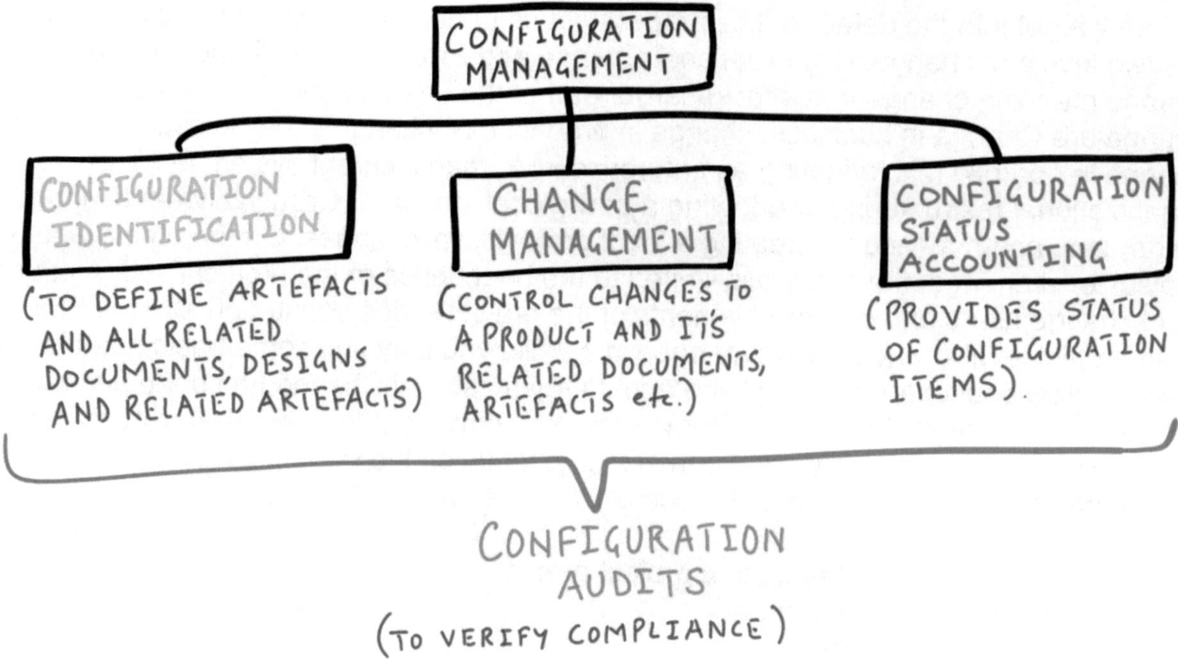

There are many reasons why there could be unnecessary Change Requests in a project, the biggest and most prominent reason being "Bad or improper stakeholder management". You will see whenever stakeholder management is conducted hurriedly, a lot of stakeholders, who were missed out earlier, become aware of the project a bit later in the project. Once they become aware of the project they wish to ensure that the project contains the requirements that they wanted. And this is what results in a large number of avoidable change requests. Therefore the best way to prevent unnecessary changes in a project is to conduct comprehensive stakeholder management in a project.

Proper and comprehensive stakeholder management in a project prevents the root cause of the change requests in a project. The no. of change requests in a project is inversely proportional to the effectiveness of the stakeholder management.

There is nothing known as "Verbal Change Request". Every change request has to be documented either by the "originator" or by the "project manager". Even if someone raises a "Verbal" change request it has to be documented in a change request form (CR Form) and duly signed and approved by the originator.

Now, let us get into the innards of this process: -

10.20.1 Main Tools and Techniques of this Process: -

Expert Judgment, in this process, is basically the Change Control Board (CCB) and others like consultants, technical experts, financial experts, legal practitioners, sales and marketing professionals and so on who could help the CCB take proper decisions on a change request.

From the point of view of the exams, these are the official steps in change request. Best to remember this exact sequence because in the exams the questions are based on this very sequence. You would be perfectly safe if you follow the sequence of steps given hereinbelow.

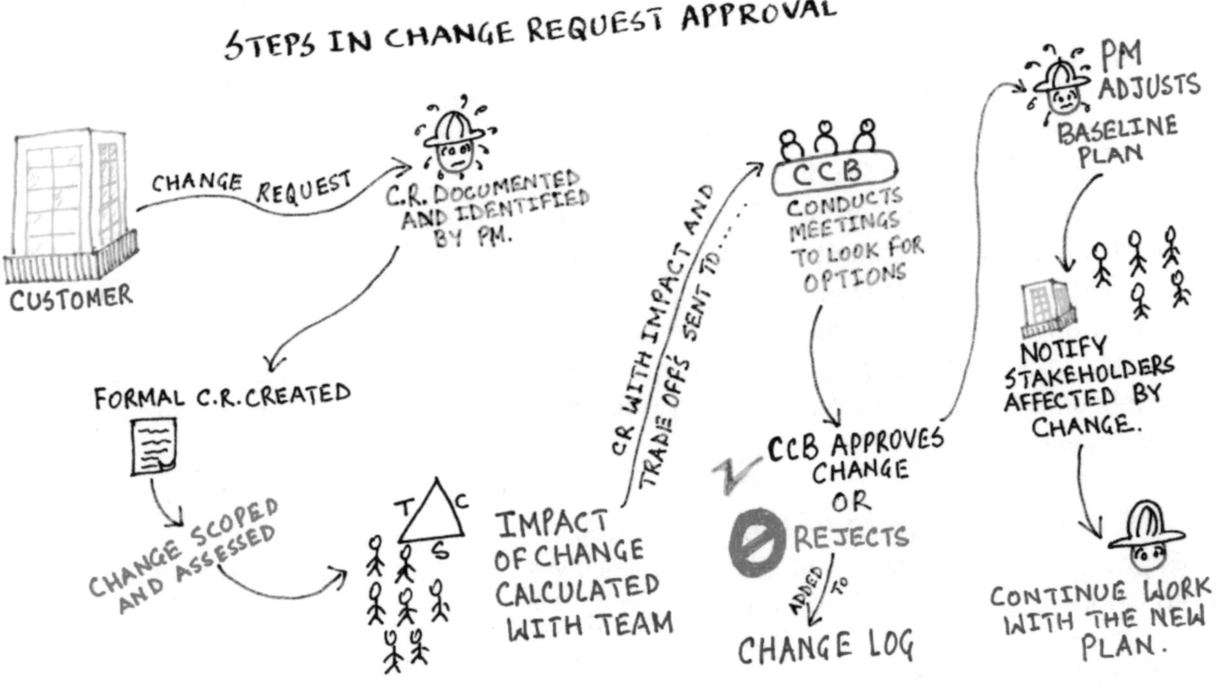

Change Control Tools are basically part of the overall Project Management Information System and they may be manual or software based and assist in documenting or conducting the change management process. One of the most common change control tools are the version control tools usually called Configuration Management Tools.

CONFIGURATION MANAGEMENT ACTIVITIES

1. IDENTIFY CONFIGURATION ITEM
    1.1. IDENTIFY CHANGES
    1.2. DOCUMENT CHANGES
    1.3. DECIDE ON CHANGES
    1.4. TRACK CHANGES
2. RECORD AND REPORT CONFIGURATION ITEM STATUS
3. PERFORM CONFIGURATION ITEM VERIFICATION & AUDIT.

Data Analysis like Alternatives Analysis (to see all possible alternatives around the proposed change request like, to fully implement the change request, partially implement the change request, reject the change request or park the change request to be taken up for decision making later in the project or next phase) and Cost-Benefit Analysis (to ascertain the benefits versus associated cost with the proposed change) are used to decide on the change request.

Meetings are the CCB meetings that have to be held formally to look at each and every change request that is raised by anyone.

It is important to remember that when it comes to agile projects:

- No Baseline as such.
- Reprioritization of Product Backlog is not a change
- Changes in Project Vision is not a change from this process point of view
- Realignment of Release Plan is not a change from this process point of view
- Reprioritization of User Stories and Iterations are not changes
- Changes in acceptance criteria is not a change
- Updated Road-Map is not a change from this process point of view.

The only time this process is applied in an agile project is when a "Change request" is made in the midst of an Iteration.

10.20.2 Outputs of this process:-

This process has 3 outputs and they are Approved Change Request, Project Management Plan Updates and Project Document Updates.

Approved Change Requests (or just Change) is the Change Requests which have gone through the ICC process and approved by the CCB and documented so. These Approved Change Requests are implemented through the "*DIRECT AND MANAGE PROJECT WORK*" process of Execution and verified through the process "*CONTROL QUALITY*". This also becomes input to the process "*CONTROL PROCUREMENTS*" to ensure that the changes are duly implemented in the contract as well in case of a vendor doing some work.

The Approved Change Request becomes an INPUT to 3 processes which are "*DIRECT AND MANAGE PROJECT WORK*", "*CONTROL QUALITY*" and "*CONTROL PROCUREMENTS*".

Project Document Updates includes a document called Change Log. **Change Log** is a document that is used to record each and every change request that was raised whether it was approved or not. If approved, all the change impacts and reasons for approval and approval dates etc. would be documented. If rejected, reasons for rejection would also be noted along with the change request.

It's important to note that this output "Change Log" becomes input to only 6 processes which are *DIRECT AND MANAGE PROJECT WORK*, *CLOSE PROJECT OR PHASE*, *MANAGE COMMUNICATIONS*, *IDENTIFY STAKEHOLDERS*, *PLAN STAKEHOLDER ENGAGEMENT* and *MANAGE STAKEHOLDER ENGAGEMENT*

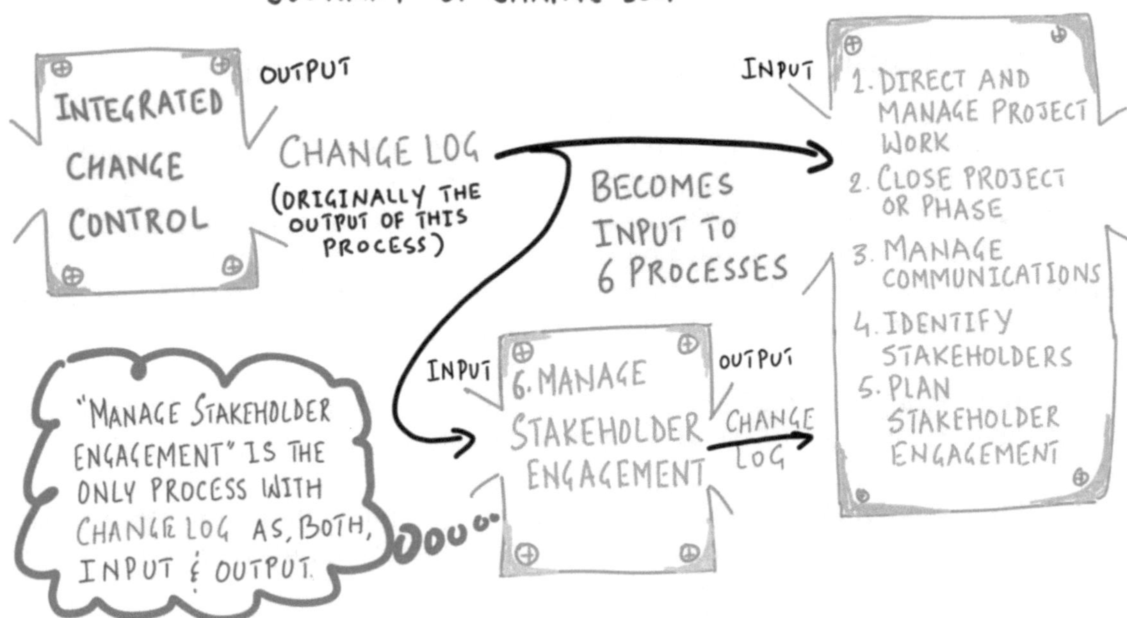

10.21 Monitor and Control Project Work

The whole purpose of this process is to compare "Actuals" with "Planned / Baseline" and generate a report about the condition of the project. The whole purpose of this process is to generate health reports, including forecasts, on every aspect of the project and present them to the stakeholders for their consumption. The actual distribution of the reports to the stakeholders is done by the process *Manage Communications*. This too is an "Umbrella Process" and more or less covers all the other 11 processes of the process group "Monitoring and Control". I hope you remember that there are 12 processes in the process group Monitoring and Controlling.

Let us look into the internals of this process:

10.21.1 Main Tools and Techniques of this process:

Alternatives Analysis: The main purpose of this process is to find out if there are any current or future deviations. These deviations would have to be corrected or prevented. The idea for this specific Data Analysis tool is to ascertain all possible "Alternatives" to correct or prevent deviations. There is always more than one way to do the right thing but each of the alternatives would have their own combinations of pros and cons. And to find out those pros and cons the other tools of Data Analysis come into the picture.

Cost-Benefit Analysis: This helps to compare the benefits obtained from each of the alternatives with the costs involved in each of the alternatives.

Earned Value Analysis: This is a method for finding the health of the project at any given point of time as well as forecasted health as well. This would be explained in details in the Knowledge Area Project Cost Management.

Root Cause Analysis: This helps in fishing out the main underlying cause of the problem or problems (in this process case, "deviations") to help the project manager and the project team focus on the right area to get the project back in shape.

Trend Analysis: Trend Analysis helps identify a forecasted performance based on current performance. Trend Analysis also helps identify if there is a "Trend" among the various deviation. *E.g., In a project there has been a clear past trend of missing milestones more than cost variances, therefore it would make sense to focus on techniques to get the project back on schedule more than other possible deviations.*

Variance Analysis: This is most of what this process does. Compares the plan with the actuals. The actual conditions are provided by the input "Work Performance Information" which is compared with the plan. Variances are done for each of the elements of the project and not just the three baseline elements.

Various kinds of **Decision-Making** techniques could be used (voting, cluster voting, majority rule, plurality, multicriteria analysis or autocratic) to take decisions about the alternatives for corrective or preventive actions. Usually, there are 7 steps in decision making.

During this process, the team may even look at the wastages being made in one or more of the project processes. The best way to do that is to use the concept of **Value Stream Mapping**. In this concept, the process under investigation, is completely mapped with all details and then the team tries to figure out exactly which steps of the process could be optimized or made leaner.

If you carefully look at the following value stream map:

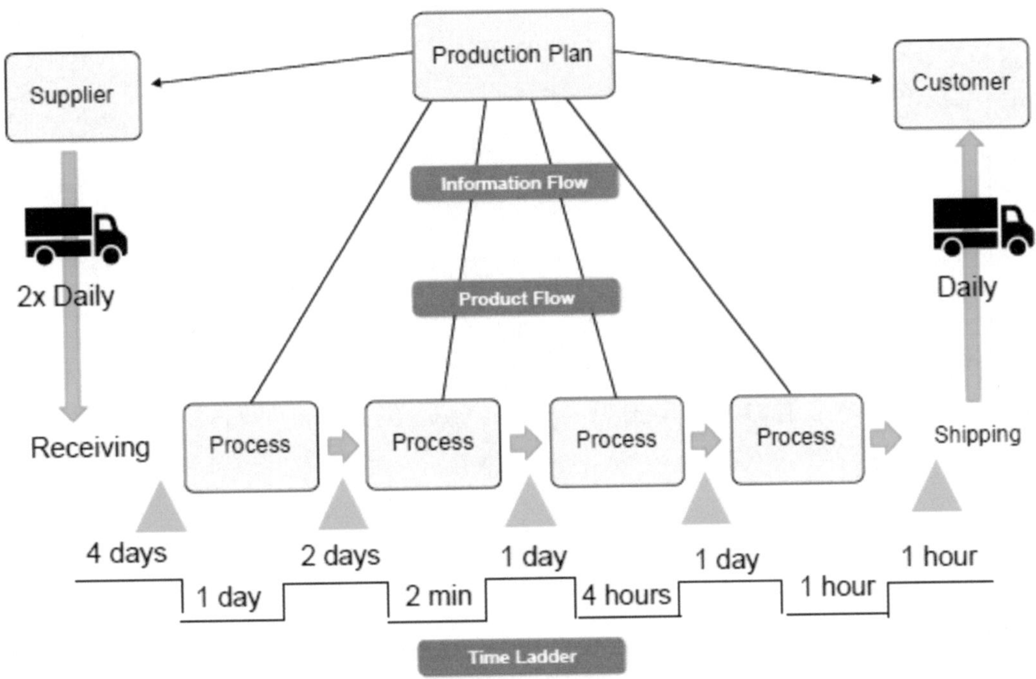

you can very well see that the first place to optimize this process is to reduce the waiting time of 4 days (after receiving the material from suppliers). This alone will make the entire process much shorter. Later we can look at the 2 days holding period between the first and the second manufacturing processes, and so on. Value Stream Map is called so because it lays bare those steps that are not adding value to the end outcome. This concept is one of the primary concepts of Lean Management.

The daily standup meeting as well as the backlog grooming (in Agile projects) are all part of this process *MONITOR AND CONTROL PROJECT WORK*.

All the agile charts and information radiators are also created in this process.
Another chart you should know about (similar to Combined Burn Chart) is the **Cumulative Flow Diagram [CFD]**. This chart indicates features completed over time, features in development, and those in the backlog. It may also include features at intermediate states, such as features designed but not yet constructed, those in quality assurance, or those in testing.

Another chart that is gaining popularity now a days is the **Cycle Time Chart**.
This diagram shows the average cycle time of the work items completed over time. A cycle time chart may be shown as a scatter diagram or a bar chart. I hope you remember what a Cycle Time is.

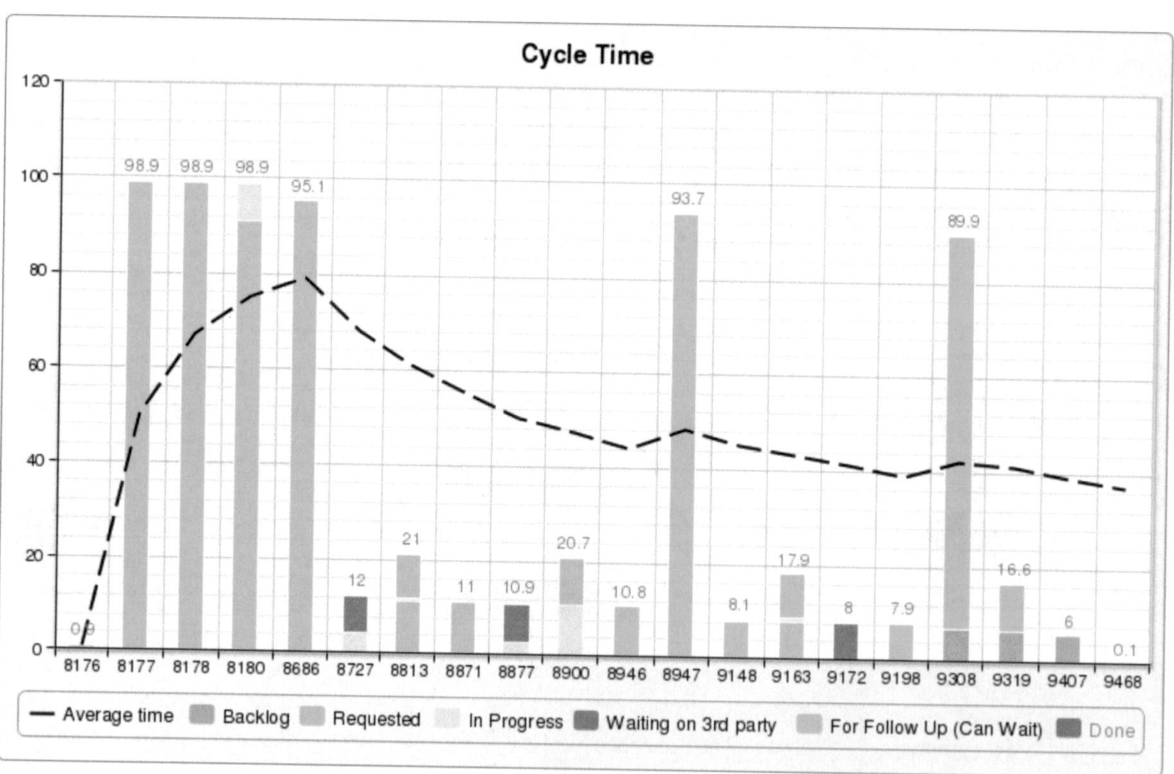

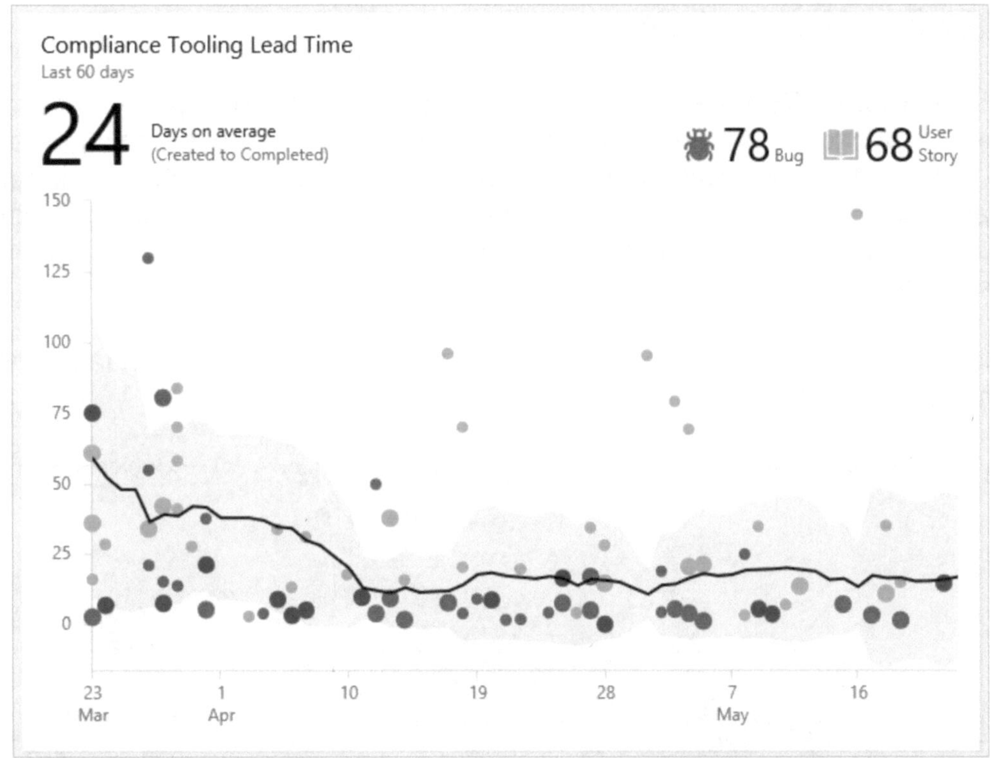

Velocity Chart is used for showing the rate at which the deliverables are produced, validated, and accepted within a predefined interval.

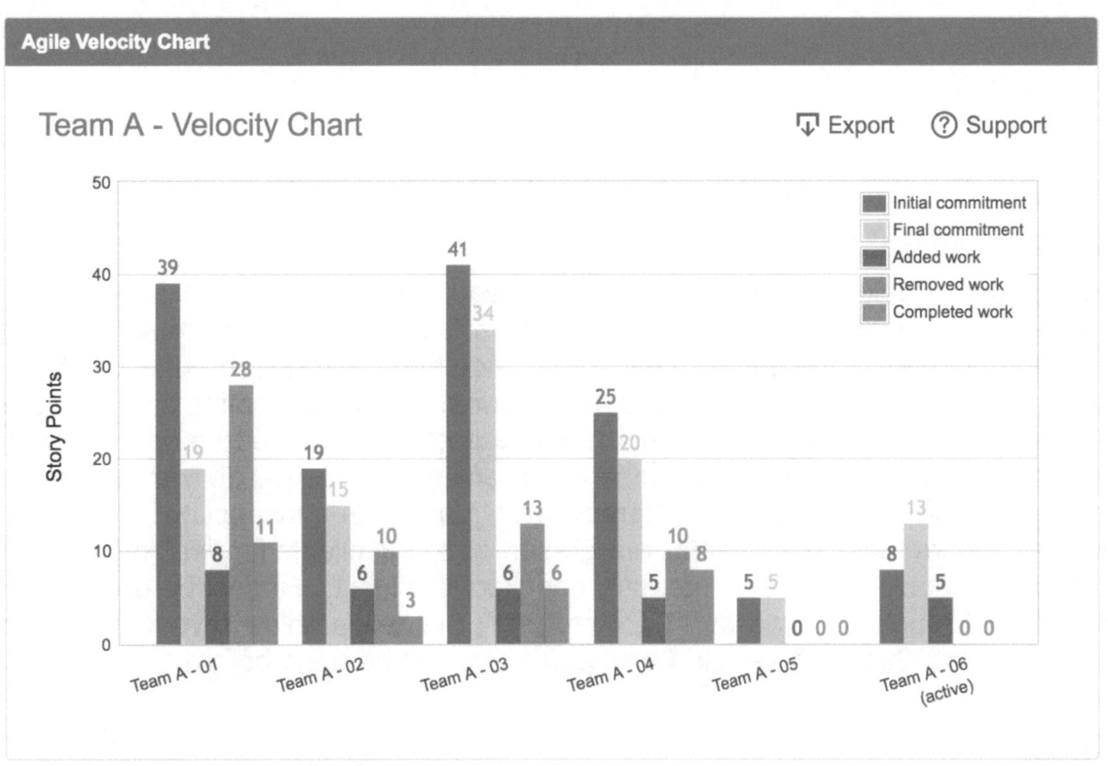

10.21.2 Main Outcome of this process:

Work Performance Reports are the electronic or paper-based reports that are compiled from various "Work Performance Information" which was the input to this process. This is the primary output of this process. These reports are generated to help the stakeholders take the necessary decisions and actions. This is nothing but turning information into consumable reports and dashboards for easy analysis and decision making *e.g., Status Reports, Progress Reports, Forecasts, Quality Metrics and so on.*

The diagram next shows the overall journey of the Work Performance Data to Work Performance Reports.

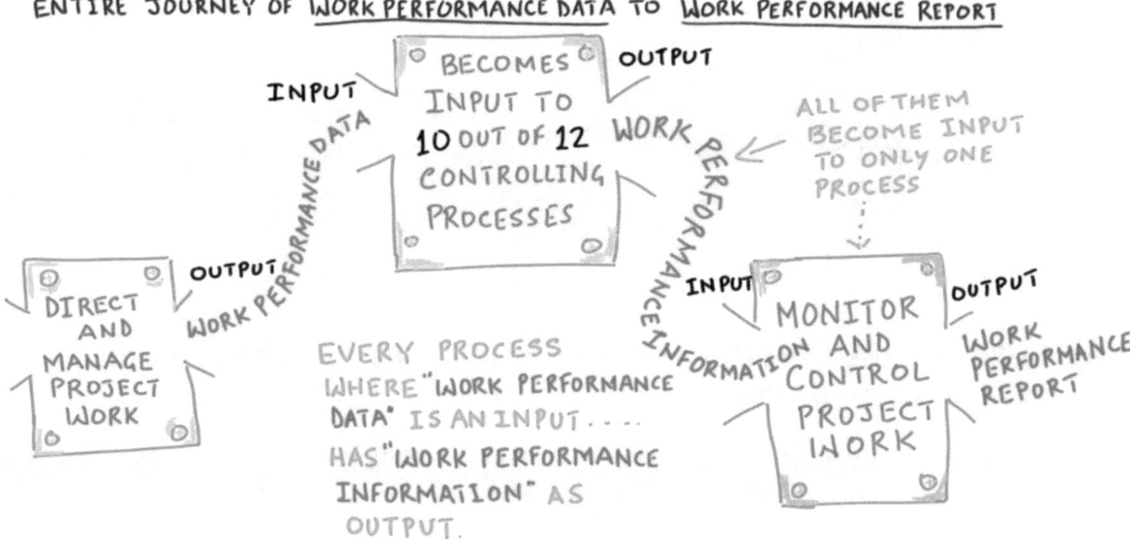

10.22 Validate Scope

Once the deliverables are ready the customer would like to check (Validate) if the deliverables are actually as per the requirements. Tests and checks would be conducted by the customer keeping the deliverables on one side and the requirements document on the other and a thorough inspection would be conducted before accepting final deliverable. If the deliverables are found lacking the performing agency would have to redo the portions that were not fit. This process of acceptance, or otherwise, of the final deliverables by the customer is called "*VALIDATE SCOPE*". **Remember!** "Validation = Inspection".
However, before these deliverables are presented to the clients for final inspection these deliverables should have been internally checked for Quality. Hence, before the deliverables are passed through this process, "*VALIDATE SCOPE*", the deliverables have to be verified by the process *CONTROL QUALITY*. As a rule *CONTROL QUALITY* must be done before *VALIDATE SCOPE*.

Verification before Validation. *VALIDATE SCOPE* is a formal acceptance of deliverables. *CONTROL SCOPE* is prevention and *VALIDATE SCOPE* is inspection.

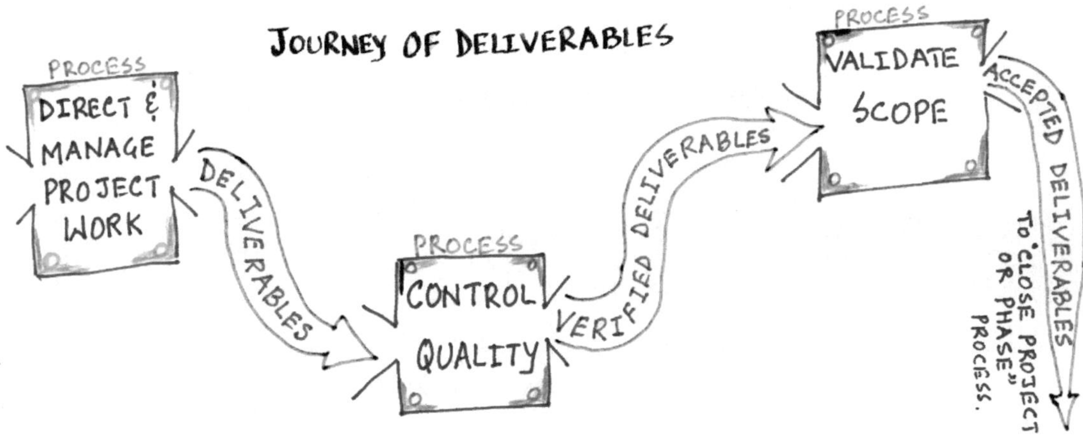

Deliverables also become input to the process *MANAGE KNOWLEDGE* along with "*CONTROL QUALITY*" but that does not become part of the flow of the deliverables and hence not shown in the diagram above.

This process is also used internally for closing a project phase. If the project is done in phases than each of the phases have to be formally closed using the process "*CLOSE PROJECT OR PHASE*" and just before that process it would have to be validated if the deliverables of the phase are completed or not and hence the process of "*VALIDATE SCOPE*" would be conducted just before the process "*CLOSE PROJECT OR PHASE*" while closing a specific Phase of the project before formally starting with the next phase.

This process may also be used to figure out the extent of completion of deliverables when the project is terminated.

Let us get into the innards of this process.

10.22.1 Main Tools and Techniques of this process: -

This process has two tools and techniques and they are **Inspection** and group tools and technique of **Decision Making.** This group tool and technique only contains one sub tool and technique in this process and that is Voting.

Inspection is a "Post Facto" analysis of deliverables. Which means that the deliverables have to be completed before they can be checked for completeness. Which also means, if the deliverables are found to be incorrect or incomplete, the deliverables would have to be made all over again or corrected, which is rather expensive. Such inspections are usually done by the Customer or on their behalf. User acceptance testing, Final inspection, Final Audit, Acceptance Testing, Final Review, Customer review are some of the other terms used for this term "Inspection".

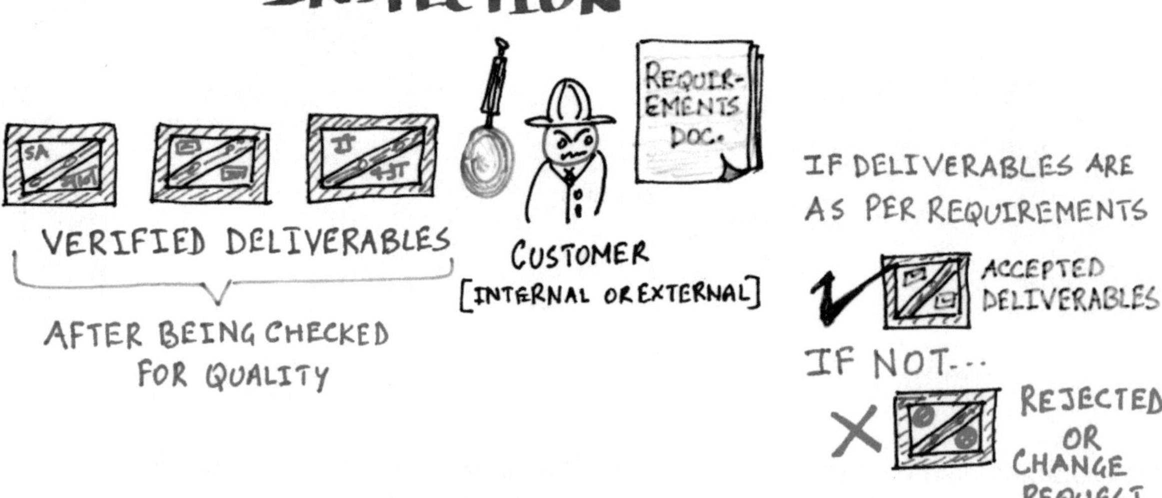

Stakeholders need to discuss and negotiate about the level of completeness and correctness of the deliverables and this is done through the various **Decision-making techniques** the main one being "Voting". Voting could be a "One person – one vote" or a "Cluster Voting" as well. Voting may be needed among the approving stakeholders to suggest if the deliverables satisfy their needs/requirements or not.

10.22.2 Main Outcome of this process:-

The whole purpose of this process is to formally accept deliverables. Once accepted these **Accepted Deliverables** become input to the process "*CLOSE PROJECT OR PHASE*" (and no other process). These deliverables are usually formally signed off by the customer/sponsor/ Single point of contact, as accepted.

It's not necessary that all the deliverables are accepted. Some may not pass the inspection and hence would not be accepted. These unaccepted deliverables would have to be corrected/redone/discarded and started afresh. This can only be done through a **Change Request**. Hence Change Request is one of the outputs (and not "Rejected Deliverables") of this process.

This process generates a lot of information in the form of **Work Performance Information**, about the kind of defects, defect density, conformity to scope, which of the deliverables have been accepted and which have been rejected and which have not been completed. During termination, this would also contain the degree of completeness of the deliverables. Remember! All Work Performance Information become input to one and only one process viz., *MONITOR AND CONTROL PROJECT WORK*".

10.23 Ninja Drill – Implementation - 5

In this Ninja Drill you will find the most important notes and pointers that are important from the point of PMP Exams and covers Integrated Change Control, Monitor & Control Project Work and Validate Scope.

S. No.	Drill Points
1.	Common causes of change: • Inaccurate Initial Estimates • Specification Changes • New Regulations • Missed Requirements • Unidentified Stakeholders • Changes In Business Environment
2.	The best way to prevent unnecessary changes in the project is to conduct comprehensive stakeholder management.
3.	There is nothing known as a "Change" in Agile projects. The whole purpose of Agile is to be able to keep adapting to changing situations and requirements.
4.	The only time formal change management may be used in Agile when a change is to be effected within a running Iteration / sprint.
5.	Steps in Organizational Change Management: 1) Formulate Change 2) Plan Change 3) Implement Change 4) Manage Transition 5) Sustain Change
6.	The five steps of ADKAR Model are: 1. Awareness 2. Desire 3. Knowledge 4. Ability 5. Reinforcement
7.	The Virginia Satir's Model of How People Cope With Changes? 1. Late status quo. 2. The foreign element. 3. Chaos. 4. The transforming idea. 5. Practice and integration. 6. New status quo.
8.	Change Vs Transition • Change is situational and happens whether or not people transition through it. • Transition is a psychological process where people gradually accept the details of the new situation and the changes that come with it.
9.	William Birdges' Transition Model: 3 Steps in Transition Model 1) Ending, losing, and letting go. 2) The neutral zone. 3) The new beginning.
10.	Change Control System is a set of procedures and processes that describe how the modifications / changes to any part of the project and its documentation would be managed and controlled in the event of a change.

11.	Change Control System usually consists of • Forms / Templates • Tracking method • Approval method • Constituents of CCB (Change Control Board)
12.	Specific steps in Project Change Management: 1. Change Identification 2. Change Documentation 3. Analysing The Impact Of Change 4. Submission To CCB For Approval 5. Approved Action 6. Update Change Log 7. Updating Related Plans 8. Informing Relevant Stakeholders
13.	Remember: Backlog grooming and Backlog refinement is not Change management.
14.	There is nothing known as a verbal change request.
15.	Every change request has to be documented.
16.	In certain projects there may be an emergency provision for change requests to be approved by a single stakeholder in lieu of the CCB.
17.	The main outcome / output / artefact of the process "Integrated Change Control" are: 1. Approved Change Request 2. Change Log.
18.	Projects using a predictive approach have a change log that demonstrates changes are being evaluated holistically with consideration for scope, schedule, budget, resource, stakeholder, and risk impacts.
19.	Projects using an adaptive approach have a backlog that shows the rate of accomplishing scope and the rate of adding new scope.
20.	Change log is the register where each of the change requests are logged with date stamping along with details and impact analysis and finally if it was approved with reason or disapproved with reason.
21.	"Monitor and Control Project Work" is concerned with the following: - • Comparing actual from planned • Assessing performance and recommending any preventive or corrective actions • Analyzing, monitoring and tracking project risks • Maintaining accurate and timely project documentation • Provide the inputs and support for generating Project Reports etc. • Identifying new risks and analyzing the previous ones • Monitoring implementation of change requests (Approved ones) as and when they happen
22.	Corrective Actions realign the performance of the project work with the project management plan.
23.	Preventive Action ensures the future performance of the project work is aligned with the project management plan.
24.	Defect repair is the correction or modification of a non-conforming product or product component.
25.	The Seven Steps of Decision Making are: 1. Identify the decision to be made 2. Gather relevant information 3. Identify alternatives 4. Weigh evidence 5. Choose among alternatives 6. Take action 7. Review decision
26.	Value Stream Map / Mapping is a lean technique and extensively used in visually mapping the process of the project in way that clearly marks each step of the process thus enabling the reviewer to easily point out points of wastages (time, cost or resources) in the entire process.

27.	Spike: A spike is a user story for which the team cannot estimate the effort needed. In such a case, it is better to run time-boxed research, exploration to learn about the issue or the possible solutions. As a result of the spike, the team can break down the features into stories and estimate them.
28.	Swarming / Mobbing: In Agile projects when a team member is lagging behind in work the other team members that have surplus time / ahead of their work, come to the rescue of the lagging team member and together they ensure that the work is completed well within time.
29.	Swarming or Mobbing increase team trust and bonding.
30.	During Agile projects the servant leader would work with the team to identify, assess and help remove / overcome Impediments, obstacles and blockers that are preventing work to happen at the planned velocity.
31.	Stand up meeting is for 15 Minutes. Every team member should be present. Can be done in co-located manner as well as across a virtual team.
32.	Questions / discussions during Stand up meeting: 1. What has been done since the last meeting? 2. What needs to be done till the next meeting? 3. What does anyone need help with?
33.	Cumulative Flow Diagram (CFD) This chart indicates features completed over time, features in development, and those in the backlog. It may also include features at intermediate states, such as features designed but not yet constructed, those in quality assurance, or those in testing.
34.	Cycle Time Chart: This diagram shows the average cycle time of the work items completed over time. A cycle time chart may be shown as a scatter diagram or a bar chart.
35.	Velocity Chart: This chart tracks the rate at which the deliverables are produced, validated, and accepted within a predefined interval.
36.	A project is healthy and progressing well when a performance review of project results against the project baselines and other measurement metrics demonstrates that the project is progressing as planned. Performance variances are within thresholds.
37.	The very last process of Implementation is "Validate Scope".
38.	If the customers accept the final deliverables then the project is deemed completed and the project moves to closure.
39.	In Agile projects Validate Scope is done towards the end of each iteration and it is called Iteration Review / Sprint Review / Demo.
40.	The main Tool and Technique of the process "Validate Scope" is Inspection.
41.	Just before release for implementation (whether it is Predictive or Adaptive lifecycle) there is a period of Go Live Black-Out time during which period no changes are further allowed into the system.
42.	The main outcome of the process Validate Scope is Accepted Deliverables.
End Of Ninja Drill	

11 Closing.

11.1 Close Project Or Phase

Look at the name of this process again and you will realize that this process is used for formally closing phases of the project as well as closing the entire project as such.
A project may be made up of phases (which are essentially related project activities that are grouped together under a heading, making it easy to track and estimate the project). Now during execution when a project phase is completed then it must be formally closed (which means that this process must be run) to ensure that all that was needed to be achieved in that phase has, more or less, been achieved and that from schedule and budget standpoint it's ok to move to the next phase. This allows the project manager to have some insight into the project at the end of each phase, to take an informed decision if the project should be carried on or stopped now. This practice allows the project manager and sponsor to kill the project earlier on if it's giving indications of going haywire, instead of wasting money by going all the way to the end and then finding that it failed.

Once all the phases are completed or a termination decision has been taken then this process is used for closing the entire project as such.

Many times during the exams it may not become immediately clear from the questions if the situation warrants Closing a Phase or Closing the entire project. For this remember that when closing a "Phase" terms like "Kill Point", "Phase End Review", "Go-no-go decision" and "Toll Gate" would be used. However to indicate that this process is being used for closing the entire project than it would be termed as "Administrative Closure" or "Project Closure".

Please note that most of the exams questions on this process would be based on "Closing the project".

A project can be closed either due to "Termination Decision" or because of "Successful completion". And in both the cases of project closure, this process has to be used.

I find that a lot of people are not really sure (some of the other rather popular books on this subject has not helped either) as to when exactly do you enter Project Closure. What really happens while closing a project? A lot of people think that "Deliverables' are approved during project closure. I will try and answer these and more, as simply and practically as possible.
Project Closure is more of an internal process for the performing organization. It has less to do with the customer/client.
So when do you start this process? This process is triggered the moment the customer approves the deliverables in the process "*Validate Scope*" (in the Monitor and Control Process Group). The process *Validate Scope* has an output called "Accepted Deliverables" which become an input to this process "*CLOSE PROJECT OR PHASE*". This means that the customer must have approved the deliverables and accepted them BEFORE this process of project

closure may start. I hope you remember that the process "*VALIDATE SCOPE*" is part of the process group called "Monitoring and Controlling".

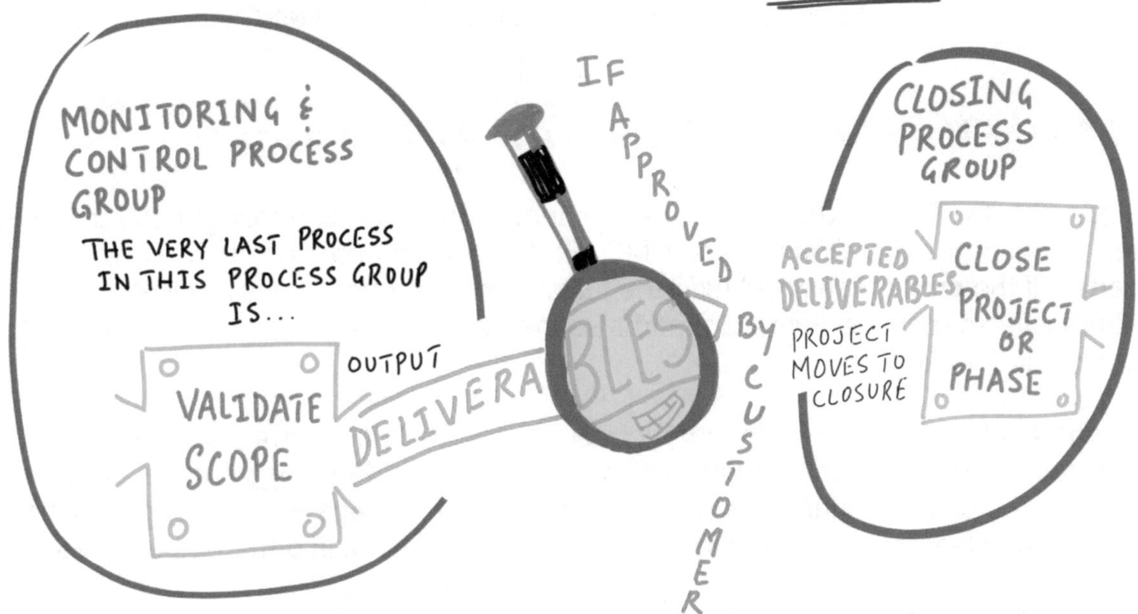

Here is an exhaustive list of all things that may be/are done during "Administrative Closure or Project Closure": -

1. Ascertain if the project met its justification as was stated in the Project Charter by the Sponsor.
2. Ensuring that all the pertinent costs are charged to the project.
3. Noting the performance of the team members and their contribution to the project and project team.
4. Award and recognitions for teams or specific team members.
5. Documenting lessons learned with the team members
6. Having team celebrations (depending on how the project went)
7. Financial post mortem and financial closure.
8. Time sheet and final efforts calculations for historical records.
9. Dealing with excess project materials.
10. Training the operations team on the product
11. Handing over of the project to operations
12. Measuring the satisfaction level of the stakeholders' vis-à-vis the project.
13. Releasing the project team from the project
14. Project documents archival.

EXAMS SPECIAL

If in the question it's asked "What is the most important activity to be done during project closure?" the answer is "Lessons Learned". The term "important" does not mean first or last, it simply means what is a must to be done during project closure. However, at times in questions, you may be asked "What is the very last activity to be done in a project closure?" and the answer is "Archiving". Once the project documents are archived, there is nothing left of the project, no costs can be booked against it, no resources can work on it, no efforts can be billed against it. Remember "Most Important", its Lessons Learned…"Last Activity" it's Archival.

Let us now look into the details of this process "*CLOSE PROJECT OR PHASE*": -

11.1.1 Main Tools and Techniques of this process: -

In this process, the **Expert Judgment** are the ones who were expert judgment for Project Charter. Sponsor, Project Consultants, PMO, Portfolio Managers and such. They are needed to ascertain if the project really did fulfill the justification (business case) as well as the benefits (business management plan) and also the objectives (end goals) for which the project was undertaken.

Document Analysis deals in going through all your project documents and project communication to find (actually "Hunt" out) all possible gaps, learnings and new knowledge that were there / created during this project. The idea is to scrape every aspect of the project not miss out any learnings whatsoever so that the organization, in general, becomes smarter.

Regression Analysis: This sounds very statistical (which it is, actually), but in project closure, it has a much simpler meaning. This is akin to how the famous detectives like, Byomkesh Bakshi, Hercule Poirot and Sherlock Holmes who look at a crime scene and then start asking questions and reviewing evidences. This is done to recreate the crime scene mentally and to try and knit together all the incidents in the past that lead to that moment of crime. After that they try and look at the most important or relevant (called motive) past event that could have a direct bearing on this incident. Well, something similar is done here for the project, though a lot less dramatic and lot less violent. This is where we could look back and see "what was the effect of one project variable on another one?". Let us take an example. Let's say by the time the project ended you realized that you went heavily over budget. Now you would have to find exactly the reasons why this happened. This has to be investigated so that you are not assuming things. Through regression analysis, you could look at the various elements like "Change in material rates", "Lack of productivity", "The project methodology" or something else. And then you look at your project data to work backward to find the most influential variable affecting budget. This specific variable has to be identified so that other projects in the organizations do not commit the same mistake. Regression is not only used for mistakes, but it could also be used for finding the "project variables" that gave some additional benefits which you would like replicated in other projects as well.

Looking back into the project one could also be able to find some clear trends that lead to certain anomalies. This is called **Trend Analysis**. There could have been a trend of delays in meeting milestones due to delay in "Management approvals". If this happened just once or twice it's not a trend. However, if you can see that this management delay in approvals happened repeatedly, then, in that case, it's definitely a trend. This trend has to be documented so that "preventive actions" could be taken for other projects.

Variance Analysis: This means all aspects of project plans and baselines are compared with the actuals done. This can be used to figure out which areas of project have given higher variances than others. Please understand that these techniques and tools do not have to be done in isolation but together. You could conduct the variance analysis and then for the higher variance elements you could see some trends and also conduct regression analysis to figure out which were the main variables (Culprits) that were most instrumental in the given variances.

11.1.2 Main Outcome of this process: -

The output **Final Product Service or Result Transition** is the handover of the product of the project to the operations. This handover could be a service, product or intellectual property rights.

Final Report is the last report about the project that is circulated to the relevant stakeholders stating how the project performed on key parameters.

Some of the possible elements of the Final Report are: -

The **organizational process assets updates** consist of things like, Lessons Learned, Audit reports, postmortem reports, sponsor observations on success of the project, project document archival and so on.

11.2 Ninja Drill

In this Ninja Drill you will find the most important notes and pointers that are important from the point of PMP Exams and covers Close project or phase.

S. No.	Drill Points
1.	Project is completed once the customer accepts the final deliverables. But project closure starts after project completion to administratively close the project.
2.	List of things that are usually done during the process "Close Project": • Ascertain if the project met its justification as was stated in the Project Charter by the Sponsor. • Ensuring that all the pertinent costs are charged to the project. • Noting the performance of the team members and their contribution to the project and project team. • Award and recognitions for teams or specific team members. • Documenting lessons learned with the team members • Having team celebrations (depending on how the project went) • Financial post mortem and financial closure. • Time sheet and final efforts calculations for historical records. • Dealing with excess project materials. • Training the operations team on the product • Handing over of the project to operations • Measuring the satisfaction level of the stakeholders' vis-à-vis the project. • Releasing the project team from the project • Project documents archival.
3.	Regression Analysis: Analysis and interrelations between all the different project variables that contributed to project outcomes (good or bad) so that such interactions and relationships may be used to control the outcomes of other projects.
4.	The most important activity of Project Closure is Lessons Learned
5.	The Last activity ever done in any project is Archival
6.	The main outcome / output / artefact of the process "Close Project" is Final Report.
	End Of Ninja Drill

12 PM Video Platform – For The Most Authentic And Dependable Video Lessons On PMP

If you are looking for video lessons for mastering all PMP concepts in a way that it makes you understand it completely, then do visit our Video Platform dedicated to the world of Project Management.

There are 3 packages for PMP at this platform. Choose and subscribe to the one that you most need.

Our PMP Dash and the Full PMP training for 35 contact hours are the best sellers. The reason why they are so is because we focus on making sure that the users understand the concepts instead of just reading stuff from a slide. Yes slides are used but the focus is practicality and understanding. Once you understand the subject you would not have to mug up anything. It makes you more confident and also lowers your stress and fear factor significantly.

The 35 Contact hours training at PM Video platform is the most comprehensive and the largest package anywhere in this industry globally.

To know more, visit this platform: https://pmvideo.pm-pulse.com/

To know more about the amazing packages on this platform, visit this platform and view the details of the packages. It will pleasantly surprise you.

13 Exams Simulator Access

As a buyer of this book, you are entitled to access the simulator for PMP®.

For this series, you are entitled to "question sets" of all the Knowledge areas and all of the full-set of PMP® simulation exams to understand your other improvement areas.

To access the simulator you would need to type the following address on the browser: -

exam.pm-pulse.com

This is what you will find once the site loads.

The *Pulse* of **Project Management**

The **Engine** For Certification

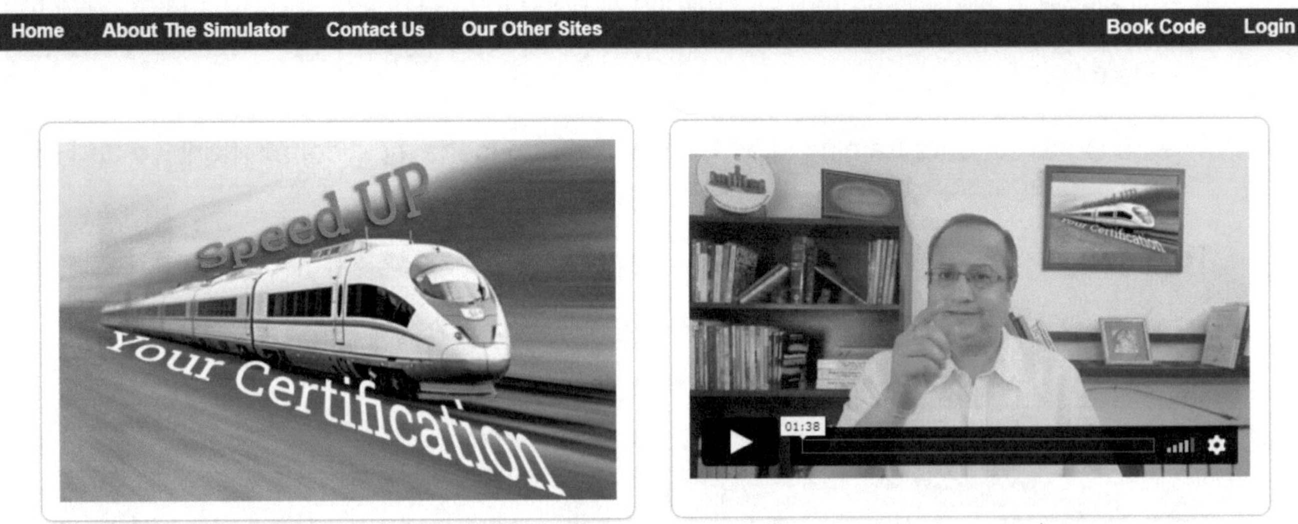

Click the menu label "Book Code" and you will be prompted to fill in a book code and the Amazon order id (without any gaps and without any special character).

The book code for this specific book is **PMP28061968** and you will get your Amazon purchase order code from the "Orders" section (enter the purchase order number without "-" or ":" or any other special characters and gaps) of your Amazon account.

After entering both you will be taken to a page where some information about yourself need to be entered. Please only use your personal email Id. Many official email sites have excessively stringent security setting thus blocking emails with links. The access to this site would be sent to your email. At times, depending on the kind of security settings and the kind of email provider the email from our exam simulator ends up being in spam folder. Hence do look up your spam folder in case you are unable to find the email in your main Inbox folder.
After that, you will be able to use the "Login" at the top right corner of this page to access your simulation.

Please only use LAPTOP or DESKTOP **to access this site as the simulator has been made almost identical to the real exams which happens only on a desktop at a prometric center.**

14 About PM-Pulse

With over 120 Training and Engagements only focused on Strategy, Program Management and every single aspect and tools and techniques around Project Management, PM-Pulse brings to you "Every Thing" on Project Management and "Only" on Project Management. Complete customization and creation of "Brand New" training only for your Project Management Needs is a hallmark of PM-Pulse. Being a REP of PMI we give PDU's on each of these training.

Practical, Effective and Interesting Engagements.

Get to know us more at www.pm-pulse.com

Join us on Facebook. https://www.facebook.com/PMPulse.a2zpm/

Connect on Linkedin. https://www.linkedin.com/in/maneeshvijaya/

Check out our videos on Youtube. https://www.youtube.com/c/PMPulse

15 Did You Know That You Can Now Listen To PMP® Audios To Prepare?

PM-Pulse has launched a one of a kind initiative to help utilize your time better while preparing for PMP® Exams, viz., PM Dhwani. Dhwani, in Sanskrit, means the celestial sound. Hence PM Dhwani is the celestial sound of Project Management. PM Dhwani is an "AUDIO" platform which contains bite-sized audios on every single topic on PMP® Exams and recited in such a way that one does not need to have a book in front of them while listening to them. Listen to them while on your way to work, while in the loo, while taking a break from work or even while working.

Listen the variety of Free Audios as well which will enrich you and your knowledge, nonetheless.
Utilize your time well.

You can subscribe to the different packages regarding PMP at this audio platform and listen to them on the go.

Know more about it use this link:

https://pmdhwani.pm-pulse.com/

I would really appreciate if you could take some time to leave a review at Amazon.

If you found this book useful please do "Recommend" this book to other friends and colleagues.

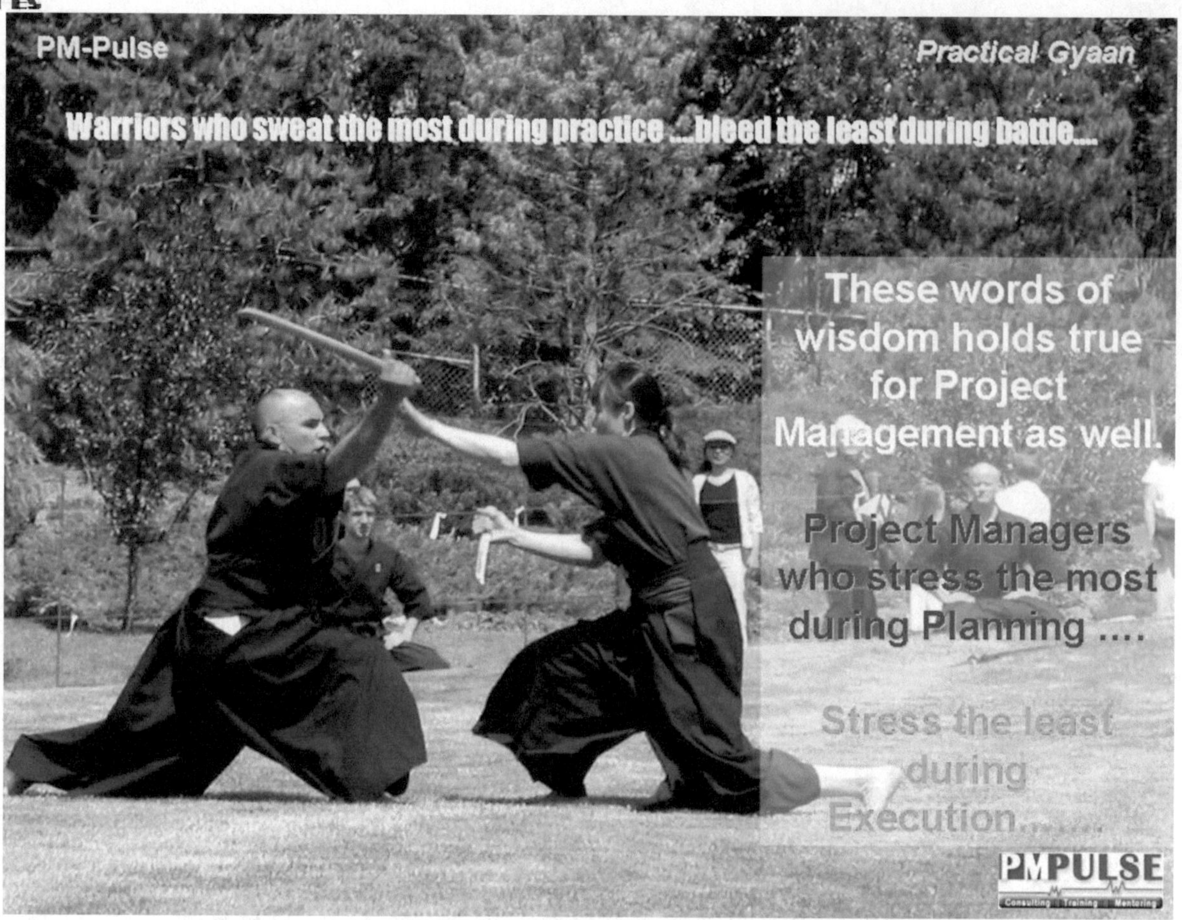
PM-Pulse
Practical Gyaan
Warriors who sweat the most during practice ....bleed the least during battle....
These words of wisdom holds true for Project Management as well.
Project Managers who stress the most during Planning ....
Stress the least during Execution.......
PMPULSE

============================== End Of Book ===========================

Made in the USA
Columbia, SC
06 November 2024